The Ukrainian National Movement in Galicia: 1815-1849

Jan Kozik

The Ukrainian National Movement in Galicia: 1815-1849

Edited and with an Introduction by
Lawrence D. Orton

Translated from the Polish by
Andrew Gorski and Lawrence D. Orton

Canadian Institute of Ukrainian Studies
University of Alberta
Edmonton 1986

THE CANADIAN LIBRARY IN UKRAINIAN STUDIES

A series of original works and reprints relating to Ukraine issued under the editorial supervision of the Canadian Institute of Ukrainian Studies, University of Alberta, Edmonton.

Originally published in Poland under the titles *Ukraiński ruch narodowy w Galicji w latach 1830–1848* by Wydawnictwo Literackie 1973 and *Między reakcją a rewolucją: Studia z dziejów ukraińskiego ruchu narodowego w Galicji w latach 1848–1849* by Uniwersytet Jagielloński and Państwowe Wydawnictwo Naukowe 1975.

Canadian Cataloguing in Publication Data
Kozik, Jan, 1934–1979.
The Ukrainian national movement in Galicia, 1815-1849

(The Canadian library in Ukrainian studies)
Translation of: Ukraiński ruch narodowy w Galicji w latach 1830–1848 and Między reakcją a rewolucją.
Bibliography: p.
Includes index.
ISBN 0-920862-40-3 (bound). ISBN 0-920862-28-4 (pbk.)

1. Ukrainians—Galicia (Poland and Ukraine)—History. 2. Galicia (Poland and Ukraine)—History—Uprising, 1848. 3. Galicia (Poland and Ukraine)—Politics and government. I. Canadian Institute of Ukrainian Studies. II. Title. III. Series.
DK511.G187K69 1986 943.8'600491791 C86–091170–5

Cover design: Sherryl Petterson
Cover Photo of St. George's Cathedral, Lviv: Andrij Hornjatkevyč
Index: Lubomyr Szuch

Printed in Canada by Printing Services, University of Alberta
Distributed by the University of Toronto Press
5201 Dufferin St.
Downsview, Ontario
Canada M3H 5T8

Contents

Foreword	xi
Editor's Introduction	xiii
Map: Eastern Galicia and Bukovyna, 1848	xxi
PART ONE: National Awakening	
1. History, Nationhood and the Slavic Awakening	3
2. The Galician Ukrainians Under Austrian Rule, 1772–1830	15
3. Polish Influences	29
4. The Ruthenian Triad	51
5. The Triad's Literary Activities	65
6. The Struggle over the Literary Language and Ukrainian Orthography	83
7. National and Social Views	109
8. Ties to the Slavic Community	127
9. The Crossroads	161
PART TWO: Between Reaction and Revolution	
10. The Dawn	177
11. The Councils	193
12. The Slavic Congress	215
13. Elections and the Austrian Reichstag	237
14. The Peasant Question	251
15. The Campaign to Partition Galicia	265
16. The National Guard and the Riflemen	287
17. Education and Culture	301
18. Polish-Ukrainian Relations	333
19. Conclusion	361

Notes	371
Appendix I: Prominent Galician Ukrainians	443
Appendix II: Place Names in Galicia	445
Bibliography	449
Index of Names	473
Subject Index	483

Jan Kozik

Foreword

The English text is an abridged translation from Polish of Jan Kozik's two chronologically sequential books: *Ukraiński ruch narodowy w Galicji w latach 1830-1848* [The Ukrainian national movement in Galicia, 1830-1848] (Cracow: Wydawnictwo Literackie, 1973) and *Między reakcją a rewolucją. Studia z dziejów ukraińskiego ruchu narodowego w Galicji w latach 1848-1849* [Between reaction and revolution: Studies from the history of the Ukrainian national movement in Galicia, 1848-1849], Zeszyty Naukowe Uniwersytetu Jagiellońskiego, vol. 381, Prace Historyczne, no. 52 (Warsaw and Cracow: Państwowe Wydawnictwo Naukowe, 1975). The translators have taken considerable liberty in rendering the Polish original into English, although every effort has been made to preserve the author's intention and thought.

Although the original works employed only Polish for Ukrainian names, the editor has followed Ukrainian usage for those persons who are identified as Ukrainians (Ruthenians). Nineteenth-century Galician-Ukrainian forms have been preserved, e.g., Iosyf not Osyp (except for the Ukrainians living in tsarist Russia, such as Osyp Bodiansky) and Teodor not Fedir. In the case of polonized Ruthenians, the so-called *gente Rutheni, natione Poloni*, who consciously embraced Polish culture, such as Kasper Cięglewicz or Julian Horoszkiewicz, Polish forms are retained. Because many Galician Ukrainians are found in the historical literature under the Polish spelling of their names, these forms are given in an appendix. Localities in present-day Soviet Ukraine are given in their Ukrainian form, and those in post-1945 Poland in Polish (e.g., Lviv not Lwów or Lemberg, Przemyśl not Peremyshl). Although the present-day boundaries correspond precisely neither to the ethnic divisions in nineteenth-century Galicia nor to the then customary distinction between Eastern and Western

Galicia, the distinction is believed to be the most appropriate way to handle this issue. An appendix showing both Polish and Ukrainian forms of key localities is also provided.

The editor wishes to express his sincere appreciation to several persons and institutions whose assistance has helped make possible the appearance of this work. Mrs. Bogusława Kozik of Nowy Sącz, Poland, generously permitted the editor to examine her late husband's notes and unpublished materials. Dr. Jerzy Zdrada of the Polish Academy of Sciences in Cracow provided helpful suggestions for merging the two Polish books into a single, cohesive volume. The Agencja autorska [Authors' agency] in Warsaw facilitated the copyright release for publication of the English translation. Sherwyn T. Carr and Anne Lalas read early drafts of the typescript. The late Ivan L. Rudnytsky, John-Paul Himka, Myroslav Yurkevich and Marco Carynnyk offered valuable suggestions and helped to resolve a number of difficult matters of translation and terminology. The generous support of the Canadian Institute of Ukrainian Studies and the Research Committee of Oakland University is greatly appreciated.

L.D.O.

Editor's Introduction

The Ukrainians, of all the Slavic peoples in the nineteenth century, were the most adversely affected in their national awakening because of division among different states. While the majority of Ukrainians lived under the yoke of tsarist autocracy and the obscurantist Orthodox church, a minority, approximately 15 per cent, had become subjects of the Austrian emperor with the first partition of Poland in 1772. Intellectual ties between the two major divisions of Ukraine largely ceased. In Left-Bank Ukraine under Russian rule, a handful of secular writers of gentry background began early in the nineteenth century to use the Ukrainian vernacular, but in Austrian-ruled western Ukraine, where the former Ukrainian nobility had succumbed completely to polonization, the entire Ukrainian intelligentsia were members of the Greek Catholic priesthood. Thus quite distinct Ukrainian national movements evolved.

To justify historically their right to rule the territory seized from Poland, the Austrians christened their new province the Kingdom of Galicia and Lodomeria (Halych and Volodymyr), making the dubious claim that these lands, which had once been subject to the crown of Hungary, had now passed lawfully to the Habsburgs. Ruthenians (as the Ukrainians in Galicia called themselves) comprised a large majority in the eastern portions of the province; Poles predominated in the western part. The arable lands throughout Galicia, however, were owned by the *szlachta* (Polish and polonized nobility). Although these Polish lords retained their possessions under Austrian rule, their previously absolute control over their peasant subjects was now tempered by the Austro-German bureaucracy.

The "enlightened" reforms of Empress Maria Theresa and Emperor Joseph II alleviated the more oppressive burdens of serfdom but made little improvement in the backward conditions of rural life in Galicia.

Although some of the reforms were withdrawn by Joseph's successors, the notion took root, especially among the Ukrainian peasants, of a beneficent Austrian ruler who was resisting the abusive power of the Polish landowners. The rural Greek Catholic clergymen, who lived closer to the peasantry than their Roman Catholic counterparts in western Galicia, were especially favourably inclined toward the Austrian ruler and his bureaucratic emissaries. This attitude was intensified by Habsburg religious policy, which sought to place the Greek Catholic clergy and rite on an equal footing with the Roman Catholic clergy and the Latin rite. Thus, when Polish forces that had attached themselves to Napoleon's banner fought to recover Galicia from Austria in 1809, the Greek Catholic hierarchy remained steadfastly loyal to the Habsburgs.

Despite the hierarchy's pro-imperial (*kaisertreu*) stance, some Greek Catholic clergymen and seminarians, influenced by the Romantic currents and calls for political liberty that infused intellectual life after 1815, sympathized with the Poles' challenge to tsarist rule in 1830-31. And in the years after the defeat of the insurrection, the Poles' conspiratorial undertakings found fertile soil in Galicia, where liberal and in some instances even radical currents permeated the lower ranks of the Greek Catholic clergy.

Although the Ukrainian clerical intelligentsia tended to use Polish in speech and writing, an interest in the Ukrainian language, especially as it had survived in folk-tales and songs and peasant speech, grew in the 1820s and 1830s. Initially it was spurred by the efforts of Polish ethnographers and writers who assiduously collected and compiled for publication examples of the Ukrainian folk heritage. Not until the 1830s, however, did a small circle of Greek Catholic seminarians in Lviv, led by Markiian Shashkevych, attempt to reproduce Ukrainian peasant speech in their writings. The publication efforts of this group, which became known as the "Ruthenian Triad," received support from other Slavic intellectuals in the empire, especially Czechs and Serbs, but within Galicia their activities were met with implacable opposition from the Greek Catholic hierarchy, which insisted on retaining the ossified Church Slavonic (or Slavo-Ruthenian) language, which was unintelligible to the Ukrainian masses. Bitter polemics ensued among the clerical intelligentsia concerning the most suitable Ukrainian literary language. Although a few proposed using exclusively the vernacular, others supported a mixture of popular speech and the ecclesiastical language. Most priests at this time, however, still sided with the hierarchy. The debate also concerned which alphabet—the Latin, the Old Slavonic or the modernized Cyrillic—was best suited to Ukrainian writing. Although modern Ukrainian literature was eventually modelled on the language used by Taras Shevchenko in tsarist Ukraine, significant variances persisted in orthography for almost a century: many writers chose to employ their own style.

The Ukrainian national movement in Galicia in the 1830s and early 1840s was limited to issues of language, literature and history. Political and socio-economic questions were avoided by the clerical intelligentsia, with the exception of those few Ukrainians who had joined the Polish conspiracies. Only on the eve of the revolutionary upheaval of 1848 did Ukrainian awakeners begin to raise political issues. Iakiv Holovatsky, a member of the earlier Ruthenian Triad who echoed the Czechs' Austro-Slavic programme, was one of them. Although a "liberal" opposition to the Greek Catholic hierarchy becomes increasingly apparent, an indication of the inherent social conservatism of the Ukrainian clerical intelligentsia is reflected in its opposition to the Poles' renewed attempts to foment insurrection in 1846.

The rapid spread of revolution eastward across Europe in March 1848 caught the guardians of the old order as well as the Ukrainian national spokesmen unawares. In Vienna the court, hoping to assuage public unrest, jettisoned Prince Metternich, but was soon pressured to abolish censorship, sanction a national guard and promise constitutional government. The street demonstrations in Vienna were repeated in the provincial capitals of the empire. In Lviv the Poles quickly advanced liberal political and national demands. A petition was drafted, and signatures were hastily gathered, including those of several Ukrainians, and submitted on 19 March to Galician Governor Franz Stadion. In a second petition on 6 April to the emperor, the Galician Poles asked for sweeping local autonomy and called for the Polish language to replace German in the schools, courts and administrative offices. These petitions contained no specific references to the Ukrainians. The Poles believed that they constituted the sole "political nationality" in Galicia and therefore could speak on behalf of all the province's inhabitants. The only concession to the Ukrainians was an oblique mention that instruction in primary schools be in the prevailing local "dialect."

Most Poles were therefore considerably surprised when on 19 April a group of Greek Catholic clergymen, headed by the Lviv suffragan bishop, Hryhorii Iakhymovych, submitted a separate petition to the emperor on behalf of Galicia's "loyal Ruthenians." Within the month, sharp differences between Polish and Ukrainian national aspirations had surfaced in Galicia. Whether Governor Stadion had instigated the Ukrainian response to weaken the Poles' position (as the Poles maintained) or not, there was a growing sense among Ukrainian intellectuals in the spring of 1848 that the Galician "Ruthenians" constituted a distinct nationality, a part of the larger Ukrainian nation, and would no longer consent to being considered a "branch" of the Polish nation.

The guiding force in this affirmation of Ukrainian cultural separateness was the Holovna Rada Ruska (Supreme Ruthenian Council), which was formed with Bishop Iakhymovych's approval in Lviv in April. Although it was dominated by the conservative Greek Catholic consistory and espoused unconditional loyalty to the Habsburg dynasty, under the pressure of its local affiliates in Galicia to take a stand on social and economic issues, the council became a vehicle for the genuine expression of Ukrainian aspirations in 1848-9. In effect, the council became a school for the political education of a broad stratum of Galician Ukrainian society.

The political and national activities of Galician Ukrainians in 1848-9 took place not only at the provincial and local levels, but in encounters at the first Slavic Congress in Prague in June 1848 and in the deliberations of the imperial Austrian parliament (Reichstag) in Vienna and later in Kroměříž. That many of the Ukrainians' hopes and aspirations were not fully realized cannot be blamed solely on the often shortsighted policies of the conservative clerical leaders in the Supreme Ruthenian Council. The spokesmen for most of the Slavic nationalities in Austria were unequally matched against the manipulative Habsburg politicians and generals once they recovered from the initial shock of March 1848.

The Ukrainian leaders' belief that the fortunes of their people depended on the good faith of Austrian officialdom had strong historical roots in the pre-March period and was reinforced by the refusal of most Poles to recognize the Ukrainians' right to separate national existence. The few advocates on the Polish and Ukrainian sides for compromise and reconciliation in 1848–9 were overwhelmed by the prevailing intransigence in both camps; they found themselves caught in an untenable position between revolution and reaction. And so the heady national aims of Galician Poles and Ukrainians alike succumbed to the triumph of counter-revolution. The Ukrainians, however, came only slowly to realize that their loyalty to the court was not to be repaid through real concessions to their nationality. Bitter recriminations then followed, and some leaders, such as Iakiv Holovatsky, decided that the future of the Ruthenians lay only in closer association with the tsarist empire and Russian culture.

Despite the disappointments and setbacks, the experience of 1848-9 did bring some long-term benefits to the Ukrainians in Galicia. It provided valuable political experience and firmly rooted the achievements of the earlier intellectual awakening. The various political and national orientations that emerged in the turmoil of 1848-9 would remain the basic alternatives for decades to come. The national movement in Galicia would undergo a period of largely Russophile orientation for almost two decades, but the freer political atmosphere in Austria after 1866 would see a return to a genuine "Ukrainian" (populist) orientation in Galicia, which would draw inspiration from the earlier achievements of the Ruthenian Triad. In the decades before World War I Eastern Galicia would supplant Russian Ukraine as the most vital center of Ukrainian national activity, becoming a sort of Ukrainian Piedmont.

* * *

The untimely death of Jan Kozik on 23 November 1979 at the age of forty-five robbed Ukrainian studies of an accomplished scholar whose work held much promise of further distinguished contributions. Like many historians, Jan Kozik had come to his field of specialization by chance, as a master's candidate seeking a suitable thesis topic in Professor Henryk Wereszycki's seminar at the Jagiellonian University in Cracow. That initial choice became a vocation. Nothing in Kozik's background suggested that he would devote his scholarly life to the history of the Galician Ukrainians and the tortuous relationship between Ukrainians and Poles. Kozik had chosen a subject definitely not easy for an aspiring scholar in the new Poland. In the immediate postwar years, Polish historians had been discouraged from exploring the history of the peoples of Poland's former eastern possessions. This task presumably would be handled by their Soviet colleagues. Moreover, for Poles the requisite sources for such study were seemingly beyond their reach.

Undaunted by these strictures and other hurdles, Jan Kozik committed his prodigious skills and energy to the study of nineteenth-century Galician Ukraine. He wrote his master's thesis on Russophilism in Galicia between 1848 and 1866, a period that saw sharp divisions in the political and national views of Galician Ukrainian leaders following the setbacks and disappointments of 1848–9. Although he was obliged to work for several years after receiving his master's degree as a secondary school teacher in the Upper Silesian town of Chrzanów, Kozik pursued in free moments his interest in Ukrainian history. Eventually, in 1963, he was admitted to doctoral study in history at the Jagiellonian University. For his thesis topic, Kozik chose the early period of the Ukrainian national awakening in Galicia, with particular attention to the activities of the Ruthenian Triad. He defended his thesis in 1967, and in 1973, after some revision, it was published under the title *The Ukrainian National Movement in Galicia, 1830-1848*. Though he had to rely largely on published primary sources and secondary works available in Polish repositories, his book represented an original synthesis and broke new ground by examining theretofore less studied figures of the Galician Ukrainian awakening and especially by demonstrating the extensive ties of the leaders of the Ukrainian movement to the burgeoning Slavic renaissance throughout the multinational Habsburg empire. In his work Kozik adopted a thematic approach to his subject within a broader chronological framework.

Quite understandably, Jan Kozik chose the ensuing period of revolutionary turmoil in 1848–9 with its attendant interplay of conflicting national and political aspirations as the subjects of his *praca habilitacyjna* (a sort of second doctorate in Poland comparable to the French *doctorat d'ètat*, traditionally seen as a prerequisite for a regular academic appointment). While serving as a lecturer in the Institute for the History of the Peoples of the USSR at the Jagiellonian University, he devoted himself to this project between 1968 and its formal acceptance in 1974.

From the outset Kozik realized that this work would require thorough examination of archival materials housed in the former Galician capital of Lviv. Notwithstanding the difficulties in using these repositories, even for Soviet scholars, Kozik persisted and in the early 1970s secured access—albeit carefully prescribed—to the State Central Historical Archives and the Library of the Academy of Sciences of the Ukrainian SSR in Lviv. There he located the files of the Supreme Ruthenian Council, long thought by scholars to have been lost. Kozik tested his findings in several articles, and then in 1975 the Jagiellonian University Press published his book *Between Reaction and Revolution: The History of the Ukrainian National Movement in Galicia, 1848-1849*. His work was not only the most comprehensive and authoritative to appear on this subject, but was also distinguished by a critical objectivity and a detachment notably lacking in earlier studies.

Although this work represented a direct continuation of his earlier book on the pre-March 1848 national awakening, it differed markedly in style and methodology. Whereas Kozik's first book (here presented as part one) paid considerable attention to literary accomplishments and cultural ties with other Slavs, the emphasis in the second volume (presented here as part two) is foremost on political aspirations and issues of historiographical controversy. In style the first part is a more fluid prose; the second work shows a more academic, less polished style. In the English version an effort has been made to smooth and obscure these differences. The contrast in style may be attributed in part to the exigencies of a particular scholarly apparatus for the *habilitacja* and its hurried publication in the Jagiellonian University's monograph series. There is also considerable difference in documentation, with the first book based extensively on literary sources and the second on multiple archival citations.

As the breadth of Jan Kozik's knowledge and understanding of the national relationships in nineteenth-century Galicia grew, he became convinced that a precondition to overcoming many years of mistrust was to provide an honest and forthright account of the Galician Ukrainians' experience. Though he did not live to complete a general history of Galician Ukraine, his profound hope was that his works nevertheless might make a modest contribution to surmounting prejudice and to fostering better understanding among future generations of Ukrainians and Poles.

With dignity and without complaint, Jan Kozik bore the pain and hardship of debilitating illness for the last ten years of his life. Rarely, if ever, did he speak in bitterness of the mishandled initial surgery and the ensuing treatment that subsequently rendered his heart ailment irremediable. In failing health and against the advice of his doctors, Kozik availed himself of an opportunity to return to Lviv in the winter and spring of 1978 to gather information on another critical phase of Ukrainian history in Galicia, the years of Michał Bobrzyński's viceroyalty on the eve of World War I. Although weakened physically, he endured the rigours of that stay and completed his researches. Upon his return, however, his condition worsened, and he was obliged to yield his teaching duties at the Jagiellonian University. He spent his last year and a half at the family home of his wife Bogusława, outside Nowy Sącz in southern Poland. Although he knew he had little time to live, he spoke to friends especially of his desires and hopes for work still unfinished and future projects in Galician Ukrainian history.

When the suggestion for an English version of his two books was made to Kozik in 1977, he responded enthusiastically and proposed that the work be extended chronologically to 1866. Steps were taken to invite Kozik for the academic year 1979-80 to the Canadian Institute of Ukrainian Studies at the University of Alberta, where he could complete his work and oversee the translation into English. Because of his illness and early death, he did not come to Canada, and the additional chapters remained unwritten. Thus, the narrative presented here stops in 1849.

Jan Kozik was by nature quiet and unpretentious. The scholarly values he cherished most were professional integrity and a commitment to the truth. He refused to make the "little compromises" that too many academics in Poland did in the 1960s and 1970s for the sake of material betterment, apparent prestige and career advancement. He never bent his scholarship to please prevailing doctrinal prerequisites. He remained faithful to the professional values and discipline he learned from his first and only mentor, Professor Wereszycki. Writing in the independent Catholic weekly in Cracow, *Tygodnik Powszechny*, shortly after Kozik's death, Professor Wereszycki noted that "Jan Kozik's pioneering works revealed his full scholarly maturity . . . [and] have acquired a recognized place in Ukrainian historiography, because of their objective judgements and exacting research. The fine qualities of Jan Kozik's character—his devotion to truth and his perseverance—moulded his scholarly approach." Not surprisingly, Kozik's scholarship earned greater recognition among historians abroad than in his native Poland. And it is especially fitting that the English version of his monumental study of the Ukrainian national awakening in Galicia now appears in North America, where he had many devoted friends and colleagues.

Eastern Galicia and Bukovyna, 1848

Map prepared by Stephanie Kucharyshyn, Cartographic Section, Department of Geography, University of Alberta. Based on maps 1, 4 and 5 in John-Paul Himka, "A Researcher's Handbook on Western Ukraine (Galicia and Bukovina) in the Late Nineteenth and Early Twentieth Centuries," prepared for the Ukrainian Cultural Heritage Village, Historic Sites Service, Alberta Culture. Used by permission of the author and Alberta Culture.

PART ONE

National Awakening

1. History, Nationhood and the Slavic Awakening

The latter part of the eighteenth century saw a crisis develop in the feudal-rural economy of East Central Europe. The gradual emergence of capitalistic elements, with an attendant increase of manufactured goods, led to increased trade; nationwide markets came to supplant subsistence production. In time new social classes arose, notably the commercial and industrial bourgeoisie and eventually a modern working class. The serfs, freed from the centuries-old bonds tying them to the soil, headed for urban areas in search of work or marketplaces for their own goods. All these economic changes had far-reaching national consequences. The various national vernaculars gradually began to compete with and displace German, which had been the primary language of commerce in the region. As the numerically superior native peoples entered the towns and cities in ever-increasing numbers, the burgher class, although it would continue to use German for a long time, began to succumb to national assimilation. To be sure, the loosening of social bonds and the increased mobility of the lower classes had to lead, especially in multinational states, to conflicts among the nationalities. Both linguistic and religious differences, assiduously underscored by young intellectuals who had maintained close ties with the common people, significantly hastened the nation-forming processes.[1]

The social and economic changes were reflected in the movements known as the Enlightenment and Romanticism. The thinkers of the

Enlightenment espoused the equality of all men before the law and broadened the concept of the nation to embrace all social classes. Assuming that the entire nation (regarded as a community of autonomous individuals) alone and exclusively was entitled to sovereign rights, these men held that the nation should decide its form of government, whose most important task would be to abolish despotic rule and feudal vestiges. These changes would, in turn, lead to new social relationships.

With the approach of the Romantic era, the problems of nationhood were viewed in a new light. In *Reflections on the Revolution in France* (1790), the conservative British statesman Edmund Burke found salvation from revolutionary ideas in the concept of the nation as a historically formed organic whole, a community of past, present and future generations. His views were further developed by the German philosophers: Johann Gottlieb Fichte in *Reden an die deutsche Nation* (1808-9) and Georg Wilhelm Friedrich Hegel in lectures on the philosophy of history. They believed that a nation regarded as a historical community had a special mission in human progress. Such a nation did not have to be created, because it had existed since ancient times; it was necessary only for it to be reborn.[2]

What were the consequences of this position for the development of the national idea among the Slavic peoples? Increased interest in the problems of historically based nationhood was evident everywhere. Everyone committed to his own country and nation, regardless of the political situation in which it found itself, made use of Hegel's ideas. For some, like the Poles, the most important element in his thought was his statement of the necessary grounds for independent national existence; others, like the Russians, saw in it a justification of their nation's future role. But everyone agreed that the historical role of the Slavic nations not only had not come to an end, but in fact had not even begun for all of them. For this reason too, an interest in national history greatly increased. Historical motifs were most important for those nations that lacked their own tradition of a nation-state, or for those that had long ago lost their statehood. History was invoked to display the continuity of the nation's life and the grandeur of its traditions, thereby to contrast the glorious past with the impoverished present and to demonstrate that a nation once capable of independence could regain it in the future. The nation might even be a model and, as the Polish messianists stated, a spiritual and political leader of other nations.

This fascination with history led to literary and scholarly works of lasting value among the Slavic nations. Enduring achievements are found in the works of the most famous poets of the age—the Pole

Adam Mickiewicz, the Slovak Ján Kollár, the Slovene France Prešeren, the Croat Ivan Mažuranić, the Montenegrin Petr Njegoš, and the Ukrainian Taras Shevchenko—while important scholarly works were produced by the "Czecho-Slovak" Pavel Šafařík, the Czech František Palacký, the Pole Joachim Lelewel and the Ukrainians Mykola Kostomarov and Panteleimon Kulish. Even forgeries were undertaken in the hasty pursuit of still more proofs of the Slavs' splendid past: the Czech Václav Hanka's *Královédvorský rukopis* [Manuscript of Dvůr Králové (Königinhof)] (1817) and *Zelenohorský rukopis* [Manuscript of Zelená Hora (Grünberg)] (1819), Izmail Sreznevsky's *Zaporozhskaia starina* [Zaporozhian antiquity] (1833-8) and perhaps even the celebrated *Slovo o polku Ihorevi* [Tale of Ihor's campaign] (1800).[3] Still, it was precisely works such as these—the products of those times and intellectual currents—that passed among contemporaries for monuments of antiquity and proofs of a magnificent culture. They played an enormous role in raising the national consciousness of all Slavs, and they became sources of poetic inspiration and intense effort in the national arena.

In addition to historicism, the cult of folk culture was characteristic of Romanticism. In the 1770s it found its greatest advocate in the German Johann Gottfried Herder, who emphasized the great value of folklore for national culture. In *Ideen zur Philosophie der Geschichte der Menschheit* (1784-91), Herder praised the Slavs as peaceful agriculturalists, lacking a quarrelsome nature, and he predicted that they would play a significant role in the future.[4] For this reason, his *Philosophy of History* contributed much to the formation of national concepts, especially among the Czech awakeners, Polish messianists and Russian Slavophiles. The Slavs had been interested in oral folk tradition since the Renaissance and Baroque periods, but Herder's influence was especially strong.[5] For most Slavic nations, oral folk literature was simultaneously a foundation for the national literary language and the national literature, and a specific cause for pride. As Ján Kollár's aphorism put it, "You foreigners claim that our people lack a culture. You sing to your people, but our people sing to us in a chorus."[6]

Almost everywhere, however, the issues of introducing the folk idiom into literature and recognizing it as the basis for the literary language caused bitter confrontations and disputes. Among the Galician Ukrainians, these disputes began in 1834 and continued for decades. The modern Slovak literary language arose thanks to the group associated with L'udovít Štúr, but only after the failure of the language formulated by Anton Bernolák (the so-called *bernoláčina*). Vuk S. Karadžić waged a campaign against the conservative Serbian Orthodox clergy,[7] and France Prešeren and Matija Čop a similar struggle in Slovenia,[8] in order to achieve acceptance for their vernaculars.

Although folk creativity evokes for us primarily the customs, beliefs and spirit of the rural populace, the Romantic Slavic enthusiasts saw it as very valuable source material. They maintained that the essential features of Slavic antiquity were reflected in the folk tradition, and therefore could be studied and identified. They imagined that folk expressions were unchanging, and accordingly that events preserved in folk songs referring to the nation's earliest history had been passed on perfectly accurately. For the "researchers" of that time, folklore was also the "shrine of the nationality," in which the national spirit was clearly mirrored. Thus the best minds in the Slavic world busied themselves with the collection, editing and publication of folk songs.

The ideas of the French Revolution, brought to Slavic soil during the Napoleonic Wars, also played a great role in the formation of a modern national consciousness. The gains of the bourgeoisie—personal freedom and equality before the law—contributed markedly to the increased mobility of the populace. Universal military service became in large measure an education in citizenship, patriotism and nationhood. For the South Slavs in particular, the creation of the Napoleonic Illyrian provinces, where between 1809 and 1813 a series of social and economic reforms was carried out, was highly significant. In this manner external forces complemented and accelerated internal changes.

Nevertheless, although the national awakenings among the various Slavic peoples had many similarities, noticeable differences were apparent owing to varying levels of economic development and diverse social structures. To a substantial degree these variations resulted from the differing political conditions in which the individual Slavic nations found themselves. Only Montenegro and Serbia, which had their own states at the beginning of the nineteenth century, could exert some political influence on the remaining South Slavs. No other Slavic nation except the Russians possessed statehood. The Slovenes, the Croats and those Serbs in lands under the Hungarian crown belonged to the Habsburg state, as did the Czechs, Slovaks, Galician Poles and those Ukrainians who lived in Eastern Galicia, Bukovyna and Transcarpathian (Hungarian) Rus'. However, the majority of the Ukrainians inhabited the compact territory that was part of tsarist Russia and known then as "Little Russia."

The Slavs of East Central Europe also adhered to a variety of religions. The Ukrainians in Russia and in much of Bukovyna were Orthodox, while the remaining Ukrainians in Bukovyna, as well as in Galicia and Hungary, belonged to the Greek Catholic (formerly

"Uniate" under Polish rule) rite. The Poles, Croats, and Slovenes were Roman Catholics; the Serbs and Montenegrins were Orthodox, and a part of the Bosnians (Serbs and Croats) were Moslem. The Czechs practiced both Catholicism and Protestantism, while the Slovaks were predominantly Catholic.[9]

Not all the Slavic nations had similar historical traditions. Some, such as the Czechs, Serbs, Bulgarians, Croats and Ukrainians (if one regards Kievan Rus' or the Principality of Halych and Volodymyr as Ukrainian states) had lost their statehood centuries before, whereas others, such as the Poles, had lost their independence only recently. And some Slavs, like the Slovaks, Belorussians and Lusatian Sorbs, had never had their own states.

From these observations it is evident that foreign powers and nations not only wielded political sovereignty, but also held social hegemony over virtually all the Slavic nationalities. This situation was the consequence of a centuries-old process, partly of assimilation and partly of repressive policies toward subject peoples. National oppression was closely linked to social oppression. In these conditions, national liberation of the majority of the Slavic nations was equivalent to social liberation. A Slavic nobility barely existed, and the national struggle had to be conducted almost exclusively by the lower, oppressed classes. At the beginning of the nineteenth century, the Czech nobility was largely germanized and, since the time of the Czech defeat at the Battle of White Mountain in 1620, not particularly numerous. The Galician Ukrainians, Slovaks, Slovenes and Serbs did not have a native nobility. (Several landholding families in Slovakia or a few Serbian feudal lords in the Vojvodina did not constitute a class.) Where the middle class of the nation was particularly weak, as was true among most of the Slavic nations, the national movements had to involve chiefly the peasantry and the intelligentsia. The latter group, which took the lead in articulating the national aspirations, was mainly of peasant descent and consequently close to the people in status, language and faith.

The national intelligentsia was composed primarily of village teachers, clergymen who were assigned to village parishes and some lesser governmental officials. The village clergy exerted substantial influence, particularly the Greek Catholic priests among the Ukrainians in Galicia and Transcarpathian Rus'; the Orthodox priests in the Principality of Serbia, Vojvodina, in the military cordon along the border with the Ottoman Empire (*Militärgrenze*) and among the Ukrainians in Bukovyna; and the Protestant pastors in Bohemia, Moravia and Slovakia. The clergymen, during their theological studies, came into contact with the remnants of the old national literatures, and they often preserved national relics in their parishes. Besides, given the catastrophic state of education in the countryside, clergymen were the villagers' only advisors and guides. Patriotic and at the same time conservative in their social and political views, clergymen thought that they alone could decide the destiny of the faithful.

A somewhat different situation existed in Serbian-inhabited Vojvodina, which was part of the Hungarian kingdom. Its advantageous geographic position and fertile soil significantly affected commerce and crafts and brought about a more rapid economic development than elsewhere. The rise of a prosperous commercial middle class heightened national consciousness among the Vojvodinian Serbs, and many young intellectuals came from this class. They held more revolutionary views and stood at the head of the struggle for the Serbs' national rights.[10]

With so many potential nation-states in East Central Europe, it was inevitable that conflicts among the nationalities and even violent social clashes would erupt sooner or later. In Bohemia, for example, the ruling class was the German and germanized Czech nobility; in the towns the German bourgeoisie was strong, and the state apparatus was in German hands. The Polish nobility held a similar position in Galicia, as did the completely polonized descendants of the old boyar families and the Ruthenian nobility. The Galician townspeople were primarily Poles, Germans and Jews. In Russian Ukraine, the Russian and Polish nobility, together with the russified or polonized former Ukrainian nobility, were the major social force. In Bukovyna it was the Romanian boyars, and in Transcarpathian Rus' it was the Magyar nobility. Needless to say, these dominant classes were, if not outright hostile, at best completely indifferent to the indigenous national movements. The national struggle thus was waged not only between oppressed and oppressing nations, but above all between the social classes of these nations. The Hungarian nobles, for example, fought for their own national liberties, but refused to meet similar demands from the other nations that composed the Crown of Saint Stephen. They saw the national aspirations of the Slavs as manifestations of particularistic separatism and their national struggles as counter-revolutionary actions designed to support the Austrian authorities. The Poles in Galicia responded similarly toward the Ukrainians. The Polish nobility and urban intelligentsia sought to reconstruct the Polish state according to the boundaries of 1772, refusing to recognize the Ukrainians' national separateness and even denying their right to their own literature in Ukrainian, which the Poles regarded as simply a dialect of Polish.

For the same reasons, the Poles were opposed to Ján Kollár's notion of Slavic reciprocity, which was in fact directed, notwithstanding the author's disclaimers, against germanization and was to be the platform of a common struggle by the Slavic nations for their rights. Kollár's original concept—that Slavic reciprocity was to be achieved in the realm of culture—did not have a political thrust, a fact which hampered its acceptance among those Slavs whose national aspirations had already gone beyond what Kollár demanded. With time, even the leaders of such smaller Slavic nations as the Slovaks and the Slovenes came to oppose Kollár's Slavism because his programme had no place for their languages and literatures; they were to subordinate themselves to their larger Slavic neighbours. Kollár recognized as literary languages only four Slavic language groups: Russian, Polish, Czech and Illyrian (Serbo-Croatian). In the future Slavic community, the right to self-determined and independent existence would belong only to Slavs who used those languages. The other, "lesser" Slavic tongues were to dissolve into them: the Slovaks were to join with the Czechs, the Slovenes with the Illyrians and the Ukrainians with the Russians. Kollár's views derived in large measure from contemporary linguistic research. The Czech linguist Josef Dobrovský also opposed excessive fragmentation of the Slavic dialects, as did Pavel Šafařík in the early stages of his academic work.

The origins of the national movements in the Austrian empire date from the second half of the eighteenth century. The imperial policy of germanization, which aimed at creating a centralized state and obliterating the national differences, raised the national consciousness of the Magyar nobility, which not only stood resolutely against Vienna's attempts to introduce German in place of Latin, but also began to demand equal rights for Hungarian. In turn, the nationalities that had hitherto supported the Hungarians' resistance to the imperial policies now categorically opposed efforts to introduce Hungarian into the schools and civil administration. This sharply defined language conflict accompanied the rise of national consciousness among the Slavs in Hungary. An analogous process occurred at the end of the eighteenth century in Bohemia and Moravia and, at the beginning of the nineteenth, among the Serbs, Slovenes and Ukrainians. This first phase of the national awakening, however, did not go much beyond matters of ethnography, literature and language.

The Slavs' growing interest in their own history also was related to the disputes over language, despite the fact that the early historians lacked appropriate models and did not write in their national languages, but rather in Old Serbian, German or Latin. However, what was important was that these researchers took a critical approach, attempting to determine historical truth on the basis of a thorough use of sources. Some, like Gelasius Dobner and his student Mikuláš

Adaukt Voigt in Bohemia, published critical editions of the sources, thereby establishing a basis for subsequent research. Others—for example, František Martin Pelcl in Bohemia, Anton Linhart in Slovenia and Jovan Rajić in Serbia—wrote historical syntheses. The title of Pelcl's *Kurzgefasste Geschichte der Böhmen*, first published in 1774, indicated the new trends in historiography, in which the real subject was the nation, not a certain geographical-historical area. Linhart's *Versuch einer Geschichte von Krain und den übrigen südlichen Slaven Österreichs* (1791) and Rajić's *Istoriia raznykh slavenskikh narodov* [History of the various Slavic nations] (1794-5) provided at least a hazy forecast of later concepts aimed at resolving the Slavic question in the Austrian monarchy: Linhart's work presented the rudiments of Austro-Slavism and Rajić's the idea of South Slavic unity. But the interest in history turned the academicians' attention primarily to that feature which most clearly characterized and distinguished individual nations, namely, the national languages. Their allure and richness were discovered in the speech of the common people; examples of folk and regional idiom were collected and published. These efforts contributed to the development of comparative Slavic linguistics, in which the Czech Josef Dobrovský, the Slovene Jernej Kopitar, the Russian Aleksandr Vostokov and Pavel Šafařík excelled. Their research led to the preparation of grammars for the individual Slavic languages, which appeared with increasing frequency in the early decades of the nineteenth century.

There were lengthy disputes whether the folk idiom could furnish the basis of the literary language. Though some held that it could, others insisted that the literary language must represent a compromise between the common speech and the language of earlier texts. In practice, the former view prevailed. Among the South Slavs its adherents were Kopitar, Karadžić, the Croat Ljudevit Gaj and the Serb Dositej Obradović; Ivan Kotliarevsky, Taras Shevchenko and members of the Ruthenian Triad employed the ordinary vernacular successfully in Ukrainian literature, and Iosyf Lozynsky was a fervent exponent of it. Adherents to the second concept—the so-called middle style—were Dobrovský and the Ukrainian Iosyf Levytsky.[11] A large number of dictionaries supplemented the work of codifying the Slavic languages. The first was Samuel Bogumil Linde's *Słownik języka polskiego* [Dictionary of the Polish language] (1807-14), upon which Karadžić modelled his *Srpski rječnik* [Serbian dictionary] (1818) and Josef Jungmann his *Slovník českoněmecký* [Czech-German dictionary] (1835-9).

The Slavic national movements also produced their own journals and organizations designed to support scholarship and culture, to stimulate education and national consciousness by expanding the school system, and to campaign against the central government's germanization policy. The first Slavic journals and newspapers in the Habsburg monarchy appeared in the late eighteenth century, but their number increased significantly in the 1830s and 1840s. On the eve of 1848, only the Ukrainians in Galicia and the Lusatian Sorbs lacked their own journals, although these groups often used the columns of Polish, Czech, Russian and German papers. The bi-weekly *Dennitsa-Jutrzenka* [Morning star], published in Russian and Polish in 1842 and 1843 in Warsaw by the Russian Petr Dubrovsky, and the journal *Jahrbücher für slawische Literatur, Kunst und Wissenschaft*, edited by the Lusatian Jan Petr Jordan and published in Leipzig from 1843, played a significant role in the propagation of Slavic concerns.

The cultural and learned societies that derived their name from the Serbian word *matica* [queen bee, home, source] were as important as the press. The Matica Srpska, established in 1826 by the Serbs in Hungary, was the first; later the Czech Matice Česká (1831), the Croatian Matica Ilirska (1839), the Lusatian Matica Serbska (in Bautzen in 1847), the Ukrainian Halytsko-Ruska Matytsia (1848) and the Slovene Matica Slovenska (in Ljubljana in 1864) were formed. Other noteworthy Slavic national institutions were the Czech Museum (from 1818) and the Learned Society in Belgrade (from 1840). The developing Slavic national movements, although initially they did not display a strongly political orientation, nevertheless forced the governments to take a stance toward the various national conflicts that were developing. In response, the Austrian government began fully to apply its policy of *divide et impera*, which pitted nation against nation and used every means possible to preserve its authority. The events of 1848 provided a glaring example of its practice.

A political component gradually emerged in the national movements, although before 1848 it had no chance of success. Croatian Prince Janko Drašković's plan of 1832 contained concrete political features regarding the unification of those South Slavic lands that were in Austrian hands. His ideas were a harbinger of the Greater Croatia programme that Gaj proposed in his journal *Danica* [Morning star] in 1836, which would have joined all the South Slavs, even the Bulgarians. This programme was opposed by the Serbs, who, having formed a state since 1815, regarded themselves as most entitled to decide the fate of their kindred. Serbian governmental circles therefore advanced their own proposals. One of them was Ilija Garašanin's *Načertanije* [Instructions] of 1844, which were drafted under the influence of the Polish émigré leader Prince Adam Czartoryski. His work expressed a Serbian policy of drawing all the Serbs together around the Principality of Serbia. Another plan was Matija Ban's *Osnovi politični Jugoslavena* [The political foundations of South Slavia] (1848), published by young Serbian enthusiasts who were supported by Garašanin. The very title of Ban's work suggested the Serbs' future political activities.[12]

On the other hand, whereas the Serbian schemes aimed to create an independent South Slavic state, the Illyrian (Croatian) programme sought to establish an autonomous country of Illyria within the framework of the Austrian monarchy. In this respect it was a forerunner of Austro-Slavic political concepts. The origins of Austro-Slavism can be traced to Kopitar's theory about the Pannonian heritage of the Old Church Slavonic language;[13] however, the actual theoretician and creator of political Austro-Slavism was the Bohemian aristocrat Count Leo Thun, who believed that the Slavs should be satisfied with gaining cultural autonomy within Austria. Moreover, they could not expect anything more: Austria's Slavs would gain nothing by looking to Russia for aid before radical political changes had taken place there. The thesis that the Slavs' future could be guaranteed only by the existence of a multinational Austrian state ultimately found expression in František Palacký's open letter to the organizers of the German parliament in Frankfurt on 11 April 1848: "Assuredly, if the Austrian State had not existed for ages, it would have been a behest for us in the interests of Europe and indeed of humanity to endeavour to create it as soon as possible."[14] Thanks especially to the influence of such Czechs as Karel Havlíček-Borovský and Karel Zap, the Ukrainians in Galicia became adherents of Austro-Slavism after 1846. As we shall see, this programme linked the Austrian Slavs in common action against the revolutionary activities of the Poles and the Hungarians during the revolutionary upheaval of 1848 and 1849. The most revolutionary programme of the time, however, was the messianic vision of the Brotherhood of Saints Cyril and Methodius (1846-7) in Ukraine, which aspired to establish a democratic federation of seven Slavic nations.[15]

All of these unrealistic schemes grew from their creators' conviction that the Slavic nations could mount a genuine mutual opposition to the systematic pressure exerted by external foes, especially the Germans and Hungarians. Kollár's ideas, the Illyrian movement, Austro-Slavism, Polish Slavism and even Russian Pan-Slavism shared this foundation; substantive differences are apparent only on specific questions. The South Slavic ideology saw its greatest enemy in the Magyars; the Poles were resolute foes of both the Germans and the Russians, and the Russian Pan-Slavist Mikhail Pogodin believed that the future of the Slavs lay in unconditional subordination to Russia, without regard to contemporary Russian social and political conditions.

The facts cited in this chapter show irrefutably that by the 1840s almost all the Slavic national movements were transforming themselves into typically political movements. This change demonstrated emphatically that the Serbs, Croats, Slovenes, Czechs, Ukrainians and Slovaks were becoming nations in the modern sense of the word.

2. The Galician Ukrainians under Austrian Rule, 1772-1830

The first partition of Poland in 1772 was a milestone in the history of both the Polish and the Ukrainian nations. The partitioning of Polish lands was simultaneously a further division of Ukrainian lands. Up to that time all of Ukraine belonged to Russia, Poland, Turkey and Hungary; now Austria annexed the Ukrainian lands between the San and Zbruch rivers. Thus, a new contestant entered the battle for domination over the Ukrainian nation. However, Austria did not add still more Ukrainian territories in the subsequent partitions of Poland. Instead, the entire area from the Zbruch eastward became a possession of tsarist Russia after 1795. For more than 120 years afterwards, Ukraine was divided between Austria and Russia (Austria obtained Bukovyna from Turkey in 1775), and this situation had serious consequences for the Ukrainian nation. The division contributed in large measure to retarding national revival and the formation of a modern national consciousness among Ukrainians. All of Russian Ukraine in the nineteenth century remained subject to the same form of government, but the Ukrainian lands in the Habsburg monarchy were variously administered. Transcarpathian Rus' belonged to the lands of the Hungarian kingdom; Bukovyna constituted a distinct administrative entity from 1775 to 1786, when it was joined to Galicia, and after 1849 it formed a separate province. The remaining Ukrainian lands were joined with the other Polish territories that Austria took in the first partition to form the so-called Kingdom of Galicia and Lodomeria, or simply Galicia. Politically and legally, Galicia unquestionably comprised a territorial whole. Ethnically, however, the western part clearly differed from the eastern. Poles inhabited the area from the Biała to the San rivers, known as Western Galicia, whereas Ukrainians predominated in Eastern Galicia.

The new political relationships had serious socio-economic and national consequences. In Galicia the ruling class was the Polish *szlachta* (nobility). In Bukovyna, it was Romanian boyars, and in Transcarpathian Rus' it was the Hungarian nobles. Indeed, in this respect nothing had changed; social oppression was still intertwined with national oppression. However, a new force had risen over these existing taskmasters: the Austrian bureaucracy, which represented the centralizing and germanizing tendencies of Viennese "enlightened" absolutism.

One result of the political changes was that the economic situation of the Ukrainian lands that became part of Austria, in particular Galicia, significantly worsened. Commercial trade between Galicia and the remaining Polish lands halted abruptly, and the domestic market was destroyed. Western Galicia, which until partition was linked by strong economic ties to the lower Vistula basin, and Eastern Galicia, similarly joined to the remaining Ukrainian lands in the former Polish Commonwealth, were forcibly incorporated in the Austrian sphere, with which previously they had had no connection. Now they had to merge economically with the Danubian basin. Galicia, which was already worse off than other Austrian areas at the time of partition, had little opportunity to improve. Galician manufactured goods, inferior to Austria's, could not conquer the markets in the empire. On the other hand, German products too easily found buyers in Galicia. Galicia's domestic market had a limited capacity to absorb goods, which had in time to lead to economic regression. The development of capitalistic relations came to a standstill; the towns declined, and the small bourgeois element could not become a powerful force in the economic and socio-political life of this new Austrian province. Instead, the dominant influence in Galician life until the revolution of 1848 remained the feudal system of obligatory peasant labour.

The exact ethnic composition of Galicia before 1849 is difficult to determine because the sources available record religion and not nationality. Furthermore, although the figures for Galicia as a whole are quite reliable, the records for Eastern Galicia alone are very incomplete. The existing data indicate that the population of Galicia together with Bukovyna rose from approximately 3,893,000 in 1820 to about 4,980,000 in 1843. The increase was fairly steady during these years, except for 1831, which showed the impact of the cholera epidemic. Approximately 65 per cent of the population inhabited the province's twelve easternmost districts, or Eastern Galicia.[1] The Galician population in 1849 was officially set at 5,290,974. It may be assumed that generally the Poles were Roman Catholic, the Ukrainians Greek Catholic and the Germans predominantly Protestant, although it must be remembered that religious affiliation did not precisely coincide with nationality. Therefore, of the 4,920,000 inhabitants of Galicia (excluding Bukovyna) in 1849, 2,258,500 (45.9 per cent) were Poles; 2,303,000 (46.8 per cent) were Ukrainians; 328,000 (6.7 per cent) were Jews; 27,000 (0.55 per cent) were Germans, and the remaining 3,000 belonged to other nationalities.[2]

The Ukrainians, who were called and referred to themselves at that time as Ruthenians (Ukrainian *Rusyny*; Polish *Rusini*; German *Ruthenen*), comprised the largest national group in the twelve eastern Galician districts. Of a total of 3,113,320 inhabitants, 71 per cent were Ukrainians; 20.4 per cent were Poles; 7.9 per cent were Jews; 0.6 per cent were Germans, and 0.1 per cent undetermined.[3] The words of a leading Ukrainian spokesman, Iakiv Holovatsky, reveal just how accurately religion reflected nationality at that time:

> A person in Galicia usually calls himself a Ruthenian only if he professes Greek Catholicism; as soon as he changes his faith to the Latin rite, which often happens now, he ceases to be a Ruthenian and is called a Pole.[4]

Holovatsky clearly pointed to the continuing polonization of the Ukrainians in Eastern Galicia, a process that had been going on since the fourteenth century. The Ukrainian boyars, in desiring to ensure for themselves the same privileges that the Polish *szlachta* held in the old Polish-Lithuanian Commonwealth, succumbed almost totally. They adopted the Polish language, Polish customs and Roman Catholicism. Because they thus became indistinguishable from the Polish upper strata, the social structure of the Ukrainian nation was transformed: it became in the main a nation of peasants. A nobleman, a land-owner—in general, a lord (*pan*)—became for the Ruthenian peasant someone nationally alien; he became a *Liakh*—a Pole—and the Ruthenian always associated national oppression with social exploitation, with the bondage of obligatory toil and humiliation. Holovatsky, writing in the 1840s, described the denationalized boyars:

> Having lost everything that constitutes nationality, they had nothing that could tie them to their compatriots. The sacred bonds of fatherland no longer bound them, because for them Poland was their fatherland, to which they

offered everything for their own advantages and freedoms, but to the detriment of the entire [Ukrainian] nation; the [Ukrainian] national literature no longer bound them; it was degraded, not aided or supported by anyone, and was limited to only clerical writers. Neither the native language, which was denied its original dignity and was displaced from schools and [administrative] offices by foreign dialects, nor the native laws bound them any more, for they had been transformed into Polish [laws]. Only the faith still maintained [our] collapsing nationality, but in time all these things overwhelmed the final remnants of [our] nationality. For such a man it only remained to change his faith. And then he immediately denied his entire nationality and became the most fervent *Liakh* and the fiercest persecutor of his [former] compatriots, who in turn renounced all of these renegades.[5]

One exception, among others, was the déclassé nobility of the Sambir district, which, though Polish in consciousness, differed from the Poles by keeping the Greek Catholic faith. They comprised the so-called group of *gente Rutheni, natione Poloni.*[6]

The peasants comprised the overwhelming mass of the Ukrainian community. They were also the only Ukrainian social class in Galicia that had retained its national distinctiveness. A separate language, separate customs and the Greek Catholic rite determined whether one was a Ukrainian. However, the consciousness of one's own distinctiveness, especially in comparison to the *szlachta*—the Polish nobility—still did not constitute a national consciousness.[7] The peasant instinctively felt that he was a Ruthenian; he sang Ukrainian songs that spoke of a great Ukraine, a land where freedom and liberty prevailed. From these songs he also knew about the past struggles with the *Liakhy*. Still, without the systematic development of education, and especially without fundamental change in the Galician social and economic structure, it was impossible for peasants to be nationally conscious as Ukrainians or, for that matter, in Western Galicia as Poles. To be sure, some "Polish" peasants also lived in Eastern Galicia, but in small numbers, and they had settled on these lands long ago. They constituted small islands among the Ukrainian rural populace, and often they differed from them only in their clinging to the Latin rite, since they had forgotten long ago how to speak Polish.[8]

What was the situation of the common people in Eastern Galicia, and how had it changed since Austria had assumed rule?[9] Contemporary accounts of peasant life are unanimous in their descriptions of catastrophic conditions. Travelling in the Eastern Galician countryside in 1842, the Czech Karel Zap saw the village of Demyche:

The low, crooked cottages are fashioned from sticks and clay, but cleanly whitewashed every Saturday; [they have] small angled windows [and] low entrances, [but are] without chimneys and covered only with corn stalks and leaves. Beside them all around are stables and pigsties full of holes and in a sorry state; behind them are haystacks, animal pens and small orchards, and around the whole of it are willows and fences.[10]

A Russian officer who passed through Galicia during the period of the Napoleonic Wars was appalled by the life and the obscurantism of the rural populace, but another Russian, M. D. Likhutin, observing conditions there in 1849, wrote, in comparing Galicia to the Volhynian countryside in the Russian empire, that "the huts in villages are ample, clean, all whitewashed; the villagers are dressed more cleanly and are apparently better off than ours."[11]

From the time of the Austrian emperor Joseph II, the subjugated peasants were obliged to labour on the manorial lands three days per week, or 156 days per year. Within the Habsburg monarchy this modified form of serfdom was termed *robot* (*panshchyna* in Ukrainian, *pańszczyzna* in Polish). Cottagers and tenant farmers performed only twelve days of *robot* per year. In practice, however, more compulsory labour was exacted; on certain estates it reached as many as six days per week. For example, in the Stanyslaviv district in 1847, *robot* was 60 per cent greater than in the 1770s. The total value of the peasants' burdens in Eastern Galicia in the form of *robot* and in sundry levies has been estimated at over 2.3 million guldens annually.[12] In 1844, the so-called rustical lands that the peasants had for their own use (in contrast to the manorial possessions on which they performed *robot*) amounted to 70 per cent of the arable land, 68.5 per cent of the meadows, and 63.7 per cent of the pastures, but only 0.7 per cent of the forests, of which the noble landowners possessed 98 per cent. In general, the rustical possessions represented 48.9 per cent of the land, and the manors owned 47.1 per cent.[13] Nevertheless, the peasantry was severely disadvantaged. Not only did the amount of *robot* demanded by the manors increase, and stratification among rural homesteads occur, but between 1787 and 1847 the peasants in Eastern Galicia lost 257,211 morgs of land. During the same period the manors added 331,482 morgs to their holdings. In Western Galicia the peasants' losses and manorial gains were slightly less.[14]

The Ukrainian peasantry's resistance to its worsening condition did not take on the character of an armed jacquerie such as occurred in Western Galicia in 1846, but it was evidence of the pressing need for change in rural conditions, especially in relations between the manor and the village. The peasants' struggle was characterized by spontaneous rather than organized actions and by a kind of naïve monarchism. They believed in the myth of a benevolent emperor whose sympathies were with the serfs, but whose good intentions were thwarted by the lords and governmental officials. This understanding of their situation was characteristic of almost all popular outbreaks during the feudal era. In Galicia this attitude was reinforced by the measures Emperor Joseph II instituted. His agrarian reforms could have had an entirely different outcome were it not for their partial renunciation during the reign of his successors. The Josephinian reforms were certainly not revolutionary; nonetheless, they aimed at significant social and economic changes. Personal serfdom (*Leibeigenschaft* in German, *poddaństwo* in Polish) was abolished, permitting landless peasants to abandon their villages. (Those peasants who possessed land henceforth were obliged to leave a successor.) Serfs no longer needed the manorial lord's approval in order to marry, and it became possible for peasants to have their children trained in a trade. Most importantly, it was stipulated that the peasants' rustical lands could not be annexed to the manorial lands. Manorial jurisdiction (which function would henceforth be performed by a so-called *justiziarius*, or *justycjariusz* in Polish) was made separate from the administration of the manor and its associated villages (now placed in the hands of a *mandatarius* [Pol. *mandatariusz*]). The increase of *robot* was forbidden. The more affluent peasants benefited most, because their obligatory labour had tended to be greater. By regulating *robot*, the Austrian government gained the permanent support of the so-called middling strata in the countryside.

The most potentially far-reaching of the Josephinian reforms was the tax and urbarial regulation of 1789, which, based on the notions of the physiocrats, aimed at eventually abolishing *robot* and levies in kind. In exchange, it stipulated the introduction of monetary payments, amounting to approximately 30 per cent of what the peasant produced. This plan provoked strong opposition by the noble land-owners and, given the feeble growth of the exchange of goods for money in Galicia, did not gain many adherents even among the peasants. Indeed, the reform was quickly repealed after the death of Joseph II. Still, the reforms meant that peasants could now appeal directly to governmental authorities in disputes between the village and the manor. The enormous number of peasant complaints that was reviewed up to the end of the eighteenth century by the *Kreise* (district administrative offices), the *Gubernium* (office of the imperial governor) in Lviv, and even the court chancellery in Vienna were telling evidence of the peasants' grievances. By allowing the peasants legal remedies in their struggle with the manors, the government also acquired stricter control over their actions. It is difficult to say precisely what effect the changes had on the Ukrainian peasants' consciousness, but as Ivan L. Rudnytsky has written, "All in all, Maria Theresa and Joseph II's peasant reforms did much to turn the Ukrainian masses in Galicia into loyal supporters of the Habsburg dynasty until the end of the monarchy."[15]

One must concede that the Austrian government exploited superbly the antagonism between the village and the manor in Galicia, even though the aim of the reforms was not to set the peasant against his lord, but to strengthen the peasant social class upon which the power of the centralized and bureaucratic state and the strength of the dynasty rested. The Viennese court, acting on the humanitarian tenets of the Enlightenment, came forward to defend its serfs; however, the manorial administrators—the *justiziarii* and *mandatarii*, the lowest chain in the state administration—exerted all of the direct pressures on the peasantry. The manor was charged with collecting state taxes, providing a suitable number of recruits for the army and resolving rural disputes. (The *justiziarii* were usually biased, since they were maintained from the manor.) Thus the myth grew of the benevolent emperor who was ensnared by the lords, and despite the apparent half-heartedness of the reforms, the peasants' sympathies remained with the government. On more than one occasion (in 1809 and 1846, for example) the Austrian bureaucracy cleverly turned this attitude to its own advantage.

The Josephinian agrarian reforms and the peasants' resulting loyalty to the Austrian authorities significantly influenced the social conflict in the Galician countryside. The reforms guided the struggle toward a legal and formal course, which undoubtedly was the purpose of Viennese policy. Though blood was occasionally spilt, the usual cause was the manors' use of army detachments to force resisting peasants to carry out their obligations. The most evident form of the social struggle was the legally sanctioned litigation between the village and the manor, which sometimes dragged on for years at the local, district, provincial and state levels of adjudication. These cases were so common that in all of Eastern Galicia there was scarcely a single village that did not take its noble landowner to court. As a consequence, a spirit of common purpose among the villages was born.[16] To be sure, these cases were not always resolved to the peasants' satisfaction.

Another expression of the peasants' struggle before 1848 was internal migration and flight beyond Galicia, particularly to Bukovyna, where until 1830 military service was not obligatory and *robot* was less severe, or to Ukraine under tsarist rule.[17] Some peasants also fled to Galicia from the lands that belonged to Russia—Podillia, Volhynia or the farther reaches of Ukraine. However, there were few of them, and one cannot ascribe any great significance to them in the formation of the Ukrainian peasantry's national consciousness.[18] Their influence seems to have been that the Galician peasants learned from the fugitives about conditions in Russia, which helped create the Galicians' averse attitude toward tsarist Russia. This hostility was underscored both by agents of the tsarist police in the Third Department of His Imperial Majesty's Chancellery and by officers of the Russian armies stationed in Galicia during the later Russian intervention in Hungary in 1849.[19]

Other forms of peasant resistance included performing various acts of sabotage, refusing to fulfill the feudal obligations, balking at additional tasks and falling into arrears with taxes and rents. These actions led to numerous disturbances, which usually ended in clashes with the manorial administration and not infrequently in military intervention at the land-owners' request. The more notable peasant disorders of this nature occurred in the districts of Zhovkva (1802), Ternopil (1803, 1838), Sambir (1819, 1833), Chortkiv (1809, 1838) and Stryi (1842). Those in the Chortkiv district in 1838, in particular, assumed serious proportions when the peasants of more than thirty villages refused to comply with *robot*. The Austrian authorities, however, quickly gained control by exploiting the peasants' naïve monarchist illusions.[20]

Mention should also be made of the "brigands" in the countryside. To judge their activities is not a simple matter since their motives were mixed. Ordinary bandits existed alongside those protesting feudal conditions.[21] Certainly, contemporaries understood that by the 1830s and 1840s the majority of the brigands consisted of army deserters and robbers who plundered the peaceful Hutsuls herding their sheep in the eastern Carpathian mountains more often than they attacked the land-owners' estates.[22] Nevertheless, the folk songs and legends about the brigands Dovbush, Marusiak and Janosik emphasized the help they gave to the poor common people.

The Ukrainian peasants in Eastern Galicia did not participate to any significant extent in the turmoil of 1846. The slaughter of the Polish nobles and insurrectionaries was carried out largely by Roman Catholic peasants in Western Galicia. It is true that in the Stryi district a proclamation in Ukrainian was distributed, urging the peasants to cease performing *robot* and to take action against the lords and Austrian bureaucrats. However, except for an armed clash with the Polish insurrectionaries in Horozhanna (Sambir district) and demonstrations in Naraiv (Berezhany district), there were no serious confrontations involving the Ukrainian peasants, whose pacific behaviour was favourably appraised by such contemporary Ukrainians as

Iakiv Holovatsky, who saw it as a manifestation of his people's positive features.[23]

Austrian social policy, which sought to limit the land-owners' power without actually endangering the institution of *robot*, was aided by other forces that helped to maintain the peasants' already rooted loyalty. The clergy played an enormous role in this respect.[24] The Austrians quickly recognized that they could take advantage of the fact that Galicia was a nationally diverse land. The nationality issue was linked to Austria's church policy, which aimed at subordinating the church hierarchy to the state and transforming clergymen into state officials. This policy necessarily fostered equal rights for all the Christian faiths within the Austrian monarchy; it therefore strengthened the Ruthenian clergy. Until the partition of Poland, the Greek Catholic clerics, dispersed among more than three thousand impoverished parishes, were virtually indistinguishable from the peasants, and, despite existing regulations that exempted clerics from *robot*, Greek Catholic priests not infrequently were forced to fulfil serf obligations. Moreover, the priests were barely able to read the liturgical books in Church Slavonic. Only the policies of Maria Theresa and then Joseph II created the conditions necessary for leaders of the Ukrainian national movement in Galicia to evolve from the clergy. As a consequence, for many years the social and political character of the Ukrainian movement was marked notably by conservatism and Austrophilism. The Ruthenian clergy lived much closer to the common people than Roman Catholic priests and enjoyed considerable respect among them. As Iakiv Holovatsky clearly put it:

> The Ruthenian cleric, inseparable from his faithful, is with them in their every need with aid and advice. Whether it is a birth or a funeral, the priest is in their hut with his blessing. He does not spurn the meagre meal that the peasant provides. In a word, he lives with the people like the people.[25]

In 1774, Empress Maria Theresa established in Vienna a seminary called the Barbareum for all Greek Catholic subjects of the monarchy. Joseph II subsequently established the first diocesan Ruthenian seminary, in Lviv in 1783, which in 1785 was transformed into a general seminary with the task of preparing candidates for the priesthood from Galicia, Hungary, Dalmatia and Transylvania. The language of instruction in both of these seminaries was so-called Ruthenian, that is, Old Church Slavonic. (It was usually called simply "Ruthenian" or "Slavo-Ruthenian.") In 1784 the Austrian government founded Lviv University, where lectures were given in this tongue. Thus, for the first time, the conditions were set for the development of the Ukrainian nationality in Galicia. A contemporary wrote: "The first day of November 1787 is and will be memorable in the national life of every Galician Ruthenian, because on this day [our] highest resolve was fulfilled: the lecturers in philosophy and theology spoke in the national Church Ruthenian language."[26] Nevertheless, this development did not ensue.

In fact, it was precisely the "national Church Ruthenian language" that acted as a brake upon the growth of Ukrainian literature and completely prevented Ukrainian publications, even though there were enlightened Ukrainian professors at Lviv University, and the printing office of the Stavropygian [Holy Cross Society] Institute was already in existence.[27] Contemporary educated Ukrainians lectured in the ossified Church Slavonic; they did not write in Ukrainian at all, and wrote very little in Polish. Instead, they sent their scholarly treatises to German journals. The later wars with revolutionary France also did not favour the development of a Ukrainian national consciousness.

The second institution that the state intended to use to influence Ukrainian society was the school system.[28] The state assumed that a peasant should be sufficiently educated to fulfill his obligations, to manage his affairs and to become a support for the authorities. Austrian policy worked at cross-purposes, however, because instruction was conducted in German and schooling was not universal. Only in the Czech schools were children taught in their native language; in the other Slavic territories, including Galicia, germanization was the most important component of Austrian policy in the pre-constitutional period.

Until 1849 there were three types of schools for the general populace in Galicia: parish schools, in which organists and cantors taught some reading and church hymns; trivium schools in towns and small cities, where the instruction was primarily in Polish; and the normal (four-year) schools, whose graduates had the right to enter the six-year gymnasium. In 1791 Ukrainian trivium schools were introduced in Eastern Galicia, but only where there were no similar Polish or German schools. However, in 1805 these schools were placed under the supervision of the Latin-rite consistories, and they consequently became to a certain degree instruments of polonization. The first two years of the normal school were called *Stube* (ground level), and instruction was in Polish, with special emphasis on acquiring a command of German. German was used exclusively in the third and fourth years, and the pupils were forbidden to use their native language, even in private conversations. These regulations were strictly enforced with the aid of the infamous *Sprachzeichen* method: a pupil who spoke in his native tongue had to learn a certain number of additional German words and wear a special placard, which he could remove only when he caught a classmate breaking the same rule. German also dominated in the gymnasium, and, beginning with the third year, Latin was used. Even in church the pupils were obliged to sing German songs, and it was not until 1834 that the Polish hymn "Królu Boże Abrahama" (Lord God of Abraham) was permitted.

In 1842 there were 1,458 parish schools in Eastern Galicia, of which 785 were in the Lviv diocese and 673 in the Przemyśl diocese. Instruction was in Polish and Slavo-Ruthenian. There were also 80 trivium schools (of which 60 were in the Przemyśl diocese) under the authority of the Greek Catholic consistories, in which instruction was conducted primarily in Polish or German.[29] However, only a very small portion of school-aged Ukrainian children actually attended any school. A directive of 1812, which abolished mandatory schooling in Galicia but not in other imperial provinces, worsened the situation. According to data gathered by Karel Zap, 73 per cent of the children in the Stanyslaviv district in 1839 received no formal instruction at all, and of the remaining 27 per cent, only a fourth regularly attended school. Matters were even worse in other areas of Galicia, where between 3.9 and 24.6 per cent of the children attended parish schools.[30] Moreover, this state of affairs existed at a time when official Ukrainian church circles were purportedly undertaking an energetic effort to improve popular schooling. After 1842, the Ukrainians also had one school for girls and two for cantors. Those who wished further education had to rely on the thirty-two normal schools and thirteen gymnasia in Eastern Galicia. Ukrainian priests were reluctant to send their sons to normal schools administered by Poles or Germans, although they readily made use of the Basilian school in Buchach. However, some Ukrainians did graduate from convent schools run by Piarists, Bernardines and even Jesuits.[31]

Lviv University was also germanized; the lectures in Slavo-Ruthenian mentioned above were given only in the philosophy and theology departments. Ultimately even this limited use generated dissatisfaction among the Ukrainians, who felt they were being wronged by not being lectured to in German like the Poles. By 1808, they had caused the government to eliminate Ruthenian from the university. Slavo-Ruthenian remained only at the Greek Catholic seminary in Lviv. At a later date, Ukrainian enthusiasts sought to explain the government's action as the result of pressure by the Poles. That was Iosyf Levytsky's opinion, expressed in the manuscript of his Ukrainian grammar, but Jernej Kopitar corrected him by pointing out that it was the Ukrainians themselves who had demanded the removal of the Ruthenian language, and Iakiv Holovatsky later confirmed the fact.[32] At that time the Austrian government had no reason to support the Polish element in Galicia, and so its decision can be explained partially by its desire to counter Russian influences. In any case, the Ukrainians had squandered a real opportunity for national development. For the next forty years, Ukrainians wrangled among themselves over the introduction of their native language into the schools and literary culture. Only the events of 1848 offered them a chance to regain their missed opportunity.

Initially, this struggle was barely noticeable, because a vehement polonization of the Ruthenian clergy occurred, and the Ukrainian language was displaced even from the deliberations of the Greek Catholic consistory. Church leaders believed that the vernacular was too coarse, and no Ukrainian clergyman was allowed to use his native language in official correspondence. He could not even issue vital certificates in that language without antagonizing the hierarchy.[33] It is not surprising, therefore, that many Greek Catholic priests did not know Ukrainian. There were instances of candidates for the priesthood, most often the offspring of village pastors, who not only could not read Ruthenian, but frequently did not even know the prayers in that language. How could such clerics teach the common people in their own language? From necessity, the clergy used Polish, which was generally understood by the Ukrainian peasants in Galicia. The result was that the Polish spirit spread among the Ukrainian intelligentsia together with the Polish language. This situation persisted until the 1830s.

The Ukrainians' ready resignation from the Ruthenian language at Lviv University is also proof that, at least until 1809, there was no awareness of a national problem in Galicia. All the Ukrainians' disputes with the Poles involved church matters; they were disputes between two religious rites, not two nationalities. Developments in 1809, when pro-Napoleonic Polish insurgents seized control of Lviv, fundamentally altered that situation. When the recently appointed Greek Catholic metropolitan to the Galician See Antin Anhelovych and his vicar-general Canon Mykhailo Harasevych (subsequently Baron de Neustern) refused to renounce their fealty to the Habsburg emperor and attempted flight, they were briefly imprisoned until Austrian troops regained control of Galicia; they then became fierce polonophobes and thereby significantly strengthened the forces favouring germanization.

That concessions were made under Habsburg rule for the Greek Catholic rite had both positive and negative repercussions. The Ukrainian clergy rose from its quasi-peasant status, gained greater authority within the society and eventually became the genuine leader of its own people. Concurrently, Austrian policy brought forth a Ukrainian intelligentsia from the peasantized clergy. As a later observer noted, the intelligentsia "became accustomed to see the force sustaining and ordering national life not in the nation, or in itself, but beyond the nation, in the government."[34] Mykhailo Harasevych perhaps best justified their attitude by maintaining that the Ruthenians fared much better under Austria than they had in the Poland ruled by the *szlachta*; everything they had, he wrote, came "from the favour of the most kindly Austrian government." It followed, therefore, that the Ruthenians were bound by a "steadfast loyalty, adherence and love for the most benevolent monarch." His words were symbolic of the political faith of the higher Greek Catholic clergy in Galicia in the first half of the nineteenth century.[35]

Political developments also tended to root monarchism more deeply among the Ukrainians. The examples of Anhelovych and Harasevych served to educate others in the spirit of loyalism. Vasyl Shchurat remarked that as early as 1813 the Ukrainian community "was inclined toward the elevated tone of Austrian patriotism and already deserved to be depicted as the 'Tyrolians of the East'."[36] Throughout Galicia Ukrainians organized celebrations of thanksgiving for the victory over Napoleon, the "enemy of the fatherland." The most pompous display was made by Ivan Lavrovsky, the rector of the Greek Catholic seminary in Lviv, but there was no lack of young people sharing in the enthusiasm. Austrophilism among Ukrainian youth in the Barbareum in Vienna began to manifest itself immediately after Napoleon occupied Vienna in 1809. It was fundamentally an expression of opposition to current plans to reconstruct Poland in its historical boundaries. A student from the Academic Gymnasium, the later professor at the gymnasium in Berezhany, Iosyf Biletsky, wrote a poem entitled "Triumfalnyi spiv Nimetchyny" [The triumphant song of Germany], dedicated to the victory by the coalition powers over Napoleon at Leipzig in 1813. Similar "patriotic" verses were written by Ivan Hromnytsky, Ivan Ostyslavsky and Roman Telykhovsky, all future Greek Catholic pastors.

After 1815, the Galician situation became more involved. The government granted permission for a Polish national-cultural foundation, the Ossolineum, which signalled the Poles' deepening interest in their own language, literature and past. Polish literary publications began to appear like mushrooms after a rain. Youthful Polish enthusiasts established a "society for educating youth in the native literature," with the aim of national regeneration through literary activity and self-education. Gradually two camps—one Polish and one German—began to form. In literary terms, on one side stood the admirers of the Polish poet Adam Mickiewicz, and on the other were grouped the admirers of Friedrich Schiller.[37] In time, the Polish camp began to manifest a longing for an independent Poland, but initially it tested its strength only in literature, professing that as the easiest way to serve the national cause.

The national accent in Polish literature was a reaction to germanization and pervasive German literary influence. The Polish writer Wincenty Pol stated that "it was not the Austrian government, not the German official, artisan or colonist who introduced and disseminated the German language in Galicia, but Kant and Schelling, Fichte and Schlegel, Goethe and Schiller."[38] These German influences seized persons in the Ukrainian community as well. The notions and slogans of liberty and nationalism flowed into Galicia together with German literature. However, the political indolence in which Galicia found itself in the Metternichian era did not favour the rapid formation of a Ukrainian national consciousness. The Polish journal *Rozmaitości* [Variety] carried articles from time to time on the national aspirations of the other Slavs, and some information filtered through the Austrian press, but only a few Ukrainian enthusiasts studying in Vienna made use of them. From this Ukrainian Viennese circle would emerge the first proponents and organizers of Ukrainian national life in Galicia: Bishop Ivan Snihursky, Canon Ivan Mohylnytsky, Rector Ivan Lavrovsky, Kyrylo Blonsky, Iosyf Levytsky and Iosyf Lozynsky.

In Galicia, the Poles and Ukrainians continued to live in harmony, despite differences of opinion (especially on matters of language), as long as there were no political goals among the Poles. Poles and Ukrainians alike accepted the preponderance of German influences, and the Ukrainian national movement was not distinct from the Polish movement. This state of affairs lasted from the Congress of Vienna in 1815 until November 1830, when the situation changed radically for both the Poles and the Ukrainians.

3. Polish Influences

Both the Polish and Ukrainian liberals in Galicia were particularly concerned with the abolition of *robot* and the emancipation of the peasants. However, the issue was especially complicated among the Poles because it was the Polish *szlachta* that exploited the Ukrainian populace, and this group was vitally interested in maintaining its power and possessions. Furthermore, any loss for the *szlachta* would be tantamount to diminishing the Poles' economic dominance in the province. And so, in the years preceding 1848, the issue of national liberation was closely tied to a resolution of the social question, especially since the powers that had partitioned Poland were opposed to any change in existing social and economic conditions. However, although the Poles clearly defined their aspiration for complete political independence, the Ukrainians before 1848 had no such programme and did not openly raise the question of regaining their own statehood. The hazy and unrealistic plans for a federation of the Slavic nations advanced by the Brotherhood of Saints Cyril and Methodius in Russian Ukraine and Mykola Kmytsykevych's vague scheme for a federated union of Poland and Ukraine were exceptions. A close tie between Ukraine and Russia likewise was not considered, or at least there is no mention of it in the Ukrainian programmes before 1848.[1]

Polish influences penetrated the Galician Ukrainian community in various ways. Polish belles-lettres played one role as the model for literary efforts by the younger generation of Ukrainians, whereas revolutionary agitation after 1831 constituted a quite different influence. Literature brought the two peoples closer, but the political activities achieved an end that the Poles had not intended. By seeking to subordinate the Ukrainian movement to their own revolutionary aspirations for national liberation, the Poles awakened and strengthened the Ukrainians' feeling of national separateness.

Polish cultural life in Lviv flourished in the 1820s and 1830s. The literary almanac *Pątnik Lwowski* [The Lviv pilgrim] appeared in 1827, and in 1830 Walenty Chłędowski published in two volumes the almanac *Haliczanin* [The Galician], which, according to a contemporary observer, was "a pillar demarcating the old and new periods in Galician literature" and "awakened our minds from a torpor."[2] The *Haliczanin* had a significant impact on the thought and literary work of Markiian Shashkevych, particularly through two articles by Jan Nepomucen Kamiński on the philosophical dimension of language; Eugeniusz Brocki's novella *Opryszki w Karpatach* [Brigands in the Carpathians]; Leszek Borkowski's poem "Kozak" [The Cossack]; several translations into Polish of Ukrainian, Serbian and Czech songs; and fragments from the *Královědvorský rukopis*. Kamiński wrote that all literary creativity must commence with study of one's native language, which was "the expression of the organism of the human soul," and especially with the elaboration of grammar. He argued that "the grammar should extract the entire thread of the language's construction from one point and through that reveal the spirit of the nation that spoke and thought and expressed its thoughts in that language."[3] His notions are strikingly similar to the propositions contained in Shashkevych's *Azbuka i abetsadlo* [The Cyrillic and the Latin alphabets] (1836).[4] Brocki's *Brigands in the Carpathians* was probably the archetype for Shashkevych's "Olena," and Borkowski's poem contributed to his writing of "Pohonia" [The chase].[5]

The extent of reciprocal influences—of Ukrainian on Polish literature and Polish on Ukrainian literature—is an immensely interesting subject, especially in regard to the so-called Ukrainian School, which played an enormous role in the history of Polish Romanticism, enriching it with motifs taken from the history and the life of the Ukrainian lands. Fascination with the open expanses, the steppe, the beauty of the land, the Ukrainian people and the Cossacks, their adventuresome and glorious past—with all the themes that Taras Shevchenko so splendidly depicted in his work—are visible in the writings of this school. For example, they are present in Antoni Malczewski's "Marja," in Józef Bohdan Zaleski's "Dumka hetmana Kosińskiego" [Ballad of Hetman Kosynsky] and "Dumka Mazepy" [Ballad of Mazepa], in Seweryn Goszczyński's *Zamek Kaniowski* [*Kaniv Castle*], and in the songs and poems of Tomasz (Tymko) Padura, a Pole who attempted to write in Ukrainian. *Kaniv Castle*, in particular, made a deep impression on Ukrainian readers, because until Shevchenko's *Haidamaky* appeared, it was the finest protest in literature against social injustice toward the Ukrainian people and the best expression of their struggle for their own rights. The creative work of these poets was not directly tied to Galicia, but some Galician Ukrainians were vitally interested in them. They attempted translations and lamented, as Ivan Holovatsky later noted, that there was among them no such singer of ballads as Józef Bohdan Zaleski. For then "the Little Russian tongue would have risen in spirit and shone more beautifully than all the Slavic currents.... [Then] neither the *Liakhy* nor the Muscovites would need to fight, squabble and argue over us; we would have been silent, but not silent in the way we now are"[6]—that is, there could have been no doubt about the distinctiveness and independence of the Ukrainian nation. The works of the Polish Romantics Adam Mickiewicz, Kazimierz Brodziński, and Michał Czajkowski also exerted a strong influence on Shashkevych.[7]

The fascination with Polish culture and literature was so great as almost to threaten the continued existence of the Ukrainian nationality. As Ivan Franko later wrote, "About the year 1830, the Poles could safely think that there is no Rus' in Galicia, that there is only one Polish nation, oppressed by the Germans."[8] In order to protect their distinctiveness and uncover their own worth, the young Ruthenian intellectuals had to make a break with Polishness. But, unable to do otherwise, they modelled their work on Polish Romantic literature. The construction of Shashkevych's verses, for example, clearly reveals a link to Polish poetry.[9]

Shashkevych was great friends with Tadeusz Wasilewski, the Polish vice-marshal of the Galician Estates diet, and indeed Shashkevych ascribed his return to the Greek Catholic seminary in 1832 to Wasilewski's efforts.[10] Wasilewski, being both learned and gifted with political foresight (in 1843 in the diet he called for freeing the peasants from serfdom and granting them full title to the land), could not fail to perceive the direction of the developing Ukrainian movement. Perhaps this inclined him to guide Shashkevych, to whom he pointed out opportunities and whom he helped educate. Well versed in the Slavic literatures, Wasilewski interested Shashkevych in Polish, Ukrainian and Serbian literature and enabled him to make use of the collections in Dykiv, where the Polish magnates, the Tarnowskis, had accumulated a beautiful library containing many old manuscripts and copies of the finest works of Slavic literature.[11] Later, in times of doubt or when Shashkevych's fragile health made itself felt, the thought of his friend spurred him to his work.[12]

Zaleski's and Goszczyński's poems were extraordinarily revered by the Ukrainian younger generation for their "Ruthenian spirit"; the works of Padura, on the other hand, were sharply criticized, although they were written in Ukrainian. Iakiv Holovatsky pointed out they were written in a macaronic Little Russian language, blended with Russian, Polish, Church Slavonic, and in large measure Padura's own invention. In spirit, his writings belonged to Polish literature; they were full of sympathy for the *Liakhy* and only "imitations in the spirit of the people." Holovatsky concluded that "Padura lacked... the heart of a Ukrainian."[13]

The publication *Rozmaitości*, edited by Mikołaj Michalewicz, a Ukrainian by descent and professor of Polish literature at Lviv University, played a significant role in Ukrainian intellectual life in the 1830s. (After Michalewicz's resignation, Jan Nepomucen Kamiński assumed the editorship.)[14] The Ukrainians learned from *Rozmaitości* about national work throughout Slavdom. In its pages they would read reviews of works concerning the language, literature, culture and history of the Slavic countries, and even such "unorthodox" works as *Paroles d'un croyant* by the French priest Félicité Robert de Lamennais. It was in *Rozmaitości* that Ukrainians first printed their learned articles: Iosyf Lozynsky published his startling—for those times—proposal for introducing the Polish-Latin alphabet in Ruthenian writing; Denys Zubrytsky wrote about the Greek Catholic Stavropygian Church in Lviv and the joining of the institute to it; Hryhorii Ilkevych (under the pseudonym "Mirosław z Horodenki") issued a series of articles about the region's antiquities; and one of the first reviews of *Rusalka Dnistrovaia* [The nymph of the Dniester] appeared here.[15] The significance of Bartłomiej Jabłoński's and Jan Milikowski's bookshops likewise cannot be overlooked. Milikowski's bookshop in particular, established about 1820 in Lviv, was often mentioned in the correspondence of the Ukrainian "awakeners." The main shop and its branch in Stanyslaviv were splendidly stocked with belles-lettres and with Polish, Czech, Russian and German learned publications, and the shop also frequently acted as an agent in the international exchange of new publications in Slavic literature.

In 1817 Józef Maksymilian Ossoliński founded the library of the Ossolineum National Foundation, which was opened to the public ten years later. Because of the friendly relations between Ossoliński and the Ukrainian scholars Modest Hrynevetsky and Mykhailo Harasevych, the library housed many Ruthenian collections which were later used by younger Ukrainian enthusiasts. The first curator of the Ossolineum Library was Mikołaj Michalewicz. Canon Ivan Mohylnytsky in Przemyśl befriended him, and his "Rozprawa o języku ruskim"

[Discourse on the Ruthenian language] appeared in the *Czasopismo Naukowe Księgozbioru Publicznego im. Ossolińskich* [Learned journal of the Ossolineum Public Library]. Mohylnytsky's treatise was the first to state unequivocally that the Ukrainian language was distinct from Polish and Russian and to insist that it be recognized as an entirely independent tongue. His work subsequently was of paramount significance in shaping the national and linguistic views of the Ukrainian activists who formed the circle known as the "Ruthenian Triad."

The scholarly and literary work of the Triad also was intimately associated with the Ossolineum's reading room and library. There its members read the first edition of Ivan Kotliarevsky's *Eneida* [Aeneid], Mykhailo Maksymovych's collection of Ukrainian songs, Oleksander Pavlovsky's grammar and the literature of the Slavs. There also they established their first contacts with the Polish writers and scholars Lucjan Siemieński and August Bielowski. Bielowski's *Ziewonia* (1834) became a model for the subsequent Ukrainian literary miscellanies *Zoria* [The star] and *Rusalka Dnistrovaia.* The influence of the Ossolineum on the Ukrainians came to an end in 1834, however, when the Austrian police uncovered revolutionary publications there. The reading room was closed and the director, Konstanty Słotwiński, was jailed. Shashkevych was himself interrogated by the police, but nothing could be proved against him except frequenting the reading room and borrowing books.[16]

The renewed scholarly interest in folk culture and the nation that began in the second half of the eighteenth century did not bypass Galicia. An interest in folk songs emerged in Galicia toward the end of the 1810s and is associated with the activities of Adam Czarnocki, known under the pseudonym "Zorian Dołęga Chodakowski," who between 1813 and 1821 undertook a series of journeys across Poland, Ukraine and Russia in order to record folk legends and songs, conduct archeological and archival searches and note the locations of old settlements and grave mounds. On the basis of his research, Czarnocki published in 1818 his treatise *O Słowiańszczyźnie przed chrześcijaństwem* [On Slavdom before Christianity] (a second edition appeared in the Lviv journal *Pamiętnik Lwowski* in 1819), in which he sought to prove the thesis of a single proto-Slavic culture subject to "common laws, rites and customs." In the same work he also proposed a programme for ethnographic research, urging those interested to go into the huts of the peasants and draw their information directly from the source. The Ukrainians appreciated Chodakowski's study all the more because it commended the Ruthenian clergy for living close to the common people and applauded the priests' gentleness and tolerance of folk customs, as a result of which the "Ruthenian areas had preserved incomparably more old legends" than the Polish regions.[17]

In 1818 Chodakowski journeyed through Eastern Galicia. In Lviv, he wrote, "having looked through the archives of the capitulary and the Ruthenian metropolitanate, I found a few items." He also met Metropolitan Levytsky, Canons Mohylnytsky and Lavrovsky, and Professor Hrynevetsky. His correspondence from this time provides an excellent source for studying and evaluating Ukrainian efforts to develop the school system:

> Metropolitan Levytsky and Father Mohylnytsky are undertaking the cultivation of the Ruthenian language here.... [They] are fulfilling an important service in this regard. Having introduced schools for the rural populace and having obtained by dint of devotion permission from the emperor, they have published books for the people in the Ruthenian dialect, avoiding as much as possible expressions from Polish.

Chodakowski took several copies of these textbooks for the use of the celebrated Polish lyceum in Kremianets [Krzemieniec] in Volhynia, as a "token of the work in respect to educating the rural populace in this region and of the desire to preserve the language, which was leaning more and more toward collapse." He objected only to the language of the textbooks. "The clergy wanted to use an entirely local language, but following the example of the old Uniates who had published liturgical books in Lviv, the languages become mixed with one another."[18] It is worth recalling that the materials that Chodakowski gathered in the Lviv area for his geographical dictionary were later used by Pavel Šafařík, who received them from Mikhail Pogodin.[19] Chodakowski also planned excursions in the vicinities of Halych, Terebovlia and Chortkiv and through Bukovyna. However, he had trouble obtaining permission from the Austrian authorities.[20]

Chodakowski became a symbol for young Ukrainians in the 1830s. They attempted to imitate him in their own work. As Ivan Franko wrote, "the image of this noble, original man, who wandered from village to village, lived on the lips of the [Ukrainian] youth, enveloped in a legend."[21] It is not surprising that later Ivan Vahylevych was described as a "second Chodakowski," and Ivan Holovatsky compared Chodakowski to the Ukrainian folklorists Hryhorii Ilkevych and Mykhailo Luchkai, and lamented that the scholarly world had lost them at so young an age.[22]

Chodakowski also exerted a significant influence on Wacław Zaleski [Wacław z Oleska], one of the best contemporary Polish writers in Galicia and an eminent authority on German aesthetics and philosophy with a lively interest in the progress of Slavic research. From the 1820s he regularly provided *Rozmaitości* with articles on the national life of the Slavs. However, Zaleski's most notable work was *Pieśni polskie i ruskie ludu galicyjskiego* [Polish and Ruthenian songs of the Galician people], published in Lviv in 1833. The volume also included an instrumental score by Karol Lipiński.[23] Zaleski justified the joint publication of the two nations' songs by pointing out that Galicia was inhabited by Poles and Ruthenians. He also provided a practical explanation for this kind of work. Because songs would substantially enrich the national language, a philologist or grammarian could draw from them, and he "will not lose his good taste on account of it; indeed, he will certainly gain." Zaleski attributed the lack of Polish historical songs to social and political conditions: "The common people,... deprived for so many centuries of the benefits of the law or any influence on the political composition of the nation, and having virtually no part in the history of the nation, could they preserve national memories and legends in songs and pass them on to posterity?"[24] Still, Zaleski recognized that the Ukrainians, though no less oppressed, nevertheless had preserved many of their historical songs. He explained the apparent anomaly:

> It was otherwise in Rus'. There a villager—in greater misery and more heavily oppressed—was nevertheless left more to himself. The petty nobility was not scattered throughout the villages in Rus' as it was in Poland; there were none of these incessant requisitions, transports, etc. On the estates of the great lords, the [Ukrainian] villager was not disturbed in his festivities and rituals by a long burdensome transport [obligation], and for that reason these festivities and rituals were preserved to this time.[25]

Zaleski's *Polish and Ruthenian Songs* was the first book published in Galicia containing monuments of folk creativity expressed in a pure Ukrainian folk idiom. It constituted a turning point for Ukrainian literature. In Ivan Franko's estimation:

> This book was the first harbinger of our national rebirth. Only then did lettered Ruthenians become convinced that in their very midst, in the mouths of the simple, enserfed peasant, there lived songs and tales of which they could be proud before the world; a language lived that was not only recorded in books, but one in which outsiders found a strange beauty of the kind an unenlightened Ruthenian had not noticed up to that time.[26]

The value of *Polish and Ruthenian Songs* was not lessened even by Zaleski's own views on the future of the Ukrainian literary language. He assumed that Galicia was inhabited not by two separate nations, but by two branches of a single nation which spoke different but mutually intelligible dialects. He postulated the merger of the two literatures:

> In higher respects, the exclusion of the Ruthenians from our [Polish] literature seems to me to be very harmful to a general Slavic literature, toward which we should eternally and always strive. The Slovaks, the Slavs in Silesia and the Moravians joined with the Czechs. But with whom are the Ruthenians to join? Or are we to desire that the Ruthenians have their own literature? What would happen to German literature if the individual Germanic branches attempted to have their own literatures?[27]

Zaleski assumed Polish-Ukrainian unity in literature and was a proponent of Slavic literary unity even before Ján Kollár formulated his principles of Slavic reciprocity. To be sure, when Zaleski wrote his foreword to *Polish and Ruthenian Songs* in 1831, the future of Slavic national development could not be foreseen. The next several years would reveal that Zaleski's categorical statements—about the Slovaks' merging with Czech literature, for example—would prove erroneous.

Moreover, Zaleski believed that the Slavic nations soon would abandon the Cyrillic alphabet, which in his opinion stood as the primary obstacle to including Slavic literature in the general body of European literature. He himself used the Latin alphabet in printing the Ruthenian songs. Only the spelling posed problems for him, the more so because the Ruthenian language still had neither a grammar nor a dictionary. As Zaleski wrote: "Wanting to keep to certain rules, I followed the principle as much as possible of writing as the people speak, even if obvious grammatical errors intruded." Zaleski saw the necessity of preparing a Ukrainian grammar, a dictionary and an orthography modelled after the work of Vuk Karadžić, who had established "the most logical orthography in all of contemporary Europe" for the Serbs.[28] At the time Zaleski's work appeared, Galician Ukrainians had no strong objections to its stipulations; Iosyf Levytsky alone was indignant over its use of the Latin alphabet.[29] Only when Iosyf Lozynsky demanded, in 1834, that the Latin alphabet be applied in Ukrainian orthography did widespread opposition to the idea emerge. Regardless of the alphabet employed, Zaleski's principle of phonetic spelling of the Ruthenian songs had permanent value, although Lozynsky, Markiian Shashkevych and many others had to struggle arduously and many battles took place in print before the principle of phonetic spelling finally won out in Ukrainian literature.

In the 1820s and 1830s the lyrics of Ukrainian songs and articles devoted to questions of folk culture appeared in such Polish journals and literary miscellanies as *Rozmaitości*, *Haliczanin* and *Ziewonia*, and in the émigré literary journal in Paris, *Północ* [The north]. Certainly all of this attention to folk culture could not help but influence the views of the Ukrainian awakeners. Shashkevych probably read in a transcript made by his friend Father Mykhailo Kozlovsky of Pidlyssia an 1835 article from *Północ* entitled "O poezji Rusi" [About the poetry of Rus']. Perhaps the ideas contained in the article are reflected in Shashkevych's poem "Pobratymovi" [To a blood brother].[30]

The Polish intellectual movement of the 1820s and 1830s would not have awakened Ukrainian national feelings had it not been for the political changes that occurred with the outbreak of the November 1830 insurrection in Russian Poland. The insurrection represented a watershed in the formation of national ideas among the Slavs and brought on a crisis for the notion of Slavic unity. The Russians' treatment of the Poles was seen as contrary to all people's aspiration to a self-determined, independent national life or, at the least, to developing freely their own nationality within the framework of a union with other nations. This reaction was especially noticeable among the Czechs, who were appalled by the Slavs' internecine conflicts and began to condemn tsarist Russia.[31]

The significance of the November insurrection for the Ukrainian national movement in Galicia is stressed in Polish historical writings and is not challenged in Russian literature and older Ukrainian historiography, but it is clearly discounted in recent Soviet Ukrainian scholarship.[32] It is not my intention to claim that the Ukrainian movement would not have been possible without the insurrection, since the general historical flow tended toward the formation of national movements, but rather to underscore the fact that the Polish insurrection hastened the crystallization of the Ukrainian national idea. The impact of the insurrection was well understood by contemporary Ukrainian leaders such as Iakiv Holovatsky, who wrote in 1844 in a letter to Osyp Bodiansky: "Not long ago, about a decade or so ago, a new spirit—a Ruthenian spirit—began to appear. Neither a genius awakened [our] somnolent nationality, nor any [internal] event that shook the nation; perhaps it was the neighbouring thunder that sounded or the example of the other Slavic nations that roused us."[33]

There is nothing surprising in this view. During the insurrection the youth in the secondary schools of Lviv and at the university, Polish as well as Ukrainian and German, sympathized with the Poles' struggle against tsarist misrule. They also attempted several times to cross the border and join the insurgents who were fighting in the Zamość region. The atmosphere at the university and the attitude of certain professors such as Józef Mauss, who considered joining the insurrection a patriotic duty, also fostered support.[34] There can be no doubt that similar views must have had a forceful effect on the Ukrainians, and there is no convincing reason to doubt Mykola Ustyianovych's statement that

Shashkevych also wanted to join the insurgents (the more so since he was at loose ends after being dismissed from the Greek Catholic seminary in February 1830).[35]

The collapse of the insurrection brought a large influx of Polish émigrés to Galicia. They were received enthusiastically, and not only by the Poles. Greek Catholic clergymen not infrequently falsified émigrés' papers, making native-born Galician citizens of them, which effectively freed them from persecution by the Austrian authorities. But once those authorities became aware of what was going on, they complained to the Greek Catholic hierarchy.[36]

Conspiratorial activities by the Poles in Galicia in the 1830s also influenced Ukrainian youth. The underground movements captivated their minds, led them to join illegal organizations and instilled a deeper social and political understanding in them. There was significant intellectual ferment among the Greek Catholic seminarians and Ukrainian students at Lviv University and among the school-aged youth of Lviv, Przemyśl and Sambir. Many political organizations, both overt and clandestine, arose, although they did not live long and accomplished little—as was usually the case with the purely Polish conspiratorial endeavours as well. The Ukrainians were won over in one of two ways: the young intelligentsia was reached through Polish literature, while the peasants were touched by direct revolutionary agitation. Klyment Mokhnatsky, a Ukrainian by descent, clearly pointed out in his "Pamiętnik spiskowca i nauczyciela" [Memoirs of a conspirator and a teacher] that before 1830, "there were no political notions among the [Galician] youth. There was debate neither over the [former Polish] Commonwealth nor on the issue of Poland's independence. Although the spirit was Polish, it did not exceed the bounds of literature. Only the November insurrection resurrected the Polish political spirit."[37] It should be emphasized that this Polish spirit also was raised among Ukrainian youth. To a substantial degree this phenomenon can be attributed to Polish belles-lettres, as well as to Polish revolutionary writings that were smuggled into Galicia or illegally printed at the Ossolineum.[38] Revolutionary proclamations in both languages and whole collections of Polish and Ukrainian revolutionary songs also circulated among young Ukrainians. The song "Kozak" [The Cossack] (contained in a collection by Dmytro Mokhnatsky), which began with the words "Hei Kozache v imia Boha" [O Cossack, in the name of God], purportedly inspired Shashkevych to write the poem "Boleslav Kryvousty pid Halychem v lito 1139 r." [Bolesław the Wrymouth at Halych in 1139], although Shashkevych substituted anti-Polish elements for the anti-Russian accent of the original song.[39]

The revolutionary writings churned the young minds, awakened sympathy for bold dreams for the future and, of course, drew them away from academic studies. It also happened that this or that student would leave his studies, take up political matters and in effect make his way into the Polish conspiratorial movement. Through this revolutionary literature, the interdependence of national and social liberation was all the more readily recognized. Klyment Mokhnatsky did not gratuitously write, "I came to the conclusion that Poland will not regain its independence until the common people are freed from *robot*."[40] Behind this statement lay the serious dilemma of the time: how was one to involve the common people in the struggle for independence, how might one make a citizen of the peasant, whether Polish or Ukrainian? Without a change in social conditions, it was impossible to count on the support of the masses for the aspirations of the Polish *szlachta*, especially when the reconstruction of Poland according to its 1772 boundaries was contemplated. That concept was virtually always linked to a repudiation of the Ukrainians' national distinctiveness.

What were the characteristic features of the Poles' revolutionary agitation? Klyment Mokhnatsky, as noted earlier, had called attention to its antifeudalism. His contemporaries, such as Henryk Bogdański and Julian Horoszkiewicz, similarly underlined this point. Bogdański wrote:

> We did not distinguish between Ruthenians and Poles in our activities.... We infused the Ruthenian priests and seminarians with our spirit, so that through selfless actions to gain completely the confidence of the peasant they would establish schools; so that as intermediaries between the peasant and the *szlachta* they would draw these two strata closer to each other and [thereby] obliterate the hatred and suspicion of the peasant for his lords, and through this rectify his perception of the *Liakhy*; and so that by preserving his nationality they would facilitate a close union of the two in the fraternal oneness that the pride of the *szlachta* and the fanaticism of the Jesuits had weakened. And we presented to the *szlachta* in Rus' the advantage and the necessity of aiding the Ruthenian priests in these undertakings, of drawing closer to them and the peasant, and of enlightening him and preparing him for self-reliance.[41]

Hipolit Ignacy Kulczyński agitated in a similar vein. About him Horoszkiewicz noted:

> His strategy was to bring all social strata closer together, to convince the landowners of the need, absolute necessity and obligation to abolish serfdom. He called upon them to do this in the name of love for the fatherland, which could not be freed without these conditions; without them it was "not worth

> its freedom." On the other hand, he stressed the need to work on the people's behalf, to enlighten the people, to elevate the people morally, to unite the people with the enlightened strata, to awaken in them the desire for and the faith in freedom, which they deserve according to divine law and human justice, but [also] to teach them how to acquire this freedom through the general goodwill and common sacrifice of all elements in the society, and to prepare them gradually for the coming essential and general struggle for common liberties through the political freedom of the fatherland.[42]

These fragments clearly present the trend of contemporary revolutionary propaganda with its positive and negative features: the abolition of feudal relations and *robot*, the necessity of the struggle for freedom, and the enlightenment of the rural populace on the one hand, and of social solidarity and paving the way for "merger of two branches [not nations] in fraternal union" on the other hand. These were its fundamental elements.

These issues are especially interesting because at the same time one discerns in the programme of the Ruthenian Triad a withdrawal from all practical social and political activity. Instead, the Triad was almost exclusively occupied with the enlightenment of the common people, which, it was imagined, would spontaneously bring about political and socio-economic change. Already at that time, loyalty to the government was not an insignificant consideration for the Ukrainian awakeners.[43]

We know the names of some of the agitators who worked among the Ukrainian common people in Galicia: Ignacy Kulczyński, Kasper Cięglewicz, Karol Kotkiewicz, Alojzy Zgierski, Mykhailo Popel and Iosyf Berehulsky. Some were also the authors of revolutionary proclamations and brochures. It was Kulczyński who called Cięglewicz's attention to the fact that "the common people here are Ruthenian, and, therefore, they need Ruthenian poetry—simple, accessible, intelligible [verse] for the village."[44] Many such works in the Ukrainian language that were distributed among the rural populace have survived; for example, Cięglewicz's *Instrukcija dla uczytelej ruskoho naroda* [Instructions for the teachers of the Ruthenian nation], Julian Horoszkiewicz's *Lysty do pryjateliw myru* [Letters to friends of the community] and Popel's *Rusyn na praznyku* [A Ruthenian at a holyday celebration]. These works stressed the social bondage of the common people, demanded that the *szlachta* free them from *robot* and criticized the lords' rights to harass and oppress the peasants. They called for a struggle for social and national liberation and for battle with the Germans in the name of an understandable—so it seemed to the contemporary activists—Polish-Ukrainian solidarity. The conclusion to Cięglewicz's *Instructions* was typical: "We will shout 'down with the bondage of the emperor and the lords,' and we will follow the common people who are showing us the path to happiness and freedom."[45]

Horoszkiewicz's *Letters to Friends of the Community* was bitter against *robot* and the government and exhorted the peasants to organize resistance to *robot* and to remember the injustices committed against them. The director of the police in Lviv tersely judged it in saying, "This is a hellish publication." Horoszkiewicz envisioned a mythical Poland in which all classes lived in harmony and unity and there was no social oppression. In his Poland, "Ruthenians and Poles lived like brothers; they did not know serfdom . . . , [and] there were no kings, no taxes, no rents, no tributes, no military impressment."[46]

The Polish agitators also voiced a programme for unity among the Slavic nations and a plan for the unity of the Ukrainians inhabiting Galicia, Transcarpathian Rus' and Ukraine of the Dnieper region. They were markedly pro-Polish, anti-German, and anti-Russian. Their attitudes were clearly evident in Popel's "Ruthenian at a Holyday Celebration":

Słowianszczyna nasza maty,
A nasz bat'ko so nebes.
Wsi Słowiane sut' nam braty,
Tilko Nimeć to je pes.

[Slavdom is our mother; our father is from heaven. All Slavs are brothers to us; only the German is a dog.] In his *Adzow k bratiam* [Appeal to my brothers], the pamphlet in which this verse appeared, Popel asked all inhabitants of the region of the Dnieper, Dniester and Buh rivers, regardless of descent, religion or nationality, to live in peace and harmony: "We shall extend our hands to the just *Liakhy*, and the *Liakhy* will give us their hands, and together we shall exclaim: 'Long live freedom! We are with you, you with us; down with tsarism and the lords, down with bondage in our lands.'"[47] Popel resolutely opposed any attempt to fashion a positive stance toward tsarist Russia, in his opinion the greatest enemy of freedom; he sharply condemned the members of the Stavropygian Institute in Lviv who reportedly wished "to deliver the Ruthenian people into the bondage of the Muscovite tsar for medals and roubles." Popel thought that "the Polish nation has matured more toward freedom than the Russian [nation]; . . . it has already experienced a bloody struggle for liberty." Accordingly, he rhetorically asked the Ukrainians,

> Is it better to join with those who are so far removed from freedom, that is, with the Muscovites, or with the Poles? Is it better to join with those who in their blindness fight against freedom, because such are the Muscovites, or

> to fraternize with those who fight for freedom, that is, with the Poles? To disperse the kings and the emperors, let us not only fraternize with the Poles, but with all the nations that struggle for freedom, and we shall become stronger.[48]

Let us now look at the national programme of a major faction of the Polish democratic revolutionaries who carried out conspiratorial activities in Galicia in the mid-1830s—the Stowarzyszenie Ludu Polskiego (Association of the Polish People). Its principal goal was the reconstruction of the Polish state of 1772. Its ranks included Poles, Ukrainians, Lithuanians and Belorussians, whom it regarded as components of the "Polish nation." The association's programme unequivocally stated that the future Poland would be a federated republic, with no one nationality predominating.[49] Kasper Cięglewicz also "defended in revolutionary circles the equal status of the Ukrainians with the Poles," though it is not known whether he had in mind full and equal political rights or only equal status for their culture and language.[50] The Polish historian Marceli Handelsman rightly wrote in this regard, "Polish propagandists advanced the thesis of the unity of all the Ruthenian branches—from Galicia, from beyond the border and beyond the Carpathians—though in the name of a higher Polish-Ruthenian unity, or rather an all-Polish [unity] embracing both nations."[51] There was serious disparity, therefore, between the Polish position and the purely Ukrainian position of the circle of the Ruthenian Triad.

The Poles did not achieve their intended goal; the effect of their revolutionary propaganda among the common people was considerably less than they had expected. Given the current level of national consciousness among the Galician peasantry, striving to reconstruct an independent Poland elicited little interest among the Polish peasants. The Polish revolutionaries had even less success among the Ukrainian peasants, for whom social bondage was always associated with Polish oppression, especially since persons who could recall the times of the *szlachta*'s "Republic" were still living. The peasants' response to the agitation to abolish *robot* was somewhat different, although instances did occur, as Klyment Mokhnatsky noted, when the peasants even defended that onerous burden.[52]

Ukrainian participation in the clandestine Polish organizations in Galicia has been carefully examined in the historical literature. This scholarly interest is due primarily to the Ukrainian historian Kyrylo Studynsky, who devoted a special study to the issue, which he complemented by publishing extensive source materials.[53] Rather than present here a detailed account of these Ukrainian revolutionaries, I shall only call attention to certain aspects of their involvement in the

Polish movement that had a direct bearing on the further development of the national question in Galicia. At the outset, it must be noted that the Ukrainians not infrequently contributed a greater social radicalism to the Polish conspiratorial organizations than did the Poles themselves, and that the Ukrainians were not given to any kind of chauvinism in their national views. These characteristics should not be surprising if one considers that the Ukrainian revolutionary youth shared the social background of the common people, and that their mounting national consciousness—the sense of their own national distinctiveness and their aspiration for the independence of the Ukrainian nation in Galicia—turned them against national discrimination.

Besides belonging to many of the major conspiratorial organizations, such as Stowarzyszenie Ludu Polskiego, the Konfederacja Powszechna Narodu Polskiego (General Confederation of the Polish Nation) and Młoda Sarmacja (Young Sarmatia), many Ukrainians took part in the secret societies of young, Romantic-minded Poles that had sprung up in practically every major town in Galicia. For example, in the Towarzystwo Uczonych (Learned Society), also known as the "Senate," established by Kazimierz Turowski, an admirer of Ukrainian poetry, in Przemyśl, the following Ukrainians participated: Mykola, Iuliian, Teofil and Lev Kmytsykevych and Antin Luzhetsky, who later became a poet and was closely tied to the Ruthenian Triad. The leading Ukrainian agitators among the youthful conspirators in Sambir were Mykhailo Popel and Iosyf Berehulsky; in the short-lived Towarzystwo Starożytności Galicyjskich (Society of Galician Antiquities) in Lviv, founded by the future historian Karol Szajnocha, one might find A. Shashkevych (Antin, the brother of Markiian?), Danylo and Petro Tavrashkevych, Hryhorii Bodnar, Ivan Levytsky, Antin Lozynsky and Oleksa Luchakovsky.

Conspiratorial activities among the Greek Catholic seminarians were noted as early as 1833.[54] Ivan Seletsky was a key instigator, and even after his withdrawal from the seminary he maintained ties with the seminarians. In 1834 he formed a secret society devoted to reconstructing Poland as a republican federation within its pre-partition boundaries. His organization also agitated for an end to *robot* and for giving the peasants free title to the lands they tilled. The youthful conspirator endeavoured to raise the consciousness of the common people to the degree that the conspirators could rely on their participation in a struggle for liberation. However, the latter aims were seldom attained. For example, the priest Father Dezyderii Hrechansky, annoyed at seeing that the land-owner of the village in which he worked often expounded views on liberty and equality but himself tyrannized over his serfs, decided in 1838 to denounce the conspirators agitating in his area. A commission of inquiry determined that the leader of the local conspiracy was Ivan Seletsky, who had been in close contact with the Polish underground in Galicia. Although Seletsky managed to escape to France, the other Ukrainians involved were less fortunate and received prison sentences ranging from one to four years. Two of the Ukrainian conspirators, Iosyf Konstantynovych and Venedykt Kushchykevych, against whom charges were dropped in 1838, were rearrested six years later for their part in another conspiracy and received the death sentence, although it was later commuted to a prison term.[55]

Despite the extent of the conspiracies, in 1835 the clerical authorities still had no conclusive evidence against the seminarians with revolutionary leanings, although the hierarchy suspected that even seminary instructors might be involved.[56] The hierarchy's greatest concern was that the conspiracies not compromise the reputation of the Greek Catholic clergy with the Austrian authorities. Metropolitan Levytsky was particularly anxious that those "who are attempting to place our clergy under the government's suspicion" not be able to exploit the situation. In fact, Levytsky noted that nine seminarians were under suspicion, "and among them was [Dmytro] Mokhnatsky, now in his fourth year of theology, [who] is considered the most dangerous."[57] In fact, Mokhnatsky, who was expelled soon after, gave a lengthy deposition during the inquest against the alleged *russische Partei* [Russian faction] of Markiian Shashkevych and his colleagues.[58] The church authorities' counteraction pleased the Austrian officials. The metropolitan ordered that thorough searches be conducted to confiscate all revolutionary writings. In 1837, Levytsky wrote indignantly about the purported conspirators: "The government has taken note of them. . . . Therefore, the question arises if it is proper to dismiss them, even though no revolutionary journals or books were found among them. Because of such, if I may say so, nitwits, the reputation of our seminary has been marred."[59]

In 1841, Father Mykola Hordynsky, who between 1830 and 1837 had been the prefect of the seminary, was actually imprisoned. He had become acquainted in 1833 with the Polish émigrés' emissary Napoleon Nowicki and joined his Związek Węglarzy Polskich (Union of Polish Carbonari). Three years later Hordynsky represented the Ukrainians in the executive council of the Association of the Polish People. Later, however, he was excluded from the council after a bitter exchange with one of the Polish members, Leon Korecki.[60] For this reason the Ukrainians who were members of the Association of the Polish People submitted a resolution to the council to change the organization's name to the Association of the Polish *and* Ruthenian People. When the council, supposedly not wishing to elicit national quarrels, refused, the more radical Ukrainian members broke away and created the Kolo Ruske (Ruthenian Circle). From that time on, the differences between the Polish and the Ukrainian conspirators steadily increased.[61]

Hordynsky's role in the Association of the Polish People had been extremely valuable for the Poles. He was personally acquainted with the leading Polish conspirators, and as the prefect of the Greek Catholic seminary he was in the best position to know the convictions prevailing among the Ukrainian youth and their attitude toward the clandestine Polish organizations. He could advise whom it would be worthwhile to recruit, with whom one could speak and whom one should avoid. Hordynsky also acted as an intermediary, receiving the revolutionary literature designated for the seminary that entered Galicia by way of Hungary. The consequences of the conspiracies were tragic for him, but despite this he remained loyal to the Polish cause to the end. Because he was also a member of Young Sarmatia, Hordynsky was given the death penalty, which in 1845 was commuted to twelve years in prison. The revolution in Austria in 1848 eventually brought his freedom.[62]

In 1838 the Ukrainians Mariian Lapchynsky, Venedykt Kushchykevych and Vasyl Podolynsky formed the clandestine organization Vilni Halychany (Free Galicians), with such a radical, bluntly terrorist programme that it alienated even the Poles, notwithstanding its support for an independent Poland. (In 1848, as we shall see, Podolynsky advanced a programme for the full independence of Ukraine, toward which the Ukrainian nation should strive "straight and direct or through the Slavic community.")[63] Discussions of Poland's independence in Polish conspiratorial circles compelled the Ukrainians to concern themselves with their own nation and its future. Essentially, there were three paths from which to choose: joining with Poland, independence for Ukraine or union with Russia. Understandably, the Poles firmly insisted on the first course, although among themselves they differed substantially on the essence of a Polish-Ukrainian union. The anti-Polish Ukrainians, such as Denys Zubrytsky, contemplated the unification of the entire "Ruthenian" nation, and they included in this nation all the "Ruthenians" inhabiting the area from the Carpathians to the Urals and from the White to the Black seas. On the other hand, Mykola Kmytsykevych attempted to reconcile the Polish cause with obtaining the greatest assurances for his own nation. He wrote about this hope in a letter to his friend Kazimierz Turowski:

> Some kind of great spirit of freedom has overwhelmed me.... I dreamt that I had liberated the Ruthenians and given them independence. This has become such a mania with me that I can think of nothing else.... In my opinion, it would be best if Poland rises; I have great plans.... The Ruthenians are most on my mind; let the Poles think about themselves, and I shall think about my own kind. No one will think the worse of me for that.[64]

On the other side, the church hierarchy attempted to counter the seminarians' involvement in Polish conspiratorial organizations. The new rector of the Greek Catholic seminary in Lviv, Venedykt Levytsky, concluded that it was necessary to turn the seminarians' attention away from free thinking and revolutionary literature, which, as Mykhailo Mynchakevych later admitted at his inquest, had undermined the foundations of religious belief and led to the conviction that a republican form of government was better than a monarchy.[65] In his lectures on moral theology, the rector explained the perniciousness of such views in political matters and, if one is to believe Mynchakevych, at least among some students he achieved his goal.[66] However, Levytsky also tried to obtain more money to increase the seminary's library collection. He encouraged the seminarians to attend additional classes in agriculture and the Polish language; he charged them to study their native history and the Ukrainian language, and to gather materials for a Ukrainian dictionary. He recommended preparing homilies in Ukrainian for the people, as well as translating into Ukrainian books for use in the primary schools and works pertaining to economics.

The results of the rector's and the metropolitan's initiatives were not long in coming. Ivan Vahylevych collected materials for a dictionary and translated *The Imitation of Christ* by Thomas à Kempis from the Latin original and a German translation. Markiian Shashkevych prepared a reader for the parish schools. Rector Levytsky eventually even came to believe that all the achievements of the Ruthenian Triad were due exclusively to his efforts. Unfortunately, his successor, Hryhorii Iakhymovych, did not appreciate the work of the seminarians in the national arena in the same way.[67]

Wishing to deflect the government's suspicion of the seminarians' alleged subversiveness, Metropolitan Levytsky ordered the rector to require the most capable seminarians to deliver addresses on the obligations toward the monarch and the authorities in the presence of their superiors and colleagues. Between 1834 and 1841, fifty-seven such addresses were given in the seminary, of which nineteen were in Latin, sixteen in German, eleven in Polish, and only four in Ukrainian (by Shashkevych, Roman Pasichynsky, Antin Mohylnytsky and Rudolf Mokh). Shashkevych's address, entitled "Slovo k pytomtsem" [A word to the seminarians], was the first public presentation by the young poet. Unfortunately, only a fragment, published in verse form in 1835 under the title "Holos Halychan" [The voice of the Galicians], is preserved. Essentially, it honoured Emperor Francis I, whose birthday coincided with the day the address was delivered. From Mykola Ustyianovych's later account, we know that Shashkevych's presentation, the first to be delivered within the walls of the seminary in a beautiful Ukrainian language, commanded great admiration among his listeners and "raised the Ruthenian spirit by a hundred per cent." This account is probably accurate, because the poem countered the Polish conspiratorial underground and its attempt to subordinate the Ukrainian national movement to the Polish cause. The substance of Shashkevych's verse probably did not differ greatly from that of an address by Roman Pasichynsky, who stressed the Ukrainians' loyalty to Austria, which, he maintained, since 1772 had invariably given them happiness and facilitated their free national development. Ukrainians should be grateful to the emperor for the benefactions he had bestowed; they should renounce even the shadow of a lack of reverence for his name and his instructions. In conclusion, Pasichynsky exhorted: "Remember, brothers, that we are Ruthenians [*Ruslany*], and shall never sully the Ruthenian heart with such disgrace." Pasichynsky clearly posed the issue of the national separateness of the Ukrainians by calling them *Ruslany*; it follows that the name Shashkevych adopted—*Ruslan*—meant the same as Ruthenian or Ukrainian and that his *Psalmy Ruslanovi* meant simply "the psalms of a Ruthenian." These first addresses by the Ukrainian seminarians testified that the Ukrainian national movement from the very outset was in its essence directed against the Polish dominance in Eastern Galicia, but before the movement became purely Ukrainian, it was already Austrophile. It seemed that in the pre-March 1848 conditions there was no other course to choose.[68]

Shashkevych and all those Ukrainians who thought similarly were suspected by the Poles of pro-Russian sympathies. Henryk Bogdański and Klyment Mokhnatsky wrote about these suspicions, and Dmytro Mokhnatsky bought his freedom by testifying to this effect at his inquest. Sheets with the names of alleged Russian sympathizers circulated among the Polish revolutionaries. The lists included Markiian Shashkevych and his brother Antin, Roman Pasichynsky, Semen Pleshkevych, Mykola Ustyianovych, Tselestyn Skomorovsky, Iuliian Velychkovsky, Antin Liubych-Mohylnytsky, Mykhailo Bulvynsky, Ivan Studynsky, Havrylo Seroichkovsky and, of the older generation, Rector Hryhorii Iakhymovych, Professor Mykola Napadiievych and Denys Zubrytsky. The Poles attributed Ukrainian pro-Russian sympathies to the influence of Mikhail Pogodin, who in 1835 was in Lviv, where he met some of these men. Later he maintained a lively correspondence with them. However, in the 1830s and 1840s, Shashkevych's group in fact displayed no sign of Russophilism, whereas Zubrytsky's pro-Russian outlook, shaped much earlier, was only, in Vasyl Shchurat's words, a "private dream."[69]

All in all, however, the metropolitan's directive that the seminarians deliver speeches about obligations toward the authorities and the frequent searches to find forbidden literature were of little avail; indeed, they became a curtain behind which the youths could carry out activities quite contrary to the hierarchy's wishes. For example, Dezyderii Hrechansky was the first to deliver an address, on 4 October 1834, at a time when he was already a member of a secret organization in which he would continue to participate for several years. Shashkevych and the group of young Ukrainians associated with him, to be sure, pursued a different course. They exploited these convenient occasions to commence entirely legally work on the rebirth of the Ukrainian language and literature. Their way was not as attractive as the path of plots and conspiracies that counted on an armed struggle for national independence; it was a long, laborious path, but entirely legal, and for that reason practicable in the existing political circumstances. By assuring the authorities of their loyalty, these young Ukrainian enthusiasts were able in turn to rely on government backing. At the time they did not foresee that their work, by rejecting the ossified Church Slavonic, would elicit fierce resistance from the defenders of that language.

It is difficult to say what influence Western literature, especially revolutionary writings, had on these youthful enthusiasts. Indeed, Iakiv Holovatsky stated that Ivan Vahylevych became well acquainted with Polish and German literature in the gymnasium, and Volodymyr Kotsovsky suggested that Shashkevych was quite familiar with the literature of Western Europe. However, Ivan Franko has maintained that the entire contemporary current of Polish and European literature left virtually no trace on the intellectual life of the Galician Ukrainians, arguing, "We know not at all whether Shashkevych really did become acquainted with the literature of Western Europe.... In his writings... Shashkevych never reaches beyond the bounds of the Slavic world."[70]

Yet while it is possible, it is difficult to imagine that the students of Lviv University and seminarians who were associated with the Polish revolutionary movement were the only ones acquainted with Western European belles-lettres and social and political writings. Mention has already been made of the reading that took place illegally within the walls of the seminary in Lviv. Most popular at that time were the works of Shakespeare, Scott, Richardson, Byron, Dumas, Goethe, Schiller, Kotzebue, Caroline Pichler and the German philosophers Schelling, Schlegel and Hegel. In the 1830s Hegel's work was widely accepted and appreciated by the seminary authorities, and not until later was it conceded that "he [Hegel] cast the seed of religious misunderstandings through his precepts."[71] Lamennais's book *Paroles d'un croyant*, condemned by Pope Gregory XVI in 1834, circulated in a Polish translation entitled *Słowa wieszcze* and generated among the youth distaste for existing political conditions and respect for republicanism and democracy. The popular German encyclopedia, *Allgemeine Enzyklopädie der Wissenschaften and Künste*, by Johann G. Ersch and Johann G. Gruber, and *Les Ruines, ou méditation sur les révolutions des empires*, by Constantin Volney (the Polish title was *Rozwaliny, czyli uwagi nad rewolucjami narodów*), stirred religious doubts. Ludwig Börne's *Briefe aus Paris* and Heinrich Laube's *Das Junge Europa* shaped the liberal views of contemporary youth. Also in this spirit was the enormously popular *Allgemeine Geschichte* by Karl Rotteck, in which the author stood for a state based on law, healthy reason and a constitution corresponding to the general will of the people.[72] Among the Ukrainians, Iosyf Levytsky was a specialist in German philosophy and literature; in his Ukrainian grammar he cited Schlegel's views and attempted to translate the poetry of Goethe and Schiller, though into a rather poor Ukrainian. It is also known that Hryhorii Bodnar translated Byron.

Thus it seems that Shashkevych, Vahylevych, Holovatsky and their comrades could not pass indifferently through the intellectual and cultural scene of those years. It is simply too hard to believe that these movements could have been completely foreign to them. However, they did not openly write about or discuss these matters in order not to cause unnecessary suspicions. Furthermore, in the early 1830s they already had linked their hopes to the general aspirations of Slavdom, and the currents that emanated from that direction clearly shaped their national individuality. This statement applies not only to the South Slavic community, but also to Ukraine along the Dnieper, although later the Triad sometimes presented the issue differently. In his university lectures, Iakiv Holovatsky stated that "separated from Ukraine, without association and an understanding, under different influences, a Ruthenian national literature began to develop in our Galician land."[73] However, in this case Holovatsky was concerned with emphasizing the highly significant role played by Joseph II and later Austrian authorities on behalf of the national emancipation of the

Ukrainians in Galicia. As a good subject of the Habsburg monarchy, he did not want to speak of other influences, but we nevertheless cannot ignore them.

4. The Ruthenian Triad

The elimination of "Slavo-Ruthenian" from university courses in 1808 created a complicated and difficult situation for the Ukrainian nationality in Galicia. Knowledge of Ukrainian began to fall abruptly. Clergymen were trained exclusively in Latin and German and in private life spoke Polish; they were barely able to read Church Slavonic liturgical texts. A proficient knowledge among them of Church Slavonic, let alone of the folk idiom, seemed out of the question. The situation worsened in 1812, when mandatory schooling ended in Galicia, resulting in a sharp decline in the enrollment of Ukrainian children in the parochial, trivium and normal schools. The use of children for farm labour and the popular dislike for schools that taught in a "foreign" tongue also deterred Ukrainians from educating their offspring. Therefore, in 1813 the Austrian authorities issued a directive authorizing the villages themselves to organize Ukrainian schools. Instruction in these schools was to be "in the mother tongue" [*in der Muttersprache*], whereas in the town schools instruction was to be "in German and in the national language" [*in deutscher und in der Nationalsprache*]; in the principal schools, however, instruction must be "entirely in German and Polish" [*durchaus in deutscher und polnischer Sprache*].[1]

The Greek Catholic leadership in Galicia was able to use this situation to improve the educational system. Mykhailo Levytsky (the future metropolitan of Lviv) was appointed bishop of Przemyśl in 1813. Although privately he spoke Polish and publicly German or Latin, under the influence of Canon Ivan Mohylnytsky, who was responsible for school affairs at the Przemyśl consistory, Levytsky launched a broad campaign to expand parochial schooling. Over the next several years, he became its staunch defender. He was also the first person in Galicia who ventured openly to raise the issue of educating the Ukrainian people along national lines.[2] With this aim, the metropolitan called upon the Greek Catholic clergy to open parochial schools and to establish an appropriate school fund and appealed to the authorities to introduce Ukrainian in village schools.

The *Gubernium* in Lviv responded negatively. In justifying their position, the Galician authorities wrote to Vienna:

> For such an enlightened, liberal and just government as the Austrian, there are no political grounds to advise against teaching reading and writing in Polish in Galicia. Perhaps this will bring forth a spirit of factionalism. But, if political considerations are taken into account, there is certainly less reason to propagate Ruthenian instead of Polish, since it is only a variant of the Russian language [*nur eine Abartung der russischen ist*].[3]

The *Gubernium* replied to the metropolitan that the Ruthenian language was little used in writing and no governmental decrees were issued in it; besides, few teachers were proficient in the language. Therefore, the Ruthenian language would only be a burden for the pupils and consequently could not be used in school instruction, except in the teaching of religion. Because a majority of the population in Galicia understood Polish, the *Gubernium* proposed continuing with Polish for instructional purposes and eventually to consider whether it would be possible to use the Latin alphabet in Ruthenian writings, which would be more beneficial to the common people. Finally, the *Gubernium* proposed calling a special commission to resolve these contentious problems.[4] In response, Levytsky sent a grievance to the emperor, who in 1816 ordered a school commission to be established.

The commission was assembled the following year by Governor Franz Hauer. Besides eleven gubernial counsellors, the commission included representatives of the Latin (Roman Catholic) consistory (Bishop Andrzej Alojzy Ankwicz and Canon Minasiewicz) and the Greek Catholic consistory (Metropolitan Levytsky and Canon Mohylnytsky). By majority vote the commission recognized Polish as the language of the land (*Landessprache*) in Galicia and accordingly decided that, with the exception of religious instruction, teaching would take place in that language. Schools using the Ukrainian language were to be regarded as private and could not draw from the school fund. Supervision of the school system was placed in the charge of the Latin consistory. In opposition to these decisions, Levytsky and Mohylnytsky lodged a *votum separatum* and then sent to the authorities in Vienna a comprehensive memorandum in which they steadfastly defended Ukrainian as the *Landessprache* for the Ukrainians, basing their position on legal, historical, national and cultural grounds.

Ultimately, in 1818, partly as a consequence of the Greek Catholic hierarchy's pleading, the central Austrian authorities decided that 1) religious instruction for Ukrainian youth was to be conducted in Ukrainian; 2) in the bilingual schools instruction was to be in Polish, but the schools were obliged to teach Greek Catholic children to read and write in Ukrainian; 3) in those schools where the enrolment was exclusively Greek Catholic, instruction was to be in Ukrainian, although reading and writing in Polish as well was mandatory; 4) in localities with existing "mixed" schools, the communities (*gminy*) would be allowed to establish and maintain Ukrainian schools at their own expense; and 5) supervision over the schools belonged to the church authorities of one or another of the rites, depending on the national composition of the school; supervision over mixed schools was to be exercised by the consistory of the rite to which the majority of the children belonged.[5] The Galician school system established on the basis of this directive undoubtedly represented a compromise between Polish and Ukrainian demands, and it was preserved until 1848. Although the regulations of 1818 favoured Polish education, they were still a clear step forward for the Ukrainians in contrast to the earlier programme.

Intense action was begun to develop a Ukrainian school system for the common people. The Societas Presbyterorum [Clerical Society] had already been established in Przemyśl in 1816; it represented the first formal attempt to co-ordinate the efforts of the Ukrainian intelligentsia to publish books with educational and religious content.[6] The initiator of the society was Canon Ivan Mohylnytsky, who prepared its statutes, which were accepted by Metropolitan Levytsky and confirmed by the emperor in July 1816. Only clergymen were invited to membership: Ivan Mohylnytsky, Ihnatii Davydovych, Danylo Kachanovsky, Petro Nazarevych, Vasyl Sozansky, Ivan Trylovsky, Ivan Turchmanovych and Ivan Snihursky. But of this group, only Mohylnytsky and Snihursky laboured diligently on behalf of the Ukrainian national revival in Galicia.

Mohylnytsky understood perfectly well the peasants' hostile attitude to the land-owners. He pointed out in the statutes that the peasants often manifested their opposition to *robot*, to the hereditary lords and to estate officials, whom they regarded as tyrants and oppressors and whose properties were the "legacy of [the peasants'] sweat." The Clerical Society therefore intended, through appropriate literature, to explain to the common people that

> the emperor's authority comes from God, and the imperial decrees, state taxes, military service and decisions of the higher courts are bases absolutely essential for the well-being of society.... The noble landowners cannot be regarded as oppressors and tyrants [*oppressores et tyrani*], but rather as fathers of a family, guides and protectors [*ductores et protectores*] of the people who live on their manors. The villagers should feel love toward them and sincerely fulfill their due obligations, guard and defend their property, and all the more refrain from damaging these possessions.

Mohylnytsky also emphasized that the society would explain that the people's own possessions, gained through hard work, "should be put toward the needs of their homes, to improve their life [and] to insure the welfare of their children, and [that] the excess should be given to the poor or donated for the needs of the church, rather than drunk away at the tavern for the enrichment of the Jews."[7] The contents of the statutes thus make clear that the founders of the Clerical Society interpreted social phenomena in the spirit of the reigning feudal ideology in Austria. They believed that improving education and raising the people's morality were sufficient to safeguard the existing social relationships from class conflict.

The principal aim of the Clerical Society was to prepare religious and pedagogical books for the Ukrainian common people. These books were to be so written that the "uneducated peasantry" [*rudis plebecula*] could use them; that is, they should be written in the vernacular. However, the society was determined to avoid the grosser "errors in peasant speech" and prepare the books so that they would approximate "a more perfect formulation" [*ad elegantiorem sermonem*] and thereby enhance the popular idiom.[8]

The result of this search for an "intermediate" literary form was the mixing of the folk language with Church Slavonic, a style that Zorian Dołęga Chodakowski had so severely criticized.[9] Nevertheless, Mohylnytsky and his associates had recognized, for the first time in the history of the Ukrainian nation in Galicia, the language of the simple people as the essential foundation for national education and literature. The Clerical Society should not be faulted for inconsistency, since contemporary opinion in Slavic studies (notably in Josef Dobrovský's view) held that the literary language was not to be identified with the folk idiom. It was not only the nobles who were biased against the popular speech. In Ivan Franko's characterization, there was widespread conviction in the 1820s that it was "a boorish dialect full of errors and demanding refinement and growth in the direction of assimilation to the Church Slavonic language."[10]

This first Ukrainian society concerned with education in Galicia undertook a broad publishing programme, including school texts and books on farming, hygiene, church history and canon law. The Greek Catholic hierarchy appealed to the clergy to submit works that could be approved by the episcopal synod and rewarded with money. There is no evidence to show whether this campaign produced the expected results, but the recommendations concerning instruction in the parochial schools, prepared by Ivan Lavrovsky and Mykola Torbatsky and preserved in manuscript form, indicate that Ukrainian intellectual life had genuinely come alive.[11] All of the society's efforts were intended to enlighten the Ukrainian peasantry and improve the education of the Greek Catholic clergy. Special attention was devoted to fostering patriotism and loyalty to the Austrian dynasty and the state. Between 1817 and 1821, several textbooks were published through the efforts of the Clerical Society, most of them written by Ivan Mohylnytsky himself. His opponents spread rumours that "Mohylnytsky, as the diocesan inspector of the village schools, had a monopoly on the school texts and did not permit anyone else to write them."[12] However, that was not the case; there simply was no one else to write textbooks in Ukrainian.

The society's activities provoked some opposition among Poles, who did not approve of a publishing campaign aimed at providing the Ukrainian community with only Ukrainian books. Ukrainians associated with the Basilian Order also were ill disposed toward the society, and the pope sharply criticized its statutes and personally admonished Metropolitan Levytsky, who was compelled to reply to these charges in Vienna. Levytsky, for his part, maintained that he had been accused before the Papal Curia by Dorotei Mykhalsky, the hegumen of Saint George's Monastery in Lviv, and Professor Modest Hrynevetsky, both of whom wished to become bishops in Galicia. The Austrian interior ministry, however, backed the metropolitan. Still, it is difficult now fully to understand the details of this episode. Hrynevetsky's published letters to Ivan Snihursky, for example, reveal that he apparently was pleased with the creation of the Clerical Society, and he even promised to help prepare a Ukrainian grammar, despite not having been honoured by society membership.[13] But perhaps Hrynevetsky merely sought to ingratiate himself with Snihursky, who had been newly appointed bishop of Przemyśl.

It is not known for certain how long the Clerical Society continued to operate and what brought its efforts to a close. After becoming Greek Catholic archbishop in Lviv, Metropolitan Levytsky radically altered his attitude toward national work and abandoned his interest in the society. Still, in the 1830s Jernej Kopitar, who was well informed about Galician matters through correspondence with Snihursky and the grammarians Iosyf Levytsky and Iosyf Lozynsky, asked Iakiv Holovatsky about its ongoing activities.[14]

Przemyśl was the only centre of Ukrainian intellectual life in Galicia between 1815 and 1830. There the Clerical Society was established, and there the plans for Ukrainian publications were prepared; from there came the first attempts to defend the Ukrainian language. The most eminent contemporary Ukrainians were there: Mohylnytsky, Snihursky (the Greek Catholic bishop of Przemyśl from 1818 and the patron of Ukrainian literature), Ivan Lavrovsky (professor at Lviv University and rector of the Greek Catholic seminary in Lviv until 1820, then a professor at the lyceum in Przemyśl and a member of the Society of Learning in Cracow), and the grammarians Levytsky and Lozynsky. Their work was closely associated with the efforts of the Ukrainian circle in Vienna that met at the church of Saint Barbara, and for this reason the historical literature speaks of a Vienna-Przemyśl circle of Ukrainian scholars.[15]

Vienna had been a vigorous centre of Slavic studies since the 1810s. Scholars from throughout Slavdom met there, and they often came to Saint Barbara's Church, whose pastors were known for their broad scholarly interests. Frequently the discussions touched on academic topics or the national aspirations of the Slavic nations under the Habsburg monarchy. The participants shared information that later was published in the columns of the *Wiener Allgemeine Literatur Zeitung*. The pastor of Saint Barbara's was Iosyf Striletsky, whose textbook of Ukrainian grammar had been used at the beginning of the nineteenth century by the Greek Catholic seminarians who boarded in Vienna;[16] he also possessed a substantial library, which later became the basis of the capitular libraries in Przemyśl and Lviv. Perhaps more importantly, Striletsky introduced at Saint Barbara's the custom of delivering sermons in Ukrainian, a practice which Snihursky continued after 1813,[17] and which Petro Paslavsky steadfastly observed after 1820. This tradition led to broadening interest in Ukrainian and to the first literary attempts in that tongue. Between 1820 and 1822 Iosyf Levytsky and Kyrylo Blonsky published in Vienna a work entitled *Domoboliie prokliatykh* [Nostalgia of the damned], a translation of *Das Heimweh der Verbannten*. However, the language of *Domoboliie* was a macaronic mix of the folk idiom, Old Church Slavonic and Russian, and it could not offer an effective model for future endeavours.

The most important activity of the so-called Vienna-Przemyśl circle was its work on linguistic matters and the closely associated national question. Kopitar's knowledge about Ukrainian, for example, in large measure came from his Ukrainian informants Ivan Olshavsky, the pastor of Saint Barbara's between 1804 and 1812, and Ivan Mohylnytsky, who spent some time in Vienna in 1816. Nevertheless, in reviewing a treatise by Dobrovský on the etymology of the Slavic languages in 1814, Kopitar revealed little understanding of Ukrainian, which he regarded as "plattrussisch" or "eine Varietät der russischen." However, two years later, in "Rusniakische Literatur," a review of Mohylnytsky's *Nauky parokhialni* [Parish sermons] (Buda 1816), Kopitar stated explicitly that Ukrainian, though not a literary language, lived on the lips of the simple Ukrainian people of Galicia and Russian Ukraine and was distinct from both Polish and Russian. About nine million people spoke Ukrainian, and accordingly it merited nurturing.[18] Kopitar's attitude must have strengthened Mohylnytsky's views on the essence and role of the Ukrainian language and encouraged him to defend it resolutely in his memoranda of 1818 and 1822, as well as in his 1829 "Discourse on the Ruthenian Language."

In 1821, Metropolitan Levytsky made plans to issue a circular in Ruthenian, which the Greek Catholic consistories had not done for many years. The *Gubernium* opposed this step with the argument that it was not possible to use a language that lacked the appropriate literary traditions and was unintelligible to the people. In reply, Mohylnytsky penned a comprehensive memorandum in which he showed that Ruthenian was not a mixture of Polish and Russian, but rather a separate branch of the proto-Slavic tongue. It was close to the Slavonic language preserved in ecclesiastical books, and in no way could it be identified with Russian. Basing his argument on old documents, Mohylnytsky demonstrated that Ruthenian was as old and well developed as the other Slavic languages and actually surpassed several of them. He also accorded the Ruthenian nation an independent place among the other Slavic nations.[19]

Mohylnytsky's endeavors during the 1820s had enormous impact on the linguistic and national views of those who came after him, particularly on Levytsky, Lozynsky and the Ruthenian Triad. Yet in his eloquent insistence on the separateness and independence of the Ukrainian language, Mohylnytsky committed a serious error by not drawing a clear distinction between the popular idiom and Church Slavonic. He thought that combining these languages in literature would in effect produce a Ukrainian literary language and thus unwittingly contributed to unleashing the long-lasting linguistic and literary disputes. Ivan Lavrovsky, an eminent contemporary expert on Church Slavonic and the folk idiom, held similar views. He left a "Ruthenian-Polish-German Dictionary" in manuscript form. The language of his commentaries "approximates to a maximum the folk idiom."[20]

The Vienna-Przemyśl circle, however, did not limit its efforts to matters of education and language. Members of it also gathered materials on the history of the Greek Catholic church and of the Ruthenian lands and Ruthenian printing, and old documents. Zorian Dołęga Chodakowski noted that he saw in Lviv, in Father Hrynevetsky's possession, a Graeco-Slavonic grammar dating from 1591, which was entirely "unknown to the general scholarly community." He tried but failed to persuade Hrynevetsky to offer the book to the collection at the lyceum in Kremianets, because Hrynevetsky "himself is an admirer of such things and the Uniate clerics here are diligently collecting books for their seminary library." Instead, Ivan Lavrovsky presented to the lyceum a "gold coin [with the image] of Stanisław August, minted in 1774."[21]

Lavrovsky himself assembled an extensive library in Przemyśl, numbering about thirty thousand volumes and containing many rare works, incunabula and Ruthenian manuscripts. He also organized the well-endowed capitular archive. Bishop Snihursky, who was very concerned with improving the parochial schools and had opened an institute for cantors and village teachers in Przemyśl in 1818, possessed a similar library. In 1829 Snihursky also established an episcopal printing shop in Przemyśl, which published books valuable to the rebirth of the Ukrainian nation in Galicia. Snihursky himself often gave financial help to Ukrainian youth and, according to Iakiv Holovatsky, "encouraged them to work at uplifting the native literature." Lozynsky maintained that Snihursky "was a true and, at the time, the only patron of [Ukrainian] writers."[22]

The Ukrainian scholars in Galicia took a lively interest in the broad spectrum of Slavic questions. They were well acquainted with the pertinent academic literature and corresponded widely with the most eminent Slavic scholars. The anonymous author of the article "Moloda Rus'" [Young Rus'], which appeared in the newspaper *Zoria Halytska* [Galician star] in 1850, linked the beginnings of Ukrainian national thought in Galicia with the spread after the Napoleonic wars of the idea of nationality:

> I still recall as though it were yesterday, because my young years saw those moments when my peers at Lviv university often spoke about the Ruthenian world, about the past, about our sacred homeland, and tears streamed down many pale faces. They longed for something; they desired and expected something; they wanted to say something to the world, proclaim it to their neighbours, but words could not yet convey the feelings that were bursting from the depths of their hearts. Indeed, here and there a voice was raised; however, it was frightened, weak, like a child that begins to whimper. The bard had not yet appeared; the nightingale had not sung [*ne bulo shche pivtsia, ne bulo soloviia*].[23]

These dreams were fulfilled and given tangible form by Markiian Shashkevych, who organized the national endeavours among his young friends from Lviv University and the Greek Catholic seminary. In the early 1830s, Iakiv Holovatsky and Ivan Vahylevych formed an educational circle which was jokingly called the "Ruthenian Triad" by their friends. Their efforts opened a new era in the history of the Ukrainian nation in Galicia, the era of its national consciousness.[24]

The precise date of the formation of the Triad is not known because of significant discrepancies in Iakiv Holovatsky's memoirs and notes. Apparently, it took place in 1832.[25] The main figure in the group was undoubtedly Shashkevych. The son of a village pastor, who from childhood knew intimately the Ukrainian common people and their needs, of engaging appearance and with a poetic nature, and possessing an extraordinary gift for persuasion, he became the group's true organizer and recognized leader. His enthusiastic work for his nation and his straightforwardness in communicating with people gained him general admiration and respect. Holovatsky later recalled:

> When he [Shashkevych] unwound about Ruthenianness, about nationality, about the native language and the native literature, then the power of his spirit became apparent.... His eyes glistened keenly, and with a kind of holy inspiration his brow became wrinkled and his face took on a kind of fierce seriousness. He spoke with sincerity; he was powerfully persuasive because his thoughts flowed from his heart; all of him lived and breathed this [Ruthenian] spirit.[26]

During his studies at the gymnasia in Lviv and Berezhany, as well as later, Shashkevych acquired a substantial knowledge of classical, German and Polish literatures and of Slavic studies and linguistics. He became acquainted with the works of Karadžić, Dobrovský, Šafařík, Linde and Ignacy Rakowiecki, and with Pavlovsky's Ukrainian grammar. They revealed to him "a great world—the Slavic world."[27] That which Shashkevych acquired he plumbed and passed on to his colleagues, both in direct and frequent conversations and through his poetic works, in which he exhibited a gift for expressing the thoughts, feelings and desires of contemporary Ukrainian youth. He achieved and made known a synthesis of their aspirations.

Ivan Vahylevych possessed entirely different merits. He was distinguished by his extensive knowledge of history, ethnography, mythology and Old Ruthenian literature. He was above all else a scholar. He tested his powers in poetry and in literary translations, but without great success; his was a ponderous, rough style that did not particularly lend itself to this type of creative effort. However, he laid down the historical foundation for the Ukrainians' national aspirations through his encyclopedic knowledge. He linked the present with the past traditions of an independent Ukraine-Rus', and he armed Ukrainian national thought with logical and firm historical arguments.

Among the three men, Iakiv Holovatsky was the most practical and the best organizer. He did not retreat from difficulties; he successfully brought to fruition his own and his colleagues' plans, the best example of which was the publication of the *Rusalka Dnistrovaia*. In the 1840s, when the ties that bound these young friends had loosened, he renewed efforts in literature and publishing. The best proof of his energy and indefatigable activity was his extensive correspondence with virtually all of the leading national spokesmen among the Slavs.

Mykhailo Bulvynsky, N. Kushlyk, Iosyf Lovytsky, Iuliian Iaminsky, Mykola Ustyianovych, Semen Pleshkevych, P. Lukashevych, Porfyrii Bilynkevych, Iosyf Skomorovsky, Antin Mohylnytsky and Lev Treshchakovsky eventually joined the circle of the Triad. It was precisely these men whom Dmytro Mokhnatsky named in his deposition as members of the "russische Partei" at the seminary.[28] From other sources we know that Ivan Holovatsky, Viktor Lopatynsky, Iosyf Ostrozhynsky, Iosyf Okhrymovych, Roman Pasichynsky and Ivan Pokynsky,[29] as well as Ivan Biretsky, Hryhorii Ilkevych, Iosafat Kobrynsky, Rudolf Mokh and Ivan Vendzilovych, also belonged to Shashkevych's circle. In joining, everyone adopted a Slavic first name, signed his name to the album called the "Ruska Zoria" [Ruthenian star], and took a solemn oath that henceforth he would work intensely for the well-being and enlightenment of the Ukrainian nation. From that moment they appeared in literature under their adopted names: "Ruslan" Shashkevych, "Dalibor" Vahylevych, "Iaroslav" (Iakiv) Holovatsky, "Bohdan" (Ivan) Holovatsky, "Velymyr" Lopatynsky and "Myroslav" Ilkevych, for example.[30] Among all those mentioned, only Ilkevych, a teacher in the trivium school in Kolomyia, and Ivan Holovatsky, a doctor in Vienna, were laymen. Therefore Ivan Franko was correct in saying, "To speak of the intelligentsia among us before the abolition of *robot* means to speak of the clergy; there was no other intelligentsia."[31] Ivan Vahylevych frankly acknowledged, "The worst thing is still that among us South Rus' people, there is no one of any other class besides the clergy.... Luchkai, Levytsky, Lozynsky.... Vereshchynsky—they are all priests! And I am studying to become a priest!"[32]

The national rebirth among the Galician Ukrainians before 1848, in contrast to the analogous process in Russian Ukraine, was the work of the young clerical intelligentsia. Ukrainian publications offer distinct proof: between 1837 and 1850, of forty-three published works, forty were written by clergymen. Among these publications, there were seven religious titles, seven works of poetry and homilies for various occasions, four translations and six journals (and it should be remembered that the Ukrainian journals in Galicia did not begin to appear until 1848).[33] Nevertheless, the efforts of this generation of Ukrainian intellectuals had little in common with the majority of the Greek Catholic hierarchy and with the church's activities. They were concerned almost exclusively with laying a foundation for a national literature in the language of the common people. The path toward this goal led the young national awakeners through folklore and the publication of Ukrainian literary miscellanies, as well as through linguistics and history. Most of all, they came to know the older documents and relics of their nation's past.

The young Ukrainians recognized the difficulties of their enterprise. As Iakiv Holovatsky noted, since most were more proficient in Polish than in their native language, they probably would have won greater literary success by writing in Polish. But this step would have meant embracing Polish literature and Polish intellectual life, and thus renouncing their aspirations for national independence and joining with the Polish nation. Such a choice seemed a crime to them.[34] Necessarily, they chose their own course. Having through heated discussion come to the conclusion that they knew little about the Ukrainian nation and nothing about the language or life of the common people, they followed the example of the Poles Zorian Dołęga Chodakowski and Wacław z Oleska. As Iakiv Holovatsky wrote, they decided

> to go among the people, to do studies on the spot, from their very lips to collect songs of which thousands have been preserved in the memory of the nation, to record their proverbs and adages, their tales and legends; in a word, we philosophers must go among the people and learn their wisdom. After such reflections the question arose in turn, who is prepared to overcome all the obstacles and difficulties of this purpose? And I first decided to go to the people.[35]

Several Ukrainians earlier had undertaken to collect songs. Hryhorii Ilkevych gathered many that found their way into the *Polish and Ruthenian Songs* of Wacław Zaleski. Iakiv Holovatsky maintained that before he began his methodical journeys through Galicia (which could have taken place in the summer of 1833 at the earliest), he already possessed a fair collection of Ukrainian folk songs, copied partly from Maksymovych's collection and partly from Wacław Zaleski's, but he also had noted down many original songs from various localities, initially in Polish orthography because "no one knew the Ruthenian script."[36]

In the 1830s several persons began to collect songs: Markiian Shashkevych and his brother Antin in the Zolochiv district; Ivan Vahylevych in the Chortkiv, Stanyslaviv, Stryi and Zolochiv districts; Iakiv Holovatsky in virtually all of Galicia and in Transcarpathian Rus'; Ivan Holovatsky and his wife Mariia among the Hutsuls in the Pokuttia region; Ivan Biretsky in the Sanok district; S. Semenovych in the Kolomyia district; Mykhailo Tymniak in the Zolochiv district; Ivan Bilynsky in the Berezhany district; and Markyl Kulchytsky in the Stryi district. Among the older generation, Iosyf Levytsky collected songs in the Zhovkva district and Iosyf Lozynsky in the Przemyśl district. Other collectors were Stepan Petrushevych, the father of the historian Antin Petrushevych, Mykhailo Mynchakevych and Mykhailo Hnidkovsky. In addition, Vahylevych personally won over several other individuals to the same task.[37]

Ethnographic excursions produced extensive folkloristic materials that were only partially exploited in the Triad's later publications. Iakiv Holovatsky eventually gave a substantial portion of the songs to Osyp Bodiansky, which were not published until the 1860s and 1870s in Moscow. However, the creative works of the Triad circle indicate that, except for Shashkevych, no one had a fundamental command of the folk idiom and no one used this speech in his writings. All of their attempts were various compromises with Church Slavonic and Russian. Iakiv Holovatsky's correspondence provides ample evidence of this fact.

Ethnographic research convinced the young Ukrainians that they were part of a very limited group of persons who were seriously interested in the artifacts and oral tradition of their own nation. Holovatsky wrote in his work, "Podróż po Halickiej i Węgierskiej Rusi" [A journey through Galician and Hungarian Rus'], "We have no writers and men of learning among us as in other lands, neither in the countryside nor in the cities and towns, who love the objects of their homeland [and] who, by gathering [national] relics in their region, could teach a traveller and aid him with good advice.... [We] do not have a single work that contains the precious local artifacts."[38] Thus, this group had to rely all the more on its own strength. The substantial impact of folk creativity on the social, political and national views of the Triad and their contemporaries cannot be ignored, and indeed folklore may have been the principal source of their endeavors.[39] The common people often sang of their difficult fate and complained of *robot* and other feudal obligations. They decried the taxes and long-term military service imposed on them and criticized the lords, officials and priests. But they praised the legendary brigands and sang songs about the battles of the Cossacks and about Ukraine, which was presented as a land of freedom and liberty. These songs demonstrate that the Ukrainian people living on both sides of the Zbruch River had preserved a sense of ethnic and national unity.

Their common work drew the Ukrainian enthusiasts very closely together. Holovatsky's correspondence shows that it was precisely in the Romantic era that a love for national work was born, and it was recognized that Shashkevych had achieved a breakthrough in this area. Mykola Vereshchynsky called for retaining Shashkevych's rules in writing Ukrainian because "he directed us to the correct path."[40] Ivan Biretsky said that everything that concerned the Ruthenian nation and its glory pleased Shashkevych.[41] Antin Petrushevych believed that it was Iakiv Holovatsky who lit in his heart "the flame of love for the homeland" and led him onto the path without which "the glory of the Ruthenian nation would have been foreign to me, the graves of [our] ancestors would have been silent, and [my] heart would not have beaten so fiercely in [my] breast at the thought of the fate and lot of Ukraine."[42] Even the Polish *mandatarius* Kilarski fell under Holovatsky's sway, as is evidenced in his letter to Holovatsky:

> For the three years of our inseparable life together—the most exuberant, most intense, richest in dreams and hopes in the epoch of the life of a man—I became so accustomed to you and intimate with you that, if you were the pope and I was a swineherd or vice versa, my meeting or conversation with you would be the same as in 1836 or 1837.... May God bring back the days so that we could live somewhere close to one another even for a year.[43]

5. The Triad's Literary Activities

The most important facet of the Ruthenian Triad's activity was indisputably its literary efforts. Everything else was to be subordinated to them; even scholarly work was aimed at codifying Ukrainian grammar with a view to applying it to belles lettres. The Triad realized that it could best reach the common people through literary works in their own idiom. Simple, easily understood poems, stories, novellas and fables modelled on folk tales were intended, on the one hand, to raise the nation's literacy and, on the other hand, to help entrench national consciousness. However, there was little or no notion that such changes were virtually impossible without a fundamental alteration of the prevailing social and economic system. Some may have considered this prerequisite, but no one spoke openly of it and no one proposed reforms. In their literary work the Ukrainian enthusiasts expressed themselves on national rather than social issues, and despite sharp protest against social inequality, injustices toward the common people and *robot*, they did not suggest fundamental change.

The first anthology of Ukrainian poetry in Galicia, though not intended for publication and actually prepared before the Triad was formed, was entitled *Syn Rusy* [The son of Rus']. It is generally believed to have been compiled in 1833, simply because that year appears on the cover of the work.[1] Nevertheless, many facts speak for an earlier date. First of all, Iakiv Holovatsky was apparently unaware of *Syn Rusy* until it was reprinted in 1887. Furthermore, when he undertook his first journey through Galicia in the summer of 1833, he was already a member of the Triad. At that time, he met Hryhorii Ilkevych in Kolomyia, whose collection of folk songs included M. Muchynsky's poem "Kohut rozsvit vypivaie" [The cock sings at dawn], which also appeared in *Syn Rusy*. This poem may have found its way into the anthology from Ilkevych's collection, but it is equally possible that the anthology indirectly furnished it to Ilkevych, because it became a very popular folk song.[2]

It is doubtful, however, that *Syn Rusy* dates from early 1830 or that Shashkevych was dismissed from the seminary on 28 February 1830 for being its compiler, as has been suggested.[3] There is no evidence for this in the seminary authorities' correspondence of 1830,[4] or in the later correspondence of the church and gubernial authorities regarding Shashkevych's case. From the extant correspondence, it is apparent that the seminarians were severely punished for disciplinary infractions;[5] in Shashkevych's case there was no reason to expect a lesser punishment. Still, how Shashkevych occupied himself during the year and a half from his dismissal until October 1831 is not known, although he was certainly not inactive.[6] Therefore it can be assumed that *Syn Rusy* was compiled during 1830-31, and that the November 1830 insurrection exerted a considerable influence on it. Moreover, certain anti-Polish accents in the work may have stemmed from the reports then circulating about the self-centred national and social policies of the leaders of the Polish insurrection.[7] There was a significant difference in tone and emphasis between *Syn Rusy* and the later literary miscellany entitled *Zoria*, which the Triad submitted to the censors in May 1834. The distinction is so marked that considerable time must have passed between the appearance of *Syn Rusy* and the editing of *Zoria*. The dates 1830-31 for *Syn Rusy* are also buttressed by the fact that there were no works by Holovatsky or Vahylevych in the anthology.

Syn Rusy contained no allusions to the existing social conditions; it even sought to present Ukrainian life in an idyllic manner. However, it did not sidestep the national question, and therein lay its value and significance. The Ukrainian authors were aware of their national distinctiveness; they regarded their country as the Ruthenian land inherited from their forefathers, over which Ruthenian princes had once ruled and where battles were fought with their enemies. Seeing the centuries-old bondage of their nation, the young writers called for a national awakening, the pooling of efforts for the development of literature, and national enlightenment. One contribution, Mynchakevych's "Satyra" [Satire], was the first literary expression of Polish-Ukrainian antagonism in Galicia. It depicted a dispute between two brothers—a stubborn Ruthenian and a proud Pole—who could no longer endure each other, "like salt in the eye," and whom even a third neighbour, Austria, could not reconcile. The Pole, fearing his Austrian brother, humbled himself somewhat, and despite his malice he could do nothing evil against the Ruthenian, who only now, under the rule of Austria, felt truly fortunate. It is difficult to assess the significance of *Syn Rusy* in the further moulding of the national aspirations of Ukrainian youth. It certainly awakened an interest in the national issue, but since it remained in manuscript, it could not circulate widely in the Ukrainian community, and for that reason it was quickly forgotten. Even the contributors to it did not recall its existence.

The young Ukrainians became convinced that it was very difficult to write in a national language that lacked developed literary models, that many obstacles had to be overcome, and that great effort was required to introduce an appropriate orthography. Much self-denial and sacrifice was necessary, and not many were willing to endure such a course. From the moment when Holovatsky and Vahylevych joined the circle of admirers of the Ukrainian language, however, the Triad occupied itself in earnest with literature.

On 4 May 1834 the Triad submitted to the Lviv censors the literary anthology entitled *Zoria, pysemtse prysviashchenoie ruskomu iazyku* [The star, a note dedicated to the Ruthenian language]. Because there was no censor for Ruthenian books in Lviv, the manuscript was forwarded to the police authorities in Vienna, where the censor of Slavic books was Jernej Kopitar. He was already familiar with some works by Ukrainian writers from Galicia, because he as censor had reviewed the grammars by Mohylnytsky, Levytsky and Lozynsky, as well as Lozynsky's *Ruskoje wesile* [Ruthenian wedding].[8] However, for Kopitar *Zoria* was an exceptional phenomenon. He appreciated its literary merit, but he also recognized its political significance. Political considerations—concern for the welfare of the Austrian monarchy, to which Kopitar was wholeheartedly attached (he hoped Vienna would become the centre of the spiritual life of the Slavs)—prevailed, with disastrous consequences for *Zoria*. Kopitar was convinced that the moment it was published, this new Ukrainian literary anthology would have a strong impact throughout Ukrainian intellectual circles and would awaken Ukrainian national consciousness in Galicia. He also believed that it would have at least some influence among Ukrainians in Russia. This could elicit Polish opposition, and certainly opposition by the Russians, who were averse to any kind of separatism. The appearance of *Zoria* could strengthen the Ukrainian intellectuals in Russia against "the wielders of power in Saint Petersburg" [*Petersburger Machtgewalt*]. Since only under extraordinary circumstances might the Ukrainians in Russia join with the Ukrainians in Austria, the Russian authorities would find a way to steer their opposition against the Austrian state. Ultimately, Kopitar did not want to decide by himself whether to allow *Zoria* to be printed; he advised asking the opinion of the censor in Lviv, who was more familiar with Polish-Ukrainian relations and could "later explain his political judgement."[9]

The necessity of a censorial review of *Zoria* hastened the nomination of a censor for Ruthenian books in Galicia, a matter that had been dragging on since 1832, when Iosyf Levytsky had submitted his Ukrainian grammar to the censors. There were many candidates for this position, including Mikołaj Michalewicz,[10] although finally Venedykt Levytsky, a professor at Lviv University and later rector of the Greek Catholic seminary, was the government's choice. Until 1848, he presided over the cultural and national life of the Galician Ukrainians, resolutely opposing any progressive tendencies.

Levytsky issued a negative judgement on *Zoria*, because, in his opinion, its content and language were indecent and because it openly espoused the idea that the Ruthenians were oppressed, politically and religiously, by the Poles. Reminding the public of these facts, Levytsky maintained, was most inadvisable. Moreover, the very fact that one of the authors signed himself "Russland" [Russia] (or so Levytsky read the name "Ruslan") could raise the suspicion that the Ruthenians, theretofore loyal to Austria, were gravitating toward Russia.[11]

What was it in *Zoria* that could have so upset Levytsky that he disallowed its publication? Unfortunately, the manuscript of the anthology has not been preserved. In Kopitar's earlier evaluation, however, we read:

> The content of the manuscript is basically all right; in its entirety in respect to language, materials and opinions, it is rather thorough and adequate, sometimes even ingenious. The essence of the booklet is Ruthenian folk songs, a biography of Khmelnytsky in prose, a popularly written short story about him, a humorous and satirical complaint about a new pastor which presents his office in detail, etc. All of this is in good Ruthenian. However, the recorded fragments of the songs about the Cossack leader Khmelnytsky are hostile toward the Poles.[12]

Iakiv Holovatsky indicated that all the materials contained in *Zoria*, with the exception of the article about Khmelnytsky, which Shashkevych had subsequently lost, were later included in *Rusalka Dnistrovaia* in 1837. Nothing more regarding the contents of *Zoria* is known.[13]

The prohibition against *Zoria* had a depressing effect upon Shashkevych. His hopes collapsed for the rapid development of Ukrainian literature and through it the awakening of the Ukrainians' national consciousness, leading him to a pessimistic assessment of the possibility of further national work. He termed such efforts "children's games and fantasies that are impossible to realize." He relied instead on German benevolence for the Ukrainian cause and reform from above. Shashkevych also confided in Holovatsky that the director of the Lviv police had invited him to dinner, questioned him about the Ukrainians' aspirations, and promised much on condition that the Ukrainians not co-operate with Polish conspirators. Holovatsky, who had just returned from studying philosophy at the university in Budapest, told his friend about the national movements among the other Slavs, and he identified the Germans as their greatest enemies. Holovatsky's words restored Shashkevych's faith in his own powers, and he began to busy himself anew with literature. He wrote and encouraged others to write; the group of admirers of national literature grew, and Mykola Ustyianovych, among others, joined the circle of the Triad.[14]

The result of these renewed efforts was *Rusalka Dnistrovaia*, the first Ukrainian literary anthology in Galicia, which was printed in Budapest in late 1836 and carried a publication date of 1837.[15] By publishing in Hungary, the Triad hoped to circumvent the censor in Lviv who had been so hostile to *Zoria*. Besides, *Rusalka* could not be printed in Galicia because neither the presses at the Stavropygian Institute nor the episcopal print shop in Przemyśl possessed the requisite modern Cyrillic font. Although it could have been printed in Vienna, that would have required permission from Kopitar, and the Triad feared that he would again defer to the censor in Lviv. Iakiv Holovatsky, who had lived in Budapest in 1834 and 1835, was quite familiar with conditions there and had established ties with Ján Kollár and several Serbian and Croatian national awakeners. The Serb Georgij Petrović submitted the manuscript of *Rusalka* to the censorship board in Budapest, which issued a favourable opinion. Printing was complete by early December 1836. The costs were covered largely by the great friend of the Triad and the patron of Ukrainian literature in Galicia, Mykola Vereshchynsky; Shashkevych paid the rest.[16]

In April 1837, Petrović sent most of the copies of *Rusalka* to Vienna, where the police authorities seized a substantial number of them and ordered a critique by the censor in Lviv. In spite of the Triad's manoeuver, Venedykt Levytsky was to decide the anthology's fate. His review was devastating. *Rusalka* undermined the foundations of the state, religion and morality, and special police permission should be required to read it.[17] On the other hand, Kopitar in Vienna conceded that *Rusalka* could be sold and cited in catalogues, but could not be discussed in the press. He defended the editors, noting that although they introduced their own dialect into literature, they had not exceeded acceptable limits. Kopitar did not understand Levytsky's animosity.[18]

The Viennese police also requested the critique from the Hungarian censor. Because of this, Petrović could report to Holovatsky that "*Rusalka* is saved"; it would soon be approved and then "we shall triumph." After a while he wrote that "*Rusalka*, ab excelso Consilio Regio sub sessione dto 26 Juni, is approved and may be sold publicly."[19] However, permission was not given for its sale in Galicia. Thus a book intended for the Ukrainian reader—a first-rate work of crucial importance for the development of Ukrainian literature and the formation of a Ukrainian national consciousness—was unavailable in Galicia until 1848. On the other hand, it could be distributed and purchased in the rest of the monarchy.

Was the reason for this paradoxical situation that the book "undermined morality"? Definitely not. The Hungarian censor believed that it arose from a desire to prevent the growth of any kind of Ruthenian literature.[20] *Rusalka* was written in a simple folk idiom, such as the Ukrainians used in the areas surrounding Chortkiv and Kolomyia. The book elevated this speech to a literary language, a point that Kopitar had underscored. The editors had also employed a phonetic spelling and used the modern Cyrillic alphabet. These features represented significant innovation in Ukrainian writings in Galicia and could not have pleased Venedykt Levytsky, all the more because he was an important dignitary in the Greek Catholic church, for which the only literary language was Church Slavonic. The Triad circle also realized that the new orthography was the reason *Rusalka* was suppressed in Galicia,[21] although its fate may also have been affected by the fact that the editors had not sought the support of the ecclesiastical authorities, who certainly knew about its preparation. (For example, Spyrydon Lytvynovych wrote to Bishop Snihursky that he had learned from Father Mykhailo Malynovsky that Shashkevych "is supposed to have some kind of Ruthenian publication at hand for the New Year.")[22]

It was not only churchmen who reacted aversely to *Rusalka*. Iakiv Holovatsky noted that it was

> conceived at an inopportune hour. Instead of aid and encouragement, there were only jeers, dissatisfaction, even hostility. It became apparent that there were as many opinions as minds. There were those who would have welcomed it happily, but not in that garb [the modernized alphabet]. One did not like this, another did not like that. There was no lack of those who completely disowned such a wonder and looked at it with the eye of a devil.[23]

The sharpest objections, however, were raised by Iosyf Levytsky, who had been regarded as an oracle on matters of language and orthography since 1834, when his Ukrainian grammar was published. He did not care for the pagan names (Dalibor, Ruslan and Iaroslav) adopted by the editors of *Rusalka* or for the orthography, which "offended the eye with its barbarism." He also disliked its contents and grammar. Finally, he expressly endorsed the authorities' position: "Let there be thanks to the government, which keeps a vigilant eye not only on political conditions, but on unnecessary novelties, and has not allowed *Rusalka Dnistrovaia* to be disseminated in the form in which it issued from the hands of the triumvirate [Triad]."[24]

The rector of the seminary in Lviv, Venedykt Levytsky, who as late as November 1836 had boasted that it was on his initiative that the seminarians became interested in Ukrainian literature, now took a resolute stand against the Triad. In mid-June 1837, he sent to the consistory a "Report Concerning the Work *Rusalka Dnistrovaia* Published in Hungary," as a consequence of which Shashkevych, Vahylevych and Holovatsky were obliged to remain in Lviv during the academic vacation. Next a detailed inquiry was conducted regarding the publication of *Rusalka*, and its findings were submitted to the metropolitan and the gubernial authorities. The young writers ably defended themselves. Shashkevych stated clearly that his intention was to lay the foundations of a literary language and a national literature. Convinced that the Ukrainian language differed fundamentally from Church Slavonic and Russian, he had chosen to write in the vernacular. He had even financially supported the printing, because he wanted to be able to learn readers' reactions before proceeding with further work. He persuasively refuted the charge of disregarding the censorship board by noting that identical principles of censorship were mandated throughout the Austrian state; the standards applied in Hungary, where the manuscript had been submitted to the censor, were the same as in Lviv or Vienna. Vahylevych, for his part, disclaimed any involvement in preparing the publication, declaring that his works had been included without his knowledge and that they were the same ones he had given to Holovatsky for the earlier *Zoria*. Holovatsky, however, assumed full responsibility for publication, emphatically declaring that he had submitted the manuscript to the censor in Budapest in 1835, when, as a student of philosophy at the university there, he was not subject to the clerical authorities in Galicia. He further noted that *Rusalka* was published in 1836, not in 1837 as was printed on the title page.[25]

As a result of the inquiry, all three men received reprimands. The investigation revealed complete co-operation between the Greek Catholic church and the state authorities. The director of the police, having the national aspirations of the Ukrainian activists in mind, was heard to remark: "We are up to our ears in trouble with one [Polish] nationality, and those hotheads [*Tollköpfe*] still want to awaken the dead and buried Ruthenian nationality."[26] In fact, despite the ban, *Rusalka* did awaken the "buried nationality." Today there can be no doubt that *Rusalka* launched modern Ukrainian literature in Galicia and was a milestone in the formation of a national consciousness.[27] Its revolutionary role in shaping the Ukrainians' national and social values was no less important than its contribution to literature, language and orthography.

On the reverse side of the title page of *Rusalka* appeared Ján Kollár's epigram:

Hope flourishes
Not when eyes are saddened,
But when hands are busied.

Another of his epigrams was placed at the beginning of the first chapter: "Folk songs are the firmest foundation of education, the element of culture, the buttress of nationality, the defence and pillar of the language." These words captured virtually the entire programme of the Triad—the precept to act for the welfare of the nation, for its enlightenment and its national consciousness, as well as to indicate the means toward this goal by making use of the nation's achievements and language. *Rusalka* was intended to fortify these aspirations and direct them on their proper course. The authors pointed to the nation's difficult situation, extolled its struggle for social and national liberation, glorified the former splendour of Ukraine-Rus', stressed the national unity between Ukrainians in Galicia and Russia,[28] evoked a sort of Slavic federation in which all the Slavs "will join in brotherhood in the full, bright sun," and buoyed the Ukrainian community's hope for a better future.

Rusalka was not a large book. Folk songs and scholarly and literary works of the Triad were presented on 135 pages. Shashkevych's contributions included the introduction and poems ("Zhadka" [Remembrance] and "Pohonia" [The chase] among others), the short stories "Olena" and "Starovyna" [Olden times], a review of Lozynsky's

Ruskoje wesile, translations of Serbian songs and fragments of the Czech *Rukopis královédvorský*; Vahylevych wrote *Peredhovor k narodnym ruskym pisniam* [An Introduction to Ruthenian songs] and some poems; Holovatsky contributed poems, translations of Serbian songs and an article entitled "A Brief Account of Slavic and Ruthenian Manuscripts Found in the Library of the Monastery of Saint Basil the Great in Lviv." Holovatsky also prepared for publication a Ruthenian document dating from 1424.

For the present-day reader, *Rusalka* has no great literary value. Only Shashkevych's poetic work can still move us. *Rusalka* was a child of its times, the expression of an awakening nation, and that was the way in which friends of the Triad understood its role. As Ivan Holovatsky wrote, "Having now read *Rusalka*, I learned what zealous Ruthenians prepared it. However, pitifully they were not allowed to take pleasure in it. It was like an aromatic flower in the wilderness, but it was not allowed to come into full bloom."[29]

Rusalka's fate had serious consequences for Ukrainian literature. The young Ukrainians, disillusioned by their lack of success, lost hope and the desire to continue their work,[30] and Shashkevych's circle gradually dissolved. He himself, after abandoning hopes of advancement in the church administration, completed his theological studies in 1838 and moved to the countryside. To the end of his life he fulfilled the duties of a village pastor in the Zolochiv district. Thus Lviv lost an organizer who could inspire the young generation. Just what Shashkevych had meant to his colleagues is apparent in Mykhailo Kozanovych's words: "From the time [our] countrymen began to criticize, flog and drive away your innocent daughter [*Rusalka*], I fell into melancholy; my feelings remained hidden in a heart full of pain, and, separated from you by the world, I remained without consolation, family and a friend."[31]

Shashkevych, preoccupied with his pastoral work and financial troubles and mortally ill with tuberculosis, did not, however, abandon his literary interests. He kept abreast of Ukrainian poetry; one expression of his continued interest was the poem "Pobratymovi," which he dedicated to Mykola Ustyianovych. It demonstrated the further crystallization of Shashkevych's national views, for in it he stressed the national unity of the Ukrainians living on both sides of the Zbruch River and the necessity of creating a homogeneous Ukrainian literature for that entire nation.[32]

Historical writings on the national awakening of the Ukrainians in Galicia frequently emphasize that the Triad acted as one and held common views before 1848. However, Holovatsky's correspondence reveals a more complex reality. To be sure, Shashkevych's ideas and the direction he laid out in the 1830s were preserved. Vereshchynsky, for instance, insisted that it was necessary to preserve Shashkevych's orthography in Ukrainian publications, writing, "Since we praised Markiian for his Ruthenian heart, let us preserve in memory the principles in writing that he left behind. He guided us onto the right path; why should we grasp at foreign prattle when we have our native speech? Let the monument erected to Markiian not amount to pharisaic incense."[33] By 1849, however, those orthographic principles were no longer observed.

After *Rusalka*, personal contacts among the members of the Triad also began to lessen. Ivan Holovatsky was even convinced that Shashkevych's departure for the countryside meant he was lost to Ukrainian literature, and he reacted somewhat harshly: "And even more [than for *Rusalka*] I am sorry for our Ruslan [Shashkevych], who seems so wastefully to have succumbed to parasitism [*shcho lebon tak marnisinko na darmoida pustyvsia*] and forgotten about everything that was just. Now I recognize him, when I see that he has already been brought to ruin."[34] Ivan Holovatsky was wrong, however. He could not have known much about the later fate of the editor of *Rusalka*, because the other members of the Triad did not remain in touch with him. Each pursued his own affairs. Vahylevych in the late 1830s established a close association with the Poles and became involved in academic work. Iakiv Holovatsky took advantage of his situation as an extern in the seminary and in 1839 travelled widely through Galicia and Transcarpathian Rus', after which he stayed at Vereshchynsky's home in Kolomyia and began to prepare for publication an edition of Ukrainian proverbs that Hryhorii Ilkevych had collected. For the next several years Holovatsky was the real co-ordinator of Ukrainian literary and publishing work in Galicia.

Holovatsky's association with Ilkevych dated from 1833, when they had collaborated in gathering folk songs with the intention of publishing them later. It was probably with this aim in mind that Ilkevych gave his collection to Holovatsky. Although for the time being nothing came of the project, their association continued, and Holovatsky made annual visits to Ilkevych in Kolomyia.[35] Some of the folk songs Ilkevych collected did eventually appear in anthologies published by the Poles Wacław Zaleski and Żegota Pauli, as well as in *Rusalka Dnistrovaia*,[36] but Ilkevych's collection of Ukrainian proverbs, which Iakiv Holovatsky hoped to publish in 1840,[37] was far more significant. Holovatsky, fearing difficulties in Galicia, hoped to circumvent the Lviv censor and enlist the help of his brother Ivan, a student of medicine in Vienna, who "accepted [the task entrusted to him] all the more eagerly, because he had the national cause in regard, and it delighted him all the more that he could bring to fruition... his brother's labour."[38]

Iakiv Holovatsky confided his plans only to his closest friends: Vereshchynsky, who would cover the printing costs despite the losses he incurred when *Rusalka* was banned, and Ivan Biretsky, whom he asked to send his collection of folk riddles and proverbs in order to supplement his own collection. Biretsky responded gladly, assuring Holovatsky that he would keep the publication plans a secret from those who would want to impede work on behalf of the Ukrainian nation and its glory.[39]

Having undertaken his assignment, Ivan Holovatsky suggested to his brother that he use the Latin alphabet in the projected work. Iakiv, however, would not agree. Ivan asked for something to study so that he could familiarize himself with the proposed alphabet and orthography, "which surely have certain peculiarities, and who knows whether these peculiarities would coincide with the Serbian ones." He also wanted to know why Iakiv wished to adopt the modern Cyrillic alphabet. (Ivan was concerned to be able to prove himself innocent to colleagues with whom he lived, if they suspected him and his brother of joining with the Russians and isolating themselves from the Poles, Czechs and others.)[40] Ivan also transmitted suggestions to his brother that were offered by his Czech acquaintances Josef Podlipský and František Kampelík. They urged that the proverbs be arranged thematically not alphabetically, on the model of the songs published by František Čelakovský and Ján Kollár, which would underscore their national, cultural and political significance.[41] Neither of these ideas was accepted: it was too late to change the arrangement, and Vereshchynsky would not agree to print in the Latin alphabet. He stated categorically, "We shall gain nothing by writing in Latin letters, and for that reason we cannot adopt them, even though the Czechs and Illyrians, whom we admire, write and print with them. Still, we cannot imitate them."[42] Ivan Holovatsky, therefore, submitted the proverbs to the censor in the form in which Iakiv had prepared them. Iakiv had augmented Ilkevych's collection by about one-third with his own and Biretsky's additions, and he had fundamentally revised Ilkevych's introduction.

The manuscript, however, did not escape the pen of Venedykt Levytsky, because the director of the Viennese police sent it to Lviv. It was not until February 1841 that Levytsky approved the manuscript for publication, after having deleted everything "where even the words *liakh*, *pop* [priest] and *nimets* [German] appeared." As Ivan Holovatsky noted, Levytsky's action pleased the Poles in Vienna very much. The Lviv censor, however, left in those proverbs aimed against the Jews and the Muscovites.[43] The proverbs finally were published in the same year at the Mekhitarist priests' printing shop in Vienna as *Halytski prypovidky i zahadky zibranii H. Ilkevychom* [Galician proverbs and riddles collected by H. Ilkevych], in an edition of five hundred copies, of which Ivan sent four hundred to Denys Zubrytsky in Lviv. He also sent fourteen copies to Czech acquaintances in Prague, six to Croats in Zagreb and eight to Slovaks in Bratislava.[44]

Ilkevych's *Galician Proverbs* was the first book to be published legally by the young Ukrainians whom Markiian Shashkevych had inspired to undertake national work. This victory convinced them of the necessity for further developing Ukrainian literature. Stepan Petrushevych, for example, who was later known as the author of the play *Muzh staryi, zhinka moloda* [Old husband, young wife], in 1842 intended to publish in Lviv an anthology, "Proverbs and Parables of the Ruthenians in Galicia." However, although the censor approved it, the collection was not published until 1857, when it appeared in the Polish journal *Przyjaciel Ludu* [Friend of the people], but with a Polish title and a foreword written in Polish.[45]

Encouraged by his success, and while Ilkevych's proverbs were still being printed, Ivan Holovatsky asked his brother whether he intended to publish the Ukrainian songs that he had collected, and which Levytsky could review in the course of three months. If so, Ivan would try to have them published in Pest or in Vienna.[46] Bishop Snihursky also encouraged Iakiv to publish the songs: he gave Holovatsky fifty guldens toward the expense of preparing the manuscript for publication and promised to print it at the episcopal press in Przemyśl. Holovatsky, however, did not ready the manuscript, though several years later he was completing it with the aim of sending it to Bodiansky in Russia. The songs collected by Holovatsky never did appear in Galicia. He also failed to publish the literary miscellanies he had projected for 1843 and 1845, which were to include articles devoted to folk songs and which he entitled *Halychanka* [The Galician woman].[47]

From 1843 until 1848, Iakiv Holovatsky lived in the Kolomyia district, where, having completed his theological studies, he fulfilled his priestly duties, first in Pistyn and then in Mykytyntsi and in Khmeleva. It was also from Kolomyia that he directed further publishing efforts. The result was *Vinok Rusynam na obzhynky* [A wreath for the Ruthenians at the harvest feast], published by Ivan Holovatsky in two parts in Vienna (1846-7). The material for this work had been collected in part in 1842 and 1843, when the Austrian authorities had proposed the publication of a Ukrainian journal and suggested Ivan Holovatsky as its editor. These plans had come to nothing, but the materials did become useful. Ivan Holovatsky secured financial support for the printing costs of *Vinok* in various ways. He expected money for the first part from the Prince of Lucca,[48] to whom the work was dedicated, and from the Serbian patriarch Josip Rajačić for the second part. However, the prince never sent any money, which resulted in serious financial troubles for Ivan, especially because the 140 advance subscriptions did not meet his expectations. The remaining costs, as usual, were borne by Vereshchynsky.[49] On the other hand, Rajačić—who harried Serbian literature in his own archdiocese and who did not want to accept the New Testament in Karadžić's translation—eagerly accepted the dedication of the second part of *Vinok* and sent Ivan Holovatsky five hundred guldens.[50] Evidently Ukrainian literature had found support in the leader of the Orthodox church in Serbia, but could not count on the same favour from the dignitaries of the Greek Catholic church in Galicia. Still, as Liubych-Mohylnytsky wrote to Iakiv Holovatsky, the Ukrainians were pleased that "in dedicating *Vinok* to the metropolitan of Karlovci, your brother shamed our Herod [Metropolitan Levytsky], through whom we have borne not infrequently such torments and sufferings for uplifting our mother tongue and a sensible literature."[51]

On this occasion there were no difficulties with the censor. The authorities did not ask an opinion from the Lviv censor, and the Slovene Fran Miklošić, who had become the censor of Slavic books in Vienna after the death of Kopitar, had no particular reservations. He expurgated only certain fragments from Iakiv Holovatsky's discourse "Velikaia Khorvatiia ili Halytsko-Karpatskaia Rus'" [Great Croatia, or Galician-Carpathian Rus'] concerning the last years of independent Poland, and he did not allow the publication of Ivan Holovatsky's poem "Pinie radostnoho holosa" [The singing of a joyous voice]. That work was a panegyric in honour of Nicholas I, written during the tsar's stay in Vienna in late 1845 and delivered by Ivan himself to the Russian embassy in Vienna.[52]

According to Ivan Holovatsky's plans, *Vinok* was to be an anthology of Ukrainian writers from Galicia and Russian Ukraine, including Ivan Kotliarevsky, Petro Hulak-Artemovsky, Levko Borovykovsky, Halka [Mykola Kostomarov], Mohyla [Amvrosii Metlynsky], Oleksander Shpyhotsky and Taras Shevchenko. Holovatsky received or was to receive their works from Izmail Sreznevsky.[53] As it happened, Holovatsky could not entirely achieve his aim. There are no works by writers from Russian Ukraine in either part of *Vinok*. Perhaps their works were to have been included in a third part, whose publication Ivan Holovatsky was seriously considering in spring 1847. (He also contemplated a separate edition of Kvitka-Osnovianenko's *Marusia.*)[54] Yet Holovatsky was reasonable in seeking first to make available to the

Ukrainian reader in Galicia the works of local writers and in postponing until later the publication of Ukrainian writers from beyond the Austrian frontiers.

Certainly *Vinok* was of no small significance in the development of Ukrainian literature in Galicia, especially because it contained a cross-section of the achievements of local Ukrainian literature up to that time, in poetry and prose and in scholarly and journalistic works. Among the latter, of special distinction were Antin Dobriansky's "Kreshchenie Rusy" [The baptism of Rus'], Ivan Danylovych's "Istoricheskoe rozsmotrenie zakonodatelstva Litovskoho" [Historical survey of Lithuanian legislation], Mykola Markevych's "Litochyslitelnyi spys derzhavtsiv Malorossii (Iuzhnoi Rusy)" [Chronological list of rulers of Little Russia (Southern Rus')] and Iakiv Holovatsky's "Velikaia Khorvatiia." Iakiv also contributed reminiscences of Shashkevych. Among the belles lettres in the first part of *Vinok*, there were Shashkevych's poems, translations, and his "Olena," Iakiv Holovatsky's translations of Serbian songs and his essay on Serbian folk poetry. The second part included works by Antin Liubych-Mohylnytsky, Vahylevych, both Holovatskys (Iakiv Holovatsky's pseudonym was Iatsko Balahur), Luka Dankevych, Antin Luzhetsky, Tselestyn Skomorovsky, Ustyianovych and Mykhailo Tymniak. Ivan Holovatsky's national views at that time are especially evident in his "Pryhovor chytateliam" [Foreword to the readers], printed in the first part of *Vinok*. Holovatsky espoused the immortality of the Ukrainian nation and embraced the idea of the "national integrity" of the Ukrainians inhabiting the territories "from the San, Vistula and Buh to the Don and Donets rivers, from beyond the Beskyd mountains, the Dniester River and the shores of the Black Sea far, far up to the Pripet and Desna rivers."

It is difficult at this time to estimate the social impact of *Vinok* in Galicia. Both parts were published in editions of only five hundred copies, and there were serious difficulties with their sale, which was undertaken by, besides Ivan and Iakiv Holovatsky, their closest friends Vereshchynsky, Kobrynsky, Zubrytsky, Mokh, Biretsky, Bodnar, Ivan Proskurnytsky, Ivan Doskovsky, Malynovsky, Mykola Terletsky, the vice-rector of the seminary Ivan Ilnytsky and the bookseller Jan Milikowski. There were few readers of Ukrainian literature, since the Ukrainian peasants were ill-educated and the high Greek Catholic clergy, with the exception of Bishop Snihursky, was indifferent, if not actually hostile. As Vereshchynsky noted, "We hear nothing of what the elders are saying in Lviv about *Vinok*, but I am afraid that probably no one there will want to sell it, in order to keep from falling into the hands of our zealots."[55] Apparently the proponents of new currents in Ukrainian intellectual life continued to be viewed askance by the Greek Catholic consistory in Lviv. And the other clergymen? In the same letter Vereshchynsky complained about the priests for whom it seemed that four twenty-kreuzer coins (*tsvantsygery*) were too high a price for one copy of *Vinok*. Mokh wrote that it was impossible to distribute copies because no one wanted to take them. He was able to collect only eleven subscribers, all of whom were priests. Petro Holovatsky encountered similar difficulties in Bukovyna.[56] The barely 140 subscriptions to the first part were proof of the scant interest in literature. Iakiv Holovatsky attached greater hopes to the second part, writing to Doskovsky, "I expect that this year's harvest of *Vinok* will be more abundant... than last year's. God grant that there be a greater demand than for the first and that it stir a greater love for [our] nationality."[57]

Of course, among Holovatsky's close friends, *Vinok* was enormously popular. Having read it, Mokh fell upon the idea of a special kind of promotion. "I couldn't help but share with others the beauty that is found in it [the collection]. For that reason, I invited some people in order to read to them a little of it, and you ought to know that more was done through this than through all kinds of notices."[58] The list of subscribers Mokh recruited indicates that those who attended these literary soirées were exclusively country priests. Therefore, Liubych-Mohylnytsky's remark that "already all of Galicia has read your brother Ivan's first and second part of *Vinok* and [then] perhaps torn them up," applied primarily to the Ukrainian parochial clergy.[59] Even if this were so, it would still bear witness to a substantial increase of interest in intellectual life and literature by this social group, which had the power to exert great influence on the peasant masses—and this, after all, was the editors' first concern.

By publishing the works of a host of young Ukrainian writers in *Vinok*, the editors wanted to prove that the Galician Ukrainians fully deserved a separate name among the Slavic nations and were capable of developing their own intellectual life in all its aspects. They simply wanted, as Iakiv Holovatsky rather coarsely put it to Doskovsky, "just to make it stick in the throats of our enemies; let them not lie [*ne breshut*] that we are creating nothing in literature."[60] Holovatsky undoubtedly had the Poles in mind. To a significant degree, the Ukrainians did achieve their intended goal.

Vinok inspired Liubych-Mohylnytsky to renew the literary endeavours that he had interrupted in 1839. In a short time, they would earn him the reputation of one of the best Ukrainian poets in Galicia.[61] Moreover, besides the Ukrainian contributors to *Vinok* already mentioned, new names emerged. One of them was a close acquaintance of Holovatsky, Father Hryhorii Bodnar (Bednarz, Bodnarenko), the author of the allegorical poem "Lis Dubina" [Oak forest], which Petro Holovatsky tried to have published in Chernivtsi, though without success. It was not until 1849 that it appeared in print.[62] Bodnar was also for his time a splendid translator of Byron and Schiller and a strong advocate of education for the Ukrainian common people. He fervently appealed to Iakiv Holovatsky, "For God's sake, write a Ruthenian history for our nation and physics and natural history [texts], in order to raise this obscurantist people from their superstitions."[63] He was not only concerned with eliminating superstitions, of course; the study of history necessarily would have had a significant influence on the national consciousness of the Galician Ukrainian community.

In the 1840s other lesser-known writers also began their literary activity: Luka Dankevych (Luka z Rakova), Mykhailo Kozanovych, Pavlo Leontovych (Pavlo z Shutkova), Rudolf Mokh (author of the collection *Motyl*, 1841), Tselestyn Skomorovsky (translator of Aleksei Khomiakov's *Ermak*), Iosyf Shukhevych (translator of Vergil, Herder and Scott) and Iuliian Velychkovsky.[64]

The role of the Ukrainian theatre in shaping the national consciousness also cannot be ignored. The earliest theatrical performances were associated with the Greek Catholic seminary in Lviv, where in the late 1820s and early 1830s amateur performances took place in Polish. (They were highly regarded by the organizer of the Polish repertory theatre in Lviv, Jan Nepomucen Kamiński.) Performances in Ukrainian did not begin, however, until 1837, during the rectorship of Hryhorii Iakhymovych, who not only gave permission for them, but also encouraged and supported a variety of theatrical activities by young people. But in 1841, after Iakhymovych left the seminary to become suffragan bishop of the Lviv diocese, the theatrical movement at the seminary came to a standstill, and Ukrainian amateur theatre in Galicia did not revive until 1848.[65] A permanent, professional Ukrainian theatre was not established in Lviv until 1864.

Much less effective, though very necessary, were the Ruthenian Triad's efforts to improve education and disseminate knowledge of modern agricultural methods among the Ukrainian common people. Shashkevych prepared a "very sensibly structured" *Chytanka* [Reader],[66] but unfortunately it went unpublished during his lifetime. Its publication in 1849 (a second edition appeared in 1853) gained widespread attention. The primer by Kobrynsky, published in 1842 under the title *Sposob borzo vyuchyty chytaty* [A quick way to learn to read], was the first Ukrainian text to teach pupils to read the modern Cyrillic script. Kobrynsky was also the author of a series of articles on agrarian matters, and in 1847 he prepared a study called *O prychynakh nedostatku hnoiu i o sposobakh iak sobi na toie pomochy* [On the reasons for insufficient manure and ways to remedy the situation], which was highly esteemed in his circle of friends.[67] This work was the first treatise on agriculture in Galicia written by one of the associates of the Ruthenian Triad. Recognizing that such works were necessary to improve the agrarian economy, Kobrynsky wanted a large edition—five thousand copies. He asked Ivan Holovatsky to undertake the publication and assumed all of the costs himself.[68] Ivan accepted this task and obtained the approval of the censorship board, but he had reservations about the orthography. He asked his brother Iakiv, "Do you think Father Kobrynsky would not agree to have this work published in the old Cyrillic script and not the new, because it is intended for the common people?"[69] Ivan obtained Kobrynsky's approval, corrected the manuscript in his own way, and delivered it to the printer. The events of 1848, however, prevented Kobrynsky's work from appearing in Galicia until March 1849. Besides this project, Ivan Holovatsky also oversaw the publication of *Nauka o upravi tiutiunu* [The science of the cultivation of tobacco], a study which he regarded as "very useful for our nation."[70]

This survey of the literary and publishing activity of the Ruthenian Triad indicates clearly that Markiian Shashkevych played the principal role in it until 1837, and Iakiv Holovatsky in the 1840s. Ivan Holovatsky, to whom we owe the actual publication of Ilkevych's *Prypovidky*, both parts of *Vinok* and other Ukrainian literary works, was only the instrument of his older brother's will, and he subordinated himself entirely to Iakiv's decisions. Contemporaries, with the probable exception only of Vahylevych,[71] fully appreciated Iakiv Holovatsky's leading role. Neither the attitude of the higher church authorities nor a life of hardship and financial insecurity caused Holovatsky to abandon his sense of obligation toward the nation. Indeed, some believed that it was precisely difficult circumstances and isolation from the main centre of intellectual life in Galicia that fueled Holovatsky's persistent literary activity. As Denys Zubrytsky wrote to him,

> You long for your friends, and I am pleased that fate has transported you to another place. Your destiny is to be the centre of your corner [of the world], to awaken among your fellow brothers [the clergy] and the people a love for the native literature, for olden times. Thoroughly complete your mission.[72]

Zubrytsky understood the need for a firm bond between the literary and national activities and the life of the people—the necessity to awaken an interest in literature, history and the nation's heritage on which to create a broadly based national consciousness. However, his letter to Holovatsky did not reflect his real attitude toward a literature moulded on national principles and based on a systematic development of the popular idiom. For the time being, he masked his aversion to the language of *khokhly* (the Russian pejorative for Ukrainians) and *skotopasy* (herdsmen), but by the beginning of the 1850s he openly called for the Ukrainians' linguistic and literary merger with Russia.

The purest tribute to Iakiv Holovatsky, however, came in 1848, when the Austrians authorized the establishment of three chairs of Ukrainian language and literature in Lviv, one at each of the gymnasia and at Lviv University. The more sober-minded Ukrainians, in appreciation of his services to the national literature, urged Holovatsky to assume the position at the university. As Ivan Borysykevych wrote to his friend, "Everyone is in agreement that they cannot do without you, because who is more worthy of this position?"[73]

6. The Struggle over the Literary Language and Ukrainian Orthography

As Ivan Vahylevych completed his "Rozprawy o języku południoworuskim" [Treatise on the South Rus' language] in 1843, he felt obliged to include the following bitter words:

> God grant that the South Rus' learn in time to make use of this writing and employ it properly. I say in time, because on the one hand indifference and on the other a twisted perception threaten them with the loss of their own language, and through that their own individuality as a nation. Now you do not have a South Rus' upper class; it belongs to the Polish or Russian nation. The middle class, not knowing the language of literature, either considers Old Bulgarian [Slavonic] in the (terribly maligned) ecclesiastical books as pure Ruthenian and disdainfully calls the language of the common people the language of manure, or uses a muddle of Polish, Russian, German and other languages.[1]

The more than ten-year activity of the Ruthenian Triad had little impact on knowledge of the literary language in the Ukrainian community. Even after the "official" conclusion of the war over the alphabet, the orthography and the literary language, certain writers, including Vahylevych and Iakiv Holovatsky, continued to use their own individualized languages, which often represented a mixture of Ukrainian, Russian, Church Slavonic and Polish, or simply wrote in

Polish. The issue of the Ukrainian literary language would remain open for many decades, and Ukrainian orthography in Galicia would not be codified until the end of the nineteenth century.

In the 1830s the literary language could have developed in various directions. The traditional view was that the only literary language was Church Slavonic, which was also called Slavo-Ruthenian. Although its usage had brought no advantages to the Ukrainian nation, every effort by the Ruthenian Triad to introduce the vernacular into literature met indignant opposition from conservatives. Even Ukrainian intellectuals who genuinely desired to develop a national literature could not agree on a particular approach to the language. Each attempted to justify his own approach by invoking the findings of contemporary Slavic studies.

The most important problem, therefore, was to resolve the disputes over basic principles. It was generally recognized that popular speech should play a fundamental role, but specific proposals varied markedly. During the years the Triad was active, two schools of thought collided on this issue. The Czech scholar Josef Dobrovský believed that the literary language differed from the folk idiom because it had been elaborated in a scholarly way and was capable of expressing all states of the human spirit. Common speech was inapplicable to scholarship; at the most it could enrich the literary vocabulary. Jernej Kopitar represented another position. Because of his peasant background, he fully understood the linguistic and literary needs of the masses, and he thought that their speech should be the foundation of the literary language. Kopitar accepted the possibility that every dialect might evolve independently, and he respected all literary attempts in the folk idiom, although he did not always support them unconditionally. His reaction to Shashkevych's *Zoria* provides a case in point.[2]

The future was to prove the validity of Kopitar's concept. The Slavic national movements necessarily were compelled to seek mass support; they could not ignore national education, which could only succeed with the emancipation of the folk idiom, the language intelligible to the common people. As the Czech scholar Frank Wollman has stated, the inclusion of folk speech and writings in the "process of creating a national literature became a measure of the true nationalization of literature."[3] Introducing the folk idiom into Ukrainian literature in Galicia would not only strengthen the national aspirations of the Ukrainians, but would also lead in the future toward an intensification of the social struggle and its close association with the national question.

The Triad circle fully appreciated that using the folk idiom was the only path to a truly national literature. However, the situation was very complicated. There were no generally accepted principles of orthography and grammar, and earlier efforts to establish them were not satisfactory. Ivan Mohylnytsky, in his (unpublished) "Discourse on the Ruthenian Language," took the position that in the Slavic languages it was necessary to distinguish the "book" dialect (otherwise called the "church" dialect, since it was originally used in church literature) from the folk dialect used in common speech. According to Mohylnytsky, the folk idiom was the true national language. Yet it differed substantially from the everyday speech of educated persons, which had all the properties of a "book" dialect. Mohylnytsky wrote, "Among us Ruthenians language can be divided into oral and bookish forms. The book dialect in Little, White and Red Rus' has indeed gone unchanged from the twelfth century to the present."[4] He thought that the folk idiom could not simply be adopted into literature. Instead, he advocated a "middle style," used by some educated Ukrainians in writing. He thereby established the basis for applying the church language to literary work and, in the end, of applying Russian, though he explicitly stated that the Russian language was not the Ruthenian language. (Denys Zubrytsky would later attempt to prove that there existed only one literary language in Rus', and that was Russian.)

Iosyf Levytsky followed a similar path with his *Grammatik der ruthenischen oder kleinrussichen Sprache in Galizien* in 1834. He intended to prepare a grammar of the language that the Galician Ukrainians actually spoke, but he failed to attain his goal. In attempting to reconcile the rules of the church language with the patterns of the folk idiom, and in citing examples from old documents, from Kotliarevsky's *Eneida* and from folk songs, he came to the conclusion that common speech differed grammatically from the church language and that this was a basic error. Therefore, instead of systematizing the rules of the folk idiom, he attempted to make this language conform *a priori* to grammatical rules. There is nothing odd in the fact that Levytsky's grammar did not meet with the approval of Kopitar, who interpreted his approach as "service to two lords."[5]

Iosyf Lozynsky apparently followed yet another course in preparing a grammar of the Ukrainian language and in his folkloristic publication *Ruskoje wesile*. In reviewing these works, Kopitar praised the author for preparing a grammar of the folk idiom, but he also advised him to adopt a phonetic orthography, to write as the people speak.[6] As it happened, however, the 1833 redaction of Lozynsky's grammar was not published, although the censor granted permission. Perhaps this was Lozynsky's fault, because he wanted to incorporate Kopitar's suggestions and publish it in the Latin alphabet. But it is difficult to be certain, because the manuscript has been lost. However, we do know the fate of the 1837 redaction of the grammar. The Lviv censor, Venedykt Levytsky, did not allow it to be published and did not even offer a justification for his decision. Perhaps it was because, as a grammar of the living folk idiom, the book would have demonstrated a complete break with the church tradition in philology. Lozynsky's grammar could have been a splendid supplement to *Rusalka Dnistrovaia* and a linguistic substantiation of the Triad's views.[7] In refusing permission to publish it, Levytsky did as much harm to Ukrainian literature and the Ukrainian national movement as when he forbade the distribution of *Rusalka.*

It was not until 1844 that Lozynsky gathered the courage to submit the manuscript of the third redaction of his grammar to the censor. It did not, however, vary significantly from the previous redaction. Again Levytsky opposed its publication and completely expurgated the introduction, in which Lozynsky substantiated his linguistic and national views. The author appealed to the censorship board in Vienna, which received his request favourably. As a result, the grammar was finally published in Przemyśl in 1846, under the Polish title *Gramatyka języka ruskiego*, and with the introduction unchanged.[8]

I shall analyze Lozynsky's views elsewhere in this book, but it is worth noting here that Venedykt Levytsky objected primarily that he had dared to question the beneficial influence of the ecclesiastical language on the preservation of the purity of the Ukrainian language. In his introduction Lozynsky had written: "[The Ukrainian language] was protected indeed to some degree by the language of the church against the influence of Polish, but could a dead language, which was heard only from time to time in church, preserve its purity?"[9] Lozynsky also believed that the everyday language of the common people was considerably purer than the language in the writings of the old authors, and the purest language was that of the folk songs, which represented the permanent legacy of the nation and were a treasury for the developing literary language.

The so-called first linguistic war in Ukrainian literature in Galicia—the struggle over the alphabet and orthographic principles—was closely tied to the censor's review of the first redaction of Lozynsky's grammar and his *Ruskoje wesile*. It was but one of a series of similar struggles that took place in those times in various Slavic lands, such as Serbia, Croatia and Slovenia. Lozynsky's plan to employ the Latin alphabet in Ukrainian literature in Galicia was not new. Similar proposals had been made by August Schlecer (Schlözer) in his 1802 work on the early chronicler Nestor, and a year later by J. Voltigi in his *Illyrian-Italian-German Dictionary*. Kopitar, in his *Grammar of the Slavic Language in Carniola, Carinthia and Styria*, also had posed the idea that using the Latin alphabet would be advantageous for the whole of Slavic literature, and the Czech scholar Antonín Puchmajer even devised a Latin alphabet for all the Slavs, a scheme which Dobrovský sharply criticized. The Ukrainians were widely familiar with Karadžić's struggles to introduce phonetic spelling and the "štokavian" dialect into Serbian literature, as well as with the vehement linguistic struggles in Slovenia at the beginning of the 1830s, when the young generation of Slovenian writers, headed by France Prešeren and Matija Čop, sought to establish the bases of a uniform literary language and to apply a uniform orthography.[10]

Lozynsky was acquainted with the linguistic struggles among the South Slavs through the foreign press and the journal *Rozmaitości*. He also understood Kopitar's goals. Kopitar, discussing Wacław Zaleski's *Polish and Ruthenian Songs* in the Viennese newspaper *Oesterreichischer Beobachter* on 8 December 1833, maintained: "The Polish as well as the Ruthenian songs were written in Latin characters, the latter for the first time in this manner. We wish and expect that the grammars announced by Levytsky and by Lozynsky for the eight million speakers of the Little Russian language will take for their model the fidelity of the gentleman from Olesko [Wacław Zaleski] in respect to the grammar."[11] Kopitar's words prove that he was indeed the spiritual father of Lozynsky's project. All the rest, such as the linguistic battles in the Slavic countries and the path indicated by Zaleski, were merely influences that hastened Lozynsky's decision.

In early July 1834 at the latest, he submitted to *Rozmaitości* his "Rozprawa o wprowadzeniu abecadła polskiego do piśmiennictwa ruskiego" [Discourse on the introduction of the Polish alphabet into Ruthenian writing].[12] It represented the beginning of the battle over the alphabet and the orthography for the Ukrainians in Galicia. In it Lozynsky stressed Kopitar's inspirational role. After reading Kopitar's comments in *Oesterreichischer Beobachter*, Lozynsky had begun to reflect "whether it would indeed be well to introduce the Polish alphabet to the evolving Ruthenian literature. The result of this research was the conviction that the Polish characters are the most adequate to convey every Ruthenian sound and for that reason should be used in writing." He based his judgement on the fact that until then there had been no appropriate grammar of the Ukrainian language; therefore, authors had adapted their writings to the rules of Church Slavonic, using the old Cyrillic alphabet. The result was not a pure Ukrainian language. Thus, up to that time the Ukrainian language was not a written language and perforce did not possess its own literature. Lozynsky further noted, "And from this I conclude that the Ruthenian language, not yet being a written language, has the freedom to choose for itself an alphabet that would be most adequate to express its sounds and most advantageous to moulding it, and the Polish alphabet is such."

Lozynsky compared the old Cyrillic script with the Polish Latin alphabet to demonstrate "how much more suitable the latter is for Ruthenian than the former," and finally he stated that adopting the Polish alphabet would bring great advantages to the Ukrainians, because "it would serve to propagate the Ruthenian language among the other Slavic branches and would facilitate the learning of Ruthenian among the [foreign] nations." With Latin letters, the Ruthenian language could develop more rapidly, and Ukrainian children could both learn to read more quickly and learn Polish more easily. However, Lozynsky believed that the old Cyrillic alphabet should be taught as an optional subject in parish schools, while being mandatory for all those who were studying to be priests, village teachers or cantors.

Applying the Latin alphabet to Ruthenian writing actually had long traditions in Galicia. Between 1821 and 1834 alone there were eight instances of so using the Latin alphabet.[13] However, we do not know to what extent this practice was tried before 1821. Lozynsky's decision in 1835 to publish *Ruskoje wesile* in the Latin alphabet was known to Bishop Snihursky, who encouraged him to announce his plan in print and wished to learn how public opinion received it.[14]

Lozynsky's project was intended to assure a more amicable coexistence between the Ukrainian and Polish nationalities in Galicia. The Poles presumably would take an active part in Ukrainian cultural life; in turn, Ukrainians would participate more vigorously in Polish culture. To be sure, Lozynsky did not explicitly state these conclusions, but the thesis of his article warranted such expectations. Thus Marceli Handelsman made a valid point when he wrote that applying the Latin alphabet in Ukrainian publications was equivalent to "preserving in the language the initiated Polish-Ruthenian solidarity." Still, one cannot entirely agree with his argument that it was precisely for this reason that it was attacked so sharply.[15] In fact, it was only much later that anyone suspected that Polish intrigue was involved in Lozynsky's decision. Iakiv Holovatsky, for example, in a retrospective evaluation of the events between 1834 and 1836, pointed to Lozynsky's having been inspired by the Poles Wacław Zaleski and Gwalbert Pawlikowski, ignoring the fact that Lozynsky did not meet Pawlikowski until 1836, when he became the pastor at the Pawlikowski estate of Medyka. Indeed, Holovatsky depicted the controversy over the alphabet as involving the very existence of the Ukrainian nation: "Had the [Ukrainian] Galicians adopted the Polish alphabet in the 1830s, a distinctive Ruthenian nationality would have perished [and] the

Ruthenian spirit would have disappeared."[16]

The leading Ukrainian spokesmen in Galicia—Iosyf Levytsky, Denys Zubrytsky and Markiian Shashkevych—were all opposed to Lozynsky. They were united by a single aim: defence of the Cyrillic alphabet. However, their arguments were as different as their individual views. Levytsky was the first to respond to Lozynsky, in "Odpowiedź na zdanie o zaprowadzeniu abecadła polskiego do piśmiennictwa ruskiego" [Reply to the opinion on the introduction of the Polish alphabet into Ruthenian writing], which Mikołaj Michalewicz distributed as a supplement to *Rozmaitości*.[17] (It was probably because Michalewicz, a Ukrainian by descent, supported Lozynsky's opponents that he was removed as editor of *Rozmaitości*.)[18] Levytsky regarded the Cyrillic alphabet as indispensable for Ukrainian writings, pointed to its superiority over the Latin alphabet and explicity stated that the Ukrainians should not make any orthographical reforms. They should write just as their forefathers did, modelling their efforts on Church Slavonic and the monuments of Ruthenian literature. He also attempted to prove that the Ruthenians had possessed their own grammar from the beginnings of Ruthenian writing, that is, from the ninth century, and he offered the grammar of 1591 as an example. Levytsky saw no difference between the language of Old Ruthenian literature and Church Slavonic and the contemporary Ukrainian language used in Galicia and concluded that even if Ukrainian books had at one time been printed in the Latin alphabet, it was done only to benefit those who sold worthless devotional scribblings. He even charged Lozynsky with wanting to support the writings of such hucksters.

Lozynsky's reply to Iosyf Levytsky's accusations has been preserved only in manuscript, because Venedykt Levytsky did not allow its publication.[19] Lozynsky argued that the relics of Ruthenian literature had the stamp of Church Slavonic, and therefore could not provide the foundation for the national language. He called for linguistic reforms along the lines set by Mikhail Lomonosov in Russia, who "distinguished the national language from Church Slavonic and was the first to elevate it to dignified literature." He further argued that if two million Ukrainians in Galicia had been unable to preserve their literature, then they certainly would not preserve it by using the old Cyrillic alphabet. Ukrainians should adopt the modernized Cyrillic alphabet, which was much more correct than old Cyrillic and was used by the Russians and Serbs. This last proposal was completely novel within Galicia. Not long afterward, Shashkevych took it up in *Rusalka Dnistrovaia*, although during the dispute with Lozynsky, he defended the old Cyrillic alphabet.

The polemic between Lozynsky and Levytsky over the choice of alphabet became, in fact, an argument over the principles of orthography and the literary language. Two concepts clashed: the traditionalist, which propagated etymological spellings and the use of Church Slavonic as a model and basis for the Ukrainian literary language, and the progressive, which favoured phonetic spelling and the elevation of the folk idiom to a literary language.

Of immense interest in this regard was Lozynsky's manuscript "Some Remarks on the Orthography of the Ruthenian Language," which probably dates from 1834 and is preserved in Żegota Pauli's papers at the Jagiellonian Library in Cracow.[20] (This work suggests that the phonetic spelling adopted by the Triad for *Rusalka* had a much earlier propagator.) In this work Lozynsky aimed to establish Ukrainian orthogaphy on solid principles; he considered phonetic spelling the most important of these. Because writing was used to record the spoken language—to be its image—the best writing was that which most faithfully conveyed the spoken language. "For that reason," Lozynsky maintained, "the first and principal law of writing is: write just as is commonly spoken." Writing should reflect the characteristics of the language and underscore the differences between one language and another; phonetic spelling was preferable because etymological orthography erased these differences. Accordingly, Lozynsky proclaimed that "first of all we should remember that the foundation of spelling is pronunciation, and recourse to etymology is but an exception, which has a place only for [special] needs"; for example, if "through abandoning etymology, the written word would lose in meaning." If, however, the need arose to rely on etymology, it was essential to know in which language to search for the root of the appropriate expression. The Ruthenian spoken language must be relied upon in Ruthenian writing, and no others such as Church Slavonic, Russian or Polish, because "from there would flow only absurdities." Indeed, at an earlier date writing was done in that way, "because, without a grammar of Ruthenian, the orthography of the ecclesiastic language was used as a model; but this practice does not authorize us to do likewise when we feel and recognize that this was not appropriate for our language." Therefore, in such instances Lozynsky advised relying on intuition, because the Ukrainians lacked appropriate earlier writers or accepted traditions in this area.

Lozynsky resolutely opposed all those who, like Levytsky, advocated writing as in the past and leaving reforms to their successors, noting that if his forebears had kept to that principle, "we should still not have even letters." Thus, if one believed that the older orthography was not applicable to Ukrainian, a better orthography should be adopted.

Lozynsky concluded by appealing for new principles and earnest efforts to develop the native language:

> We should have sinned against ourselves if we had not progressed, but kept to the old errors; we shall have sinned against our successors if we place on their shoulders what we ourselves can and ought to do. But if our successors still wish to keep to the rules inherited by us, then our language will never become formed. Therefore, we must cast aside pedantry and strive toward progress.

His final words reformulated Kopitar's direction to himself. Kopitar's review of *Ruskoje wesile* instructed Lozynsky to abandon pedantry in orthography and not only to write as one speaks, but to print faithfully as well.[21]

Lozynsky's views made him the most eminent and progressive philologist of his time among Ukrainians in Galicia. The conditions then prevailing in Ukrainian cultural life and the impossibility of publishing his articles and grammar of the Ukrainian language, however, meant that his contributions went unappreciated for many years. His works could have provided a permanent foundation for the evolving Ruthenian literature, but fate dictated otherwise.

Denys Zubrytsky advocated diametrically opposite theses in defence of the old Cyrillic alphabet in "On the Introduction of the Polish Alphabet instead of Cyrillic into Ruthenian Orthography."[22] He firmly condemned the contemporary revolutionary currents, criticized the Carbonari, the proponents of "Young Europe" and the Polish society of "Philomaths" at Vilnius University, and denied any value to Lamennais's views. He maintained that "this unfortunate spirit of the times" had stolen into the pacific lives of the Ruthenians and "made itself heard in the Lviv *Rozmaitości*" (a specific allusion to Lozynsky's article). These harmful currents had generated confusion among the Ruthenians, who up to that time had resisted "these frivolous novelties and products of a rankled and inflamed imagination"; they had caused the fall of what until then had been "to the credit of the Ruthenian." Among these values Zubrytsky listed unvacillating loyalty to the throne, attachment to religion and one's native soil, respect toward parents and superiors and love for the customs and language of one's forefathers.

Of special interest are Zubrytsky's ideas regarding the Rus' nation, which he did not specifically identify with the Ukrainian nation. On the contrary, he believed that the Rus' nation embraced all the peoples inhabiting the territories from the White Sea to the Crimea, from Courland to the "lands of the Kazan tsardom and the Volga Hills, from the Pechora River and the boundaries of Northern Asia to the source of the Tisza River in the Hungarian kingdom." This nation professed one faith, the Greek rite, and spoke "one and the same language," which was divided into various dialects that were still undescribed and not distinguished by scholarship. It also possessed two literary languages: Great Russian and Church Slavonic. Zubrytsky further noted that the differences between the dialects of the Rus' language "do not constitute a fragmentation of its unity"; similarly, the one German language had ninety dialects. The external and formal bond between the individual branches of the Rus' nation was, for Zubrytsky, the old Cyrillic alphabet. Thus the struggle to preserve that alphabet was for him a struggle to limit Polish influence, which had contributed to despoiling the Ruthenian language in the borderland areas. At the same time, this struggle was to open the way for the influence of the Russian language, which he believed would be the only language of Rus' in the future. For the time being, however, the creation of works in local tongues would be permitted. It should be noted that Zubrytsky's opinions were formed independently of direct Russian influence. Only later, after his outlook crystallized under Mikhail Pogodin's overpowering influence, did Zubrytsky join the ranks of the Russophiles. In the meantime, Mykhailo Maksymovych persuaded Zubrytsky that literature in the native language could exist and develop in Galicia since the "phase involving the Polish language has passed long ago and the time of the Great Russian language has not yet arrived for them [Galician Ukrainians]."[23] Despite the fact that Zubrytsky's article remained in manuscript,[24] it was immensely popular among Ukrainian youth and circulated in numerous transcriptions. One may also assume that other manuscripts concerning this "alphabetic madness" (as Vahylevych called it) were widely circulated.

Shashkevych's circle took another position. Shashkevych himself wrote *Azbuka i abetsadlo*, three thousand copies of which were published in Przemyśl, an enormous edition for those times.[25] This work had a significant effect on Ukrainian intellectuals, although Shashkevych did not understand some of Lozynsky's ideas. He accused Lozynsky of trying to introduce alien terms and a foreign means of expression into Ukrainian. Shashkevych did not agree that Ruthenian had not earlier been a literary language, because the existence of *The Tale of Ihor*'s *Campaign*, Nestor's *Chronicle*, the *Ruska Pravda* [Rus' justice] and the Lithuanian Statute contradicted this thesis. He believed that the language of these literary treasures was more akin to the language of the common people than to Church Slavonic; the seventeenth century, however, had been a period "of the spoilage of the Ruthenian language under the influence of a corrupted Polish tongue."

According to Shashkevych, Lozynsky saw the old Cyrillic alphabet as an obstacle to the incorporation of Slavic writings into the general body of European literature. That indeed was the view of Wacław Zaleski, who had encouraged Lozynsky to apply the Latin alphabet to Ukrainian literature. Shashkevych replied with the argument that the literature of every nation was an "image of its life, its manner of thought, its soul." Literature was absolutely essential to national education, and for that reason no foreign expressions should be introduced into the language, for they would not adhere to it. "In that case," he warned, "literature will become the property of only a few so-called European literati and will therefore miss its primary goal." Shashkevych also held that the Latin alphabet would not make the Ukrainian language more familiar among other peoples, because every nation possessed its own orthography and alphabet and would, therefore, read Ukrainian according to its own rules. If the Latin alphabet were used, "a not particularly favourable judgment would issue about the Ruthenian language." Shashkevych maintained that grammar should be "not a lawgiver to the language, but its most faithful image;... all the properties should be pointed out and the nature of its changes and rules, according to which... it functioned and functions. We await such a grammar with impatience."

All in all, Shashkevych's views on the role and nature of grammar really were not far from Lozynsky's; after all, Lozynsky also believed that grammar should reflect faithfully the principles of the common language. It was actually Iosyf Levytsky who had attempted in his grammar of 1834 to make grammar "the lawgiver of the language" and to bend it to the rules of Church Slavonic. Shashkevych, using punctilious linguistic arguments, pointed out the impossibility of applying the alphabet of Polish to Ukrainian writing. In conclusion, he cited the words "of a certain not shallow-thinking Pole: 'Is it conceivable that the alphabet of Polish is adequate to express all the Ruthenian sounds, when it is not [even] perfect to convey all Polish [sounds]?'"

Lozynsky responded to Shashkevych's objections and also wrote a reply to both Levytsky and Shashkevych.[26] The latter piece is interesting because it clearly identified Levytsky's gross error in acknowledging Ukrainian and Church Slavonic as one and the same language. Lozynsky advised using "either the [modern Cyrillic] *hrazhdanka* as more correct and living, or even better, the Latin [alphabet] in its Polish form." By adopting the *hrazhdanka*, the Ukrainians would make Serbian and Russian literature accessible to themselves, and by adopting the Latin alphabet they would share in Polish literature and draw closer to the Slavs and "to all of enlightened

Europe." Only the future would tell which of these alphabets would emerge victorious, but in the meantime both could be used with greater advantage than the old Cyrillic. These remarks indicate that Lozynsky's position had undergone a significant evolution since 1836. He no longer insisted on the exclusive adoption of the Polish [Latin] alphabet, although he was consistent in resisting the old Cyrillic—much as all his opponents were consistent in defending it.

At the end of his reply, Lozynsky appealed to Ukrainian writers to stop criticizing and take up literary creativity instead. "Let us first write, so there is something to criticize. Woe to the nation that has critics rather than writers. Therefore, without wasting time on such disputes, let us write and let us leave criticism to those who are incapable of writing anything else." He continued: "So, let us write, each one according to his opinion, and let victory remain in the hands of time. And even if both of our opinions do not survive, the results of our work, nevertheless, will not be fruitless. They will remain as monuments for the language." Time has demonstrated, in fact, that neither Lozynsky's proposal to apply the alphabet of Polish nor his opponents' desire to preserve the old Cyrillic won out. A third view, arising in the heat of the bitter debates and proposed by Lozynsky himself—namely, the adoption of the *hrazhdanka*—ultimately triumphed.

Lozynsky's disputes with Levytysky, Zubrytsky and Shashkevych continued for two years, until July 1836. They did not resolve the issue of which alphabet to employ in Ukrainian literature, but Lozynsky's appeal to end the quarrelling and begin to work brought immediate results. In August 1836 the manuscript of *Rusalka Dnistrovaia* was completed and sent to the censor in Budapest. Perhaps it was because of Lozynsky that Shashkevych, who not long before had defended the old Cyrillic alphabet against Lozynsky, used the *hrazhdanka* alphabet in it. Shashkevych had even defended old Cyrillic when reviewing Lozynsky's *Ruskoje wesile*, at a time when he himself was no longer using it. In this review Shashkevych characterized the old alphabet as "the impregnable fortress and bedrock" upon which, despite a series of adversities, holy Rus' arose; he concluded, "[The old Cyrillic alphabet] has made it possible that we are Ruthenians to this day."[27] It is not surprising, therefore, that under his sway, Ivan Vahylevych wrote to Mikhail Pogodin, "Now no one doubts the burning need for the Slavic [Cyrillic] alphabet for the Ruthenian language, and everyone acknowledges its superiority over an inadequate and alien alphabet."[28]

It is characteristic, however, that the "polemic over the alphabet" was carried on exclusively in Polish. This fact illustrates perfectly the state of writing at that time: the limited development of the Ukrainian language and the overpowering influence of Polish on the Galician Ukrainians. Moreover, not once during this extended debate was there any reference to the national unity of the Ukrainians on both sides of the Austro-Russian frontier or to the need to preserve a uniform alphabet in Galicia and Russian Ukraine in order to maintain the cultural unity of a divided nation. The absence of such references probably offers distinct evidence of the prevailing state of national consciousness among the leading Ukrainians in Galicia. Only Zubrytsky proclaimed the unity of the entire "Ruthenian" nation, in which he included the Russians, Ukrainians and Belorussians, although he did not mention them by name. A homogeneous Ukrainian nation appeared out of the question. Even Shashkevych's *Azbuka i abetsadlo*, in addressing the Ukrainians' ties to Slavdom, cited only the Czechs and the South Slavs. It is not known whether he did not wish to or could not write about the Ukrainians in tsarist Russia.[29]

One thing, however, is certain. Lozynsky's contentions upset the Galician Ukrainians, creating a ferment in the previous cultural stagnation. In no small way, he contributed to the development of Ukrainian literature.[30] No matter how one may evaluate his proposals, it was in large measure thanks to Lozynsky that the later literary and linguistic successes of the new Ukrainian literature in Galicia did occur.

Lozynsky's arguments and the discussion they unleashed by no means concluded the war over the alphabet. In somewhat different circumstances, on the occasion of the publication of Ilkevych's *Galician Proverbs*, Ivan Holovatsky also proposed adopting the Latin alphabet for Ukrainian literature (though apparently at the prompting of the Czechs František Kampelík and Josef Podlipský). The revolutionary-minded Polish students in Vienna likewise had a certain influence on him. An examination of his plan is especially worthwhile, because both he and his brother raised new arguments.

In advancing his proposals in a letter of 13 April 1840 to Iakiv,[31] Ivan Holovatsky assumed that the adoption of the Latin alphabet was essential for the more rapid development of education and culture in Eastern Europe, because the old Cyrillic alphabet had not contributed to raising the intellectual level of the Ukrainian nation. He therefore rejected all historical evidence as justification for preserving it as the universal Slavic alphabet. Ivan maintained that in Russia itself only tsarist rulers, striving for new territorial gains at the expense of other nations and entirely unconcerned with Slavic liberation, were seeking to preserve the alphabet. He even suggested, erroneously, that many noted authors, including Nikolai Gogol and Mikhail Pogodin, desired union with Europe and the adoption of the Latin characters. Thus he argued that the Ukrainians, once they adopted the Latin alphabet, could act as pioneers by skilfully exploiting the circumstances favourable to them, especially the benevolence of Austrian authorities. The people had no advantage in using the Cyrillic alphabet, which was convenient only for the Muscovite tsar and the Orthodox priests. Ivan Holovatsky's progressive views, therefore, are evident not only in his criticism of tsardom and its objectives, but also in his attitude toward the democratic elements in the Polish community. In condemning the Polish *szlachta* as well as everyone "who does not believe in Slavdom" and "wishes at all costs that we regard Poland as our fatherland and adopt the Poles' orthography and perhaps their language," Holovatsky hoped that the Ukrainian nation would ally itself with those Poles who aspired to liberation and social justice.

Ivan Holovatsky presented his brother with a plan for a "Latin-Ruthenian" or "Latin-Slavonic" orthography based on the principle of using whatever was best in the individual alphabets for a new Ukrainian alphabet. For a time he employed it in his correspondence in the Polish and Ukrainian languages.[32] The Latin alphabet was to be a link between the Polish and Ukrainian nations, "because when the Ruthenian peasant begins to read, he will be indifferent whether he reads Polish or other characters," as long as he reads in Ukrainian. Holovatsky also believed that it would be easy to incline the Greek Catholic clergy to alphabetic reform and that the Poles would pose no obstacles.

Needless to say, Ivan Holovatsky's plan was not well received in Galicia. The members of the Triad, including his brother Iakiv, Mykola Vereshchynsky and the instigator of the entire matter, Iosyf Lozynsky, opposed it.[33] Iakiv even issued a fierce defence of the Cyrillic alphabet,[34] maintaining that it had been devised "by Cyril for the Slavic language" and adopted by the Slavs beyond the Danube, of Pannonia, of Kievan Rus', "and even by the Czechs and the Poles." It was an all-Slavic alphabet. On the other hand, the Latin alphabet was "introduced later with the Latin [Roman Catholic] faith, (voluntarily and compulsorily) in greater part by the Germans, the Poles and God knows what foreigners (missionaries)." He accused his brother of separating himself from his native land and encouraged him to inquire more deeply into the history and nationality of the Slavs, which certainly would convince him that they had preserved "the political arrangements of patriarchal Slavdom, as well as their ancient customs and traditions. Their songs are inexhaustible, their folk creativity is richer, and their education is more highly developed than among western nations."

Iakiv Holovatsky asked whether in the East "there is a Europe and the traces of an, as you call it, enlightened Europe, or just Asiatic barbarism? Here I only want to reflect on the bygone and present governments of the Slavs . . . , and I shall demonstrate whether in their laws one cannot, in fact, find that there is and was more love toward the people, more national fervor, than among the western [peoples]." He had concluded from reading Byzantine historians that "then, when in enlightened Rome and Greece countless numbers of slaves wore manacles, then, I say, the Slavs under the patriarchal system did not know slavery." The early Rus' chronicles had convinced him that ancient Novgorod had republican institutions, and he also valued highly the organization among the Zaporozhian Cossacks and the patriarchal structure still found in Montenegro and Serbia. All of this, in his opinion, proved the superiority of the Slavs and their system of rule and commended the preservation of the Cyrillic alphabet, which would lead the nation to education along the shortest path. Appropriate books and a developed literature, and not unity with Europe, were needed in order to provide the people with knowledge. The Cyrillic alphabet itself did not pose an obstacle, because anyone could learn it, just as he could learn Sanskrit or Arabic. Iakiv advised his brother to familiarize himself with the Serbian songs of Karadžić, the Ukrainian songs of Maksymovych and the Russian songs of Kireevsky and Sakharov to convince himself of this. He also reproached Ivan for professing the fictitious view that "the Ukrainians (Kvitka-Osnovianenko, Kotliarevsky and others) were writing for the tsar, the Muscovite magnates and the priests." Iakiv Holovatsky maintained that the writing of good books for the people in their own language and not a link with Europe was important.

Clearly then, Iakiv Holovatsky's views reflected the ideas of the Slavophiles, which were transmitted to Galician soil through the works of Khomiakov, Kireevsky and Pogodin, as well as through Pogodin's personal acquaintance with several leading Ukrainian spokesmen. Iakiv opposed ties with Western Europe and advised instead union with all of Slavdom. He also ascribed a significant role to religion, which he regarded as an inseparable attribute of nationality; he felt that adopting the Latin alphabet would both suit the Jesuits and separate the handful of Galician Ukrainians from all of Ukraine. "What would ancient Kiev, the city of the nation's old tales, the centre of our South Rus', have said? What would the people beyond the Dnieper say, where our entire—as much physical as moral—strength lies, where the memory of the old Cossack times is alive?" No resolute Ukrainian could agree to adopt the Latin alphabet.

In the heat of the battle over the alphabet and the principles of orthography, the notion grew that a uniform development of Ukrainian literature in the entire territory inhabited by the Ukrainians was essential. A conviction that the main centre of Ukrainian intellectual life was to be found along and beyond the Dnieper, in Kiev and Kharkiv, also gathered strength. This view was frequently modified later, but no one dared to undermine its substance.

Iakiv Holovatsky's Slavophile arguments did not convince his brother, who, being at that time an adherent of revolutionary and democratic ideas, understood the issue of the national culture in broader terms. Ivan replied that no product of the human mind, even one of foreign origin, should be considered alien. He believed that one could not know the true philosophy of the common people, its creativity and the great dignity of Old Slavonic literature without the general knowledge that would permit him to compare foreign literatures with the literature of the Slavs. All nations had evolved according to similar laws, regardless of their geographic position. As Ivan explained,

> The aspiration of nations is one and the same, because the spirit of the age does not depend upon time and the wind, but comes from man as man and permeates all of us. You know of the French Revolution, and you have read about the Serbian Revolution (perhaps in Leopold Ranke's work). Is it not the same course of governments in the one and the other, although (in Serbia) there were neither French books nor Frenchmen? Nations and their true national enlightenment are not so distant from one another as you believe. You cannot measure them in miles. My aim is the same as yours, but also [the same as] all Europe's.

Ivan concluded that if the Latin alphabet were adopted, the Ukrainians would not acquire more foreign books; rather, Ukrainian books would become more accessible to foreign nations. "In this way, having come to know us, they will study our language at foreign universities." However, Ivan did not wish to renew the war over the alphabet, and he agreed to use the orthography Iakiv and Vereshchynsky proposed in Ilkevych's *Galician Proverbs.*[35]

At that point it seemed that the lengthy debate over the alphabet and orthographic principles had finally ended. However, in the 1840s Iosyf Levytsky took the discussion beyond the borders of Galicia to the columns of Petr Dubrovsky's *Dennitsa-Jutrzenka* in Warsaw and Jan Petr Jordan's *Jahrbücher für slawische Literatur, Kunst und Wissenschaft* in Leipzig. We have already noted the attitude Levytsky expressed toward Shashkevych's *Rusalka Dnistrovaia* in his first *Listy tyczące się piśmiennictwa ruskiego w Galicji* [Letters regarding Ruthenian literature in Galicia], written in 1841 and published two years later in Przemyśl.[36] Another letter, written in 1843 and unfavourably reviewed by the censor, was never published. This second letter was a critique of two translations into Ukrainian of Metropolitan Mykhailo Levytsky's pastoral letter of 10 March 1841, written to protest abolition of the church union in Russian-ruled Volhynia. It appealed for unity with the Roman Catholic church and contained an appraisal of a bull by Pope Gregory XVI.[37] Iosyf Levytsky sharply condemned the translations because they had little in common with either the ecclesiastical Slavonic language or the Ukrainian vernacular (the latter of which Levytsky called southwestern or Galician-Ruthenian language). Through close analysis of the language of both translations, Levytsky decided that "only he can write to some purpose for the Galician Ruthenians who uses forms of the living language and intelligible expressions in his works." He was convinced that the literary language was evolving gradually from common speech and folk songs. It did not depend upon the linguistic despotism of certain people. "It is necessary first," Levytsky wrote, "to study the national tongue and then to judge it.... Who will take the Galician-Ruthenian language under his care, if [our] clerical superiors have renounced it and speak to their flock in a foreign and unintelligible language?" Levytsky also claimed that the Ukrainian language was declining among the Greek Catholic clergy in Galicia, and he blamed the church hierarchy, which had not permitted the publication of his *Biblioteka besid dukhovnykh* [Library of spiritual homilies], despite the fact that it was intended to "awaken the somnolent spirit of the Ruthenian clergy in Galicia."[38]

Iosyf Levytsky took a similar position in an 1841 letter to the metropolitan concerning a small liturgical book published in Przemyśl, *Molytvoslov dlia parokhiian shkolskykh* [A prayer book for parishioners in schools]. He wrote that he hoped that "every Galician could come to know the ecclesiastical as well as the Ruthenian folk language." To achieve this end it was essential that the clergy should use only Ruthenian. Levytsky himself published a Slavonic-Polish dictionary and a German-Ruthenian grammar in order to facilitate the teaching of Ruthenian. He also wished to eliminate the use of Latin in the consistory, because it was understood only by priests, "and what can two thousand clergymen do compared to two million Ruthenian people?" Finally, the Ruthenian schools, which existed largely on paper, had to become schools that truly served the nation. In ten years, Levytsky contended, "the whole of Galicia can be transformed."[39]

In the 1840s, Iosyf Levytsky seems to have become an advocate of employing the folk idiom. Iakiv Holovatsky wrote to Osyp Bodiansky: "Levytsky did praise a mixed style in his grammar—what he called 'higher' [*höhere Stil*]—but from his later poems and translation it is apparent that he tended completely toward the popular speech."[40] However, much evidence indicates that it is necessary to modify Holovatsky's statement. In 1843 an anonymous article appeared in *Dennitsa-Jutrzenka* entitled "Dolia galitsko-russkago iazyka" [The fate of the Galician-Ruthenian language], which undoubtedly was written by Levytsky.[41] His linguistic views at that time were splendidly characterized in a letter to the editors of *Dennitsa-Jutrzenka* that accompanied his article.

> I attempted to write in a manner that they could understand in Galicia. However, it is necessary to observe closely my [rules of] orthography. My goal is to make the Little Russian language coincide with [the dialect in] the northeast [Great Russian] in its orthography, even though they differ in pronunciation. However, this is not an obstacle to my nation, and whoever wishes may pronounce according to Little or Great Russian [practice] and quickly and easily make progress.

Editor Petr Dubrovsky seized upon these words, commending them as "a thought most worthy of attention in respect to literary unity among the Slavs."[42] He certainly had in mind literary unity between the Ukrainian and Russian languages.

The journal usually required that all articles appear in either Polish or Russian. On this occasion, however, the editors made an exception and published Levytsky's piece in his own language and orthography. Although the author himself believed that the "Galician-Ruthenian language can develop and is entirely in agreement with the folk idiom," the editors remarked: "We venture the opinion that such a language as the one in which this article is written, in time and through the gradual drawing closer of Galician writers to Russian literature, could easily pass into our contemporary literary language."

Levytsky's aim in his article was to point out the many achievements of Ukrainian literature in Galicia, which had become possible because of his own initiative and example. He also assumed credit for the fact that young seminarians were beginning to practice in the Galician-Ruthenian language, and that the editors of the *Rusalka Dnistrovaia* had emerged from their circle. Levytsky, seeking to combat misconceptions about Ukrainian, chided the Russian scholar Stepan Shevyrev for considering the Ruthenian in Galicia to be a "Polish-Ruthenian language." He also criticized the Poles Samuel Linde and Kajetan Jabłoński for calling Ruthenian "provincialized Polish," but he did not mention that the author of this term was the Russian linguist Nikolai Grech. Levytsky himself believed that "the southwestern Ruthenian language is as old as the nation which speaks it," and that "it is still preserved in Galicia and in Hungary... under the rule of the Austrian two-headed eagle." He did not say, however, that this same language was also preserved in Russian-ruled Ukraine, although he had expressly stated this in his grammar.

Above all, Levytsky's article was a caustic attack on the metropolitan and every Ukrainian activist who had ever dared to hold an opinion at variance with his own. He charged the metropolitan with not knowing the Ukrainian language and keeping the manuscript of Mohylnytsky's grammar too long because "he could not bring himself to pay two hundred guldens in silver to publish it." He further argued that the metropolitan had made a Latin version of his pastoral letter "to demonstrate to the Roman pope that he was a fervent defender of the [Brest] union," and especially that he had sabotaged the publication of *Biblioteka besid dukhovnykh.* Levytsky also accused Ivan Mohylnytsky of writing his grammar "not for the benefit of the nation, but only for personal profit, because he did not publish it at his own expense despite his easy circumstances."

Levytsky, however, reserved his most severe criticism for Lozynsky's use of the Latin alphabet in his *Ruskoje wesile* and his endorsement of that alphabet for Ukrainian literature. It appeared to Levytsky that Lozynsky wanted "to gratify the wishes of Wacław z Oleska" and "provide grist for the Polish mill." Levytsky also credited himself with having defeated this scheme.

Levytsky was not yet content. He continued by criticizing the Ruthenian Triad, accusing Shashkevych and Ustyianovych of "muddling up the orthography" and Vahylevych of "wanting, but failing, to elevate the Galician-Ruthenian language to a high aesthetic degree," because he created a jumble of "the southwestern language with the Russian of the northeast," a mixture which "is neither the old written southwestern [language] nor the current folk [idiom]." It therefore does not seem odd that he named Venedykt Levytsky, Mykhailo Hnidkovsky, Kyrylo Blonsky and Iosyf Sokulsky among "the fervent defenders of the natural [*pryrodnyi*] Galician-Ruthenian language, although their works were not published." His list gives a clear indication of what he thought the Ukrainian literary language should be, since it includes the infamous censor of Ukrainian books in Galicia, Venedykt Levytsky.

The end of Levytsky's article suggests that by the spring of 1843, the idea of relying on Austria had already taken root in the Ukrainian Galician community. He wrote: "Austrian rule does not pose obstacles to Galician Rus' in regard to its religious rites, language and customs, but the polonized Ruthenians are undoing themselves."

Levytsky carried a further discussion of these issues to the columns of Jordan's *Slawische Jahrbücher*, where several articles appeared between 1844 and 1846 regarding Ukrainian literature in Galicia.[43] Levytsky repeated the objections he had raised in *Dennitsa*, and he also attacked the prelates of the Lviv capitulary. He accused Mykhailo Kuzemsky of "professing confused ideas and eagerly wanting to mould a Galician-Ruthenian language, which is neither Great Russian nor Little Russian." Iosyf Levytsky now charged Venedykt Levytsky, whom he earlier had praised, with tendencies toward "Muscovitism." Venedykt Levytsky and other prelates of the Saint George group (the Greek Catholic cathedral church in Lviv), he maintained, intended "die galizisch-russische Sprache zu Grabe tragen" by regarding Vahylevych's grammar as the best.[44]

For his part, Iosyf Lozynsky regarded Iosyf Levytsky's articles as harmful to Ukrainian literature in Galicia, defended Ivan Mohylnytsky (who, he said, had done nothing for his own profit because he had bequeathed his entire estate to impoverished Ukrainian youth), and defended Metropolitan Mykhailo Levytsky. Of himself, Lozynsky noted that he had collected the songs published in *Ruskoje wesile* and had suggested using the Polish alphabet out of the conviction that it would be advantageous to the Ukrainian nation, not to please Wacław z Oleska.[45]

During the entire debate on the issues of the alphabet, orthography and literary language we can distinguish three tendencies: pro-Polish, Ukrainian national or all-Slavic, and pro-Russian. Lozynsky in the 1830s and Ivan Holovatsky at the beginning of the 1840s represented the first view. The proponents of the second view were Shashkevych, Iakiv Holovatsky and their associates from the circle of the Ruthenian Triad. Initially the pro-Russian trend had an adherent only in Denys Zubrytsky (who remained faithful to this view to the end); it was not until 1843 that Iosyf Levytsky, in advancing a scheme to make the Ukrainian and Russian orthography conform to the language used in his article "Dolia galitsko-russkago iazyka," allied himself with Zubrytsky. It was precisely because this language had tendencies toward uniformity with Russian that Levytsky's article elicited the admiration of the *Dennitsa* editor. Dubrovsky, accepting Kollár's idea of Slavic reciprocity and of developing literature in only certain Slavic languages, did not believe in the independent development of Ukrainian. He expressly stated in his journal that "the Little Russians are writing in their folk dialect (for effect or out of need?) and endeavouring to raise it to the level of a literary language; God knows, how far will they go?"[46]

The exchanges regarding Ruthenian writing in Galicia, the article "Dolia galitsko-russkago iazyka," and the later discussion surrounding these works aroused Ukrainians, who were sensitive about everything concerning their language and literature. On the one hand, this debate convinced the Ukrainian enthusiasts that Iosyf Levytsky's course of criticizing everything that did not conform to his concept of a southwestern Ruthenian language, supposedly identical or in accord with the popular speech, the results of which could be seen in *Dennitsa*, would not lead to their objective. On the other hand, the discussion gave them great satisfaction, because someone had finally openly opposed the Greek Catholic hierarchy in Galicia, the principal force blocking Ukrainian national literature.

The Ruthenian Triad decided to ignore Levytsky's criticism of *Rusalka*. Vahylevych himself, who had borne the brunt of Levytsky's attack, stated that he did not intend to reply.[47] The editors of *Rusalka*, he continued, obviously were in the right, and Levytsky's criticism was both bitter and disloyal. Response would have only further inflamed the discussion and strengthened the opposing camp. In any case, the circumstances were not favourable to broadening the polemic. Shashkevych had died six months earlier, Iakiv Holovatsky had remained away from Lviv, and Vahylevych was not well regarded by the church authorities.

The surviving correspondence does not permit us to ascertain precisely the young Ukrainian enthusiasts' reception of Levytsky's articles, but it was probably not favourable. Karel Zap warned the Ukrainians against this type of debate and its eventual consequences. "I read Levytsky's reply to the Saint George priests in Jordan's *Jahrbücher*. If only he had let the matter lie in peace, because by widening the scandal he helps neither himself nor [Ukrainian] literature. The metropolitan should now be converted [to the other point of view], since he already has the [order of] Leopold. What else could he want?"[48]

Ivan Vahylevych was the first to reconcile himself with his clerical superiors. He undertook at Iakhymovych's recommendation the preparation of a grammar of the "South Rus'" language, written in Polish according to the Grech orthographical system, which he considered the most suitable for school instruction. Through this work Vahylevych earned the metropolitan's favour and his own ordination.[49] However, he did not gain sympathy in his circle of friends. As Iakiv Holovatsky wrote to Osyp Bodiansky, "he played the sophisticate in his own way; he twisted [his grammar] so that nothing came of it."[50] One should recall that the same Bodiansky had recommended that Vahylevych prepare a grammar of the folk idiom spoken in Galicia instead.[51]

Still, Vahylevych's grammar illustrates his linguistic theories. He gradually departed from the principles that the Triad accepted during the first phase of its activity. In the introduction Vahylevych stated that the "Little Russian language is a separate, middle language in Slavdom," divided into two dialects: "Galician and Kievan, [which] have so much in common that it is impossible to consider them two separate languages." (In this he agreed with the linguistic scholarship of his day.) He then emphasized that in preparing the grammar he had followed the guidelines established by Grech and Vostokov and sought to apply his own orthography, which resembled that used in the sixteenth and seventeenth centuries and hence reflected a different pronunciation from that of contemporary common people. He had done so in order to liberate the Ukrainians from the "frenzy over the alphabet," and also because he had decided that Ukrainians, "by establishing a link to their past literature, will be able to develop their language on a historical basis." He believed that "this bookish language is the pure Ruthenian and began to be corrupted only subsequently [after the seventeenth century].[52]

Vahylevych's stance made it clear that the lengthy struggles over orthography had produced very little. Virtually every writer continued to use his own orthography, not infrequently adapted the language in his own way and was convinced of the validity of his position. In the 1840s the orthographies of Kotliarevsky, Pavlovsky, Maksymovych (Iakiv Holovatsky employed his system for Ilkevych's *Galician Proverbs*), Borovykovsky, Metlynsky, Hulak-Artemovsky and Oleksander Korsun, and the Galician Ruthenians Shashkevych, Lozynsky, Iosyf Levytsky, Ivan Zhukovsky and Iakiv Holovatsky were known; Vahylevych also usually used his own orthography.[53] Echoes of the struggle over the alphabet continued until the end of 1847, by which time there was a general desire for agreement.[54]

One of Shashkevych's first Ukrainian verses, entitled "Slovo do chtytelei ruskoho iazyka" [A Word to the Lovers of the Ruthenian Language], includes the following stanza:

Razom, razom, khto syl maie,
Honit z Rusy mraky tmavi,
Zavyst nai nas ne spyniaie,
Razom k svitlu, druhy zhvavi.

[Together, together, whoever has strength / Expel from Rus' the dark fog. / Let envy not hold us back. / Together toward the light, lively friends.][55] These lines foretold the direction of further national endeavours. They called for unity, with the aim of enlightening the

Ukrainian nation. It was precisely toward this objective that the further linguistic and literary work of the Triad was dedicated. The concepts of national enlightenment were formed in the heat of the bitter linguistic disputes beginning in mid-1834 and continuing through 1848; in later years this conflict assumed other features, although in large measure it was a continuation of the disputes from the pre-revolutionary period.

Shashkevych first formulated the programme of national enlightenment in his *Azbuka i abetsadlo.* Believing that Ukrainian literature should develop on a national basis, he repudiated all foreign influences, which he thought would have been unavoidable had the Ukrainians adopted the Latin alphabet. He defined the aims of the new national literature democratically: "Literature is essential for the entire nation. Its endeavour and principal aim is to spread education among one and all." From this he argued for developing only literature that would "cling to the people," becoming the property of all citizens and not just "a few so-called European literati through whom it will miss its primary aim."[56]

The Ukrainian enthusiasts, including Shashkevych, believed that the path toward the general education of the people led from the alphabet through the language to a literature that was generally accessible and intelligible to the masses. But they deluded themselves into thinking that it would be possible to resolve socio-economic and perhaps even political problems through education. On this ground was constituted the statute of the Societas Presbyterorum. Its founders believed that through education the Ukrainian peasant could be persuaded to work more productively and to respect the existing social order. The Ukrainian enthusiasts of the 1830s and 1840s had gone considerably further. In explaining to his brother Ivan the problems of developing national education, Iakiv Holovatsky wrote:

> At the very outset I want to consider what we understand by enlightenment and education.... I do not understand either the current fashions, or sweet (but praiseworthy) noble speech, or the jabbering in foreign languages, or the rich, comfortable apartments, buildings, inns, etc. For me, European enlightenment is the aspiration of nations to the attainment of natural rights by the entire nation; it is the spread of true humaneness, true love toward people, through the spread of science and so forth.[57]

The two Holovatsky brothers, however, had different interpretations of the principles by which one ought to be guided in reaching this goal. Ivan educed the aspirations of nations toward the expansion of their rights from the ideas of the French Revolution; he was convinced that

Ukrainians should be guided by the same principles, since the "aspiration of nations is identical," regardless of other dissimilarities. Accordingly, he easily concluded that it was necessary to unite with democratic groups and support those activists who desired socio-economic and political changes. Ivan himself was involved in 1840 and 1841 with revolutionary-minded Poles, such as Karol Moszczański, and progressive Czechs, such as Josef Podlipský and František Kampelík. He was also a proponent of an alliance between the Ukrainians and those Poles who wanted to liquidate the great landed estates. On that basis he wished to build the future of his nation.[58]

Iakiv Holovatsky thought otherwise. He rejected all revolutionary ideas and a Ukrainian-Polish alliance, asserting that the Slavs should rely on their own traditions. He pointed out the superiority of Slavic legal and political institutions, the greater social democracy, the absence of slavery and the republican system of ancient Novgorod; he could not see in the cultural traditions of Western Europe the continuity that he observed among the Slavs. What was European literature? Was it classical Greek and Roman literature, altered by the descendants of the Romans and their neighbours, or a new literature formed on the old Latin foundations? From his reflections on these questions he concluded that Ukrainian literature could develop only on the basis of native traditions.[59]

Several years later, Ivan Holovatsky came to embrace the same views. Having become more closely associated with the leading Slavic spokesmen—from the Habsburg monarchy as well as from Russia—to whom all revolutionary social change was foreign, he gradually accepted their ideas. In this spirit he wrote to Iakiv in the first days of February 1844.

> My acquaintance with Kollár, Vuk [Karadžić], Sreznevsky, and Miklošić has taught me much and pointed me in a better [direction]. Thanks to them I recognized that our nations and the spirit of the time do not demand political changes that are not inherent in their lives, feelings and level of enlightenment. But they do demand that we study and present everything that is characteristic and native only to the nation. We are to plant this field and expect from it only a copious harvest. The politics will change and find its own balance, as was ordained.[60]

In his contention we see a marked convergence with Iakiv Holovatsky's earlier rejection of great political endeavours and attention to educational matters.

The absence of a literary language was the main obstacle to the realization of this programme. Once the language of the common people had been accepted as the basis of the literary language—which the Ruthenian Triad believed to be a necessity emanating from the social structure of the Ukrainian nation[61]—it was essential to decide which dialect should be its foundation. Ultimately it was decided that the dialect of the Chortkiv and Kolomyia areas in Pokuttia best fulfilled this role, "because this part of the country lies in the middle of the Ukrainian lands from Kiev to Sącz."[62] All that was necessary was to supplement it with vocabulary from other Galician dialects and from Ukrainian writers (especially Kotliarevsky) and to adapt some Serbian, Czech, Polish and Russian expressions. Although each member of the Triad wrote in a language of his own, the folk idiom, which they mastered during numerous journeys through Galicia and by diligent study of folklore, clearly had an impact on all of them.

The conviction that the folk idiom was valuable for literature was so strong that in the mid-1840s Iakiv Holovatsky could reply to a sceptic:

> You say, my friend, that in our simple language one can only speak of domestic, everyday matters, that the Ruthenian folk idiom is completely incapable of expressing loftier notions. Shashkevych provided you a living example of how easy it is to express the loftiest ideas about God in one's own dialect, without foreign admixtures—much more strongly, wisely, sober-mindedly and to the point! It is not the folk idiom that is at fault, but you yourself, because (strike your breast) you are not familiar with it; you do not know Ruthenian. Shashkevych did not spend just a year or two studying and analyzing the speech of the common people.... Do not be lazy. Work, and it will go better for you. But know that without work you will never reach that other shore.[63]

Similarly, immediately before the congress of Ukrainian scholars in Lviv in 1848, Vereshchynsky implored Holovatsky "in the name of human reason" that no new learned language be created, but that the folk idiom become the foundation of Ukrainian literature. He added: "We are seeking illumination and [material] abundance for our nation; let its language be the organ by which we speak to it and impart to it the eternal truths."[64] Unfortunately, by then Holovatsky had already come to a somewhat different opinion.

That the Ruthenian Triad possessed valid goals for national enlightenment cannot be denied. But it was very difficult to realize them; indeed, before *robot* was abolished, it was quite impossible. Contemporary education for the common people, particularly in the parish schools, was so poor that the masses generally were illiterate. The situation in the average Ukrainian village was well characterized by Ivan Biretsky, who became a priest in Bachórz in the Sanok district. He wrote in a letter to Iakiv Holovatsky that, although his was supposedly a Ruthenian parish, his parishioners did not know Ruthenian. Even in church they sang in Polish; only the older people used Ruthenian in private, whereas the young people "mostly jabber in Polish." There were no Ukrainian songs to be heard "because their place has already been taken by the Polish 'Krakowiak'."[65] Biretsky himself initiated the construction of a school building, attempted to obtain appropriate textbooks and requested through Holovatsky a copy of Kobrynsky's *Bukvar*. Obviously conditions were not as bad everywhere; Bachórz lay on the ethnic boundary between the Poles and Ukrainians and therefore was more vulnerable to assimilation.

Iosyf Levytsky, the pastor in Sklo in the Przemyśl district, had similar concerns. In his letter to the metropolitan in 1841, he had stipulated the necessity of earnest attention to education. He maintained that in each of the previous seven years he had had approximately a hundred pupils in his school, and he believed that if every Greek Catholic clergyman made an effort similar to his, within ten years the educational level of the Ukrainian people would be raised substantially.[66]

The Ukrainian activists recognized, however, that it would be hard to achieve a broad readership for good literature. There were few publishers; editions were small, and there were no distributors except friends and clerical acquaintances. The lack of bookshops was painfully felt. "Could it not somehow be arranged," Iakiv Holovatsky asked bitterly, "that if a supply of books cannot be kept with every dean, at least one copy of each book be in every district? Otherwise, nothing will come of our literature."[67]

7. National and Social Views

The Ukrainian Galician awakeners, and the members of the Ruthenian Triad in particular, wrote extensively about the national question in their works concerning the Ukrainian language. Although they themselves viewed national issues as peripheral to their linguistic and literary endeavours, for those times they had a good grasp of the place of the Ukrainian nation among the other Slavic nations. As Ivan Vahylevych noted, "In my philological investigations I was not infrequently compelled to search out specific historical data to support my findings."[1] Writings that were primarily philological, such as the many articles and treatises on the Ukrainian language by Vahylevych, Ivan Mohylnytsky and Iakiv Holovatsky, as well as the Ukrainian grammars of Levytsky, Lozynsky and Vahylevych, are especially important to our understanding of their national views.

The Triad circle regarded the nation as a community shaped in the course of its history; they recognized the national language as the primary feature of nationality; and they associated its loss with the disappearance of the national character. Iakiv Holovatsky, like all Romantics, believed that folk songs were an expression of the national spirit. There existed a period in the spiritual development of every nation when all the members of the society were identically educated, all were creative, and "the spirit of all—the national spirit—functioned as one for all—in place of all—and this spirit defined the form and nature of song."[2]

Iakiv Holovatsky and Ivan Vahylevych attempted to offer a definition of "nation." In Holovatsky's opinion, "the nation is a moral person, who, having settled himself, must remain in one place for many years to grow accustomed to the land and the climate, become familiar with nature, cleave unto it, know and love it, so that it speak unto him and so that he himself create songs [and] conceive and discover for himself the appropriate form to express his feelings."[3] Vahylevych believed that "a nation is a people who, having entered upon political life, has evolved for itself its particular character—or, I should say, distinct type—and to this character language most belongs."[4] Political life, which every nation could develop if it were given favourable circumstances, nevertheless was not an indispensable condition for national existence. Vahylevych noted explicitly that "it is self-evident that every nation possesses or had to possess a political life, even if [only] for a short time. That political life is an external manifestation of the inner life." He further maintained that "the South Rus' people are a nation, because they possess a distinct type of nationality or, in other words, an individuality that manifests itself in customs and traditions. In addition, they speak one language. That they had a political life is well known."[5]

The Ukrainians, therefore, constituted a nation, although they did not then have a political life. It was sufficient that they had had one in the past. The members of the Triad did not demand an independent Ukrainian state. Did they, however, contemplate one? After all, *Rusalka Dnistrovaia* speaks of a Slavic federation, however hazily and unclearly. What role was destined for Ukraine in it? No answer can be found in the writings of the Triad.

The most important element in both Holovatsky's and Vahylevych's definitions of a "nation" (despite the fact that they did not explicitly mention it) was the recognition of a certain individuality that differentiated nations from one another. That individuality lay in their distinctive national consciousness, expressed through songs and the native language. The Triad circle also voiced the thesis of the literary and linguistic unity of the Ukrainian populace that inhabited the lands of Galicia, Hungarian Rus' and Great (i.e. Russian) Ukraine. This was obviously not a new idea in the 1830s and 1840s; its origins could be found in the pronouncements of learned Ukrainians, Slovenes and Czechs, such as Mykola Hoshovsky, Ivan Mohylnytsky, Kopitar and Šafařík.

In the early 1840s there was still no agreement about what the Ukrainian nation in Galicia was officially to call itself. The territory inhabited by the Ukrainians was commonly referred to as Little Russia (literally, Rus') and its inhabitants as Little Russians; in Galicia they were variously called *Rusyny*, *Rusnaky*, *Ruśniaki* or *Rusini*. Eventually, at the request of Metropolitan Levytsky in 1843, the

Austrian authorities established the official name as *Ruthenen* (Ruthenians).[6] However, this name included only the Ukrainians under Habsburg rule, and not all the Ukrainians on both sides of the Zbruch River.

Mykola Hoshovsky, a professor at the Jagiellonian University and a known informer to Josef Dobrovský on Ukrainian matters, noted in 1815 in a letter to Jerzy Samuel Bandtkie that "the Little Russian living in Galicia calls himself a *Rusyn* or a *Rusnak* but never a *Rus̀niak*," and that nothing had been done since the thirteenth century to develop the language of this nation. Hoshovsky said that no written works had yet appeared in it, with the exception of one translation of a German exegesis of the Gospels and some homilies. Nevertheless, a reasonably pure spoken Ukrainian had been preserved. Hoshovsky discerned traces of the Ukrainian language in Nestor's *Chronicle*, and he offered the opinion that it should be read according to Ukrainian pronunciation.[7] Thus, without addressing directly the issue of the unity of the entire Ukrainian nation, Hoshovsky substantiated the continuity of the historical and linguistic traditions in Ukrainian literature from the times of Kievan Rus'.

The question of the national distinctivenss of the Ukrainians was not clearly posed until 1817 and 1821, by Ivan Mohylnytsky in his memoranda regarding the legal status of the Ukrainian language in Galicia. He buttressed his arguments more precisely in his 1829 "Discourse on the Ruthenian Language," in which he maintained that Ukrainian was not a mixture of individual Slavic languages, but a separate branch of the primeval Slavic language, much as the Ukrainian nation was an independent part of the great primeval Slavic people. "The Ruthenian language or the Ruthenian dialect," he wrote, "has a place of similar rank alongside Polish, Russian, Czech, Illyrian and Carniolian [Slovenian]; it is equal to them, just as the Ruthenian nation is equal to the other Slavic nations."[8] Mohylnytsky believed that the development of the Ukrainian language was inseparably tied to the fate of the nation that inhabited the Ukrainian lands in Russia, among which he included Ukraine proper (the former Polish palatinates of Kiev, Bratslav and Chernihiv), Podillia, Volhynia, and White and Black Rus'. (Thus he denied a separate nationhood to the Belorussians.) He attempted to prove "that the Ruthenian language was always distinguished from the other [Slavic] languages, and especially from Polish and Russian," and he devoted a separate section to substantiating the differences between the Ruthenian and Russian languages.[9]

The spokesmen in the 1830s provided more precise data on the areas of Ukrainian settlement. Iosyf Levytsky wrote in his Ruthenian grammar that "the eastern part of the Carpathians and the plains between the rivers San, Wiara, Dniester, Buh, Boh [Southern Buh], Pripet and Dnieper are inhabited by a Slavic branch which in its mother tongue calls itself Ruthenian (*Rusyn*) and calls its country Rus'."[10] He also stated that in 1831 the Ukrainian nation numbered more than 8,000,000 people, of whom more than 5,000,000 lived in Russia, 1,874,148 in Galicia, more than 500,000 in Hungary and 100,271 in Bukovyna.[11]

Iosyf Lozynsky's *Gramatyka języka ruskiego* [Grammar of the Ruthenian language] of 1846 says that "the Ruthenian (Little Russian) language stretches from the centre of northern Hungary and Galicia through all of southern Russia as far as the Kuban River." Lozynsky included the Belorussians in the Ukrainian nation, thereby increasing its number to 15,870,000. He provided other data on the basis of Pavel J. Šafařík's *Slovanský nârodopis* [Slavic ethnography].[12]

The members of the Ruthenian Triad held similar beliefs. Vahylevych wrote in *Rusalka Dnistrovaia* that "the Ruthenian nation, one of the principal Slavic formations, at the Slavs' centre, stretches over the fertile expanses from beyond the Beskyd mountains to the Don River."[13] In his foreword to the first part of *Vinok*, Ivan Holovatsky extended these boundaries to the Donets River in the east and the Desna River in the north.[14] A summation of the Triad's national views was Iakiv Holovatsky's *Rosprava o iazytsi iuzhnoruskom i ieho narichiiakh* [Treatise on the South Rus' language and its dialects], which he presented at the congress of Ukrainian scholars in 1848. This discourse was a systematic exposition of contemporary Slavic research in the Ukrainian language and nation. Holovatsky did not go beyond Šafařík's works, culling data on population and the precise boundaries of the Ukrainians' settlement according to the first edition of *Slovanský nârodopis* of 1842. He also echoed Šafařík's conclusion:

> The South Rus' (Little Russian or, as we say, *ruskyi*) language stretches over both slopes of the Carpathians, over all of southern Russia on both sides of the Dnieper, from the Ondava and Poprad rivers in [northern] Hungary and the Wieprz in [Russian] Poland to the middle Don, indeed as far as the Kuban River in the Caucasus, from the estuaries of the Dniester and Dnieper rivers, from the Black Sea as far as the Pripet and not far from the sources of the Desna, Seim and Donets rivers.[15]

Holovatsky again relied on Šafařík in stating that, of a total of 13,144,000 Ukrainians, 10,370,000 lived in Russia and 2,774,000 in Austria, of which 625,000 were in Hungary. "From this survey," Holovatsky concluded, "one can see that the nation that speaks the Little Russian language is the most numerous, after the Great Russian, among all the Slavic nations."[16] And this nation "speaks one and the same language," which is called "Ukrainian, Little Russian [South Rus'], or simply Ruthenian."[17] Holovatsky believed that all those who said that Ukrainian had evolved from Church Slavonic and was a dialect of Polish or Great Russian were in error. Rather, Ukrainian was a distinct and independent language. In substantiating this view, Holovatsky once more turned to Šafařík's findings:

> The degree to which our South Rus' language differs from Great Russian and Belorussian can easily be recognized by the features that Šafařík indicated and described. Apart from their close proximity, their common early history, the long contacts between them, and the similar influence of the [Slavonic] ecclesiastical language on each of them, [these languages] differ very significantly, both in their grammatical forms and in pronunciation. The Belorussian and Great Russian languages are closer in pronunciation to Polish than to Ukrainian.[18]

Obviously, then, the leaders of the Ukrainian national awakening in Galicia regarded the Ukrainians as a separate, entirely independent nation among the Slavs, clearly distinct from the Polish, Russian and Belorussian nations. By contrast, the Russian Slavophiles, like Mikhail Pogodin, explicitly tried to blur the differences between Russians and Ukrainians (as the Galician Ukrainians were well aware) and pronounced the "oneness" of the Russian nation, from the San River and the Black Sea to the Pacific Ocean and the seas of the Arctic.

Although they acknowledged the linguistic and national unity of the Austrian Ukrainians and those under tsarist rule, the Galician Ukrainians drew no political conclusions before 1840. To be sure, in 1774 Bishop Lev Sheptytsky, in a memorial delivered to the Galician governor Count Pergen, alerted the Austrian government to the possibility of exerting political influence on tsarist Ukraine through the Ukrainians in Galicia. However, he did not have in mind national unity, but the religious unity of Greek Catholics on both sides of the new state border. He expected in this way to guarantee some advantages for himself as bishop and for the Greek Catholic church in Galicia.[19]

Mykhailo Harasevych likewise had dissociated himself from any political aims in a report concerning the Jesuits in 1836. He simply stated that, although the Ukrainian nation in Galicia "is of the same extraction as the Ukrainians of Podillia, Volhynia and Ukraine, who first belonged to the Kingdom of Halych and Volodymyr, [and] although it is associated with them through its literature and language,... it has never exhibited a yearning to join with those fellow kin and come under Russian rule."[20]

The possibility of Austria's acquiring political influence upon Ukraine through the Galician Ruthenians, however, did not escape the attention of Jernej Kopitar, who clearly emphasized this notion in his review of Shashkevych's *Zoria*. At that time Kopitar held that exploiting the possibility was not in Austria's best interests. In 1842, however, perhaps at Kopitar's suggestion, Bishop Hryhorii Iakhymovych made an official proposal to the Austrian government on this question. Iakiv Holovatsky noted the bishop's action in an 1846 article on conditions among the Galician Ruthenians: "Several years ago Bishop Iakhymovych drew up a paper for official use concerning political support for the Ruthenian nationality and its influence on Little Russia. [This document] came by chance into our hands. Apparently it had been consigned to oblivion."[21] Although Holovatsky believed that Iakhymovych's "paper" had been forgotten, it should be recalled that in 1842 and 1843 Austrian police officials began to support the national aspirations of the Ukrainians in Galicia. Proof of this lies in the projected publication of an official Ukrainian journal with the explicit aim of countering Russian propaganda.[22]

Iakiv Holovatsky made a similar offer of Ukrainian-Austrian co-operation in his article, although in entirely different political circumstances (namely, following the suppression of the Polish insurrection in Cracow and the peasant jacquerie). Holovatsky drew a picture of broad political advantages for Austria, both in domestic policy (capitalizing on the Ukrainian-Polish antagonism) and in foreign policy (acquiring influence over tsarist Ukraine).

By regarding the Ukrainians in Galicia as part of the larger Ukrainian nation, the Ruthenian Triad recognized its own Galician literature as part of Ukrainian literature in general. In his introduction to *Rusalka Dnistrovaia*, Shashkevych defined the anthology as a continuation of works that had appeared in Russia and Austria.[23] In other ways as well the Triad pointed to the literary unity between Galicia and Ukraine: in Shashkevych's "Pobratymovi" and Vahylevych's and Holovatsky's treatises on the "South Rus'" language. They ascribed literary leadership to the Ukrainians in Russia. Iakiv Holovatsky, for example, maintained that Ivan Kotliarevsky pointed the way for literature based on the folk idiom; he also knew that "in Little Russia the Kiev-Pereiaslav language is regarded as the primary, purest and most depictive variety of the South Rus' language."[24] It was unfortunate that this knowledge was not exploited in literary work in Galicia. Ustyianovych quite simply conceded, "If we want to enjoy the charming affability [of the Ukrainian language], let us take Osnovianenko's *Marusia*; if we desire to study the beauty of its hues, let us turn our eyes to the rising sun (Osnovianenko's description); if we want to arm ourselves in strength, let us listen to the sonorous Shevchenko; if we want to amuse ourselves and joke, let us take Kotliarevsky."[25] For the Ukrainian writers in Galicia in the 1840s, Ukrainian literature was an ideal worthy of emulation and an unexploited model. In Vahylevych's opinion, Russian Ukraine itself had played the decisive role in the development of Ukrainian literature in the Austrian monarchy.[26]

Arguments based on folk songs and historical data were advanced in support of national views. The Galician Ukrainians saw the songs, particularly historical songs, as a means of learning about the past. Shashkevych wrote in *Rusalka*: "The old epos [*staryna*] is a good, sonorous song that speaks to our times in different ways and appeals with different moods to us from before the ages.... The epos is a great picture, a mirror like clear water in which the unclouded image of the centuries appears."[27] Ivan Vahylevych regarded the folk songs as equally important for the poet, the historian and the archeologist: "In them are found recollections of events from the eighth century and perhaps even earlier, from the primeval Slavic era, and about Constantinople, about Halych; there are also mythical [songs]. This is the spirit of the life our ancestors preserved in the shadow of the Carpathians."[28]

The question of the ethnic differentiation of the Slavs and the beginnings of the state of Rus' occupied a leading place in Vahylevych's and Holovatsky's historical reflections. They studied this question against the background of contemporary historiography and Slavic studies, using learned studies by Russian, Czech and Polish scholars, especially those of Zorian Dołęga Chodakowski, Joachim Lelewel, and Pavel Šafařík. Their sources were based on archeological remains, ancient Greek and Roman documents, the native linguistic material and folk legends. (The latter were taken as "historical phenomena" only cautiously and critically.)[29] On the basis of linguistic evidence, Vahylevych concluded that in the distant past the Slavs had comprised one nation that spoke a single proto-Slavic language. He also sought an answer to the question of the Slavs' origins. For a while he believed that they had come from India; later, under Šafařík's influence, he acknowledged that the original homeland of the Slavs was the Danubian basin; therefore they were native to the region they now inhabited. He maintained that in the Greek sources there were proofs "that the Dacians and the Illyrians are one nation in respect to language and customs, and if the latter were Slavs, then so were the former."[30] In accordance with the then prevailing historiographical theory of the Varangian, or Norman, origin of the state of Rus', Vahylevych maintained that the name Rus' itself came "from there, whence the 'Russes' came, that is, from Scandinavia, where a part of Sweden to this day is called *Roszlagen*.... To this day the Chudians [Finns] call Sweden *Ruotzonia*, that is, 'Rus' land,' and the Swedes *Ruotzolainen*, that is, 'Rus' people'."[31]

Iakiv Holovatsky took a more specific interest in the lands inhabited by the Ukrainians in the Habsburg monarchy. The product of these investigations was his article "Great Croatia or Galician-Carpathian Rus'," published first by Pogodin in the journal *Moskvitianin* in 1841, and later in Ukrainian in the second part of *Vinok*.[32] "It is not known to us what nation originally settled the region around the Carpathians," he stated. However, referring to Zubrytsky's *Rys do historii narodu ruskiego w Galicji* [Outline history of the Ruthenian nation in Galicia], published in 1837, Holovatsky contended that the Slavic presence in those lands was so ancient that the Slavs doubtless could be called its first citizens. The proof lay in the fact that "history nowhere speaks of the Slavs' migration to or settlement in these lands." Thus, he concluded, "a nation about which there is an absence of information concerning when it might have come and settled in its fatherland—a nation which in addition has itself sent out numerous groups for settlement [elsewhere]—indeed must be very old. It increased adequately in that place; it was primeval, a nation that lived in savage, barren mountains, places not conducive to habitation."[33]

Holovatsky's contention was a basic ingredient in the general outlook of the Ruthenian Triad, because it held great contemporary significance. If the Ukrainians were original inhabitants, then they should be the masters. Holovatsky believed that the first Slavic states—of Riurik in Novgorod and his descendants in Kiev, of the Lekhites in Gniezno, and of Rastislav in Pannonia—arose at virtually the same time and extended their boundaries through subjugation of neighbouring tribes, which, belonging to the same ethnic and linguistic group, gradually "grew from clans into one nation." In this manner the inhabitants of White Croatia, the ancestors of the contemporary Ukrainians in Galicia and Hungary, were subordinated to the rule of the Kievan princes. Holovatsky agreed with Lelewel's concept of "internal conquest," according to which major changes occurred in the social and proprietary structures in the captured lands. He pointed out that before the Slavs of the Carpathians became subjects of the Kievan prince, they lived "in a patriarchal state under the leadership of their native elders of the clan or princes. They carried on farming and herding, without doubt, and the mining of ores and trade."[34]

The thesis of the pernicious influence of Western ideas upon the Slavic countries in general and upon Rus' in particular—a notion emphasized by the Russian Slavophiles in dealing with Russian history and by Lelewel in some issues in Polish history—found a firm adherent in Holovatsky.[35] It was precisely Western ideas that caused the fall of Rus', which was divided up into small principalities, infected by Western feudalism, rent by internal conflict and devastated by foreign incursions. On the other hand, the Greek rite, voluntarily accepted by the Bulgarians, Moravians, Czechs, Silesians, Polanians and Rus', played a salutary role in their history.[36]

In emulating Chodakowski and Šafařík, Vahylevych similarly praised the role of the Greek rite. He opposed August Bielowski's thesis that the Slavic nations could not have become civilized through their own efforts and that civilization was brought to them through the Latin rite. Vahylevych maintained that "all these nations and peoples were sedentary; they worked the fields and had numerous towns where artisanship flourished." What is more, the Slavs even had religious books, among which Vahylevych included "law-giving tablets in the [ancient Slavic] assemblies, [such as] the so-called prophecy of Libuše, a poetic literary find from the tenth century that Šafařík and Palacký published."[37] To be sure, Vahylevych's assumptions were based on false premises, and he was convinced that the prophecy of Libuše was authentic. However, Šafařík and Palacký also accepted it, and only Kopitar had reservations.

Vahylevych felt that the Latin language had brought only harm to the Slavic nations and made them strangers to one another, because civilization and literature had developed only where "the yoke of Latin" was cast off and the native languages were introduced. It was precisely the influence of Constantinople, Vahylevych asserted, that allowed the Slavs the benefits of their native language. The spiritual life of the Slavs, modelled on Byzantium, had evolved "on the basis of nationality"; thence had come religious, theological and law books.[38]

Holovatsky and Vahylevych had clear practical objectives: they presented theses in support of Slavdom's distinct historical route, opposed to the West's allegedly undemocratic road of development, and they stressed the ancient Slavs' republican ideals, patriarchal social structure, the great role of the *viche* (popular assembly) and its bell, and the absence of feudalism. On the other hand, they were concerned to oppose every revolutionary tendency that justified social and political change with the slogans of the French Revolution (although Ivan Holovatsky, as we saw, for a while advocated such "alien" views).[39] The Ukrainian enthusiasts, especially Iakiv Holovatsky, instead expected legal change—reform instituted and carried out by the Austrian authorities.

Evocation of the ancient and glorious history of Ukraine-Rus' was of major importance in the Galician Ukrainians' national movement. They based their thesis of the continuity of national history and traditions on historical materials; they pointed to history as the source of national memories and moral examples worthy of imitation; they used the past to defend the Cyrillic alphabet and to argue for the necessity of an independent national life in 1848; they searched the past for reasons for the present condition of the nation. Iakiv Holovatsky's speech at a Ukrainian gathering in 1848 in Chortkiv reveals this commitment. He described his remarks in a letter to Kyrylo Blonsky:

> I spoke about the situation of our nation as the first master of this land from the most distant times, about the splendid period of Rus' and our princes, about its collapse during the Tatar incursions, about how Poland lay in wait for Rus' and conquered it, about its fate under the rule of the Polish *szlachta* and under Austria's reign up to this date, about the freedoms granted by the constitution [of April 1848], about our significance, about [our] new, free life, about the need to show ourselves as a nation before the world—a nation free in itself and equal to other nations according to the law, in the schools, the offices, etc. In several images I underscored in what the constitution consists. I said that other nations may also demand their due. We are not crossing anyone else's path, but let no one degrade us. We will not permit it, we will not submit; let no one dare to control us or humiliate us, because behind us stands the law.[40]

Just such an appeal to the Ukrainians' historical traditions was essential for the awakening nation in the circumstances of that time. The past reminded the nation that if it was once capable of an independent political existence, it could be again. Emphasizing ancestral heroes was meant to prompt the present generation to action. For that reason Shashkevych had juxtaposed former glory with the sad present. He had written of the joy of their ancestors' victory over Bolesław the Wrymouth and described the strength of the Cossack armies in the verses "Khmelnytskoho obstuplennie Lvova" [Khmelnytsky's siege of Lviv] and "O Nalyvaiku" [On Nalyvaiko].[41] Vahylevych also touched upon the struggle for national independence in his poem "Madei" and in his introduction to the Ruthenian folk songs in *Rusalka Dnistrovaia*.[42] The Ukrainian spokesmen often turned to the history of Kievan Rus': to the splendid achievements of its culture, to the *Ruska Pravda* and the *Tale of Ihor's Campaign*; to the glory of the Principality of Halych and Volodymyr; to the wars for the national independence of Ukraine during Khmelnytsky's times.

History, however, was not treated critically, which led to an excessive idealization of the Ukrainian national character and distorted facts.[43] Yet in this respect the Galician Ukrainians acted no differently than the other Slavic nations—and, indeed, not only the Slavs.

In the social and political conditions that prevailed in Galicia before 1848, it was difficult openly to voice any call for change, because this would have been regarded as spreading revolutionary propaganda. The fate of the Polish conspiratorial movement and the decidedly hostile attitude of the Austrian authorities were clear warnings. The Ukrainian spokesmen were compelled to choose another course, for these and other reasons as well. Their activity was essentially anti-Polish in that it led toward liberation from Polish influences, and consequently they had to seek to resolve social issues in other ways than Polish revolutionaries. In fact, there was only one possibility: to merge national work with loyalty to the Habsburg monarchy. One could freely accuse only the Polish *szlachta* of oppressing the Ukrainian people. Moreover, this approach suited the Austrian bureaucrats, who eagerly exploited class and national antagonisms for their own ends.

The circle of the Ruthenian Triad was socially conservative. One of Iakiv Holovatsky's closest friends, Antin Liubych-Mohylnytsky, when speaking in 1839 to a group of colleagues in the Greek Catholic seminary, stated that the clergymen were not only sons of the fatherland, but also state officials discharging a secular authority imparted to them by the emperor. Accordingly, they should instill in the people the conviction that the authority of the emperor and the imperial officials came from God and explain to them that all the decrees, levies and labours, although they seemed too difficult, were imposed "for our own advantage." Mohylnytsky's speech could lead one to conclude that the entire social and political programme of the Galician Ukrainians in the 1830s was limited to preaching loyalty and obedience to the emperor and his officials (in the Austrian system the estate owners also fulfilled administrative functions) and the patient bearing of *robot* and reconciliation to a fate dependent on the will of God.[44] But should views such as those that Mohylnytsky espoused necessarily be taken absolutely seriously, especially since they were expressed in extraordinary circumstances and with a prescribed objective? After all, many of the Greek Catholic seminarians who gave similar speeches in fact took part in the Polish conspiracies.

In addressing social conditions in Galicia, the young Ukrainians chose a middle course: in speaking of past events, they connected them to the present. If in his poem "Zhadka" Shashkevych juxtaposed the "joyous" life of the past to the "sad" present,[45] the reader could interpret his words in two ways: he could either associate his words with the national life of the Galician Ukrainians or with the people's social position. Most readers probably joined the two interpretations, recognizing the interdependence of the national and social issues. Antin Liubych-Mohylnytsky wrote similarly in his poem "Zhadka staryny"

[Recollection of antiquity], dedicated to the memory of the Ukrainians who perished during the times of the Tatar incursions; it ends with an effective comparison:

Tilko vsypani mohyly,
Shcho ottsiv kosty pokryly,
Spomynaiut smutnyi chas,
Hirshu doliu, jak u nas![46]

[Only the raised burial mounds / that cover our forefathers' bones / recall the sad time, / a lot worse than ours.]

The members of the Ruthenian Triad sharply criticized *robot*, which they treated as a historical phenomenon and, therefore, transitory. It had arisen along with the rooting of personal property rights and was the consequence of a historical process—the nature of which, however, they were unable to explain. *Robot* had not yet arisen in the world of Shashkevych's and Mohylnytsky's historical poems. These liberal concepts are reminiscent of the theses of Lelewel's later discourse *Stracone obywatelstwo stanu kmiecego w Polsce* [The loss of citizenship by the peasants in Poland], in which the distinguished Polish historian asserted that common ownership was the original proprietary form in Poland and individual ownership only later.

Vahylevych wrote in *Rusalka Dnistrovaia* that the Poles, after having occupied Rus', introduced greater national and social oppression than had the Tatars. They made the populace perform *robot* and forced those who resisted to comply, not sparing the "wire knout." Ruthenian traitors aided the Poles in oppressing their own nation.[47] In "Olena," the first Ukrainian novella in Galicia, Shashkevych wrote about that bygone era, but the work also contained many issues related to current actions by brigands in Galicia. "Olena" tells of a willful noble land-owner who has been invited to a village wedding and has abducted the bride. On the way back to his castle, he is killed by brigands. Shashkevych presented the brigands as avengers fighting for their rights by trying to end the land-owners' abuses against their serfs. In fact, in this work Shashkevych expressed ideas that appear to have been taken from the leaflets issued by the Polish conspiratorial movement. For example, the leader of the brigands orders his subordinates: "Vanka, take six men with you to the castle. Remove whatever will be useful to us; whatever you don't take, let the fire destroy together with the castle! You won't have much difficulty there, but let us know how you fare. And you, Semen, will take us to the wedding, where we'll dance a round with the plunderers, those sons of our old foes."[48]

The Ukrainian writers in general focused on the actions of such brigands, though they evaluated their role in various ways. Admittedly, the subject was not unusual in contemporary Polish Galician literature. We noted earlier that Eugeniusz Brocki placed his short story "Brigands in the Carpathians" in *Haliczanin*, August Bielowski wrote about Dovbush, in the 1830s *Rozmaitości* devoted a series of articles to the brigands, and in 1839 Kazimierz Turowski published his "Dumy o zbójcach na pograniczu Polski i Węgier" [Tales about the brigands of the Polish-Hungarian borderland] in the periodical *Słowianin* [The Slav].[49] In Vahylevych's opinion, the Carpathians were the "cradle for the rebirth" of the Ukrainian nation, and in those mountains "from the beginning of political life, brigandry evolved." Vahylevych compared these events to analogous processes in Ukraine, where "in the meadows along the Dnieper there arose out of brigandry a political life of the mother Sich—great, splendid, and wild—until it merged into one political body with Rus' in 1775."[50]

Iakiv Holovatsky, on the other hand, treated brigandry somewhat ambiguously. In preparing an introduction to a collection of folk-songs, he wrote that the Ukrainian nation "never toyed with that disgraceful trade," because it was a pacific, calm and industrious people. Instead, he said, the Polish *szlachta* had taken up brigandry, organizing incursions and forays. He asked: "Is it any cause for wonder that in certain corners, amidst the tumult and confusion of old Poland, brigandage also appeared among the Ruthenians?" Moreover, the Poles were guilty of spreading it. However, in the same article Holovatsky stated: "In the mountains they considered it an honour to be a brigand. That is why a girl, if a suitor was courting her, asked if he had been among the brigands and would not marry him if he could not prove that he had been with the brigands."[51]

Like Vahylevych, Holovatsky compared the brigands to the Haidamaks and Cossacks in Ukraine and the uskoks (anti-Turkish guerrillas) in Serbia and Montenegro and stressed particularly the social nature of their struggle.[52] Holovatsky pointed out that the contemporary Ukrainian community was hostile toward the brigands, who often were criminals or deserters from the Austrian army and who usually robbed poor shepherds—the Hutsuls—of their goods. However, the Ukrainians did glorify those brigands who "lived in song," such as Marusiak and Dovbush, and pointed to Dovbush's hut as a shrine. Holovatsky wrote: "The descendants of Stepan Dzvinka, who shot Oleksa Dovbush, live to this day in the village of Kosmach, isolated and condemned by the people as outcasts [*pod narodnoi opaloi*]; no one befriends them or keeps company with them."[53]

The Triad circle opposed the exploitative burden of *robot*. Mykola Vereshchynsky's words in 1848—"I thank God that He permitted us to live to see the fall of *robot* and slavery, to enjoy liberty and better times"[54]—reveal this attitude, but Iakiv Holovatsky's impassioned criticism in an 1842 article, "Journey through Galician and Hungarian Rus'," does so even more vividly. In his discourse "Great Croatia" Holovatsky already had decried the polonized Ukrainian nobility, whom he accused of oppressing its own people. In the ranks of "the ardent persecutors of their own countrymen" Holovatsky listed the best known Galician families: the Potockis (of Kaniv), Komarnickis, Lewickis, Paparas and Turkuls.[55] He accused the Galician *szlachta* of illegally increasing *robot*, of wresting the better pieces of land from the peasants and annexing them to the manorial lands, and of concluding cunning agreements according to which the peasants ("swindled by deceit and alcohol") were obliged to work every day of the year. Holovatsky wrote: "What benefactions! The peasant now has nothing to worry about, not about taxes, nor about tilling the land, the garden. He pulls his yoke like an ox.... What Machiavellian perversity! They take away the peasant's last freedom and make a slave out of him." Holovatsky further pointed out that the Polish noblemen and the Armenians were one of a kind in this exploitation. Armenians were a true "scourge of God" toward their serfs, because they were purportedly guided by the principle, "Beat the peasant (they murmur) like an ox; let him work for you like an ox; let him eat like an ox."[56]

"Journey through Galician and Hungarian Rus'" presented a broad panorama of the Ukrainians in Galicia. Holovatsky was wholeheartedly on the side of the often starving common people, among whom a rich man was one who did not go hungry before the first harvest and "who has enough of his own bread through the winter and the spring until the new bread, and needs neither to overpay nor to borrow for grain or flour." These people paid taxes, served in the army, and fulfilled a series of obligations for the manor besides *robot*. The highlanders, who raised cattle, sheep and goats and did not possess their own land, were compelled, Holovatsky noted, to pay the land-owner for fodder: "four silver crowns for an ox or a cow; three silver crowns for a heifer; one silver crown for a sheep and a calf. Next, they pay rents for their huts and homesteads." In addition, they were obliged to cut trees and float them down to the Dniester three times a year. Still, "the governmental taxes are very small."[57]

The peasants in Podillia were in a worse situation, because they were forced to work for a whole week, sometimes a long distance from home, "for half a pound of meat or potatoes." A particularly perfidious method of exploitation was to call villagers for the so-called *toloka*, or special harvest labour, for which their sole reward was a quarter litre of vodka. Holovatsky commented, "Thus, for an entire day's bloody work, [they received] a quarter measure of poison! A truly noble reward! And then you are to be surprised by the poverty of the Galician villager. And yet there is no more industrious a people in Galicia than the Ruthenians."[58] For it was the Ruthenian people who worked the soil in Galicia, sowed the grain, gathered the harvest, planted the potatoes that the land-owners later turned into vodka, and raised the herds of cattle that were driven each year to Olomouc, Prague and Vienna. At what expense? Holovatsky answered:

> Turn [your] ears to the voice of the people and you will hear how much this costs in wailing, how much in lamentation, how much in innocent tears, how much in the beatings of an enslaved people! And the so-called assigned labour, that is, either to dig up in one day five bushels of potatoes, or to reap and grind one and a half stacks of grain, or to tie three stacks of grain into sheaves! All of this is against Austrian law, which explicitly forbids burdening a person with more than his strength will endure. How much bloody sweat this squeezes forth! God have mercy on them.[59]

In this enormous machine of oppression, Holovatsky (and not only he) ascribed a large and not especially honourable role to the Jews, who in the fall bought the peasant's possessions for almost nothing, so that during the time of scarcity before the next harvest, they could sell or lend them back at an enormous profit.[60] Holovatsky blamed the Jews for the economic backwardness of the country and accused them of stirring up the landowners against the peasants. "The Jews who nested [here] for so many centuries have eradicated all ingenuity in the nation and with their claws have buried all crafts and industry. This perverse tribe with its deceitful actions is able to keep the peasant continually dependent and does not permit him to act on his own strength.... Finally, the Jew stirs up the land-owner or the steward of his estate against the peasant, since he expects to fleece him of something."[61]

Unfortunately, before 1848 the Ukrainian spokemen did not have an adequate plan for changing existing conditions. They opposed *robot*, which they considered to be a historical phenomenon that would one day be terminated. But Iakiv Holovatsky, for example, was not appalled by the fact that *robot* was legally established and sanctioned; what concerned him was the additional burdens introduced by the land-owners "contrary to Austrian law." Like the Ukrainian author of an anonymous letter to the Austrian emperor in 1834, he was willing to let *robot* continue so long as there was no such merciless exploitation.[62] Holovatsky's extensive correspondence, in which until the revolution of

1848 one could search in vain for any criticism of the institution of *robot*, supports this interpretation of his social views. As a loyal imperial subject and a man of established liberal views, Holovatsky expected changes from above in the social and economic system. He expected and was even bold enough to propose that the Austrian government ameliorate the fate of the Ukrainian peasant, rely on the middle rural strata (as Joseph II once had done), and do away with *robot* or transform it into a system of rent payments.[63] (The anonymous letter writer also counted on reforms from above.)[64]

For the time being, however, the Ukrainian activists propagated certain half-measures, which could improve the peasants' lot slightly. In particular, in the 1840s they engaged in the widely propagated abstinence movement in Galicia by organizing brotherhoods of sobriety. Luka Dankevych wrote a sketch from the life of the common people for *Vinok* under the title "Besida o horiltsi" [A talk about whisky], in which he decried drunkenness, advocated sobriety, and urged the peasants to become true "makers of their own destiny."[65]

Even Denys Zubrytsky, who in 1819 had published an article in praise of *robot* in *Rozmaitości*, in 1844 wrote to Iakiv Holovatsky:

> Extricating our people from the satanic, that is Jewish, grasp is the first and most important step toward [national] renascence. It is precisely at this moment, when the Russian government through legislation is attempting to wrest the Slavic tribes from the degradation of inebriation, that the Almighty gave our [government] the salutary thought of saving [our people] from this abyss through moral and religious strength. In the Lviv consistories they write much about this; they print and make decrees; Malynovsky sweats over his sermons, and the metropolitan and the bishops have hidden themselves like dachshunds in a hole. The Latin rite bishop in Tarnów acts the best, and he already has several tens of thousands of proselytes. With your mind and eloquence, you could accomplish much for the common good.[66]

It seems that Zubrytsky did not sense the antifeudal thrust of this temperance movement, but it did not suit the land-owners, who thought only of income from the distillation of alcohol, or the tavernkeepers who sold the whisky. The tsarist government, which in 1844 increased the price of whisky in the Polish kingdom and taxed its production, took the step for fiscal reasons. The parochial priests, however, seriously thought that by these means they could lift the peasant out of his misery, and therefore in their sermons they specifically attacked tavern-keepers, and thus the Jew and indirectly the land-owner. For this reason the Russian governor in Warsaw, Prince Ivan Paskevich, warned the Austrian authorities in Lviv that the work of revolutionaries was visible among the brotherhoods of sobriety, and he himself forbade their activity in the Polish kingdom.[67]

8. Ties to the Slavic Community

The Poles

Various ties between the Galician Ukrainians and the Poles played an immeasurably important role in the Ruthenian Triad's activities. The two peoples lived side by side, were subject to similar external influences and had many common characteristics, although they differed in their social and political circumstances. Until the 1830s any Polish-Ukrainian antagonism was almost entirely limited to religious and cultural issues. The unavoidable national conflict seemingly went unnoticed until the November 1830 insurrection in Russian Poland made its existence apparent to everyone. Alongside the great enthusiasm for the struggle for Poland's liberation, there surfaced in the Ukrainian community aspirations toward a more independent development, the result of which was the activity of Shashkevych's circle. The year 1830 also revealed the earliest manifestations of open Polish-Ukrainian antagonism, one of which was a poem ascribed to Spyrydon Lytvynovych, "Kto Lach, ma strach" [Whoever is a Pole is scared], published in Vienna in 1832. Because the author called the Poles traitors, praised Paskevich, the new Russian commander in Warsaw, and regarded the tsarist government's repressive actions there as legitimate and just, the Austrian authorities forbade its distribution.[1]

Obviously, opinions such as Lytvynovych expressed did not stem exclusively from sympathy for Russia. They must have had deeper causes, especially because later Lytvynovych was not an adherent of Russian autocracy. Perhaps the poem was inspired by some notion of Slavic unity, the fragility of which was clearly proven by the Polish insurrection, or by the national policies of the Polish insurrectionary government in Warsaw, which ignored the Ukrainian nation's right to an independent state existence, or at least to a separate cultural development.

The Polish uprising fundamentally shaped the views of the young Ukrainian intelligentsia in Galicia and influenced its attitude toward the Polish nation in general and toward Polish-Ukrainian relations in particular. Thus it is not irrelevant to provide at least a cursory description of the different Polish positions on the Ukrainian question. The Polish "middle" strata—that is, the intelligentsia descended from the nobility and the burgher class—were of one mind, while the magnates were of another; the attitude of the Polish inhabitants of Western Galicia also differed markedly from the attitude in Eastern Galicia.

During the period of conspiratorial activity, the Polish revolutionary democrats espoused the unity of the entire populace of Galicia; they therefore regarded any emphasis on national differences as stemming from a desire to cause national strife. One result of this attitude was their sabotaging of the Ukrainians' demand that the Association of the Polish People change its name to the "Association of the Polish and Ruthenian People." In general, before 1848 the Poles regarded the Ukrainians as an offshoot of their own family tree, differing only in adherence to the Greek Catholic rite. The Ukrainian language was regarded as a dialect of Polish, and Ukrainian culture and literature were viewed as part of Polish culture and literature. As the Polish historian Stefan Kieniewicz put it: "In those times the assimilation of Rus' was an indisputable, natural and generally understood fact."[2] It is therefore not surprising that the Polish intelligentsia strove to unite the two nations and carried on conspiratorial agitation among the Ukrainian common people. At the same time, it was hostile toward the Ukrainian national leaders, the Ukrainian intelligentsia. This antagonism stemmed not only from the firmly rooted tradition of a Poland of the *szlachta* "from [the Baltic] Sea to [the Black] Sea," but from the fact that the "Polish intelligentsia saw in this new intelligentsia, being created directly from the Ukrainian common people, a dangerous economic competitor to itself." Concern about vested interests caused the Polish intelligentsia in Eastern Galicia to treat the entire Ukrainian national movement as essentially inimical to the Polish nation and to regard support for it as tantamount to national treason.[3]

The Polish magnates, too powerful to fear economic competition, viewed the Ukrainian national movement differently. Some, such as Prince Leon Sapieha, grasped its future significance and thus favoured an accord in 1848 and later supported compromise.[4] Others, such as his son, Prince Adam Sapieha, were committed to a more elastic policy, involving confrontation as well as accord and compromise, and they believed that they could assume the leadership of the Ukrainian movement themselves. Prince Adam Sapieha's idea that the Polish aristocratic families of Ukrainian descent should convert to Greek Catholicism and create a Ukrainian upper stratum—a new group of leaders of the Ukrainian nation—was intended to serve this objective. However, official Ukrainian circles, with Bishop Hryhorii Iakhymovych at their head, would have nothing to do with his scheme.[5]

A typical representative of the Eastern Galician Polish intelligentsia was Julian Horoszkiewicz, a conspirator whom the Austrians imprisoned for some time. His 1848 *Nauka obyczajności dla dzieci* [The science of morality for children] openly argued that differences in speech within a single country "should fuse into one [language] and be perfected in a written language proper to the fatherland of the nation." He had in mind Ruthenian, which he considered a dialect of Polish.[6] The prominent Polish political activist Florian Ziemiałkowski also believed in the national unity of the Poles and Ukrainians.[7]

Therefore, one can see that virtually nothing had changed in Polish national views from Wacław Zaleski's first pronouncements up to 1848, although this period of some fifteen years should have convinced the more sober Polish observers that some change was necessary. A comparison of Prince Leon Sapieha's attitudes with those of Julian Horoszkiewicz is exceedingly revealing. Horoszkiewicz meticulously noted in his diary:

> When I told him [Leon Sapieha]... that we [Poles] are demanding the Polish language in schools and governmental offices, he remarked: "This is foolish, because the Ruthenians will demand the same thing for the Ruthenian language." This statement surprised me, and I remarked that of course all educated people in Eastern Galicia speak Polish within the family. The Ruthenian priests deliver their sermons in the churches in Polish; the Ruthenian seminarians always belonged to Polish patriotic societies and conspiratorial circles; the Ruthenian prelates are for the most part descended from the Polish *szlachta*...; the Ruthenian peasants understand and, in large measure, speak Polish. Therefore, for whom would it be necessary to consider Ruthenian schools? "All of this may have been true enough," said

> the prince, "as long as the German language dominated all of us, but since today we demand the Polish language, obviously it would be unjust to the Ruthenians if these same freedoms were not given to the Ruthenian language." The discussion continued in this way, but the prince persistently explained away my contentions by arguing that this is a Ruthenian country and that the Ruthenians deserve at least equal rights, which, he believed, they will undoubtedly demand if such claims are made by the Poles.[8]

However, Prince Leon Sapieha's beliefs were atypical.

Everyday matters were important to the Ukrainian activists, and their experiences could not lead them to favour the Poles' nationality policies, although the Ukrainians did not object to amiable contacts with individual Polish spokesmen. The Ukrainians found the problems of schooling and literature especially irritating. Contemporary observers, and not only Ukrainians, testified to the Polish *szlachta*'s general reluctance to establish village schools because "the peasant who learns to read and write becomes impudent toward authority; that is, contrary to the will of the lords, he is able to defend his human and civil rights, which are protected by the authorities."[9] Moreover, as the Czech Karel Zap noted, those Ukrainian priests who attempted to teach the peasants "are scolded by the local *szlachta* for being rebellious and headstrong." Zap felt that the social and national oppression of the Ukrainian common people had caused Ukrainian separatism, which manifested itself in a "mistrust of anyone who differed from them [the Ruthenians], even in dress."[10]

In "Journey through Galician and Hungarian Rus'," Iakiv Holovatsky blamed the Poles for completely neglecting culture in Galicia: "The aristocratic Polish literature indifferently shuns this land of which it is rather a stepmother than a mother."[11] Iakiv Holovatsky, in fact, was the most anti-Polish member of the Ruthenian Triad. His opinion was clearly evident in a letter to his brother Ivan:

> It was hard for me to read your words, "The Poles want us to regard Poland as our own fatherland at all costs and to adopt their orthography and perhaps even their language; the Poles do not believe in Slavdom." Such words are painful to a Ruthenian heart and, moreover, [express] what I have heard time and again about the *szlachta*, about those fleecers [*deruny*] who cling to the nobles. Mindful of all of this and looking with open eyes at the misery of millions, reviewing my own activity, [seeing] who was the cause of it, you will not be surprised that I expressed myself so bitterly in my letter. This was only a faint reply of a friend of the common people [*narodoliubets*] to such heinous words, to such wrongs that have been done to us, are being done, and have no likelihood of abating. I did not then have in mind either "more enlightened" Poles (when and where can one be found?—I have been fooled by the best more than once and now can hardly believe them) or other

Slavs I know well whose good intentions [and] sincere hearts love their heritage [*rodoliubivoe*].[12]

The Holovatsky brothers reacted strongly against the Polish uprising in Cracow in 1846, but they praised the Polish peasants who turned against the insurrectionaries. Iakiv compared their action to the earlier *koliivshchyna* and *paliivshchyna*, eighteenth-century peasant uprisings against the Polish nobles.[13] However, the brothers did not praise the "Mazurians" (Polish peasants) for their social and anti-*szlachta* stance, but for their opposition to those Poles who dared to oppose the ruling political order. The Holovatsky brothers saw no social revolution aimed at abolishing feudal vestiges and *robot* in the Cracow uprising, but only a threat to the Austrian authorities, whose fervent adherents they were in the 1840s. Only in this way can we interpret the overtones of the sonnets from the cycle "Semaia na chuzhyni vesna" [A seventh spring in a foreign land], contained in the second part of *Vinok.*[14]

A similarly anti-Polish, but at the same time anti-revolutionary tone marked Iakiv Holovatsky's 1846 article "Conditions of the Ruthenians in Galicia," in which, for the sake of preserving an equilibrium between the various nationalities of the Austrian monarchy, he proposed to the government that it support the Ukrainians. Holovatsky maintained that the Ukrainians "in fact are prepared to stand always as a strong bulwark against revolutionary machinations in Galicia, which already have shattered many times against the rock of Ruthenian loyalty" [*an den Felsen der russinischen Treue zerplatzten*].[15]

The year 1848 would bring basic changes in the progressive Ukrainians' attitude toward the Poles. Iakiv Holovatsky no longer would place his faith in the Germans and would reject the insinuations that the Ukrainians aspired to unite with Russia. Rather, he would embrace Ukrainian-Polish cooperation, while yet knowing well the difficulties of it. As he wrote to his brother Petro in May 1848: "The Poles, enthralled by the voices of European nations and the consent of courts that Poland will be and must be [re-established] within its former boundaries, have forgotten about us Ruthenians; they desired only Poland and called our language only a dialect, denying us even the name Ruthenians."[16] As we shall see, both the Ukrainians and the Poles were at fault. Mykola Kmytsykevych's former dreams of an independent Poland and a Ukraine federated with it were forgotten.[17] And not until mid-1848 would new concepts, presented in Vasyl Podolynsky's *Słowo przestrogi* [Word of warning], begin to crystallize.

The problem of the Ukrainians' attitude toward the Polish cause was but one side of the question of Polish-Ukrainian ties in Galicia. No less important were the Ukrainians' personal contacts with many Poles, ranging from members of the Polish conspiratorial movement to pro-Russian "conciliators" such as Wacław Aleksander Maciejowski. Scholarly and literary interests usually formed the basis of these ties. Therefore, it is worthwhile considering what advantages they brought the young Ukrainians and what they contributed to the treasury of Polish culture and scholarship.

Markiian Shashkevych, who often visited Tadeusz Wasilewski in Pidlyssia, must have come into contact, although perhaps by chance, both with Polish conspirators and with writers such as Seweryn Goszczyński and Lucjan Siemieński. Goszczyński, for example, sojourned for a time in the villages adjacent to Pidlyssia, and Siemieński also visited them. This sort of acquaintance is suggested by Goszczyński's strong literary influence on Shashkevych as well as by Siemieński's remark in his introduction to the Polish edition of *Královédvorský rukopis* that Shashkevych had already translated the work into Ukrainian in 1832. Goszczyński himself, an eminent member of the conspiratorial underground, maintained personal contacts with the students at the Greek Catholic seminary in Lviv, where Shashkevych was studying. Although it is difficult to determine whether the Triad drew its organizational model from the circles of the Carbonarist association Przyjaciele Ludu (Friends of the people), their practices were so similar as otherwise to be an extraordinary coincidence.[18]

I have already spoken of the reciprocal literary influences between the Poles and Ukrainians. But it is worth describing a few more important associations. One of the finest chapters in the history of Ukrainian-Polish contacts in Galicia, for instance, was the sincere friendship between Shashkevych and Wasilewski. Wasilewski convinced Shashkevych to return to the seminary in 1832 and also offered him scholarly guidance in familiarizing himself with Slavic literature and gathering information about old Ruthenian documents at the Tarnowski estate in Dykiv [Dzików].[19] Count Jan Feliks Tarnowski had asked Wasilewski to send several students with a knowledge of Church Slavonic to Dykiv to catalogue Slavonic and Ruthenian manuscripts. Shashkevych could not undertake this work because of his health, and so he recommended his comrades Iakiv Holovatsky and Vahylevych to Wasilewski. During their first stay at Dykiv, the young researchers made a series of observations regarding the Ukrainian language and Polish-Ukrainian relations in the ethnically mixed borderland regions. The documents in Dykiv helped the Triad provide a scholarly foundation for Ukrainian national aspirations. Recalling his stay in Dykiv, Holovatsky wrote,

> Our joy knew no bounds. We discovered relics of the language of statecraft and governance from such distant times, and on the basis of these discoveries we determined that these documents were nothing less than the continuation of the political and material life of that Ruthenian (Galician) nation which lived and flourished during the time of the independence of the Principality of Halych under Volodar, Vasylko, Iaroslav, Roman, Danylo and Lev. In our imagination we saw a powerful state stretching along the whole of the Carpathian highlands, from the source of the Neman River to the mouth of the Dnieper and the Black Sea.[20]

Scholarly interests drew Ivan Vahylevych closer to scholars at the Ossolineum Foundation, including August Bielowski. Bielowski and his colleagues saw Vahylevych as a man of encyclopaedic knowledge, of whom they eagerly made use; he was an expert on the history of Poland and Slavdom and an eminent specialist in the genealogies of the Polish noble families.[21]

The result of Vahylevych's historical interests was a series of scholarly works. He translated and annotated Nestor's *Chronicle*, included in *Monumenta Poloniae Historica* published by Bielowski; he proofread the second edition of Linde's *Słownik języka polskiego*; he was the author of *Dzieje narodu polskiego od r. 1058 do 1090* [History of the Polish nation from 1058 to 1090] and the study "O uprawie języka starosłowiańskiego w Polsce" [On the cultivation of the Old Slavonic language in Poland]. Vahylevych also left in manuscript form translations of *The Tale of Ihor's Campaign* into Polish and Ukrainian. In his historical research, he propounded the thesis that the Slavonic rite was "the dominant rite in Poland during the reign of Bolesław the Bold, and the hypothetical discrimination against the Latin rite provided the bishop of Cracow, Stanisław, his initial reason for breaking off with Bolesław."[22]

Vahylevych's close contacts with the Poles, however, aroused indignant opposition among the other Ukrainian activists. Denys Zubrytsky wrote to Pogodin: "The outcast Vahylevych has become completely polonized and in hanging about with the *Liakhy* nourishes himself on fantastic dreams."[23] His closest comrades, Iakiv Holovatsky and Ivan Biretsky, also were apprehensive. The extant correspondence is sparse, but probably they were afraid that Vahylevych might go over entirely to the Polish side.[24] Iakiv Holovatsky also reminded him that he was neglecting the Ukrainian cause. "I asked you to be good enough to send some article to my brother in Vienna for his literary miscellany, but I see nothing has come of it. You support all the Polish journals with your articles. It would be fitting to aid our Ruthenian orphan with something; after all, you have plenty of little articles."[25] The events of 1848 would prove that their fears were justified, because

Vahylevych became one of the most active members of the so-called Polish-Ukrainian party and the editor of the pro-Polish *Dnewnyk Ruskij* [Ruthenian daily]. From then until the end of his life, Vahylevych remained closely associated with the Polish intellectuals in Lviv.[26]

The Triad circle made significant contributions to compiling and supplementing the collections of Ukrainian folk songs published by the Poles. We have seen that Wacław Zaleski used materials provided by Ilkevych and Shashkevych in his *Polish and Ruthenian Songs of the Galician People*, and when Żegota Pauli published *Pieśni ludu ruskiego w Galicji* [Songs of the Ruthenian people in Galicia] in 1839-40, he used manuscript collections of various Ukrainian writers. This was the basis for the later accusation that Pauli was guilty of a literary theft in publishing songs already collected by others. However, it is puzzling that Iakiv Holovatsky accused Pauli not in the 1840s, when the issue was most current, but only after several decades, in the 1880s. The available sources prove that Holovatsky's relations with Pauli in the 1830s were cordial, because Wacław Maciejowski sent his regards to Pauli through Holovatsky.[27] The correspondence surviving from that period also fails to suggest any coolness between Pauli and the Ukrainians.[28]

Iakiv Holovatsky's later memoirs about Shashkevych and Vahylevych, however, contain a long discussion of Pauli that is worth quoting because of its oddity:

> A man of medium height named Ignacy Pauli, a Mazurian, who came to the university from the gymnasium in Sącz, attended classes together with us. He tried to make our acquaintance, expressed a fervent desire to learn Ruthenian and [Old] Slavonic, acted like a Slav and even signed his name "Zhegota" Pauli. I distrusted him, but Vahylevych was more open, and Shashkevych was pleased that the Slavic idea had taken root on Polish soil and that Pauli stood on the ground of democratic principles, because he gathered songs of the Polish common people. [Shashkevych] regarded him as innocuous, believing that the democratic *Liakhy* are not dangerous to us. Pauli not only tricked us out of notebooks of folk songs, but he also copied Maksymovych's songs from me and later sold them to the bookseller Kajetan Jabłoński, who published them in two volumes under the title *Pieśni ludu ruskiego w Galicji, zebrał Żegota Pauli*, Lviv, 1839, although he did not collect songs at all, but transcribed them.[29]

I shall not reiterate the scholarly disputes that Holovatsky's contentions provoked, because Mykhailo Vozniak has analyzed them thoroughly and determined that Pauli indeed used the song collections of Antin and Markiian Shashkevych, Vahylevych, Holovatsky, Bilynsky, Kulchytsky and Blonsky, as well as the published Ukrainian collections of Maksymovych (1827 and 1834) and Platon Lukashevych (1836).[30] Still, relations between Pauli and Shashkevych must have been especially close. This is evidenced by the transcriptions in Shashkevych's own hand that are preserved among Pauli's papers at the Jagiellonian Library in Cracow, in particular the copy of Maksymovych's collection of Ukrainian folk songs from 1827 and the beginning of a fable entitled "Droniuk" written by Shashkevych in the Latin alphabet and, therefore, presumably dating from the early 1830s.[31]

Ultimately, in judging the Triad circle's attitude toward the Poles and the Polish cause, it must be conceded that, despite frequently maintained close personal contacts, despite much goodwill and not infrequent friendships, they were generally antagonistic, particularly toward Polish national concepts. The Poles themselves were at fault for not taking into account the Ukrainians' national aspirations.[32]

The Czechs and the South Slavs

The Ruthenian Triad also sought legitimation for its aspirations among the other Slavs. The vigorously developing field of Slavic research played a significant role in this regard. Dobrovský, Kopitar, Šafařík, Palacký and other eminent Slavists provided a scholarly foundation for the Ukrainians' national endeavours. The Slavic and Ukrainian activists shared common concerns, and national awakening followed basically the same course in all the Slavic nations. The Ukrainians thus could compare their own efforts with those of kindred nations. Scholarly interests and the associated development of a national literature based on folk creativity, together with the interest in Kollár's concept of Slavic reciprocity, provide the best examples of this process. On the other hand, the notion of reciprocity, so successful in the inaugural phase of the national awakening, had surrendered by the 1840s to a growing awareness of national distinctiveness among the individual Slavic nations.

The fact that the different Slavic countries did not experience the same degree of social and economic development provided broad opportunities for comparisons and influences. Czech scholars were especially influential. As Iakiv Holovatsky wrote to Karel Zap in 1848: "Through your impartial researches you were the first to discover our nation among other nations [and] to define its strength. [Šafařík's] *Slovanský národopis* was the first work to show the world [our] nation of fifteen million, to describe and identify it. It was from you that the thought first came that our nation's literary language could exist independently."[33]

It seems odd that there is no trace of Markiian Shashkevych's contacts with foreign scholars. He was keenly interested in the growth of the Slavic researches, knew the Slavic literatures and translated from Czech (notably *Královédvorský rukopis*),[34] Serbian (his own translations of Serbian songs appeared in *Rusalka Dnistrovaia*),[35] and Polish (excerpts of Seweryn Goszczyński's *Zamek Kaniowski*). The reminiscences of his friends, particularly of Holovatsky, prove that Shashkevych was fascinated by the Slavic world. He dreamed of the Ukrainians' keeping pace with the Slavic nations in national and cultural development. He maintained lively contacts with the Czechs Karel Zap and Jan Koubek, who were living in Galicia. Koubek called him his friend and published excerpts from Shashkevych's translation of *Královédvorský rukopis* in *Časopis Českého Museum* [Journal of the Czech museum] in 1838.

Iakiv Holovatsky was the ambassador of the Ruthenian Triad in its contacts abroad. In the 1830s and 1840s he personally met many eminent Slavic spokesmen, including Ján Kollár, the Slovaks Karol Kuzmány and Michal Miloslav Hodža, the Croat Fran Kurelac, and the Serbs Georgij Petrović, Todor Pavlović (the publisher of *Srbske Narodne Novine* [Serbian national news]), Jovan Popović (who later became the Serbian minister of education), and the patron of Serbian literature, Josip Milovuk. The first encounter took place in 1834, when Holovatsky went to Hungary to continue his studies in Košice and Budapest. He later remembered his time there as one of the most beautiful and happiest periods of his life.[36] He acquired a knowledge of the Slavic languages, and the contacts he made then were useful later in carrying out the Triad's publishing plans. The young Serbs, especially Petrović, contributed greatly to the publication of *Rusalka Dnistrovaia*, displayed concern over its distribution and even told the Ukrainians why its distribution was prohibited.[37]

In 1841 and 1842, Ivan Holovatsky renewed his brother's acquaintance with the Serbian national awakeners when he moved from Vienna to Budapest to continue his studies. Pavlović made a disagreeable impression on him, although Petrović and Vuk Karadžić promised to seek financial support for him from Serbian Prince Mihajlo Obrenović to permit him to complete his studies. In return for this aid Ivan Holovatsky would work later for a time in Serbia as a physician.[38]

The South Slavic developments were avidly followed by both of the Holovatsky brothers, partly because the Serbian and Ukrainian literatures were in comparable situations. Karadžić's works, known and valued in virtually all of Europe and also highly prized by the Ukrainians, had given rise to modern Serbian literature and a Serbian literary language based on the living language of the common people (the štokavian dialect). These efforts had broken the tradition of using the Slavo-Serbian language, based on Old Church Slavonic, in literature. Karadžić's works, like those of the Ukrainians, had provoked persecution of the new literature by the Serbian church hierarchy.[39] Karadžić's activities thus were a kind of weathervane for the Triad; they were also models that they wished to approximate and emulate. Like Karadžić, they believed that folklore studies would help to create a national literature, draw them closer to the common people and become familiar with their language and needs, and thus allow the activists to begin working toward their enlightenment.

The Triad circle also fervently sympathized with the Croats, who, in rallying around Ljudevit Gaj's Illyrian programme, were forced to wage a difficult struggle with the Croatian pro-Hungarian camp (the so-called Magyarones). In 1841 and 1842 this conflict led to clashes in the streets of Zagreb, which resulted in a prohibition by the Austrian authorities on the use of the word "Illyrism."[40]

There is insufficient information to assess the extent of the ties between the Ukrainians and the young but vigorous Slovak national movement. Iakiv Holovatsky was acquainted with Karol Kuzmány and Michal Hodža, but whether he kept in direct contact with them in later years is not known. The Slovak national awakeners in northern Hungary especially interested the Galician Ukrainians because their social and political conditions were similar to the Ukrainians'. Knowledge of the Slovak situation usually came indirectly, through Karel Zap and Karol Moszczański, or from reports emanating from Vienna. During his stay in Budapest Ivan Holovatsky personally observed the so-called Magyar freedom, and he returned from Hungary with unpleasant impressions.[41]

The essential question in assessing ties between the Ukrainians and the other Slavs is to determine what views and ideas the Ukrainians adopted and who represented these ideas. The noted Czech Slavist Josef Dobrovský, as I noted earlier, maintained that the literary language could differ from the vernacular. But because Ukrainian was not a literary language during Dobrovský's time, he did not see it as an independent language; instead he included it with Belorussian in the Russian language group.[42] This stance elicited opposition among the Galician Ukrainians, who, starting with Ivan Mohylnytsky,[43] had begun to regard Ukrainian as an entirely independent language, differing from Russian and Polish. Several Ukrainian spokesmen, however, had accepted Dobrovský's concept of a "middle style" in literature.

The Ukrainians based their claim to an entirely independent language on the works of Jernej Kopitar, who as early as 1816 had explicitly separated Ukrainian from Russian and Polish.[44] The Ukrainians also adopted from Kopitar the thesis that the literary language should develop on the foundation of the folk idiom. And, as we have seen, the Ruthenian Triad successfully applied this concept. As Ivan Vahylevych wrote in a letter to Pavel Šafařík, "For us literature can be none other than the [literature] of the people..., because we have no other language (as there is in Poland, for example) except the peasant speech or, should I say, besides the popular vernacular."[45] Kopitar's belief that Ukrainian was an independent language in the end was substantiated by Šafařík; the idea that the vernacular should be the basis of the literary language eventually took root through further development of the national literatures.

Šafařík's first major work, *Geschichte der slawischen Sprache und Literatur nach allen Mundarten* (1826), said little about the Ukrainians. He did note, however, that "in a linguistic and historical respect they are a *terra incognita*"; he also estimated the number of Ukrainians at 10,780,000, of whom 10,430,000 were in Russia and 350,000 in Hungary. Šafařík recognized the oneness of the Ukrainian nation that inhabited the area of northeastern Hungary, Galicia and Russian Ukraine, and he divided the east Slavic languages into three dialects (*Mundarten*) of equal status: Russian (Great Russian), Ukrainian and Belorussian.[46] He substantiated and expanded his theses in a widely known and extraordinarily popular work of 1842, *Slovanský nârodopis*. This book legitimized the Galician Ukrainians' national and linguistic aspirations. Section eight, entitled "Nářečí maloruské" [The Little Russian dialect], was devoted to Ukrainian matters. In it Šafařík precisely delineated the range of spoken Ukrainian and determined the number of Ukrainians (Little Russians) at 13,144,000, of whom 10,370,000 lived in Russia and 2,774,000 in the Austrian empire, and, further, that 2,149,000 lived in Galicia and 625,000 in Hungary. It is apparent from his data that the Ukrainians were the most numerous Slavic nation after the Russians (35,314,000) and considerably outnumbered the Poles (9,365,000).[47]

In 1830, the Czech historian František Palacký similarly wrote in "O národech polských" [On Poland's nations] that the "Ruthenian nation" differed in language from the Russians and the Poles and that the Hungarian, Galician and Ukrainian Ruthenians composed this nation.[48] Karel Zap, who lived in Galicia from 1830 to 1845, notwithstanding his personal ties with the Poles, formed sincere friendships with the Triad circle, especially with Iakiv Holovatsky, Vahylevych and Biretsky.[49] Zap was not only the intermediary in the exchange of correspondence and books among the Czechs, the Ukrainians in Russia and the Galician Ukrainians, but was also the first to provide a clear presentation of the national conflicts in Galicia. In 1843 he published *Cesty a procházky po Halické zemi* [Travels and wanderings through the Galician land], in which he described the actual conditions prevailing in Galicia and uncompromisingly accused the Polish *szlachta* of social and national oppression against the Ukrainian peasants. He revealed the misery, alcoholism and lack of education among the people. Zap also pointed out that the same *szlachta* that discoursed so much about freedom and national rights and sang Polish patriotic songs did not even want to consider recognizing the Ukrainians' national distinctiveness and opposed everything that aimed at their national emancipation. His book aroused Polish indignation and unleashed a heated polemic in Bohemia with the more radically oriented Czech leaders, who well understood that Zap had not only exposed the national conditions in Galicia (thereby indicating the feebleness of Kollár's concept of Slavic reciprocity), but had also endorsed the limited and legal programme supported by the liberal Ukrainian national movement in Galicia, in opposition to the revolutionary undertakings of the Poles.[50] In 1843, discussing "Rzeszów i jego okolice" [Rzeszów and its environs] by Józef Borkowski-Dunin, Zap wrote to the Czech journal *Květy* that

> we read in it with amazement that the Ruthenians who settled in Eastern Galicia are not Ruthenians, but Poles. [The Ruthenians] were amazed when they read this. If the author wrote in this way for patriotic reasons, then we must be surprised at how similar this kind of Polish patriotism is to the acquisitive patriotism of the Magyars. The Little Russian nation numbers twelve million. Are these only Poles, which the author does not doubt? Let us then add nine million Poles and together there will be twenty-one million. What sort of great nation is this? Besides, the gentleman did not fail to reproach Šafařík for counting differently and separating the Ruthenians from the Poles. *Difficile est satiram non scribere* [In these circumstances it is difficult not to write satires] (Juvenal).[51]

From the time of Zap's observations, the problem of Polish-Ukrainian relations was clearly reflected in the views of other Czechs living in Galicia. Their anti-revolutionary and anti-Polish views were adopted by the Ukrainian activists, especially Iakiv Holovatsky. Among such Czech liberals as Zap, Jachim and Havlíček-Borovský the opinion strengthened that the Czechs had their "best friend at the moment" in the Ukrainians. In the latter half of the 1840s, the Czechs, and in particular Zap, regarded the Ukrainians as "natural national and political allies."[52]

By 1845, the Czech liberals were becoming disillusioned with Russia, largely because of Havlíček-Borovský's writings.[53] Accordingly, the liberal Czechs came to believe that because Russia would offer no genuine aid, the Austrian Slavs had to rely on their own strength and Austria's help. Thus Austro-Slavism was accepted as a political concept. Originated by Kopitar, substantiated in the journalistic work of Count Leo Thun, and eventually refined by Palacký in 1848, it was the doctrine that Iakiv Holovatsky espoused in his article "Conditions of the Ruthenians in Galicia" in 1846 and that was adopted in 1848 and 1849 as the policy of the Holovna Rada Ruska.[54]

Ján Kollár influenced the views and activity of the Ukrainians in another way. His *Slâvy dcera* [Daughter of Slava] (1824) was an ardent manifesto that was a call to labour for the nation's welfare, but at the same time it seemed to retreat from the issues and disputes of everyday life, because Kollár wrote that the "name of the fatherland cannot be ascribed to the country in which we live, because we carry the true fatherland only in our hearts."[55] Kollár's messianism, which proclaimed the superiority of the Slavs over other nations, was borrowed in large measure from Herder and passed on to Iakiv Holovatsky, who from a Slavophile's position argued the superiority of Slavic social, political and institutional structures over similar structures in West European countries, as well as the superiority of the Cyrillic over the Latin alphabet.[56]

However, the Ruthenian Triad could not accept unreservedly all of Kollár's ideas; in particular, it disagreed with the ideas in his treatise, *On Literary Reciprocity between the Various Branches and Dialects of the Slavic Nation.* Kollár regarded the Slavs as one nation that spoke four "dialects" of one language: Polish, Russian, Czech and Serbian (Illyrian). According to Kollár, these four were entitled to develop independently; the remaining Slavic tongues could evolve only to a limited degree. As a result, the latter should blend with the dialect that they most resembled. Kollár detailed these views in *Journal of a Journey to Northern Italy*, published in 1843. "We praise the Slovaks for having ascended [to the use of] the Czech language, the Croats and Carinthians [Slovenes] the Illyrian language, and the Little Russians the Great Russian language."[57] In the name of his ideal, Kollár condemned all national egoism and separatism. He reprimanded the Galician Ukrainians: "The scholarly author of the Ruthenian grammar published in Przemyśl in 1834, Iosyf Levytsky, asks in wonder on page 88: 'How can Wacław z Oleska write Ruthenian songs with Polish characters?' And for God's sake, why not? Are characters bound to a dialect by some sort of privileges, monopolies, legal stipulations or bans? Is it not enough that states, dialects, religious rites, orthographies divide us? Are letters also to stand like an unpenetrable, fortified wall? How empty and unreciprocating."[58]

Iakiv Holovatsky translated Kollár's *On Literary Reciprocity* into Ukrainian, and it quickly became known to the circle of the Ruthenian Triad. The Ukrainians tended to see little practical benefit for their own objectives from Kollár's scheme; their correspondence with him broke off after 1836. Iakiv Holovatsky himself probably judged Kollár's work unfavourably, because, despite Shashkevych's suggestion that he turn to Kollár for aid in the publication of *Rusalka Dnistrovaia*, he turned instead to his colleague from his student days in Budapest, the Serb Georgij Petrović.[59]

The Slovaks L'udovít Štúr and Karol Kuzmány (in the latter period of their activity) and the Slovenes (in particular France Prešeren) were also hostile to Kollár's notions of Slavic reciprocity, perceiving in it a threat to their own national existence. In general terms, Kollár's concept was diametrically opposed to Šafařík's. Šafařík acknowledged the right of all nations to develop their own literature and thereby underscored the presence of national differences. Moreover, he recognized the existence of national antagonisms as normal and even beneficial, stating that the Ukrainian-Polish conflict in Galicia during the revolutionary years 1848 and 1849 was proof of "an awakening of Slavdom in general."[60]

The Slovak-Hungarian antagonism to a significant degree served to radicalize the views of certain Ukrainians. Iakiv Holovatsky's travels had familiarized him with the conflict in northern Hungary, and he wrote bitterly of the Hungarian land whose representatives "bark so much about liberalism" and at the same time mercilessly persecuted the Slovaks.[61]

Ivan Holovatsky, who began his studies in Vienna in 1839 and was associated with radical Polish and Czech circles, was well acquainted with the prevailing attitude among the Slovak intellectuals who had drawn around Štúr in Bratislava. In a letter to his brother Iakiv he said that the young Slovak enthusiasts, including clergymen, were opposed to the Magyars and agitated among the Slovak common people during their vacations. He was surprised that the Slovaks were favourably disposed toward the Czechs, Poles and other Slavs, despite the fact that "in their hearts the first sense of independent existence had awakened."[62] Holovatsky himself believed that the crystallization of national consciousness led to an exclusive nationalism, which would impede the unity of Europe's various nations.[63] In 1840 and 1841 he believed that tsarist rule must collapse because it opposed strengthening Russia's ties with Europe and sought only to expand its own empire at the expense of other nations. Russia did not in the least intend to liberate the Slavs, and Holovatsky therefore believed that the Ukrainians in Galicia should try to draw closer to the West and join their national aspirations to the endeavours of those Poles who wanted to liquidate the landed estates of the privileged classes. Still, he realized that Polish nationalists denied the existence of a Ukrainian nationality.[64]

Ivan Holovatsky gave a splendid characterization of Austria's nationalities policy, which in his eyes fomented national hatred, particularly in Hungary. "The Magyar diet, which still convenes, is a squabbler's den; the Magyars' demands [*postulationes*] take on more and more importance for Austria, as a consequence of which [Austria] patronizes the Hungarian Slavs, sets the Hungarians against the Slavs, and vice versa, in order to weaken both sides and protect itself."[65]

By the early 1840s Ivan Holovatsky had come to embrace democratic opinions, whereas his elder brother Iakiv held a more moderate, liberal position. The subsequent years, however, brought a marked change in Ivan's outlook. His personal ordeal (he was suspected of belonging to a secret Polish organization, while his roommate Karol Moszczański was sentenced for belonging to it), his subsequent hope that the Austrian authorities' attitude toward the Ukrainians had changed (the editorship of a proposed Ukrainian journal was offered to him), and, finally, his contacts with eminent pro-Austrian or pro-tsarist Slavic spokesmen led him to conclude that political changes could be achieved by educating the common people, and hence did not require revolutionary action.[66] In this sense, he completely renounced any kind of actions aimed at changing social, political and national conditions. The course of time, he came to believe, would resolve the issues.

The help that the Czech awakeners accorded the Galician Ukrainians was also expressed in concern over the development of Ukrainian literature. The Czechs made the columns of their literary and scholarly journals available to Ukrainian writers. Šafařík in particular eagerly accepted Ukrainian works while he served on the editorial board of *Časopis Českêho Museum.* Thanks especially to his efforts, Ivan Vahylevych and Iakiv Holovatsky were able to publish on a number of Ukrainian topics in this esteemed journal between 1838 and 1843. Iakiv and Ivan Holovatsky also published in the Czech periodicals *Poutník* and *Květy*. These articles were usually translated from Ukrainian into Czech by Karel Zap. As was noted earlier, Jan Koubek included in *Časopis Českêho Museum* fragments of *Krâlovêdvorský rukopis* in Shashkevych's and Vahylevych's translation.[67] In addition, the numerous articles devoted to the Ukrainian question by Šafařík, Zap, Jachim, Jan Vocel, Jan Slavomír

Tomíček and Ludvik Rittersberg that appeared between 1837 and 1847 in *Časopis Českêho Museum*, *Květy* and *Českâ Včela* evidenced the Czechs' deep interest in the Ukrainian nation and its literature.

The Czechs also offered advice on contentious and difficult issues. Vahylevych apprised Šafařík of the linguistic disputes in Galicia between 1834 and 1836 and introduced him to the orthographic systems then in use, including his own, which "coincides with Kotliarevsky's [orthography], with the difference that it is guided everywhere by the spirit and the need of our language." He assured Šafařík that he was always prepared to abandon anything that would interfere with the creation of a Ruthenian literature.[68] Because no letters from Šafařík to Vahylevych from this period are preserved, it is difficult to know what suggestions Šafařík in fact did make. Ivan Bryk believed that Vahylevych, at Šafařík's behest, subsequently changed the phonetic spelling of *Rusalka Dnistrovaia* to a more etymologically based system, which, Bryk thought, was to the detriment of the language. Vahylevych took this step, however, as he himself wrote, with the aim of saving his countrymen from a further controversy over the alphabet.[69] It is also worth noting that Shashkevych cited Šafařík in his defence of the Cyrillic alphabet in his 1836 brochure *Azbuka i abetsadlo*.

Iakiv Holovatsky elected not to make use of the advice of Podlipský and Kampelík in preparing and publishing the anthology of Ukrainian proverbs and riddles collected by Ilkevych. The Czechs advised arranging the proverbs thematically and not alphabetically, because a collection published in this format would have cultural and political as well as national significance and could point out that the Slavs were second to none in life's wisdom. In addition, the Czechs suggested preparing "two editions of the proverbs—one in the Latin alphabet for the Czechs, Poles and Illyrians, and a second in the Cyrillic alphabet for the Ruthenians, Russians and Serbs"—or using both alphabets in a single edition. Podlipský and Kampelík thought that "in this way the realization of a great idea—the unification of Slavdom and all of Europe—would draw nearer."[70]

Czechs also served as intermediaries in the exchange of books and correspondence between the Ukrainians in Galicia and such Ukrainian and Russian scholars as Ivan Sreznevsky, Osyp Bodiansky, Mykhailo Maksymovych and Mikhail Pogodin. The intermediaries in this exchange were Šafařík, Zap, Hanka, Jan Dvořáček and Karel Štorch. Books were sent by various means: through the mail, through booksellers in Lviv, Brody, Prague, and Leipzig, through persons travelling to Russia or returning, and through the Russian embassy in Vienna.[71] During his stay in Moscow, Karel Havlíček-Borovský played an important role by acting as a go-between on matters that could not be arranged through normal correspondence.[72]

Nevertheless, the ties between the Ukrainians and the Czechs were not, as is frequently believed, only those between students and teachers. To be sure, the Czechs were the mentors on basic issues concerning the shaping of Ukrainian national and political thought, but on specific questions Ukrainians contributed significantly to the development of Czech scholarship. Vahylevych and Holovatsky, for example, influenced Šafařík, who was interested in everything related to Slavdom. While preparing his major work *Slovanské Starožitnosti* [Slavic antiquities] in the 1830s, he quickly realized that the young Ukrainians' scholarly achievements could further support his own position. In 1836 he read in the journal *Moskovskii nadbliudatel* [Moscow observer] that Vahylevych had found in the Rozhirche caves in the Carpathian mountains old inscriptions, which he regarded as proof of the high culture of the early Slavs. Vahylevych turned to Petr Koeppen and Pogodin in this matter,[73] and the latter advised him that he should write to Šafařík about his research. In this way the correspondence between Vahylevych and Šafařík began. It continued until the mid-1840s. In his first letter, Vahylevych sent Šafařík a reproduction of the inscriptions, which the latter at first glance took for distorted Cyrillic letters.[74] He also gladly included, in *Časopis Českého Museum* in 1837, an article by Vahylevych on the discoveries in Rozhirche entitled "O zemí jmenované Bojky" [Of the land called Boiky]. Šafařík made extensive use of it.[75] Still, Vahylevych himself was apparently not entirely satisfied, because he took up a similar subject in a second piece that Šafařík also had published in *Časopis Českého Museum.*[76]

Šafařík learned from Vahylevych of the early sixteenth-century manuscript "Kormchaia kniga" [Nomocanon] in the collection of Count Tarnowski in Dykiv. He requested that a transcribed copy be sent to Prague, but he was told that this was impossible for the time being because of Vahylevych's difficulties in leaving for Dykiv. Count Tarnowski was not familiar with Church Slavonic orthography and consequently could not make a copy himself. Šafařík therefore turned to Iakiv Holovatsky, who for reasons similar to Vahylevych's could not send the needed copies. After several years of waiting, Šafařík finally received the original manuscript from Count Tarnowski himself.[77] At the request of the Archeological Commission in Saint Petersburg, Šafařík sent a copy of the manuscript there. It was returned to Prague after it had been examined.[78]

From *Rusalka Dnistrovaia* Šafařík learned about other manuscripts housed in the university library and the monastery of Saint Onufrii in Lviv. For more precise information Šafařík turned to Iakiv Holovatsky, who sent him a detailed description of the Serbian Chronicle from the time of Archbishop Daniel II (1325-1338). Šafařík needed this document for the *Monumenta Serbica* he was then preparing. Ivan Biretsky made a copy of the chronicle for Šafařík, and Holovatsky personally verified its conformity with the original. Šafařík also received from Holovatsky other Ruthenian documents whose titles are not known to us.[79]

Šafařík's *Slovanský národopis* stimulated the greatest interest among the Ukrainians. In preparing this work Šafařík appealed to many eminent Polish, Russian and Ukrainian scholars for materials. He particularly valued the observations regarding the demarcation of the areas inhabited by Ukrainians and their neighbours, which he obtained from Bodiansky, Wacław Maciejowski and Vahylevych. Šafařík assayed this information very critically, recognizing that his informants were biased. As the Czech Slavist Josef Hůrský has noted, it was curious that Maciejowski, in a letter to Šafařík, "gave a very precise demarcation between the Poles and Ukrainians, and, if one takes into account the polonization that occurred in the ensuing decades, perhaps even to the detriment of his own countrymen." Maciejowski traced the western boundary of the "Rusniaks" along the Wisłoka River and a line between Szczebrzeszyn and Lublin in Russian Poland. On the other hand, he regarded the area to the south of Hrodna, in present-day Belorussia, as inhabited largely by Ruthenians, although the area to the north, he believed, had a Polish majority. Šafařík was sceptical. "This is impossible. It is Lithuanian [territory]; not in the least is it Polish. The basis for me is the peasant, not the *szlachta*."[80] Vahylevych also provided Šafařík with information about the ethnic and linguistic boundaries of the Ukrainian populace in Galicia and Bukovyna. He based his information on Denys Zubrytsky's data, which likewise did not entirely satisfy Šafařík. Accordingly, Vahylevych, relying on information provided by the rector of the seminary in Chernivtsi, sent more credible data, which Šafařík then incorporated in *Slovanský národopis* with only minor alterations. However, on the ethnographic map accompanying the volume, Šafařík left many areas of Bukovyna that Vahylevych considered to be Ruthenian in the Romanian-language area.[81]

The first edition of *Slovanský národopis* in 1842 was barely sufficient to meet the subscribers' demand, and a second edition was prepared the same year. Šafařík took the opportunity to write to Karel Zap and Iakiv Holovatsky in Galicia requesting that they point out the more important factual and typographic errors. Holovatsky's observations, included in the second edition, were particularly valuable because they came from a man who was very knowledgeable about Galician and Hungarian Rus'.[82] Holovatsky also prepared for Šafařík a list of German settlements in Galicia, as well as the names of towns and cities in Eastern Galicia, Podillia and Volhynia, according to an ordered chronology of historical acts and documents dating from the fourteenth century to his own time. Šafařík needed the material to prepare the historical maps.

In Galicia, the Ukrainians enthusiastically received Šafařík's work, but the Poles were cool. Zap wrote that the Poles "are angered that [the geographical names] of the old Polish lands in Rus' are not given in Polish."[83] However, it seems that this was not the most important reason for the Poles' dissatisfaction; rather, they were displeased that such an eminent scholar had recognized the independence and distinctiveness of the Ukrainian nation.

These observations offer conclusive proof that the Ukrainian national movement of the 1830s and 1840s, and particularly its leading activists Iakiv Holovatsky, Ivan Vahylevych and Ivan Biretsky, contributed vitally to the development of Czech Slavic studies. This was indeed one of the most significant achievements of the Ruthenian Triad.

Ukrainians in Russia and the Russians

The development of Ukrainian literature in the area under Russian rule and the contacts between the Triad circle and Ukrainian and Russian scholars and writers were as influential in moulding the Ukrainian national movement in Galicia as Czech-Ukrainian ties. This interaction was both ideological and literary-scholarly. Before 1848, literary and scholarly influences were more important; later pro-Russian ideology became more significant, which retarded the Ukrainian national movement in Galicia.[84]

The Galician Ukrainians frequently mentioned that Ukrainian literature from beyond the border had considerable influence on the development of Galician literature. They pointed to its models and regarded their own work as a continuation of the development of all-Ukrainian literature. This message was emphasized by Shashkevych in his introduction to *Rusalka Dnistrovaia*, by Vahylevych in his "Uwagi o literaturze ruskiej" [Notes on Ruthenian literature], and by Iakiv Holovatsky in an article about Ivan Kotliarevsky and in "Try vstupytelnye prepodavanyia o russkoi slovesnosty" [Three introductory lectures on Ruthenian literature], which he had delivered at Lviv University. Ustyianovych apparently held the same opinion when he addressed the congress of Ukrainian scholars in Lviv in 1848.[85]

These views are entirely understandable if we recall that Ukrainian literature in Russia began to develop almost forty years earlier than in Galicia. Developments among the Ukrainians in Russia had followed a pattern similar to the one in Eastern Galicia. The Ukrainian upper classes succumbed to russification to the east of the Dnieper (so-called Left-Bank Ukraine) or to polonization in the territories west of the river (the Right Bank). A pure Ukrainian speech was preserved only among the common people, but Ukrainian was cultivated in a deformed Ukrainian-Slavonic form by the clergy. Among the upper classes in Left-Bank Ukraine at the end of the eighteenth century, a local Ukrainian patriotism began to emerge, which harkened back to the times of the Cossacks and their hetmans. Interest grew in the Ukrainian language, songs and folk heritage. An expression of this Ukrainian patriotism and sense of autonomy was the *Istoriia Rusov ili Maloi Rossii* [History of the Rus' or Little Russia], probably the work of Oleksander Bezborodko or Hryhorii Poletyka (although earlier attributed to Bishop Hryhorii Konysky). Before its publication in Moscow in 1846, numerous copies of it had circulated in the Ukrainian community, thereby endowing it, as Mykola Kostomarov stated, "with quasi-nobiliary Little Russian patriotism." This work pointed out the necessity for a constitutional government for Russia and identified such a structure with the former Cossack order.[86]

It was in this atmosphere that Ivan Kotliarevsky's *Eneida* appeared in 1798. It was in fact a travesty of Vergil's epic, placed in a Ukrainian setting. Kotliarevsky drew upon the folk idiom and for the first time elevated it to the rank of a literary language, while also presenting a splendid panorama of social life. His sympathies were clearly on the side of the oppressed Ukrainian common people, and he criticized the upper classes caustically and humorously.[87]

The social and intellectual ferment permeating Left-Bank Ukrainian society at the turn of the nineteenth century contributed significantly to the development of cultural life. Most notably, the theatre emerged. Permanent companies were formed in Odessa (1804), Kiev (1805), Poltava (1810), Kharkiv (1812) and Nizhyn (1826). At the same time gymnasia were established in Kharkiv, Nizhyn, Odessa and Poltava, and universities were founded in Kharkiv (1805) and Kiev (1834). From its inception the university in Kharkiv became the centre of Ukrainian literary and intellectual activity. There the first journals in Ukraine appeared: *Ukrainskii vestnik* [Ukrainian herald] (1816-19), *Kharkovskii Demokrit* [The Kharkiv Democritus] (1816) and *Ukrainskii zhurnal* [Ukrainian journal] (1824-5), each of which published works of Russian and Ukrainian writers as well as translations from Western European literature. *Kharkovskii Demokrit* was the first satirical journal in Ukraine, which scathingly unmasked the hypocrisy, falsehood, greed, arbitrariness and corruption of the privileged classes. The literary activities of the celebrated Ukrainian writers Hryhorii Kvitka-Osnovianenko, Petro Hulak-Artemovsky, Levko Borovykovsky, Amvrosii Metlynsky, Kyrylo Topolia, Mykhailo Petrenko, Viktor Zabila and the young Mykola Kostomarov were all associated with Kharkiv.

Ukrainian literature by Kotliarevsky, Hulak-Artemovsky, Kvitka-Osnovianenko, Ievhen Hrebinka and others already exhibited national features. Their works touched upon matters pertaining to the life of the entire nation and did not avoid social questions, although the issues of serfdom and *robot* were treated circumspectly, the more so because the Ukrainian writers who preceded Shevchenko, despite their local Ukrainian patriotism, supported the official ideology of tsarist Russia.[88]

The collections of folk-songs published by Mykola Tsertelev, Mykhailo Maksymovych, Izmail Sreznevsky and Platon Lukashevych, however, were particularly significant in the development of Ukrainian literature in Russia. They uncovered the wealth of native folk poetry and the charm of the Ukrainian language. Without this knowledge of folk creativity, the poetry of Taras Shevchenko and the splendid melodious quality of his literary style would be unthinkable. The appearance of Taras Shevchenko was the single most important event in directing Ukrainian literature onto a national and revolutionary course. His poems "Prychynna" [Bewitched], "Na vichnu pamiat Kotliarevskomu" [To the eternal memory of Kotliarevsky] and an early fragment from *Haidamaky* were published in Hrebinka's literary miscellany *Lastivka* [The swallow] in 1841. In the 1840s there appeared his works *Kobzar* [The minstrel], "Tryzna" [The funeral feast], the full version of *Haidamaky* and *Hamaliia*. Shevchenko's innovative literary work consistently developed the wealth of the folk idiom and became a model for national literature. His poetry was critical of the enemies of the Ukrainian nation, the Polish *szlachta* and tsarist Russia, and of those who exploited the Ukrainian populace. His work constituted a call to struggle for social and national liberation. Thanks to his remarkable sense of language, Shevchenko was able to resolve the problems of Ukrainian orthography. After Shevchenko, orthographical disputes were superfluous, although they did not cease.[89]

Nevertheless, many scholars in Russia did not believe that Ukrainian literature could develop along national lines. They regarded Ukrainian as a dialect of Russian and treated it as material to enrich the Russian language. Maksymovych, Sreznevsky and Bodiansky held similar views, and Oleksii Pavlovsky, the author of the first grammar of the

Ukrainian language, published in Saint Petersburg in 1818, called the Ukrainian language "neither living nor dead, [but] a disappearing dialect."[90]

In discussing Ukraine in the first half of the nineteenth century, one cannot neglect the revolutionary and political currents that began there about 1820. Between 1818 and 1825 the centre of the Decembrist Union of Welfare, with Pavel Pestel at its head, was located in Tulchyn on the Boh River. Vasylkiv, Kamianka and Poltava were also centres of its activity. In Kiev, Pestel's programme "Russkaia Pravda" [Russian Justice] was accepted. The Society of United Slavs, which aimed at the creation of a democratic and republican federation of Slavic countries, was also active in Ukraine. Both of these organizations belonged essentially to the Russian revolutionary movement, and in their programs the name Ukraine was not even mentioned. Hence the revolt of the Chernihiv Regiment under the leadership of Sergei Muravev-Apostol in Vasylkiv in the Kiev district did not gain great support from the local community.

The Polish revolutionary and insurrectionist movement likewise was not favoured in Ukraine. It is true that the Polish *szlachta* drew some Ukrainian peasants into the campaigns of the November Insurrection in the Volhynia, Podillia and Kiev gubernias, but the vast majority of the populace was indifferent, if not hostile, to the insurrection. Promises of liberty, the abolition of serfdom and land distribution did not help, because the Poles sought to re-establish the boundaries of 1772. In any case, the Polish detachments that fought in Ukraine were too weak to oppose the Russian forces. The Poles' struggle against tsardom was criticized by Artemovsky and Bodiansky, who, like the native Russians Pogodin and Pushkin, applauded the Russian victories. After 1831 the tsarist government dealt severely with the Poles. Polish schools in Right-Bank Ukraine were closed and Russian schools created in their place. Russian also became the official language in the courts.

The peasants also mistrusted Polish efforts led by Szymon Konarski to organize conspiratorial activities and revolutionary agitation in Right-Bank Ukraine after the suppression of the November Uprising. Even though it proclaimed abolition of serfdom, this was a movement of the *szlachta* without broader social support. However, Konarski's and Mickiewicz's ideas did influence measurably those Ukrainians who in 1846 established the Brotherhood of Saints Cyril and Methodius in Kiev. Creation of the brotherhood evidenced the growing national consciousness of the Ukrainians and the beginning of a new stage in their national development. Only then was the Ukrainian national movement transformed from a national-cultural movement into one that was truly political. The brotherhood's program, as expressed by Kostomarov in *Knyhy bytiia ukrainskoho narodu* [Books of the genesis of the Ukrainian people], was actually very hazy. It contained messianic notions and voiced the need to create a democratic federation of the Slavic nations, based on principles of broad autonomy, in which Ukraine would play a leading role and Kiev would be the capital. However, the demands to abolish serfdom, establish complete social equality and introduce universal education offer proof of the brotherhood's progressive nature. A split soon developed between liberal (Kostomarov and Kulish) and radical (Shevchenko, Mykola Hulak and Mykola Savych) wings. In 1847 the authorities eliminated the brotherhood and sentenced its leaders to harsh punishments, despite seeing in their activities only the "erudite delirium of three young people." Shevchenko was exiled as a simple soldier to the citadel in Orsk "under the most severe supervision, with a prohibition against writing and sketching." Thus tsardom attempted to break the poet whose work had become a symbol of the national renascence of the Ukrainian people and had stood at the foundation of Ukrainian political and national thought. The destruction of the brotherhood caused the collapse of Ukrainian national life for some fifteen years.

Other contemporary conditions, particularly the prohibition (in effect since 1822) against transporting books from Russia to the Habsburg state, without question also contributed to the marked absence of Ukrainian and Russian books among the Galician Ukrainians. Biretsky, in fact, pointed this out in a letter to Iakiv Holovatsky, and Vahylevych mentioned it to Pogodin.[91] The Galician Ukrainians eagerly used everything that could be obtained in Lviv at the Ossolineum and in the university library. By the mid-1830s the young Ukrainian enthusiasts knew of Kotliarevsky's *Eneida*, Tsertelev's and Maksymovych's collections of songs (which Shashkevych and Holovatsky transcribed personally), Sreznevsky's, Kvitka-Osnovianenko's and Hrebinka's works, Pavlovsky's Ukrainian grammar and Bantysh-Kamensky's *History of Little Russia.*[92]

In about 1835 a regular exchange of books between Galicia and Ukraine and Russia began. Initially Pogodin played the most important role in this exchange, but in the 1840s he was succeeded by Sreznevsky, Bodiansky, Maksymovych and Lukashevych. The extant correspondence from those years allows one to follow precisely the paths by which Ukrainian and Russian books made their way to Galicia in exchange for locally published works and copies, or sometimes even the originals, of old documents. The bookshops of Hartenstein in Brody and Radyvyliv and of Milikowski in Lviv were used as legal intermediaries. This form of consignment was not particularly convenient, however, because the books went from there to the Lviv censors, where they were kept for several months. Moreover, especially large or frequent shipments could not be made lest the authorities become suspicious. Indirect channels therefore were developed with the aid of such private individuals as Maciejowski in Warsaw and the Czechs, who sent books either through Milikowski's and Pichler's bookshops in Lviv or through persons travelling to Galicia. Packages of books were also sent from Galicia to Russia via Prague.[93] Sometimes the Galician Ukrainians even availed themselves of official help by the Russian authorities—for example, by the Russian embassy in Vienna, where initially the secretary, Adelung, occupied himself with these matters, and, after 1842, the embassy chaplain, Archpriest Mikhail Raevsky.[94]

As a result of the exchange of literary and scholarly works, virtually complete editions of the works of Kotliarevsky, Kvitka-Osnovianenko, Hrebinka, Kostomarov, Metlynsky, Bodiansky, Sreznevsky, Maksymovych and Shevchenko, as well as the Russian works of Pogodin, Shevyrev, Vostokov, Venelin, Khomiakov, Gogol, Iazykov and Sopikov, were to be found in Galicia. The Ukrainians acquired a complete collection of the early Rus' chronicles, Karamzin's *Istoriia gosudarstva rossiiskogo* [History of the Russian state], Dmytro Bantysh-Kamensky's and Mykola Markevych's histories of "Little Russia" and the anonymous *Istoriia Rusov.* These books, however, could not satisfy all the needs of the Galician Ukrainian community, since very few copies were sent. For that reason Iakiv Holovatsky decided to publish a new edition of Kvitka-Osnovianenko's *Marusia.* In 1843 he delivered a manuscript copy to the censorship board, which rejected it, as Zap noted, "not because of its content, but because of the orthography and Ukrainian words." (It was not published in Galicia until 1849.) For these very reasons Kyrylo Blonsky sought to publish Kotliarevsky's *Eneida* in Vienna and even announced a subscription, but he never followed through on the plan.[95]

On the other hand, Kotliarevsky's plays *Natalka-Poltavka* [Natalka from Poltava] in Ivan Ozarkevych's adaptation and *Moskal charivnyk* [The soldier-sorcerer] in Stepan Petrushevych's adaptation enjoyed great success and were constantly performed on Ukrainian stages in Galicia from 1848. Taras Shevchenko's poetry was known to the Ukrainian enthusiasts in Galicia at the beginning of the 1840s. And it is likely that Iakiv Holovatsky possessed first editions of *Kobzar* and *Haidamaky.*[96]

The Ukrainian and Russian learned men were often informed of the progress of Ukrainian literature in Galicia. Maksymovych gave a precise account of *Rusalka Dnistrovaia* in *Kievlianin*, expressing the opinion that Ukrainian literature in Galicia could develop further only on the basis of the popular speech.[97] Works by the Galician Ukrainians appeared in Russian journals. In *Moskovskii nadbliudatel* in 1836 Vahylevych's *Pismo iz Lemberga* [Letter from Lviv] was published, and two years later, in *Zhurnal Ministerstva narodnogo prosveshcheniia* [Journal of the Ministry of Public Education], a Russian translation of Ivan Mohylnytsky's "Discourse on the Ruthenian Language" appeared. In it the translator obliterated the semantic difference between the terms "russkii" (Russian) and "ruskyi" (Ruthenian), which even caused a scholarly misunderstanding as though Mohylnytsky combined the Ukrainians and the Russians. The same journal reprinted Holovatsky's "Journey through Galician and Hungarian Rus'" in 1844, and Pogodin published Holovatsky's "Great Croatia or Galician-Carpathian Rus'" in *Moskvitianin.* Works by other Galician Ukrainian authors also appeared in learned journals in Russia.[98]

Holovatsky's correspondence with Bodiansky began from their common interest in Ukrainian folk-songs. Bodiansky had turned in this regard to Havlíček-Borovský, who was in Moscow at the time, and he had recommended Zap. Zap then informed Holovatsky that Bodiansky needed Ukrainian songs from Galicia for a Slavic chrestomathy and a collection of "Little Russian" songs. In return for a collection of Galician folk songs, Zap promised to send Holovatsky books valued at between two hundred and three hundred roubles, and even agreed to Holovatsky's publishing the same songs in Austria.[99] Thus began a correspondence between Holovatsky and Bodiansky that continued for more than thirty years. In his letters, Holovatsky carefully informed Bodiansky about conditions in Galicia, about the development of Ukrainian literature there, and about the efforts of the Triad circle. He identified the causes and the directions of development and pointed out the differences between the younger generation, which propagated the folk idiom, and the older generation, which defended Church Slavonic. He underscored the similarities in the situation of the Galician Ukrainians and the other Slavic nations.

The surviving sources also indicate that Holovatsky was especially anxious to publish the Galician Ukrainian songs in Russia. In 1844 he wrote, "I shall gladly give you my entire collection.... I give you my word that I will not publish the songs myself until you publish them there, and perhaps it may come about that if you wish I will not publish them at all. We can discuss that later." Holovatsky's only stipulation was that he intended to send some of the songs to his brother, who was preparing a new literary annual in Vienna, and he told Bodiansky that he would try to have the collection ready by the following spring. Nevertheless, he delayed putting the songs in order, because it was not until the end of the following year that he informed Bodiansky that he had sent the completed collection to Prague.[100] Zap, Šafařík and Karel Erben studied it closely, and, according to Zap, Šafařík tried to persuade Holovatsky to publish it as soon as possible because every delay would be a great loss. Šafařík doubted that Bodiansky would publish the songs quickly, because "this is a person who intends to do a great deal, but brings nothing to a conclusion."[101] Time proved that Šafařík was right. *Narodnye pesni Galitskoi i Ugorskoi Rusi* [Popular songs of Galician and Hungarian Rus'] in fact did not appear until 1863 to 1877 in the Moscow journal *Chteniia* [Lectures]. A separate four-volume edition was not published in Moscow until 1878, thirty-three years after the songs were sent to Russia.

Pogodin had a substantial influence on several of the Galician Ukrainians, especially Vahylevych, Zubrytsky and Holovatsky. In the fall of 1835 he visited Lviv in the company of D. Kniazevich, Nikolai Nadezhdin, Petr Kireevsky, and Prince Dmitrii Kropotkin. He became acquainted with the superior of the monastery of Saint Onufrii, V. Kompanevych, and with the Poles Jan Nepomucen Kamiński, A. J. Rościszewski, Kazimierz Turowski and Aleksander Zawadzki. However, on that visit he did not meet any of the younger Ukrainian activists. It was not until the spring of the following year that Vahylevych began to correspond with Pogodin. Eventually, it was through Pogodin that the Ukrainians established ties with other scholars in Russia as well as with Šafařík.[102]

Vahylevych informed Pogodin of the early literary activity of the Ruthenian Triad, about the disputes over the alphabet and the language and especially about his own works, aspirations and projects. He boasted of his own achievements, even those that he would never accomplish (for example, that he was preparing a dictionary of the Little Russian language in Galicia, which he intended to publish according to Karadžić's model). Vahylevych also mentioned that he had prepared a "South Rus'" translation of *The Tale of Ihor's Campaign* and repeatedly requested the newest publications in Ukrainian and Russian literature. Pogodin not only sent the books, but interested the Russian Academy of Sciences in Vahylevych's projects. The academy promised financial support to complete them, with the proviso that it receive detailed information about the projected Ukrainian dictionary.[103]

Pogodin also strongly affected Zubrytsky, and their correspondence certainly contributed to Zubrytsky's joining the ranks of the Galician-Ukrainian Russophile party in the 1850s. Zubrytsky gained a great deal personally from their association, and his scholarly work was highly regarded in learned circles in Russia. He received honoraria for his writings and was also accorded honorary positions. In 1842 he became a corresponding member of the Archeological Commission, two years later a member of the Kievan Commission for the Study of Ancient Documents, in 1846 a member of the Imperial Society of Russian History and Antiquity, and in 1855 a member of the Imperial Academy of Sciences.[104]

During his first trip through the Slavic countries in 1835, Pogodin had no official mission. However, through the Academy of Sciences and the Ministry of Education, he attempted to give a political purpose to the journeys abroad of Russian scholars. In a letter to the academy, Pogodin proposed that he act as intermediary in relations with Slavic scholars, "particularly in matters that for various reasons cannot initially be conducted officially." Pogodin believed that the Slavic dialects (he purposely did not use the term "Slavic languages") that were not yet known to Russian writers could constitute excellent material "for enriching the Russian language." Accordingly, he thought that the Imperial Academy of Sciences should support all scholarly endeavors aimed at preparing grammars and dictionaries of these dialects. It was in this context that he mentioned the dictionary supposedly in preparation by Vahylevych and a Little Russian dictionary, on which Bodiansky was working, pointing out that it was in the academy's interest "to hasten the completion of such essential works."[105]

Four years later, after returning from a second trip to the Slavic countries, Pogodin reported to Minister of Education Count S. S. Uvarov on the Slavs in Austria. From his observations of their national renascence, he concluded that "such a movement occurs only before great events." Consequently, "the Austrian empire, even more than the Turkish [empire] should tremble for its own existence." Because it was composed of a mosaic of nationalities, it would disintegrate in the next war. Austria was most afraid of Russia, because "all the Slavs to the Adriatic Sea sympathize with her" and "gaze at Russia as the three kings [gazed] at the star from the east," seeing in her the fulfillment of their desires and hopes. Finally, Pogodin said, the Austrian Slavs believed that after Russia had delivered them from their enemies, they would "come into the world and fulfill their destiny."

By right, Pogodin maintained, "Galicia, which is inhabited by pure Russians [*chistymi russkimi*], followers of the Greek rite, virtually belongs to Russia." Not only the Galician and Hungarian Ruthenians were drawn to Russia, but also the Slovaks, the Austrian Serbs and the Czechs. Only after the Slavs were joined to Russia would a federated Slavic state arise, "with Russia at its head, from the Eastern [Pacific]

Ocean to the Adriatic Sea, a state unlike any in history which will rule the entire remaining world." Indeed, it was Russia's obligation to aid the Slavic countries, in particular the Galician Ruthenians, who "are pure Russians," like the inhabitants of Poltava and Chernihiv: "They bear our name, speak our language, profess our religion, share the same history with us,... groan under the triple yoke of the Germans, Poles and Jews as well as Catholicism, and complain bitterly of our indifference." Therefore Russia should subsidize and otherwise support Slavic scholarship, furnish Russian books to Austrian libraries and open Russian schools for the Slavs so that their graduates would later propagate "the Russian spirit" in their own countries.[106]

Minister Uvarov, in reporting to Tsar Nicholas I on the Russian scholars' journeys in the Slavic countries, pointed out that these travellers were not only providing scholarly materials, but "full particulars on the situation in the Slavic world," whose development was linked to the "emergence of sympathy for Russia." Therefore, these journeys were "advantageous not only to the tsar, but to the whole Russian nation; they are contributing to tightening the bonds of the Slavs to Russia and... gain new friends for Russia."[107] At about the same time, in 1840, Count Mikhail Muravev, following a journey through Galicia to Karlovy Vary in Bohemia, also suggested in a report for the tsarist authorities entitled "Vzgliad na Avstriiu" [A look at Austria] that they needed to take a greater interest in Slavic affairs. He conjectured that the Austrian empire would eventually fall apart.[108]

Nevertheless, Pogodin's assertion that the Slavs had great sympathy for Russia and wanted to unite with her and his suggestion that Austria would quickly collapse were nothing but wishful thinking; neither was borne out by Vahylevych's or even Zubrytsky's correspondence. To be sure, Vahylevych, not seeing any opportunity for work in Galicia and banned from holy orders by the church authorities, voiced his intention to emigrate to Russia. He wrote to Pogodin: "Perhaps I shall move to your country if our government favours my request. Always suggest me for a position in a library or a professorship, for which I would gladly prepare as necessary."[109]

These intentions were never fulfilled. Either the Austrian authorities did not agree to Vahylevych's departure or Pogodin did not attempt to find him a suitable post in Russia, but in any case, Vahylevych's correspondence with Pogodin seemed to confirm Austrian suspicions that the Galician Ruthenians were in league with the tsarist administration. In finally conferring holy orders on Vahylevych in the mid-1840s, the Greek Catholic church authorities stipulated that he not return to his old ways and cease all contacts with foreign, particularly Russian, writers.[110]

Amicable ties linked Vahylevych and the Holovatsky brothers with Izmail Sreznevsky, who, returning from a trip abroad, sojourned in Lviv in July 1842. Sreznevsky had met Ivan Holovatsky in Vienna, and in Lviv Karel Zap introduced him to Vahylevych, Iakiv Holovatsky, Denys Zubrytsky, Iosyf Levytsky and the Poles Kamiński, Bielowski and Zaleski (Wacław z Oleska). He did not like Levytsky—"a poor grammarian, even though he wrote a grammar," as Sreznevsky noted—but he maintained a lively dialogue with the other Ukrainians. For the Galician Ukrainians Sreznevsky was "one of the better literary guides." He was regarded as a Ukrainian, although he was in fact a Russian who was enamoured of the language and history of Ukraine.[111] Sreznevsky influenced the political views of the Holovatsky brothers to no small degree. He was no revolutionary, and he merged his political conservatism with tolerance for other nations. His motto was "To respect political authority while remaining a loyal subject of the fatherland, and to respect nationality."[112] Iakiv Holovatsky likewise harboured no revolutionary inclinations, as the following excerpt from a poem he dedicated to Sreznevsky illustrates.

Izviazhymsia ridni dity,
Chas vzhe nam vidmolodnity!
Svoiu pisniu zaspivaimo,
Svoiei syly dobuvaimo
Ta vse pide v lad.[113]

[Let us join together, my children; / it's time to be rejuvenated! / Let us sing our song; / let us gain our strength; / all will then go well.]

In sending Sreznevsky the first part of *Vinok*, Ivan Holovatsky wrote: "Your instructions have become deeply ingrained [in me]; they are inbred in my soul and in my desires, [and] they will become unforgettable comrades and guides, because they have awakened my activities and animated the idea of Slavdom." Holovatsky also pointed to the direction of this revitalization.

> I am also sending you several of my songs; they are a faithful reflection of my experience, thoughts, regrets and hopes. I wanted to present "Pinie radostnoho holosa" to His Highness, Your Emperor . . . , but not having the opportunity to do so, I am placing it, together with the remaining songs, in your honourable hands. It was thanks to your influence that they were written.

He further requested that Sreznevsky find an appropriate place to have them published, "and perhaps [a place] for me as well? That would make me even happier."[114]

The Triad circle shared Platon Lukashevych's intense love for Ukraine, its history and its Cossack past. Through Lukashevych the circle also became acquainted with Shevchenko. Lukashevych's letter to Vahylevych in autumn 1843 offers interesting evidence of Shevchenko's interest in Ukrainian affairs in Galicia. Both Shevchenko and Lukashevych read Vahylevych's "Madei" as printed in *Rusalka Dnistrovaia* and expressed regret that such poetry, written in "a pure Beskydian language," has been prohibited, especially because that language was "our ancestral tongue." Lukashevych encouraged the Galician Ukrainians to undertake ethnographic investigations of the Ukrainian common people inhabiting the Carpathians; he also noted that he would forward the manuscript copy of the Lviv Chronicle, which Iakiv Holovatsky had sent to him, through Shevchenko to the censors in Saint Petersburg, where he would try to have it published. The most important part of Lukashevych's letter, however, was the passage, "During Shevchenko's stay with me I proposed to him that we borrow some of your words and linguistic forms, to which he consented."[115] Perhaps Shevchenko's familiarity with *Rusalka Dnistrovaia* influenced the naming of *Knyhy bytiia ukrainskoho narodu*, the programme of the Brotherhood of Saints Cyril and Methodius in Kiev, "Podnistrianka" [The girl from the Dniester region].[116]

Lukashevych's attachment to the Ruthenians' past and the monuments of their literature induced him to make a series of suggestions concerning orthographic principles to Vahylevych, advice that did not benefit Ukrainian literature in Galicia. In Lukashevych's opinion,

> the best orthography is that which, without [anyone's] playing the wise man, is taken directly from the Church Slavonic language or from our Old Ruthenian, from the chronicles of Nestor, of Kiev and Volhynia.... Until we, like the Great Russians, adopt it, we shall never have our own literature. We should examine and clarify the individual dialects, but we should write in only one [dialect] and alike, otherwise confusion will result.

Accordingly, Lukashevych believed that the eastern Ukrainians should borrow many words and linguistic forms (only not Polish) from the Galician Ruthenians. He also expected that Vahylevych would follow his suggestions in the grammar that he was preparing and that it would therefore be the best Ukrainian grammar yet written.[117]

Mykhailo Maksymovych, who had enjoyed enormous popularity from the time his Ukrainian songs were published and was seen as a scholarly authority among the Galician Ukrainians, tried to influence them with official Great Russian ideology. His advice probably appealed only to Zubrytsky, and it was only to him that Maksymovych conveyed his true thoughts. In a letter of 1840 he indicated that he was fascinated by Zubrytsky's assimilation of the Russian language and the letters he had written in Russian. Maksymovych realized that it was more difficult for the Galician Ukrainians to write in Russian than in Polish. He called the Polish language an abomination, completely unfit for the Ukrainians, maintaining that "for the Ruthenians of the Austrian empire, the living language is the South Rus' language. The time of the Polish language is long past, [and] the time of the Great Russian language has not yet arrived.... In my opinion, your Red Ruthenian literature should be in your own South Rus' language, and only in Galicia can it be in this language."

Maksymovych advised adopting his own orthography (later called the *maksymovychivka*), and he criticized Shashkevych's orthography in *Rusalka Dnistrovaia.* He believed that the orthography should be uniform, because the Ukrainians otherwise would not successfully develop their national literature. (Iakiv Holovatsky, of course, did take these suggestions into account in publishing Ilkevych's *Galician Proverbs.*) However, Maksymovych viewed the future of Ukrainian literature in Russia differently. In Ukraine, he stated, "there can be no literature in the South Rus' language, but there can be and are individual works by Kotliarevsky, Kvitka-Osnovianenko, Hrebinka and others in this language. The South Rus' language is for us only a monument through which the Great Russian language can be enriched." For Maksymovych, this Great Russian language was the real "Ruthenian language," the language "in which we speak, write and think, the universal language used in Ukraine among the educated class of the nation." Everything written in Ukrainian in Ukraine was artificial.

In closing his letter, Maksymovych asked Zubrytsky to communicate his suggestions to other Ukrainian writers in Galicia. He also asked him to send articles concerning Austrian Rus' to *Kievlianin,* which he published and of which he enclosed three copies from 1840 for Holovatsky, Vahylevych and Zubrytsky.[118] Zubrytsky fulfilled these requests. Nevertheless, we do not know how the Galician Ukrainians reacted to Maksymovych's auguries about the Ukrainian literary language and literature, because there is no reference whatsoever to them in their correspondence. The Ukrainians could reach only one unpleasant conclusion from Maksymovych's theorizing: Ukrainian must yield its place in literature to Russian. Still, they did agree with his resolute criticism of the Polish language.[119]

In 1846 disillusionment grew among the Galician Ukrainians toward Russia and its official ideology as represented by Pogodin,

Maksymovych, Sreznevsky and Bodiansky, and contacts with them slackened substantially. As I have already mentioned, the Czech spokesmen, especially Zap and Havlíček-Borovský, had a significant impact on the Ukrainian liberals' changing attitude. In his 1846 "Conditions of the Ruthenians in Galicia," Iakiv Holovatsky severely criticized Pogodin's aspirations toward unity and his contemptuous attitude toward Lukashevych's Ukrainophilism. Holovatsky condemned the tsarist authorities' policies toward Ukrainian literature, and he remarked of Russia's social policies that

> nowhere can a land-owner maltreat his peasants with such impunity as there.... The Ruthenian peasants know how it goes for a serf in Russia.... Under Russian rule they could not hope for anything. And that is indeed why they are so bound and devoted to their [Habsburg] emperor![120]

9. The Crossroads

In the mid-1840s the Ukrainian national movement stood at a crossroads. The situation ultimately was the consequence of both disillusionment with Russia and the appeal of the Polish cause after the events of 1846. All of the Russian and Ukrainian scholars to whom the Galician Ukrainians were closest adhered to "autocracy, orthodoxy and nationality," the basic tenets of official Russian ideology formulated by education minister Count S. S. Uvarov. On the other hand, those activists in Russia who could have been true allies of the Ruthenians, such as the founders of the Brotherhood of Saints Cyril and Methodius, were in tsarist prisons by 1847, and they were to do penance for their "disloyal" views for many years. In Galicia there was a growing understanding of what Ivan Holovatsky had already written in 1840: tsarist Russian policy had reactionary, annexationist aims and wanted to unite the Slavs only to the extent that they would be completely subordinated to the Romanov monarchy. The Ukrainians, of course, were most imperilled by this policy. Familiarity with social problems in Russia and with the fate of Ukrainian literature beyond the Austrian border only reinforced the liberal Galician Ukrainians' antipathy to Russia, thus inclining them all the more toward the Habsburg monarchy.[1]

Only the Poles could have been allies of the Ukrainians in Galicia, and then only if Ukrainian-Polish understanding were rooted democratically. However, by the 1840s the Polish cause had lost its appeal. The Austrian authorities indicated several times that the Ukrainians could not expect the government's backing if they collaborated with the Poles. The Poles themselves could not alter this state of affairs. Their conspiratorial movement was too weak, and legal efforts toward social and political change could not succeed. The best example of the futility of lawful activities was the behaviour of the Galician estates diet, which between 1843 and 1845 attempted to resolve the peasant question. In the diet itself the proponents of reform, with Prince Leon Sapieha and Tadeusz Wasilewski at their head, had to wage a pitched battle with the conservatives led by Władysław Sanguszko. The noble reformers sought peasant support for the Polish national cause (including the support of Ukrainian peasants in Eastern Galicia) and at the same time wished to draw them away from the conspiratorial emissaries and from the Austrian government. They believed that the system of *robot* was unproductive and should be changed in the interests of the manorial estates themselves. However, the Austrian government voided all of the diet's reform proposals. It saw growing social upheaval in the 1840s and was determined to bring the peasants to the Austrian side. To be sure, the government could not officially refuse to accede to certain changes in *robot*, but neither could it allow the Poles to initiate such reforms. The events of 1846 in Western Galicia proved that the Austrian authorities had won, thanks to the class antagonism in the Galician countryside.[2]

The discussions on the peasant question in the Galician estates diet found no echo in the correspondence of those Ukrainians associated with Iakiv Holovatsky and Ivan Vahylevych, nor did Metropolitan Levytsky write anything on the subject.[3] Yet it is virtually impossible that information from the diet did not reach the Ukrainian leaders. How then do we explain their silence? It seems that they did not wish to discuss publicly non-literary issues. For the metropolitan and his associates, the matter was straightforward: loyalty to the authorities did not allow them to join the discussion on issues that did not have the resolute support of the Austrian ruling circles.

The year 1846 brought further disadvantages to the Poles in Galicia. The disaster of the Cracow uprising and the peasants' turning against the *szlachta* in Western Galicia definitively discredited the Poles in Ukrainian eyes. Even old Zubrytsky was pleased that among the Ukrainians "no one was involved in the conspiracy" and "not one [Ukrainian] is under suspicion."[4] Platon Kostetsky appraised events most concisely: "The year 1846 made a laughing stock of the Poles in the eyes of the Ruthenian peasants."[5]

Still, the liberal Ukrainian intelligentsia also could not reconcile itself to what the higher Greek Catholic clergy represented. In proposing in 1843 the official name "Ruthenians" for the Ukrainian nation in Galicia, Metropolitan Levytsky probably did not consider that a distinct name suggested the existence of a separate nation, even though the Galician Ukrainians were but a part of a fifteen-million-member nation with its centre in tsarist-ruled Ukraine. And although Bishop Iakhymovych pointed out to the Austrian authorities that they could gain political influence over the Ukrainians in Russia by enhancing the Ukrainian nationality in Galicia, the Greek Catholic hierarchy completely accepted the status quo in Galicia and was even inclined to regard the local Ruthenians as a separate nation different from their kinsmen in the east. The church leaders linked their fate entirely to the Habsburg monarchy and, completely satisfied with their personal advantages and honours, did not expect any major national or cultural concessions.

The decidedly hostile attitude of the metropolitan toward the Triad's literary activities, the prohibition in the seminary against reading the works of the most eminent contemporary writers and the ban on literary endeavours by the seminarians themselves set them against their own clerical hierarchy. Ivan Vahylevych wrote to Wacław Maciejowski that he would not want to publish his works in Lviv for various reasons, but primarily to be free from the booksellers and, most importantly, "from the metropolitan's order, according to which priests must be idiots."[6] The Ukrainian national movement quite simply could not submit to clerical leadership. In such circumstances the Ukrainian liberals had to turn to the one real force able, as it seemed to them, to guarantee the future of the Ukrainian nation in Galicia: Austria.

The Austrian authorities themselves had for many years been interested in the Ukrainian question in Galicia, understanding that they should exploit the awakening Ukrainian national life. In a multinational monarchy in which Germans were only a minority, the Austrian authorities had to support the most loyal nationalities. But when one nationality made too far-reaching demands, Vienna countered its aspirations by manipulating the other nationalities. The year 1848 demonstrated that the Austrian strategy of *divide et impera* was an extraordinarily useful policy.

In the 1830s, Austrian bureaucrats had not been favourably disposed toward the young Ukrainian national movement. Their negative attitude stemmed, among other things, from their vigorous repression of the Polish conspiratorial underground. The appearance of the Ruthenian Triad in those circumstances was seen as an attempt to resurrect a "buried nationality." Nevertheless, the Austrian attitude was modified as the Ukrainian national movement gained strength and its literature developed, despite the ban on printing *Zoria* and distributing *Rusalka Dnistrovaia*. This change occurred at the beginning of the 1840s, not without the notable influence of Jernej Kopitar, an adherent of the Austrian solution for the future of the Slavs, who dreamed of making Vienna the political and cultural centre of Slavdom.[7]

The first clear proof of the authorities' changed attitude toward the Ukrainians was the proposal by the Viennese Polizeihofstelle in 1842 to Ivan Holovatsky to assume the editorship of a government-sponsored Ukrainian journal. Evidently, the Austrian police were more interested in making national concessions to the Ukrainians than were the administrative authorities. The police expected that in this way they could draw the Ukrainians away from the Polish underground. Because of the importance of this issue for the Ukrainians and Austrian governmental circles, we must take it up in more detail.

Politically, the proposal was essentially anti-Russian, and that is how Ivan Holovatsky judged it in relaying to his brother Iakiv a precise account of his conversation with the commissioner of police. Apparently the Austrian authorities had learned that a pro-Russian party was beginning to emerge in Galicia. Its purported members included the Greek Catholic priests Mykhailo Malynovsky and Spyrydon Lytvynovych and the elders of the Stavropygian Institute. Ivan Holovatsky wrote to his brother, "The kindred language [and] literature draw some under the mantle of Russian Pan-Slavism, the faith and the rite [draw] others, and the Russian authorities directly bind others perhaps through their emissaries—roubles."

To counter these tendencies, the Austrians intended to entice the Galician Ukrainians to the side of Austrian Slavdom, to detach them from "the Great Russian whole, which would be pleased to make every shoe fit its foot, to russify [*pomoskovshchyty*] and to bring them into schism [*poshyzmachyty*]." Austrian governmental circles further let it be known that all Slavic nationalities would be allowed to develop freely, and the proof was that Count Leszek Dunin-Borkowski was to publish a Polish weekly in Vienna to counterbalance the pro-Russian, Polish-language *Tygodnik Peterburski* (Saint Petersburg weekly). Ivan Holovatsky concluded, "They are asking me if I would undertake publishing in Vienna a similar journal in the Little or Galician Ruthenian language, whether I would find enough contributors in Galicia, and whether you [Iakiv] or other Ruthenian acquaintances [would contribute]." The journal was to consist initially of two or three printer's sheets and would be published quarterly. It was to be written in a "pure folk idiom, not mixed with either Polish or Muscovite." In Ivan Holovatsky's opinion, its aim would be

> to treat the language [and] nationality of Galicia and of all Little Russia as a genuine branch of Slavdom, to have it decide upon its own [fate], to break away from Muscovitism and the [Pan-]Slavic spirit that is rising among the Galicians, [and] to incline [the Ruthenians] over to the Austrian Slavs and concentrate [them] here.

Vienna, as the centre of Slavdom, was the place to publish; the journal was to be "printed with Latin typeset according to the best orthography." This journal, Ivan added, was to have a varied content, but "not reaching too far"; there would be descriptions of national life, customs, manners, superstitions and folk rituals, articles that aimed at "comparative research between the national language and other Austrian Slavic dialects," folk legends and tales concerning ancient times, descriptions of individual localities, "and other information in the fields of ethnography, geography, statistics, the history of Little Russia, etc. Also some better stories and poetry, and sometimes even reprinted Little Russian works could find a place in it."[8]

Ivan decided to exploit the opportunity that had presented itself and began to consider the publication seriously. The only obstacle was the Austrian authorities' decision to require Latin characters. He tried to convince them to permit the Cyrillic alphabet, but without success. However, regardless of the kind of characters used, the journal would be to the Ukrainians' benefit. Ivan also informed his brother that governmental circles wanted him to obtain enough material for one year and then submit a publication plan. He urged his brother to send his own materials and induce other Ukrainian enthusiasts to do the same, although he noted that they would not be paid, "because it is hard to expect such an honorarium... from the authorities." He himself would be pleased if the authorities covered only the journal's printing costs. In concluding, Ivan warned Iakiv against undue optimism, encouraged him to collaborate and expressed his belief that together with Fran Miklošić they could convince the authorities to allow the Cyrillic alphabet.[9]

Publication of the journal remained in abeyance, even though Ivan Holovatsky energetically set to work. He prepared materials, translated Czech and Illyrian works and complained about his inability to obtain needed Polish, Russian and Little Russian books. Actually, with the exception of Mykhailo Maksymovych's collection of Ukrainian songs, the first part of a story by Hryhorii Kvitka-Osnovianenko and a few minor pieces sent by Izmail Sreznevsky, he had nothing at all. However, Ivan expected to bring the matter to a satisfactory conclusion. If his intentions eventually came to nothing, "the materials could serve the publication of some kind of Little Russian anthologies."[10]

How did Ukrainians in Galicia receive these plans? We know from Ivan Holovatsky's letters that he provided his brother precise information on the government's ideas, and Iakiv did not conceal his own satisfaction when informing his friends and acquaintances about the matter. The news coming from Vienna must have caused quite a stir. In reporting to Pogodin, Zubrytsky was convinced that publishing a Ruthenian journal in the Latin alphabet would conclude the long-standing disputes over Little Russian orthography.[11] The first impressions, therefore, were positive.[12] Only in time did doubts surface, especially with respect to the Latin alphabet. Iakiv Holovatsky wrote to Bodiansky: "It seemed as though something was to come of a Little Russian journal that was to have been published in Vienna, but since it is so difficult to solicit its publication in Cyrillic, there is little desire for it. The Ruthenians definitely would prefer that there be no literature at all if it has to be written in Latin (Polish) letters, and it is apparent that this [project] will amount to little, or, more likely, nothing will come of it at all."[13]

Evidently, Iakiv Holovatsky was less than candid, and in his letter to Bodiansky he exaggerated his reluctance to use the Latin alphabet. Rejecting the journal proposition would have been an unpardonable mistake at the expense of the further development of Ukrainian literature. He was prepared to agree to the form proposed by the government, but he also wanted to sound out the Ukrainians in Russia in regard to the proposal. Because of the censorship, he could not send a letter by mail, and Iakiv therefore took advantage of Karel Havlíček-Borovský, who visited Lviv between November 1842 and January 1843 en route to Moscow, to send a letter to Sreznevsky. In addition, Havlíček was to tell Sreznevsky in detail of the Austrian authorities' intentions.

Havlíček, for his part, informed Sreznevsky in a special letter that the Austrian authorities, in desiring to separate the Galician Ukrainians from their "Orthodox Pan-Russian [*vseruských*] brothers," had charged Ivan Holovatsky to publish a Ruthenian journal with the aim "of convincing the Galician Ukrainians that they are a completely separate nation from the other Little Russians," and he added that Kopitar had devised an orthography for the journal that was completely different from the Czech and Illyrian orthographies.[14] Havlíček's letter contained substantial inaccuracies. The Austrian authorities did not wish to create a separate nation of the Galician Ukrainians, but only aspired to cut them off from Russian propaganda. The author of the new orthography was not Kopitar but Miklošić, as Ivan Holovatsky had specifically noted.[15] It is not known how this news was received in Russia, but probably not very well, if Iakiv Holovatsky had to explain to Bodiansky in the fall of 1843 that the Ukrainians in Galicia did not want a literature written in a romanized alphabet.

In any case, the project never materialized, perhaps because after Kopitar died in 1844, the Ukrainians no longer had a champion in Vienna to defend their interests.[16] However, the idea had some effect, notably the awakening of certain hopes in the Ukrainian community. Iosyf Levytsky intended to exploit this favourable atmosphere and announced plans to publish *Biblioteka besid dukhovnykh.* In articles in *Dennitsa-Jutrzenka* and Jordan's *Jahrbücher* in 1843, he pointed to the Austrians' favourable attitude toward the Ukrainian movement and Ukrainian literature. Thus, for the first time, a Galician Ukrainian came forward publicly with an offer to rely upon Austria. Nevertheless, his proposal had to await suitable conditions, which came eventually as a consequence of the events of 1846 in Galicia.

On 25 June 1846, Iakiv Holovatsky completed his article entitled "Zustände der Russinen in Galizien. Ein Wort zur Zeit. Von einem Russinen," which appeared shortly thereafter in Leipzig, in Jordan's *Jahrbücher für Slawische Literatur, Kunst und Wissenschaft*, under the pseudonym Havryło Rusyn. The article, "written upon the ruins of the former capital Halych," represented the end of the literary and linguistic stage in the development of the Ukrainian nation in Galicia and guided the Ukrainians toward politics. From this time forward, the Ukrainian national movement in Galicia began to take on political features, which would become fully apparent during the revolution of 1848-9.

In his article Iakiv Holovatsky presented the past, present and future of the Ukrainian nation in Galicia in its close association with the Habsburg monarchy. He criticized the Poles' past policy of denationalization, and he bitterly spoke out against the Ukrainian upper classes, which had succumbed to complete polonization. However, Holovatsky reserved his sharpest criticism for the leaders of the Greek Catholic church, whom he described as "sogenannten *predstojateli ruskaho naroda*" [so-called leaders of the Ruthenian nation]. Holovatsky noted that when Mykhailo Levytsky assumed the position of metropolitan, the Ukrainians had expected a better future and regarded him as a sincere Ruthenian. However, his convictions had changed completely from the time he became related through kinship to the Polish Stankiewicz family. The money the metropolitan used to purchase the Zbora estate, Holovatsky maintained, "could in the course of time have accounted for an entire body of literature," and, after all, this money represented "the bloody sweat of his subjects and the faithful." Levytsky could have done much for his own nation, but he did nothing except sow discord between the *szlachta*, to which he was accommodating, and the Greek Catholic clergymen "with whom he dealt virtually like a despot." Holovatsky accused him of surrounding himself with individuals "without character, [who] were ready to do any service on behalf of his dark aims," and blamed him for the collapse of the Greek Catholic seminary, which once was the hope of the Ukrainians. It could not have been otherwise, wrote Holovatsky, because "jesuitical hypocrites, Polish renegades, vile toadies, relatives of Levytsky" governed the seminary. The seminary had become an institution that educated people "without a soul and without an idea," in which reading books was forbidden and young men of talent were under suspicion.

In presenting a series of examples of the church hierarchy's antagonism toward Ukrainian literature, Holovatsky asked bitterly, "How can literature develop here? In what spirit and in what way are authors to write?" Holovatsky concluded: "It is sad for a nation when villainous people of other nations trample upon its nationality; but it is much, much sadder still when a profligate son claws open the breast of his beloved mother."

After describing the Galician Ukrainians' current situation, Holovatsky stated that their condition would be much improved if Ukrainian intellectual life could develop as among the other Slavs. After all, the Ukrainians were not worse subjects, and they would like to keep pace with other nations of the monarchy. It was time, Holovatsky wrote, for the government to take the Ruthenians under its protection. The Ukrainians in Galicia could represent a "strong bulwark against revolutionary machinations..., which already have shattered many times against the rock of Ruthenian loyalty." Austria therefore must support the Ukrainian nationality; it must introduce instruction in the native language in the schools and establish a university chair of Ukrainian language and literature. The Ukrainians had fully earned this kind of concession, having demonstrated their loyalty and devotion many times—in 1809, in 1833-4 and in the very year in which Holovatsky wrote. Especially at the present time, "when so many Roman Catholic priests have been compromised," two thousand Ruthenian clergymen and millions of Ukrainians had remained faithful. Ukrainians fully merited what Emperor Francis I had said of them: "Die Russinen in Galizien sind meine Kinder" [The Ruthenians in Galicia are my children].

It was not right that until that very time the education of these children was "entrusted to Polish and Jewish care." The year 1846 should have opened everyone's eyes. If Austria had taken the lesson of 1809 to heart and followed the example of Emperor Joseph II, the catastrophe that occurred at the beginning of 1846 could have been avoided. Holovatsky added, "If Austria wants to fortify its rule in Galicia, it must follow the political principles of Emperor Joseph II." That great emperor had known well that all of Austria's power in Galicia rested upon the Ukrainians; for that reason he had cared for them and "advanced Ruthenianism." The present situation was no different. Above all, it was essential to see to the rapid development of education in the native language, so that the community's "culture, industry and prosperity should rise." Besides, by introducing the native language into governmental offices, the authorities could avoid the misunderstandings that often occurred in district offices and in courts. The officials themselves would gain the confidence of the people by using the language intelligible to them. The enhancement of literature and the development of periodicals would uplift the Ukrainian nationality, and consequently Polishness would gain far fewer adherents. "Then Austria will have in its civil and military service Galicians as faithful as the Czechs, Croats, etc. and as loyal as the Ruthenian clergy and simple people."

Holovatsky determinedly countered assertions that the Ukrainians were a threat to Austria because of their close proximity to Russia. "Empty chatter!" he said indignantly, because the Ukrainians could not gain much from a Russia that had achieved its conquests at the point of a bayonet. Besides, the Ukrainians in Galicia were Greek Catholic, whereas in Russia everyone was of the Eastern faith; there could be no accord between them, just as there was none between the Greek Catholic and Orthodox subjects in Bukovyna or Dalmatia, who, after all, were under Austrian rule. Religious conditions in Orthodox Russia would not suit the Galician Greek Catholics, inasmuch as educated Ukrainians did not care for the poor life of the Russian priests, deprived of property and leading an eremitical existence. In addition, Ukrainian literature in Russia lacked the right conditions for development. Individual works had to appear there anonymously or under pseudonyms, and the government looked with a jaundiced eye on Ukrainian literature. Accordingly, Holovatsky maintained, "the Ruthenian nationality's entire hope lies in Austria, in which every nationality has been safe and secure." Austria could exploit this awareness and influence Russian Ukraine by supporting Ukrainian literature in Galicia.

It appears that Iakiv Holovatsky was not only familiar with Aleksander Wielopolski's condemnatory *Lettre d'un gentilhomme polonais sur les massacres de Gallicie adressée au Prince de Metternich*, but fully understood the feelings this letter aroused among the *szlachta*, because he wrote explicitly that only the *szlachta* could hope for much from Russia, where a landowner could oppress his serfs with impunity. Holovatsky also indicated that some Galician estate owners likewise would be willing to submit to Russia if certain reforms were enacted there. He himself believed that abolishing *robot* or replacing it with a system of rents would be most desirable in Galicia, because it would give strength to the oppressed Ukrainian peasants, who, being aware of the Russian serfs' conditions, could not hope for anything from Russia and would be even more bound to "their emperor."

Holovatsky concluded:

> Austria must actively pursue the task begun on behalf of emancipating and uplifting the Ruthenian peasantry, without impairing the national life, faith and language of the common people. Austria stands and endures by safeguarding various nationalities. It has become strong by an always continuing toleration of religious confessions and nationalities. But for every departure from these maxims Austria has also been made to atone heavily. Hence, it should remain true to this principle and not allow itself to be led astray from its ancestral track by Russian centralization, the Prussian system of germanization or the Jesuits' proselytizing. The Ruthenians in Galicia have not lost faith in Austria. Austria will finally become convinced from so many examples of the rights of the loyal and honest Ruthenians and will implement them in schools and in everyday life, in church and in governmental service, as it has with the other Slavs: Austria first and foremost, if it only has the will [*denn, Oestreich über alles, wenn es nur will!*][17]

Thus, Iakiv Holovatsky's article contained an offer of resolute co-operation between the Galician Ukrainians and the Austrian monarchy, an agreement that promised Ukrainian opposition to the revolutionary and anti-Austrian activities of the Poles in exchange for minor language and national concessions. At the same time, it was in a way the last and most important link in a chain of loyal declarations offered, over many years, by the church hierarchy and the young liberal intelligentsia. However, up to that time these pro-Austrian declarations were not purposely anti-Polish; Holovatsky's remarks represented a significant stride in that direction. He expressed an increasingly discernible Ukrainian separatism in Galicia, a decisive break with Polish society,[18] and at the same time rejected any return to a revolutionary course. Such, in any case, were his intentions. Holovatsky's "Conditions of the Ruthenians in Galicia" constituted the first political programme of the Galician Ukrainians, to which they would basically remain loyal until the end of the Austrian empire.

The anti-Polish and anti-revolutionary sonnets in part two of *Vinok*, mentioned previously, were only a logical consequence of the position in Holovatsky's article. Another series of sonnets in *Vinok*, entitled "Torzhestvo" [Celebration] and dedicated to Emperor Ferdinand, was similar. The author strongly implied that the fate of the Slavs depended exclusively upon the emperor's will, an expression of divine truth, and suggested that God had entrusted the worldly life of the Slavic nations to Austria. It was only in the Austrian monarchy that the cordial bond of the nations inhabiting the lands of the Vltava, Elbe, Vistula, Dniester, Danube and Sava rivers was strengthened.[19] Contemporaries accepted the political implications as obvious.

Havryło Rusyn's article caused a stir in the Galician Ukrainian community. Insulted by its personal attacks, the Greek Catholic hierarchy suspected Father Levytsky of Hrushiv of being the author.[20] Ultimately, the church leaders appealed to the gubernial authorities to ban the distribution and sale of Jordan's *Jahrbücher* in Galicia.[21] The young Ukrainian activists, however, took an entirely different attitude, although whether they completely accepted Havryło Rusyn's political notions or were merely pleased by the bitter criticism of the metropolitan and his supporters is not known. Ivan Holovatsky certainly agreed wholeheartedly with the sentiments his brother had expressed, writing to him: "As regards Havryło Rusyn, his article is marvellous, beautiful; the Slavs [in Vienna] loved it, even Miklošić. As for myself, I was truly electrified to the depths of my heart and soul; if only I could meet him and press him to my bosom! Tell me, do I know him?"[22] Others esteemed the article highly, but regretted that it was not easily available in Galicia. Still, they trusted that it would bring positive results for the Ukrainian nation.[23]

These conjectures proved unexpectedly accurate. In 1847 the Austrian authorities pointedly began to back the Ukrainian element in Galicia. An indication of this new attitude, though never formally implemented, was a scheme to divide Galicia into two distinct parts, with seats in Cracow and Lviv. The emperor's decision came on 27 February 1847, and a ministerial rescript of 9 March directed that gubernial announcements for the districts of Eastern Galicia be printed in Ukrainian, using the Cyrillic alphabet. The issue of this administrative division would drag on for several years, gaining impetus in 1848 when the newly formed Holovna Rada Ruska [Supreme Ruthenian Council] endorsed the plan and Denys Zubrytsky wrote a scholarly attempt to legitimate historically the ethnic boundaries between the Ukrainians and Poles in Galicia.[24]

The evolution and shaping of the Ukrainian national movement in Galicia before 1848 stemmed foremost from social, economic and ideological changes that occurred in the Ukrainian community itself, but not exclusively. In large measure, the process also depended on external forces, notably other Slavic national movements. Political considerations—the division of Ukrainian lands between Austria and Russia and the ban in 1822 on the importation of books from the Russian empire—inhibited the natural development of the Ukrainian national movement and caused its leaders to seek aid from without. Polish national endeavours, heightened by the events of 1830, stimulated the formation of a Ukrainian national consciousness. But because the Poles insisted on the reconstruction of their state according to its historical borders before 1772, which implicitly denied the national separateness of the Ukrainians, the Polish movement could not represent a base of support for the Ukrainians. Thus, the activities of the liberal Ukrainian intelligentsia that gathered around the Ruthenian Triad in the 1830s were inherently anti-Polish. Still, until 1846 this was not an intentional and consistent anti-Polish programme, although such sentiments occasionally were expressed. Instead, the Ukrainian spokesmen consciously emphasized their nation's linguistic, cultural and religious distinctiveness, which would ultimately result in the emergence of a Ukrainian national consciousness and a political definition of the Ukrainian nation during the revolutionary events of 1848 and 1849.

The development of the Ukrainian national movement in Galicia basically followed the pattern of the other Slavic nations in the Habsburg monarchy, a point that the Ruthenian Triad, particularly Iakiv Holovatsky, frequently stressed. Among both the Serbs and the Ukrainians, to take the clearest analogy, the clerical hierarchy thwarted the development of a truly national literature rooted in the heritage of the common people. The attitude of the Orthodox metropolitan of Karlovci, Josip Rajačić, toward Vuk Karadžić and his adherents was virtually identical with the policies of Metropolitan Mykhailo Levytsky toward the circle of the Ruthenian Triad. Likewise, both nations were divided between different states and their main political centres were outside the Austrian imperial boundaries: the former was in the Principality of Serbia, and the latter was in Ukraine, a part of the Russian empire. A notable difference in their situations, however, was that the centre of Ukrainian intellectual life was beyond the Austrian frontiers, while the Serbian was located within them.

The social and economic dependence of the Ukrainians in Galicia upon the Polish element and the denial of their rights as a nation also invites a comparison with the situation of the Slovaks in the Hungarian kingdom. This would explain the extraordinary popularity before 1848 of the political writings of Count Leo Thun among Ukrainian intellectuals.

The national awakening of the Ukrainians in Galicia was typical of national and cultural movements in East Central Europe before 1848. Attention was concentrated on moulding a Ukrainian literary language and a literature written in that language, whereas political matters largely were set aside for the future. The events of 1846, however, represented a turning point for the Ukrainians; their programme moved toward political issues. The Ukrainians had come fully to perceive themselves as a nation and consciously intended to guide their own destiny. The year 1848 would bring an even more radical change; the Ukrainian national movement would become a political movement *par excellence*, even with decidedly nationalistic overtones.

Prior to 1848, the rise of a national consciousness affected only a small portion of the Ukrainian community, of which very few were laymen. Ivan Snihursky, the bishop of Przemyśl, had called attention to this situation when he advised Ivan Holovatsky to dedicate the second part of *Vinok* to some eminent Ruthenian official or lawyer, in order to "show the world that not only the clergy are righteous Ruthenians but also secular persons of high rank, who do not deny [their] Ruthenianism but aid in its consolidation and in setting it right."[25] Ultimately, it was the abolition of *robot* that would create the conditions in which a Ukrainian national consciousness could envelop the whole of society. However, this required enormous political work. The politically ignorant and inexperienced Ukrainian peasants responded to all political activity with distrust, fearing an eventual return to feudal conditions. They mistrusted not only the Poles, but even their own leaders. It was among the peasants that the Ukrainian national leaders would face their most demanding challenge and test in 1848.

PART TWO

Between Reaction and Revolution

10. The Dawn

The spring of 1848 was exceptionally early and lovely. It seemed as if nature itself, assuming a brilliant green—the colour of hope—was encouraging the people to assert their rights, to eradicate the Vienna settlement of 1815 and to usher in independent national life. In February reports of revolution had come from Italy and France and, filling the courts of Europe with disquiet, had awakened the hopes of liberals and revolutionaries. "Down with despotism!" and "Long live constitutionalism!" were the most popular slogans in Europe.

The nineteenth of March 1848 was warm and sunny in Lviv. From early morning, crowds of lightly clad people poured into the streets, feverish with excitement. The day before, startling news had arrived from Vienna: Emperor Ferdinand I had dismissed Metternich, authorized the formation of a national guard and promised to establish a constitutional government. Was it possible? Had the absolutist and bureaucratic system really fallen? Would one no longer awaken at night with a pounding heart, afraid of unexpected arrest?

Seeking answers, the crowds instinctively headed toward Ferdinand and Halych squares. At the Hotel George and at the offices of Ignacy Kulczycki's newspaper *Dziennik Môd Paryskich* [Journal of Parisian Fashions], they would know what was happening. News reached there the fastest. The crowds were right. From the balcony of Kulczycki's building the journalists Jan Dobrzański and Józef Dzierzkowski in ringing voices were reading and commenting in turn on an address to the emperor by the inhabitants of Galicia. Dzierzkowski's sonorous bass pronounced the demands: preservation of the Polish nationality; a separate provincial administration; a general amnesty for all political prisoners; the abolition of censorship; the creation of a national guard and national army; general education for all classes; complete civil and political equality; native administrators; a public judiciary; and total abolition of *robot* and all feudal obligations. Citizens (the word had now taken on a different meaning) who supported these demands were urged to sign the address.

From the balcony blank sheets of paper were thrown at the feet of those assembled below. Enthusiasm gripped everyone. They signed, one eyewitness recalled, "on the steps and walls of the building, on one another's backs; children and the unschooled made the sign of the Holy Cross."[1]

In the general excitement not everyone heard the words of protest. Dr. Kyrylo Vinkovsky, a member of the Stavropygian Institute, spoke to the clerics of the Greek Catholic seminary:

> Do not forget that you belong to the Ruthenian branch of the Slavs, distinct from the Polish, and that you have a different nationality, a different history and a different language; in a word, you are Ruthenians. If you still wish to sign this address, do not do so before additional points are made that would safeguard your separate existence, nationality and language.[2]

Furthermore, not everyone grasped the significance of his warning. It was the first public utterance in 1848 by a representative of the Ukrainian nation who was conscious of his distinctiveness. At the same time, unfortunately, it expressed a nascent Ukrainian-Polish antagonism that would cast a dark shadow over the common aspiration for liberty. Only the most perceptive observers could guess that from this moment Polish-Ukrainian unity in Galicia was a thing of the past. But did even they fully comprehend the consequences of this fact? Did they understand that if there was no unity in Galicia, there could be even less chance for it among the peoples of the multinational Austrian monarchy? Would the oppressed nations of the Habsburg state have sufficient strength and will to oppose through concerted action the government's policy of *divide et impera*, and thereby achieve full political, social and national rights? Could they forge and maintain unity in the face of domestic reaction and the danger of outside intervention, which mortally threatened every thrust toward liberation? The fate of the peoples of the Austrian Empire in this memorable year of hope, emotion and illusions depended on their successful resolution of these problems. But let us not anticipate the facts.

The prospects for Ukrainian national life had improved somewhat after Count Franz Stadion, an Austrian bureaucrat, was appointed the new governor of Galicia in 1847. To be sure, the initial impression was not especially agreeable, for he accused the Greek Catholic clergy of demonstrating too little concern for the education of the common people. Stadion also announced that he favoured introducing the Latin alphabet in Ukrainian writings and criticized the conservative instruction given the seminarians, who, he recommended, should read the works of Schiller, Goethe and Voltaire in order to "make them aware of what evil lies in them." The governor's suggestions were opposed by Metropolitan Mykhailo Levytsky, who feared a repetition of the debates over the alphabet and language that had taken place in the 1820s.[3] Levytsky's fears proved to be unfounded. There was no debate because the governor made an about-face and on 3 February 1848 agreed to allow the publication in Cyrillic characters of the Ukrainian journal that had been planned since the fall of 1847 by the Stavropygian Institute. Stadion even encouraged the organizers, but insisted that they meet the expenses of publication.[4] In making concessions to the Ukrainians and offering them the chance to publish a journal, both the provincial authorities and the central government had certain objectives in mind. In the face of an imminent uprising, the authorities were depending on the Ukrainians not to join forces with the Poles or to support the "revolutionary party." These facts were not hidden from the Ukrainians.[5]

The Ukrainian movement was revitalized. For the first time in the history of the modern Ukrainian national movement, laymen became actively involved. In discussing them—"the secretary of the *Gubernium*, [Iakym] Khomynsky; the fiscal adjunct, [Kyrylo] Vinkovsky; the municipal physician, Kerechynsky; the owner of a confectionery, Tovarnytsky; and others"—the Lviv suffragan bishop Hryhorii Iakhymovych noted that they nonetheless "preferred to have a priest as the editor in order to avoid any affront in matters of religion or morals." The church leadership concurred and proposed a priest, Professor Ivan Herovsky.[6] A decision on "the aims and the means to publish" the journal was supposed to be made on 19 February 1848 at the Stavropygian Institute, but no agreement could be reached. Denys Zubrytsky was offered the editorship, but he declined, citing his advanced age and lack of practice in Ukrainian. At the insistent urging of the prelates and Khomynsky, however, Zubrytsky agreed to serve for six months. The clergymen—Iuliian Velychkovsky, Mykhailo Malynovsky, Ivan Zhukovsky and I. Kulchytsky—and the laymen—Ivan Hurkevych, Teodor Leontovych and Ivan Borysykevych—promised to help him.[7]

Actually, other considerations influenced Zubrytsky's decision. Most important was the fact that the new journal, *Halytska Pchola* [Galician bee], was intended to oppose Polish activities. This fact is known from a letter of the Lviv director of police, Leopold von Sacher-Masoch, to the authorities in Vienna, although Zubrytsky himself only mentioned that "the conditions, which I really cannot write about, are so important that I decided to offer my services for the common national benefit, ... since no one else in Lviv dared to undertake this project."[8] Zubrytsky's candidacy was approved by Metropolitan Levytsky, and the Stavropygian Institute officially requested permission to publish the journal, agreeing to assume all costs.[9] On 2 March 1848 a delegation from the institute, headed by Zubrytsky, presented the journal's programme to the governor. Stadion received the delegation warmly, "encouraging them ... to work actively on behalf of the Ruthenian nation." He promised his support but added, "Laziness, however, I will not countenance." His only demand was that the journal be published in "the Ruthenian language."[10]

The planned journal was to maintain a literary character, but also to address itself to questions of agriculture, industry, commerce and "the moral and intellectual development of the Ruthenian nation and language." Above all, it was "to strengthen an unwavering fidelity and love among the people for His Majesty the Emperor and the House of Habsburg." Zubrytsky defined its policy:

> Our *Pchola* will accept all forms of contributions, including prose and verse; only political themes and quarrelsome polemics will be unacceptable. The editors desire neither to stoop to the trivialities of the common people's speech nor to rise to the manner of expression employed in Great Russian literature. We intend to follow the ancient adage of our people to "keep to the mean" [*seredyny derzhysia*]. If we lack certain words or expressions of our own, we shall adopt them from our kindred [Russian] language or from the church dialect. We shall not create new words, because so bountiful a language as our Ruthenian does not generally require invention. The biblical history by Father Venedykt Levytsky, the introduction to the second part of *Vinok*, the ancient documents of the fifteenth century and the Volhynian Chronicle may in particular serve as models. If we follow this path, then we can expect in time to create a pleasant and harmonious literary idiom accessible to all Ruthenians.[11]

The orthography Zubrytsky proposed was a step backward in relation to the principles adopted by the Ruthenian Triad; introducing it could not contribute to the development of a Ukrainian literary language. This would explain why Zubrytsky apprised only Antin Petrushevych of his plans and bypassed Iakiv Holovatsky, whose criticism, in all likelihood, he feared.

Zubrytsky's most immediate task was to attract enough contributors to supply *Pchola* with literary and scholarly works. Realizing that he could not rely solely on the representatives of the church and the

Stavropygian Institute, Zubrytsky turned to Petrushevych and ultimately to Iakiv Holovatsky, hoping that they could interest others in collaborating. The old associates of the Ruthenian Triad were enlivened, especially since they hardly expected such favourable news. *Pchola* could become a platform and centre of Ukrainian intellectual life in Galicia. When Holovatsky recommended working with Antin Liubych-Mohylnytsky, Kyrylo Blonsky, Hryhorii Bodnar and Hryhorii Savchynsky, some observers thought that it would finally be possible to write and publish without fear "of antagonizing... the faint-hearted [Greek Catholic] consistory," which was largely at fault in neglecting the development of the national literature.[12]

The first issue was to have appeared on 1 May 1848, but the March events radically altered the situation. On the spur of the moment, Zubrytsky wrote to Iakiv Holovatsky:

> We received permission (16 March), but it is already too late. The outbreak of the revolution in Vienna on 13 March and the revolutionary demonstrations here on 19, 20 and 21 March have changed the shape of things. Here everything rings Polish—Poland and not Rus'. The Ruthenian seminarians have pinned [Polish] cockades to their clothes and are chasing that good man [Vice-Rector] Ilnytsky from the seminary because he was encouraging them to use Ruthenian and making them study it. The students are armed, guards and patrols are dispatched at night, and a national guard is being formed; in a word, there has simply been nothing like it before. *Robot* has been abolished, and so on. But aside from all this, my dear friend, go on working calmly on *Vinok* because it will be awfully difficult for our poor little bee [*Pchola*] to appear in Lviv.[13]

This chain of events had come unexpectedly, even though reports of the disturbances in Italy and France had already filtered through in February, causing anxiety and uncertainty. The conservative Greek Catholic leadership was concerned lest this revolutionary unrest spread to Galicia and warned its clergy against conducting services commemorating "fallen revolutionaries." The hierarchy believed that the outbreak of war in Italy and the ensuing departure of Austrian troops from Galicia could provide a "good opportunity for renewed stirrings in Galicia, where even now many émigrés are said to be scattered." It also suspected that emissaries were inciting the rural populace because "here and there the peasants are becoming impudent toward the district commissioners."[14] The fluctuating value of the currency added further to the mood of uncertainty. There were even fears that Galicia might be occupied by Russian armies.[15] A sense of unease also gripped the Poles, who were more apprehensive of a recurrence of the events of 1846 than of a general European conflict. Indeed, they even almost hoped for war.[16]

No one, however, expected that the revolutionary events would so quickly envelop the Austrian monarchy, disrupt Vienna and open new possibilities for Galicia. The Poles exploited the opportunity almost at once. Encouraged by reports from Prague and Vienna,[17] they drafted an address to the emperor on 18 March, which held basically to a programme of moderate bourgeois liberalism. It called for Galician autonomy; a guarantee of rights for the Polish nationality; the use of Polish in the schools, courts and government offices; the establishment of a provincial administration; the expansion of the Galician Estates to include representatives of all social classes; fortification of the cities "in order to safeguard peace and order and the safety of persons and property"; trial by jury; selection of officials from among the native population; the organization of a national army; a statute on municipal self-government; abolition of censorship; provisions for a general system of popular education; "complete civil and political equality before the law for all classes and religious denominations of Galicia's inhabitants"; and abolition of *robot* and other feudal obligations, "which the Galician land-owners wish to make a gift of to their former subjects."[18] Undoubtedly this last point was the most significant stipulation in the address. It recognized the necessity of abolishing *robot* and simultaneously liquidating the "servitudes" [the traditional right of the peasant to free use of his master's woods and pastures for fuel and grazing]. Consequently, the rights of the lord in relation to the peasant, as well as the peasant's right to use freely the manorial lands, were to cease.

The address represented a compromise between the liberal intelligentsia and the nobility.[19] It was signed by twelve thousand inhabitants of Lviv without distinction of their class, nationality or religious confession, in an atmosphere of unprecedented enthusiasm.[20] Considering that it was written on behalf of the entire Galician population, the address could have become a platform for action by the Ukrainians as well, although it contained no mention of their national rights. It was understood that civil liberties, equality of religious rites and the abolition of censorship could serve both nationalities in equal measure, but the eradication of feudal conditions in eastern Galicia benefited especially the Ukrainian peasantry, which comprised a considerable majority of the population. The address thus was not as anti-Ukrainian as it might seem at first glance, even though its authors accepted Polish-Ukrainian union as an accomplished fact. They certainly gave no thought to safeguarding the rights of the Ukrainian nation as such; they simply saw no need to do so. The Poles regarded Dr. Kyrylo Vinkovsky's action as treacherous, and he was accused of "wanting to throw a bone of contention among us."[21]

The authors of the address were mindful of Polish national aims. The formulation of the passage regarding *robot* and later Polish propaganda efforts in favour of a voluntary remission of it were intended to demonstrate a "reconciliation with the common people" and to establish neighbourly relations with them, with the idea of guarding against social upheaval.[22] The Poles wanted to obtain national concessions and to protect the future of the country, thereby increasing their strength for an anticipated war with Russia. They hoped that news of the abolition of *robot* in Galicia would provoke an anti-Russian reaction from the Ukrainian peasantry beyond the border.[23]

Polish aspirations were even more emphatically expressed in a second address to Vienna on 6 April, in which the Poles demanded not merely autonomy for Galicia, but also the creation of a separate state entity of Galicia in federation with Austria (on the model of Hungary). The new address expressly indicated "the need for the restoration of a whole and independent Poland" under the leadership of a national committee, which was to deal with the "internal organization of the country according to the national principle" and to draft a constitution and voting regulations for a future national assembly. Other demands included those for a national army, equal civil and political rights regardless of status or religious faith, polonization of the civil administration, courts and school system (with the exception that in the primary schools instruction would be "in the dialect that predominates in the locality"). The national committee was to decide on abolishing *robot* and distributing the rustical, nonmanorial lands to the peasants, but the Galician diet would resolve the issue of servitudes.[24]

Although its demands were characteristically bourgeois-democratic, the Vienna address adhered strictly to the principle of legality: the emperor would not decide, to be sure, on the form of government for Galicia, but he would sanction the national committee. Since the address in fact made some minimal concessions for using Ukrainian "in the schools for the common people," it represented an improvement over the Lviv address of 18 March, even though the Ukrainians' aspirations were not fully satisfied.

Polish agitation against *robot* did not lose sight of the peasants; efforts were made to convince them of "the good intentions of the lords" and to sway them from the Austrian bureaucrats, who were averse to Polish aspirations. It soon became evident, however, that even liberal-minded nobles were not particularly eager to renounce voluntarily their rights over the peasantry. The *szlachta* hid behind a literal reading of the Polish addresses and advised the peasants to fulfill their obligations and await the emperor's ruling, which alone would be legally valid. Nobles were appalled at the idea of losing their feudal privileges without recompense, and they therefore welcomed the subsequent address of 6 April, which promised indemnification.[25] The Galician democrats, on the other hand, urged the immediate abolition of *robot* without regard to the emperor's decision.[26] They tried to reach the Ukrainian peasants through appeals in their own language, which pointed to the Germans as the principal enemies of "the lords and the peasants"—that is, of the Poles and the Ukrainians. The democrats called upon the Ukrainians to preserve and strengthen Polish-Ukrainian unity, which would make possible a determined opposition to the bureaucracy and German reactionism and at the same time alleviate social tensions. To this end, the appeals stressed that only the nobles, not the emperor, could remit *robot* and that to all intents and purposes they had already done it. However, the appeals warned against any repetition of the disturbances of 1846, pointing out that the "Mazurians" (i.e., Polish peasants) had not gained by them.[27]

Governor Stadion, seeing that authority was slipping from his hands, was at first uncertain how to proceed. But once he had recovered from the initial shock, he set out to nip the Polish movement in the bud by launching plans of action both in Galicia and in Vienna. He came out against the Polish address and on 21 March dissolved the "Committee of Forty," which had been formed to organize a national guard. The following day he established his own committee for this purpose, and on 23 March he created the so-called Citizens' Committee (Committee of Twelve), which was to serve as a liaison between the people and the government and present written projects and demands.[28] Stadion's circulars of 20 and 29 March and 5 April made it virtually impossible for the landed nobility to remit *robot* on its own initiative. At the same time, they proved that the authorities were worried that voluntary remissions would stir thc pcasants' hopes and lead to revolutionary disturbances. The governor advised, therefore, that the peasants be made aware that the nobility had no right to remit *robot* and directed that all agitators should be turned over to the district offices. The surviving records indicate that these recommendations were put into practice, a fact that considerably increased Polish fears of a repetition of the "slaughter" of 1846 and therefore slowed the incidence of remissions.[29] In order to forestall spontaneous actions by the peasants and yet avoid pushing them into the revolutionary camp, on 28 March Stadion presented to the government a plan to reduce *robot* that would go into effect on 1 July 1848. But then, on 13 April, he declared himself in favour of totally abolishing *robot*, and two days later he even suggested granting indemnification to the landed nobles.[30]

The protocols of the Austrian Council of Ministers show that Stadion had little faith in the possibility of "maintaining Galicia in its present relationship to the monarchy." Either the monarchy had to abandon Galicia or it had to agree to a "national government under Austrian protection." Stadion preferred the latter solution.[31] The Council of Ministers, however, could not accept this approach, since to turn the administration of Galicia over to the Poles would risk war with Russia. Therefore, the council decided to take advantage of the peasant question, abolish *robot* and offer indemnification, while at the same time retaining the former serfs' rights to servitudes. Succumbing to Stadion's alarming reports, the council immediately sent the appropriate instructions to Lviv.[32]

Stadion meanwhile attempted to organize the conservative elements in the province. He forbade the formation of a national guard in the villages and ordered the Estates Diet to convene on 26 April, but this action had the effect of consolidating the democratic and liberal forces, which established the Rada Narodowa (Polish National Council).[33] In its proclamation "Do właścicieli dóbr" [To the estate owners], the Rada Narodowa appealed for the remission of *robot* on Easter Sunday (23 April) and declared the Estates Diet to be unlawful and invalid.[34] Fully empowered by the government in Vienna, however, Stadion on 22 April had pre-empted the Polish action by announcing the abolition of *robot* with indemnification to become effective on 15 May. The servitude rights were to remain in force. In this manner the Austrian conception, together with all its social and political consequences, triumphed completely.[35]

There was widespread indignation. The Rada Narodowa demanded that Stadion publish an addendum to his circular of 22 April informing the people that "*robot* had been abolished upon the demand of the land-owners themselves," and that he publish the full imperial patent from which the circular had been extracted.[36] The land-owners regarded the governor's way of terminating *robot* as most unscrupulous, and they expected that opposition to the government in Galicia would increase.[37]

The peasants reacted with mixed feelings. They accepted remission gratefully from some nobles,[38] and with reserve from others,[39] but as a rule they believed the government.[40] Stadion paid little heed to objections. He distributed instructions to the district commissioners that "it is not the citizen land-owners, but His Most Gracious Majesty who remits *robot*, and this he does in a continuing expression of his promised favour for their loyalty shown in 1846."[41] Both Stadion and the government in Vienna were convinced that by settling the peasant question they had succeeded in "strengthening the attachment of the rural populace in Galicia to the Austrian government" and diverted the peasantry from the Polish cause.[42]

Despite his failure to dissolve the Rada Narodowa, Stadion effectively split the Polish community. He won over the large land-owners, who abandoned their broader, all-Polish stand and limited their aims to "supporting the interests of only one province." To protect their property, on 3 May they organized the Stowarzyszenie Ziemiańskie (Land-owners' Society). Its very conservative programme did not find much support even in aristocratic circles.[43] At the same time, Stadion had "solved" the Ukrainian issue by uniting the leaders of the Greek Catholic church in support of Austrian plans and by promoting the idea of establishing the Holovna Rada Ruska. These measures became the grounds for the later accusation that Stadion "invented" the Ukrainians.[44]

We should explore as well how Ukrainian society perceived the demands in the Polish addresses. The fragmentary and controversial sources do not permit us to determine conclusively what influence Kyrylo Vinkovsky's reservations had on Ukrainian youth. Whether "the seminarians signed the document without exception" or whether "the seminarians and some Ruthenian lay people were too proud to sign" is now difficult to determine.[45] It would seem that the more knowledgeable individuals did not sign the address, yet even this is uncertain, considering that many Ukrainians in full awareness later joined Polish organizations and favoured Ukrainian-Polish co-operation. Besides, the clear division in the Ukrainian community between the liberals and conservatives considerably complicated relations with the Poles. It became evident that the March incidents caught the Ukrainians unprepared and without a clear-cut plan. In late March, Mykola Vereshchynsky wrote to Iakiv Holovatsky: "All of our people have lost their heads, some from grief, others from overwhelming joy. It seems to me that they all have lost their wits for no reason, because nothing being said is true, and it will not work out as people think."[46]

The former supporters of the Ruthenian Triad were scattered all over Galicia; they were not especially well informed about developments, and they did not have the strength or capability to take control of national affairs. They were pleased, in fact, by the Poles' success and advised against trusting the Germans. Instead of taking action themselves, they considered what advantages the Ukrainian nation might gain from the existing situation.[47] On the other hand, there was considerable unease among the more active Ukrainians, such as Ivan Biretsky, who not only called for work in the national domain, but vigorously defended Ukrainian rights against the stance taken by the Polish journals.[48] Biretsky disagreed with Denys Zubrytsky's view that publishing a Ukrainian journal had now become impossible. Biretsky argued that the abolition of censorship significantly facilitated publication, and that possessing their own newspaper unquestionably was necessary; above all, the Ukrainians needed to launch a broad campaign to raise national consciousness. In point of fact, however, many Ukrainians, even among the intelligentsia, failed to understand the political changes.[49]

After the experiences of the first weeks following the March events, liberal-minded Ukrainian enthusiasts concluded that all Ukrainians henceforth would have to rely on Austria. Biretsky maintained in a letter to Iakiv Holovatsky: "Now, Brother, is the time to write and with sensitive words to awaken the nation from its slumber and to lead our fervent young people on the right path; we cannot permit anyone to rule over us, except the true emperor of Austria, the constitutional king of Galicia."[50] It seems that this concept also appealed to those Ukrainians who supported co-operation with the Poles, and especially to Antin Liubych-Mohylnytsky and Vasyl Podolynsky, who realized that constitutional freedoms could be secured only by presenting a united front against reactionism.

A few Ukrainians reached totally opposite conclusions. Ivan Holovatsky, for example, judged the revolutionary upheaval negatively, as though foreign to the Ukrainian nation. He advised against placing any hopes on the Austrian Slavs, who, "judging by the present young generation, will go the way of the Poles." He would rely on Russia instead. "As to our concerns," he wrote to his brother Iakiv, "I believe our Rus' will not perish. Even a blind man can sense the wholeness of Ruthenia!!—*tutta quanta*, as it's said in Italian—not by means of violent upheaval, as in the west, but humbly and quietly [*smyrenko tykhenko*], as Rus' has evolved to this day."[51]

The conservatives favoured absolute allegiance to and co-operation with the Austrian government. Many liberals thought that national concessions could be obtained through an understanding with Austria, but conservatives did not desire any changes at all. The March events appalled them, and in the general confusion they sought a way out, "in order not to sully their conscience and to avoid compromising the interests of the government and the [Greek Catholic] faith."[52] Stadion's position caught them by surprise. Not only did he permit the Greek Catholic seminarians to sign the Lviv address, but he also instructed the rector to sign it. Only because of pressure from the street and "in order not to exacerbate matters, which His Excellency the governor advised avoiding,"[53] did Bishop Iakhymovych agree to illuminate on 19 and 20 March the seminary and consistory buildings.

The bishop did not, however, make any concessions to the Polish movement. He forbade the seminarians to wear Polish cockades or to join the Academic Legion, since carrying weapons was contrary to their status and seminary regulations. He advised Iuliian Vyslobotsky, the director of the Stavropygian Institute's printing office, to refuse or at least to delay publishing the Polish address in the Ukrainian version prepared by Fathers Mykola Ustyianovych and Tselestyn Skomorovsky. "Its distribution could raise much misunderstanding among the common people, and perhaps such an announcement could be interpreted as already granting them the right to cease carrying out their obligations under *robot*."[54] Iakhymovych had no intention of "betraying the government in any way," though he did wonder how the Ukrainians could avoid a situation in which the Poles proclaimed a republic and then pressed the Ukrainians to join them. The canons of the Greek Catholic consistory posed similar questions. Iakhymovych, realizing that such a step would constitute "an obvious renunciation of allegiance to the government," advised invoking the bans of the consistory and his own prescriptions in such an instance.[55]

Meanwhile the Greek Catholic leadership moved decisively against such Ukrainians as the priests Terletsky, Ustyianovych and Onufrii Krynytsky, who favoured co-operation with the Poles and had taken an active part in the Polish movement. Ustyianovych, a member of the central Polish Rada Narodowa, was ultimately assigned to a monastery. Iakhymovych prided himself "on having thus removed a complication, in which the Basilian Order might easily have been enmeshed." However, the metropolitan was afraid that Ustyianovych might continue to agitate at the monastery and set a bad example for the other clergy.[56] The situation was more difficult with Father Krynytsky, who took part in the Polish delegation to Vienna. The church hierarchy deemed the delegation itself to be illegal, not knowing by whom or in whose name it was sent.[57] Metropolitan Levytsky wrote to Iakhymovych on 30 March: "Earlier no delegation was ever allowed to go to Vienna without the prior permission of His Imperial Majesty. Now, however, the delegation that Canon Krynytsky joined without a word to anyone can be received in Vienna, and in such cases it will not be possible to criticize any of the delegates."[58]

Bishop Iakhymovych's loyalty to the Austrian authorities, his willingness to co-ordinate all his decisions with them, and his solicitation of "orders in respect to future conduct" meant that he was much in Stadion's confidence. For example, the governor received in Iakhymovych's presence a delegation of former prisoners who had been released in line with the demands laid down in the 18 March Polish address.[59] These facts permit the assumption that the Ukrainian address to the emperor on 19 April was to some degree inspired or at least arrived at after consultation with the governor. This is discreetly suggested in Iakhymovych's report to Metropolitan Levytsky:

> I believe that the Father Scholastic will enclose the text of the petition that we signed in the name of the Ruthenians and that was graciously accepted by His Excellency the governor. It will be at least a sign that here, besides the Poles, there are still Ruthenians, ever faithful to the government, who are impelled by a very modest desire to safeguard their freedoms.[60]

The Polish question undoubtedly played a role in the formulation of this address. The disregard of the Ukrainians in the 18 March Polish address and the decidedly unfavourable attitude toward them in the Polish press accelerated Ukrainian activities.[61] Obviously this does not mean that Ukrainian-Polish solidarity would have become an accomplished fact if the rights of the Ukrainian nation had been recognized. There were equally serious differences in the political objectives of the two nations and in the means employed to gain those objectives.

The Ukrainian address, written on 19 April by Father Mykhailo Kuzemsky after consultation with dignitaries of the Greek Catholic consistory, was delivered to the governor the following day by a delegation composed of members of the higher clergy and three laymen, who requested that it be sent to Vienna.[62] The address attests to the Ukrainians' reluctance to propose social or political changes in Galicia. They demanded neither political freedoms nor relief for the lower strata of the Ukrainian peasantry. Instead, they expressed their gratitude for the benefactions bestowed on the Ukrainian nation under Austrian rule, which had contributed to the "universal development of our beloved homeland." This flourishing could have been quicker, but the Ukrainians, "the original inhabitants of these... lands, had not been represented in the Estates Diet or to the government." Starting with historical data, the authors pointed to the splendid past of the principality of Halych, which lost its independence after conquest by the Poles. Although social oppression and religious persecution had led to the denationalization of the Ukrainian nobility ("the natural representative of the nation"), "the kernel of the nation, the Ruthenian common people," had victoriously persevered and preserved "its language and writing, its customs and rituals,... and had passed on the faith of our fathers and our nationality as the only precious thing rescued from all these storms." The authors felt duty-bound to preserve and develop the Ukrainian national character, and they requested that the government extend its protection by permitting instruction in Ukrainian in both primary and higher schools in those Galician districts where a Ukrainian majority prevailed. They also asked that all state acts be published in Ukrainian and that the Ukrainians be assured access to all governmental offices and positions. Clergymen of all denominations were to have equal rights, and seminary training was to be changed so that future priests would be able to teach the people in their mother tongue. The address ended with the vow that the Ukrainian nation would remain faithful to the emperor and the dynasty.[63]

These very modest demands could not satisfy the general Ukrainian community, and the official clerical circles had difficulty justifying their position. Iakhymovych pointed especially to the necessity of calling attention to the presence of the Ukrainian nation in Galicia; he justified the modesty of the demands by the Ukrainians' loyalty to Austria. Stressing this point, *Zoria Halytska* stated that in their address the Ukrainians had requested and had not threatened "with disturbances and bloodshed" like the Poles, because such behaviour "is not ... in the nature of the Ruthenian people." They fully expected, however, to achieve their objectives more quickly by maintaining a mild and loyal demeanour.[64]

This explanation was unsatisfactory to younger, more determined and progressive clerics. Kyrylo Khomynsky's immediate reaction to the petition was "It seems to me, as they say, 'too little, too late [*pozdnym Ivanom*].' Besides, the terms are too general. It contains nothing that is not already a matter of course. As far as I am concerned, it is of little value."[65]

The Poles were saying the same thing. Their council's newspaper *Rada Narodowa* [National council] criticized the narrow-mindedness of the address, which derived from the fact that "it praises past Austrian rule. Thus it fails to raise the matter of political freedoms ... as though its authors were unaware that political freedoms are the only guarantee of nationality."[66]

It seemed to contemporaries, and perhaps rightly, that the address had been prepared in concert with the reactionary Austrian party. That group, which opposed constitutional rule, wanted only to underscore that the Ukrainians had been satisfied with Austrian rule and expected no political changes. They desired, however, safeguards for their language and the Greek Catholic rite. *Rada Narodowa* was correct in emphasizing that control of the Ukrainian national movement by the church hierarchy deprived the movement of political independence, which was a misfortune for the Ukrainian nation. History proved that the higher Greek Catholic clergy had "never come out in defence of the people and the Ruthenian nationality, but stood as an obstacle." The lower clergy, on the other hand, more than once had embraced the common people's cause and waged fierce struggles with the spiritual authorities.[67]

The entire experience of the Ruthenian Triad bore witness to the hierarchy's intransigence. But was it perhaps possible in 1848 to shape Ukrainian forces capable of assuming control of the struggle for political and national rights? After *robot* was abolished, the progressive elements found it difficult to convince the peasants that supporting a revolution was in their interest. It was even more difficult in eastern Galicia, where social and class problems inhibited the formation of Ukrainian consciousness among the peasantry. The Greek Catholic lower clergy understood the problem at the outset and tried to find a way out of the impasse by attempting to overcome the peasants' wait-and-see attitude.

On 27 April 1848, a group of Greek Catholic clergymen from the Berezhany deanery wrote to the metropolitan consistory requesting that it assume leadership of the Ukrainian national movement in Galicia. The authors did not know how to proceed in the existing conditions, because the Polish nobility considered them "disrupters of the peace, destroyers of unity and, in a sense, traitors to the government." They asked, "To what end do we direct our energies, at what point do we come together, and which minds do we obey?" In concluding they stressed the danger of further inactivity. "Thus, like children we scurry under your wings, asking and demanding firm advice as to how we should proceed, how we should act. We do not believe that we should remain silent, since silence could lead us to ruin. We expect that you will fulfill our request quickly, as time is of the essence and we believe that danger threatens us. *Hannibal ante portas. Roma deliberante, Saguntus perit.*" These clergymen failed to impose a course of action on the consistory. Only Father Ippolit Kashubynsky of Lisnyky proposed that "the clergy should endorse the [Galician Polish] petition of 6 April 1848, because the political principles expressed there, ... correspond to the needs and desires of the Ruthenian nation."[68]

It took the pressure of Ukrainian public opinion to compel the church leaders to act. They realized that a spontaneous movement, arising from the masses, could threaten them, especially considering the increasingly discernible pro-Polish (and therefore revolutionary and anti-Austrian) sentiments. These sentiments might undermine the principles that they wanted to impose on their own society, and the Ukrainians would not be satisfied with steps that would merely buttress the pro-governmental party or acknowledge the Polish national councils as illegal and forbid the Ukrainians to join them.[69] The participation by Bishop Iakhymovych and the priests Mykhailo Kuzemsky and Mykhailo Malynovsky in the tasks of the Beirat (Auxiliary Council) created by Stadion in April also was not enough. Basically, the Beirat was an advisory body that in no way impinged on the governor's will or power; it could only convey appeals to "the ministry [in Vienna], which does not hesitate to enact his decisions."[70] For this reason, as Maurycy Kraiński noted in a letter to Prince Leon Sapieha, the Beirat "has garnered ... no popularity; most certainly general opinion condemns it, and daily its members are withdrawing, one after another."[71] For Iakhymovych, however, participation in the Beirat was a form of anti-Polish political demonstration. He wrote to Metropolitan Levytsky,

> I shall not be able ... to give much advice, but I must be there, so that it does not appear that I, too, like certain citizens, became frightened by the terrorism of the Rada Narodowa, which has inspired an anonymous letter to me, summoning me to come to my senses and abandon this council of this godless man [Stadion], for I have little time left."[72]

Circumstances demanded the creation of a Ukrainian organization modelled on the central Rada Narodowa that would lead the Ukrainian national movement, especially since Paragraph 22 in the constitution granted by the emperor on 25 April 1848 permitted the formation of such associations.[73] For the Greek Catholic higher clerics, who conformed strictly to the letter of the law, it was an extremely propitious situation.

11. The Councils

The origins of the Holovna Rada Ruska are unclear. The fragmentary and conflicting nature of the sources has significantly affected later historical interpretations.[1] It is known that in late April 1848 there prevailed among the Galician Ukrainians a common desire to establish their own political organization. The older leaders in particular were dissatisfied with Polish objectives and wary of the reconstruction of the Polish state within its 1772 borders. They looked to Bishop Iakhymovych to "summon the Galician Ruthenians to a national gathering and become our leader."[2]

The discussions about creating the council were kept secret because the Ukrainian spokesmen "waited until they could act lawfully"[3]—that is, until the constitution was proclaimed and they had obtained the governor's permission. Only then did Iakhymovych inform Metropolitan Levytsky about the preparations. In his reply, the metropolitan stated, "I agree to a committee that would watch over our interests, the more so because it will be formed in accord with the intentions of His Excellency the Governor, and this committee will not undertake anything that would be averse to the present government."[4]

The council was convened by a group of Bishop Iakhymovych's supporters, who enjoyed the governor's backing. They secretly summoned Ukrainian representatives to a gathering at six o'clock on 2 May 1848 in the conference room of the Saint George's capitulary. The course of this meeting proved that everything had been determined in advance, including the make-up of the council itself. More than three hundred Ukrainians were present, representing various social groups (except the peasantry). Canon Mykhailo Kuzemsky, the scholastic of the capitulary, presided. Those present honoured the memory of Markiian Shashkevych and indicated that they intended to carry forth his work. Next Father Ivan Zhukovsky spoke of the necessity of moulding a council that would devote itself to enhancing the Ukrainian nationality in Galicia, but a representative from the central Rada Narodowa, a lawyer named Suski about whom no more is known, opposed a separate Ruthenian council. One "Polish" nation, in his view, required but one council. However, his assertion that the Poles wished to resurrect Poland in its old boundaries caused indignation among the Ukrainians, who unanimously affirmed their wish never again to belong to a Polish state. Suski defended his position, citing the necessity of consolidating national forces in order to gain constitutional freedoms and oppose the Germans. He accused the Ukrainians of consciously fanning national dissension. Oleksii Zaklynsky emphatically rejected this charge and declared that the Ukrainians alone should decide the issues pertaining to their own nation.

The Holovna Rada Ruska was constituted in only one hour. It comprised thirty members under the temporary leadership of Father Kuzemsky. They decided to ask Bishop Iakhymovych to become the chairman. The council was to act in the spirit of the Ukrainian petition of 19 April; its specific programme would be announced in a special proclamation. The inaugural session closed with the singing of "Mnohaia lita" [Long life] in honour of Emperor Ferdinand I.[5]

At the next meeting, Iakhymovych presided. He called upon the Ukrainians to remain faithful to the government and the dynasty. Committees were established to draft a proclamation to the Ukrainian nation and to prepare for the publication of a journal in Ukrainian. Ivan Borysykevych presented the council's draft statutes, which were endorsed and on 6 May submitted to the Galician authorities for approval.[6] The statutes provided that a council member must be a Ukrainian born in Galicia and of the Greek Catholic rite—that is, "a person admitting, by his faith [religion], to the Ruthenian nationality"—elected by a two-thirds majority of the members in attendance. Council sessions were to be public, but at the request of at least three members they could be declared closed. Established policies could be changed by consent of three-fourths of the members. The chairman of the council, his two deputies and the two secretaries were chosen for life, and new elections could take place only in the event of death or resignation, although the council could remove a member if he acted contrary to the accepted principles. Article I—concerning the composition of the council—demonstrated the organizers' lack of foresight, because in effect it prohibited members of the Latin rite. In practice, however, this rule was not rigorously enforced.[7]

The Holovna Rada Ruska eventually consisted of sixty-six members, of whom twenty were state officials and one a private clerk; there were also nineteen clergymen, ten students of theology and four of law, five Lviv burghers, one land-owner, three teachers, two writers (Denys Zubrytsky and Ivan Borysykevych) and one journalist (Antin Paventsky).[8] The council's executive committee included Iakhymovych as chairman, Kuzemsky and Borysykevych as deputy chairmen, and Malynovsky and Leontovych as the secretaries. Since the majority of the members belonged to the urban intelligentsia, the council was not representative of the Ukrainian nation in Galicia. The absence of peasants and the fact that the most important officers were ecclesiastics meant that the council, despite its bourgeois-liberal appearance, sympathized from the very beginning with the reactionary elements in the Austrian monarchy. Council meetings occurred each Monday and Friday, at first in the facilities of the Greek Catholic consistory at Saint George's Cathedral, but later in a hall, suitably converted at the council's expense, at the Greek Catholic seminary.[9]

The council's organizational structure developed gradually, in response to the needs and problems with which it had to contend. On Zhukovsky's motion, four committees were initially established: external and internal correspondence, administration, and a court of honour. Later seven departments were created: the central executive, which directed the council's work; correspondence; finance; national affairs; constitutional issues; education; and clerical matters. In addition, Antin Paventsky, Teodor Rozheiovsky and Teodor Leontovych proposed the formation of an informational department to handle private affairs, which became known as the "section for conciliation."[10] This department played an important role in settling agrarian matters. It heard complaints from peasants regarding the annexation of arable lands, meadows, pastures and forests, and it interceded on their behalf on the nobles' estates and in governmental offices. The department prepared appropriate memoranda that were delivered to the governor, the emperor and the Reichstag.

The proclamation to the Ruthenian people was prepared very carefully. After a discussion in closed session, the council decided to publish three thousand copies in Ukrainian, two thousand in Polish and a thousand in German and to include it in the first issue of *Zoria Halytska*.[11] The council realized that the proclamation must underscore the separateness and political self-determination of the Ukrainian nation and lay out the council's goals in representing the nation. The authors started from a national, "all-Ukrainian" standpoint, justifying their views historically.

> We Galician Ruthenians belong to the great Ruthenian nation that speaks one language and counts fifteen million people, two and a half million of whom inhabit the Galician land. This nation was once independent and equal in glory to the most distinguished nations of Europe. It had its own perfected language, its own laws and princes. In a word, it was flourishing, prosperous and powerful.

They went on to describe how the loss of independence had brought about the denationalization of the Ukrainian upper class and a social decline that even the "gentler tutelage" of the Austrian government could not remedy. Only the April constitution had enabled the Ukrainian community to revive. "Arise, brothers!" the proclamation now ardently appealed.

> Rise from your long sleep. It is time! Arise! But not to quarrels and disharmony. Let us stand together and elevate our nationality, safeguard our liberties. Let us take advantage of this opportunity, [but] not to cover ourselves with shame before the world or bring down upon ourselves the complaints of future generations. Let us behave toward other nations with love and harmony! Let us be what we are capable of and what we should be: let us be a nation!

On the one hand, the proclamation called for steadfast fidelity to the constitutional emperor and king, Ferdinand I, in the conviction that "under Austria's mighty protection our rights and our nationality can develop and grow in strength." But on the other hand, in order not to provoke the Poles, it urged the Ukrainians, while still defending their own nationality, not to nurture any hatred toward the Poles, but to live with them "as sincere neighbours on the same land, in harmony and unity." The Holovna Rada Ruska took upon itself the tasks of preserving the Greek Catholic faith and rite; achieving rights for the Greek Catholic church equal to those of the other churches; strengthening the Ukrainian nationality by perfecting its language and introducing it in the schools and administrative offices through the publication of journals and books; maintaining contacts with scholars of other Slavic countries; and defending constitutional rights—that is, fostering concern for Ukrainians needs and striving to improve the "national well-being along the constitutional path."[12]

The proclamation demonstrated that the Ukrainian leaders still had not moved beyond the postulates of their 19 April address, which, except for the language issue, had not improved the lot of the Ukrainian peasantry. The future would prove that the Holovna Rada Ruska would have to move far beyond the programme outlined in the proclamation.

From the moment the council was established, however, the Ukrainians organized rapidly. In a pronouncement on 10 May, the council appealed to local Ukrainian leaders "to assemble in smaller councils," and its proclamation of 18 May 1848 contained concrete organizational stipulations. The Holovna Rada Ruska reasoned that "only with the aid of the entire Galician nation" could its intended objectives be realized, since the Ukrainian peasants "will still not be able to organize themselves to the extent that the constitutional law and our common interest demand." Therefore, it proposed establishing local councils in every Greek Catholic deanery in whose districts the majority of the inhabitants were Ukrainian. Each council should be composed of thirty members drawn from all social groups, including "three rural representatives possessing the peasants' backing, three burghers, three lesser noblemen who rent [the land they work] (if such nobles can be found) and three cantors, which comes to twelve members. To this number eighteen more are to be added from among our learned men, who have earned the confidence of the Ruthenian nation. But there should not be more than ten clergymen among them." The councils thus chosen were to act in accordance with the Holovna Rada's statutes, "with modifications that local needs may demand." The structure of the deanery councils was to be similar to that of the Holovna Rada; individual departments were to prepare issues in their area of competence and present them to the council for discussion. There are a little or no data on whether all the local councils established the departments of school affairs, indigence, rural economy, artisans and burghers, nationality and correspondence proposed in the proclamation. This last department, however, played a special role, "because to preserve unison in our actions it is absolutely essential to be in agreement with us [the Holovna Rada] in every important matter." To achieve this aim each council chose a correspondent in the Holovna Rada; in special circumstances, a local council could delegate its own representative to the Holovna Rada, where he was obliged to present the position of his own organization.

In addition to providing for the local councils, the proclamation of 18 May placed special emphasis on promoting the education of the common people:

> Do not fret over what you will deliberate. Because the Ruthenian has so many needs, he does not know where to begin. If you concern yourselves just with the enlightenment and teaching of our people in the villages and consider how to establish schools in every parish and find teachers and the means of supporting them, these measures will be so great a service that you will be rewarded with the gratitude of our grandsons.

The local councils were to function in accordance with existing legal regulations and the constitution. They were also supposed to explain to the common people the blessings accruing from the constitution and to teach them devotion and sacrifice for the good of the Ukrainian community. "It is high time that we stop being children and start to make do without outside tutelage and decide our needs by ourselves.... For if all nations must now care for themselves, who will concern himself with our fate? Who could care more honestly than we Ruthenians ourselves?"[13]

The proclamation clearly reveals the motivations impelling the Holovna Rada during the first phase of its existence. The leadership wished both to emancipate the Ukrainian national movement from Polish influences and to subordinate it to the Greek Catholic church and thereby assure the clergy's influence over the activities of the local councils. (Priests and cantors, it will be recalled, were to constitute approximately 43 per cent of the members of the deanery councils.) The first matter raised particular misgivings. It soon became apparent that the parochial clergy disapproved of the wait-and-see tactic and was eager to undertake concrete projects. Some Ukrainians, such as the clergy of the Berezhany deanery, called for the church leaders to direct the movement, but others, who were more venturesome, endorsed the Polish cause and took an active part in it. Those Ukrainian clergymen justified their stance by arguing that the two nationalities had to co-operate to defend the liberties already gained. Nevertheless, they insisted on safeguards for Ukrainian national rights within the scope of the 19 April address.[14] It is known that for a time Greek Catholic clergymen participated in virtually every Polish district council, even though the sources that have been preserved do not always confirm this fact.[15] This fairly common situation did not reflect well on the Ukrainian movement in Galicia, especially since the well-known Galician Ukrainians, Iakiv Holovatsky, Antin Liubych-Mohylnytsky and Ivan Vahylevych, who enjoyed the general respect of the Ukrainian intelligentsia, favoured co-operation with the Poles.[16]

These "defections" caused unease not only in the church hierarchy, but also in the Austrian bureaucracy that supported it. At the governor's request, Iakhymovych issued a directive on 12 May (curiously, in German) in the name of the consistory, which forbade the Greek Catholic clergy to join Polish national councils. The bishop explained this ban by pointing to the clergy's duty to fulfill its pastoral responsibilities and remain absolutely faithful to the government.[17] His directive greatly distressed the liberal Ukrainian clergymen, who were compelled by ecclesiastical discipline to withdraw from the Polish organizations and to account for their actions. Some clergymen in Berezhany indicated very clearly that they wished to remain in their district's Polish council because it was legal and constitutionally sanctioned and because it kept strictly to the laws and had not acted against the government, the emperor or the Greek Catholic faith. Their Polish council's attitude toward the Ukrainians was friendly, and it had not sought to restrain the Ukrainians in any way. It desired unity only on the basis of equality. The representatives of the clergy in Berezhany asked the consistory to respect their will.[18]

On the other hand, the more anti-Polish clergymen in Berezhany were dissatisfied with their colleagues' position. Even though the Polish council had not opposed the Ukrainian nationality and the Greek Catholic rite, these men felt that its Ukrainian members "should not only know the Ruthenian language and the [Greek Catholic] church ritual, but also embrace them." Yet they were conferring in Polish and were concerned exclusively with Polish affairs and needs.[19] The result was that all of the Greek Catholic clergy in Berezhany decided to withdraw from the Polish council.[20]

More clear-cut cases of opposition also occurred. The clergy of the Husiatyn deanery, a significant number of whom belonged to the Polish council in Zalishchyky, sent a letter to the central Polish council's newspaper, *Rada Narodowa*:

> If the Most Reverend [Greek Catholic] Consistory understands the Ruthenian question as the awakening and preservation of [the Ukrainian] nationality, we openly declare that we will support and defend such a cause by every conceivable means, because we love our nationality. But if by the national question . . . the political life and material welfare of the Ruthenian nation are understood, then we believe, on the basis of unity and brotherhood, that these objectives can be attained only together with, and by our embracing the aspirations of, the Polish nationality. Where does our isolation lead, when alongside us there is another nationality, further evolved than our own, which publicly does not . . . pose any obstacles to the development of our spiritual and material strengths? Therefore, side by side we should preserve our nationalities and together defend the freedoms that have been gained.

The Husiatyn clergymen "perceived the salvation of the nation in the combined forces of all of Galicia" and regarded the Poles not only as neighbours, but as brothers. They were intent on pursuing the union of all the Polish and Ukrainian national councils "in one camp." However, they criticized the Ukrainians in the government-sponsored Beirat for "not raising one voice" in defence of the Ukrainian nationality when some members spoke out against it during the sessions.[21]

The Greek Catholic consistory's attitude toward the dissident clergymen and seminarians who supported co-operation with the Poles also disturbed the former supporters of the Ruthenian Triad. Iosafat Kobrynsky wrote to Iakiv Holovatsky on this issue:

> I enclose Father Kuzemsky's letter. Read it and pass it among the reverend fathers. Let them know of what "Saint George's hill" smacks. Iakhymovych has stated that he will know who should be ordained. The deans also have secret instructions to watch those who side with the *Liakhy* and not to admit them until the Holovna Rada in Lviv has entrenched itself (that is, until the local councils are formed). This is the way the world turns: a few years ago they would not have ordained someone because of his Ruthenianism, and now because of anti-Ruthenianism.[22]

In certain districts of Eastern Galicia the Greek Catholic clergy's participation in the Polish councils catalyzed the decidedly pro-Austrian and anti-Polish forces of reaction. In Stanyslaviv a group of officials of Polish and German extraction joined the clergymen Hryhorii Shashkevych and Petro Shankovsky to create, on 14 May, the so-called Austro-Constitutional Association (commonly called the Stanyslaviv Beirat). This body decried the activities of the Polish national council in Stanyslaviv, "which was not and is not lawfully empowered to give any authority to anyone," because its principles were contrary to the constitution and the will of "the majority of the people in the Stanyslaviv district." The presence of some clerics in the Polish council—clerics who were "not authorized by their colleagues, estate or office"—is not evidence that "the entire Ruthenian clergy of the Stanyslaviv district is joining *in corpore* this [Polish] society or professing its avowed political principles." The Austro-Constitutional Association insisted that it was not a Ruthenian or German committee; rather, the association was an organ "based on the constitution and inner conviction, having as its purpose to combat any usurpations, limitations on the expression of public opinion or imposition of unwelcome proxies."[23]

In answer to the Holovna Rada's proclamations of 10 and 18 May, a movement to create Ukrainian councils at deanery, district and village levels was launched throughout Eastern Galicia. The organization of these councils, which lasted most of 1848, followed a common pattern. The Greek Catholic deans issued special appeals and notices regarding the times and places for the meetings; on the specified day representatives drawn from the various strata of Ukrainian society convened. After listening to an address by a clergyman on the need to establish a council, goals and guiding principles, they proceeded to elections. The council members then selected a chairman, deputies, secretaries and a treasurer. Sometimes only the clergy participated at an initial meeting and selected their representatives to the council. Then, at the next session with broader social representation, the deanery-level council was chosen.[24] Special founding committees were formed in only a few cases. For example, this occurred in Stanyslaviv, where a "committee of four," established at the initiative of Father Petro Shankovsky, organized the inaugural ceremonies.[25] However, it is not known whether this preparatory group actually carried out any functions, because on 16 May several representatives of the Ukrainian community, composed of both clergymen and lay persons, issued a special programme for a national rally, which they scheduled for 30 May 1848. The group included members of the Stanyslaviv Beirat, notably Shankovsky and Hryhorii Shashkevych. However, the liberals Stepan Ilnytsky, Ievstakhii Prokopchyts and Mykhailo Kozanovych dominated the gathering. Ukrainians from the entire Stanyslaviv district were invited to participate. The stated objectives of the rally were to select a Ukrainian council in Stanyslaviv, to underscore the distinctiveness of the Ukrainian nationality and to demonstrate the strength, cohesiveness and solidarity of the Ukrainian community.[26]

Vasyl Ilnytsky successfully captured the atmosphere:

> On the square in front of what is now the court house (the old Trinitarian Church) and the military hospital, an altar was raised at which . . . a priest accompanied by two other clergymen said the Mass. It was a beautiful day. . . . A countless throng of Ruthenians filled the spacious square and nearby streets. Church and national banners (a golden lion on a field of celestial blue) protruded upward among the assembled people, and an echo resounded all around. Lofty national feelings, unbeknownst for centuries to the downtrodden Ruthenian, radiated forth . . . from the genial Ruthenian breast and brought a moment of joy and happiness. . . . In a clear, soaring and strong voice . . . the priest sang: "Blessed is the kingdom," and then "Christ has risen!" . . . It seemed that these words portended the resurrection of the nation.[27]

In his sermon Father Shashkevych attempted to substantiate historically the need for the independent development of the Ukrainian nation in an alliance with Austria.[28] Ilnytsky recalled that the sermon made a significant impression.

> Just when Shashkevych intoned, among other words, "And the Ruthenian lion shakes its golden mane with displeasure at these injustices," . . . a light wind rose and before everyone's eyes the Ruthenian banner unfurled . . . , and the golden lion shone in all its beauty. . . . The people reacted in a single voice of amazement, as though a signal had been given, and the soldiers who stood in rows behind the people—supposedly to add splendour to the

> ceremonies, but actually to provide protection from the exasperated Poles—fired a salvo.[29]

After the service, the clergy, the lay intelligentsia and the representatives of the rural communities assembled at the Fraenkel building, where a Ukrainian council was formally established, but even this did not occur uneventfully. Antin Liubych-Mohylnytsky, who urged moderation and political co-operation with the Poles, was not allowed to finish his speech. On the other hand, Shankovsky's anti-Polish remarks (Ilnytsky called him a black-and-yellow zealot)* caused indignation among those Poles who had also gathered in the hall. Shankovsky then appealed to the peasants for help, but Shashkevych prevented bloodshed by quieting the crowd.[30]

Similar gatherings were held in Drohobych on 22 May and in Zhovkva on 7 June. In certain localities in Eastern Galicia, Ukrainian district councils were chosen at popular rallies. Such was the case in Chortkiv on 4 July and in Stryi on 3 August, where Iakiv Holovatsky, Mykola Ustyianovych and Luka Dankevych figured prominently.[31] A characteristic trait of all of these assemblies was their pro-Austrian orientation, due primarily to the key role of the Greek Catholic clergy. Ordinarily, this attitude was directly tied to an anti-Polish stance. Moreover, one may risk the supposition that the Ukrainian nation's pursuit of emancipation from Polish influences was the main cause of its leaders' Austrophile tendencies. Addressing the members of the Ruthenian Council in Hlyniany (which was also called the Univ council), Rudolf Mokh stated that history showed that Ukrainians always had respected their rulers and had not disgraced themselves with treachery. His conclusion then followed logically:

> Are we to be such vile creatures and betray our benevolent monarch Ferdinand II [*sic*], under whose rule millions of our brothers were freed from the yoke and from bondage? A Ruthenian ought to be grateful and loyal, and the world will see that our nation has nothing precious that it would not offer gladly to our most merciful and benign father and emperor Ferdinand. We offer to him our property and our lives to the last drop of our blood.[32]

That his sentiments were widespread is evidenced by the fact that virtually every meeting of the Ukrainian national councils and every ceremonious occasion closed with the singing of the Austrian state anthem or the song "Mnohaia lita" (May he live many years!) in honour of the emperor.

---

* Black and yellow (*Schwarz-gelb*) were the colours of the Habsburg emblem.

Ultimately fifty deanery councils were established in Galicia: at Berezhany, Bibrka, Bircza, Bohorodchany, Bolekhiv, Brody, Buchach, Chernivtsi (in Bukovyna), Chortkiv, Drohobych, Dynów, Halych, Hlyniany, Horodok, Jarosław, Jaśliska, Kalush, Khodoriv, Kholoiv, Kolomyia, Komarno, Kosiv, Łabowa, Lubaczów, Mokriany, Naraiv, Olesko, Perehinsko, Pidbuzh, Pidhaitsi, Przemyśl, Rohatyn, Rozdil, Sambir, Sanok, Skalat, Sniatyn, Stanyslaviv, Stryi, Terebovlia, Ternopil, Turka, Ustia Zelene, Zaliztsi, Zatwarnica, Zbarazh, Zboriv, Zhovkva, Zhuravno and Zolochiv. In July, the district Ruthenian councils began to organize. There were eventually thirteen of them: Berezhany, Chernivtsi, Chortkiv, Hlyniany, Kolomyia, Przemyśl, Sambir, Sanok, Stanyslaviv, Stryi, Ternopil, Zhovkva and Zolochiv.[33]

The district Ruthenian council in Berezhany was formed somewhat unconventionally. The chairman of the deanery council in Berezhany, Sylvester Lezhohubsky, convened a conference of delegates from the deanery councils in the area to form a district council. According to his plan, each deanery council was to delegate its chairman and three members (one of whom was to act as the spokesman) as representatives to the district council, which would be presided over alternately by the chairmen of the various deanery councils. The secretary of the Ruthenian council of the Berezhany deanery would retain that position in the district council, which would meet once a month. On 2 August, at its first session, the statutes of the district Ruthenian council in Berezhany were confirmed.[34]

Representatives from the Holovna Rada Ruska frequently presented its position on political matters at the founding meetings of the district councils. The chancellor of the metropolitan curia, Iuliian Velychkovsky, represented the Holovna Rada in Stryi, and Vice-Chairman Ivan Borysykevych was present in Chortkiv. The latter spoke of the constitution, the freedoms emanating from it and the meaning of the constitution for the Ukrainian nation. At the same time, he urged "fidelity to the emperor, the necessity of providing recruits, the payment of taxes and obedience to the authorities."[35]

The final phase in establishing the Ukrainian councils was to have been the formation of the village councils, which were planned in the autumn of 1848, after the Viennese parliament had approved the laws granting land to the peasants and the patent of 7 September was issued. This plan was linked to the reorganization of the then existing system of local self-government, but precise details of it are not known. Ivan Borysykevych wrote, "It would be good to prepare and publish in *Zoria* the proclamations to the people that were resolved by our council for establishing village councils, because the continued organization of the Ruthenian councils will be built on this foundation."[36] His advice was not followed before the events of November 1848 ultimately made the Ukrainian village councils impossible.

Thus, the Holovna Rada Ruska intended that a four-tiered council system be established in all of Eastern Galicia, as well as in other areas of the province inhabited by a Ukrainian population. Unquestionably the deanery councils played the most important role in this scheme, particularly because of their close contact with the populace, and in fact they did become spokesmen for the lowest strata of society. Some of them, such as the council in Halych, were composed not only of Ukrainians, but also of Poles and Jews, and exercised considerable authority among the latter two peoples. The Halych council was the only one whose chairman, Kłosoń, was a priest of the Latin rite and whose secretary, Krasuski, was an official of the local magistrate. The membership of the council clearly influenced its objectives; it assumed that equal rights for all nationalities in Galicia were essential, and, therefore, the official language of administration must be the language of the majority. In Halych that language ought to have been Ukrainian. Unfortunately, the Holovna Rada did not accept the principles of the Halych council, because they contravened the guidelines.[37]

Nevertheless, despite mandates regulating the composition of deanery councils, in only a few cases did the number of members equal thirty; instead, the figures ranged from a dozen or so to several score, and in rare cases even exceeded one hundred. In Brody, for example, there were 106 members; in Stanyslaviv, there were 90 clergymen and 450 members from other social groups, including peasants. The social composition of the affiliated Ukrainian councils was quite varied. The leading elements ordinarily consisted of clergymen, which is understandable because of the lack of a secular intelligentsia in the Ukrainian community. However, this was not always the case, for to cite one instance, in the Turka deanery Ruthenian council, Stepan Tsybuliak, the *viit* (mayor) of Sianky, was chosen chairman at the general insistence of the local peasantry.[38]

It appears that the participation in the councils by villagers and the lower strata of urban dwellers depended in large degree on how much confidence they had in the Ukrainian parochial clergy. Adequately publicized rallies, coupled with nationally oriented celebrations, patriotic speech making and campaigning among the peasants enabled many councils to boast a very diversified membership. The deanery Ruthenian council in Berezhany consisted of twenty-nine burghers, ten peasants, three governmental officials and two teachers, besides the clergy. The Ternopil council included twelve clergymen, nine members of the lay intelligentsia, thirteen burghers (including artisans), three cantors and thirty-three peasants. The Kalush council consisted of thirteen clergymen, five burghers, four impoverished nobles (who were in fact reduced to the status of peasants), twenty peasants, three cantors and two teachers. The Zhovkva council had forty-four clergymen, twenty-four peasants, three burghers and one "private official."[39]

Where the peasants were reluctant to participate, as for example in Sambir, Kolomyia and Przemyśl, the councils summoned them to attend. In a special proclamation, the Hlyniany council called upon the Ukrainians to support the "holy Ruthenian cause" and encouraged peasants to join in its work. The Kolomyia council, which consisted almost entirely of clergymen, issued a similar appeal.[40] The fragmentary sources do not permit us to ascertain the number of peasants who were actually members of the Ukrainian councils. There were certainly several hundred. It is known that in the festivities celebrating the formation of the councils, thousands of Ukrainians participated, among whom the peasants were certainly the most numerous group. This was particularly true in Stanyslaviv, Chortkiv and Stryi. It can be said with full certainty that the councils, as the genuine representatives of Ukrainian society, were destined to play an enormous role in the political circumstances of the period. Let us therefore consider what expectations contemporaries had for the councils.

First, there was no one view in the Ukrainian community as to the councils' immediate tasks. This was good to the extent that they did not function according to a superimposed scheme. Their activities were shaped by local conditions, but the closely knit ties between the local councils and the Holovna Rada permitted mutual interaction and compelled the Holovna Rada to address itself to basic problems. At the same time, the local councils had to act within a strictly legal framework. However, the Greek Catholic church leaders proposed one set of objectives for the councils, and the liberals another, while the Ukrainian peasants held a variety of opinions of the councils' role, and governmental officials intended them to serve yet other, markedly different purposes. But to some degree all of these groups contributed to shaping the councils' character, as did external pressures, among which Polish attitudes and the governmental policies took on special significance.

The position of the higher Greek Catholic clergy was reflected principally in the proclamation of 10 May and in later appeals. They confined council activities within strictly legal bounds—that is, according to the constitution and in step with the monarchy. When Bishop Iakhymovych told Metropolitan Levytsky about the Holovna

Rada, he outlined its aims:

> The Ruthenian committee has been constituted. Its chief task will be to educate the Ruthenian people through the publication of journals, to provide them with useful information, correct errors, refute biases against us, indicate needs, etc., while always striving to reinforce goodwill toward the government. Consequently, we shall stay apart from anything that could jeopardize the peace.[41]

This attitude entirely pleased the Austrian government, which was inclined to see the establishment of the Holovna Rada as the fulfillment of its nationalities policy. The protocols of the Austrian Council of Ministers indicate that Governor Stadion reassured the government with reports that the Ukrainian association (*ein ruthenisher Verein*) would oppose the Polish Rada Narodowa. Similarly, he emphasized that the Ukrainian council would not pursue union with Russia. Stadion assured Vienna that he intended to use the Holovna Rada to support the government's determination to paralyze the Poles' programme, and he therefore requested a subsidy to promote the council's activities and, especially, to use the press against the Poles.[42]

The establishment of the Holovna Rada and the Stowarzyszenie Ziemiańskie, together with Stadion's suggestions, considerably eased the government's anxiety. Minister President Franz Pillersdorf applauded the governor's shrewdness and recommended that he maintain close ties with the two organizations, and with the Holovna Rada Ruska in particular.[43] The church leaders and the Austrian government were pursuing the same ends, and it seemed that these goals could be achieved in concert.[44] Stadion himself adhered closely to these principles, but after he left Galicia, the Polish vice-governor, Agenor Gołuchowski, forbade officials to join the councils. The Ruthenian council of the Berezhany deanery protested and asked the Galician authorities to reverse his decision. It argued that the success of the Ukrainian councils and the fulfillment of the national goals by the "Austro-Ruthenian" people were impossible without the participation of governmental officials, who comprised the only lay Ukrainian intelligentsia.[45]

The Ukrainian liberals, both those directly connected with the Holovna Rada and the former associates of the Ruthenian Triad, although they did not question in principle the pro-governmental course, did interpret the councils' tasks somewhat differently. Ivan Borysykevych attempted to link them with the universal aspirations of man and thus to avoid extreme reactionism.[46] Others, who were familiar with the political intricacies of the church leadership and its adverse influence on the Holovna Rada, thought that the nation's general aims should not be subordinated to private interests or personal grudges, because "our own well-understood interest counsels us not to multiply the number of our enemies close at hand, when we have other, more harmful ones who would like to build castles in the air out of all our constitutional freedoms, so that what was so beautifully promised may be left on paper forever."[47]

One should recall, however, that the liberalism of the young Ukrainian spokesmen before 1848 had led them to embrace Austro-Slavism. During the revolution of 1848, Austro-Slavism became a platform for co-operation between liberals and conservatives in the Holovna Rada Ruska and the local Ukrainian councils; indeed, it was mentioned in virtually every speech. Neither Iakiv Holovatsky and Ivan Borysykevych in Chortkiv, nor Rudolf Mokh in Hlyniany, nor Iosyf Krushynsky in Zhovkva avoided the subject. Krushynsky said, most concisely: "Only in close union with Austria can we raise up our nationality and show the world... that we are capable of constitutional life."[48] The liberals wanted to serve their nation without expecting personal advantage. The secretary of the Holovna Rada, Teodor Leontovych, stressed that the councils should serve the people; council members Ivan Vitoshynsky, A. Radykevych and Ivan Hushalevych, when they departed on holiday, pledged themselves to defend and support the Ukrainian cause wherever they might be.[49] Ivan Krynytsky, when he appealed to the Greek Catholic clergy to become involved with the purposes of the Holovna Rada and "to submit suitable projects to it,"[50] probably meant that the clerics should take an interest in the needs of their local Ukrainian communities.

It seems that the leaders of the Holovna Rada did not expect that its programme would have to be substantially expanded and modified. Changes occurred primarily because the Ukrainian peasants began to regard the national councils as fully competent to take care of their social and economic interests, and they deluged them with a multitude of complaints, grievances and petitions in matters of land ownership. The councils thus soon became intermediaries between the Ukrainian common people and the Austrian authorities. To the extent that they could, the councils tried to use these opportunities for social and political work. However, in only a single case, in the statute of the district Ruthenian council in Zhovkva, was it officially noted that one of the council's activities was to hear the demands of town-dwellers (both Ukrainian and Jewish) and villagers and to see to it that the peasants retained their rights of servitudes.[51]

As a rule, the councils tried to consolidate the Ukrainian community. In a speech before the district Ruthenian council in Przemyśl, Iosyf Lozynsky stressed that constitutional existence required the participation of the whole nation, which ought to manage "its own needs." Otherwise, "some others will appear to take care of us, but certainly not according to our ideas and not for our good." Furthermore, he believed that the councils were the essence of the nation's constitutional life. As democratic organizations, they achieved the principle of equally shared public life:

> Here a lord and a farmer who had been the lord's subject sit together. Here at one table there is room for clergy and lay persons, for learned and simple people, for officials and servants, for the wealthy and the poor. All take counsel together, encircled by a ring of people who hang on every word. This assembly joins . . . those who once stood far apart. Here the haughtiness of the unapproachable aristocrats evaporates, together with that submissiveness demeaning for a man—the hat-in-hand manner from afar and boot-licking near the lords. By means of the national councils, the division between upper and lower is levelled and smoothed. Everyone here, although clothed differently, genuinely and sincerely fraternizes. Here all the estates melt away and flow as into one mass, because all have a single matter in mind: the commonweal of the nation.[52]

Putting aside this rather idyllic portrait of the councils, we must point out that a significant number of Ukrainian peasants did in fact congregate at the open meetings. They also participated at the sessions of the Holovna Rada, where they not only were attentive to the discussions, but also spoke out on issues of vital concern to them.[53]

In effect, the councils were schools for the peasantry. Contemporaries correctly pointed out that it would have been impossible to achieve a national consensus on basic questions or a constitutional life for the Ukrainians without councils. Thanks to the councils, "the nation is becoming conscious of itself and developing a sense of its freedom and dignity." The liberals likewise believed that the councils were helping them regain the confidence of the people, "who are being deceived about their needs." Through their well-meaning activities and concern for the peasants' interests, the liberals expected to acquire many seats in the future Galician diet.[54] However, in Rudolf Mokh's opinion, in order to secure and keep this confidence the councils would have to be transformed into the genuine "heart and pulse of our Ruthenian life,"[55] which was possible only if they waged a determined struggle to preserve the peasants' rights to the lands they had tilled and to maintain the servitude rights in their existing form. Hence, the liberal stance was that "one should not say: *robot* is no more, therefore nothing further is required. Rather, our needs are still great."[56] By this, they meant that the Ukrainians could not be satisfied either with the rights already gained or with the land enfranchisement carried out by the government. Instead, they had to fight for complete national, social and political equality.

The activities of the Ukrainian councils were multifaceted. In evaluating them one should remember that throughout their existence, there was a close relationship between the Holovna Rada and its affiliates, which functioned according to instructions issued in Lviv. Appointment of the correspondents who were members of the Holovna Rada and looked after the deanery councils assured unified action. The Holovna Rada's proclamation no. 218 of July 1848 obliged each lesser council to inform it of all events that took place in its assigned domain as well as of its own activities.[57] This proclamation made a principle of the then current practice of informing the Holovna Rada of the time and place of the formation of local councils, their composition, the circumstances and substance of their inaugural sessions and the national symbols they had adopted. The local councils also reported the kind of impression they had made on the Ukrainians in their areas.[58]

Strict centralization and hierarchical subordination, however, did not preclude the possibility of independent local action, especially in the matters of schooling and social aid—in a word, affairs that did not require a decision by Galician or Viennese authorities. In the latter instances the Holovna Rada did intervene, since it was the only means by which to represent the Ukrainian national movement to the outside world. The source materials that have been preserved lack information about whether local councils ever undertook actions that were not consonant with the positions of the Holovna Rada. Therefore, if I call the local councils more radical than the Holovna Rada, one should remember the reservations cited here. Only with them in mind can we agree with the view that "by involving the broad popular masses in energetic social action and by representing their basic interests, the local councils impelled the Holovna Rada to take more active measures and to democratize its programme."[59]

The councils were concerned with the full scope of the socio-political and national life of the Ukrainians, ranging from the most minor matters, such as arranging living accommodations for the duration of the sessions, to efforts to partition Galicia.[60] At the outset, the greatest attention was devoted to organizational work, which included both internal and public propaganda and informational activities. During this period virtually every proclamation and pronouncement of the Holovna Rada explained the rationale and objectives of its policies and contained an appeal for support. They also indicated how those policies would be implemented. The council's message of 1 June reads:

> Brother Ruthenians! In the proclamation of 10 May we informed everyone of our meeting and announced that our intention and earnest endeavour will be to support and protect by all legal means the Ruthenian nationality and the well-being of all Ruthenians on Galician soil. In order to realize this intention we ought to print and distribute all kinds of writings, correspond with the numerous and constantly growing affiliated councils, submit various proposals and requests to high offices, and see to it that necessary information appears not only in our newspapers here at home, but also in foreign newspapers.[61]

Zoria Halytska was the first Ukrainian political newspaper, and it became an important instrument in the cultural and political rebirth of the Ukrainian nation. The first issue appeared on 15 May 1848, and thereafter it appeared once a week (in 1849 twice weekly) on Tuesdays, in a four- to six-page smallish format. Since it was the organ of the Holovna Rada Ruska, it carried notices of the council's activities, published certain of its proclamations, instructions and admonitions and explained its principles and the government's policies. It reported on events in the Austrian monarchy and in the world at large, with special attention to the Slavic nations, except Russia. It included information about economic matters, in particular what might be useful in agriculture. In this way the newspaper attempted to become popular with the Ukrainian peasants. Ukrainian men of letters found an opportunity to publish their works in its columns.

It would be a mistake to underestimate the influence of *Zoria Halytska* on the masses. Thanks to the priests and cantors who were familiar with it, its contents reached virtually every corner of Eastern Galicia. It was read and commented on in taverns, at council meetings and not infrequently from pulpits. This latter agitation caused fierce attacks against the Greek Catholic clergy in the Polish press, but these pulpit discussions were necessary since the peasants, who were generally illiterate, seldom subscribed to it. Instead the Greek Catholic deaneries received copies. On Stadion's initiative the Galician authorities distributed at their own expense five hundred copies of *Zoria Halytska* to the poorest Ukrainian village communities. This was no small number, considering that a half-year subscription cost one gulden and fifteen kreuzers in Lviv; a mail subscription to the provinces cost thirty kreuzers more. *Zoria Halytska* had a printing of four thousand copies, of which twenty-one hundred were distributed in the Lviv diocese, twelve hundred in the Przemyśl diocese and two hundred fifty in Bukovyna.[62]

In May a propaganda campaign was launched beyond the borders of Galicia. Through articles placed in Viennese and Prague journals and in the prestigious *Augsburger Allgemeine Zeitung*, as well as through brochures written in German, efforts were made to focus European public opinion on the arduous history of the Ukrainian nation and its distinctiveness among the Slavic nations and to win support for its national aspirations.[63] To a certain extent, the *Denkschrift der ruthenischen Nation in Galizien zur Aufklärung ihrer Verhältnisse*, a lengthy disquisition prepared and discussed by the Holovna Rada and issued on 31 July, and *Deutsche Brüder! Allgemeine Stimme der Ruthenen in Galizien*, issued on 23 August, fulfilled this role. Eight hundred copies of the first address were sent to the Ukrainian deputies in Vienna and, as Lev Treshchakovsky wrote, it gained many Germans in the cities for the Ukrainian cause.[64] Simultaneously, however, it provoked a violent polemic from the Polish side and enflamed the already strained Polish-Ukrainian relations in Galicia.

The council's programme was most fully presented in Iosyf Lozynsky's brochure, *Geliebteste ruthenische Brüder! Die Wünsche der ruthenishen Nation in Galizien dürften auf dem künftigen Reichstage in folgenden Punkten, die uns besonders am Herzen liegen, gewürdig werden*, which was dated 19 June in Lviv and signed "Ein Ruthene."[65] Lozynsky called for the abolition of the remnants of feudalism, a guarantee of land ownership for the peasants and improvements in their holdings. He demanded freedom of action in industry and commerce, the formation of industrial enterprises and the organization of a credit system. He postulated the equality of all citizens before the law and called for an improvement in education, the regularizing of health care, and safeguards for the freedom of national development. These thoroughly progressive demands became the basis of a nationwide discussion, the results of which the Holovna Rada included in numerous memoranda to the government. The most important of these concerned the normalization of land relationships in favour of the Ukrainian peasants, education and the partition of Galicia.[66]

The Holovna Rada recognized that the government's favourable response to the Ukrainian address of 19 April was an unprecedented success for its policies and obvious proof of the authorities' goodwill toward the Ukrainian movement. The Ukrainians did not fail to exploit the government's support in their propaganda, especially after Stadion wrote personally to Iakhymovych:

> On this occasion it is with special satisfaction that I inform Your Reverence of the highest respect that I feel for the Ruthenian people, who distinguish themselves in faithful adherence to the emperor and the Austrian government by their rightful thinking and peaceful, lawful behaviour, and especially for the Greek Catholic clergy, who take their apostolic mission . . . to the communities . . . entrusted to them and upon whom . . . gratitude must be bestowed for the peace and order that hitherto

has been preserved in the communities, despite the tumult prevailing elsewhere.[67]

From Minister President Pillersdorf's response of 9 May, which Stadion enclosed with his letter, it was apparent that the emperor and the government had received the Ukrainian nation's expression of fidelity and gratitude with satisfaction. In order to meet the Ukrainians' demands, the government had decided to introduce Ukrainian-language instruction in primary schools and, in those districts where a Ukrainian majority existed, to establish a chair of Ukrainian language "to give the youth who are at study the means to learn the fundamentals of their native speech and thereby to prepare the perfection of that language." The government charged the church authorities to teach students in the Greek Catholic seminary in Ukrainian and pledged equality under the law for all rites. At the same time, Pillersdorf confirmed that admitting Ukrainians to administrative offices was assumed "in paragraph 24 of the constitutional patent... and will be the object of the government's close scrutiny." He also offered assurances that the issues of publishing laws in the Ukrainian language and requiring local officials to know that language were being attended to.[68]

By complying in theory with all the postulates of the Ukrainian address, the Austrian government pleased the Ukrainian community in general and won the support of the Greek Catholic clergy in particular. The future would show that not everything that had been promised would be realized. However, a satisfied Bishop Iakhymovych told the metropolitan that "the village populace is demonstrating everywhere its favour for the government. The common people and the priests of our rite are seen as the strongest supporters of the government, so much so that only thanks to them is there the peace that still prevails in this land."[69] (What the bishop did not admit was that this was Stadion's opinion; he presented it as his own.) In informing the clergy of the interior ministry's rescript of 9 May, Iakhymovych directed that it be announced and explained to the people in such a way as to strengthen their loyalty to the constitutional monarch.[70]

The events of May in Vienna and the emperor's flight to Innsbruck presented the Holovna Rada with an opportunity to underscore its loyalist sentiments. On 26 May the council sent a letter to Stadion stressing that "the Galician Ruthenians learned with grief and dismay the news" about the "lamentable events" and expressing the hope that the episode would "pass without a trace." The letter further stated, "And may Your Highness most graciously permit us for this reason to express the unchanged feelings of fidelity and allegiance of the

Galician Ruthenian to Your Highness and to the Exalted Imperial House, the more fervently so, in that we were gratified so quickly and most graciously by the most generous consent to our petition of 19 April 1848."[71]

On 6 June in Innsbruck, Ferdinand I issued a "Manifesto to My Faithful Galicians" in response to the Ukrainian address, in which he announced that these new proofs of adherence and loyalty obliged him to announce his intentions to his faithful Galician subjects. In appreciation for their display of gratitude, he promised shortly to convene a constitutional parliament to reconstruct the Austrian governmental system so that deputies could confer on the future state laws.[72]

12. The Slavic Congress

Ukrainian political activity in Galicia had just begun when outside events turned Ukrainian aspirations to an international platform. The premises of the Ukrainian movement as embodied in the address of 19 April did not take into account the possibility of co-operation with the other Slavic nations in the monarchy. Therefore, the news from Prague, particularly the proclamation of 1 May by the Preparatory Committee of the Slavic Congress that called upon representatives of the Ukrainian nation to participate in joint deliberations, stirred public opinion. To the same degree that the liberals greeted the news with joy, the conservatives in the Holovna Rada were cautious and watchful. Still accustomed to subordinating all their actions to Stadion, the conservatives wondered whether the government would look favourably on the congress or would regard the participation by Ukrainian delegates as a hostile act. They decided to answer these questions as simply as possible—they asked the governor. His reply would be binding upon the Holovna Rada.

Actually, their move was superfluous, since the proclamation unambiguously stated that the congress would undertake nothing contrary to the interests of the dynasty and the integrity of the Austrian state. The initiators of the congress (the Ukrainians could not have known that there were Poles from Poznania among them) stated in the proclamation that the present misfortunes had been caused by the past isolation of the Slavic nations. Moreover, there was a need for mutual understanding and agreement on a common stand by the Austrian Slavs in regard to the Frankfurt Parliament, which in the name of "German unity" was seeking to incorporate Austrian lands into the German empire. The authors were convinced that "such a step would not only violate the integrity of the Austrian state, but would break the binding link and autonomy of the Slavic peoples and consequently endanger their very nationhood." The Slavic nations had to defend their own interests. To meet requests emanating "from various Slavic countries," the organizers invited representatives of "all the Slavic nations of the Austrian state"—guests from beyond the boundaries of the monarchy were "cordially welcome"—to the congress commencing in Prague on 31 May, "where we shall together take under consideration those matters that the welfare of our nation demands and what we should do in these important times."[1]

The proclamation clearly reflected the influence of the Czech policy formulated in František Palacký's celebrated reply to Frankfurt.[2] Aside from preserving the monarchy, however, the proclamation did not indicate what demands the Slavic nations should pursue and how their vital interests should be protected. Thus, it is important to consider what hopes and expectations the Ukrainians attached to the congress. The Holovna Rada formally received copies of the proclamation, as did privately Iakiv Holovatsky, Ivan Borysykevych, Ivan Biretsky, Mykhailo Malynovsky and possibly Denys Zubrytsky. Certainly the signatures of the well-known "Czech awakeners" Palacký, Pavel Šafařík and Karel Zap were reassuring.[3]

It was actually Zap who, on behalf of the Preparatory Committee, publicized the congress idea among the Galician Ukrainians. Well aware of the Ukrainians' attitude toward Austria, Zap wrote to Holovatsky on 3 May that there was no danger in participating in the congress, and therefore he urged sending a large number of delegates, "because Galician-Ruthenian interests require resourceful defenders." Zap clarified the purpose of the congress in the spirit of liberal Czech politics: opposition to the German bureaucrats, who, by not wanting to relinquish their control, "are gradually treading onto illegal, revolutionary soil"; safeguarding the interests of each Slavic nation; common defence; and, most importantly, "the transformation of Austria into a Slavic state, free and independent of all alien politics." Zap promised the Ukrainians more than they had been demanding, saying, "What [the emperor] has given to us Czechs, he must give to all the remaining Slavs. Toward this end we shall strive."[4]

The Ukrainian liberals firmly endorsed the proposals contained in Zap's letter, especially since he had addressed the protection of political liberties.[5] It seems, however, that while attaching so much importance to the congress itself, some had failed to recognize the difficulties in sending delegates. The Ukrainian activists launched a campaign in favour of the congress. On 19 May, Iakiv Holovatsky, Ivan Antonevych, Iosafat Kobrynsky, Mykhailo Terletsky and Denys Burachynsky sent a letter in the name of the Greek Catholic clergy from Pokuttia, who had assembled in Rozhniv, to the metropolitan consistory, in which they announced the selection of Father Tadei Vyrsky, a priest from Popelnyky, as their delegate to Prague. They expressed "complete confidence in his ardour for the general welfare of Galician Ruthenians" and requested permission "for his release from his parish" for the duration of the congress. Meanwhile Holovatsky asked Zap to acquaint Vyrsky with the issues that would be discussed there.[6]

Ivan Biretsky was more pessimistic. He was sceptical about sending delegates because he saw two obstacles: the Ukrainians' delayed national development and the complicated Ukrainian-Polish relations, which had caused the separatist tendencies of the Holovna Rada set up "under the governor's patronage." Biretsky wanted an understanding with the Poles, but he stressed the necessity of preserving the autonomy of the Ukrainian nation. Unable to think of anyone who could represent the Ukrainian cause at the congress, he asked if Zap would wish to speak there on behalf of the rights due the Ukrainian nation.[7]

The Holovna Rada discussed the congress at its meetings on 12 and 16 May. The Preparatory Committee's call was read at the first session, where it was decided to seek "official information whether the congress was indeed sanctioned by the government."[8] This step suggests that the council did not entirely agree with the ideas of the organizers of the Prague gathering. Zubrytsky confirmed this impression indirectly in a letter to Iakiv Holovatsky: "The deputation will go to Prague, even though their [the Czechs'] objectives are different."[9] Certainly Zubrytsky not only had in mind the government's failure to endorse the congress, but he also feared antagonizing the authorities by demanding too much, especially in the area of political rights. But, after receiving an affirmative reply from Stadion, the council decided in a secret session on 16 May to send its own delegates. Their presence would counter the fact that the Ukrainians were often considered a part of the Polish or Russian nations.[10]

The designated delegates were Ivan Borysykevych (vice-chairman of the Holovna Rada), Hryhorii Hynylevych (a doctor of theology and canon in Przemyśl) and Oleksii Zaklynsky (a fourth-year student of theology). Each received a letter of recommendation and specific instructions by which to act in Prague. The instructions stressed that the delegates "were to hold especially to the 10 May proclamation of our council."[11] In theory, this meant that they were to call for equal language and cultural rights, equality of religious rites and a guarantee of constitutional rights for the Ukrainian nation, while preserving a harmonious Polish-Ukrainian coexistence in Galicia. However, practice did not always follow theory. The cost of the delegation's sojourn, in the amount of two hundred florins per person, was borne by the council, which decided to turn to the Ukrainian community with a request for financial assistance.[12]

In its authorization of the delegates to the congress organizers, which was at the same time an appeal to the Slavic brothers, the Holovna Rada justified its decision to attend:

> Like you, brothers, we want to continue to enhance our national strength and to develop the freedoms and fortune of our nation in concert with the Austrian state. But we surely feel that we shall not achieve our goal and we shall not safeguard ourselves from circumstances inimical to us if we remain separated from other Slavic nations.

The document strictly limited the Ukrainian delegation's authority "to all actions that do not oppose the integrity of the Austrian state and our expressed loyalty to the imperial House of Habsburg, our constitutional liberties and our forever beloved nationality."[13]

Nevertheless, the matter of Vyrsky's departure came to a standstill. Kuzemsky proposed considering whether a fourth delegate was necessary: although the council appreciated the value of a sizeable Ukrainian representation, it had already decided to send only three representatives from Galicia.[14] When he conveyed this decision to his colleagues, Iosyf Levytsky of Zabolotiv, citing unconfirmed reports that the congress had been postponed until 7 June, suggested calling a meeting of the clergy of the Kolomyia deanery on 29 May in order to choose a "fourth venerable and sensible delegate."[15] These efforts came to nothing for unknown reasons.[16]

This whole issue of the congress sheds a great deal of light on both the liberal and the conservative approaches toward the national and political aspirations of the Ukrainian community. Both sides adhered to strictly legal means of obtaining constitutional and national rights. But whereas the liberals included political rights within the concept of constitutional freedoms and based their activities on the constitution of 25 April, the conservatives limited their demands to linguistic and cultural rights, and they made all their efforts subject to the constituted authorities. Before leaving for Prague, the Ukrainian delegates paid a visit to Stadion, and perhaps under his influence they were persuaded to act in an anti-Polish spirit. Stadion gave them a letter to the governor of Bohemia, Count Leo Thun, in which he described them as the true and exclusive representatives of the Ukrainian nation.[17]

The Ukrainian delegates were cordially welcomed to Prague on 29 May by the Czechs, who hoped to bring about an understanding between the Ukrainians and the Poles. Their intention was a logical consequence of their liberal policies, the success of which depended in large measure on Polish attitudes. Certain Polish spokesmen had declared that they wished to remain with Austria, and the Czechs hoped that this might be possible if the concept of Poland's independence were recognized. As František Rieger announced, the Czechs' task was "to mediate between Austria and Poland. Poland's present status is unnatural, and it cannot remain so."[18] The Czechs, however, understood the difficulty of winning the Poles over to a settlement with the Ukrainians, especially because reports emanating from Galicia gave no grounds for optimism. Letters from Galicia by the Czechs František Jachim and Čeněk Vrba and articles by Karel Havlíček-Borovský severely criticized the Poles.[19]

Jachim wrote that they desired to restore an independent Poland according to its old boundaries and thereby to continue to oppress the Ukrainians. They did not accept Slavic reciprocity; their conduct was contrary to it. The Ukrainians, on the other hand, comprehended the concept much better. They accepted the call to the congress "with real enthusiasm," supported attempts to achieve an understanding among the Slavs and were "our forever faithful allies." Therefore, "the Czechs will always recognize in [the Ukrainians] honest and faithful brothers, and in the future we shall join them in a close alliance that will grow ever stonger.... But the Poles, the Poles! They are not drawn to us or to the other Slavs; their present allies—God grant that we are mistaken.... "

Jachim did not finish, or did not want to finish, the sentence. Vrba did that for him. He compared the Galician situation with conditions in Bohemia. "Just as the German oppresses the Czech nationality, so do the Poles and the bureaucracy oppress the Ruthenian nationality. One feeling links the Ruthenians to the Czechs: to protect the liberties obtained from His Imperial Majesty from an alien onslaught. For this reason the Ruthenians understood the importance of the Slavic Congress." Therefore, it was necessary "to support and advise" the Ukrainian delegates, especially since the Polish newspaper in Lviv, *Dziennik Narodowy* [National daily], was suggesting that "the Austrian authorities are prepared to satisfy all the wishes of the Polish nation and will recall Governor Stadion if the Polish nation does not send its deputies to the Slavic Congress in Prague." The Poles themselves, Vrba maintained, "have made an alliance with the Magyars..., the most menacing enemy of the Slavs." It was therefore apparent

> what can be expected from this chivalrous nation on the Slavic question. That is the way the majority of the Polish nation thinks; that is, the nobility (the burgher class is little developed and the peasants stand very lowly). Nay, [the Poles even] do not hesitate to profess before the united Slavs that Poland should not recognize the independence of the Ruthenians nor limit its concerns to itself. What would [in that event] become of all of Poland in its [former] boundaries?

In these circumstances, Karel Pichler's correspondence from Lviv, which was unfavourable to the Ukrainians, was not taken seriously by the Czech liberals.[20]

There was a meeting with the Ukrainian delegates on 30 May at Jan Neuberg's home, at which Prince Jerzy Lubomirski represented the Poles.[21] The initial discussions revealed that it would be difficult to reach an understanding. "I submitted my proposals there," wrote Hynylevych, "but the idea of partitioning [Galicia] was not at all agreeable to him. But the Czechs and the Croats acknowledge the justness of our cause and are ready to defend it." Even though Lubomirski did not wish to acknowledge the Holovna Rada's delegates as Ukrainian representatives, Hynylevych expected "to maintain before the world what is most dear to us: our recognition." From his letter of 30 May to the Holovna Rada we learn that, after an exchange of views, the Ukrainians approved the agenda that the Preparatory Committee had drafted; in so doing, they already had exceeded the authority granted by the Holovna Rada.

Political conditions in the monarchy, Hynylevych continued, indicated that "the Austrian state cannot maintain its unity in any way except as a union of many nationalities, as a *Staaten Bund*"; the Slavs, as the most numerous, had to reach an agreement to maintain the union and defend the dynasty. The Magyars, Wallachians (Romanians) and Germans might belong to it, but not as nations ruling over the Slavs. Under the influence of the Czechs, he also advised accepting a common constitution with the Poles (on the model of the Bohemian charter, a copy of which he included with his letter). However, the Czechs (together with the Moravians and the Slovaks), the South Slavs, the Hungarians and the Germans would have separate constitutional charters. The provincial diets would also be separate, but there would be common ministries of war, finance, commerce and foreign affairs, as well as a federal assembly of representatives from the individual provincial diets. Hynylevych emphasized that the Slavic Congress would endeavour to safeguard constitutional liberties and to establish an alliance for defence and resistance (*Trutz und Schutzbündnis*), "even if it should come to war."

Hynylevych next presented to the Holovna Rada the Ukrainian delegation's programme, which included the partition of Galicia into two gubernias (not provinces), with a joint Polish-Ukrainian government and a common diet. Use of the province's two native languages would be mandatory in the schools and administration, with the stipulation that until the Ukrainian language was fully perfected, it would be permissible in the Ukrainian portions of Galicia "to employ also Polish alongside the principal language, Ruthenian." The common government would be seated in Lviv and composed equally of Ukrainians and Poles. The working languages of the diet would be Ukrainian and Polish. Hynylevych realized the difficulties of forcing such a programme through the congress and therefore requested that at least one lay delegate be sent to Prague. He appealed to the Holovna Rada:

> Do not be surprised by our so bold declaration. Currently, in this period of anarchy in the Viennese government, when every province should strive to remain loyal to the crown and attend to establishing order in the state..., we Ruthenians—by constitutional means and on the strength of the monarch's recognition of the Holovna Rada Ruska as our national organ—should also think of ourselves, put our country and nation in such order as seems to us to be beneficial to its welfare and submit this reorganization... to the monarch with a request that he permit his faithful Ruthenians, like other nations, to constitute ourselves.

Hynylevych was especially concerned to gain rights similar to those the Czechs had attained. At the same time, under the influence of the Czechs' programme, he declared himself opposed to sending representatives to the Viennese parliament until Galicia's affairs had been resolved. He was fearful of the recent revolutionary demonstrations in Vienna, "because we could hardly deliberate there, if we were to find ourselves between the barricades." He advised the Holovna Rada to convince the governor to delay elections to the Reichstag. The Ukrainians ought first to organize themselves, as the Czechs had done; then they should explain to their people the necessity of dividing Galicia (as the emperor had already decided prior to March 1848), raise the people's consciousness of their nationality (with the reservation that they be "understanding and just toward the Poles"), teach them the importance of elections, and pave the way for Ukrainian representation. They should not trust those officials who could lead "a loyal Ruthenian on the wrong path." Hynylevych asked:

> Are we to be different from our Slavic brothers? Let us be loyal like others, but let us not be the last. Let us identify ourselves also as Ruthenians; let us embrace our [national] emblems with a Ruthenian guard; let us awaken all our fellow Ruthenians; let us be liberal, progressive and constitutional, and those Ruthenians who have hitherto renounced us will return and give us moral strength. The Germans, who have patronized us until now only for appearance's sake and reared us little by little like a child in order to tease the Poles, should now return to us full justice, safeguarding our nationality through the partition [of Galicia] and a genuine constitution. They should reward us and strengthen our loyalty to the monarch.

The letter is evidence that Hynylevych (and certainly the remaining Ukrainian delegates) did not escape the illusions of the Czechs' liberal policy. Hynylevych embraced its principles and wanted to persuade the Ukrainian leaders in Galicia to the Czech position. However, he did not receive a reply until after the congress had ended. Both a rough draft of Teodor Leontovych's reply, preserved in the records of the Holovna Rada, and an emended version indicate that the council did not reach a consensus in regard to many issues concerning the future of Austria and Ukrainian-Polish relations in Galicia.[22] Leontovych wrote that the council agreed on the partition of Galicia, but into two provinces, not gubernias, and had submitted a request to that effect to the province's executive authorities (actually to the emperor through that body) because a common government would undoubtedly be Polish and would not guarantee equal rights to the Ukrainians. He stated further that it would be impossible to create a Ukrainian national guard prior to partition, since the people considered the present guard to be Polish, and the Holovna Rada, as the people's ministry, did not wish to, and indeed could not, act contrary to the people's will. The people adhered to monarchism and wanted to stay with Austria. "The eyes of our nation have been opened [*poniav sia*], and it will not permit itself to be led blindly; instead it desires to act for itself, to comprehend with its own mind and to wait until it is able to understand what it does not now understand. It no longer wishes to know of guardians, leaders [*vodyteliv*] or, even less, agitators."

Consumed by illusions concerning the pro-Austrian and monarchistic outlook of the Ukrainian peasantry, the Holovna Rada thought that it had enormous influence on Ukrainian society. It believed itself to be "recognized throughout Rus'," and alleged that some members of the Sobor Ruskyi, or Ruthenian assembly (pseudo-Ruthenians, in Leontovych's opinion), had converted to its camp. But no such defections had occurred, although negotiations on this matter were actually going on. It was in fact the Ukrainian populace, in the council's opinion, that inhibited its taking a decisively progressive stance. "Let us be for progress, but let us endeavour that our nation knows what it has to do [*postupav znaty*]; therefore, it is better to wait for our people than abandon them just because they are cautious and cannot keep pace as we desire. After all, we exist for the nation, and not the nation for us."

From the emendations to Leontovych's letter we learn that the Holovna Rada agreed to the proposed reorganization of the Austrian state as a *Staaten Bund*, suggesting that "it should be more Slavic," should defend the dynasty and throne with all its might and should establish a Slavic ministry and present it to the emperor for confirmation. The council also agreed to accept the projected constitution and to postpone elections in Galicia until internal matters there were settled. In regard to a Slavic alliance, the council wrote: "We shall join the union with all the Slavic branches of the Austrian state against all nations inimical to us Slavs, from whatever side they may come. We guarantee to each of them its nationhood, and we accept this guarantee from them for ourselves."

The council also agreed in theory that it was necessary to send the largest possible delegation to Prague; however, Leontovych explained that sending a fourth delegate would cost too much. This explanation was not necessarily true, for Leontovych wrote at the same time that "fifty, sixty and a hundred guldens" flowed from the deanery councils for the Holovna Rada's purposes. Probably the council did not want to send the fourth delegate, whom the clergy in Pokuttia had designated, but whom the council found unsuitable.

Several points that had been crossed out in the emended draft offer proof of the pressure brought to bear by the more anti-Polish and pro-Austrian wing of the council, which feared that too explicit formulations might be frowned upon in governmental circles or could obstruct the line of action adopted earlier. While affirming in principle the Czech liberals' programme, the council thus stripped it of the substance that the Poles, among others, had accepted. The Holovna Rada did not approve the following postulates:

1. We desire and agree that the Slavic congress in Prague should be independent of the present [Austrian] ministry.

2. The Germans, if they so desire, may remain in this union, but cannot rule over the Slavic peoples.

3. There will be one provincial diet for the Lviv and Cracow gubernias. The place of assembly may be in Jarosław. The Ruthenians may speak only Ruthenian (in the diet).

The programme for restructuring Austria was widely publicized through the Holovna Rada's affiliates. However, the contents often depended on the personal views of the local councils' correspondents. For example, Ivan Ilevych informed the Berezhany council that Austria would be transformed in a Slavic spirit, and the Germans, who represented one-third of the monarchy's population, would no longer be the ruling nation. He also announced that Galicia would be divided and that the Ukrainian language would be mandatory in the schools, administrative offices and all institutions in the Ukrainian portions. In effect, all officials would be Ukrainians. He widely publicized the principles and the role of the current elections to the Viennese parliament, and he advised everyone not to place confidence in either the Poles or the German officials.[23]

Meanwhile, the congress was taking shape in Prague. From the outset it was apparent that each delegation, notwithstanding the many declarations made in the spirit of Slavic reciprocity, had only the interests of its own nationality in mind. The first misunderstandings occurred over procedural issues during the establishment of the Polish-Ukrainian section. Who exactly represented the Ukrainians, the delegates of the Holovna Rada Ruska or the delegates of the Sobor Ruskyi? And then there were the "Ruthenian" delegates of the Polish Central Rada Narodowa and five clerics from the Greek Catholic seminary in Vienna.[24] In fact, a sizeable portion of Galicia's delegates claimed to represent the Ukrainian community, and on 31 May the delegates from the Holovna Rada were formally acknowledged only as representatives of the Greek Catholic clergy. Of course both sides had the requisite authorizations. Hence, when greeting the students and guests from Vienna, the polonized "Ruthenian" Jan Dobrzański spoke in the name of all Galicia without even mentioning the Ukrainians. It was left to Oleksii Zaklynsky to mention their rights. Ultimately, on Zaklynsky's motion that the delegations unite and jointly represent the Ukrainian nation, a compromise was reached.[25] More than twenty so-called Ruthenians joined the Polish-Ukrainian section, along with the Poles, the itinerant Russian revolutionary Mikhail Bakunin and a Russian Old Believer priest from Bukovyna, Olimpii Miloradov.[26] Elections to choose the section's officers took place the same afternoon. Karol Libelt, a Pole from Poznań, was elected chairman, Hynylevych vice-chairman, and the Pole Antoni Walewski secretary. Zaklynsky became the deputy secretary. At that moment, Jerzy Lubomirski, Ivan Borysykevych and Maurycy Kraiński, who had been designated the previous day by the Preparatory Committee as organizers of the section, had fulfilled their role. In assigning the section's officers, a first step had been taken in the direction of a mutual understanding.

In his first formal remarks as chairman, Libelt assured Karel Zap (who had served as secretary of the Preparatory Committee and had overseen the organization of the sections) that he would strive to maintain harmony and to support the principle of respect for every nationality. He pledged to the Ukrainians that Poland had broken with its old policies, that "it wishes to be [but] one part of a free, federated Slavdom" and that Ukrainians therefore had no reason to be apprehensive. At the same time, however, Libelt underscored the common aspirations and goals of both nationalities.[27]

On 1 June elections took place for Polish-Ukrainian representatives to the Czecho-Slovak and South Slavic sections, for members of the congress's executive bodies, and for speakers to address the ceremonial opening of the congress on 2 June. It became apparent at that time that the Holovna Rada's delegates themselves had not reached a common position. Borysykevych opposed Bakunin's candidacy as representative to the South Slavic section, because "his lack of familiarity with the Galician situation is an obstacle." On the other hand, Hynylevych saw no difficulty in this choice, since it would facilitate mutual understanding. On Borysykevych's motion it was agreed that the representatives to other sections would remain subject to the control of the Polish-Ukrainian section and could, therefore, at any time request pertinent clarifications. In the elections that followed Witalis Grzybowski and Lesław Łukasiewicz were chosen as representatives to the Czecho-Slovak section, and Wojciech Cybulski and Bakunin to the South Slavic section.[28]

The afternoon session was devoted to selecting the congress leaders. Jerzy Lubomirski was the Polish-Ukrainian section's candidate for president, Antoni Walewski for secretary and Borysykevych for deputy secretary. Hynylevych and Zaklynsky were among the section's sixteen members of the Congress Plenary Committee.[29] Finally, after lengthy discussion, Lubomirski and Hynylevych were chosen to address the opening session. It then became obvious just how much the Poles distrusted the Ukrainian delegates. Karol Malisz warned Hynylevych against voicing hostile opinions "regarding the other Slavs"—namely, the Poles. Zaklynsky protested, "Inasmuch as the Ruthenians do not rebuke the Poles, but on the contrary feel confident that the Polish delegate will speak with the best intentions, this suspicion of the Ruthenians is unjust. The Poles have not met with hostile measures from the Ruthenians, either in Galicia or in Prague." In the end Chairman Libelt reconciled the parties.[30]

Both addresses maintained a conciliatory tone. Lubomirski spoke of the Slavs' great role in the future and demanded equality for all people and nations. He stressed that pursuing federation evidenced "the purity of our thoughts," and he called for avoiding struggles that could be exploited by the despots. At the same time, he emphasized, "we do not want peace at the price of liberty." Speaking of the Polish issue, Lubomirski maintained that the Poles were the first to attempt federation, but "it had failed because it was not kneaded together by general freedom."[31]

Boryskykevych spoke for the Ukrainians, since Hynylevych had suddenly taken ill. According to him, the Ukrainians were so oppressed as a nation that they did not even exist on paper. Although they lived together with other peoples in a single state, they had never taken action independently, but "invariably only behind a German veil." Despite the fact that "we faithfully gave Austria our all and spilt our blood, we have not found that fortune which other nations possess." Borysykevych demanded guarantees of independence and liberty for the Ukrainian nation as well as national equality.[32]

On 3 June the Polish-Ukrainian section proceeded to select standing commissions to discuss its procedural rules. The differences in the programmes, goals and aspirations of the two sides quickly became clear. If the congress were to be successful, concessions would have to be made. The problem was to reconcile the Poles' aspirations for the reconstruction of their state in its 1772 boundaries (or, as a minimum, a special autonomous status for all of Galicia within Austria) with the aspirations for national emancipation of the Ukrainians, who were demanding the creation of an autonomous, Ukrainian Eastern Galicia. Libelt proposed a compromise: the election of four committees—a Polish, Ukrainian, Great-Polish (Poznanian) and an all-Slavic—with the stipulation that the first two would have to deliberate together on Galician affairs. He argued that "our concerns require separate treatment," owing to which each "nationality will be represented." He did not preclude the possibility of unity, but rightly judged that "the Polish and Ruthenian committees can comprise one Galician committee" and thereby contribute to a "mutual and in every respect desirable understanding." Libelt was supported by all the Ukrainian delegates and some of the Poles. Antoni Zygmunt Helcel proposed creating a joint committee that would be divided into two parts. Initially, Lubomirski favoured the selection of a single committee, but later yielded on the understanding that no final decision would be reached on the Galician question unless both parties agreed. Erazm Zaremba favoured a single committee ("since the [Polish] cause is one"), as did Jan Janiszewski, Seweryn Celarski, Leon Sapieha ("the interests of both nationalities are common for the whole country") and Feliks Buchwald ("there is no district that is purely Polish or purely Ruthenian"). Buchwald chastized the Ukrainians for mistrusting the

Poles, who he said were prepared to make all sorts of concessions to the Ruthenians. "We do not wish concessions," Borysykevych objected. "We demand only our rights." He spoke for creating a separate Ukrainian committee, basing his arguments on the historical traditions of Ukraine and on ethnic grounds. Galician particularism, he said, was foreign to him. The Ukrainian nation numbered fifteen million people, and the Galician Ukrainians desired to create conditions in Galicia to elevate the entire Ukrainian nationality, not simply the Galician part.

Libelt reconciled the interests of both sides by favouring the creation of two committees, Polish and Ukrainian, which would deliberate as one on political issues. In his opinion, this procedure "would facilitate and hasten a decision." Ultimately, three committees were selected: 1) the Galician committee, composed of two sections—a Polish (with Helcel, Lubomirski, Kraiński, Malisz, Buchwald and Józef Midowicz as members and Wojciech Brandys and Paweł Stalmach as substitutes) and a Ukrainian (Ruthenian) (with the polonized Ruthenians Sapieha, Julian Dzieduszycki and Ludwik Stecki and the Holovna Rada's delegates Borysykevych, Hynylevych and Zaklynsky as members, and the polonized Ruthenians Zenon Pogłodowski, Kasper Cięglewicz and Jerzy Wołoszczak as substitutes); 2) the Polish committee (largely Poznanian) (Janiszewski, Cybulski, Jędrzej Moraczewski, Cięglewicz, Libelt and Ryszard Berwiński as members, and Adam Gorczyński, Edmund Chojecki and Kalist Horoch as substitutes); and 3) the so-called Slavic committee, consisting of the members of the other committees and Bakunin, making a total of nineteen persons.

Borysykevych proposed that "Ukrainians" not be chosen for the "Polish" committee. Dzieduszycki disagreed: "We are acting as representatives of fifteen million Ruthenians. Therefore, we must join with the Polish section in order also to represent Rus' beyond the borders of Austria—Rus' in its entirety." Finally, after a lengthy debate in which the Ukrainians proposed choosing an equal number of representatives from both sides to the Polish committee, Borysykevych relented, stating that "the deliberations on the Slavic question [will] depend entirely on the integrity of the Poles."[33]

Two points of view stood out in the discussion concerning the rules governing the Polish-Ukrainian section. A committee composed of Sapieha, Helcel, Janiszewski, Berwiński, Borysykevych, Pogłodowski and Andrzej Kotula was formed to make recommendations. Whereas Sapieha, Lubomirski and Janiszewski favoured limiting the number of persons to be admitted to the section's deliberations, others, such as Berwiński, Hynylevych and Zaklynsky, opposed setting limits. According to Zaklynsky, each person had the responsibility of providing advice on the congress's aims, even if only two members remained in the section. Hynylevych formulated this thought more tersely: "The section remains until the aim is achieved."[34] The section's rules, as approved on 4 June, stipulated that "the number of members is unlimited"; any Pole or Ukrainian past the age of twenty-four could become a member with the mandate of his country or by the section's approval. Resolutions were passed by a majority vote with a quorum of two-thirds of the members. Meetings of the various committees could be attended exclusively by their own members and the chairman and secretary of the section. However, others could be invited "for consultation." Paragraph 27 stipulated that "the section will cease to be a part of the membership of the Slavic assembly at such time as it no longer contains at least half the members registered as of this day, of which there are thirty in number."[35] The lengthy debate over organization and rules caused alarm not only among some members of the section (notably Bakunin), but also among the representatives of the other sections, who properly insisted on proceeding to a discussion of the congress's programme.[36]

The necessity of reaching an agreement with the Ukrainians influenced the Poles' position on the question of the South Slavs, who had requested support in their dispute with the Hungarians. The Poles recognized that the means proposed by the South Slavs were inadequate. Therefore, they suggested that the congress, besides sending a deputation to the emperor and providing support for Jelačić, should dispatch a mission to Hungary (Celarski's motion) in the hope that the Magyars "could be persuaded to be just toward the Serbs and the Slovaks." As a matter of fact, more impatient Poles (Zaremba, for example) proposed sending a deputation to Hungary and to the emperor, but with a threat instead of a request. Lubomirski was more cautious: "Let us not display sympathy for seeking help among the Hungarians, because otherwise we might find it in Moscow. Let us speak loyally to the Hungarians. Our duty is to extend a hand to the weaker [peoples], that together we might be stronger. Therefore, I propose that Poland mediate between the two nations." His position gained the support of Hynylevych and Borysykevych, who demanded "to speak on behalf of the Slovaks and the Ruthenians in Hungary."

These differences in approach caused the matter to be referred to the Slavic committee, which, after an hour's deliberation, recommended that the deputation from the congress to the emperor include Polish representatives, who, "in the name of the two most oppressed nationalities in Austria—in the name of the Slovaks and the Serbs being stifled by the Hungarians—as well as in the name of the Poles and Ruthenians who are persecuted by the Germans, [should] demand the elimination of [these national] abuses." The Slavic committee also decided "to support the address to the Croatian *ban* [Jelačić] to give him greater moral strength." Borysykevych protested against linking the Galician question to the activities of the proposed deputation, at which Helcel threatened that the Poles would leave Prague. Libelt, however, did not accept Borysykevych's protest, noting that he failed to see "in what way the present resolution could harm the Ruthenian nationality."[37]

The discussion proved that until the Ukrainian-Polish dispute was settled, any kind of freer action by the Poles was impossible. Thus the work of the section continued methodically, with the aim of preparing proposals on mutual relations and drawing up both nations' demands. On 4 June, at a meeting of the Ukrainian section of the Galician committee, the Ukrainians' demands for the partition of Galicia into two administrative districts with a common central authority and a common diet, the introduction of the Ukrainian language into the schools and administrative offices, and separate national guards in both districts were endorsed, but only narrowly. Borysykevych, Hynylevych, Zaklynsky and Pogłodowski cast affirmative votes; Dzieduszycki and Sapieha were opposed.[38] This decision was not the worst possible for the Poles. A common diet and common government would guarantee the Poles' influence over conditions in Eastern Galicia. Nevertheless, they undertook a determined campaign against the agreement. Only then, seemingly, did the members become aware that these agreements were too far-reaching and that they had exceeded their authority. The section—and the entire congress for that matter—was not a constitutional organ. It could not, as Sapieha wrote, "encroach on the prerogatives of the Constituent Assembly, which alone has the right to rule on these requests." The agreement had assured the Ukrainians equal national rights and aid in developing their Ukrainian nationality, the creation of two departments in the *Gubernium*—for Ukrainian affairs and for Polish affairs—which would be filled by officials fluent in both languages; it was also agreed that half the officials in the "Ruthenian districts" would be Ukrainians.[39]

Probably because of pressure from other members of the Galician committee, Pogłodowski retracted his vote on the following day, 5 June, explaining that he lacked authorization to partition Galicia and considered such a division harmful for the province. Pogłodowski therefore supported Sapieha and Dzieduszycki, who endorsed equal language rights in the schools and administration and a common government and diet. Pogłodowski added a paragraph on equal rights for the clergy of both rites and changed the paragraph concerning the national guards. In his opinion there should be a common guard throughout Galicia, bearing both eagle and lion emblems. The language of command would depend on the will of the majority.[40]

The repercussions of Pogłodowski's position became apparent on 6 June during the discussion regarding the third item of the new congress programme proposed by Libelt, the issue of concluding a Slavic union or federation, which the congress's Plenary Committee had accepted the previous day. Libelt's programme unquestionably stretched the rather confined bounds of the Austro-Slavic programme that the Preparatory Committee had drafted, and it evoked the opposition of more moderate circles.[41] It was commonly known that the Poles did not want this union to restrict their national aspirations and that they therefore regarded Galicia's association in such a union as temporary. When Poland was revived in its historical boundaries, it would become the "Federation of Northern Slavs," but "it would not cut its ties with the Southern Federation."[42] The Poles, though they agreed to equal rights for Ukrainians, sought to contain them within the framework of a Polish state and nation. The Ukrainians, of course, could not agree. They rejected common statehood and again demanded the partition of Galicia.[43]

During the debates in the Polish-Ukrainian section on 6 June, Helcel proposed establishing yet another committee "to prepare ideas that could serve to clarify the Polish question in relation to the concepts and principles that the other Slavic sections of the congress have in this regard. These efforts could result in the formation of an alliance."[44] Borysykevych then insisted that reference also be made to the Ukrainians. Helcel responded that such a reference would apply to the Galician question, whereas the issue was a declaration pertaining to all of Poland. The discussion revealed that the Ukrainians did not wish to raise a political issue, but rather demanded a resolution of the national question. In Hynylevych's opinion, they had gathered in Prague to consider the national question, not the Polish question. He declared: "Indeed the Ruthenians are a nation. We were bound and oppressed for a long time; we make this painful admission. However, we do not blame the Poles for this past oppression. Those are historical misfortunes. But today, when there is hope for liberty, we demand that Rus' be mentioned in all the records; otherwise, we shall have to demand that the [Polish-Ukrainian] section be divided." From the Polish side Dobrzański insisted that the Ukrainians were not a nation, and Zaremba stated that he could not conceive of a nation within a nation; to separate the Ukrainians from Poland was an affront to the Ukrainians themselves. Libelt once again attempted to mediate, saying that the future Poland "will be federated and will respect and assist its peoples and nationalities." Nevertheless, he believed that complying with the Ukrainians' wishes would provoke the Lithuanians and the

Mazurians to similar claims. For Libelt, the Polish question was also the Ukrainian question, and therefore the Ukrainians must declare "whether they wish to be our brothers or to be with the tsar." Poland "must rise together with Rus'," but Rus' must be federated with Poland. He appealed to the Ukrainians to propagate the idea of this "sincere and indivisible union of [our] two nationalities."

Zaklynsky answered: "We wished to show Europe that we desire to live not subject to Poland, but as a separate nation. We ought to have been asked if we wish to be separate. Many of us have come here in order not to remain with Poland under any circumstances. We do not know how this will occur, but we want complete separation." In reply, Cięglewicz spoke out with unusual vehemence, saying, for example, that there had been no oppression in Rus', that the Ukrainian language was in fact Polish, that Poland's union with Rus' was eternal and that the Greek Catholic priests wanted to sever that union because they desired a theocracy. Cięglewicz insisted that to break away from Poland was a disgrace and a wrong to the Ukrainians, concluding, "I, too, am a Ruthenian, but no less a Pole."

Borysykevych was the most unyielding of the Ukrainians. He said that they had come to Prague because they had been unable to reach agreement with the Poles in Lviv. If the Poles accepted the Ukrainians' conditions, an accord would ensue. "If not, then perhaps we shall demand a separate section." The Ukrainians had been wronged, and the greatest injustice was the failure to recognize them as a completely separate nation. Responding to Cięglewicz's assertions, Borysykevych recalled that at the time of the historical grandeur of their "joined peoples," only the nobility had acted. "But today the people act, and they desire to act as a nation." The Ukrainians were laying claim to their own language because they wished to elevate their own nationality, and they would convey it "on the path of freedom and progress." He ended by stating that "the chairman demands a declaration on how we are to relate to one another. You are set on determining your [own] relationship to the [other] Slavs, while we inquire about our relationship toward you [Poles]. But to submit to your unconditional demand for unity would be a disgrace."[45]

The debate showed that neither side could make concessions without renouncing its position. As the Polish historian Władysław Wisłocki has pointed out, a renunciation would have been equivalent to cancelling one's national programme.[46] At the same time, however, the members understood the need to proceed as quickly as possible with the committee's work. Early on 7 June, an accord was reached, the result of which was the Galician committee's acceptance of a document entitled "Żądania Rusinów w Galicji" [Demands of the Ruthenians in Galicia].[47] This document was significantly more comprehensive than the tentative understanding reached on 4 June. Accepted were equal rights for the Ukrainian language in administrative offices (paragraph 1) and in the schools (paragraph 2); the establishment of a common national guard (paragraph 3); a common central authority and common diet (paragraph 4); equality of rites and privileges of the clergy (paragraph 5); and a guarantee of national and political rights in the future constitution (paragraph 6). Finally, paragraph 7 stipulated that "decision on the need and the time to divide Galicia into two separate administrative districts is a matter for the legislative diet." The document was accepted by a vote of eight to four, because Pogłodowski, Malisz, Midowicz and Lubomirski voted against the first paragraph but accepted the remaining points. The four dissenters, as Lubomirski wrote, insisted "that the introduction of the Ruthenian language, as well as Polish, into the schools, offices and the diet is a matter for the legislative assembly [to decide], and for that reason both the Ruthenians and the Poles should strive with all their strength to achieve an assembly that would place the relations between these nationalities on an equal footing."[48]

The agreement of 7 June was the only real effort, as it turned out, at a Ukrainian-Polish understanding, and this fact explains its significance.[49] Nevertheless, its authors did not go beyond the framework of the prevailing liberalism; its postulates were limited to national and political issues, and social problems were disregarded. In fact, socio-economic issues were never even discussed at the congress.

How does one explain so sudden and radical a change in the Ukrainians' position and their unexpected concession which permitted the agreement? Contemporary observers and later historians agree that it stemmed from the intervention and mediation of the Czechs,[50] who were afraid that if an accord was not reached the congress would end in a fiasco. The Ukrainian-Polish compromise, therefore, was also a Czech-Polish compromise. The Czechs, although they did not believe that the Polish state would be restored within its historical borders,[51] did not rule out such an eventuality, and in return the Poles supported the Czechs' aspirations. A modern-day Czech historian, Vladimír Hostička, has aptly called the agreement "a compromise between the Czech Austro-Slavic concept and the Polish proclivity toward liberation from Austria."[52]

Less, however, has been written about the influence of the Hôtel Lambert, the centre of the conservative Polish émigrés in Paris, on the one hand and of Mikhail Bakunin on the other. Prince Adam Czartoryski, through his intermediaries Leon Sapieha and Antoni

Walewski, inclined the Slavs toward "justice and reconciliation" while maintaining good relations with the Hungarians, who were to support Galicia in the event of a conflict with Russia. Unless the quarrels between the Poles and the Ukrainians and between the Slavs and the Hungarians were settled, it would be impossible either "to direct the congress's aims in a political direction" or to advance the Polish cause, which especially concerned the Hôtel Lambert circle.[53] Bakunin saw the danger that threatened the Slavs from the German side as well as from tsarist Russia. He urged hastening the deliberations and putting an end to the disputes in the Polish-Ukrainian section, which would then facilitate a federation of the Slavic nations based on democratic principles. Bakunin also expected that such a federation would be an important means of spreading revolutionary propaganda to Russia itself.[54]

From the moment the agreement was signed, the attitude of the Ukrainian delegates changed markedly, which meant that further deliberations could proceed freely. Moreover, it became clear during the discussion over Helcel's proposal on the Polish question and Lubomirski's amendments to it that the Poles themselves were in disagreement, whereas the Ukrainians were voicing a conciliatory spirit.[55] Helcel moved that the members acknowledge that "the Slavic Congress regards the division of Poland as the greatest violation of the law of nations and, in order to comply with that law, and also for the future well-being and peace of Europe, deems the earliest possible restitution of independence and integrity of the nation as indispensable."[56]

Lubomirski modified this motion by adding a reference to Rus': "The Slavic Congress considers the division of Poland as the greatest transgression against the law of nations, namely, against the Polish nation and the Ruthenian nation that is joined with it. In order to comply with that law and to insure the order and peace of Europe in the future, [the congress] deems indispensable the speediest rectification of these wrongs and the restoration of independence to both united nations."[57] Lubomirski had two objectives: a defence against Russian policies and the creation of a Polish-Ukrainian federation. He assumed that a resolute and forthright statement of the issue of federation did not contravene the principle of Poland's unity. Moreover, it created the conditions that made it possible for the Ukrainian nation to favour such unity. Lubomirski hoped that the Ukrainians would not want to break away before being liberated and that the Poles, if they understood their role, ought not in principle to oppose it. "Whoever fears the splintering off [of Poland's peoples], does not understand the Polish question," he stated.[58] A federated Poland had to unite nations by its moral strength and, by guaranteeing them the freedom of national life, ought to make them adhere to one another. Therefore, recognition of the Ukrainians' right to "splinter off" (today we would say the right to self-determination), would not threaten the Polish nation.

Nonetheless, the Polish delegates opposed Lubomirski's motion, accusing him of confusing the state question with the national question. Helcel even tried to prove that Lubomirski was being unfair to the Ukrainians by prejudging their state affiliation. "According to the motion you are joined [with us], but if you can manage it, you may nevertheless become a separate nationality," Helcel called out to the Ukrainians.[59]

In the meantime, the Ukrainians responded favourably to the motion. Having agreed with the substance of Helcel's original motion, they supported Lubomirski's modifications. Zaklynsky stated, "I protest in favour of the version by Prince Lubomirski, who has only changed the text in the intent of its content by adding to [the word] Poland a reference to Rus'."[60]

Unfortunately, we do not know the fate of the motion. Perhaps, as Wisłocki believed, it was approved in the Polish and Czech sections, and only the South Slavic section was afraid to support it for fear of antagonizing Russia.[61] There is no mention of the Ukrainian question in the final version of Palacký's "Manifesto to the Nations of Europe."[62] However, the Ukrainians are referred to in the "Address to the Emperor," in which the conditions laid out in the Polish-Ukrainian agreement of 7 June are found in their entirety.[63] Yet neither these documents nor Helcel's and Lubomirski's draft proposal, "The Act of Austro-Slavic Union,"[64] exerted any real influence on Slavic politics.

Nevertheless, the Ukrainian-Polish accord was a genuine achievement—or rather it could have been if its principles had been carried out. Its authors were perfectly aware of its value. In Libelt's opinion, the conditions "will be . . . of mutual satisfaction and pride to us";[65] Lubomirski believed that thanks to the accord, "the Galician difficulties between Poland and Rus' are resolved."[66] Although Seweryn Celarski expected a permanent understanding after the agreement was ratified,[67] Antoni Walewski considered it only a tactical manoeuver.[68]

The Ukrainian delegates esteemed the agreement very highly. Hynylevych wrote that it represented the basis for "the closest federation" of both nations and the foundation for ukrainization of national life—for introducing the Ukrainian language into the schools and for extirpating German influences and the bureaucracy. A Galician provincial diet with legislative power could open the way to political rights.[69] To be sure, Borysykevych's draft proposal, "Galiziens

Forderungen für das Manifest des Slaven-Congresses an den Kaiser" [Galicia's demands for the Manifesto of the Slavic Congress to the Emperor], did not mention the agreement. However, drawing on its assumptions, he insisted that the central authority for Galicia be based on the model granted to the Czechs and that the Galician legislative diet be convened before the start of deliberations by the all-Austrian Reichstag.[70]

Unfortunately, circumstances evolved otherwise. The Polish Rada Narodowa made its decision on the Polish-Ukrainian agreement dependent upon the position of its executive department and then "concurred in its resolution,"[71] the text of which is not known to have survived. On the other hand, the Holovna Rada Ruska did not even debate the agreement. Its stipulations did not suit the Ukrainian clerical leaders. On 4 June, while the fate of the agreement was being weighed in Prague, the Holovna Rada submitted the question of Galicia's division into two provinces to a general national discussion, and then on 9 June submitted a resolution in favour of partition to the emperor.[72] An answer to the question whether reservations of the Polish Rada Narodowa about the Prague agreement were caused by the actions of the Holovna Rada Ruska hangs in abeyance.

I mentioned earlier that in the discussions pertaining to the Slavic question, Borysykevych had requested mediation on behalf of the Slovaks and Ukrainians in Hungary. His voice was the harbinger of the Holovna Rada Ruska's interest in Hungarian (Transcarpathian) Rus', where the Ukrainian national movement was just beginning to awaken. Although the Ukrainians in Hungary did not have representatives in Prague, the Slovak spokesmen successfully defended their interests. Their achievement was the acceptance by the congress and the inclusion in the address to the emperor of "The Demands of the Hungarian Slovaks and Ruthenians," which requested recognition of their national distinctiveness and equal rights within the framework of the Hungarian state.[73]

The outbreak of the Prague Uprising on 12 June interrupted the deliberations of the congress. The majority of the delegates hurriedly left the city. Only a few, such as L'udovít Štúr, Mikhail Bakunin, Ryszard Berwiński, Edmund Chojecki, Jędrzej Moraczewski, Josef Václav Frič, Karel Sabina and Karel Sladkovský, took part in the fighting. We know nothing certain regarding the Ukrainian delegates, except that they remained for a short while in Prague, where Borysykevych wrote his draft demands of the citizens of Galicia, which was dated "16 June [1]848." However, the Ukrainians did not participate in the conflict. Characteristically, *Zoria Halytska* wrote nothing about the Prague events, and there is no mention of them in

Iakiv Holovatsky's correspondence. Furthermore, there are no letters whatsoever to or from him from 13 June to 10 July 1848.

It must be said in conclusion that the Slavic Congress and the Austrian Reichstag were the only international forums in which the Ukrainians appeared as a distinct nation in the family of Slavic nations and were acknowledged as such. The congress contributed to a proper understanding of the Ukrainian question in the international arena, strengthened the position of the Ukrainians and accelerated significantly the formative process of Ukrainian national and political consciousness.

13. Elections and the Austrian Reichstag

The victory of reaction in Prague and the dispersion of the Slavic Congress made it impossible to settle Galician affairs before deliberations began in the Reichstag in Vienna. In these circumstances, postponing the elections no longer made any difference. Although the Holovna Rada Ruska agreed in theory with the rationale of postponement, it did not intend to urge abstention from the elections. What, then, did the council expect from them, and how did it attempt to influence attitudes in the Ukrainian community in general and among the peasants in particular?[1]

It was generally understood that the peasants, who comprised over 80 per cent of the Galician population, would vitally affect the outcome of the elections, despite the fact that they were held in two stages—the populace selected electors, who in turn voted to choose a deputy. The Poles through their Rada Narodowa, the Ukrainians through the Holovna Rada and the Galician bureaucrats—all campaigned for the peasants' vote. When the Austrian bureaucracy saw that it was unable to organize a majority on its own, it began to support those Ukrainian candidates who were pro-governmental.[2] The Polish national councils, on the other hand, initially intended to boycott them, but they finally joined the campaign because they did not want the Poles to be outvoted in the Reichstag.[3] The Poles especially feared the peasants' attitude in the eastern part of the province. They assumed that the Ukrainian villagers would not back the Polish candidates, and it was for this reason that all the Polish proposals in the pre-election discussions on voting procedures aimed at limiting the suffrage.[4]

In contrast to the Poles, the Ukrainian leaders generally were satisfied with the electoral regulations. Closely adhering to the principles prescribed by higher authority, the Ukrainians explained them to the common people in their own terms, although sometimes with rather naïve monarchist illusions. Ivan Ilevych, for example, directed the deanery council in Berezhany to explain the electoral act to the peasants:

> Until now the emperor has issued laws to us; we have had to observe these laws, whether they were convenient for us or not. Therefore, more than one of us has complained of injustice. The illiterate, especially, who could not read the laws that were issued, have been much oppressed. In these circumstances, the people came before the emperor [and] presented their cause to him, and he most graciously...granted them such rights that they themselves, since they best know their own needs, may determine the laws together with the emperor. And to this end, the elections are to take place. Ask the people this: can they expect any benefit in their country unless they have representatives next to the emperor who will take to heart the fate of the Ruthenian people? Will representatives unsympathetic to the Ruthenian nation seek the welfare of the Ruthenians or their own welfare? Please explain this to them with examples and demonstrate to them the importance of these elections.

Ilevych also appealed to the national spokesmen in Berezhany to show the people that the Ukrainians, like other nations, had a right to claim what is their own and not permit themselves to be wronged, "either by the German officials or by the Poles. The former filled their bellies on our lands; and after stirring us up, they blamed us [for the unrest] and stripped us of our last possessions.... The Poles, having drunk enough Ruthenian blood, will drop off like leeches." When the Ukrainians, in agreement with the emperor, made the laws and decided their own fate, then "there will be Ruthenian officials, Ruthenian schools; everything will be Ruthenian, because that is as it should be on Ruthenian soil." Ilevych maintained that it was necessary to establish a Ukrainian national guard in order to safeguard these laws. For, if "the emperor demands an army, who will defend our rights and who should defend them, if not every husbandman who lives in the countryside?"[5] Ilevych's letter of instruction thus expressed some of the contradictions within the Holovna Rada leadership. The negative attitude toward the German bureaucracy reflected Ilevych's private opinion, not the official view.

One thing was certain. All the Ukrainian spokesmen, even those not connected with the council, counted on the peasants in the elections.

Their expectations coincided with the government's hopes; the Austrians expected to form a pro-governmental majority in the Reichstag thanks to the peasants.[6] The government, however, did not want to arouse suspicions that it was attempting to influence the elections. It ordered officials to refrain from any pressure on the voters, although it recommended explaining the meaning of the constitution, the rights that issued from it and the importance of the electoral act itself, "provided that this explanation and instruction of the peasants be entrusted to calm and temperate persons who have the confidence of the people and that it not be conducted secretively, but entirely openly and publicly."[7] Individual *Kreishauptmänner* and district comissioners, however, carried out their own policies. In some electoral districts they opposed the Polish candidates, while in others they supported them against the Ukrainians.[8]

The local Polish national council in Stanyslaviv issued a Ukrainian-language appeal, "Do bratei mishchaniv, selianiv, zhydiv" [To our brother burghers, villagers and Jews], recommending the choice of "wise clergymen, sound, good-hearted and God-loving country lords [who are] now your neighbours, as well as upright men of property, just and humane *mandatarii*, kind-hearted leaseholders, and merchants—in a word, literate people." If there were none, then the electors were to choose from among the peasants "a wise, honest, conscientious man who cherishes the law, for such a deputy will better defend your rights than some stranger."[9] It is apparent from this and other documents that the Poles were not so much afraid of the Ukrainian candidates as of the possibility of a unified Ukrainian-Austrian electoral platform, which could lead to the election of very anti-Polish officials. The Poles assumed that "the nation's" interests were by then in complete opposition to the government's; "the bureaucratic caste" wanted a return to the pre-March status quo, which it called "order and authority."[10]

On 30 May, the Holovna Rada Ruska issued its first electoral directive, which was distributed among the local councils.[11] After explaining the principles of the electoral law, the council advised selecting persons who were favourable to the Ruthenian cause; these should be literate individuals, preferably clergymen, though if they could not be found, then rural husbandmen. The council emphasized that the good fortune of the Ukrainian nation depended on its representatives, and therefore the people should vote. However, since many of the affiliated councils did not receive the directive and initial reports about the peasants' attitude toward the elections were not satisfying, the council launched an electoral campaign in the press.[12]

The result was disappointing. Ukrainian leaders had not anticipated that the peasants would be unreceptive. As Iosafat Kobrynsky wrote, "We are in terrible trouble. The peasants do not believe anyone and there is little hope that someone wise will go to Vienna. But what is to be done? First, we shall try to sway the people to our side."[13] The Ukrainian peasants, partly from inexperience and partly as a result of Polish countermeasures, largely stayed away from the primaries and then from the elections themselves.[14] In such circumstances the council's candidates lost and the Polish candidates were elected, even though on more than one occasion the latter had not obtained the required number of votes. In Berezhany only forty-three electors were chosen instead of the requisite one hundred, even though it was necessary, according to paragraph 48 of the electoral act of 9 May 1848, that a quorum of three-quarters of the entire number of electors be present in the second round in order to choose a deputy. Of the twenty-six assembled electors, twenty-one voted for the candidate of the Polish Rada Narodowa, Józef Zajączkowski, to represent them in Vienna.[15] In Dynów, Ivan Biretsky wrote,

> our people are in the majority; I don't know whether it is the Jews or . . . the devil who has stirred them up, so that they left the voting room like madmen and did not want to vote. The intelligentsia, gladdened at this, elected as expected a Pole . . . , and even though he did not have as many votes as necessary, he will be accepted by the National Assembly.[16]

The Holovna Rada received complaints from different parts of Galicia and from various Ukrainian councils about electoral fraud. To a certain degree the Holovna Rada itself inspired these complaints by appealing to the deaneries and the affiliated councils, in the event of any irregularities, to make a record that could be the basis of protests directed to the Galician high officials. The council suggested sending copies of such protests and precise information on the conduct of the elections to Lviv, promising for its part to intervene with the Austrian authorities.[17]

Thus, peasants from various villages protested against irregularities in the electoral primaries; they complained at meetings of the Ukrainian councils and wrote to the district authorities. The deanery council in Berezhany lodged a protest with the *Kreis* and sent a copy to the Holovna Rada and to other Ukrainian councils. Andrii Shushkevych prepared the German text and Teofil Pavlykiv drafted the Ukrainian version.[18] The protest makes clear that the deanery had received the electoral ordinance only on 26 May, although the primaries were scheduled for 4-6 June. Obviously there had been no time to prepare the common people, and most did not participate in the voting. The *mandatarii* conducted the primaries by arbitrarily establishing an electoral commission composed of persons dependent upon the estate owners. In Adamiv, for example, the primaries took place even during Greek Catholic church services, and the members of the commission had spoken out against the clergy.[19]

The *Kreishauptmann* in Berezhany replied to such protests by saying that the obligation to instruct the people belonged to the district commissioners, the *mandatarii* and the village mayors, although the clergy could have taken an active role. The charge that the electors were adherents of the nobility, he maintained, was invalid because the peasantry and the petty bourgeoisie had comprised the majority. Since the elections had to be concluded within several days, he declined to repeat the primary elections.[20]

The Ukrainian councils' protests were based primarily on the absence of the requisite number of electors during the elections themselves. Stressing this point in a protest to the *Gubernium*, the Berezhany council emphasized that of the twenty-one persons who had voted, twenty belonged to the "revolutionary party" (*Umsturzpartei*), and therefore the election did not reflect the actual social composition of Berezhany. Besides, the *Kreis* had not set the proper election date—the electors' identification papers had indicated either 14 or 15 June—and the name of a candidate whom they did not desire was recorded for some electors.[21]

The Holovna Rada forwarded the protests that it received from the local councils to the Viennese and Galician authorities and also informed the Ukrainian representatives in Vienna.[22] The results were varied. In certain electoral districts orders were given to repeat the elections. This occurred in Berezhany, Naraiv, Kryvche, Horodok, Dynów, Lutowiska, Drohobych, Sambir, Stryi, Skalat, Zbarazh, Oliiv, Sokolivka, Lubaczów, Maidan and Zolochiv,[23] although the repetition of elections ordered by the Galician authorities violated the constitution and the prerogative of the Reichstag.[24] The new elections, however, increased the Holovna Rada's hope of obtaining additional parliamentary seats. It appealed to the Ukrainians to try to elect "genuine and just Ruthenians of honest character who would not be swayed by promises or intimidated by threats." From its ranks the council supported the candidacies of Ivan Borysykevych, Ivan Hushalevych, Oleksii Zaklynsky, Ivan Zhukovsky, Amvrozii Ianovsky, Mykhailo Kuzemsky, Spyrydon Lytvynovych, Teodor Leontovych, Ivan Konstantynovych, Toma Poliansky, Ivan Slymakovsky, Mykhailo Malynovsky, Mykola Ustyianovych, Vasyl Khomynsky and Antin Paventsky.[25] As it turned out, not a single one of them obtained a mandate; only in Horodok was Iosyf Savka elected, in a repeat election.

However, the Reichstag did not recognize his election, just as it did not recognize the majority of the electoral protests by the peasants and the Ukrainians.

In many electoral districts the peasants did not want to vote for the Holovna Rada's candidates, instead backing the peasant representatives, among whom were some Poles. From among those candidates proposed by Iosafat Kobrynsky, only Kyrylo Blonsky became a deputy. In contests with the peasants' candidates, Sylvester Drymalyk, Mykola Vereshchynsky and Spyrydon Lytvynovych were defeated.[26] In Zbarazh, Ivan Borysykevych lost, even though his candidacy was fervently supported by the local Greek Catholic dean and Ruthenian council. Borysykevych's opponent was a Polish peasant named Matiasz Mazurkiewicz, a small landholder from Kretivtsi, who was backed by all the Poles "because, though uneducated, at least he is not a Ruthenian." Borysykevych's case was not helped by his speech to the electors "in a liberal, Ruthenian spirit." He explained his defeat by noting that he was unknown to the local electors, that the peasants lacked confidence in those who wore "frockcoats," and that he had only a weak knowledge of the Ukrainian folk idiom.[27]

The repeated elections in Berezhany did not take place until 7 July. Sylvester Lezhohubsky, the Greek Catholic dean and the chairman of the local Ruthenian council, issued a special circular to the faithful on 3 July, advising them to vote. The Berezhany council also approved sending a special deputation to the *Kreishauptmann* to discuss the elections; however, he informed the council on 5 July that there was not enough time for new primaries and that it would be best if Zajączkowski, the Pole selected earlier, went to Vienna. If the Ukrainians wanted a different deputy, then let those electors selected in the previous primaries choose him. If it were the case somewhere that a primary had not taken place, then the local inhabitants should pick the electors. Despite the *Kreishauptmann*'s recommendation, the *mandatarii* responsible for the primaries in Kozivka and Potutory did not conduct them, and the *Kreis* refused to recognize those electors whom the inhabitants of these villages had chosen. The Holovna Rada learned that the local peasants also did not participate in the elections because they thought that the imperial electoral patent, on which the initials "L.S." were printed differently from those on the patent of 1846 (which had abolished some abuses of the serfs), was counterfeit. Pointing out the emperor's signature had little effect.[28]

The Berezhany election was not repeated, however, because the electors thought that it would take place in the afternoon, as it had the first time, and they had not yet appeared when the commissioner closed the elections at eleven o'clock in the morning. The Poles, therefore, confirmed Zajączkowski's election in the official record, a decision with which the *Kreishauptmann* in Berezhany concurred. The Ukrainians protested and announced that they would carry their protest to higher authority.[29] The outrage felt in the Berezhany deanery council was so great that the Holovna Rada was forced to appeal for moderation.[30] When the Polish district Rada Narodowa in Berezhany proposed to the Ukrainian council that they "come to an understanding on whether to provide some instructions to the elected representatives to Vienna," the Ukrainians declined, saying "we did not choose them and therefore we have no reason to instruct them."[31]

The election of the only Austrian official from Galicia, Governor Stadion, took place without any problems. Gołuchowski had written to Iakhymovych that the governor wished to be selected as a deputy, and the Holovna Rada then appealed to the clerics of Zolochiv, Berezhany and Zhovkva to encourage their parishioners to vote for him. The council also raised the matter with the peasants who had been attending its sessions. "The reminders were not without success," Iakhymovych wrote, "since His Excellency the Governor was to be chosen from two precincts of the Zhovkva *Kreis*."[32] Accordingly, Kuzemsky withdrew Stadion's candidacy in Berezhany, proposing instead Antoni Dąbczański, the candidate of the Sobor Ruskyi, who, he noted, "favours the Ruthenian cause, has a good understanding of the issue and is quite eloquent."[33]

The outcome of the elections could have been worse for the Ukrainians.[34] Of the one hundred mandates allotted to Galicia (not including Bukovyna, which elected eight deputies), the Ukrainians gained twenty-five. Fifteen peasants were elected: Hryhorii Andrusiak (Skole), Iosyf Dynets (Sokal), Andrii Dzivakovsky (Zhydachiv), Stepan Hoi (Zalishchyky), Vasyl Harmatii (Mykulyntsi), Iosyf Hryhoruk (Deliatyn), Ivan Kapushchak (Solotvyna), Panko Kozar (Zhovkva), Ivan Krukhovsky (Horodenka), Stefan Lesiuk (Kolomyia), Hryhorii Nychyporuk (Sniatyn), Hryn Petryshyn (Tysmenytsia), Konstantyn Posatsky (Rozhniativ), Ivan Ryshko (Kuty) and Iosyf Savka (Horodok);[35] eight Greek Catholic clergymen: Kyrylo Blonsky (Iabloniv), Oleksander Dobriansky (Sanok), Mykhailo Hankevych (Radekhiv), Mykhailo Hnidkovsky (Voinyliv), Hryhorii Iakhymovych (Przemyśl), Hryhorii Levytsky (Zolochiv), Ivan Lomnytsky (Turka) and Hryhorii Shashkevych (Monastyryska); and two members of the lay intelligentsia: Ievstakhii Prokopchyts (Mariampil) and Kyrylo Vinkovsky (Iavoriv).[36] To be sure, the Ukrainian clerical leaders had expected a greater success. They could get over the defeat of their candidates by Poles, but it was more difficult to reconcile themselves to the defeat of the Greek Catholic priests by the Ukrainian peasant candidates in the same district: Father A. Dutkevych by Ivan Kapushchak in Solotvyna, Father Sylvester Drymalyk by Stefan Lesiuk in Kolomyia, Father Spyrydon Lytvynovych by Hryhorii Nychyporuk in Sniatyn and Father Mykola Vereshchynsky by Ivan Ryshko in Kuty.

These reversals demonstrated clearly the decline of the peasants' confidence in the Ukrainian clergy in general and in its pro-Austrian policy in particular.[37] There was consternation among the conservatives. They began to wonder how they could possibly direct the actions in Vienna of the peasant deputies, who, after all, were unacquainted with politics; moreover, the majority were illiterate and did not speak German. Thus the Greek Catholic church leaders, as Iakhymovych wrote, wanted to "find reliable and competent advisors in Vienna, since many opponents will gather there." He recognized the simplest and most desirable means: Stadion was among the deputies from Galicia, and he "could effectively support our interests . . . , since he is very well aware of the situation here."[38]

On the other hand, the liberals were much more critical. They openly conceded that the Holovna Rada's policies had caused the crisis. The Ukrainians, deceived in their hopes, had lost confidence in the clergy and the Austrian authorities. The liberals blamed the council's leaders for "caring as much about the people as a dog cares for a fifth leg. Just give them lots of money and titles, and they would even sell their own fathers. We are in need of great reform, especially at the top. But we do not know how and when that will occur." However, they did not despair. They called for more intense work in preparing the common people for the anticipated elections to the Galician diet, which, they felt, could become the foundation for further development of the Ukrainian nation.[39] They agreed with the conservatives only in regard to the negative influence of Polish electoral propaganda on the Ukrainians. As Iakiv Holovatsky remarked, "The peasants do not believe anything from the Poles [*Liakhy*], [and] now they do not trust the German commissioners. They hold to the saying: don't believe anyone, then no one will deceive you," which was just a way of masking their distrust of the Ukrainian leadership, because of the latter's co-operation with the government during the elections.[40]

The peasants' withdrawal from the elections in many districts of Eastern Galicia seems to show that they believed at least some of what the Poles were saying. The propaganda was not particularly subtle, even proclaiming that there would be fighting in Vienna and that signatures would be collected there to restore *robot*.[41] Father A. Dutkevych, who had been thwarted in his hope to become a deputy, wrote:

> [The Poles] in their newspapers . . . dishonoured, fouled and blackened the Ruthenian clergy, Bishop Iakhymovych, *Zoria Halytska*, the Holovna Rada, and its affiliates. . . . They threatened the zealous Ruthenians with death, they instilled suspicion and distrust in the peasants' minds toward their priests and divided parishioners from their pastors; by these means they separated the unlettered part of the nation from the intelligentsia, the result of which has been that the Ruthenian nation, misled about the general assemblies, has sent uneducated and illiterate peasants to Vienna.[42]

Ivan Biretsky's appraisal of the elections even suggested—aptly, it seemed—that the Ukrainian common people followed the example of the Polish peasants, "who now do not want to trust either their priests or their commissioners."[43]

The sources indicate that the Ukrainian peasants demonstrated markedly independent action, the result of which was a relatively large number of peasant deputies in the Reichstag.[44] The peasants' position caused concern not only in Polish circles,[45] but also among the Ukrainian leaders. With the Ukrainian masses in mind, Teodor Leontovych, the secretary of the Holovna Rada, wrote to the delegates of the council in Prague:

> We have, to be sure, the greatest influence on the nation. God, the emperor and the Holovna Rada are the nation's byword. But we can only consider ourselves to be its ministry, which fails if it does not act in the spirit of the nation. Our nation now has its own existence; it is monarchical and desires to remain with Austria as the Ruthenian nation; we can do all things together with our nation, but we do not want to do more than we are able.[46]

But the data already cited show that in reality the Ukrainian spokesmen were not able to act; they were simply afraid of the peasants.

The final act of the elections was played out in Vienna. Efforts had to be made there to resolve the electoral protests. In the Holovna Rada's reasoning, this matter was one of the elements of its struggle with the hegemony of the Poles in Galicia. Otherwise, it would be difficult to understand the Ukrainians' accusations that the Polish electors in Berezhany belonged to a "revolutionary party" hostile to the government, or the insinuations that Franciszek Smolka was "a pardoned traitor to the state, neither an aristocrat nor a democrat, but a veritable republican."[47]

The Austrian interior ministry, however, either returned the protests and complaints over the elections or directed that they be sent to the Reichstag for verification. The Ukrainians counted most on the decision in the Reichstag.[48] The protest against Zajączkowski's election in Berezhany seemed to have a chance for a favourable resolution, but it was doomed to failure because the councils concerned, the Holovna Rada and the Berezhany deanery council, could not form a united front.[49]

The divisions within the Ukrainian community during the elections were reflected among the Ukrainian deputies to the Reichstag. Their lack of cohesiveness was particularly important because the 190 Slavic deputies comprised the most numerous group of the 383 members of the Reichstag. The Slavic politicians, especially the Czechs, hoped that they would be able to fulfill their programme along the lines laid out at the Slavic Congress, but success depended on support by the hundred Galician deputies, both Poles and Ukrainians. The Poles expected to gain self-rule for Galicia and the possibility that it could break away from Austria if the Polish state were restored. The Ukrainians, however, adhering closely to the Austrian monarchy, wanted to bring the partitioning of Galicia to a successful conclusion. They certainly did not think of being included within the borders of a Polish state. Again the Czech liberals had to mediate the Ukrainian-Polish dispute.[50] When Kyrylo Blonsky informed Iakiv Holovatsky that the Germans wanted the Ukrainians to join with Germany ("inniger Anschluss an Deutschland"), he added, "They will not succeed." He also remarked, "we are at constant odds with the *Liakhy*, but when it is a matter of the common welfare of the Slavs, then we, the Poles, the Czechs and the Illyrians [South Slavs] stand by one another." The Czechs' support, and not only theirs, seemed like a saving grace to the Ukrainians. "If God grants it, our cause will go well. The only bad thing is that we have few of our intelligentsia here, only the peasantry [*muzhychnia*]. But Stadion and others are behind us. All the Czechs back us—God grant them health. Palacký, Havlíček and other famous names."[51]

Havlíček played a special role. As a particularly active deputy, he defended the Ukrainian peasant deputy Stepan Hoi when attempts were made to stop him from addressing the Reichstag because he did not know German. Havlíček rightly maintained that forty other deputies who did not know German also had to vote; the business at hand needed to be explained to them. Havlíček, along with František Rieger, also supported the peasant deputies' successful request that resolutions before the Reichstag be translated into appropriate national languages. (Hryhorii Shashkevych first acted in the role of both Ukrainian and Polish translator on 4 October.[52]) *Zoria Halytska* emphasized the Czechs' "honest, fraternal generosity," noting with pride that Havlíček "even sits among our deputies."[53]

Such attempts at translation were meant to unite the peasant deputies, who did not always follow their leaders. Blonsky's initial assurances that "all the Ruthenian peasants and all the Mazurians

[Polish peasants] are keeping with us," were proved wrong the moment debate opened on the question of abolishing *robot*.[54] Bishop Iakhymovych, for example, complained that the rural deputies, because they did not know German, voted for resolutions that they would certainly have rejected "if they knew what the matter concerned. But they do not want to trust anyone at all who could lead them, though they listen to the promptings of enemies with false pretenses."[55]

It became apparent that both the pro-governmental party and the opposition forces had to take the peasants' votes into account, because there were ninety-two peasant deputies in the Reichstag (of whom thirty-eight were from Galicia). Characteristic in this regard were the results of the votes on indemnification for the land-owners and on the resolution by the Bohemian German Ludwig Löhner that the decision of the Reichstag on the abolition of *robot* did not require the emperor's sanction. When the first of these matters was raised on 31 August, the Ukrainian peasant deputies, with the exception of Andrii Dzivakovsky, who abstained, voted against providing indemnification. Hryhorii Shashkevych also abstained, but Dobriansky, Iakhymovych, Levytsky and Vinkovsky supported the motion to pay indemnification for the loss of *robot*.[56] This was the only occasion on which the peasants voted with the leftist wing of the Reichstag.

The second issue provoked an even greater divergence in the voting. Hankevych, Hryhoruk and Ryshko came out against the need for imperial sanction, while Blonsky, Dobriansky, Dynets, Hoi, Hnidkovsky, Harmatii, Iakhymovych, Krukhovsky, Levytsky, Lomnytsky, Nychyporuk, Petryshyn, Posatsky, Shashkevych and Vinkovsky voted against Löhner's motion. The remainder either abstained or did not participate in the vote. The majority of the deputies from Bukovyna, however, supported the motion, with only Mykhailo Bodnar opposed.[57]

Given this division in the voting, the Polish deputy Marian Hubicki's protest that Stadion had influenced the outcome by swaying the peasant deputies to the government's side was only partly justified. Hubicki did not know that the Czech deputies were even more influential. This vote had already indicated that Polish-Czech-Ukrainian co-operation in the Reichstag could not last. Its final collapse was an outcome of the Hungarian issue.[58]

A deputation from the Hungarian diet arrived in Vienna on 17 September with a request for aid from the Reichstag to repel the incursion into Hungary by Croatian *ban* Jelačić's army. A tempestuous debate ensued two days later on whether the Reichstag should receive this delegation. The German left wing and a majority of the Poles, who appreciated the Magyars' value as political allies, favoured the meeting; on the other hand, the political right, led by the South Slavs, who considered the Hungarians oppressors of the Slavic nationalities, opposed it. The South Slavs maintained that the Magyars not only intended to be masters of the Slavs, but also to break up Austria, aims which jeopardized the plan of transforming Austria into a federated monarchy. The issue was decided on a roll-call vote in which the majority opposed receiving the Hungarians. Among the Galician Ukrainian deputies only three—Dobriansky, Hankevych and Vinkovsky—voted for the meeting.[59] The Hungarian issue led both to a collapse of co-operation between the Poles and the other Slavs and to a final consolidation of the Reichstag factions. Blonsky wrote on 5 October to Iakiv Holovatsky: "There are three parties in the Reichstag: ultra-radical, reactionary and democratic-monarchist. The Ruthenians belong to the last with the exception of Vinkovsky, Fedorovych [Federowicz] and Dobriansky."[60]

After the outbreak of the Viennese uprising on 6 October, when the local populace sought to block the sending of a battalion of grenadiers against the Hungarians and the minister of war, Count Theodor Latour, was killed, the Reichstag was the only organ of state authority left in Vienna. (Philip Krauss was the only member of the ministerial council remaining in the city, and the emperor escaped with his court to Olomouc in Moravia.) This situation persisted until the end of October. During this entire period the Reichstag continued to deliberate under the leadership of Franciszek Smolka, first in his capacity as vice-president (the president, the Bohemian Anton Strobach, had left), and from 12 October as the newly elected president. Smolka sought to keep the Reichstag from dissolving. He forbade the remaining deputies to leave Vienna, and, when the Czech deputies who had gone to Prague called for transferring the Reichstag to Brno, he caused the Reichstag to accept a resolution that it was "the only legal, constitutional and legislative authority."[61]

Many Czech and Ukrainian deputies, particularly the peasants, left Vienna during the October Revolution. The stenographic record, however, proves that Blonsky, Dobriansky, Hankevych, Iakhymovych, Shashkevych and Vinkovsky remained. Vinkovsky unquestionably played a role in the efforts to aid Minister Latour, and he authored a resolution that Anton Doblhoff and Theodor Hornbostl be included in the new ministry. Shashkevych was chosen as a Galician representative, together with the Pole Leszek Borkowski, to the commission charged with drafting the legislation that was to follow Emperor Ferdinand's manifesto of 7 October. On 17 October he proposed establishing local land commissions to resolve the peasant question.[62]

With the one exception of the Bukovynian deputy Lukian Kobylytsia, who took an active part in the October Uprising, the remaining Ukrainian deputies did not support the revolution, and the majority also were opposed to the further functioning of the Reichstag. The surviving correspondence shows that the fighting on the streets of Vienna appalled the Ukrainians. Danger from the revolutionary elements and the proletariat, as Iakhymovych stressed, prompted them to stay in their lodgings, and eventually they decided to leave Vienna. Iakhymovych himself departed for Brno on 19 October. It was in his rooms there, on 22 October, that a meeting took place among Bohemian, Moravian and Galician deputies who, in reply to the Reichstag's threat that they return to Vienna or have their mandates invalidated and new elections called, resolved to go instead to the court at Olomouc. There they secured the emperor's decision to terminate the proceedings of the Reichstag in Vienna and to transfer the deliberations to Kroměříž. Iakhymovych received this news with delight: "In such conditions it was impossible to conceive of free deliberations in the Reichstag, which was increasingly departing from a legal course. The majority of moderates had [already] left."[63]

The moderate Ukrainian deputies thought that the Magyars had planned the Viennese Revolution in accord with the Poles and German republicans. In Blonsky's opinion, they desired to "abolish the monarchy, annex Bohemia, Moravia, Silesia, Austria, Styria, the Tyrol and Illyria to Germany, and create a Magyar republic with its subject territories and a Polish republic with the Ruthenians subordinated. Meanwhile, in Germany [the Slavs] would be germanized, in Hungary magyarized and in Poland polonized." Blonsky was pleased by the rout of the insurrectionaries and the role played by the Nassau and Parma regiments, composed largely of Ukrainians, in the capture of Vienna and the ensuing counter-revolutionary terror. He was most pleased by the defeat of the Polish cause: "Now the whole world knows what the Poles are like; the Czechs and the other Slavs especially have become convinced of this."[64] He also viewed the November events in Lviv as a continuation of the Viennese Revolution, and he based this contention on the deputies' appeal of 19 October, directed at Galicia and signed among others by the Ukrainians Dobriansky, Hankevych, Kobylytsia and Vinkovsky, which called for refraining from an untimely outbreak there.[65]

The Ukrainians' attitude toward the rump Reichstag in Vienna and the Viennese Revolution was reflected also in the later results of the election for president of the reconstituted Reichstag in Kroměříž and especially in their vote for the motion to declare invalid the Reichstag's meetings during the last days of October (that is, from 22 October, the day of the emperor's order to transfer the deliberations). Smolka's victory over Strobach in the new election for the presidency of the Reichstag particularly displeased the Ukrainians,[66] and so they voted, with the exception only of Dobriansky, to invalidate the final deliberations of the Viennese Reichstag. Nonetheless, it should be noted that Vinkovsky, Dynets, Hankevych, Kozar, Hoi and Stavarsky, who were not then present in Kroměříž, did not participate.[67]

The Ukrainians', and especially Bishop Iakhymovych's, antipathy toward the Reichstag deepened when it became apparent that it would not fulfill the fundamental postulate of the Holovna Rada: it would not decide on the division of Galicia. The bishop laid the burden of responsibility for that failure on the Poles, the German centralists and the Czech deputies, upon whom he had placed great hopes until that time.[68]

It is therefore hardly surprising that the Ukrainian leaders were relieved when the government dissolved the Reichstag in March 1849. According to Shashkevych, the Reichstag had become such "a fool that the [Austrian] ministry sent it home to reflect."[69]

14. The Peasant Question

Before 1848 the Galician peasants used approximately two-thirds of the arable land, meadows and pastures, but less than one per cent of the forests. Nevertheless, their situation had worsened significantly since the time of Joseph II. The amount of land they possessed in Eastern Galicia had diminished by 7.4 per cent (or 257,911 morgs). Moreover, the peasant's traditional practice of subdividing his holdings among his male heirs had continued, so that in certain districts three-fourths of the peasant holdings amounted to fewer than ten morgs, or a little over seven acres. At the same time, the peasant's obligations under *robot* had increased.[1]

The situation of the peasants in Eastern Galicia was further complicated by the ethnic difference between the nobles and their subjects. The Poles failed to appreciate this distinction: they were not interested in the Ukrainian national movement, and before 1848 they were virtually unaware of it, especially because the national movement had barely penetrated the Ukrainian masses, which were still subject to the conditions of *robot*. Although the Ukrainian peasants retained their distinctiveness in religion and language and were conscious of their separateness in relation to the Polish *szlachta* (*Liakhy*), these feelings still did not constitute a national consciousness. For them, as one contemporary wrote, "the name 'Pole' always meant nobleman, a lord. It . . . was not the name of a people, but of an estate."[2] In other words, the social question clearly dominated the national question in the Eastern Galician countryside. Yet these two issues were indissolubly linked. Not until 1848 did the Polish activists become cognizant of the social question, and even then they did not fully grasp its meaning.

Before March 1848, the conservative Ukrainian leaders avoided saying anything that might dissuade the peasants from fulfilling their *robot* obligations. They refused to publish the Polish address of March 1848 in Ukrainian, and initially they did not contemplate making any socio-economic demands. The Ukrainians' address of 19 April did not contain any references to social conditions; it did not mention the liquidation of *robot*. It seemed as though the authors, even though they had signed the address in the name of the Ukrainian nation, were afraid to antagonize the government. They held to the belief that the government alone was competent to change the conditions of serfdom.[3] Inwardly, the conservatives desired no changes at all. They bore the abolition of *robot* painfully, fearing loss of income.

From its inception, the Holovna Rada Ruska also had no set programme on socio-economic issues. It seems that the vague programme outlined in the council's proclamation of 10 May was to have remained unchanged; the leaders did not imagine that the peasants would demand that the local Ukrainian councils and the Holovna Rada deal energetically with economic problems. Thus, when the Ukrainian councils gained recognition and the peasants began to regard them as competent to mediate between themselves and the Austrian authorities, the Holovna Rada's programme had to be substantially broadened.

The Holovna Rada, however, did not have a single peasant member. It realized that this was an unnatural state of affairs and that it was not sufficient occasionally to invite peasants to attend an open session, seat them in a place of honour next to Bishop Iakhymovych and chat with them.[4] It was necessary to involve them actively in national and political life. With this aim in mind, the Holovna Rada recommended that at least three peasant representatives be included in its locally organized affiliates and that one section in each of these councils concern itself with "matters of the rural economy."[5] However, because the established guidelines concerning the number of members were not strictly observed, in certain councils from a few to several score peasants participated. It is known that hundreds of Ukrainian peasants took part in the ceremonies establishing the various councils and that large numbers attended their sessions. Thus, it can be stated without exaggeration that the local councils became genuine schools of the Ukrainian peasantry, a point that contemporaries underscored on more than one occasion.[6]

Both the conservatives and the liberals counted on the peasants' support, especially during the campaign for the Reichstag elections. At the same time, the peasants' attitude toward the elections surprised everyone. The peasant deputies' behaviour in the Reichstag clearly demonstrated that, out of concern for their own interests, they had no intention of listening to instructions from, or siding unconditionally with, the government.[7] Their position became evident during the debate over the abolition of *robot* and on the government-backed scheme for indemnification. The Ukrainian peasants in the Reichstag generally favoured (1) preserving the so-called servitudes (evident in Kapushchak's proposition that while serf obligations were to be abolished, their right to gather wood from the forests was not;[8] (2) land enfranchisement without indemnification (forcefully expressed in Kapushchak's celebrated speech on 17 August against indemnification);[9] (3) the return of the peasants' confiscated lands (to be done according to the Josephinian cadastre of 1786 and not the land registers of 1820); (4) the creation of commissions to resolve land disputes, with broad participation by village representatives; (5) the introduction of instruction in the native languages; (6) the staffing of public offices by their countrymen; (7) the reduction of taxes; (8) some equalization of wages; (9) permission to keep weapons for the defense of every property owner's home and land; (10) the shortening of military service to four years; (11) forbidding fairs to take place on Sundays and holy days (both Roman and Greek Catholic); (12) a prohibition on the sale of rustical lands; (13) securing the right to use the grist mills; (14) the assumption by the village communities of the right of presentation [advowson] of their pastors; (15) equal remuneration for the clergy of both rites and their payment in coin so that they might have more time to fulfill their obligations; and (16) the division of Galicia into two gubernias—one Ukrainian, with its seat in Lviv, and the other Polish, with its seat in either Tarnów or Cracow. The Galician peasant deputies included all these demands in their formal proposal to the Reichstag, which was signed in Vienna on 3 September and which indicated the close co-operation among the Ukrainian and Polish peasants. It was signed for the Ukrainians by Andrusiak, Hoi, Hryhoruk, Kozar, Nychyporuk, Posatsky and Ryshko.[10]

To this day the authorship of the document remains an open question. Perhaps it was drafted by the Polish radical Julian Maciej Goslar, who remained in Vienna after 7 August, conferred frequently with the peasant deputies, served informally as their parliamentary advisor and certainly exerted an influence on their attitudes during the debate over indemnification.[11] It has also been maintained that Kapushchak's philippic—a ringing denunciation in broken German of the land-owning nobles—was written either by Stadion or Hryhorii Shashkevych. The former can be excluded, but nothing conclusive can be said about Shashkevych's role, although he did refrain from voting during the balloting on indemnification, and on 17 October he introduced an excellently reasoned motion on forming land commissions to resolve the issue of the servitudes.[12]

Stepan Hoi had also intended to take part in the debate over Kudlich's proposal on indemnification, but he was not permitted to do so because he did not know German. His prepared speech was treated, therefore, as a petition. It was unfortunate that he did not speak, since he demanded the consolidation of all lands and the return to the peasants of the rustical lands, which were not to be inferior in quality to those to be apportioned to the manorial estates.[13]

The peasant deputies maintained contact with their constituent electors, corresponding with them on a range of issues.[14] They also enjoyed the confidence of their electors, as is evidenced by the large number of complaints from villages and individual farmers about the seizure of their lands and the loss of their right to use forests, meadows and pastures that were addressed to the Reichstag deputies. Hundreds of such cases were noted in the stenographic record of the Reichstag. Unfortunately, they had no impact on the resolution of the peasant question.

The significant number of peasant deputies and their position in the Reichstag caused all the political factions to bid for their favour. The so-called peasant-catching (*łapichłopstwo*) was by no means just a Polish specialty;[15] the Czech liberals alerted the Ukrainians to the threat posed to the Slavic cause if the governmental party Stadion directed should be supported by the peasant deputies.[16] In order to unite those deputies and draw them away from the Poles, the members of the Holovna Rada courted and counselled them. They discussed indemnification, wrote letters to the deputies and tried to convince them of the necessity for partitioning Galicia. Iuliian Velychkovsky wrote that, as a consequence of these actions,

> the Polish peasant deputies asked if our [Ruthenian] council could not publish something in Polish for the Mazurians. They said that the Jews and the lords were confusing them, but I answered that it was not possible, since the Ruthenians are poor and such a publication requires considerable expenditure. I told them that when Galicia is divided, they will be able to set up a Polish journal under the editorship of some professor.... With this they were very satisfied.[17]

While the peasants' support was being solicited in Vienna, in Galicia attempts were being made to depict the election of peasant deputies as inappropriate. In describing the debate over indemnification and the unfortunate incident in which Hoi had been denied the right to speak, the editors of *Zoria Halytska* added the caustic comment:

> So the peasants, in choosing only peasants as deputies, thought that they would best defend their rights. But meanwhile, it turned out just the opposite. And what will happen when the deliberations over schools begin?... But the peasants can rest easy, because there are other deputies who stand behind them and for their rights, and, even though they are not peasants, they are far better than the peasant deputies, who have only remained silent.[18]

The peasants' stance and the election results forced the Ukrainian councils to become more attentive to rural concerns. Even though the Greek Catholic consistories expressed anxiety over the peasants' boycott of further work on the landed estates,[19] other developments in the Ukrainian countryside generated still greater concern. On 30 June the Holovna Rada, through *Zoria Halytska*, resolved to warn the peasants against selling their meagre holdings.[20] The council pointed out that land—the principal means of sustaining rural families—should not be sold hastily, even if the new owner permitted the peasant to continue to till the land he had sold. This arrangement would constitute a new form of *robot*. The council appealed to the peasants to "preserve their hereditary holdings for themselves, their families and their heirs." The council's effort probably had little effect, since a similar warning was issued in February 1849, and the Ruthenian council in Buchach asked the government to prohibit land sales.[21] The Holovna Rada also proposed a plan to organize communal granaries in order to safeguard the peasants from starvation during the period before the next harvest, to allow a reserve of grain to be set aside and to designate any profits for the purchase of land or forests for common use. The council also warned the peasants not to borrow with their lands as collateral, or to commit themselves to work two days a year for each ten guldens borrowed, or to place themselves in the land-owners' debt for the use of pastures or forests.[22] *Zoria Halytska*, for its part, sought to prepare the peasants for the future system of rural self-government, the dismantling of the large landed estates and the removal of *mandatarii* and their replacement by elected village elders.[23]

In many parts of Galicia the peasants regarded the Holovna Rada and its affiliates as the only intermediaries between the countryside and the government,[24] a situation which the Austrian authorities tolerated. The Holovna Rada therefore had to settle hundreds of complaints sent through the local councils from Ukrainian hamlets and individual peasants. These complaints concerned the annexation of rustical lands, communal forests, pastures and huts, and the peasants' long-standing litigations with the nobles. There also were requests for aid in demarcating the boundaries between the rustical and manorial lands. The patents of 17 April and 7 September 1848 had addressed these problems only in general terms, making reference to later, more specific regulations that were to be uniformly applied throughout the Austrian state. But until this occurred, these patents confirmed as belonging to the peasant only those rustical lands registered in the cadastre in 1786, if they had still been in the possession of the peasants in 1820. In this way, the seizures of peasant holdings that had occurred between 1786 and 1820 were legally recognized. Nor were the peasants given title to those manorial lands "that they had been allowed to use by the land-owner under a formal agreement."[25] The issue of the servitudes was not conclusively regulated, although they were to be abolished with some compensation to the peasants.

In order to reduce the rival claims, on 10 June the Polish central Rada Narodowa issued a proclamation encouraging all parties to use the "courts of conciliation," whose findings then "could not be appealed to a higher court" in resolving land disputes.[26] The affiliated Ukrainian councils intended to form similar courts.[27] The authorities responded immediately. The *Gubernium*'s ruling of 4 July reads: "Because the peasants are beginning to apply to the courts of conciliation in considerable numbers, a valid fear arises that they will lose their confidence in the *Kreis* administration."[28] The circulars, some in Ukrainian, issued by the *Kreise* warned the villagers against "participating in this illegal action" and announced that penalties would be meted out.[29] Under these circumstances an informal system of courts of conciliation could not develop.

There was a certain consistency in the conduct of the Ukrainian councils in settling the villagers' disputes with the manors. For example, the Ruthenian council in Univ referred to the Holovna Rada those matters that pertained to rustical lands and the interests of whole villages, but it sought to resolve private disputes directly with the estate owner. The Univ council also negotiated with him when the villagers' interests demanded it, but the settling of any matter actually depended entirely on the good will of the lord. If, however, the fault and ill will of an estate owner was obvious, the council forwarded the matter to the *Kreis* authorities.[30] The Ruthenian council in Berezhany acted similarly: if the dispute concerned rustical lands, it was referred to the Holovna Rada, but when an arrangement depended on the will of the estate owner, the interested parties were referred to him.[31] Matters concerning the persecution of the Ukrainian nationality by the Poles, officials and *Kreishauptmänner*, as well as cases of injustice toward the peasants in collecting taxes, also reached the Holovna Rada. In connection with the latter, the Ruthenian council in Kolomyia formally proposed that the demarcation of lands and the assignment of taxes be entrusted to the villages. The villagers of Horshova in the Chortkiv district even delivered a memorandum protesting against the oppression of the peasants by the manor and the *Kreishauptmann*.[32]

The Holovna Rada was in a delicate situation. It wanted to protect the peasants' rights, but it certainly did not want to overstep legal bounds. It therefore tried to control the mood of the people and the more impetuous elements in the countryside. On 8 August Mykola Ustyianovych published in *Zoria Halytska* an article in which he took issue with Baltazar Szczucki's brochure *Vidky sia vziala shliakhta, pany, panshchyna i piddani* [Whence came the nobility, the lords, *robot* and the serfs].[33] Ustyianovych argued that all lands that had belonged to the peasants at any time should be given to them. Seizing the opportunity, the editor of *Zoria Halytska*, Antin Paventsky, in the name of and upon the recommendation of the Holovna Rada, wrote that it would be erroneous to conclude on the basis of this polemic that "the villages have the right to take back the cultivated lands, forests and pastures that are in the possession of the lords. They have not this right and cannot have it, because it expired long ago." Nevertheless, lands which the manors took "either by deceit or force" and about which the villages had taken the matter to court should belong to the peasants, who could, however, regain them "only by legal recourse and without the least violence." Paventsky advised the peasants to be patient and promised them that the disputes would be settled in their favour. He added that the peasants' plundering of the forests, meadows and pastures "disgraces the Ruthenian name,... undermines the authority of the law, [and] increases the turbulence and disorder in the country." For such actions they would be held accountable.

For the most part, such warnings produced no results, and by summer 1848, the Holovna Rada had come to recognize the need for establishing commissions to resolve land disputes. The council believed that Ukrainian lawyers should participate in them, especially since the *Kreis* commissioners were not looking after the peasants' interests. The Holovna Rada also decided to petition the Reichstag for the return of lands formerly belonging to the peasants.[34] In its pronouncement of 4 August to the Ukrainian councils, it submitted for discussion "statutes according to which the villages that were previously enserfed and are now free should guide themselves while maintaining order and safety [*Comunal Verfassung*]" and "new regulations concerning the forests with provisions for unfettered clearing by entire villages, as well as by individual organizations or persons."[35] The appeal did not fall on deaf ears. The Ruthenian council in Bolekhiv sent a letter indicating that it was considering how to prevent the annexation of peasant lands by their former lords and acknowledged the necessity of requesting the Reichstag to establish special commissions to regulate and record property titles, "once and for all to put a stop to all disputes."[36]

The Holovna Rada therefore directed "that every rural community ready its grievances,... accompanied by a large number of signatures and the appropriate village seals, for submission to the local councils, which in turn will forward them to the Holovna Rada with a notation whether the issues concern private property or lands under state administration." The number of complaints preserved in the files of the Holovna Rada testifies to the extent of the problem.[37] However, the council decided not to act on the requests until the Reichstag approved on 7 September the resolution abolishing *robot*. Five days later, *Zoria Halytska* informed the Ukrainians of the substance of the patent, and on 19 September it printed the entire text in Ukrainian.[38] Thus, there were no legal obstacles to initiating action in Vienna; on 13 October the Holovna Rada announced that it had submitted a request to the Reichstag that it resolve the land disputes.[39]

The council expected the issue of the servitudes to be settled in the peasants' favour, since otherwise the peasants' situation "would become impossible to bear" with their holdings diminished and with no other means of support. The council also noted numerous court proceedings that it regarded as illegal and demanded settlement of the conflicts, since "the laws themselves do not yet provide protection." According to the Holovna Rada, litigations of this kind were occurring in Galicia because there were no up-to-date cadastres and land registers. Except for tax inventories and returns between 1772 and 1776, the only evidence of land ownership in Galicia was presented by witnesses. The council believed that the imperial rescripts from Joseph II's time should take precedence over the tax registers of 1820, because "they are signed by the lords and the villagers" and possess "the full burden of proof." The 1820 lists bore witness against the lords, who, since they possessed these lands illegally, should be punished. However, in those cases where ownership could not be determined, "the conditions of ownership [ought] to be investigated from a political perspective and a temporary arrangement arrived at, since a decision regarding legal ownership of the lands is in the domain only of the political offices." Finally, the council observed that the lords also should be anxious to settle the disputes, in order to prevent future violations. The Holovna Rada therefore requested the Reichstag to examine the relevant ordinances, institute permanent procedures in land disputes and establish commissions composed of impartial individuals familiar with conditions in Galicia. It also presented these matters to the emperor during an audience in Olomouc on 6 November. It requested the introduction of a new form of village government, the replacement of the *mandatarii* by state-appointed officials and the creation of land commissions.[40]

In the wake of the popular disturbances in November 1848 in Lviv, the Viennese and Galician authorities demanded support from the Holovna Rada to "maintain peace and order in the Ruthenian villages." Their aim was twofold: to suppress revolutionary fervor and to guard "that the village folk do not prey upon the property of the landed nobility and so that the loathsome incidents of 1846 are not repeated." The *Kreise* also received appropriate instructions. The Holovna Rada, recognizing in the government's actions "proof of its consideration for the Ruthenian nation," issued an appeal to the people in which it professed its commitment to "peace in the country and security for individuals and [their] property." The appeal stressed that the Ukrainian nation had not infringed on the peace in the past and would not do so in the future, "regardless of whatever kind of instigators—who on the ruins of Austria and in a breach of faith with the emperor... desire the old Poland within its former boundaries—may try to persuade them." A nobleman seldom could prove that a Ukrainian peasant had committed an injustice, since he chose rather "to suffer wrongdoing than to cause harm." Those rights that the Ukrainian peasants attained had come through the courts, and only as a consequence of lengthy litigations "did individual instances take place here and there of lawless opposition and reprehensible vengeance." In 1846 the Ukrainians in the Sanok and Jasło districts had even stood in defence of their Polish lords, which was evidence of "the deep-rooted principles of Christian love in the hearts of Ruthenians." The Holovna Rada expected that, this time as well, the Ukrainians "would not disgrace the Ruthenian name" and would prove to the world that "they are being judged unjustly." The future constitution would insure their rights and not permit injustices against them. In conclusion, the Holovna Rada appealed for maintaining loyalty to the emperor and recommended to the affiliated councils that they fortify the Ukrainian community in this spirit.[41]

However, the peasants no longer wished to suffer, especially because by the fall of 1848 the Polish landowners had begun to co-operate with the government, hoping to obtain favourable settlements for themselves in land matters.[42]

Meanwhile, the *Kreise* had undertaken to resolve the land disputes. In the Reichstag, Shashkevych urged repeatedly the preservation of the servitudes,[43] and in February 1849 the Galician authorities also appealed that they be honoured, because spoliation of the forests had been intensifying since November 1848.[44] Only then did the Austrian authorities seem to recognize the danger, and therefore the *Kreise* began to take decisive measures. The ringleaders were placed in jail; the villages were threatened with criminal prosecution and summary justice, and *Kreis* commissions were dispatched to the sites of the "crimes." Agenor Gołuchowski was compelled to announce that the servitudes would remain in force. Only the "willful destruction of forests" was forbidden. The Holovna Rada also appealed for the protection of the hereditary lords' private holdings, proclaiming: "One's own is sacred, but what belongs to someone else is even more sacred [*Svoie sviate, a chuzhe shche sviatishe*].... That the former serf owners and the nobles call attention to this wrongdoing is entirely just." The Poles in the Reichstag formally queried the government as to its intentions to protect the former hereditary land-owners' possessions and avert their total impoverishment. However, the Poles did not mention the injustices against the villages that were also occurring.[45]

In the spring and summer of 1849, Ukrainian peasants in large numbers refused to work on the manorial fields for fear that *robot* would be revived, and as a consequence less land was cultivated than in previous years.[46] The Holovna Rada, never having received a reply from the Reichstag to its petition of 13 October 1848, made a direct request of the Viennese authorities on 20 April 1849. Stressing the government's concern to that date for the material well-being of the common people, the council suggested that the government was being deceived by the Polish *szlachta*. One-third of the rustical lands in Galicia had been illegally seized by the nobility since the time of Joseph II, "half of the serfs were unjustly denied the right of cutting wood in the forests and using the pastures, [and]... half again as many burdens and levies" had been exacted from the peasants as the lords had a right to demand. Therefore, the council suggested that payments from the indemnification fund be withheld until the peasants' complaints were settled. It demanded that the peasants be awarded a third of the indemnification quota, because many a time "not the lord, but the serfs have the right to demand recompense." The council favoured preserving the servitudes and opposed any reimbursement for them because of the low rates for users' rights prevailing in the Galician countryside. In conclusion, the council stated: "Peace and order in the country, the welfare of the [former] serfs and the power of the government demand that the serfs' complaints be examined equitably and as quickly as possible and that their just requests be satisfied and their property returned to them."[47]

In a proclamation to the Ukrainian village communes at virtually the same time, the Holovna Rada attempted to justify the authorities' delay in replying to its earlier petition by noting the real difficulties facing the monarchy:

> God grant peace to our Austrian monarchy; then we may expect that the high imperial government will inquire into our misery, and the more loyal and more patient that you are and do not cause any new troubles, the more benevolent toward you will be the heart of His Majesty, our Emperor and King, who is glad to gratify all the nations of his monarchy. And when the diets are formed, your representatives, whom you will select, will call attention to the injustices committed against you.[48]

In June 1849 the Holovna Rada sent a deputation to the governor regarding the peasant question. But it too met with no success, and on 16 June the council decided to make yet a fourth request, this time to the Austrian Ministry of Justice. Kuzemsky was entrusted with drafting it. The petition emphasized that any further leniency by the authorities toward the hereditary land-owners could result in a loss of confidence in the government. As an example, the council cited an official circular sent to the Greek Catholic deaneries that had ordered them to warn the peasants against any demonstrations, but had not reminded the land-owners not to encroach on their property. The Holovna Rada insisted that the status quo of 1786 be the basis for demarcating the rustical and manorial lands.[49]

The Holovna Rada resolutely opposed Governor Agenor Gołuchowski's circular of 12 July 1849, which not only had called upon the peasants to refrain from striking and to agree to work for hire on their former lords' lands, but also ordered the *Kreis* officials to use force against resisters.[50] This circular provoked unprecedented indignation among the Ukrainians, caused reverberations throughout Austria and met with stout resistance from the peasants, who even began to fight with the strike-breakers.[51] On 27 July the Holovna Rada sent Emperor Franz Josef a special memorandum, in which it accused the Galician government of forcing the peasants to work the nobles' fields.[52] The council regarded Gołuchowski's circular as contrary to the patent of 7 September 1848 and the new constitution of 4 March 1849. The council was convinced that the governor's directive could lead to further conflict, and it accused the nobility of wronging the peasants, who had turned over much grain for the army's needs while the nobles were aiding the Hungarian insurrectionaries. Despite this, the council argued, the nobility received indemnification payments in advance, while the peasants, who had provided the country with recruits, were forced to work for them and military detachments were sent against those who resisted. Furthermore, no one had asked the peasants about the reasons for their demonstrations. Finally, the council noted that all its previous requests regarding the peasant question had gone unanswered. Therefore, not wishing to oppose the government during this critical period for the state, it felt obliged to suspend its activities.

Many Ukrainians were seriously frightened by the peasants' loss of confidence in the government and in the Holovna Rada. Petro Holovatsky conceded that the Holovna Rada's insistence on trying to obtain the peasants' rights through legal means, while offering unconditional support and loyalty to the authorities, had been a disaster. He wrote to his brother Iakiv: "People! For heaven's sake, confidence in Gołuchowski and the present government is collapsing; do something, help as best you can, because the people so far had hope, and now they see the sad truth, and we can no longer pull the wool over their eyes. That is why the council is dissolving itself."[53] Despair gripped the liberals because the dissolution of the Holovna Rada would signify the end of the Ukrainians' organized activities. It was all the more tragic that they had not received an answer to their many appeals concerning the peasant problem.

However, the authorities retreated. In late July, Gołuchowski issued a new circular in which he directed that the peasants be persuaded to work during the harvest, but without force or coercion.[54] Then, on 15 August, he issued a patent granting the peasants title to those manorial lands that they had possessed (not those that they held as temporary leaseholds) and abolished the unremunerated work by cottage workers and tenant farmers under *robot*. The matter of redemption for the servitudes was postponed.[55]

The Austrian minister Alexander Bach assured a delegation that had come to Vienna from the Holovna Rada—Shashkevych, Vyslobotsky, Iakiv Holovatsky and Lytvynovych—that he would institute a separate commission for Galicia to settle the complaints over land. Holovatsky informed his brother Petro that Bach indicated that "a law regarding redemptions for the termination of *robot* will be issued before long; it has already been accepted by the ministry in a form prepared by our trusted associates Lytvynovych and Counsellor Stroinovsky."[56]

The Ukrainian leaders again began to expect that their wishes would be fulfilled, and they called for intensifying activity in all areas of national life and for an uncompromising attitude on their demands, hoping thereby to regain authority and recognition within the Ukrainian community.[57] The land commission began its work in Vienna in September 1849. The Ukrainian leaders seemed certain of ultimate victory.[58]

In the Vienna delegation's report of its activities, presented on 16 November 1849, Kuzemsky expressed the conviction that the government genuinely favoured the Ruthenian nation and the contributions of the Holovna Rada on its behalf. The proof was the government's invitation to the Ukrainian delegates to participate in land commission deliberations, at which "our particular intention was to safeguard the villagers' property and to remove all the encumbrances except those imposed by the provincial and imperial authorities, so that the peasant can be the master of his possessions and proceed freely along a constitutional and legal path." Kuzemsky also noted that the former owners would receive a just settlement for losses caused by the remission of *robot*. The commission also aimed at repeal of the decree of 1846, which set 1820 as the basis for demarcating between manorial and peasant holdings. Kuzemsky's report concluded:

> We wholeheartedly defended the interests of the villages, and with God's help we managed to pass this law through the commission. And if the Lord God permits this law in its present form to pass through all the [subsequent] deliberations and be enacted, then we expect that our villagers will be completely satisfied with it. We, the Holovna Rada, would then be convinced that we have contributed to the worldly happiness of our peasants.[59]

Unfortunately, relying on the government's favour produced no results. The case could not have been otherwise, since the government represented the interests of the propertied classes. The Holovna Rada was unable to grasp that enfranchisement occurred not as a result of the goodwill of the Austrian authorities, but was a consequence of objective necessities—the result of competition with the forces of revolution for the minds and support of the peasant masses.

The agrarian problem had marked repercussions on Ukrainian-Polish relations during this period. The liquidation of the nobility's *folwark* (manorial) system and the remnants of feudalism in the Galician countryside could have occurred through revolutionary change. However, at that time there were neither Ukrainians nor Poles able to turn events in that direction. The defeat of the 1846 insurrection was at the same time the end of the activities of the Polish revolutionary democrats, the only force capable of effecting profound socio-economic changes. Ultimately, no settlement that did not bring such changes could win the peasants' support.

15. The Campaign to Partition Galicia

> With . . . the obviously antagonistic tendencies of the Poles and Ruthenians, it is clear that they cannot live together in peace.
>
> The partition of Galicia is a vital issue for the Ruthenians, because only through it can one finally limit the Poles' encroachments onto the Ruthenian land and end all their hopes of restoring the former Polish state with the help of the Ruthenians. Only in this way can the country be freed from the terrorism under which it now groans and the Ruthenians be permitted freely to develop their nationality.[1]

These excerpts from the memorial of 28 October 1848 by the Holovna Rada Ruska to the Austrian interior ministry indicate the primacy of partitioning Galicia. The council was willing to admit any arguments and means of action to achieve that end. At the same time, the passages testify to a significant evolution in the council's views since the events of March 1848.

The demands in the first Ukrainian address of 19 April did not allude to the separation of Eastern Galicia. This issue emerged only in the course of the mounting Ukrainian-Polish antagonism in May and June 1848. There is no clear evidence whether the Ukrainian delegates to the Slavic Congress were empowered to demand the division of Galicia in their negotiations with the Poles, or whether the idea of partition developed under the influence of the plans for federalizing Austria, which the Czech liberals proposed and which had found clear expression in Hryhorii Hynylevych's letter of 30 May from Prague to the council. The Holovna Rada did not totally approve the proposals advanced by its delegates there, although it later made decisions that revealed their influence.[2]

In making its case for dividing Galicia, the Holovna Rada referred to the emperor's decision in 1847 that had envisaged partition. However, that plan had not been put into effect because Governor Stadion, who insisted on a unified administration for the province, blocked it.[3] It may be assumed that Stadion's opposition was the reason the Holovna Rada initiated action to divide Galicia only after he had left the province. On 4 June, the day Stadion left Galicia, the Holovna Rada issued a circular to the local Ukrainian councils that suggested, among other things, a discussion of the issue. Without awaiting replies, on 9 June the council sent a special address about it to the emperor. It is evident, then, that from the very beginning the Holovna Rada did not intend to honour the compromise reached at the Slavic Congress on 7 June, which had deferred the decision on this matter to the Galician diet. Citing paragraph 4 of the constitutional rescript of 25 April, the Holovna Rada demanded that partition be implemented "for reasons of state." It based its arguments on ethnic grounds (the distinctiveness of the Ukrainian nation was manifested "in its writings, language, literary development, religion, customs, traditions and national temper"), historical grounds (the eastern part of Galicia had once been independent as the Principality and Kingdom of Halych and later as the province of Red Ruthenia [*Woiwodschaft Rothreussen*, in the German text]), and political grounds (the Ukrainians' attachment to "the beloved imperial house").[4]

The imperial decision on 19 June 1848 to proceed with the division of Galicia into two gubernias (not provinces), to become effective as of 1 August,[5] caused anxiety among the Poles and stirred the hopes of the Ukrainian leaders. Iosafat Kobrynsky wrote:

> Perhaps God will grant that henceforth there will be peace among us, and without especially involving ourselves in political matters, we can peacefully concern ourselves with the instruction and education of the people and our own selves, both morally and materially, particularly since through this division our nationality will arise from the ruins that are crushing it.[6]

The Holovna Rada, therefore, was incorrect in arguing that its request of 9 June had not been fulfilled and that accordingly, on 17 July 1848, it had felt obliged to send a separate memorial to the Austrian ministry.[7] The immediate reasons for this step were Agenor Gołuchowski's negative attitude, expressed in his comments attached to the council's address to the emperor,[8] and the countermeasures taken by the Sobor Ruskyi and those Ukrainians co-operating with the Poles who had written to Vienna opposing partition. The council's memorial of 17 July to the government contained a host of new arguments designed to refute these opponents. It called attention to the fact that, although Ukrainians comprised a substantial majority of the population in Eastern Galicia, Polish was the official language in many courts, while Ukrainian was being displaced. The Ukrainians were demanding partition in order finally to free themselves from Polish influences, which, because of the Poles' revolutionary aspirations since 1831, had brought only misfortune. Partition would guarantee the Ukrainians pursuit of their own national development under the protection of the Austrian government, which the Poles attempted to thwart. Worse, the Poles were aided by polonized Ukrainians, who were more dangerous than "the true Polish party itself." The memorial maintained:

> The national development of these two nations, which the constitution has as an objective, is impossible without the division of Galicia because of their conflicting inclinations.... The Ruthenians, freed from all harmful Polish influences and protected against similar enticements, would try to demonstrate with all their might further proofs of their traditional loyalty and adherence to the loftiest [Austrian] Throne.[9]

In sending copies of both the 9 June address and the 17 July memorial to the local councils, the Holovna Rada recommended that they begin educating the people and encourage them to sign in large numbers a petition of endorsement. The lists of signatures sent to the Holovna Rada were to be conveyed in turn to Vienna.[10]

Feverish efforts were launched throughout Eastern Galicia. The Ukrainian councils discussed partition at specially convened open meetings.[11] The council of the Hlyniany deanery wrote: "It is a matter of the utmost concern, upon whose resolution depends whether we Ruthenians shall find happiness. We shall be happy—with God's help—if we join with the Holovna Rada and are willing to support it according to our strength, because it works indefatigably for the good of our nation in this pure and just matter."[12]

The councils used the clergy to persuade people to lend their signatures in support of partition. However, the peasants complained that their former lords were pressuring them to join the opposition, forcing manorial servants to sign a petition against partition, and threatening to dismiss or turn over to the authorities those who refused.[13] The peasants also heard rumours that the signatories would be forced to pay off the remitted *robot*. In many parts of Eastern Galicia, therefore, people hesitated to sign. To ease their anxieties, the Holovna Rada prepared a new petition that would still constitute an endorsement of partition without including individual signatures. It was only necessary to indicate that the people feared that their signatures would be exploited for hostile purposes and to have reliable witnesses and the local pastor confirm the popular sentiment.[14]

A delegation from the Holovna Rada went to Vienna on 18 July to submit the new memorial concerning partition to the Reichstag as well. This document categorically rejected any suspicions that the Ukrainians were gravitating toward tsarist Russia. The Holovna Rada maintained that "one ought to distinguish between a nation and the government, between kinship and political welfare," and consequently the council unequivocally embraced the Galician Ukrainians' remaining within the framework of the Austrian monarchy.[15]

Rolls containing the Ukrainians' signatures reached the Viennese Reichstag in a steady stream. On 29 August, Franciszek Smolka noted: "One now reads that the Ruthenians submitted a second petition with 15,000 signatures."[16] On the previous day Hryhorii Shashkevych had written that thirty-two large sheets of signatures had arrived from Ternopil; on 1 September he received rolls containing 40,000 signatures. By 5 October the number had grown to 65,000, and by the end of 1848 to 100,000. Eventually, by the end of January 1849, 200,000 signatures had been gathered.[17]

This campaign was conclusive evidence of the prevailing mood in Ukrainian society and represented a serious danger to the Poles in Eastern Galicia. The Poles responded with a multifaceted campaign, undoubtedly instigated by the Polish deputies in Vienna, who feared that the Reichstag might be transformed into an arena for debate on the partition issue. Such a situation could represent a serious obstacle to the Poles' plans and could also affect the possibility of restructuring Austria along the lines proposed by the Czechs. Galicia and Bohemia together possessed 191 votes in the Reichstag. However, no understanding was reached because the deputies had no common purpose. Some Czechs also responded critically to the Ukrainian position. As František Jachim wrote to Iakiv Holovatsky,

> Your Ruthenians... were accorded equal rights [in Prague]. I cannot, therefore, commend the discordant behaviour of many Ruthenians here, who have now found a strange liking for bandying words and crying out against the Poles. After all, the Poles have already sunk enough; they can do you no more harm. On the other hand, it is absolutely essential that all the Slavs in the Reichstag join without delay with the other nations of our state to attain equal rights.... In Vienna, it seems that attaining predominance depends only on harmony among the Slavs. Therefore, seek everywhere to act in accord. The Poles have already conceded everything to you that provides equality, and all of us need only unanimity against our common foe. Your

> Ruthenians, the so-called Saint Georgites [*sviatoiurtsi*], include many old and stubborn enemies of Poland who lack judgement, political sense and any knowledge of our general needs.[18]

The Poles' endeavours caused Austrian minister president Anton Doblhoff to declare, on 27 July, his opposition to the immediate partition of Galicia. He proposed a delay and suggested the possibility of referring the matter to the provincial Galician diet.[19] Thus the partition issue returned to its stage at the Slavic Congress. Smolka surely had the minister's decision in mind when he wrote: "One reads now that a petition of 'Ruthenian Subjects for the Division of Galicia into Two Gubernias' has been submitted. You know that, *brevi manu*, we have broken the neck of the intended division of Galicia." Smolka urged that a counterpetition of Ukrainians opposed to partition be sent from Galicia. He also recommended preparing a written clarification of the Ruthenian issue that could be distributed to the Reichstag deputies.[20] The response was immediate. The Rada Narodowa took charge of the Polish campaign in Galicia. With its knowledge and approval, the Sobor Ruskyi came forward first, sending to the deputy Marian Dylewski a petition against partition signed by 577 persons. Citing paragraphs 3 and 45 of the constitution of 25 April, the petition pointed out that partition could be accomplished only by the Reichstag and in any case would bring no advantages in the present circumstances. Division would cost money, and, being "more a political move than an administrative one," it jeopardized the Ukrainians, because a geographic demarcation between the Ukrainian and Polish nationalities was not possible. The editors of *Dnewnyk Ruskij*, the newspaper of the Sobor Ruskyi, even suggested that "the Ruthenian intelligentsia knows well that if the Ruthenian language is not introduced in the administrative offices, then only German newcomers will be installed here, and in the end it will come to our Galician Rus' being annexed to Germany."[21]

On 26 July the Rada Narodowa directed Józef Dzierzkowski to draft a protest by the Poles, which would be distributed throughout Galicia and published in the press. A commission was set up to oversee the collection of signatures. On Tadeusz Wasilewski's recommendation, the Rada Narodowa decided to send a delegation to Metropolitan Levytsky to solicit his signature as well. The Poles expected that Levytsky, who had lived outside of Lviv for years and stood on the periphery of the Ukrainian political movement, could be induced to sign. They were mistaken. The metropolitan declared that he would not sign because he was indifferent to whether there would be one or two gubernias. He allegedly stated in regard to the protest, "This one is the same as the other, and I will not sign it either, because, to tell you the truth, I have already signed the request to the ministry in support of partition."[22]

After Wacław Zaleski was named governor of Galicia, the Ukrainians became even more worried about the efficacy of their efforts in Vienna. It seemed likely that the matter of partition would be deferred indefinitely.[23] Given these circumstances, Ievstakhii Prokopchyts proposed trying to get some Poles to come forward with a petition favouring division. Several Ukrainian deputies were to write home regarding the matter, in the expectation that there would be "a protest against the protest."[24] However, there is no proof that this plan was carried out, although the peasant deputies' programme included the demand to divide Galicia and the contemporary Polish press reported that there were Polish advocates of partition in some parts of Galicia.[25]

The Holovna Rada Ruska expressed its concern over Zaleski's appointment as governor in a pronouncement of 19 August, to which it attached a letter from the Ruthenian district council in Stanyslaviv that was decidedly hostile to the new governor:

> The Ruthenians deem it essential to renew their request regarding a division of the country, because the newly appointed governor, although an imperial official, is a Pole and consequently offers no guarantee of even such impartiality as could be expected until now.[26]

Kasper Cięglewicz's *Rzecz czerwono-ruska 1848 roku* [The question of Red Rus' in 1848] and Antoni Dąbczański's *Wyjaśnienie sprawy ruskiej* [An explanation of the Ruthenian issue] were intended to counter the Holovna Rada's arguments and demonstrate that the Galician Ukrainians did not constitute a separate nation and that the Ukrainian language was a dialect of Polish.[27] Both authors emphatically rejected the imputation that the Ukrainians' rights had been restricted in the old Polish state, maintaining that Ukrainians even had sat on the Polish throne (Kings Sobieski and Wiśniowiecki, for example) and that the Ruthenian nobility had had equal access to all Polish state offices. Without judging the merits of their arguments, let us examine their opinions regarding partition. Dąbczański wrote: "The breach between Ruthenians and Poles is accordingly a betrayal of humanity most deserving of punishment, because it raises the banner of the reactionary aristocracy, as much by disrupting unity as by diminishing the democratic forces, which are precisely the most united [with the Poles] among the Ruthenians." More importantly, Dąbczański thought that the districts of Eastern Galicia would not be able to remain with Austria or to form a state of their own. "*Nolens volens*, [they would] become disloyal to the House of Austria and join with their co-religionists and compatriots in Russia."[28] Cięglewicz offered similar arguments: "Because this intended separation of the eastern and western parts of Galicia will lead ultimately to the annexation of the western part one day—perhaps to the Congress Kingdom [of Poland]—the eastern part, cut off from Austria (for only through Hungary could it touch upon Austria), would fall to Russia, and Austria would be compensated with something else."[29]

Cięglewicz's response pleased the Polish deputies, particularly Smolka, who caused a German translation of it to be published in Vienna in 1848. This pamphlet, together with a German translation of Dąbczański's work, was distributed among the deputies in Kroměříž.[30] The two publications accentuated the Ukrainian-Polish debate in Galicia. *Zoria Halytska* published Iosyf Levytsky's "On the Division of Galicia," which restated the Holovna Rada's views. Levytsky contended that any understanding between the Ukrainians and the Poles was practically impossible. He realized that Ukrainian efforts to achieve partition prevented the Poles from maintaining their dominance and also delayed indefinitely a reconstructed Polish state. He remarked, "It is not [the Poles] who will be asked what they wish for themselves on our land, but we, the original and more numerous nation." A separate gubernia would guarantee the Ukrainians' administrative autonomy and national development, and it would constitute the strongest barrier against Polish rule. Levytsky added, "Whether [Poland] will exist someday is of no concern to us. But we do know that thousands of noise-makers, singing the Polish anthem 'Poland has not yet perished,' will not now manage to raise a corpse or drown out [Tadeusz] Kościuszko's prophetic words, '*finis Poloniae*'." Levytsky thought that the fratricidal struggle among the Polish factions was proof that "disharmony is like an hereditary trait of the Polish nation"; therefore he reproached his pro-Polish compatriots who had embraced "the ideal of discord and disorder." It would be a disgrace for the Ukrainians to continue to submit to the Poles and a disgrace for the Poles to maintain their domination. Levytsky concluded:

> Let them [the Poles] learn from other nations upon what freedom and equality depend; let them read the Croatian and Slovenian deputies' manifesto of June of this year, in which it is said, "Those nations that seek to usurp dominion over others understand the true meaning of liberty and equality as little as those that continue to remain under such rule; neither the one nor the other has yet matured to the higher notion of humanity."[31]

However, in the circumstances of 1848—circumstances of a decisive struggle between the revolutionary forces and reaction—did the position of the Ukrainians serve this idea of liberty and equality? The answer perhaps is provided in the Holovna Rada's new memorial of 28 October to the Austrian interior ministry: "Not only the Ruthenians desire partition, but also everyone... of sound mind in the country." Although the Poles in Eastern Galicia did not constitute a nation, the council did not oppose the development of their nationality, as long as they did not act to others' detriment. The Poles in Eastern Galicia were isolated, dispersed among the villages as former hereditary lords and leaseholders; only in Lviv did the "Polish party" have a somewhat stronger base of support. Strengthened by the influx of émigrés, the Poles did not want to understand that Lviv was not a Polish city. The Holovna Rada added: "And so there was created in this Ruthenian country one clan made up of country squires, their *mandatarii*, leaseholders, writers and soldiers of fortune [*Glücksrittern*], who in modern times took on the name of the Polish nation. [These persons] not only exploited and sucked dry [our] country for their own aims, but in addition tried to wrest away the name of its original inhabitants, the Ruthenians." Under these conditions, the Ukrainians were unknown in Europe, and the Poles depicted every manifestation of Ukrainian national life as favouring Russia. During the events of March 1848, the Poles propounded the thesis that "Galicia is a Polish country, and there are no Ruthenians" [*Galizien sei ein Polenland, und es gebe keinen Ruthenen*]. The Ukrainians understandably took exception to being identified with the Poles. They were fully aware of "what Polish equality and fraternity mean and where a union that the Poles desire will lead." The Ukrainians sought union with Austria not from fear, but "by free choice and with the conviction that... it gives them sufficient guarantee of free national development and displays the honest will to assure the welfare of each citizen." The Holovna Rada's memorial was a conscious indictment of Polish revolutionary aspirations:

> The recent events in virtually all the capitals of Europe revealed the Polish machinations and showed that a Polish hand was chiefly involved in every upheaval. The sad occurrences in Vienna made clear how closely the Poles are linked to revolutionaries in all countries and nations. The Poles did not provoke or themselves take part in these disturbances out of sympathy for people with like sentiments. No, the Poles do not know the meaning of sympathy. Nor do they care about the freedom of nations, although they call themselves defenders of liberty. They care for none of these things; they have only one idea, to which they aspire with a tenacity the like of which history has never seen: the reconstruction of their former kingdom. They sacrifice everything for this idea; no cost is too dear for them. They shed their blood on every barricade and they would enter into an alliance even with the savages of America [*mit den Wilden Amerikas*], if with the aid of such an

alliance they could rebuild their own state.

According to the Holovna Rada, the Poles were not guided by love of country, but by selfish aims and the desire to rule over others. After their unsuccessful outburst of 1831 and later in Poznania and in Cracow, they desired to see Austria "brought to collapse" and Galicia "reclaimed as their own possession." By contrast, "the most important task of the Ruthenians is to preserve the integrity of the Austrian monarchy. The Ruthenian desires that Austria be set in order, strengthened internally, and respected externally.... He wishes to remain in close alliance with a constitutional Austria, so that he may develop freely, preserve his own inviolable nationality and assure his spiritual and material well-being."[32]

The Holovna Rada's delegates broached the issue of partition during an audience with the emperor on 6 November, at which time, presumably, they were already aware of the contents of the rescript of 4 November that had been sent to Galician Governor Wacław Zaleski. The rescript required the governor to "protect the country from revolutionary movements and peasant disturbances," praised the Greek Catholic clergy for its allegiance to the government and directed that the influence of the Holovna Rada Ruska be exploited in the interests of "maintaining peace and order in the Ruthenian rural communities." It also directed that control of the Gubernial Commission in Cracow be transferred to Hofrat Ettmayr, who, "acting for the governor," was to administer the western Galician districts of Rzeszów, Jasło, Tarnów, Sącz, Bochnia and Wadowice.[33]

This appointment was a first step toward an actual division of Galicia; thus Zaleski understood it, and he protested to the ministerial council.[34] Together with some conservative citizens and deputies, he organized a campaign against the policies of the central government and the Holovna Rada. The group decided to prepare an address to the emperor and a memorial to the ministerial council, requesting that the Galician diet convene and demanding that the partition question not be decided without the diet's concurrence. A deputation headed by Gwalbert Pawlikowski was to present these documents. It was also decided that Galicia's urban representatives, in view of "the recent catastrophe in Lviv, should come forward... with clarification and explanations and not with complaints." The final version of the address was worked out at a meeting on 20 November, and both the address and memorial were ready a few days later.[35] But the change on the Austrian throne delayed the entire campaign. Instead, on 9 December the governor's circle prepared an address of homage, which was delivered to Emperor Franz Josef in January 1849. This message—an expression of loyalty by the conservative elements in Polish society, which did not allow any persons associated with the Polish central Rada Narodowa to figure among the signatories—uttered the timid hope of preserving the territorial unity of the country and "our indivisible, province-wide [*całokrajowa*] nationality," and promised in exchange its complete support for the monarchy.[36]

The Polish conservatives also decided to submit their previously drafted address to the government and the Reichstag, and so Pawlikowski left for Olomouc and Kroměříž.[37] The Polish demands were in keeping with the settlement reached in Prague on 7 June 1848, although the argumentation strove to discredit the Ukrainians, stating that partition was justified by neither political nor national necessity and that most of the people did not desire it. The notion of partition "had been served up only by a passion incapable of judging its consequences." Polish-Ukrainian discord, "already completely erased among the educated," was also disappearing among the common people. The popular aspirations in both parts of Galicia, therefore, were the same. The Ukrainians' adherence to the Galician Polish address of 19 March 1848 testified to this.

Furthermore, the Ukrainian tongue could not become an independent language in such a short time. Therefore, the Ukrainians could not be permitted to force their language on three-fifths of Galicia. In any case, the Ukrainian agitation was not of a national nature, but exclusively religious. These Poles saw it as an attempt to establish the supremacy of the Greek Catholic clergy in Eastern Galicia—which would be a step toward a closer union with the Ruthenians under Russian rule and the foundation "of the spiritual rebuilding of the Ruthenian State as it existed in the middle of the fourteenth century." Political and religious considerations, therefore, demanded that the government prevent "the strong and natural inclination of the Ruthenians toward the east" and not allow the administrative division of Galicia.

If partition became a reality, the Ukrainians would attempt to impose the Ukrainian language and the Greek Catholic rite upon the entire populace of Eastern Galicia or to remove people from the country, which in turn would invite oppression of the Ukrainians in Western Galicia. The squires and wealthier citizens in particular would be persecuted in the predominantly Ukrainian districts; the villagers who wanted to carve up the lords' lands would support such actions. Eventually, land-owners would flee, leaving only Ukrainian clergymen and peasants in the new Ukrainian province; certainly the government did not intend that result. Preserving the unity of the country would also uphold the state's political principles in regard to Galicia up to that time: uniform legislation, a single estates diet, common state and economic institutions. Moreover, the administrative difficulties and financial costs of partition had to be considered. The Polish conservatives concluded: "For these reasons we appeal eagerly to the opinion of the entire country and shall submit unconditionally to its decision. Here again we repeat our most humble request contained in our address to the throne, that the High Ministry not deign to decide this vital issue for our country before hearing our provincial diet's opinion on this matter."

The further course of the debate over partition is tied to the work of the Reichstag's Constitutional Commission in Kroměříž.[38] However, before the deliberations there commenced, the balance of power in the Reichstag changed to the disadvantage of the Ukrainians, who unexpectedly no longer found support even among the Czechs. But in November 1848 there were still no indications of this change. The Ukrainian delegation, after attending to its affairs in Olomouc, arrived in Prague on 10 November in the company of its own Reichstag deputies (Kuzemsky, Borysykevych, Zaklynsky, Lomnytsky and Shashkevych) and the Czech deputies. The Ukrainians were very cordially received, conducted talks aimed at reaching a common understanding with the Czechs and familiarized themselves with the state of education and with the Czechs' national life and institutions. As Borysykevych noted, the Czechs made quite an impression upon the Ukrainians: "Prague is not Lviv; it is nationally Czech, yet we still have Polish barricades."[39]

The Prague talks contributed to consolidating the Slavic rightist faction in the Reichstag. The Slavic Club of deputies was formed on 22 November in Kroměříž. It included Czechs, Ukrainians, Moravians and South Slavs, but not Poles. The newspaper *Slawische Central-Blätter* began publication in Prague, in the hope of influencing the other Slavs in the monarchy. Nonetheless, the Slavic Club was not able to prevent the election of Franciszek Smolka as president of the Reichstag.[40]

It seemed as though a split among the Slavic deputies was impossible. However, the overly pro-governmental and anti-Polish policy of the Holovna Rada and the Ukrainian deputies created such a schism. The Czechs did not expect that the Ukrainians would be willing to make concessions to the bureaucracy at the expense of curtailing their own rights. Their position made the struggle against German domination more difficult. Eliminating Polish-language instruction from schools in Eastern Galicia and introducing German, with the knowledge and consent of the Holovna Rada, had to provoke opposition in segments of the Ukrainian community and among the Czechs, especially since the latter continued to oppose the

Schwarzenberg government, which the Ukrainians supported.[41]

Full Czech support for the plan to partition Galicia thus appeared impossible. Besides, the Czechs had never unequivocally favoured partition. Although they recognized the need for equal rights for both nationalities in Galicia, they were inclined to support division into two gubernias while preserving a common administration and provincial diet. Essentially, the Czechs were for preserving the unity of the country, while granting the Ukrainians full rights.

The Galician question in the Reichstag's Constitutional Commission represented part of the broader subject of restructuring the Austrian monarchy. Three alternatives were advanced: maintaining strict centralization; dividing the state on a historical-political basis; and reorganizing it as a federation along ethnic-national lines. The first solution was not seriously considered, but the other two had a chance of being implemented by the Reichstag. The desire to maintain traditional, historical-territorial units—strong among the aristocracy—met with resistance among the numerous nationalities endeavouring to safeguard their rights. The principle of federation on a national basis, however, did not appeal to everyone, since some stood to lose their predominance in provinces with a mix of nationalities. Such was the case with the Poles and the Czechs; compromise was essential.

The Constitutional Commission, chosen on 31 July and composed of thirty members (three from each traditional province (*Land*), an arrangement that underrepresented Bohemia and Galicia and dissatisfied the Czechs and Poles), prepared two projects: František Palacký's federalist plan, which divided Austria into a new arrangement of lands with their own governments and diets that had the right to choose their deputies to an all-Austrian parliament; and the Silesian German Kajetan Mayer's centralist plan, which proclaimed that Austria was an indivisible hereditary monarchy composed of the traditional crown lands (*Kronländer*).[42] Mayer's proposal was the basis of the discussion that began on 22 January 1849. The Czech Adolf Pinkas criticized its premise and advocated a compromise between historical and ethnic-national considerations.[43] The Galician Pole Florian Ziemiałkowski emphasized the necessity for uniform treatment of all the provinces, because it was not possible to apply historical principles to one (Bohemia) and national principles to another (Galicia). Ziemiałkowski thought Galicia was a Polish land, and he ascribed the breach between the Ukrainians and Poles to religious, not national, causes. Rudolf Brestl, a representative of the German left, explained the issue in similar terms.

The Croatian deputy Matias Kaušić, Iakhymovych and the Czechs Palacký and Rieger held different opinions. Kaušić argued that only the principle of nationality should be considered in dividing territories. Therefore, he called for treating Western Galicia, Eastern Galicia and Bukovyna as separate provinces.[44] Iakhymovych stressed that until 1809 the Austrian government had differentiated between Western and Eastern Galicia and that the division of Galicia had become essential after the annexation of Cracow. Stadion had supported this view; the emperor had made his decision, and only the change in the government had delayed its ratification and implementation. In Iakhymovych's opinion, the mutual hostility of the nations, the intensification of religious conflict since March 1848, linguistic differences and the necessity of retaining the Ukrainian language in the schools and administrative offices all argued for partition.[45]

Palacký's and Rieger's remarks in defence of the Ukrainian nationality rested on thorough familiarity with the problem and the recent findings of Slavic scholars. They did not defend partition, since in their opinion political factors were deciding the issue. Palacký hoped that "Austria's nations would get along well together," and to this end he offered a compromise between historical and ethnic approaches. He divided the monarchy into national-historical groups of countries (*Länder*) with smaller national state districts (*Reichskreise*). Austro-German, Czech, Polish, Illyrian, Italian, South Slavic, Magyar and Wallachian lands would comprise a number of districts. He included Galicia, Cracow, Bukovyna and Transcarpathian Rus' among the Polish lands. He acknowledged the separateness of the Ukrainian nation and expressed the hope that it would quickly merge with Western European culture and become an instrument against the monarchy's enemies.[46]

Rieger supported Palacký's position. According to him, sixteen million Ukrainians constituted a nation, whether separated from Galicia or not. Furthermore, the development of Ukrainian literature in a democratic spirit would contribute to the disintegration of Russian absolutism and inspire Ukrainian serfs in Russia to break away from it. Consequently, "the collapse of the despot inimical to European liberty will be close at hand." Turning to the Poles, Rieger declared that

> the time has passed when the lettered classes dictated the tone to the national masses. You know the hateful meaning of the word *Liakh* on the lips of a Ruthenian.... The concessions made in the teaching of religion in the village schools are no longer sufficient. The Poles and the Ruthenians understood one another best at the Slavic Congress in Prague.... I should be saddened if my words, which are only intended to mediate, are ignored and no concessions are made to the Ruthenians. If the Ruthenians are not aided here, they will know where else to turn. And, gentlemen, take this to heart, not only the Poles, not only Austria, but also freedom will be

endangered if this occurs.[47]

Nevertheless, Rieger did not favour the division of Galicia. His scheme for dividing Austria into *Reichsländer*, or state lands, allowed for their subdivision into districts, thus preserving historical rights and taking the nationalities problem into consideration. Each district would have its own diet.[48] Rieger's plan was similar to Palacký's, though it did not allow for the possibility of uniting all the Ukrainians inhabiting the Austrian monarchy.

Ultimately, the commission opted for Brestl's plan, which provided for the retention of the old division into provinces. Galicia remained undivided, and Bukovyna was to be joined to it. In the vote of 25 January 1849 on the partition of Galicia, only three members of the commission—Iakhymovych, Pinkas, and Kasper Ratz—supported division, while Palacký and Rieger abstained.[49] The commission's decision caused anxiety among the Ukrainians. At the meeting of the Holovna Rada on 16 February, Borysykevych proposed establishing a special council committee to consider methods to achieve division. The motion passed, although Kuzemsky declared that "in essence, the division of the country is already taking place." Lev Treshchakovsky offered a more radical solution. He stipulated that if the Reichstag accepted the principle of an undivided Galicia, the Holovna Rada should appeal to the nation to recall the Ukrainian deputies. Any deputy who remained in the parliament would be deemed a traitor. The Holovna Rada also approved this motion.[50] Thus the Holovna Rada did not decide to boycott the Reichstag, although the Ukrainian deputies played no further role in it. Bishop Iakhymovych did not participate in the Constitutional Commission during the supplementary debate regarding Galicia, Bukovyna and the Tyrol that began on 28 February 1849. However, thirty-five petitions for and against partition sent by the Holovna Rada and individual villages were presented. In reporting on the Galician question, Joseph Scholl proposed that the petitions be given to the commission for examination and that the Reichstag be informed of this action, but that the issue not be debated. His resolution was passed with Iakhymovych's tacit approval. Scholl postulated that the part of Galicia inhabited by the Ruthenians had never existed independently within the Austrian empire and had never had a separate state constitution; the Ruthenian nationality was protected by paragraph 21 of the fundamental law. Scholl's resolution also stated that dividing the country would obstruct the national spirit and that the government's recent decisions concerning the language of instruction in schools nullified complaints about polonization of the educational system.[51]

Smolka reported on the status of Bukovyna for the Constitutional Commission. He presented four petitions in favour of union with Galicia and four against. One of the petitions, signed by Lukian Kobylytsia among others, suggested that if Bukovyna became a distinct entity, the peasants' association with Austria would be lessened, and they would be forced to work off the cost of ending *robot*. Smolka personally supported separation, whereas Pinkas and Rieger initially favoured maintaining the region's union with Galicia. In Rieger's words,

> The aristocracy and the bureaucracy, not the people, are in favour of separating Bukovyna from Galicia. I heard from first-hand observers that the Romanian boyars in particular are oppressing the peasants.... Among Bukovyna's nearly 340,000 inhabitants, there are approximately 100,000 Ukrainians.... We must recognize them as a nation and protect them in Bukovyna; this will be far easier to accomplish if we leave them with Galicia. On the other hand, if we separate Bukovyna, the inhabitants will fall prey to the influence of the Turkish system. Meanwhile, we could easily lose Bukovyna to Moldavia and Wallachia, which perhaps are destined to become a Russian inheritance some day.[52]

In the final analysis, Rieger was anxious not to strengthen Russia's position.

The proponents of a separate status for Bukovyna advanced similar arguments, as is apparent from Kaušić's remarks.

> I must favour the separation of Bukovyna, if only because this step weakens Galicia and in particular the Ruthenians, who harbour sympathy for Russia. Austria must turn its main attention to the Danubian basin and attempt to draw the region of Moldavia and Wallachia nearer to itself. This can be best accomplished by separating Bukovyna [from Galicia] and establishing its own diet. The majority of the inhabitants of Bukovyna would not be understood at the [Galician] diet in Lviv.[53]

These arguments also convinced the Czechs, and the commission therefore unanimously recommended a separate status for Bukovyna. In sum, the constitutional draft of the Kroměříž Reichstag provided for redividing Austria into semi-autonomous lands, or *Länder*, among which were a separate Bukovyna and the separate Kingdom of Galicia and Lodomeria with Cracow. To protect national minorities, the draft postulated the creation within the individual countries of smaller territorial entities with their own district diets, of which there were to be ten in Galicia.[54]

The Kroměříž constitution was a victory for the proponents of decentralization and national autonomy, a victory that unfortunately came too late and consequently could not be exploited. Before the constitution was voted upon by the full Reichstag (planned for 15 March), the emperor dissolved the body and proclaimed in its stead an octroyed constitution.

The Ukrainian activists were basically satisfied with this turn of events. Iahkymovych wrote about the rumours that the Reichstag was to be dissolved, "which would have made no one happier than myself, since I will have been relieved of the most distasteful situation in the world." Iakhymovych blamed the Poles, Czechs and German centralists for the failure of the Holovna Rada's policies. "Thus, the seeds of new conflicts will remain in the provincial diet, which will be all the more harmful if legislative powers are to be granted to it."[55] The leader of the Holovna Rada showed himself to be an Austrian centralist out of conviction. His conclusion was simple: the Ukrainians should put all their faith in the government. The Reichstag, which had not fulfilled their demands, was unnecessary.

Despite Iakhymovych's stance, the dissolution of the Reichstag caused even more uncertainty among the Ukrainians about whether the government sincerely wanted to support their cause.[56] The more cognizant Ukrainian leaders realized that the dissolution of the Reichstag and the failure to ratify the liberal constitutional draft were victories for reactionism, and the octroyed constitution not only failed to mention the division of Galicia, but provided no guarantee of the rights of the Ukrainian nation. Some members of the Holovna Rada were also dissatisfied. On 16 March Ivan Borysykevych sharply criticized the new constitution and thereby antagonized the authorities and the conservative clerics in the Holovna Rada, who issued a public disclaimer of his position. Borysykevych thereupon broke with the Holovna Rada and left Lviv.[57]

The issue of Ukrainian-Polish relations remained to be settled. The policies of the Holovna Rada and those deputies who represented it in Kroměříž had strengthened germanizing elements in Galicia, which seemed to some Ukrainians to be a lesser evil than Polish hegemony. With the apparent failure of the council's programme, a group of Ukrainian deputies turned to the Czech František Brauner with a request that he mediate between them and the Poles. Brauner attempted to assuage their anxieties. He explained that the national rights of the Ukrainian majority in Eastern Galicia were constitutionally guaranteed and that their rivalry with the Poles, which was prompting the Ukrainians to take more decisive action, would work to their advantage in all respects.[58]

Still, the Holovna Rada did not set aside the issue of partition *ad acta*. The decision of the Austrian ministerial council on 28 January 1849 that Galicia's six western districts would be administered separately did not satisfy the council. Recognizing this step as a beginning toward the real division of Galicia, *Zoria Halytska* added nonetheless that "we should be heartbroken if the Ruthenian portions of the Jasło, Sącz and Rzeszów districts were not separated and joined to us; however, we should not want the Mazurian [Polish] parts of the Sanok district to be joined to Cracow. In this way, the Mazurians and we would be freer."[59]

The Holovna Rada issued its last memorial on the question of partitioning Galicia on 29 March 1849. It stressed that no decision up to that time had satisfied the Ukrainian people; the octroyed constitution "does not clarify adequately whether the Ruthenian land, under the name 'Kingdom of Galicia and Lodomeria,' constitutes a separate land in relation to the 'Grand Duchy of Cracow with the Duchies of Oświęcim and Zator,' [and] whether this [Ruthenian] land is to receive a separate constitution and its own diet or will remain in a common provincial union." The Holovna Rada postulated the formation of a Ukrainian crown land out of Eastern Galicia, an end toward which it would always aspire. The council was prepared, however, to accept the authorities' decision, even if it were unfavourable to the Ukrainians.[60]

The ideas in the Ukrainian memorial conflicted with the territorial division of the monarchy envisaged in the new constitution, which Stadion as minister of the interior had drafted for the emperor. Stadion instructed Gołuchowski in Lviv to inform Kuzemsky confidentially that partition and public discussion of it were now "premature" and "untimely." It was necessary to avoid debates, calm the Ukrainian populace and reinforce its confidence in the government. Stadion noted that "legal decisions concerning a constitution for the Kingdom of Galicia and Lodomeria, as well as the political division of the country, will be issued after a thorough review of the specific conditions."[61]

All attempts to alter the legal status of Galicia, however, were successfully sabotaged by Gołuchowski, who had replaced Zaleski as governor in late January 1849. On 9 May he announced his opposition to the plan to divide the Galician diet. He saw in it the seeds of political division, and he feared that the growth of national consciousness and popular education would contribute to ending clerical influence and increasing tendencies "geared either to joining with the Polish nationality or—which is more probable—to drawing closer to kindred peoples under the Russian sceptre." In both instances Eastern Galicia would become the scene of political conspiracies dangerous "to maintaining peace with the neighbouring power and even to preserving that part of the country within the monarchy."[62]

Because Gołuchowski viewed the Ukrainian question as a social issue with political tendencies dangerous for Austria, he did not go beyond the formulation of the Polish conservatives' earlier address. He either did not perceive or did not admit a third possibility—that in favourable political circumstances, the attainment of national equality by the Galician Ukrainians (not necessarily through the separation of Eastern Galicia) would have a salutary effect on liberal change within Russia.

In the course of the campaign on behalf of partition, especially as the Hungarian-Austrian conflict intensified, the idea of uniting all the Ukrainian territories in the monarchy into one crown land took shape in the Holovna Rada. The Ukrainian leaders assumed that the government, having enough problems with the Hungarians and the Poles, would be favourably inclined to this concept. But the very foundation of Austria's policy demanded that no nationality be unduly strengthened, and it used its power to maintain an equilibrium among the nationalities that would guarantee the integrity and unity of the monarchy. The Habsburgs did not consider that this policy was unsound in the long run, since its immediate results were advantageous. The official Ukrainian circles that collaborated with the government did not want or perhaps were unable to understand this truth, and, what is worse, they exploited for their own ends the real, progressive aspirations of the Ukrainian masses.

In this light, perhaps, one ought to explain Iakhymovych's silence during the Constitutional Commission's debate on the future of Bukovyna, the separation of which was demanded by the Romanian boyars and the leadership of the Greek Orthodox church. At their initiative, Bishop Eugene Hakman and the conservatively disposed deputies Antoni Kral and Mykhailo Bodnar submitted, in January 1849, a declaration in support of an earlier petition of June 1848 that had called for the establishment of a separate crown land of Bukovyna. On the other side, the representatives of the peasantry, the deputies Ivan Dolynchuk, Vasyl Kirste, Lukian Kobylytsia and Vasyl Morgosh (Morgotz), supported maintaining Bukovyna's association with Galicia. Their position was backed at a popular assembly in Chernivtsi on 1 November 1848. The concerns of the propertied classes and Iakhymovych's excessive caution, however, won out. In this instance national issues were not paramount for the Galician Ukrainian leaders, since a victory by Kobylytsia, whose radical activities were sufficiently well known, indirectly would have strengthened the revolutionary camp and significantly facilitated Polish-Hungarian co-operation.[63]

In February 1849, the Ukrainians established closer ties with the Romanians in Bukovyna, whose delegation en route to the emperor had stopped in Lviv. Borysykevych, in introducing the Bukovynian emissaries to the Holovna Rada, stressed the traditional ties that bound the Ukrainians with the Romanians. He expressed the hope that both nations would continue to live "in peace and amity," and Bishop Hakman responded by echoing his sentiments. Under the impact of this encounter, Antin Petrushevych wrote "Polshcha, Rus' i Romyny, ocherk istoricheskii" [Poland, Rus' and the Romanians: A historical sketch], in which he sought to prove that "*Lekhia* [Poland] intended to subordinate the Romanians to itself as well."[64]

The Holovna Rada placed more importance on the fortunes of the Ukrainians in Transcarpathian Rus', where in the council's opinion, the national situation was most disturbing. Although the Hungarian Revolution had not fully satisfied the Ukrainian peasants, the national question had not played a substantial role because of the pronounced influence of the pro-Magyar Greek Catholic clergy. Anti-Magyar Galician Ukrainians at first had only marginal effect. However, the national conflict, which had mounted sharply in Hungary since the autumn of 1848 because of the Magyars' policies, began to affect attitudes in Galicia, where the Habsburg authorities found growing support for their Hungarian campaign in the Holovna Rada.

On 21 November the council appealed directly to the Ukrainians in Hungary to assist the Austrian army. It drew a striking parallel between conditions in Galicia and Transcarpathian Rus', where the Ukrainians, oppressed for centuries, still could not develop their nationality. The Poles and the Hungarians, contrary to the will of the monarch, sought to trample the Ukrainian nationality; they aspired to self-rule at the price of destroying the monarchy, "and, having put their own illusions in the place of law and lawless arbitrariness in the place of justice, they have clouded the peace and upset order." They had joined together "for our doom" and brought about the events in Vienna and Lviv, thus "sowing fear and trepidation." Therefore, the council's appeal continued, the government had stepped forward "to defend the weaker peoples" and send its armies from Galicia into Hungary. These troops "set foot on your land not to harass you, but to bring and establish peace and lawful order; not to destroy your freedoms or to constrain them, but to extend them to everyone; not to do you harm, but to humble the willfulness of the unrestrained and to shield the righteous with their breasts." The Holovna Rada stressed that these were in large part Ukrainian troops who had freed the Galician Ukrainians from Polish terrorism. "Your affair is their affair, and as they freed us here from Polish willfulness, so they are prepared to shield you from Magyar pride and [Lajos] Kossuth's terrorism."[65]

The Holovna Rada also undertook to safeguard the border against Hungarian influences and organized a popular defence and a mountaineers' rifle battalion. At the same time, a group representing the Ukrainian liberal intelligentsia in Hungary, with Adolf Dobriansky and Oleksander Dukhnovych at its head, began efforts to have Transcarpathian Rus' joined to Galicia. In January 1849 its deputation delivered a petition to the emperor with a request to "unite the Ruthenian crown districts in a single administrative and political entity." However, it gained no promise that its wishes would be fulfilled. These Hungarian Ukrainian spokesmen also prepared a special memorandum, which, endorsed by the Holovna Rada and containing numerous signatures, was delivered to Gołuchowski to be transmitted to the authorities in Vienna.[66]

Dukhnovych's article, "Sostoianie Rusyniv v Uhorshchyni" [The situation of the Ruthenians in Hungary], which appeared in *Zoria Halytska*,[67] reflected the Austro-Slavic and anti-Hungarian sentiments among the liberal-bourgeois Ukrainian intelligentsia in Hungary. The author accused the Hungarians of oppressing the Ukrainian nation for many centuries and blamed them for the present persecution, for not permitting the use of Ukrainian in offices or allowing Ukrainians to hold responsible positions, for taking the better lands and forests from them and for compelling them to perform *robot* and to accept the Hungarian language and the "Calvinist religion." He concluded that the only salvation for the Ukrainians was to declare on the government's behalf. Dukhnovych was convinced that the entire nation was prepared to defend the emperor. And yet the state constitution did not formally recognize 700,000 Ukrainians in Hungary who wished to claim their rights and join their Galician brothers. "[They] hope that the government..., which has promised equal rights to all the nations of Austria, will permit this [pledge] to extend to the Hungarian-Ruthenian people."[68]

Meanwhile, Gołuchowski laid before the government the dangers that he believed would issue from the unification of the Austro-Ukrainian lands. Thus strengthened, the Ukrainians in the end would turn "to their kindred peoples living under the Russian sceptre with the aim of creating a powerful, homogeneous state organism." Galician Rus' then would become a "balefire of conspiracies and activities" aimed at unifying these peoples. "In short," Gołuchowski concluded, "the same kind of struggle... could develop concerning Rus' as has, with interruptions but with iron persistence for many years, continued over the reconstruction of a free and independent Poland."[69]

Ultimately, Transcarpathian Rus' remained with Hungary. The goodwill of the Austrian government proved to be a delusion. Were there, however, no other possibilities? Some historians have maintained that "the unification of the western Ukrainian lands could have been achieved only by revolutionary means, by involving the broad masses of Transcarpathian Ukrainians in an active struggle."[70] This judgement seems too simplistic. Taking the path of revolution in the prevailing balance of forces and political conditions meant securing the support of the Poles and the Hungarians. But such a step was contrary to the inclinations of those Ukrainian circles that placed national aspirations above revolutionary struggle.

16. The National Guard and the Riflemen

According to the provisions of the Austrian statute of 8 April 1848, the national guard was to be a territorial formation, established to defend the constitutional monarchy, maintain peace and internal order, and protect the independence and integrity of the state against foreign threats. Guards were to be organized in localities numbering more than a thousand inhabitants, and all men between the ages of nineteen and fifty were to serve (with the exception of craftsmen's assistants, servants and day labourers), regardless of nationality.[1]

The statute was provisional and did not envisage a guard organized on the basis of nationality, but the Reichstag never passed permanent regulations. In these circumstances, the Galician authorities deemed illegal every attempt to establish a separate Ukrainian guard, even though at that time the national guard in Galicia was almost entirely Polish. The Poles had simply begun to organize a guard immediately after the events of March 1848. Disturbed by their action, Governor Stadion dissolved the guard organizing committee and forbade such organizing in the countryside. But he changed his position upon receiving the statute, and on 16 April issued special instructions in this matter.[2]

The Ukrainians initially had not intended to create their own guard; indeed, legally they could not. The Holovna Rada was suspicious of the Polish guard and therefore greeted with satisfaction the reports that a "significant number" of governmental officials belonged to it in Lviv.

In Iakhymovych's opinion, this development was "very advantageous since [their presence] offers assurance against abuses."[3] Response to the guard varied throughout the Ukrainian community; however, the Greek Catholic seminarians enthusiastically welcomed its public appearances, and Ukrainians in many places actually joined it.[4] On the other hand, in the eastern Galician countryside, where the Polish element was negligible, no Polish guard was organized. The Ukrainian movement could have exploited this situation and begun its own organizing efforts without conflict with the regulations. Instead, governmental circles pre-empted the Ukrainian activists and in fact supplanted them. According to Stadion's circular of 16 April, organizing the guard was to be undertaken by the *Kreishauptmänner* and commissioners appointed by them. Special instructions in this regard issued by the *Gubernium* on 21 April revealed that the authorities feared revolutionary disturbances. The rural guard was to insure the peace and property, as well as to aid the government "in enforcing measures aimed at the well-being of the country."[5]

These measures, however, failed to bring the hoped-for results, chiefly because of the negative attitude of the peasants themselves, who had little confidence in either the bureaucrats or the Holovna Rada. That the local authorities reacted rather sluggishly also was significant. It seems that the peasants' stance during the elections had made Ukrainian leaders reluctant to organize the guard along the legally established principles, but violating the regulations appeared to be impossible. The proof was the Polish-Ukrainian agreement of 7 June in Prague. According to paragraph 3, the "Galician national guard" (hence neither Polish nor Ukrainian) was to decide by a majority vote on the selection of its officers and on whether to issue commands in Polish or Ukrainian. Its emblem was to be the coats of arms of both nations.[6]

In concluding the agreement in Prague the Ukrainian delegates certainly had in mind a Ukrainian guard, because conditions in Eastern Galicia favoured its Ukrainian character. The terms of the Prague agreement, however, did not suit the Holovna Rada. In the draft of Teodor Leontovych's response to the delegates in Prague, we read: "It is out of the question to establish a Ruthenian guard before the division of Galicia, since our people do not want to form a guard for the Poles."[7] Within the Holovna Rada itself, however, there was no agreement either. Ivan Ilevych, for example, in a letter to the Ruthenian council of the Berezhany deanery, urged it to propagate the need for a Ukrainian guard in the community.

This did not mean that the Holovna Rada did not hope to form a Ukrainian guard at a later date, but that it was first essential to demonstrate that the existing Polish guard did not fulfill the tasks for which it had been established. The council intended to exploit the Corpus Christi celebrations in Lviv toward this end. As the Pole Karol Forster noted, Bishop Iakhymovych, contrary to the usual practice of the Greek Catholic church, gave permission for a festive procession accompanied by the guard, believing that the predominantly Polish guard would refuse to participate. Iakhymovych thought that there would then be grounds to ask the authorities for permission to organize a Ukrainian guard. However, when the guard accepted the invitation, Iakhymovych sought to cancel the festivities. Neither the guard nor the public permitted this to happen. Polish and Ukrainian banners were carried during the procession and were unfurled from the Lviv town hall when the festivities concluded. The public interpreted these actions as a sign of Ukrainian-Polish rapprochement in Galicia,[8] which the Holovna Rada firmly denied.[9]

Nevertheless, it appeared that the council was putting some kind of suggestions to the authorities, since Mykhailo Malynovsky wrote in *Zoria Halytska* on 11 July 1848 that "a national, not a Polish, guard is permitted in the villages."[10] Actually, none of the Holovna Rada's efforts in the summer of 1848 produced results. The Galician authorities adhered strictly to the letter of the 8 April statute. The Ukrainians therefore attempted to employ a policy of *faits accomplis*, with the understanding of the military commanders of the individual districts. The local councils as a rule instigated the action. In July 1848, the Ruthenian council in Kolomyia sent the other councils a manual in Ukrainian of the drills mandated for the national guard. Their use, the council believed, could contribute to the ukrainization of the guard in Eastern Galicia.[11]

There was no lack of organizing efforts. In July and August especially, in numerous localities in Eastern Galicia standards were festively consecrated for the still nonexistent Ukrainian guard, and, with bureaucratic support, attempts were made to create it. Festivities of this nature took place in Drohobych in July, in Stryi on 3 August and in Zhovkva on 14 August.[12] During these celebrations the close ties between the Ukrainian nation and the Austrian monarchy and the Ukrainians' loyalty to the government and the house of Habsburg were stressed, and an Austrian army detachment usually was present to add splendour to the festivities. *Zoria Halytska* noted that in Stryi the speaker, Luka Dankevych,

> roused everyone, not excluding the military garrison, composed of Ruthenian offspring from the Stryi district, who understood the native words better than any others. One saw how tears formed in the eyes of more than one soldier. After the singing of the national anthem, "Myr Avstrii" [Peace to Austria],

> the consecrated banner was given to the army garrison for safekeeping. In its name the commanding captain expressed his thanks for their confidence, and, amid shouts of "Long live the emperor," the garrison went, with the banner being carried high by a corporal and accompanied by a peasant dressed in the Ruthenian colours, to the commandant, where it was received with all military honours. A single spirit infused everyone, and it was a pleasure to see how the hearts of the army and the peasants had not ceased to understand one another. "We are with you, we will always be with you!" shouted the military garrison.[13]

Situations such as this one generated an alliance among the Ukrainians, the bureaucracy and the army, which was directed against the revolutionary and libertarian tendencies that inspired Polish society and some Ukrainians. This alliance found expression in attempts to form guards in Lviv, Stanyslaviv and Berezhany, which were called "Ruthenian-German" by the Polish press, since the guard was Ukrainian and the command was German.[14] As a rule these attempts failed, and it could not have been otherwise as long as the Galician authorities remained opposed to them.

Finally, on 7 August 1848, the Holovna Rada addressed a formal request to the provincial authorities for permission to establish a Ukrainian guard in Galicia. The response, on 14 August, was negative. In thanking the leaders of the Holovna Rada for inculcating loyalty and fidelity to the government and the crown among the Ukrainians, Gołuchowski emphatically stressed that he could not agree to the organization of a separate Ukrainian guard, because he did not have the necessary authorization. However, he stated that he did not see any obstacle to introducing a Ukrainian command in both the municipalities and the rural areas at the request of a majority of the guard. His response could hardly satisfy the Holovna Rada, which decided to carry its request to the ministerial council and the emperor. However, it decided for the time being not to publish a proclamation to the nation "on the need for a national guard," as Ivan Borysykevych and Ivan Herovsky had proposed.[15]

It was not the slowed tempo of agricultural work, as has been contended,[16] that was behind the vigorous campaign for the guard in the last ten days of September 1848 (indeed, fall planting was in full swing), but rather events that affected the entire state. After 11 September, a general war among the nationalities broke out in Hungary. When on 18 September the Slovak "diversion on Austria's behalf" (*Diwersion für Oesterreichs Sache*) took place, and the Slovak leaders appealed to the Ukrainians in Hungary to take sides against the Magyars,[17] the Ukrainian leaders in Galicia had to have known of these developments. On 20 September the Holovna Rada issued a proclamation, popularly known as Number 464, calling for an accelerated organizational campaign, and six days later it dispatched specific instructions on how to organize the guard.[18] The Holovna Rada unreservedly approved of the fact that only "property holders and lettered townsmen" could belong to the guard, since they alone were capable of preserving order and knew what to defend. The proclamation advised the Ukrainians to rely on the guard officers and to choose their leaders from among them. The guard's task, according to the Holovna Rada, was to maintain a watch in the villages, detain guilty parties and aid in repelling any attack. It was not possible to depend exclusively on the army, which might be occupied elsewhere. The proclamation explained to the peasants: "And think for a moment, when could aid for us arrive from our soldiers if some disturbance occurred in the country? Might it not be too late?" It was precisely now, when there was time to prepare a defence and when reports were spreading that "certain restless persons seek to create disturbances in the country," that it was necessary "to hasten as quickly as possible to enlist in the national guard." This step was "absolutely essential.... You will show the world that there are Ruthenians still living who are always ready to defend their nationality on their own soil, that they wish to remain with their constitutional emperor and that they desire peace and are capable of maintaining order and obedience to the laws on their own Ruthenian land."[19]

The guard's aims were presented more openly in their instructions: "Reports are reaching us from everywhere that certain boisterous persons are cooking up some disturbance in [our] country. From every quarter we are asked for advice as to how to avert this [danger] and safeguard the nation from a severe storm. The actions and strength of the government give us every guarantee that it will crush every lawless movement, but still it cannot contain every mindless outburst." The Holovna Rada urged its affiliates to select, at the meetings of the district councils and in the presence of representatives from the towns and villages, commissions that would be concerned with the guard, naturally together with the district officials and the army command. The Holovna Rada proposed choosing representatives of the clergy and laity, including peasants, to these commissions. It expected thereby to gain the confidence of the rural populace and to secure the services of a Ukrainian officer who would organize the guard. The council added, "In the event that there is no such Ruthenian officer in the entire district, we ask that you inform us, and we shall seek to find such an organizer for you in the General High Command." It instructed the commissions to follow strictly the statute of 8 April. (Whether this actually was possible everywhere was not mentioned.) In concluding, the

Holovna Rada wrote: "We demand, finally, of every Ruthenian who joins the national guard that he behave in accordance with the provisions of the statute and that he always use his weapon for the glory of the name of Rus', for the defence of the innocent, for the preservation of peace and order, for insuring our constitutional rights and the respect of provincial statutes, and for protecting all property and the security of the throne of the constitutional monarch."[20]

Thus, upholding social order, defending the nationality and resolutely opposing libertarian currents was allied with the monarchy and reactionism. Ivan Borysykevych wrote from Lviv to Iakiv Holovatsky that "they are saying something here about revolutionary unrest; perhaps it will happen one day—it is really too bad that we do not have our own guard." His words captured the full meaning of creating a Ukrainian guard.[21] In its endeavour to insure national separation from the Poles at any price, the Holovna Rada did not perceive that by autumn 1848 the main issue was not nationality, but the freedom of peoples.[22] This point is of decisive importance in evaluating the role of the Ukrainian movement in 1848. An anti-revolutionary attitude in Galicia at that time was an anti-Polish position. The authorities feared that the revolution would spread in Galicia, which could become a natural support and ally of the Hungarians.

In autumn 1848, *Zoria Halytska* carried several articles informing the Ukrainian community of the guard's objectives. On 26 September, "Pro narodnu hvardiiu abo storozh" [About the national guard] explained that the government was not opposed to a Ukrainian guard and permitted the drills to be conducted in the native language. The author insisted that the guard should assist the army, which was not always nearby. The lack of weapons should not be an obstacle for the time being; after all, it was possible "to arm oneself with long, though not reinforced sticks, scythes, and so on.... The army could give aid with firearms and swords." But a guardsman "does not stop being a husbandman." When the Ukrainian guard was formed, "the malevolent people [would] become afraid, and, even in the event something happens, the guard can immediately come forth." So, "form a guard," *Zoria Halytska* implored, "to safeguard your rights, for peace and order, to put fear into the evil ones! Every village for itself.... Otherwise, you will have only yourselves to blame when some enemy does you harm."[23]

The October disturbances in Vienna provided an ideal opportunity for the Holovna Rada to renew its efforts and confirmed its belief in the validity of its position regarding the guard. On 17 October *Zoria Halytska* wrote:

> Unruly persons who sought to sow disharmony have destroyed the established order. They took to fighting, and a great misfortune has occurred. The minister of war was killed, much blood was spilt, and this assault was so terrifying that the monarch had to withdraw and leave his capital. Brothers! Our land and the monarch are in danger! The war in Italy has barely concluded, and already a second one has begun in a neighbouring land with the Magyars, who have wronged our Ruthenians and the other Slavs in Hungary. And now we again have unrest in Vienna. Who knows if those soldiers who have protected us until now and maintained order here won't be called there? Who knows if such a storm won't strike our country? For that reason, brothers, we warn you and earnestly exhort you to join the national guard and quickly arm yourselves under the guidance of our deanery councils. Brother townsmen and farmers! In this situation, we ourselves must maintain the peace and order, so desired by us, on Ruthenian soil. We ourselves should stand in defence of our holy nationality and our constitutional rights, because our gracious emperor, by granting us these rights, said that he places them "under the protection of our national guard!"[24]

The crowning argument for the Holovna Rada in favour of a Ukrainian guard was the Ministry of Education's decision of 29 September 1848 concerning the language of instruction in schools. The Holovna Rada called upon all the villages, towns and local councils "to display their unshakeable will in protests that we will never renounce the Ruthenian language in the schools or the courts and that in our Ruthenian land we demand the same kind of respect for the Ruthenian language as the Polish language has in Mazuria."[25]

Still, the organization of the guard progressed very slowly. The Galician authorities continued to oppose forming it on the basis of nationality. This position was evident in the gubernial decree of 8 October, which stated that the newly established guard units were to be subordinate to the general command of the guard in Lviv. No distinctions were made between a Polish and a Ukrainian guard.[26] The new governor, Wacław Zaleski, adhered to this policy, declaring to a Ukrainian delegation that he "did not oppose introducing the national guard in the towns and Ruthenian villages on a legal basis."[27]

The Polish central Rada Narodowa was of a similar opinion. On 24 October the delegate from its district affiliate in Berezhany, Wiktor Wiśniewski, recommended using the Polish district councils to influence the local units of the national guard not to oppose the formation of a Ukrainian guard and to avoid any clashes. The assembled members of the Rada Narodowa, however, rejected his motion with the argument that "arming the peasants is not the formation of a guard; it threatens danger." As one member stated, it was essential "to call upon the government to ward off this [eventuality]." Another member, Piotr Wasilewski, remarked: "If we consider that there is one nation [in Galicia], then should there not be only one guard?" Marian Sroczyński added that a Ukrainian guard "is not national, but Saint Georgite [*świętojurska*]."[28]

Nevertheless, in line with the Holovna Rada's proclamation 464, the Ukrainian district councils proceeded to try to form local guard units. Special meetings of representatives of the Ukrainian community took place, for example, in Brody (4 October), Bolekhiv (9 October), Buchach (12 October), Univ (12 October), Stanyslaviv (17 October), Ternopil (19 October) and Kalush (23 October).[29] The Ruthenian district council in Berezhany even issued a special appeal regarding the guard to the deanery councils in Naraiv, Pidhaitsi, Rohatyn, Bibrka and Khodoriv.[30] Virtually all of the Ukrainian councils complained that the civil authorities were hostile. In Berezhany the *Kreishauptmann* simply declared that the guard could not be divided according to religious rite and nationality, but only according to locality. Therefore, there could be a Berezhany, Rohatyn or Bibrka guard, but never a Polish, Ukrainian, German, Armenian or Jewish guard. It was the Ukrainians' own fault, he added, that they had not joined the Berezhany guard in large enough numbers to determine its structure and the language of command and to select its officers. A multiplicity of guard units would have led only to confusion and conflicts. The negotiations by the Greek Catholic dean Sylvester Lezhohubsky and Father Teofil Pavlykiv with the *Kreishauptmann* did not produce the expected results. The latter declared that "to avoid discord and embittering everyone's mind," he could not allow the guard to be formed on the basis of nationality.[31]

The Ukrainian councils in Kolomyia, Zhovkva, Ternopil and Bolekhiv found themselves in a similar situation. On the other hand, the Ukrainian district council in Sanok wrote that "the *Kreishauptmann,* E. Uherek, is not completely opposed to it."[32] Because of the various difficulties, the Holovna Rada's delegation requested the emperor and the interior minister to intervene on the Ukrainians' behalf. The reply was, as usual, general and noncommittal. The emperor promised to take up the matter and charged the government, "as much as possible, to realize satisfactorily these aspirations."[33]

The active assistance of the military commands in the festivities surrounding the establishment of the guards and the consecration of their banners was evidence that by autumn 1848 the military had become the decisive element in Galician life. In effect, a period of military rule had begun. So it was in Berezhany on 16 October and in Ternopil on 5 December, where the army honoured the festivities with salvos and at their conclusion accepted the banner for safekeeping. There was a similar occurrence in Iavoriv, where the military commander of Galicia himself, General Wilhelm Hammerstein, attended the organization of the local guard.[34] A letter by Iosyf Buchynsky, an eyewitness, captured well the atmosphere of the festivities in Ternopil:

> After the Mass, Father Dombrovytsky from Hlubichok gave a fairly good speech. Then came the ceremonial blessing of the Ruthenian banner, brought in part from Lviv and in part from Vienna, and costing 160 florins. On one side a golden lion was represented, on the other Saint Volodymyr, and at the top was a gilded Austrian eagle.... After the blessing, the banner was affixed to the staff with fifteen gilded silver nails.

The nails were driven one by one in honour of the Holy Trinity, the emperor, the empress, Minister Stadion, Governor Zaleski, Commander-in-Chief Hammerstein, his wife, the metropolitan and primate Levytsky, Bishop Iakhymovych, the *Kreishauptmann*, the general in command of Ternopil, the president of the Ukrainian council in Ternopil, the Croatian *ban* Jelačić, all the Slavs and last, all Ukrainians. "With the hammering of every nail '*Mnohaia lita*' was sung; the army fired their rifles; and beyond the town's wall, cannon were fired three times."[35]

The speeches at such occasions were patriotic and pro-Austrian. Father Ievhen Hromovych in Berezhany maintained that the banner was "a hallmark of unity," under which the Ukrainians would be "defenders of their own and the monarch's faith, fortune, glory and security. We should most be concerned," he said, "with the happiness of this land, ourselves, and our most gracious emperor, who cares for our welfare like a father and commands us to be watchful." Hromovych added: "Let us not divide ourselves and let us not desire that the larger [Ruthenian] part of the nation be joined to the smaller [Polish] part, because this is contrary to reason and even the law of nature...; the smaller part of the nation should join to the larger." Hromovych advocated an accord with the Poles based on equal rights, and not the sort of Polish-Ukrainian unity that the Polish intelligentsia promoted.[36]

Immediately after the consecration of the banners, enrollment into the guard took place. There were not very many volunteers. Initially in Berezhany 30 townsmen took part; on 12 November another 130 guardsmen were sworn in, and in December their number surpassed 200.[37] In Iavoriv, where the guard had begun rather early, two companies were formed, each consisting of over 100 men. In the Sanok district, the Ukrainian peasants saw fit to inform the representative of the Ukrainian council, "Even though we had no Ruthenian guard [here], we are all Ruthenian guardsmen. Why is it that the Polish guardsmen never stopped the hussars who were escaping to Hungary? We Ruthenians stopped them all; so we are Ruthenian guardsmen, loyal to our emperor."[38]

Several villages of the Zhovkva district did not wait for the *Kreis* officials to grant permission for a guard. The Ruthenian district council there appealed directly to the office of the governor and at the same time requested support from the Holovna Rada. The inhabitants of Kamianka Voloska in that district requested aid in obtaining nine hundred weapons. The hamlet of Stari Myslytyntsi demanded the setting up of the national guard because it "lies along the road leading from the border region to Lviv." In the Brody district nine villages that had joined the guard requested aid in purchasing banners and uniforms, or at least caps. And in the Ternopil district the peasants of twenty-four villages sent a petition to the *Kreis* asking that commissioners be dispatched who would undertake the organization of the national guard.[39]

However, the Ukrainian guards existed too short a time to play a significant role in Galician political life. They performed sentry duty, participated in celebrations organized by the Ukrainian councils (for example, during the memorial services for Latour on 8 December in Berezhany more than two hundred guardsmen took part),[40] and helped provide recruits and apprehend vagabonds and rebels. During the events of early November in the Galician capital, the Iavoriv guard asked to be sent to Lviv "to aid the army against the rebels."[41] The proclamation of a state of emergency, first in Lviv and from January 1849 in all of Galicia, interrupted these less than commendable actions. As of 10 January of that year, all units of the guard were dissolved.

This step, however, was not the end of the involvement of the Holovna Rada and its affiliates in military activities. Beginning in autumn 1848, the Ukrainian councils backed the Austrian authorities' efforts to close the Galician-Hungarian border with the aid of armed peasant detachments (*Landsturm*).[42] On 26 October the Polish press reported that the border with Hungary was manned by armed villagers, who permitted no one to cross except those with valid passports; others were apprehended and, after a brief trial, allegedly hanged.[43] On 1 December, Governor Zaleski and Gołuchowski signed a circular forbidding the export of cloth for uniforms, arms and ammunition to Hungary, "as it is in a state of rebellion."[44] The governmental commissioners of the border districts (Stryi, Kolomyia and Stanyslaviv) organized the local peasants to guard the frontier, repulse attacks by Hungarian detachments and kill suspicious persons attempting to cross the border.[45]

The Poles even thought that the government intended to order a peasant levy en masse against Hungary,[46] an apprehension which to their general satisfaction proved false. Nevertheless, in several regions along the border battles were fought, resulting in the Hungarians' taking reprisals against villages. The affair concerning the village of Studena created a considerable stir, as did the Hungarians' attacks on Zhupanie and Klymets on 6 February and Novoselytsia and Torun on 21 March.[47]

On 1 January 1849, the Holovna Rada officially became involved in the conflict with the Magyars. It issued two appeals to the Ukrainian nation: the first concerned the general arming of the populace in the borderland districts, the second the formation of the independent Battalion of Ruthenian Mountain Riflemen (Ruthenisches Bergschutzen-Corps, or Russisches Frey-Corps). In informing the Ukrainian community of these developments, *Zoria Halytska* explained that they were in response to "the general need of the state, the need of the emperor, [and] the need for order perturbed by enemies." The newspaper cited "the kindred Slavs," who were fighting "for the welfare of their fatherland," as a model for Ukrainians. The Holovna Rada especially feared a possible attack on Galicia by the Hungarians, who were being driven out from the direction of Bukovyna by Austrian regiments composed of "the brave sons of our mother Rus'." The council urged preparing a defence and expressed the hope that the Magyars would not succeed in destroying Ukrainian lands.[48]

The appeal concerning the Battalion of Mountain Riflemen revealed that the Holovna Rada Ruska had moved entirely into the reactionary camp. It refused to see that the Hungarians' struggle aimed at social and national liberation, regarding the conflict only as an attack on the integrity of the monarchy and on the freedoms that the Slavic nations had gained through the emperor's favour. Its appeal was a logical and consistent continuation of the policies initiated in September 1848.

> The arrogant Hungarians, more and more hardened in their selfishness and conceit, suddenly yearned to raise themselves up at the price of degrading the Slavic nations that are joined to them. Therefore, it is not to their taste or liking that the kindly monarch decided and proclaimed that all nations of his state would enjoy equal rights and liberties and that none would elevate itself at the expense of another. To spite this just decision, the Magyars, in their own particular implacability, were determined to achieve their selfish designs, even upon the ruins of the Austrian monarchy. They rose in rebellion against their monarch and our emperor and compelled him to take military action to defend the weaker [nations] and to enforce the appropriate respect for the law and his imperial word, and by these means to

> preserve the integrity and the glory of the Austrian state. For this reason, a terrible war flared up on our borders.

This conflict would not be so dangerous were it not for the attitude of the Galician Poles:

> And this conflagration is all the more dangerous for us, because it smoulders in our country, because here, as is known, there are those who contemplate similar unrest. Nothing could better suit their purposes than this unfortunate war in Hungary, and when their efforts here were unsuccessful, many of them went to the mountains to aid the Magyars.

The Holovna Rada was convinced that the Poles had gone to Hungary in order to return after a victorious struggle. Even defeat of the insurgents would be a threat, because then they could count on finding refuge in the mountainous regions of Galicia and "take vengeance on you [Ukrainians] for their own misery, caused by their own stupidity." The council asked, would you then have the peace that you so much desire? To secure the border, it was essential to form a regiment of volunteers under the national colours. Besides, it would be inhumane to abandon the units composed of Ukrainians that were fighting in Hungary. The new regiment was to be equipped by the government. Every volunteer would receive several silver coins, and the governmental officials who participated would retain their former posts. The appeals continued: "It is more worthy to serve the country and the monarch there (in the mountains) than to be ill-treated in service to the manor." Thus, the council turned to the peasants, the youth and the Ukrainian petty nobility living in the highlands to join in the planned enterprise, which would glorify all of Ukraine and the Ruthenian name among all nations.[49]

In the instructions to the Ukrainian councils and the clergy that were issued three days later, the Holovna Rada recommended reading the appeal in every village in the presence of an officer, who would draw up a list of volunteers and send it to Lviv for submission to the general command. The Holovna Rada expected that every town and village would provide at least several volunteers; it appealed for haste and demanded reports concerning the success of the campaign. Clearly, the Holovna Rada arranged the matter in consultation with General Hammerstein. However, these measures were probably begun without Vienna's knowledge, because permission and the emperor's acknowledgment to the council "for this new proof of its patriotic actions" was not signed in Olomouc until 10 March 1849.[50]

The campaign was conducted quickly and efficiently. Where the Ukrainian councils had been particularly active, the community supported the initiative without reservations. *Zoria Halytska* noted with satisfaction that the peasants in the Kolomyia district "understood what it was about," and at a national holiday observed in honour of the leaders of its council they shouted loudly, "We shall go beyond the mountains; everyone will go there against the Magyars."[51] In general, however, Ukrainian liberals were not enthusiastic. Iosyf Kropyvnytsky from Buchach informed Iakiv Holovatsky on 5 April 1849, "Here it is calm and quiet; but they have just introduced and ordered in the last few days a levy *en masse* (*Landsturm*)—against whom, one does not know." It seemed to Kropyvnytsky that "the Hungarian cause is already dying in nothern Hungary" and "[Polish General Józef] Bem is at the heavenly gates."[52] Hryhorii Bodnar echoed: "Here the *Landsturm* has already been introduced as far as the Dniester River; God grant that peace will prevail and it is not used."[53]

Meanwhile, volunteers for the riflemen's battalion were not lacking. By the middle of February there were 1,600, and at the beginning of April 3,460, or considerably more than the battalion was meant to include. As a result, six companies were formed and initially stationed in Berezhany, Kolomyia, Stanyslaviv, Stryi, Sambir and Lviv. Each consisted of 235 soldiers, for a total of 1,410 persons.[54] In May, to the delight of the Holovna Rada, the entire battalion was in Lviv, where it took part in the festive celebrations on 15 May of the first anniversary of the abolition of *robot*. The officers, the majority of whom were Ukrainians, were honoured by the council, and Kuzemsky explained why the council had requested the establishment of a Ukrainian unit.

> The unfortunate events of the previous year are known to each of you. Rabble-rousers, sinking ever deeper in their own blindness, finally brought about the bombardment of the Ruthenian capital city.... Fleeing from just vengeance into Hungary, where their supporters (including some [Polish] compatriots) also took up arms of wrath, they began to threaten us Ruthenians for not joining with them and not taking up weapons together against His Highness, our Most Gracious Monarch. They spread rumours that they will not remain in Hungary but, in any case, whether they triumph or are defeated, will return to Galicia. If they are victorious in Hungary, they will come [back] with the Hungarians to restore their state in Galicia and rule over the Ruthenians as before. If they are defeated and forced to retreat, in escaping before the army's pursuit they will, out of vengeance, devastate the Ruthenian populace in Galicia with fire and sword.... We [of the Holovna Rada] had...three aims: (1) to defend and protect the Ruthenian land from the aggressive Hungarian firebrands and the Polish émigrés who have joined with them; (2) to give His Highness proof that the Ruthenian nation...is prepared to show its loyalty through action; and (3) to protect the Ruthenian name from the indignity it experienced last year in its own country and in its own capital city.[55]

The Holovna Rada attempted to procure a banner for the battalion and appropriated five hundred guldens for musical instruments for a band. Ivan Borysykevych offered each company a copy of Hryhorii Kvitka-Osnovianenko's *Marusia*, which he had published.[56] However, before marching off to Hungary, the battalion did not receive either a banner (because Archduchess Sophia, the *Fahnenmutter* of the battalion, did not send her scarf until December 1849), or a band (which was not organized in time, and the unspent funds were returned).[57] The military authorities, despite the Holovna Rada's requests, did not agree to a Ukrainian command, because the riflemen, even though they were in Ukrainian national uniforms, were considered part of the Austrian army.[58]

On 6 September, nearly a month after the Hungarian capitulation at Világos, the battalion was ordered to Hungary. In Košice it paraded before the Russian general Fedor Rüdiger, and later it was assigned to occupy the towns of Senica and Kremnica. Whether it took part in any battles or joined in the pacification, which continued until the end of the year, is unknown. At the beginning of January 1850, it returned to Przemyśl. Despite the Holovna Rada's efforts to preserve it, the battalion was dissolved, and many of the soldiers, contrary to previous promises, were incorporated into the Austrian army.[5]

The Austrian authorities had tolerated the nucleus of a Ukrainian military organization as long as it was useful to them, not so much for real advantage as for propaganda purposes. This was also the reason that they did not permit the formation of a second battalion from the remaining volunteers, which the Holovna Rada proposed on 6 April 1849, even suggesting General Hammerstein as its "proprietor." The council's request, composed in an anti-revolutionary and anti-Polish spirit, was transmitted by the minister of war to Agenor Gołuchowski. He resolutely opposed this step, explaining to the authorities in Vienna that the Ukrainians were thinking of establishing a Ukrainian corps of ten thousand soldiers, which could be dangerous for the Austrian state, because the corps would be the armed representative of a nation "animated by nationalist and, in its ultimate outcome, separatist aspirations."[60] In the final reckoning, Austria deceived the Holovna Rada on this issue as well.

17. Education and Culture

Ukrainian activists were convinced that elevating the nation—almost 90 per cent peasants—depended foremost upon education.[1] They understood that only an enlightened farmer, making rational use of the land that he had come to possess, would become a conscious citizen. Enlightening the nation would guarantee its rights and constitutional liberties and provide Ukrainians the opportunity to exercise them properly. "Freedom cannot be compatible with lack of education," the Ruthenian council of the Perehinsko deanery aptly stated.[2] The proposed path to enlightenment consisted of organizing a system of general primary education (not necessarily a trade education as Iosafat Kobrynsky had proposed) and developing a written language and a literature comprehensible to the common people. Only on this basis could the ideas of the Ruthenian Triad be continued.

Although the development of a national school system depended in large measure on the state authorities, the issues of language and literature could be resolved by the Ukrainians themselves. The Ukrainian councils made this matter one of their main concerns. The difficulties were substantial. Despite improvements in education, the greater part of Ukrainian society was illiterate and consequently effectively unreachable through calls for social and national emancipation. The dozen or so years of activity by the Ruthenian Triad had only slightly enhanced knowledge of the Ukrainian language among the Ukrainian intelligentsia, most of whom continued to use Polish and German or at best, when writing Ukrainian, used the Latin alphabet.[3] The contemporary school system could not change this situation, despite the fact that it began to develop more rapidly after 1845. The appointment of Mykhailo Kuzemsky to the position of scholastic in 1842 had contributed to the improvements. Above all, efforts were made to encourage the study of Ukrainian in the primary schools. The number of parochial schools also increased substantially; between 1842 and 1856 approximately one thousand were established. But, since the Lviv diocese in 1848 could count approximately three hundred schools, the majority of them must have been established after the revolution.[4]

In early 1848, Metropolitan Levytsky attempted to convince the Galician authorities that considerable progress had been made in education. He recommended drawing up a list of books published for parochial school use, including Ivan Vahylevych's grammar, in order to demonstrate the Greek Catholic clergy's concern for the educational needs of the common people.[5] At that time, the homilies of Havrylo Paslavsky, Mykhailo Luchkai and Mikhalyts were used; Stepan Vytvytsky's sermons were published, and those of I. Hankevych had received an imprimatur. Bishop Iakhymovych wrote, not without pride, that "the very numerous discussions about the establishment of parochial schools demonstrate the resolute efforts of the clergy, notwithstanding the obstacles created by the estates owners who took a dim view [of the schools] and certain district officials who made no particular effort [on their behalf]."[6]

The leaders of the Greek Catholic church, though recognizing the need to develop popular education, disagreed with the civil authorities on two issues. They opposed the introduction of model sermons (*Musterpredigten*), which the clergy would have to follow precisely, and the adoption of the Latin alphabet for Ukrainian writings. The metropolitan was even afraid that this latter issue might lead to a controversy similar to that of 1817 and 1818.[7] Iakhymovych, on the other hand, was not worried because he believed that such attempts were based on a false tenet, "as though the Ruthenian and Polish languages completely coincided and the difficulty in mutual intelligibility came only as a result of the difference between letters." Whether the Greek Catholic leaders' arguments convinced Stadion is difficult to say.[8]

The events of March 1848 postponed the education question until the Ukrainians again raised the matter in their address of 19 April. Before a reply was received from Vienna, the Beirat in Lviv began to debate the school issue. It accepted the principle that instruction would be "in the native language of the locality (*gmina*)" in the parish and trivium (primary) schools. If the local population was mixed and there was only one school, then instruction should be available in both languages, but with no requirement that every pupil should study in both "dialects." The Greek Catholic representatives in the Beirat thought that if only one trivium school existed in an area of mixed nationality, not only should the Ukrainian language be taught, but other subjects should be taught in Ukrainian as well. The Poles in the Beirat, however, demanded that Polish be taught in the Ukrainian schools in areas with a Ukrainian majority, either as a mandatory subject (Father Karol Jabłonowski's opinion) or as an elective (Józef Widmann's and Kazimierz Stadnicki's view). Only Gołuchowski believed it inappropriate in village schools "to force the pupils to learn a language that seems unnecessary to them." Many members of the Beirat thought that the local communities should be given the freedom to choose the language of instruction, especially if they had built their own schools. Only the Roman Catholic priest Kucharski apparently feared that the issue could cause dissension between the consistories of the Roman and Greek Catholic rites.[9]

The gubernial circular of 11 May 1848 (no. 6286) was based on the outcome of the debate in the Beirat. It mandated instruction in the local language in the trivium schools and, in cases of mixed nationality, in both languages. The circular obliged the respective *Kreise* to execute the orders in agreement with the consistories, which required the teachers to offer German as an elective for "modest wages" and to transform the parish schools into trivium schools. The circular basically accorded with the government's response to the Ukrainian address of 19 April; perhaps Stadion knew the response at the time he issued it. Nevertheless, the Austrian government had not yet formed a precise opinion on secondary education. Therefore, it promised to establish a chair of Ukrainian language to provide students an opportunity to learn a language that for the time being was considered inappropriate for lectures.[10]

These decisions were the basis of further actions. On 9 May the Greek Catholic consistory deliberated the school issue, and on 16 May Bishop Iakhymovych gave the order to teach in the language of the majority or in both languages in the trivium schools.[11] Finally, on 6 June the consistory issued a proclamation to all the villages in the archdiocese on the matter of organizing Ukrainian schools.[12] These directives, in addition to the orders of the *Kreishauptmänner* on school matters, permitted the Ukrainian councils to begin organizing and aroused the local populace. The councils sought advice about how to establish and equip primary schools, appealed to the generosity of local communities and emphasized the advantages of educating children.[13] They were aware of the difficulties: the lack of teachers, school buildings, equipment and textbooks; the low standard of preparation for the cantors teaching in the schools and their poor pay, which was "less than a village shepherd's." It was proposed that the villages be obliged to build schools, introduce mandatory instruction, establish an institute to train village teachers, prepare textbooks in a language intelligible to the common people and call upon the clergy to teach in the schools.[14] The problems were all the greater because the state authorities demanded that villages maintain schools at their own expense. How the peasants reacted to this situation apparently depended in large measure upon local pastors. The peasants of the Univ deanery, under the leadership of Father Mykhailo Kozlovsky, pledged to help construct a school if their former lord would provide the materials. The Ruthenian deanery council in Univ decided to display its initiative "as a model for other villages and to publicize [the Univ peasants' action] throughout the Ruthenian land in the hope of its being imitated."[15]

Some villages possessed suitable buildings, whereas others attempted to take over the schools that had been built jointly with local Poles. The village of Vychliana requested the deanery council in Univ to support its efforts so that "our Ruthenian children, three times more numerous than the Latin [Polish] children, could study in Ruthenian," in a school built by the village. Otherwise, it would be compelled to abandon its earlier pledge. It also demanded that the teacher "be able to teach our children in Ruthenian, and the Ruthenians of the Roman rite in Polish." The Holovna Rada responded by requesting the *Kreis* officials in Zolochiv to guarantee, in accordance with the directives of the Galician authorities of 11 and 23 May 1848, instruction in the Ukrainian language, and to charge the Vychliana officials with finding a salaried teacher. If the *Kreis* did not settle the matter by 15 September, then the Holovna Rada promised to intervene with higher authorities.[16]

Not all the councils could pride themselves upon such accomplishments. The deanery council in Berezhany complained that the peasants did not want to establish schools and send their children to them. Although the peasants recognized the advantages of education—"so that one would not be fooled by the Jews or the lords"—they were convinced that learning led to betraying one's own class and surroundings, and consequently to denationalization. Fear of being called to military service also played a role, since too often literate peasants were turned over to the army.[17] The deanery council in Khodoriv pointed to the noble land-owners' aversion to establishing schools; the nobles assumed that if "the peasants do not work to pay for their release from *robot* and do not perform their duties, ... [then] the lords [too] are freed from their former obligations. Therefore, whoever needs a school, let him build it."[18]

The prevailing conditions did not please the Holovna Rada, which in the summer of 1848 addressed to the Viennese authorities a request to introduce instruction in Ukrainian. In reply, the Ministry of Education, through a decree on 31 August, reaffirmed the regulations applying to the primary schools. It recommended, however, in accordance with the decree of 28 August, that temporary teachers of Ukrainian be hired in the gymnasia. The ministry planned to establish a chair of Ukrainian language at Lviv University, which should have an impact "upon the further improvement and dissemination of Ruthenian literature."[19] The Holovna Rada maintained: "This document should fill the heart of every Ruthenian with joy. One sees from it that the ministry praises and recognizes the activities of the Holovna Rada, as well as the lesser Ruthenian councils, for the good of the nation and our beloved Galician-Ruthenian fatherland."[20]

But, as it turned out, a political change—the appointment of Wacław Zaleski as governor—brought an about-face in educational policy. On the new governor's recommendation, the Ministry of Education, through its decree of 29 September 1848 (no. 6117), decided, "in expectation of the higher development of the Ruthenian language and until such time as division is completed between the Polish and Ruthenian parts of Galicia, to introduce without delay the Polish language in the gymnasia and in the Lviv Academy." However, to safeguard the rights of the Ukrainian language, a school council was to be established to assist the governor.[21] The Polish newspaper *Gazeta Powszechna* [General gazette] wrote that the ministry had recognized "the just demands of the Poles, that a second official provincial language, i.e., Polish, be established, and not the alien German tongue," because the Ukrainians, in requesting the introduction of the Ukrainian language, had acknowledged that their language had not evolved enough to be used in the gymnasia. The ministry preferred consequently to retain German.[22]

On this basis, therefore, instruction was in Polish in the Dominican gymnasium and in the newly created university-preparatory lyceum year, and in German in the academic gymnasium. Study of the Ukrainian language was mandatory in both gymnasia, but German in the Dominican gymnasium and Polish in the academic gymnasium were to be elective. Teachers were to instruct in Polish in the provincial gymnasia and, if they did not know that language, then in German. Only in the Basilian gymnasium in Buchach did instruction take place in Ukrainian.[23]

This polonization of the school system provoked vehement protests from the Ukrainian leadership. On 9 October Ivan Borysykevych advised calling upon the Ukrainian rural communities to block the changes, and two days later the Ruthenian district council in

Berezhany even formally suggested retaining German. The Ruthenian district council in Stryi protested to the Reichstag, and a similar protest signed by twenty-two villages was sent to the Holovna Rada by the deanery council in Bolekhiv.[24] In such circumstances, agreement between the Polish and Ukrainian councils on a unified educational policy was impossible. The Ukrainians rejected beforehand suggestions from the Polish side, whereas the Poles viewed the activities of the teachers of Ukrainian with disdain.[25]

The makeup of the Galician School Council also aroused dissatisfaction among the Ukrainians, for there was no room on it for either Kuzemsky or Malynovsky, who had been proposed by Gołuchowski. However, the priests Dr. A. Monastyrsky, Onufrii Krynytsky, Ivan Vahylevych and Dr. Amvrozii Ianovsky were included all of whom were known for their pro-Polish sympathies.[26] In its endeavours to change the school system, the Holovna Rada presented its wishes to the emperor and to the Ministry of Education. It asked for the removal of Polish from the schools and a return to the arrangements prior to 29 September 1848, retaining German, since Ukrainian "is still not so developed that it could be the language of instruction."[27] The council's efforts were successful. In a decree of 4 December 1848, the Ministry of Education retracted its decision of 29 September and restored the status quo ante, acknowledging that it had been mistakenly persuaded that the change to Polish suited "the general wishes of the country."[28] The ministry issued an addendum on 8 January 1849, though it was not published in the official *Wiener Zeitung* until 21 January. Recognizing the justness of the Ukrainians' aspirations "to have their language considered in public instruction," the ministry had reintroduced German into the gymnasia because "the Ruthenians' national sentiment objects less to the German language than to Polish."[29]

Thus, German was mandated in the gymnasia of Eastern Galicia until such time as the Ukrainian language was adequately formed. Instruction in Ukrainian, however, was permitted if it was possible. In these gymnasia the study of Ukrainian was mandatory, whereas Polish was elective. The previous regulations that had made the Dominican gymnasium "Polish" were also retracted.[30] At the university, *Privatdozenten* (unsalaried lecturers) were permitted to lecture in Polish, but in all other cases lectures had to be in German until teachers were found and students were prepared to attend lectures in the "local" language. The ministry was convinced that "it had done everything it could in the present situation, without infringing on the rights and interests of others, to satisfy ... the demand for equal rights of the Ruthenian nation." The decree did not satisfy many, however, and it caused considerable trouble for the Holovna Rada. The Poles accused the council of supporting germanization. The Czechs were shocked, "unable to understand by what means the Slavic interest can be assured through the introduction of the German language." Eventually, the Ukrainians themselves admitted, according to Smolka, "that they did not want this, did not demand it and will protest against it."[31]

But we do not know whether they in fact protested. On 12 July 1849 the council asked the Ministry of Education to hasten its decision on the structure of schools in Eastern Galicia.[32] The Ukrainians demanded the immediate introduction of Ukrainian, not only in the teaching of religion, but also of geography, history and languages; the hiring of persons who knew Ukrainian to the positions of adjunct, assistant and regular teachers; making the language of instruction independent of the number of pupils in the trivium and normal schools; transferring supervision of the schools of mixed nationality in Eastern Galicia to the Greek Catholic consistories (except for the teaching of religion); remuneration for the teaching of religion in the gymnasia; and the establishment of a separate school council "for the Ruthenian land," composed of "experienced men who enjoy the confidence of the Ruthenians."

The implementation of this ambitious programme indeed would have brought genuine equality for the Ukrainian language in education. Why then had the Holovna Rada not proposed this programme in the autumn of 1848? Apparently, before 8 January 1849 it did not expect that the Austrian authorities would be inclined to revoke the concessions accorded to the Polish language. How the political situation would develop was not clear at the end of October 1848, and therefore the Ukrainians made only modest demands. They did not know whether or to what degree the government would be willing to make concessions. Vacillation and indecision had characterized the government's educational policy for Galicia up to that point; that policy depended on the general situation in the province and the composition of the frequently changing cabinets. Thus, even though paragraph 4 of the provisional constitution of 25 April 1848 recognizing the equality of the nationalities was officially respected, in reality it was variously interpreted. The strengthening of liberal forces in Vienna was advantageous for the Poles, whereas the subsequent victory of reaction brought anti-Polish tendencies and favouritism toward the Ukrainians.

The Poles naturally undertook countermeasures. In a specially prepared address, they attempted to prove that the decree of 8 January 1849 was a prelude to the actual division of the country, and in the name of the inhabitants of Galicia they asked not "for the Polish language, nor for the Ruthenian language exclusively, but... for the land's native tongue, which is unquestionably as much Polish as Ruthenian." The Poles likewise demanded a return to the status quo of 29 September 1848, though "not by derogating... the rights to which the Ruthenian language is entitled."[33] At Kroměříž, Leszek Dunin-Borkowski spoke out on this issue, and Marian Dylewski made a formal query. It seemed to Reichstag President Franciszek Smolka that the authorities "want to turn from the path upon which they have embarked... [and] withdraw the decree concerning the schools."[34] How vain these Polish hopes were became apparent on 3 March 1849, when Stadion responded to Dylewski's interpellation.[35] The minister no longer took into account the constitution of 25 April 1848—the new constitution of 4 March 1849 was already prepared—nor the Reichstag, whose days were numbered. Without mincing words, he explained the principles that guided the government's school policy and at the same time cast much light on the current Austrian policy toward the nationalities. He maintained that the government was applying the same principles to the Ukrainian nationality in Eastern Galicia as to the Poles in Western Galicia. However, in view of the weak development of Ukrainian literature, the introduction of Ukrainian into the schools must proceed slowly. The many petitions were evidence that the Ukrainians were more opposed to the interim status afforded the Polish language than to the use of German, while the Poles rejected the separateness of the Ukrainian nationality and refuted its right to independent development. The Germans, however, "accorded it full justice."

The decree of 8 January 1849 had suited the Ukrainians' wishes, as was confirmed by Rector Karlman Tangl's remarks to Gołuchowski:

> Lviv University has become entirely different, that is, Ruthenian, and Ruthenian-German only in the sense that German will be retained temporarily as the language of instruction until the full scholarly development of the Ruthenian language occurs. The whole country on this [eastern] side of the San [River] sees the fulfillment of its just desires and is carried away with joyful thanks for the wise directive of the High Ministry.

The minister's dispositions freed the Ukrainian majority from those decisions that had infringed on its rights. Stadion argued against Dylewski's view that all of the students in Eastern Galicia spoke Polish, giving as an example the departure of a significant number of young people from the Dominican gymnasium following the "polonization" decree of 29 September 1848. Stadion also contended that the government was not entirely excluding Polish. The principles of equal rights required that the minority adjust to the desires of the majority, although the minority had the right to demand that instruction in its native language be made available. The ministry intended, Stadion said, to ensure that in both parts of the country, "both in offices and in the schools, not only the majority, but also the minority would be represented as long as it possessed significant numbers." Stadion was doubtless correct, with one reservation: the deferral of Ukrainian as the language of instruction for an indeterminate period did not serve ukrainization, but germanization.[36] Just how long this period was to last depended almost exclusively on the Ukrainians themselves and on how quickly the Ukrainian language and literature developed. The years 1848 and 1849 did not augur rapid change.

The Ukrainian intelligentsia thought constantly about these problems. In the spring of 1848, at the initiative of Mykola Ustyianovych and Ivan Borysykevych, preparations were begun to convene a congress of learned Ukrainians. Even peasants from various parts of Galicia were to be invited to enable the congress to become aware of distinctions among rural dialects. But the planners quickly realized that the codification of their language required fundamental research and that the invitation of peasants was unnecessary, because many of the Ukrainian activists—for example, Iakiv Holovatsky, Iosyf Lozynsky, Rudolf Mokh and Mykola Ustyianovych—had a good command of the folk idiom.[37] The secular character of the proposed congress and the assumption that it could make decisions concerning the organization of intellectual life in Galicia irritated the conservative Holovna Rada and Greek Catholic consistory. Apparently, a Ruthenian Matytsia group was already functioning under the consistory's direction, but its work was limited to raising funds and preparing religious works for publication. Such endeavours could not satisfy those Ukrainians who wanted the congress to establish a Ruthenian Matytsia as a secular institution. Ultimately, they managed to have the existing Matytsia group declared provisional and to establish a formal preparatory committee for the congress, which would act in the name of the inhabitants of Lviv, and not the Matytsia. Understandably, the clergy wanted to cancel the congress. However, they succeeded only in placing three of their representatives on the preparatory committee.[38]

On 1 September 1848, the committee—composed of Mykola Ustyianovych, Ivan Zhukovsky, Lev Sosnovsky, Mykhailo Malynovsky, Teodor Leontovych, Ivan Zarytsky, Ivan Slymakovsky, Ivan Borysykevych, Antin Iuzychynsky, Ivan Hurkevych and Antin Paventsky—drafted an invitation to Ukrainian scholars to attend the congress, which would begin on 19 October:

> Regardless of our political convictions concerning the well-being of the nation, regardless of religious confession, all of us Ruthenians will join together in the firm conviction that the true fortune of our nation can flourish only on a foundation of enlightenment.[39]

"All political considerations" were excluded from the deliberations of the congress, which would be limited to matters of language and literature. The congress was to standardize the bases of grammar and orthography; "clarify the difference between our language and Old Slavonic as well as Russian and Polish"; facilitate the exchange of scholarly ideas and information; "organize and divide literary endeavours according to the needs of the nation"; and establish a "national institute on the model of the Czech Matice, which would assume guardianship over [Ukrainian] literature."

That institute was to be the scholarly and cultural centre of Galician Rus'. Its functions were to further ties among writers and men of learning; publish their works; collect historical artifacts and the surviving remnants of old Ukrainian writing; and maintain contacts "with learned men of all the Slavic branches and be an organ of all-Slavic reciprocity." It was also assumed that the Ruthenian Matytsia would publish a journal along the lines of the Czech and Serbian organizations, through which the Ukrainians would be informed of the progress and status of their national literature.[40] This was an entirely modern plan, laid out in a grand style and calculated for an extended period of time. The invitation further declared:

> A joint congress of Ruthenian men of learning is absolutely essential to the speedy and more vigorous advancement of our Ruthenian literature and the diffusion of useful learning and information among the people. [Ruthenian scholars] ... with their collective strengths will go to work in the field of Ruthenian literature, neglected up to this time. They will divide up their work according to their strengths and desires ... [and] establish in the oral and written language permanent boundaries and forms of the language of the entire Ruthenian nation.[41]

Ustyianovych believed that the congress should respond to the question of whether Ukrainian would endure as an independent language alongside Russian, Polish and Church Slavonic. Was a comparative grammar necessary to ensure that Ukrainian was not absorbed by these languages? Which of the existing Ukrainian grammars could be the basis for school instruction? Which members of the newly created Ruthenian Matytsia could undertake the writing or translation of textbooks? Was a national journal necessary to serve the development of Ukrainian literature?[42]

Kuzemsky opened the deliberations. One hundred ten delegates attended, with clergymen in the majority. From the laity there were members of the Stavropygian Institute and teachers from secular schools.[43] A participant, Vasyl Ilnytsky, described the atmosphere of the congress and the mood of the delegates: "At the front of the hall rose the throne of His Highness our Emperor, decked in wreaths, and along the sides hung portraits of several Ruthenian princes. The hall was decorated with blue and yellow flags and cockades of the same colour; there was nothing black and yellow to be seen." The fact that the congress took place under military protection was evidence of its political significance. The conservative group from the Holovna Rada and the Greek Catholic consistory, according to Ilnytsky, wanted to make it "an instrument of reaction... against the revolutionary aspirations of the Poles." In fact, it became the podium of the Ukrainian liberals. Ilnytsky noted that their "speeches breathed with freedom and patriotism. The canons who had come remained silent and timid. I saw that more than one bold, free word, expressed with burning patriotism, offended them."[44]

Several speeches, especially those of Iosyf Levytsky, Ustyianovych, Mokh and H. Iablonsky, made strong impressions. Levytsky spoke sharply against the denationalizing policies of the Greek Catholic hierarchy, charging it with persecuting patriotic Ukrainian youth who were seeking to develop their native literature. He further criticized the hierarchy for passing over such patriots in making parish assignments and accused it of favouring the use of Polish. "Who among us clergymen who had to know Ruthenian even received a directive or other notice in Ruthenian from the consistory? In various foreign languages, only not in Ruthenian."[45]

Ustyianovych's speech roused patriotic feelings as he praised the nation's past accomplishments and the beauty of the Ukrainian language.

> The most valuable possession of the nation is its language; it is the soul and the kernel of its life. If you add your two cents to it, you interfere in the life of the nation;... you do not kill one person, but millions!... By abandoning our speech, we commit a sacrilege against the throne of Rus'.... Who does not know the colour, the flower and the aroma of this offspring of the golden shores of Ukraine?[46]

Iablonsky, seemingly the only collaborator with the Sobor Ruskyi present at the congress, spoke of the greatness and political significance of the Ukrainian nation. He based his arguments on Ukraine's geographical position, the beauty of its folk songs and of the Ukrainian language itself, and on the glorious history of the Cossacks.[47]

Ustyianovych's and Iablonsky's speeches were infused with Ukrainian messianism and Slavic reciprocity. The speakers derived the greatness of Ukraine from its central position in "the heart of Slavdom" and its glorious and heroic historical past, written in blood and tears. Ukraine valiantly bore foreign oppression and the egoism of its own privileged classes and courageously defended other nations against "swarming Asiatic hordes." The Ukrainian nation remained faithful to its traditions and customs, preserving its language and religion and providing a model of civic sacrifice. The history and great talents of the nation predisposed it to playing an enormous role in the future "among the seven Slavic tribes," which it would gather around itself in fulfilling the principles of liberty.[48]

Rudolf Mokh called upon those assembled to work for the welfare of the nation. "A sacred cause has brought us here—a love for the common people and their enlightenment. Therefore, let this unite us in such a way that we live with one heart and one spirit. Let us in common aid one another, wherever fate may hurl us, and with the plough in hand, let us not look back nor stop."[49]

The congress deliberated in sections devoted to theology, law, philosophy, natural sciences, history and geography, agronomy, Ruthenian literature and the church language, and education. Unfortunately, combining the sections on grammar, vocabulary and orthography with the section on literature and its history had a disastrous impact on the deliberations and resolutions on the issues of orthography and the literary language.[50] This combined section was the focus of attention for all those assembled, since in it decisions fraught with consequences for the future of Ukrainian literature would be made.

Two papers of special significance were delivered: "Discourse on Ruthenian Orthography," by Ivan Zhukovsky, and "The South Rus' Language and its Dialects," by Iakiv Holovatsky. They reflected the most progressive contemporary scholarly views of Ukrainian orthography, language and literature. In acknowledging orthographical reform as the most important subject before the assembly, Zhukovsky declared himself in favour of a phonetic spelling that reflected only the language then used by the common people, although he also took into account etymology. He also recommended adapting the orthography to the dialect that had the greatest chance of becoming the basis of the literary language.[51]

Zhukovsky's paper provoked an emotional outburst. Some individuals supported introducing the vernacular into literature; others wanted to preserve Church Slavonic. The former advocated phonetic spelling; the latter adhered to etymological spelling, at most agreeing to pronounce the old forms in Ukrainian. But those supporting the vernacular were in the majority. Among them were Iakiv Holovatsky, Ustyianovych, Mokh, Zhukovsky, Lozynsky and Teofan Hlynsky. They believed that the achievements of the Ruthenian Triad should be carried forward. Mykola Vereshchynsky beseeched:

> In the name of human reason, do not create a new learned language. Let the popular speech remain inviolable and become the basis of our literature. We are seeking enlightenment and prosperity for our nation. Therefore, let its language be the organ through which we have to speak to it and impart the eternal truths.... We have already entered upon the wrong road; we are already making accommodations to Church Slavonic, Polish or Russian. We are doing little service to the other Slavs, but are doing harm to ourselves.... I highly value our Cyril and his alphabet. I acknowledge its merits, but I do not commit a sin when I cast off the "hard sign" [ъ] forever and write as I speak. Admirers of antiquity, who, in honouring the contributions of great men, do not dare to depart from the precepts established by them, are the servants of idols.... Our literature is of the common people; consequently, let us not allow historical laws to affect it. Let us be true democrats—that is, let us follow reason, nature and the truth, and let us guard against any form of elegance, which is proof of bad taste and a sign of foolishness.[52]

Mokh was especially intransigent in demanding the use of the vernacular ending "v" [в] instead of "l" [л] in the third person masculine singular form of the past tense ("buv" [був] instead of "bul" [бул] for "he was"). Mokh also wished to discard the superfluous letters "ы" and "ъ". But the opposition of Levytsky and other proponents of etymological spelling led to the defeat of his motion.[53]

The situation was similar in the congress section dealing with education.[54] The adherents of an etymological approach were afraid that phonetic spelling would displace the ossified Church Slavonic. In 1848 they could not have foreseen that by enforcing etymological orthography in the schools they would contribute to the later stagnation of Ukrainian cultural life.

Holovatsky's discourse epitomized the national views of the Ukrainian liberals. However, his talk was essentially a systematic lecture on the state of current research in Slavic studies as it applied to the Ukrainian language and nation, and did not go beyond P. J. Šafařík's earlier treatise on Slavic ethnography, *Slovanský národopis*. Holovatsky's most important achievement was his demonstration that Ukrainian could not be considered a dialect of Polish or Russian. Holovatsky believed that the distinctiveness of a language indicated the distinctiveness of the nation that spoke it. He demonstrated the ethnic and linguistic unity of the Ukrainian nation on both sides of the border.[55] His arguments were all the more significant because he expressed them at a time when Polish journalists denied the Ukrainian nation a distinctive cultural status and some Pan-Slavic enthusiasts, such as Mikhail Pogodin, proclaimed the unity of "the Russian people" from the San River and the Black Sea to the Pacific Ocean and the Arctic Sea.

What practical conclusions did Holovatsky draw? Above all, that it was essential for Ukrainians to develop their native tongue. Not without reason did he end his exposition with the aphorism, "Often of our language do we frivolously complain; we know it not, but it is a golden vein." However, he did not state clearly how and on what basis it should be developed. Only in the revised, published version of his discourse did he write:

> The speech of the common people is certainly the true and first source of the literary language, because in their mouths are preserved all the purest forms, the entire order and composition of the language, its true spirit. For that reason, it seems appropriate that we write entirely as the common people speak, just as our kindred Slovaks and Lusatians have done.

However, Holovatsky did not follow in their steps. He recognized that the vernacular was not adequate for scholarship; so he encouraged the emulation of the monuments of earlier Ruthenian literary culture, which were "the native root from which the tree of national literature must grow." On this basis, Holovatsky wrote, an elaborate body of literature "will survive the ages," and "no power will be able to dislodge or displace it."[56]

The congress adopted many resolutions that could have contributed to the development of the Ukrainian nationality if they had been implemented. Unfortunately, neither the power nor the means existed or could exist. There were nevertheless proposals to establish an agricultural society and a historical society, to prepare and publish a popular textbook of Ukrainian history and to try to preserve historical and cultural monuments. There were also proposals to strengthen cultural ties with Russia and Ukraine, to introduce the Russian language in the gymnasia, and to establish reading rooms for the common people.[57]

On 25 October, the day preceding the close of deliberations, the Halytsko-Ruska Matytsia (Galician-Ruthenian Matytsia) was formally established. Its tasks were to oversee the development of the national literature through the publication and distribution of inexpensive books, "to inculcate faith and morality, to disseminate information, to develop beautiful language and writing and to foster crafts, agriculture, pedagogy and good upbringing."[58] The Ruthenian Matytsia's officers were Mykhailo Kuzemsky, chairman; Ivan Borysykevych and Iuliian Lavrovsky, vice-chairmen; Ivan Zhukovsky and Mykhailo Malynovsky, secretaries; Ivan Lototsky, treasurer; and Ivan Hurkevych, auditor. The Matytsia, also known as the Society of National Enlightenment (on the model of foreign learned societies), was composed of two members elected from each section at the congress. They in turn could elect full, corresponding or honorary members. Borysykevych contributed most to the creation of the Ruthenian Matytsia and later sought to organize it along modern lines.[59]

The Matytsia was the only Galician cultural and educational organization accessible to all social classes. Although only lettered persons of the Greek Catholic rite who were loyal to the monarchy and "right-thinking" could serve in its administration, a so-called founding member could be anyone who paid fifty florins. Thus there were clerical and lay persons in its ranks, and the peasant deputies Andrii Dzivakovsky and Konstantyn Posatsky as well. The membership included the Czech journalist Karel Havlíček-Borovský and Governor Gołuchowski. Within a short time the endowment exceeded two thousand florins. Some money was contributed by thirty-seven village communities and ten townsmen's organizations, including craftsmen.[60]

In evaluating the congress of learned Ukrainians, one must not forget that the participants themselves were convinced that they had made a major contribution to the awakening of the Ukrainian national consciousness, mobilized the liberal and progressive intelligentsia and isolated the conservative and clerical circles of the Holovna Rada and the Greek Catholic consistory. Nevertheless, the elections to the Matytsia administration showed that the liberal intelligentsia had not managed to displace the conservatives, because the liberals' seats—vice-chairman and auditor—were in large measure ceremonial. The other administrators, all of whom were associated with the Greek Catholic hierarchy, actually decided every issue.

The first weeks after the congress witnessed renewed activities aimed at implementing the decisions reached there. Teacher-training and the preparation of textbooks of the Ukrainian language for the gymnasia began.[61] The schools were meant to play a significant role in shaping social, national and ideological attitudes; however, there were few candidates for the teaching profession who knew the native language and literature. The Holovna Rada appealed to well-known Ukrainian spokesmen for aid and prepared a list of history and geography teachers who could lecture in Ukrainian. This list was intended to be sent to Vienna, where Hryhorii Shashkevych, who had been appointed an advisor to the Ministry of Education, was to insist on their being employed.[62] Eventually, teachers of Ukrainian and religion were appointed provisionally in all the gymnasia of Eastern Galicia for the academic year 1848-9. Ivan Zhukovsky and Iakiv Holovatsky taught in the academic gymnasium and Ivan Hushalevych in the Dominican gymnasium. Petro Holovatsky was to move to Ternopil, where Ievstakhii Prokopchyts had become the director of the gymnasium.[63] In fact, the Ukrainians placed great hope on the Ternopil gymnasium, believing that it could be "ukrainized" quickly because Ukrainian teachers were in the majority there. Moreover, they could exploit the dissatisfaction of Ukrainian students, who had begun to object to the domination of German in the Lviv gymnasia and the theology faculty.[64]

However, in general, the schools roused considerable anxiety. A common complaint was that in Lviv "the teaching positions are filled with Krauts [*Nimota*]."[65] Evaluating the schools after a year's work, Iosyf Levytsky concluded pessimistically that

> the Ruthenian language, having been completely left to its own fate, has not been enhanced much in the Przemyśl schools. The new professors know very little Ruthenian, and no one demands it of them. They do not teach any subject in Ruthenian except religion. Indeed, on paper the normal schools are in the hands of the Ruthenian [Greek Catholic] consistory, but it does not especially concern itself with directing them in the spirit of the Ruthenian nationality. In a word, the Ruthenians are too lukewarm in regard to their own cause; they are not [like] the Poles.[66]

It seemed that the situation was not much better in other districts of Eastern Galicia.

The Ukrainian enthusiasts were heartened by the creation of a chair of Ukrainian language and literature at Lviv University, and they immediately tried to fill it. The chair was formally established by the imperial patent of 13 September 1848, according to which the newly appointed professor (with an annual salary of six hundred guldens) was to commence his lectures (five hours weekly) without compensation for a period of one year. The deadline for nominations to the position was 30 September. The candidates had to demonstrate, "with proofs, their completed studies, morality and knowledge of the Ruthenian language, as well as of Polish and German."[67]

The liberals wished to keep the chair open for Iakiv Holovatsky, while the conservatives had Ivan Zhukovsky in mind, in return for his "services in the Stadion-German-bureaucratic party." The polonized Ruthenians of the Sobor Ruskyi, on the other hand, attempted to assure a place at the university for Ivan Vahylevych. Holovatsky's candidacy, on all accounts, was well deserved. Borysykevych wrote to him that "your contribution [has been] an arduous effort on behalf of the Ruthenian language, a complete familiarity with all the Ruthenian literary works, and a sensible view of our national position."[68] Despite much pleading, Holovatsky delayed submitting his name, although Malynovsky did it for him. It was explained to Holovatsky that candidacy did not obligate him to anything, and if city life did not appeal to him, as a professor he could obtain an assignment in a better parish.[69] In reply, Holovatsky wrote to Borysykevych:

> I readily accede to your proposal regarding the chair of literature and the [Ruthenian] Matytsia position [the directorship had been offered to him], because what Ruthenian would not be prepared to devote his strength and health to this precious cause of his beloved nation or would not want to labour to uplift our intellectual life? Can there be a more sacred duty than to guide the youth, who are our hope, and to educate the coming generation for the glory and splendour of our people?[70]

Yet he delayed his decision for unknown reasons. Whether the efforts of the Poles and the Sobor Ruskyi influenced him, or whether he began to doubt that he would be appointed to the chair as long as Zaleski was governor, is difficult to determine. The Ukrainians, however, could not afford to lose this opportunity. After Holovatsky finally registered his application in early October, endeavours on his behalf were begun in Vienna.[71] The participants in the congress of Ukrainian scholars supported his nomination. So did the Ukrainian councils, which also protested against Vahylevych's candidacy, which was being pushed by the Polish-dominated School Council.[72] The Holovna Rada intervened with the ministries of education and the interior, which, however, seemingly could not locate Holovatsky's application. As Kyrylo Blonsky charged, "the Poles [*liashnia*] in Lviv hid it, but then they were ordered in sharp terms to send the entire file."[73]

Then, in November, the Austrian government gave its support to the Ukrainians. As we have noted, the post of counsellor in the Ministry of Education was offered to Hryhorii Shashkevych; the Galician School Council was dissolved; Holovatsky received his nomination as professor, and the decree was sent to him in Lviv.[74] The Galician authorities then sought to have Vahylevych assigned to the Dominican gymnasium, but the Greek Catholic consistory opposed this step. It was unwilling to forgive him his willful abandonment of his parish and his assumption of the editorship of *Dnewnyk Ruskij.*[75]

Because the next university session was not to begin until April 1849, Holovatsky commenced his lectures in the upper-level classes of the academic gymnasium, where Zhukovsky was already teaching. The Ukrainians anticipated rapid ukrainization of the gymnasium and, consequently, further national development.[76] Little did they know how vain their hopes were. Later, after he came to realize this, Holovatsky joined the supporters of the continued use of Church Slavonic. Late in 1849, he wrote:

> [Church] Slavonic is and always will be the treasury of our lexicon, by which we shall fortify our language. We shall not stop learning from it and interpreting the old Slavic spirit, in addition to developing forms for a living, contemporary language. [Slavonic] is a language of spiritual strength, a language of faith, higher than the vernacular, and yet it is understood by the common people.[77]

Holovatsky relied on older texts and especially S. P. Shevyrev's *Istoriia russkoi slovesnosti, preimushchestvenno drevnei* [History of Russian literature, primarily ancient], the first volume of which had recently appeared in Moscow.[78] He lectured quietly and in a monotone, "in the same muscovized Church Slavonic in which he wrote". He never went beyond the bounds of Old Rus' literature, as though he were afraid that by referring to new literary achievements of modern Ukrainian literature—the works of Ivan Kotliarevsky, Ievhen Hrebinka, Hryhorii Kvitka-Osnovianenko and Taras Shevchenko—he would reduce his linguistic and literary theories to nothing. It is not surprising that he did not have a large audience, although there were several seminarians who were obliged to attend.[79] He did not gain even their esteem. As one student later recalled:

> Professor Holovatsky came to the class unprepared; usually after half an hour had passed, he was reading [his lectures] drowsily, yawning and constantly looking at his watch, [to see] whether, God forbid, he had perhaps exceeded the allotted hour. It was apparent at every turn that he was sort of tired, as though he were sleepy or other thoughts occupied his mind. No small wonder that the youth did not cling to such a professor.[80]

In retrospect, it appears that the only effect of Holovatsky's linguistic theories was that he passed into the ranks of the Russophiles in the 1850s and, after he had broken all ties with the national trend in Ruthenian literature and intellectual life, eventually departed for Russia.[81]

The Matytsia administration was responsible for overseeing a steady supply of manuscripts for school textbooks and their preparation for publication. It also had to reject "whatever is opposed to the law and the provincial statutes." However, apart from the grammars by Levytsky, Lozynsky and Vahylevych, prepared for publication by Prokopchyts and Iakiv Holovatsky, Markiian Shashkevych's *Chytanka* [Reader], Adolf Dobriansky's *Bukvar* [Primer] and a collection of biblical stories, there was nothing to print.[82] It may be added that

Ukrainian intellectuals had little trust in their own strength. The only course seemingly was to procure Czech, Polish and Russian texts and base a Ukrainian scholarly terminology on them. Requests came from all over Eastern Galicia that such texts be furnished, with the Czech models recognized as the best.[83] Holovatsky's previous scholarly and literary contacts with the Slavic awakeners facilitated these efforts.

In the summer and fall of 1849, Holovatsky raised the matter of textbooks with Ján Kollár and P. J. Šafařík. Kollár, assuming the unity of action and purpose of all of Slavdom, favoured a uniform presentation, and therefore he recommended translating the Czech books. Šafařík, however, called attention to the necessity of preparing national chrestomathies for use in the gymnasia. Holovatsky urged the Ukrainian enthusiasts especially to turn their attention to "the national history, national life and the native country." Holovatsky also would ask Kuzemsky to convene a meeting of "professors and fervent Ruthenians" regarding "common understanding and the assignment of the work of writing those textbooks."[84] But these efforts brought no tangible results; it still was necessary to rely on foreign texts. Holovatsky therefore established contacts with booksellers in Saint Petersburg, Moscow, Kiev and Brody, asking them to send "all the gymnasium and university texts from which geography, world history and the history of individual countries, natural history, arithmetic, algebra, geometry, philosophy, etc., with the exception of foreign languages and literatures, are being taught in the Russian schools."[85]

Contemporary Ukrainian belles-lettres also could not boast of accomplishments on a par with *Rusalka Dnistrovaia* or *Vinok*. To be sure, Liubych-Mohylnytsky, Ustyianovych and Mokh endeavoured to continue the tradition of the Ruthenian Triad, and indeed Hryhorii Bodnar, Luka Dankevych (Luka of Rakiv), Mykhailo Kozanovych, Pavlo Leontovych (Pavlo of Shutkiv), Tselestyn Skomorovsky, Iosyf Shukhevych and Iuliian Velychkovsky were active in literature. However, difficulties in publishing inhibited the circulation of their work among the Ukrainians, although Ivan Hushalevych's "Myr vam brattia vsim prynosym" [Brothers, we bring peace to all of you] virtually became the national anthem of the Ukrainians in Galicia.[86] These writers espoused various views: Skomorovsky declared for the side of freedom and progress; Mokh and Ustyianovych criticized the prevailing social conditions, and Hushalevych echoed the slogans of social solidarity and bowed to the spirit of reaction.[87]

The lack of the literature that was available in Russian Ukraine was deeply felt in Galicia, especially because, for the Galician Ukrainians, that literature was unequalled, worthy of imitation and a still insufficiently used model. So, when the number of books imported from

Ukraine proved to be insufficient, reprinting of the best works was begun in Galicia. As might be expected, Iakiv Holovatsky organized this undertaking; the Galician Ukrainians were indebted to him for introducing the works of Ivan Kotliarevsky, Hryhorii Kvitka-Osnovianenko, Ievhen Hrebinka, Amvrosii Metlynsky, Levko Borovykovsky and Taras Shevchenko. Kyrylo Blonsky intended to republish in Vienna (later in Olomouc) Kotliarevsky's *Eneida* and even announced a subscription, but the project came to nothing.[88] Petro Holovatsky did translate Gogol's *Taras Bulba*, but it did not appear in print until 1851.[89] However, thanks to Borysykevych's efforts, Kvitka-Osnovianenko's *Marusia* appeared with a new introduction on the life and work of the author.[90]

The Galician Ukrainians imported writings for a broad circle of readers. They established a National Reading Club in Kolomyia,[91] and thanks to the contributions of the local Ukrainians, who were more nationally conscious than in other districts, they collected a substantial fund to buy books from Russia. Above all, they were concerned with literature that would shape the national consciousness of the common people, and in particular historical books. They even urged that more be written and quickly disseminated. Iosafat Kobrynsky suggested that the popular histories of Ukraine that Hushalevych had printed in *Pchola* (1848, nos. 1-19) be widely distributed in a cheap edition. He himself guaranteed the costs of printing and the purchase of a thousand copies for the Kolomyia district and Bukovyna. By this means, he wrote, "in a year we would flood Poland [*Liashnia*] with a Ruthenian sea." The Ukrainians' zeal in Kolomyia was also reflected in a plan to establish a Ukrainian bookshop, to exchange services in distributing already published works and to introduce dramatic productions, which in time contributed to the rise of a Ukrainian national theatre in Galicia.[92]

The beginnings of the Ukrainian theatre reached back to the 1830s and were associated with the Greek Catholic seminary, where, during Iakhymovych's rectorship, the seminarians had staged Iosyf Lozynsky's *Ruskoje wesile* and scenes from the lives of the peasants, merchants and Jews. In spite of the fact that these efforts later faded, this theatrical experience inspired young authors to undertake dramatic writing. Their efforts did not come to fruition until the end of the 1840s, when adaptations of Kotliarevsky's *Natalka Poltavka* and *Moskal charivnyk* and Kvitka-Osnovianenko's *Svatannia na Honcharivtsi* [Matchmaking in Honcharivka] were staged.[93] *Natalka Poltavka*, published in Chernivtsi under the title *Divka na viddanniu, abo na myluvannia nema syluvannia* [A maiden for marriage; or, love cannot be forced], was staged in early June 1848 in Kolomyia, where it enjoyed extraordinary success. Kobrynsky wrote to Iakiv Holovatsky:

> I am returning from the theatre, and with me several hundred happy Ruthenians. You can never have enough of the Ruthenian theatre. The performance was splendid. Then there is the matter [of hearing] the delightful native words, of seeing national events. [The play] . . . now being staged at the Kolomyia theatre is an adaptation of the Ukrainian opera known to you. The songs were well done by everyone, the music was grand, and the Germans were so ruthenized that you would say they're not Germans.[94]

It is generally assumed that this was an amateur performance. However, there is reason to believe that the actors were professionals from a German troupe. In a letter to Rudolf Mokh, Kobrynsky wrote: "In Kolomyia the local company of actors under the direction of Leitner has already staged Ruthenian plays three times. Twice they presented Kotliarevsky's *Natalka Poltavka* and once *Zhovnir* [*Moskal*] *charivnyk*. . . . Send me a copy of [Rudolf] Mokh's *Sprava v seli Klekotyni* [The affair in the village of Klekotyn], and we will stage it at the theatre before the actors leave."[95]

Perhaps the performance of *Natalka Poltavka* that took place during the congress of Ukrainian scholars in Lviv was the work of amateurs.[96] Petro Holovatsky played a significant role in the development of the Ukrainian amateur theatre. The actors, who were encouraged by the prospect of theatrical and financial success (each one received thirty gulden for each performance, and a hundred gulden were sent to the Holovna Rada), intended to establish a permanent Ukrainian theatre, but nothing came of it.[97] At the same time, a "theatrical society," composed of students and seminarians, formed in Przemyśl under the direction of Mme. Saar (the sister of Franciszek Smolka and the wife of the *Kreishauptmann* in Przemyśl). Among the female members were Poles, Ukrainians, Germans and a French woman. The director of the Przemyśl productions was Ivan Vitoshynsky, the author of the play *Kozak i okhotnyk* [The Cossack and the volunteer], an adaptation from a work by the German writer August Kotzebue. The musical accompaniment was prepared by the well-known Ukrainian composer Mykhailo Verbytsky. *Natalka Poltavka*, *Moskal charivnyk*, and Ustyianovych's *Verkhovyntsi Beskydiv* [The Beskyd highlanders] were also staged in Przemyśl.[98]

The Ukrainian theatre movement in 1848-9 touched almost all of Eastern Galicia. Performances took place in Sambir, Stryi, Ternopil and even in many villages, causing everywhere "a great resonance in society and awakening the patriotic feelings of the masses and [their] love for the native culture."[99] In Kolomyia, for example, they hoped to continue weekly performances, but the limited repertoire and the unfavourable attitude of the local authorities were obstacles.[100]

Among the few Galician Ukrainian playwrights, Rudolf Mokh distinguished himself with his comedy of 1849, *Sprava v seli Klekotyni*, which depicted a day in the life of a Ukrainian village before *robot* was abolished. The action took place in a tavern, through which a host of peasants, Jews and soldiers passed. The dialogue contained an abundance of colloquial phrases from the Ruthenian vernacular. Mokh also intended to complete a dramatic adaptation of Gogol's *Taras Bulba*.[101]

Mykola Ustyianovych made a complete revision of *Karpaccy gôrale* [The Carpathian highlanders] by the Polish writer Józef Korzeniowski. Ustyianovych introduced new scenes and songs and expanded the social content of the work. In so doing, he virtually turned his version, *Verkhovyntsi Beskydiv*, into an independent theatrical work. Because of his resolute stance against the censors' demands the play was not performed in Galicia, with the possible exception of Przemyśl. Nor was it performed in Kiev, although Iakiv Holovatsky asked P. Dolzhikov to stage it there.[102] In 1848 and 1849 S. Pysarevsky's *Kupala na Ivana* [Rites of Saint John's Eve], Aleksei Khomiakov's *Ermak*[103] and Molière's *Georges Dandin* were also adapted for the Ukrainian stage.[104]

Introduction of Ukrainian into the courts and administration and its everyday use also were connected with the struggle for national equality. The Ukrainian leaders began with themselves; up to that time Polish had prevailed in general usage, particularly among the Ukrainian intelligentsia.[105] In 1848 the conviction was expressed that the use of Polish (the sources speak of "the foreign tongue") by the common people—necessary during the feudal period in relations between the village and the manor—should be abandoned along with *robot*. The struggle for the national language was treated, therefore, as a campaign for the social emancipation of the common people. The Ukrainian enthusiasts pointed out that the existing social relationships contributed to maintaining a sort of feudal dependence, which could lead to denationalization. Too frequently young people, saturated with the Polish spirit, were ashamed of their Ruthenian origins. Appeals to the Ukrainians to speak Ukrainian among themselves and with those who understood it were made in the newspapers, at meetings of the Ukrainian councils, in sermons and in private conversations. It was every Ukrainian's obligation to use his language at home, in school and in offices.[106] *Zoria Halytska* appealed to Ukrainian mothers: "Let your children hear only Ruthenian words from you; together with your milk let them suckle love and adherence to our common Mother [tongue], so that we might at least in our grandchildren see [our language] reborn, illuminated and glorious."[107]

Chauvinism was inescapable; Ukrainian national feelings turned against the dominance of the Poles in Galicia. Lev Treshchakovsky tried to convince the Holovna Rada that Ukrainian children might be allowed to speak "all the languages that exist on earth, only not Polish," because the Poles, brothers from one mother, raised on land common to both, did not recognize the Ukrainians and were contemptuous of their language. Treshchakovsky demanded that the Holovna Rada accept the principle that any Ruthenian who was still ashamed of using his language should be recognized "as a traitor and an enemy of his nation."[108]

The Ukrainians had touched upon equality for their language in governmental offices in their first address of 19 April 1848. The government's response was that paragraph 4 of the provisional constitution of 25 April had decided the matter according to the Ukrainians' wishes. In practice, however, according to an order issued by the governor before Vienna's response to the Ukrainians' address, replies to petitions in Polish and in German were given in the language of the petition. There was no mention in the order of the Ukrainian language. The appeals court acted similarly.[109]

From all over Galicia arrived complaints against governmental officials who did not want to accept legal documents in Ruthenian. The Holovna Rada was urged "to prevent this disorder and remedy the misfortune to our language."[110] The council believed that Ukrainians should address governmental officials in Ruthenian, thereby placing a *fait accompli* before them.[111] They were most concerned with the language of the common people, because the peasants distrusted orders and patents printed in Church Slavonic, which was unintelligible to them.[112] Kuzemsky, however, assumed that it was best to write to the German officials in German, because otherwise "they will lay aside" the requests.[113]

The authorities' subsequent order permitting government offices to respond in German to Ruthenian petitions also did not satisfy the Ukrainians. Hryhorii Levytsky, of the Ruthenian deanery council in Perehinsko, wrote a memorial entitled "O movi i pysmakh ruskykh" [On Ruthenian speech and writing], which proposed that within two to three years every official should learn Ukrainian and that in the meantime the Holovna Rada should attempt to publish all the authorities' directives in Ukrainian, because otherwise Ukrainian schools existed to no purpose. Levytsky warned against the consequences of the present state of affairs: "Freedom is irreconcilable with lack of education, because whoever attempts to move about in the dark will always do some harm."[114]

Finally, in response to the Holovna Rada's petition of 14 August 1848, the Galician authorities permitted responses to be given in Ukrainian to petitions written in that language.[115] These recommendations, however, could not be followed because the Galician officials were not familiar with Ukrainian and the Cyrillic alphabet. Hence, on the basis of Borysykevych's motion of 9 October, the Holovna Rada, during an audience in November with the emperor, called for the introduction of the Ukrainian language and orthography in all government offices in Eastern Galicia, the dismissal of officials who were unfriendly toward the Ukrainian nationality and respect for Greek Catholic holy days in the schools, offices and public life.[116] Despite this request, government offices did not change their practice. In 1849 they were still requiring documents to be submitted in either German, Polish or Latin, "because neither Ruthenian writing nor speech are yet recognized as official."[117]

The victory of reaction produced a new governmental attitude toward the Ukrainian issue, a change that the Ukrainian leaders immediately noticed. Petro Holovatsky wrote to his brother Iakiv in the summer of 1849 that Stadion had believed that government officials owed their existence to "the bloody toil of the rural populace, its taxes and its poverty," and therefore they should support the common people—which in Eastern Galicia meant support for the Ukrainians. On the other hand, under Gołuchowski, "the lesser officials, who stood for Ruthenian, are now repenting, seeing that they are in the minority and that the devil hasn't carted away the ultra-*Liakhy*. We hear that the emperor is learning Ruthenian; but this will not come to anything, [since] our officials do not believe that they will have to learn [it] one day."[118] In such circumstances, popular confidence in the government and its agencies diminished markedly. Minister Bach's intervention on behalf of Ruthenian was greeted with applause, though sceptically. Petro Holovatsky wrote:

> Minister Bach's letter is very beautiful; what government official would it not move, would it not instruct, but not a Galician official.... Bach writes: "*das beste Mittel* [to gain the confidence of the people] *ist die Kenntniss der Landessprache*," etc. However, [the local authorities] have other means; they don't need the confidence of our people. They deluded us while it was necessary, but now they can even speak the truth—that our hopes are mad, that great Rus' will reduce itself to nothing! Only so much will remain as can perhaps be salvaged in the schools.[119]

Apparently, however, the central authorities prevailed. Galician officials began to take Ukrainian lessons with Zhukovsky,[120] prompted perhaps by the fact that the Ukrainian councils systematically called for knowledge of both Ukrainian and Polish by new civil servants. The councils protested against filling any posts without first demanding knowledge of Ukrainian, and they insisted that a "fixed time be designated for all officials in the Ruthenian part of Galicia, during which they must learn Ruthenian under threat of dismissal from service."[121] Demands were also made that the district physicians in Eastern Galicia know Ukrainian and that a Ukrainian-language oath be introduced in the army and the courts. There were even requests for the hiring of teachers, non-commissioned officers and army chaplains who knew Ukrainian.[122] The Holovna Rada was told to see to it that the hierarchy's circulars to the Greek Catholic deaneries were written in Ukrainian and that parish records, as well as official dealings of the Greek Catholic church, be kept in Ukrainian.[123] The Holovna Rada did endeavour to introduce Ukrainian terminology in place names and road signs.[124]

Some of the Ukrainians' wishes were met. On 23 August 1849, the interior ministry issued an order directing Governor Gołuchowski to make certain that the protocols of the Lviv Municipal Council were also available in Ukrainian, that the streets and squares in Lviv had Ukrainian signs, that the Lviv magistrate issue announcements regarding insolvencies and trial summonses in Ukrainian, and that a knowledge of Ukrainian be taken into consideration in making appointments.[125]

The role of the press in moulding Ukrainian attitudes cannot be overemphasized. The lack of a Ukrainian press before 1848 had retarded the national rebirth; awareness of this fact, coupled with the necessity of making do with foreign newspapers, spurred efforts to establish Ukrainian periodicals. In 1842 and 1843 the Viennese police had proposed to Ivan Holovatsky that he assume the editorship of a Ukrainian journal that would appear in Vienna. This was an anti-Russian effort, directed against what was perceived to be increasing Russophilism in Galicia. The police intended in this way to separate the Ukrainians "from the whole of Great Russia" and to protect them from russification and Orthodoxy. However, Ukrainians objected to the condition that the journal be printed in the Latin alphabet. Ultimately, the matter came to nothing. The initiative was not supported by the government, which did not yet fear Russian political influence on the Ukrainians living in the monarchy.[126]

In 1847 Ivan Hurkevych proposed a plan to publish a journal that might become the organ of a Ruthenian Matytsia. He obtained Mykhailo Malynovsky's agreement to edit it and the backing of Mykhailo Kuzemsky and perhaps the metropolitan. Hurkevych turned to Iakiv Holovatsky with a request that he draft the statutes for the

Matytsia and draw up a plan for the journal, which was to be submitted to the authorities. Unfortunately, the further course of this initiative is unknown.[127] The next effort to establish a Ukrainian journal likewise did not succeed. Ivan Zhukovsky, Kuzemsky and Stepan Semash undertook it, but they could not agree on the form of language to be used. Zhukovsky favoured the vernacular; Kuzemsky praised the language of the Bible that had been recently published in Przemyśl; Semash was a proponent of Church Slavonic.[128]

It was not until the Stavropygian Institute entered the field (with Stadion's determined support) that success was achieved. The events of March 1848, while delaying the publication of *Pchola*, worked to the advantage of *Zoria Halytska*, which took on the character of a political weekly. The formal programme of *Zoria Halytska* was clear and decisive, even though it was not always consistently carried out. Assuming that "journals are absolutely essential to every nation, because they enlighten it and provide beneficial and helpful advice," the editors decided to publish everything "that is of concern to the Ruthenian as a person and a citizen." *Zoria Halytska* was to report on the work of the Holovna Rada, whose press organ it would be, on political and national conditions in the country and on the Ukrainians' relationship to the Austrian state and to the other nations. "In our discussions of what was, what is and what and how it should be," wrote the editors, "we shall proceed so as never to depart from the law and justice, to preserve peace, harmony, and order in the country and to have moderate progress on a legal basis as our objective."[129]

The chief editor of *Zoria Halytska* was Antin Paventsky, a graduate in law of Lviv University and a member of the Stavropygian Institute. He was assisted by ten lay and clerical Ukrainian enthusiasts, probably the same men who had committed themselves to help publish *Pchola*: Ivan Borysykevych, Mykhailo Malynovsky, Iuliian Vyslobotsky, Teodor Leontovych, Iuliian Velychkovsky and Ivan Hurkevych, all of whom were members of the Holovna Rada. (The remaining collaborators' names are not known.) In autumn 1848, Petro Holovatsky became a permanent contributing editor.

Until May 1849, *Zoria Halytska* was printed at the Stavropygian Institute. Later, as a result of the institute's exorbitant financial demands, the editors used Michał Poremba's printing shop. (After Paventsky stepped down as editor in August 1850, Mykhailo Kossak, the new editor, and also secretary of the Stavropygian Institute, transferred the printing back to its presses.)

As the organ of the Holovna Rada, *Zoria Halytska* was supported by the authorities. Governor Stadion ordered five hundred subscriptions at the government's expense, which were distributed gratis among impoverished rural communities,[130] but this aid was terminated already in August 1848. The Polish newspapers alleged that the government's appropriation was withdrawn because the editors had published articles that aroused the masses.[131] This charge was far from the truth, even though *Zoria Halytska* was anti-Polish. Whatever one might say about the journal, it must be acknowledged that it contributed immensely to developing the Ukrainians' national consciousness and to their social and economic emancipation. The Ukrainian leaders were aware of both the shortcomings and the merits of *Zoria Halytska*. Some accused it of standing aloof from the common people and of theorizing too much; others criticized its pro-governmental stance; there were also those, such as Ivan Holovatsky, who unreservedly liked the newspaper.[132]

Antin Liubych-Mohylnytsky was perhaps the paper's most severe critic.

> If, for example, the entire *Zoria Halytska* were ground in a mill to obtain oilseed cake, would even one drop of healthy logic, of political information, of knowledge of the spirit of the times and the true need of our nation be emitted?... Our *Zoria* conducts a polemic with the Polish-Ruthenian council [Sobor Ruskyi]. The *Liakhy* do not read it, either because they don't know the Cyrillic letters or because they disdain them. Cantors and a few literate peasants read the thing. They themselves understand nothing of it and [in turn] lead the illiterate into even greater error. In a word, our coryphaei crawl into the mud and call others to follow them. But let us stand on the shore; let us wait till they are completely bedraggled; let us walk by on dry land; and we shall certainly get much further than they.[133]

The conviction grew that the leaders of the Holovna Rada (the "Lviv potentates," according to Lytvynovych) were not competent to publish a journal for the Ruthenian masses. *Zoria Halytska* could be an organ appropriate for the upper classes, but the Ukrainian common people needed a different sort of journal.[134] In May 1848, Borysykevych wrote that on 1 November he intended to start publishing a Ukrainian journal "in a Ruthenian-Slavic spirit," which was to include translations of articles from German, Czech and South Slavic journals of interest to Ukrainians. He formulated its general principles in a letter to Iakiv Holovatsky.

> I should like us to begin to view the issues of this transitory world from a purely Ruthenian and humane position and to mould our language for its future reign as the national language. I should like to conduct at least a limited polemic against the Ruthenophobes, but one worthy of a strong nation that has sensed its own essence and its destiny. You will be the censor of my language and a helper in the creation of new, but necessary words.[135]

The journal that Liubych-Mohylnytsky intended to publish in Stanyslaviv in Piotr Piller's printing shop was to be quite different. Mohylnytsky wrote that he did not want to engage in "political rumours," but rather intended to create a social and cultural journal dedicated to history, geography, demography, statistics, economic and literary issues, and the customs and traditions of the Ukrainian nation. At the same time, he intended to preserve a certain distance from contemporary events—"to apply healthy criticism to everything beneficial and harmful that happens to the Ruthenians on this earth."[136]

Still, even these projected journals were intended primarily for the Ukrainian intelligentsia. Rural issues would scarcely be considered in them, and then only as ethnography and folklore. Sylvester Drymalyk, the mayor of Kolomyia and the leading figure in the local Ruthenian council, wanted to fill the gap with a journal specifically for the common people. His plan, however, is known only from a letter by Lytvynovych, who maintained that "only activists of proven merit, who know the common people, [and who are] most familiar with their life, must publish a journal for them." He advised establishing a special association that would concern itself with matters pertaining to such a journal.[137]

Unfortunately, these projects became largely irrelevant after the fall of 1848. On the other hand, governmental circles intended to publish an official journal in Ukrainian in the form of a supplement to the Polish *Gazeta Lwowska* [Lviv gazette]. They approached Rudolf Mokh, who proposed Iakiv Holovatsky as editor and encouraged him to accept the offer, which, in Mokh's opinion, was advantageous to the Ukrainians. Holovatsky was more sceptical. He did not intend to collaborate with the reaction:

> Honestly, you have placed me in an awkward situation; bread is being offered, but I don't know how to take a bite of it and whether it will be nourishing. You ask my agreement to be the editor of the journal, but you did not write about its content. If it is not political, . . . there is nothing more to talk about. But if a political newspaper is to be published, let me be permitted to ask, of what stripe? Let it be on the side of the (constitutional) government, and I am for it, but I am only afraid that it might become necessary in the meanwhile to renounce my convictions, my just position as a Ruthenian—to betray those banners upon which I took an oath, not before some earthly office and not now, but then, when I reached [national] consciousness and before my own conscience, before God, before the court of my own race. I will not betray the [national] colours for anything; I will not sell myself for any honours. I would rather remain eternally silent . . . than have to betray or distort the nation's aspirations.[138]

We do not know why the authorities abandoned these plans for a Ukrainian supplement. Not until mid-1849 did they decide to publish a separate official Ukrainian journal, and they called upon Ustyianovych to be its editor.[139] His assistants were Ivan Holovatsky, Bohdan Didytsky and Mykhailo Kossak. The *Halycho-ruskyi vistnyk* [Galician-Ruthenian herald] appeared in Galicia from 14 July 1849 to 19 February 1850, after which it was transferred to Vienna. There it remained until the 1860s as the *Vistnyk dlia Rusyniv avstriiskoi derzhavy* [Herald for the Ruthenians in the Austrian state]. It was widely read, especially thanks to Ustyianovych's stories "Mest verkhovyntsia" [The revenge of the highlander] and "Staryi Efrem" [Old Efrem] and to the numerous articles devoted to national affairs.

Novyny [News] and *Pchola* [The bee] appeared as semi-official journals in 1849 under the editorship of Ivan Hushalevych.[140] According to Ivan Franko, *Novyny* was a "journal without a programme and without clearly expressed principles," and therefore it was insignificant. It lacked the Holovna Rada's support, and the Stavropygian Institute refused to print it. (It was printed at Poremba's press.) Hushalevych made no attempt to make the journal more appealing; he was not concerned with national affairs and published only five brief pieces on the Ukrainian question. The only items worthy of attention were Ustyianovych's play *Verkhovyntsi Beskydiv* and Liubych-Mohylnytsky's poem, "Uchenym chlenam Matytsy ruskoi novoho roku 1849" [To the learned members of the Ruthenian Matytsia on the new year of 1849]. After twenty-six issues (13 January to 11 April 1849) the journal collapsed, although ultimately lack of funds was the deciding factor. The new Austrian press code required all political journals to maintain specific cash reserves.

Pchola, which was published in its stead, was intended to be an all-Ukrainian journal, but it never became popular. Still, as the first literary and scholarly Ukrainian journal, it rendered a real service in publishing the fifth part of Kotliarevsky's *Eneida* and his "Oda do Kurakina" [Ode to Prince Kurakin], Liubych-Mohylnytsky's *Skyt Maniavskyi* [The Monastery of Maniava], Didytsky's translation of *The Tale of Ihor's Campaign*, Iakiv Holovatsky's essays on Kotliarevsky and the chronicler Nestor, Iosyf Lozynsky's work on Ruthenian orthography and Hushalevych's popular histories.

Interest in the press fell off sharply in the Ukrainian community in the second half of 1849. *Pchola* lost subscribers and stopped publishing in September. The circulation of *Zoria Halytska* also decreased because the editors continued to urge the common people to maintain peace and to advocate strictly legal means of improving the peasants' lot. Subscriptions in the countryside had already fallen off by the beginning of 1849,[141] and in August did not exceed five hundred. The editors even wondered whether it would be possible to continue publication through the fourth quarter of that year. Disagreements arose between the Holovna Rada and Paventsky, who in his difficulties with the censors and the Galician authorities (Gołuchowski and General Bordolo, who accused him of sympathy for Russia) attempted to clear himself by placing the entire blame on the Holovna Rada and his collaborators. Petro Holovatsky even suspected that Paventsky "had not only renounced the Russian, but also the Ruthenian spirit, as treacherous and incompatible with the spirit of the government." Holovatsky continued:

> All the activities [of the (Holovna) Rada] seemed to him base, hypocritical [and] false; the government's endeavours [seemed to be] an obvious withdrawal of constitutional freedoms;... the hostility of the Ruthenians to the Poles—for whom even to this day there are no Ruthenians except, as they say, the hornets of Saint George's—[seemed to be] unjust and insulting to their rights; and our fame and honour [seemed to be] an irony to all the human rights that exist in France or America.

Holovatsky concluded that Paventsky "had become an adversary of the Saint Georgites."[142] The Holovna Rada reportedly intended to renounce *Zoria Halytska* and establish a new journal. However, when it was learned that Paventsky was leaving the newspaper, the council decided to place it in Ivan Holovatsky's hands, while reserving for itself "the authority, the influence on the tone of the journal and the supervision of its revenues."[143]

Ivan Holovatsky would have eagerly undertaken this project, because the editors of the *Vistnyk* did not like him and the atmosphere there did not suit him. When Ustyianovych, in the pages of *Vistnyk*, "hinted at the [anti-Polish] bias of certain Ruthenians," the Holovna Rada accused him of wishing to "fraternize with the *Liakhy*." As Ivan Holovatsky wrote: "The Ruthenians have raised such a hullabaloo [and caused so much] dissension that one is overwhelmed with sadness." Opposition to *Vistnyk* appeared in the non-Ukrainian press as well as in *Zoria Halytska*. The Holovna Rada was especially indignant. Holovatsky continued: "Ustyianovych was barely able to assuage [the criticism] when the Holovna Rada absolutely insisted that he was inveighing against it, and in an understanding with the government [he] wants to disgrace it."[144]

Ultimately, in both instances the disputes were smoothed over and the editors remained in their respective positions. Not until September 1850 did Paventsky step down as editor of *Zoria Halytska*, nominally because of lack of time, but in fact because he was disaffected by the authorities' anti-Ukrainian policies and perhaps as well by the Holovna Rada's policies, of which he had not always approved.[145]

Under Paventsky and his successor Kossak, *Zoria Halytska* preserved a purely national character and to some extent used a Ukrainian idiom intelligible to the common people. Later, in the 1850s, it became Russophile, lost readership and in 1857 finally ceased to appear.

18. Polish-Ukrainian Relations

Our analysis to this point has shown that the Holovna Rada envisaged a resolution of the Ukrainian question exclusively through the Austrian government's support. It seems, however, that an understanding with the Poles would have been more efficacious. Both sides were responsible for the fact that this did not occur. It is probably not possible today to decide whether a Ukrainian-Polish compromise could have succeeded. There were fundamental obstacles. The agrarian question was incapable of resolution without further impingement on the nobles' manorial estates, and the Roman and Greek Catholic hierarchies, though subject to a common spiritual authority, celebrated separate rites and clashed over matters of prestige and material benefit. From these considerations alone, the hierarchies were not interested in coming to an agreement.

There is no doubt that the two nations had much in common: although their social and economic situations differed, they had been affected by similar internal changes and external influences. Until the 1830s their mutual antagonism arose almost exclusively from religious and cultural problems. Only with the November 1830 insurrection in Russian Poland and the later activities of the Ruthenian Triad did the increasing national conflict between Poles and Ukrainians beome explicit. Still, before 1848 the Polish intelligentsia deemed the assimilation of Rus' an "indisputable, natural and commonly understood fact"[1] and conducted conspiratorial activities among the Ukrainian common people in a pro-Polish spirit and in the interests of maintaining Ukrainian-Polish unity. Therefore, the Poles interpreted the breach of this "unity" in 1848 as a betrayal of their national interests.

Ukrainian separatism threatened the still vibrant traditions of the old Poland (before 1772) and struck at the interests of the Polish intelligentsia in Eastern Galicia.[2] The Eastern Galician *szlachta* likewise felt threatened. Although Agenor Gołuchowski, because of his close association with the government, was charged with having helped to create a "Ukrainian question," he consistently resisted the Ukrainian movement and accused it of pro-Russian tendencies. Consequently, a common anti-Ukrainian block of Polish liberals, democrats and nobles formed during the revolutionary period 1848-49. The Polish historian Stefan Kieniewicz has characterized this phenomenon as follows: "The difference was that, from the outset, the democrats in particular insisted that Stadion had 'invented' the Ruthenians, while in Vienna, Gołuchowski blamed the Muscovites. But on both sides Ukrainian separateness was regarded as an artificial creation, and the future of Rus' was viewed in terms of linguistic assimilation."[3] But by 1848-9 the chances of assimilation were minimal. In Eastern Galicia the Ukrainians constituted a decisive majority (70 per cent).[4]

The Polish magnates—the great land-owners of Eastern Galicia—although they saw perfectly well the adverse side of the Ukrainian movement, recommended an accord or compromise. Prince Leon Sapieha stated to Julian Horoszkiewicz in March 1848 that Eastern Galicia was a Ruthenian land and that "the Ruthenians are at least entitled to equal rights."[5] This position earned Sapieha the respect of the Ukrainian delegates at the Slavic Congress in Prague.

Prince Jerzy Lubomirski went even further. Fearing that the Ukrainian question could become for Poland what the "Irish question is for England," and warning against a repetition of the Magyars' errors, he called "for redressing the old injustices committed against Rus' by the Jesuits and feudalism." He wrote to the Polish central Rada Narodowa:

> And remember that no mortal power can oust Ruthenianism [*ruszczyzna*] from Volhynia, Podillia, Ukraine [the province of Kiev] and Lithuania. Let us remember that the entire cavalry in Russia speaks in Little Russian, and not in Russian; that Poltava, Kharkiv, the Cossack lands, Bessarabia up to Odessa, and part of Transylvania are inhabited by Ruthenians; and that the Slovaks and the Silesians, . . . our neighbours, will judge whether it is possible to be associated with us depending on the way we treat the Ruthenians. Or, do we, like the Magyars, seek freedom only for ourselves?

Lubomirski was convinced that exacerbating the hatred between the Poles and Ukrainians benefited reactionism and tsarist Russia and that open conflict could lead to the "utter destruction of the Polish element, and with it the free-thinking element in all the annexed lands [*Kraj zabrany*, i.e., the territories of the former Polish-Lithuanian Commonwealth not included in the autonomous "Congress" Kingdom of Poland, but directly incorporated into the Russian Empire]." He maintained: "Therefore, everything that binds us to the Ruthenian, that awakens in him the idea of a Ruthenian state . . . will give life to the moribund part of Poland [and] will correct what the year 1831 spoiled." In Lubomirski's judgement, it was essential to preempt the Ukrainian demands and awaken Ukrainian patriotism. Polishness (*polszczyzna*) would not perish on this account. Among the Slavic nations, that one "will have hegemony and precedence that first and most genuinely grasps this principle of equality for all nations and equal treatment for each, not only in word but also in deed." By abolishing *robot* and granting other nationalities complete equality, the Poles could calmly look to the future. Lubomirski therefore proposed that the Rada Narodowa not repel the Ukrainians, but protect their interests, demand rights for them and understand "the Ruthenian idea better, more broadly, deeply and seriously . . . than the Ruthenians themselves. They will [then] gather around [this idea], crawl and beg for it, and acknowledge its superiority." Toward this end it would be essential to establish a "Ruthenian daily (with Latin characters)" to support "honest and reliable Ruthenians, even though not from our party," and to act in an anti-German spirit.[6]

To what extent, if at all, did the Polish Rada Narodowa follow his advice? From the moment it was established, the Rada Narodowa understood that mutual accord was a precondition for a stable Galicia. The council tried to preserve Ukrainian unity of action with the Poles on political issues by recognizing the distinctiveness of the Ruthenian nation. This attempt was unambiguously apparent in the discussions at the council meeting of 14 April, when it was decided to draft an appeal to the Ukrainians and to the Greek Catholic consistories to join in mediating the Polish-Ukrainian dispute.[7] However, the appeal, published in the first issue of the newspaper *Rada Narodowa*,[8] offered an assurance of equality but no positive proposals. The Greek Catholic clergy could not be satisfied simply by a declaration of the Poles' honest intentions, evidenced by the voluntary abrogation of feudal relationships, because the appeal did not mention the Ukrainians' national rights.

It was only after the first Ukrainian pronouncement of 19 April (which caused the Rada Narodowa to accept Seweryn Smarzewski's motion calling for equal rights for the Ukrainian language in schools, courts and consistories)[9] and the creation of the Holovna Rada that the position of the Rada Narodowa toward the Ukrainians finally crystallized. Its proclamation of 7 May and its manifesto of 9 May indicated its attitude.[10] The authors of the proclamation to the Ruthenians, employing historical arguments, pointed to the voluntary character of the union between Poland and its adjoining nations, as well as to Poland's religious tolerance and respect for the Ukrainian language. According to them, the Ukrainian nobility's conversion to the Latin rite occurred "only under Austrian rule"; social oppression was not exclusively a Polish trait, and the imposition of "the Union [of Brest] was not a national, but a religious persecution," directed against religious schism, not against Rus'. These events belonged to the past, however, because "the reborn Poland... cannot stifle a kindred nationality." The proof was the Poles' address of 18 March, which demanded guarantees for the Polish nationality, but against germanization, not against the Ruthenians. The appeal of the Rada Narodowa to the Ukrainians emphasized that the expression "Polish nationality" had been understood for a long time to mean "all the nationalities that Poland embraces." The demands contained in the second Polish address of 6 April, expressed in points 4 and 9, were the best proof of this. The Rada Narodowa regarded the maintenance of fraternal ties as most important and declared its opposition to all enemies of "freedom and constitutional principles" who were seeking to cause a breach. The Rada Narodowa, therefore, "openly and solemnly declares that it regards the Polish and Ruthenian nationalities equally as its own, represents both, and wants to raise both equally with all its strength."

The manifesto issued by the Rada Narodowa on 9 May reiterated the principles expressed in the earlier appeal to the Ukrainians and, at the same time, contained an unequivocal formulation:

> Hence, the Rada Narodowa does not hesitate to state solemnly that the rights of the Ruthenian nationality are equally sacred and inviolable as its own. Far from any thought of ever hampering [the Ruthenians'] free development, the council indeed considers it as just and advantageous for our common fatherland that this Ruthenian nationality... fortify its spirit.... [But] the Ruthenian nationality cannot have needs different from those of the Polish nationality. The desires and the goals of both are today the same.... Each of them in the fullness of its rights, developing in complete freedom,... will contribute more effectively to the well-being of our common fatherland.

Therefore, the Ukrainians in Galicia, as a part of the larger Ukrainian nation, should seek to influence developments in Russian-ruled Ukraine in a pro-Polish spirit, with the aim of establishing a common state and building the strength of their common fatherland. "Its name 'Poland' will again shine like a meteoric messenger of European liberty in the east, so that by shedding its light on oppressed peoples, it becomes at once a weapon and a shield of the civilized world."

In other words, according to the Rada Narodowa, support for the Ukrainian nationality did not pertain to its political status. Contemporaries thought that maintaining national unity in Galicia was essential even if it were impossible to re-establish the Polish state, for Galicia could become the "cradle of the future Slavdom," and the "Ruthenian and Polish people, groaning under the Muscovite yoke, will have in Galicia a watchfire for their aspirations and desires, as would the Ruthenian and Slovak people in Hungary who remained under Magyar oppression."[11] Although opposed to the creation of separate Ukrainian organizations, the Polish Rada Narodowa attempted to soften the conflicts. On the one hand, it urged moderation and no aggressive actions against the Ukrainians,[12] but on the other hand, it relied on those Ukrainians who favoured co-operation with the Poles and whose efforts had led to the formation of the Sobor Ruskyi.

The origins of the Sobor Ruskyi, however, are not clear.[13] It is known that on 9 May the Rada Narodowa advised pro-Polish Ukrainians not to protest against the Ukrainian address of 19 April, but instead to submit a separate address, modelled on the various Polish pronouncements.[14] In fact, such an address was published in the newspaper of the Rada Narodowa on 11 May.[15] Its authors, although supporting in principle the Ukrainians' demands in the address of 19 April, dissociated themselves from the pro-Austrian formulations in its introduction and conclusion and declared that they recognized Galicia as the "common fatherland with the Poles," and the Poles as brothers with whom they wished to share their own fate. In their opinion the Holovna Rada did not enjoy the confidence of the Ukrainian nation and could not act in its name. The authors demanded that four Ukrainians—suggested by themselves—be accepted into the Rada Narodowa and that a separate "department of Ruthenian affairs" be established in it. Only the first demand was fulfilled;[16] the second was met by the creation of the Sobor Ruskyi. The Polish newspaper in Lviv, *Dziennik Narodowy*, described its founding:

> The instructions presently given to the delegation sent to Prague (by the Holovna Rada) became the cause of a second and extremely well-attended gathering of Ruthenians, which decided to establish a Ruthenian committee, whose mission is not only to support the general national endeavours, but in addition to nullify all dissension, to tear down and destroy all barriers to general progress, whether set on purpose or placed in the way through misunderstanding.

The writer for *Dziennik Narodowy* argued that the new organization represented "a step toward annihilating sectarianism."[17] His statement would have been true had the Sobor Ruskyi come into being spontaneously, had it been composed exclusively of Ukrainians and had it not stemmed from Polish intrigue designed to subordinate the Ukrainian movement to the Rada Narodowa. The Sobor Ruskyi was established in the second half of May,[18] but it was not until 8 June that it issued an appeal to the Ukrainian nation signed by sixty-four persons, including three Greek Catholic clergymen, fifteen land-owners, thirteen lawyers, ten officials, seven men of letters, four students, two seminarians and several citizens of Lviv.[19] Among the members were the former conspirators Kasper Cięglewicz, Julian Horoszkiewicz and Mykhailo Popel; the polonized representatives of famous Ukrainian families Aleksander, Julian and Włodzimierz Dzieduszycki, Józef and Ludwik Jabłonowski, Antoni Golejewski, Zenon Pogłodowski, Bolesław, Michał and Ludwik Komarnicki, and Prince Leon Sapieha. In addition to Popel, there were other Ukrainians: Onufrii Krynytsky, Romuald Kryzhanovsky, Kyrylo Vinkovsky and, most notably, Ivan Vahylevych, who was drawn to Lviv to be the editor of *Dnewnyk Ruskij*, the newspaper projected by the Sobor Ruskyi.

These persons, for the most part *gente Rutheni*, *natione Poloni*, were to "look after the Ruthenian nationality and contribute to its free development, and in so doing to maintain harmony and unity with the whole of the kindred nationality in our common fatherland."[20] The Sobor collaborated with the students' Academic Committee and the Rada Narodowa, in which it was represented by Golejewski.[21] In time, the conviction became widespread in the Rada Narodowa that only the Sobor Ruskyi represented the Ukrainians. This attitude contributed significantly to the failure of all efforts aimed at reaching an agreement with the Holovna Rada, which, for its part, neither desired nor made any efforts toward an agreement.

It seemed that from the moment the Sobor was established, it did not intend to pursue an independent policy. To be sure, it sent delegates to the Slavic Congress to hamper the efforts of the Holovna Rada's delegates, but at the same time Antoni Dąbczański and Zenon Pogłodowski negotiated for the Sobor with the Holovna Rada regarding a merger of the two organizations. These endeavours proved fruitless, since neither side would retreat from its political principles. Efforts to gain control of the Ukrainian movement by converting a group of Poles of Ukrainian descent to Greek Catholicism also failed. As Stepan Kachala wrote, Bishop Iakhymovych "saw through their idea [and] answered them that the Ruthenians do not have and do not need a nobility."[22] These failures finally prompted the Sobor to independent action. As an organization composed of nobles and bourgeois, it propagated the idea of social solidarity. In an address on 25 May 1848 in Sambir, at a meeting of the local Polish Rada Narodowa, Mykhailo Popel emphasized the nobility's role in abolishing *robot* and from that drew the conclusion that "henceforth there is no lord, there is no peasant; we are all lords and we are all peasants."[23] *Dnewnyk Ruskij*, which began publication at the end of August, explained the issue:

> Respect concord.... Do not encroach on another's soil or pasture.... Because today you may like someone else's pasture, tomorrow I may like your apiary, another your sheepskin, and your farmhand may take a liking to your wife. In this way there will never be concord among us.... Let us all love one another, help one another without noticing whether someone wears a nobleman's cloak or a peasant's russet coat, and there will be concord among us; as a result there will be happiness and hopefulness in our homes.[24]

An article entitled "Poradnyk hospodarskij" [Advice to farmers], published in *Dnewnyk Ruskij*, informed the peasants how to care for their homesteads and suggested that in their free moments they help their former squires who, having remitted *robot*, needed wage labourers.[25] The Sobor Ruskyi basically espoused an independent but pro-Polish position on the national question. It saw Ukrainians and Poles as two branches growing from a single trunk; trying to separate them was futile. The history of the ages and a common fate, shared glory and mutual suffering "have so fused them into a political union that through God's will they merged into one body." This opinion was voiced in *Dnewnyk Ruskij* in a proclamation calling upon the clergy to work for the enlightenment of the Ukrainian common people and to strengthen their liberties until they were equal to the freedoms the Poles enjoyed.[26]

A series of articles entitled "Słowo o Rusy i jej polityczeskom stanowyszczy" [A word about Rus' and its political position] typified the national view of the Sobor Ruskyi.[27] The author, identified only as "F. H.," criticized the Ukrainian intelligentsia in Galicia, for whom Rus' existed only within Austrian boundaries. He faulted their conservatism and their hostility "toward the current aspirations." He contrasted them to "the real Ukrainians" (he deliberately used this term), who cherished their past and were prepared to fight for the nation's welfare, "wrenched by injustice" from the common people. After the events of March 1848 in Galicia, the Ruthenians had become "a blind instrument of the bureaucracy," and the intelligentsia, instead of acting, expected salvation from the Reichstag. Meanwhile, the Reichstag was not restraining the most pernicious German influences. In the opinion of "F. H.," the division of Rus' into two parts—Russia and Ukraine—dated from the time of the Tatar incursions. The Ruthenian territory occupied by Poland developed its internal life until the time of King Zygmunt III, and even though "the *szlachta* had all the privileges, the villagers were not subjugated." In fact, the Cossacks would protect them. Poland did not aspire to polonize Rus', nor did Rus' impose its nationality on Poland. Because the Poles led in this union, the entire area was called Poland. That Rus' did not develop was the fault of foreign enemies. However, the Ruthenian nobility succumbed to polonization.

Fanaticism was the main reason for the enmity between the Ruthenians and the Poles. The Cossacks rose up many times, but they lacked the right kind of leader. Khmelnytsky was not the hero of the age; he saw nothing but the spilling of blood. "He displayed neither character nor attachment to [his] fatherland; he went over to the Muscovites [and] to the Turks." "F. H." charged that "he even converted to Islam. However, he was not bold enough to tear Rus' decisively away from Poland." Since Khmelnytsky's times, the struggle between the Polish and Ruthenian elements had continued. The political position of Rus' was based upon an alliance with Poland and resistance to Russia's influence. Only two persons really understood this point—the Cossack hetmans Vyhovsky and Mazepa, who acted accordingly. Vyhovsky concluded the Union of Hadiach with Poland in 1658, whereas Mazepa desired independence and a separate existence for Rus'. He wanted to cast off the hated yoke, but the defeat at Poltava wrecked these intentions. Tsar Peter I changed the relationship with the Cossacks: "From a guardian, he became a master and began to deal with them imperiously.... The freedom to choose their hetman was taken away, and their freedoms were restricted." As a result Catherine II had liquidated the *Sich*. To "turn the Zaporozhian Cossacks into Muscovites," a university was established in Kharkiv, and district gymnasia and lower schools were established.

"F. H." decidedly condemned the revolt of Ukrainian peasants against their Polish landlords in 1768, known as Koliivshchyna or the revolt of the Haidamaks, and the cult of its leaders Maksym Zalizniak and Ivan Gonta, the "apotheosis of banditry." However, the spirit of freedom did not collapse. "Liberalism was spreading among the Polish and Ruthenian youth along the Dnieper River. This spirit was evidenced by the conspiracy of the Little Russians recently uncovered in Kiev.... The tsar, therefore, was convinced that the Ruthenian spirit had declared war against him, that the number of his opponents had increased significantly."

"F. H." also took the position that Ukrainian was a separate language and rejected Cięglewicz's view in his *Question of Red Rus'*. "F. H." stressed the advantages of developing a Ukrainian literature based on the speech of the common people and argued that folk-songs and ballads represented inexhaustible sources. The writings of Kotliarevsky, Kvitka-Osnovianenko, Hrebinka and especially Shevchenko proved "that the moment of the Ruthenian language's entry into the body of world literature is not far off." Shevchenko's works were awakening the Ukrainian national consciousness and demonstrating that the Ukrainian language had a future and that the Ukrainian people would become free. Polish literature had not suffered through the development of the Ukrainian language, and Poland, in granting justice to the Ruthenians, would "gain for itself a nation that... will shine alongside it in the firmament of European politics." This nation would not be represented by the servile Saint Georgite party, but by "the martyrs for the national cause: Shevchenko, Kostomarov, Kulish and others."

For "F. H.," the principal objectives were the development of national consciousness and the instruction of the common people to prepare them to grasp the notion of fatherland. It was essential to introduce Ukrainian into schools of all types and into the courts. In that way twenty-two million people, who had remained largely indifferent to national and political issues, would assemble under one banner, which could carry the seed of destruction for tsardom, "because, through the example of Little Russia and Poland, White Russia and Great Russia will follow and will also demand political freedoms." "F. H." concluded:

> The Poles should take the path of justice and opportunity!... Recognizing the separateness of Rus' is just, because it signifies the recognition of the dignity in man. Separateness is possible, because fourteen million people desire it and demand it from mankind.... This is the endeavour of literature, our true goal, which cannot be achieved otherwise than by setting each group of people in its proper place. Call forth Rus' in the interests of Rus', Poland in the interests of Poland, and both in a common interest. Then the colossus of the north [Russia] will collapse and Galicia and Poznania will be saved from germanization. From this vantage point, it does not seem strange that the Poles will act in the interest of Rus'.[28]

But the hopes of "F. H." and of the pro-Polish or polonized Ruthenians of the Sobor Ruskyi had no chance of being realized in 1848. The Rada Narodowa did not change its fundamental policies, and the dissenting Ukrainians did not have sufficient strength to influence and counteract the policies of the Holovna Rada, with which it also seemed impossible to reach an understanding. Both the Ukrainian and the Polish councils saw the Prague agreement as a tactical step, taken to assuage public opinion,[29] and therefore they acted as though there were no agreement at all. The Rada Narodowa accused the Holovna Rada and its affiliates of encouraging the peasants to actions similar to those of 1846. In return, the Ukrainian councils complained that the Rada Narodowa sympathized with the "party of upheaval," was endeavouring to tear Galicia away from Austria and did not acknowledge the Ukrainians' national distinctiveness.

According to reports from Zhovkva, at the meetings of the local Ruthenian council on 26 May and 9 June, the clergymen Harasevych, Krushynsky and Bachynsky were supposed to have encouraged an attack on the Poles and called upon the peasants to repeat the events of 1846.[30] The Rada Narodowa turned to Iakhymovych and asked him to use his influence "to destroy this spirit of hatred."[31] After investigating the matter, however, the Holovna Rada discovered that Harasevych had not spoken and that the texts of the speeches of the two other men did not contain any of the statements ascribed to them. Although they had condemned Polish policies and called for elevating the Ukrainian nationality in a "close alliance with Austria," they had encouraged harmonious coexistence with the Poles.[32] Nevertheless, the Holovna Rada's reply accused the Poles of not recognizing the separateness of the Ukrainians, of interfering in the formation of the Ukrainian councils, and of spreading rumours that the Holovna Rada "had been conjured up by the government, was supported by the bureaucracy" and was inciting the rural populace, and that Iakhymovych "supposedly was bribed by the Russian government, or again by the Austrian bureaucracy." The reply further charged that the Poles considered Ukrainian a provincial dialect of Polish and labelled the entire Ukrainian movement "dissension, discord [and] a criminal intent to tear the fatherland to pieces, etc." The events of 1846 demonstrated that the Ukrainian clergy had not stirred up the common people, but that now a "certain revolutionary party," which "again lays its treacherous snares across the country and tries to produce an uprising," was doing so. This party, the Holovna Rada continued, sought to diminish confidence in the clergy and "consequently to do away with perhaps in these times the only effective force to restrain the common people." In addressing its reply to Piotr Wasilewski, the chairman of the Rada Narodowa, the Holovna Rada maintained that "the blame for the misfortunes that you fear, if, God forbid, they come to pass, will not fall on the Ruthenians because there are no revolutionary elements among them."[33] Probably no one dared to send the reply, because it was not mentioned in the report to the Rada Narodowa by the Polish delegation sent to Iakhymovych for clarification of the Zhovkva incident. The bishop, reportedly, said that he did not wish to enter into the matters or have any contact with the Rada Narodowa.[34]

What, then, prompted the Holovna Rada to such a resolute stance? It seems that it was certain of unconditional support by the army, with which it had come to an understanding about using peasants against anticipated Polish demonstrations.[35] Therefore, Karol Forster's statement that the Holovna Rada "significantly slowed its endeavours" after Stadion's departure because the authorities, fearing increasing Russian influence, had ceased to support the council,[36] showed his unfamiliarity with the Galician situation.

The statement in the response of the Holovna Rada concerning the Poles' alleged refusal to acknowledge the national and linguistic separateness of the Ukrainians is particularly striking. If this condition were not fulfilled, all of the efforts of the Rada Narodowa to find a *modus vivendi* with the Ukrainians were doomed to fail. Even though the central Rada Narodowa (though not all its local affiliates) and the Sobor Ruskyi appreciated the Ukrainians' aspirations, the Polish intelligentsia, under the aegis of the newspaper *Dziennik Narodowy*, openly denied the existence of the Ukrainian nation and considered Galicia an ethnically homogenous country. They also attempted to impose this view on European public opinion.

Following Kyrylo Vinkovsky's declaration on 19 March 1848,[37] a writer for *Dziennik Narodowy* challenged his view that the Poles and the Ukrainians were different nations. The Pole maintained that, according to historical sources, the Polanian Slavic tribes that had settled along the Vistula and the Dnieper rivers were the same people and, therefore, had comprised one nation. He argued that the Radymychians and the Viatychians had come from Poland and that the Lędzianie (Łęchowie) were joined "by the most binding tie of blood and language with the Polish clans." The Ukrainian language was a dialect, or *patois*, of Polish, and the only difference between Poles and Ruthenians was in their religious rites. His conclusion was explicit: there was no Ruthenian nation, but only the Rus' of the ruling Riurik dynasty, who spoke a Scandinavian tongue and had oppressed the Slavs.[38] National unity in Galicia had been wrecked by Stadion, who had helped create the Holovna Rada, which did not have the support of the nation.[39] Tomasz Rajski wrote in *Dziennik Narodowy* that the Ukrainian movement was not truly a national movement, because the "Saint Georgite Assembly in Lviv declares that the Ruthenians wish to write in the Cyrillic alphabet, speak Ruthenian and be German."[40]

Józef Supiński contended that three main dialects existed in Poland: Mazovian, Ruthenian and Kashubian. The common literary language arose from the first two more closely related dialects. In the beginning this literary language was closer to Ruthenian, but in time became more similar to Mazovian [Polish] speech. Because "language is the first and ultimate level of culture," to employ a dialect that was only one among others forming the basis of the Polish language meant "to retreat to a bygone era and to lead the nation into darkness, from which it had extricated itself at the cost of a dozen or so generations." Although it was necessary to speak to the common people in an intelligible dialect, it was also necessary to teach them the standard language, in order to "make all the branches of national knowledge" and "general European culture" accessible to them. Supiński also favoured the use of a common alphabet. "The common letters for these two closely related dialects will make each accessible to the other and will be the first step toward the complete fusion of the two kindred tribes." Nationality could not be allowed to obstruct social development. Supiński put it this way: "Nationality does not entail obstruction to any path toward progress. For that reason, we too, your brothers, Ruthenians like yourselves, do not stand in defence of a quasi-nationality."[41] Another writer for *Dziennik Narodowy*, Leon Korecki, maintained that the Poles rightly were demanding the introduction of Polish into the schools, courts, and governmental offices, and that "every Ruthenian is a Pole, since every enlightened Ruthenian to this day uses Polish as his customary language."[42]

Another issue that distinguished Poles from Ukrainians in those years was their extremely disparate political views. Virtually all the Polish groups (with the exception of the Stowarzyszenie Ziemiańskie) favoured the idea of reconstructing Poland within the boundaries of 1772 over the particularist and narrowly Galician interests of the Holovna Rada, which limited its endeavours to improving the national existence of the Ukrainians in the Austrian monarchy. It was precisely in this devotion to re-establishing the Polish state that the revolutionary character of the Poles' concept consisted. Realization of their aims would have to undermine the Holy Alliance. It was to be a democratic Poland, welding together the Poles, Ukrainians and Lithuanians; its rise would be a triumph of democracy and a danger to Russia. Józef Supiński believed that the oppressed Russian people, inspired by the

Polish example, would overthrow despotism and with their axes settle accounts with the aristocrats and priests who were grinding them down.[43] That is probably why Józef Cybulski stated that the development of Ukrainian separatism favoured tsarism, which represented a threat of the triumph of Orthodoxy, the knout and Siberia and which would in the final account also turn against the very leaders of the Ukrainian movement.[44]

For *Dziennik Narodowy*, the most convincing argument for maintaining unity was that Polish lands were located between hostile neighbours. The breaking away of the Ukrainian part would not bring it any advantage, and it would expose "the Mazurian [ethnically Polish] part to internal weakness."[45] In the "Proclamation to My Countrymen Who Take the Name of Ruthenians," the author, who is known to us only by the initials "R. H.," accused the Ukrainian leaders of insincerity: "You vainly say that you desire unity with us, when you are only concerned with developing your nationality. A nation is only a nation if it creates a separate entity; consequently, to be the Ruthenian nation and to be as one with Poland is a contradiction. So, if you want [your] Ruthenian nationality, you want to break away from Poland." "R.H." stated that splitting away from Poland would not be advantageous for the Ukrainians; they would not gain greater liberties, and they would be driven further from European culture and deprived of the glory that belonged to them together with the Poles.[46]

Only a few people saw the danger and warned against linking the national and political questions. During the pre-electoral debates in the Ossolineum in Lviv, August Bielowski stated:

> On the nationality question, which at the moment is the main question, we should endeavour with all our powers to grow internally stronger with every day and to consolidate the various elements among us into one powerful mass. The reconstruction of Poland within its former boundaries is a political question. To reach prematurely for the second [political end] means paralyzing the efforts on behalf of the first [national one] and driving the objectives of both further away.

On this account, Bielowski praised the Galician address of 18 March 1848, but criticized the address of 6 April. He denied the right of the Polish delegates to Vienna to have made in the earlier address the changes that had brought disadvantages. The Austrian authorities, seeing the goals of Polish policies, had done everything to forestall their realization. The Austrians had won the peasant question; they had initiated the Ukrainian address of 19 April and advised the priests "to influence the common people to sever completely from us [Poles] everything that is of the Greek Catholic rite and to cut off everything else possible from the Polish nationality under whatever pretext."[47]

Dziennik Narodowy fought against everyone and everything that opposed its concept of national unity. It accused Jan Dobrzański of not being true to the political tenets of the address of 18 March, when he admitted that he had erred in remaining silent on the Ukrainian issue and the rights of the Ukrainian language. After all, *Dziennik Narodowy* stated, that address had stipulated the equality of all classes and inhabitants of Galicia—and, therefore, of Ukrainians as well.[48] According to *Dziennik Narodowy*, the Polish Rada Narodowa had not fulfilled its mission, which was to strengthen the "national bond." It had not opposed the reaction, which denied the "unity of the Polish nation," and worse, had itself acknowledged the existence of two nationalities in Galicia and had even attempted to nurture the Ukrainian nationality. *Dziennik Narodowy* fulminated that the Rada Narodowa "not only recognized the division of the Polish nation into two nations, but even promised to support this division of the nation into two and advised others to support it."[49] The Rada Narodowa was "more harmful than helpful to the national cause."[50]

Dziennik Narodowy also reproached the editors of another Polish newspaper, *Postęp* [Progress], with dreaming of a federation of Poland, Lithuania and Rus' with the Slavic countries, because a federation with Russia would encompass two-thirds of Europe and inevitably lead to war with the states of Western Europe. But without Russia, the federation would maintain the current state of division of the country and thus bring no advantages to Poland.[51]

Dziennik Narodowy was undoubtedly correct in criticizing the Austrian bureaucracy, which preached equal rights for Ukrainian but would not accept petitions written in that language, as though "Messrs. bureaucrats had forgotten their accepted responsibility to patronize the Cyrillic alphabet, and Messrs. Saint Georgites had forgotten that the German language was to be their temporary language."[52] The newspaper also rightly condemned the consistory's order of 4 July, which aimed at elimating pro-Polish candidates from registrants to the Greek Catholic seminary. "Because the Germans have their own way of thinking, [the expressions] '*Ruthenisches Volk*, *Ruthenische Nation*, *Freundschaft mit Ruthenen*' have importance for them only when the issue of dividing the [Polish] nation arises. In all other circumstances, they acknowledge the honest truth among themselves and, pointing to the son of a Ruthenian priest, they remark '*Das ist ein Pole.*' Therefore, they will surely not give him a governmental position."[53]

On the other hand, there was no lack of spokesmen within the Polish community to support Ukrainian aspirations—for example, writers for *Postęp* and *Gazeta Powszechna*, leftist publications subsidized by the aristocrat Leon Rzewuski, who was a utopian socialist by conviction. Although for a short period *Postęp* denied the existence of the Ukrainian nationality,[54] it soon furthered the idea of Poland's independence in a federated union with Ukraine and the other Slavic states in Jan Zachariasiewicz's "Polityka czeska i narodowość ruska" [Czech politics and the Ruthenian nationality].[55] Karol Paduch took a similar position, conceding that it was futile to try to polonize the Ukrainian nation. It was in the Poles' interest to maintain and support Ukrainian national development, by which they would gain the Ukrainians' trust. Then Poland would not be an object of hatred, and the Ukrainians themselves would announce to the world that they were only a variant of the Polish nation.[56] Paduch stressed that Taras Shevchenko had urged his compatriots, "Do not allow yourselves to be oppressed by the *Liakhy*, but do not reject their fraternal hand."[57]

Gazeta Powszechna continued the tradition of *Postęp.* Emphasizing that the Ukrainians "desire a nationality," the newspaper criticized the thesis "that Ruthenian is a jargon of the Polish language and the Ruthenian nationality is a provincialism." If that were so, then refined Ruthenian speech would become Polish, but if it were an independent language, all of Ruthenian civilization would differ from Polish culture. So, the denial of the Ruthenian language was unfounded, and it was essential to allow it to develop its natural course.

On political issues *Gazeta Powszechna* agreed with the typical views of Polish activists in echoing the opinion that before partition the "Polish people" had been "the general name naturally associated with the political unity of the Polish Commonwealth, which, through association with and by occupying a place in the European framework, had become a [firm] notion.... But only if we call the people who profess this idea a "nation" in the higher meaning of this word can we also include Rus' and Lithuania under the word "Poland." Nationality in this sense is only one, and it is Polish." Therefore, the development of Ruthenianism was not dangerous for Poland; "formed into a nationality, it will merge with the ideal power that we call Poland.... Their link will be the idea of freedom, in accord with the progress of time."[58]

Let us now review and characterize the Ukrainian attitudes. In the general enthusiasm of March 1848, the Greek Catholic seminarians participated in patriotic demonstrations, wore white-and-red Polish cockades and square-tipped caps (the symbol of earlier Polish insurrectionaries) and generally supported Polish aspirations.[59] The liberal Ukrainian intelligentsia "lived by the fortune... of their brother Poles."[60] In his poem "Na chest bratei povernuvshykh z nevoli" [In honour of the brothers returned from bondage], Tselestyn Skomorovsky greeted the former conspirators as "angels of peace" struggling for truth, and advised partaking of the new freedom in harmony and for the common good. Greek Catholic priests not infrequently declared for co-operation with the Poles and took part in the Polish national councils. Dean Mykhailo Hankevych even issued an appeal calling upon the Ukrainians to support the Polish addresses of 18 March and 6 April. He proposed merging the Holovna Rada Ruska with the central Rada Narodowa and the local Ukrainian councils with the Polish district councils. According to this plan, the Ukrainian councils would become affiliates of the Polish councils and would work to shape the Ukrainian language and Ukrainian literature, to propagate the fruits of these labours, and to educate the common people. He appealed to his compatriots: "Remember that besides Ruthenian speech and Ruthenian writing, civil liberty entails something more. Be careful that in pursuing the one, you do not lose sight of the other, that in grasping the one, you do not drop the other."[61]

These Ukrainians, believing that rights for the Ukrainian language and nationality were assured, properly thought that the most important question at that moment was the attainment of political rights, which was more possible through closer co-operation with the Poles. It was also on this account that Iakiv Holovatsky regarded the establishment of the Holovna Rada as a governmental intrigue "to entrench its own bureaucracy under the cloak of the Ruthenian nationality and language, under the colours of Red Rus'." He was convinced that the Ukrainians understood this deceit and would not break with the Poles but would try "to realize all the articles of the constitution" together with them. Common needs and mutual interests would unite Ruthenians and Poles.[62]

Holovatsky's views were typical of those of a significant part of the liberal Ukrainian intelligentsia. They are especially worth examining because Holovatsky previously was always dedicated to obtaining the maximum advantage for his nation. This time he was convinced that co-operation with the *Liakhy* was the Ukrainians' best course. For the time being, even the extreme stance of *Dziennik Narodowy* did not discourage him. Unfortunately, Polish obstinacy slowly but irreversibly estranged the Ukrainian liberals. By 13 June, Holovatsky no longer saw the possibility of co-operation. He wrote to his brother Petro:

> Together with your letter, I received several others from Lviv, thanks to which things are becoming more and more clear. But I see little cause for hope. I am reading *Zoria Halytska*. Taking it all into account and comparing certain articles in the Polish newspapers, I can see that there is no point in trusting Messrs. the *Liakhy*. They would like brotherhood, but at a high price, because they want to sacrifice our language, our nationality, all

our strength, for the future Poland. Now that the Ruthenians have come to their senses and the youth itself sees that it was enticed to a precipice, everyone is drawing back and waiting.[63]

It should be clearly emphasized that Holovatsky's comments had nothing to do with political rights, since in the changed atmosphere of summer 1848 these seemed to be of little importance, but instead with the natural right, intelligible to everyone, to use and cultivate the Ukrainian language and to develop the national culture. In fact, this latter concern had come to determine the attitude of many Ukrainians,[64] for whom assurances that "a democratic Poland, a people's Poland—and only such can exist today—will not act hostilely but will join in an eternal alliance with a people's, democratic Rus'"[65] were insufficient, since everyday experience clearly contradicted them.

The conservative leaders of the Greek Catholic church and the Holovna Rada exploited this general dissatisfaction. A ban was issued on the clergy's participation in the Polish councils; disloyal seminarians were expelled, and disobedient clerics were not recommended for advancement.[66] The Holovna Rada rejected the accusation of the Polish newspaper *Rada Narodowa* that it was "established by the government as a reactionary party," explaining that the constitution and spirit of the times had created it; therefore, it "arose through freedom, and freedom does not struggle against freedom."[67] However, it did not agree to a compromise with the Sobor Ruskyi, which favoured unification of the councils in Galicia.

The Polish side carefully prepared the campaign for unification. Through the intermediacy of Iosyf Brylynsky, Antoni Dąbczański, on behalf of the Sobor Ruskyi, on 29 May presented the Holovna Rada with an appeal to the Ukrainians on the issue. He foresaw no obstacles, because both sides desired to elevate the Ukrainians, improve their lives and develop their language and literature. He suggested that the Holovna Rada by itself was not in a position to accomplish so significant a task. "You, brothers, have influence among the common people, whom you wish to enlighten. However, without an intelligentsia and wealth you cannot raise them higher." Dąbczański thought that a Ukrainian-Polish union was essential, because in the existing situation the very survival of the Ukrainians was in question. Actually, the tendency toward unification was "the only impediment to our harmony, that is, among the Ruthenians." At that time the Poles did not want to and could not break away from the Austrian government, whereas the future Poland, if it rose, could maintain itself "only in a federated union based on equal rights." The guarantee of this equality would be the current slogans concerning the equality of peoples and nations and the end of the aristocracy and Jesuitism. Those Poles who desired to maintain the territorial integrity of Poland, the appeal concluded, must be concerned about equal rights for the Ukrainians, "if only because they cannot separate from us, and life with a hostile neighbour is unbearable."[68]

The Sobor Ruskyi was inclined to make far-reaching concessions.[69] Iakhymovych wrote to Metropolitan Levytsky: "It already wishes to submit to our council and is sending a deputation with a declaration that it will accede to all conditions" if several of its members were admitted to the Holovna Rada. The Holovna Rada, following the recommendations of a commission established for this purpose, declared verbally to the Sobor Ruskyi delegates that it could not consent to their request to join, because it had to act according to its proclamation of 10 May.

What lay behind this attitude? Iakhymovych wrote that unification with the Sobor "would not be advantageous, since it would not help them, and for us it would be detrimental to the trust [placed] in us." But *Zoria Halytska* gave the real reason. "The entire Ruthenian nation must act earnestly and in common, must consult and guard diligently its needs and existence and [do this] to the exclusion of other nationalities, because they could deflect its goals and work. Least of all can [the Ruthenians] join the Poles in a common council, for they pursue separate aims and have entirely different foundations." *Zoria Halytska* also suggested that the Ukrainians' responsibility was to make their own nation and the Poles realize how illusory was the hope of reconstructing Poland within its former boundaries.[70] Later, the Holovna Rada took credit for the fact that such a Poland was not reestablished in 1848.[71]

Under these circumstances, Iuliian Lavrovsky chose to leave the Holovna Rada, recognizing that many members did not share his convictions. Kyrylo Vinkovsky was removed from the council, perhaps because he had said that the Polish-Ukrainian conflict was a "domestic affair" that ought to be settled without outside interference.[72] By June, therefore, it had become apparent that an understanding was impossible. Neither side observed the Prague agreement, and a Ukrainian campaign began on behalf of partitioning the country. The peasantry and the clergy supported it because it promised the peasants that they would be free of the Polish lords and the clerics that they would be free of Roman Catholic competitors. The split was also evident in the vehement press and pamphlet campaign conducted throughout the year.[73] At the initiative of the metropolitan, Antin Petrushevych wrote *Słôw kilka w obronie ruskiej narodowości* [Several words in defence of the Ruthenian nationality], which was distributed to the deanery libraries and gained general approval, although *Zoria Halytska* decided against publishing a Ukrainian translation.[74] Petrushevych was correct in criticizing Polish domination, which had caused the Ukrainians to become foreigners in their own fatherland, but he was mistaken in contending that only Austria had prevented their complete collapse. He asked: "By what means is this great Ruthenian nation of fifteen million to dissolve into a Polish nation of ten million and blend into one nation—into one vital fatherland? The union of Poland and Lithuania with Rus' was through the policy of the *szlachta*, and not of the peoples; therefore, they have only the nobility in common." They shared neither language nor faith, and "the faith for the simple people has one and the same meaning as fatherland." The Ukrainian people could not perish simply because their own nobility abandoned them; "through enduring constancy in the holy faith and the language of their fathers, through struggle for so many centuries against bondage, [the Ukrainians] have ennobled their entire being. For this... the presently granted constitution admits to them all the liberties of the Ruthenian nationality. Today this comforts and cheers us! Our nationality has not yet perished with the nobility." In concluding, Petrushevych addressed the young generation as the heirs of their ancestors' traditions: "Therefore, so is your flesh the flesh of the fatherland, and your spirit—Ruthenian youth—the spirit of its history."[75]

Leontovych gave a resolute reply to the Polish journalists of *Dziennik Narodowy* in "Odpowiedź na artykuł o nieistnieniu Rusinów" [A response to the article on the nonexistence of the Ruthenians].[76] He corrected the Poles' historical errors and pointed to their hypocrisy in calling for the harmonious coexistence of nations on the Swiss model, since they actually had no wish to apply the Swiss model to Poland.

The polemics were not always conducted factually and objectively, although it must be admitted that the Ukrainians' historical and linguistic arguments were more convincing than the Polish journalists' arguments. The former simply did not have to fit the facts to theory, as even Kasper Cięglewicz had done in *The Question of Red Rus' in 1848* or Antoni Dąbczański in *An Explanation of the Ruthenian Issue*.[77] Both of these authors had disputed the Holovna Rada's various pronouncements. However, instead of easing the situation, the pamplets seemed to prove that the Poles did not want to renounce their supremacy over the Ukrainians. The governmental *Wiener Zeitung* protested that "the rule of one nation over another is the greatest tyranny."[78] One can only ask whether it raised its voice in the name of justice or out of gratitude for the Ukrainians' loyalty to the monarchy.

Relations worsened during the summer of 1848, when Greek Catholic church leaders forbade the clergy to conduct services on the anniversary of the deaths of the Polish conspirators Józef Kapuściński and Teofil Wiśniowski, whom the Austrian authorities had executed in Lviv in 1847.[79] Instead, the Greek Catholic hierarchy leaders organized throughout Galicia prayers of thanksgiving for Austrian Field Marshal Radetzky's victory in Italy. The Holovna Rada even sent an address to him, joyfully hailing his victory and asking if he would

> deign to convey the gratitude and adoration of the Ruthenian people to our sons and brothers who had the honour of participating in this battle for the fatherland.... In this grand moment, in which our compatriots with their own blood confirmed their allegiance and loyalty to the monarch and the fatherland, we feel equally happy and proud that we too were permitted, in this same spirit and devotion, to do our part at home alongside Your Excellency's valiant forces.[80]

The Holovna Rada also supported a campaign to collect voluntary contributions "to defray government expenses."

The struggle over the partition of Galicia and the creation of a Ukrainian guard further embittered the two sides. An article appeared in the Polish newspaper *Gazeta Narodowa* under the title "Czarnożółty patriotyzm Świętojurców" [The black and yellow patriotism of the Saint George group],[81] which *Zoria Halytska* criticized vehemently, concluding: "It is time for [the Poles] to understand once and for all that this is Rus' and not Poland."[82] Several excesses occurred. On 25 September a group of Lviv printers attacked the printing office of the Stavropygian Institute, demanding a halt to the publication of *Zoria Halytska.* Rumours spread that a similar attack threatened the Holovna Rada itself, and consequently the council turned to General Wilhelm Hammerstein with a request for protection. The general declared that he was aware of the situation and that he had adequate strength at his disposal to crush any outburst immediately.[83] The Poles accused the Holovna Rada of inciting the peasants, and the Ukrainians accused the Poles of preparing a revolution. The Ukrainian councils demanded the dissolution of the radical Academic Legion.[84] Poles were disturbed by preparations for the congress of Ukrainian scholars and demanded explanations. The Sobor Ruskyi, desiring without success to send its representatives to this congress, demanded a public declaration of its aims to calm public opinion.[85]

The role of the Sobor Ruskyi had in fact already ended. It had failed to achieve its objectives or to gain a permanent place in the Ukrainian community, which regarded it as a Polish intrigue and an organ of the Rada Narodowa, aimed at subordinating the Ukrainian movement to itself. Consequently, in accordance with the decision at a general meeting of its members (although against the wishes its Ukrainian members), the Sobor was dissolved as an independent organization on 6 October. It became a branch of the Rada Narodowa.[86]

The events of November 1848 in Lviv changed nothing for the better. The Polish councils ceased to exist, although the Holovna Rada and Ruthenian district councils were permitted to continue to function. Only the Ruthenian deanery councils and the few village councils were abolished, because there had been difficulties in sending "official persons" to their meetings. On the strength of the gubernial rescript of 4 November, the Ukrainian councils became one of the main "pillars of the political order."[87] This made them feel confident and essential. Besides, as Ivan Borysykevych wrote on 18 November from Kroměříž, "The needs of current Austrian policy demand elevating the Ruthenians and, therefore, everything that we demanded for ourselves is permitted." At the same time, he reported, "we have broken with the *Liakhy* for as long as their policies remain contrary to the interests of the Austrian Slavs. Draw your own conclusions, and you will see what we are demanding and how we are acting."[88] Borysykevych did not complete the point. We can infer, however, that he was concerned about the retraction of the directive on education of 29 September, but did not want to admit that the Holovna Rada had agreed, in return, to the introduction of the German language. Still, the Ukrainian leaders were in the best possible spirits. It seemed to them that all the Slavs would support them and that even the Germans would join in responding favourably to the Ukrainians' demands. In these circumstances, as Borysykevych urged, "it is time to get to work; assemble all Ruthenian strengths [and] awaken the national life in all our villages. New conditions have emerged for us; new hope and a new path are before us. In the beginning we only defended and maintained ourselves; now let us act and move forward."[89]

Kyrylo Blonsky wrote to Iakiv Holovatsky that the Poles no longer mattered. The whole world had recognized what they were, especially the Czechs and other Slavs.[90] Besides, I. Baranovsky remarked, it served the Poles right. "All of Europe recognizes them as rebels, and nowhere will anyone put up with them." Those had won who had always supported the government. It did not matter that they had been labelled the black and yellow; standing on the winning side, they could be pleased with the sobriquet. "To say it in a word," Baranovsky went on, "the constitution created much trouble for the Poles: they lost money; they no longer merited the glory of a righteous nation; they were chased from France, Vienna and Galicia, and in addition they had their hides tanned; they lost the *robot*, and that is their entire gain."[91]

The Poles were blamed for all the unfortunate incidents that occurred in Lviv on 1 and 2 November. It was only thanks to the army that the Poles had not captured Saint George's Cathedral. Even the prolonged fires, Mykhailo Malynovsky explained, were caused by the Poles having damaged the fire wagons. "It is already known," he wrote with satisfaction, "who prepared the slaughter and viciousness. But the Poles place the entire blame on us." And so, "the kingdom of pride, stupidity and malice was broken apart," and "the wings of Polish dominion were clipped."[92] Ruthenian extremists thundered against Metropolitan Levytsky that he had dared request that the order of 29 September be respected and that he had rebuked his own clergy for stirring up the people, although not long before he had blessed the activities of the Holovna Rada. At the same time, many public officials were accused of favouring the Poles and of having ties to the "Polish party of upheaval."[93]

But the Ukrainians' successes were meagre. The government changed its directive on the school question, and that was all. The matter of partitioning Galicia was put aside *ad acta*. The more moderate and liberal Ukrainian leaders soon came to the conclusion that the Holovna Rada's course of action was wrong. Thus, when a large deputation of Ukrainians was sent to the emperor in February 1849 to thank him for his benefactions up to that time, Petro Holovatsky, who participated in it, was dissatisfied. He reported to his brother:

> Shame on us; we shall be ashamed of ourselves when the news [of our action] spreads around the world. Will it [the world] understand that, for the sake of [our] nation's standing, we abandoned any consideration of the sympathy of other nations and forgot about our honour? Will it forgive us this sin? . . . The Reichstag and the nations are undermining the foundations of the ministry and comforting themselves with the hope that it will collapse. Our address, then, is poor stuff—empty thanks for the past, and not an entreaty for the future. Perhaps it is an abnegation and dishonour toward those nations that wish us well. Then, God forgive us, we are making fools of ourselves. We assume that all things will collapse—but not the government. However, even if it were so, we must recognize that [our] address has served no end except to strengthen the ministry in return for nothing. It is obvious that the ministry will give us nothing more than political circumstances allow, and it will make demands. Therefore, in this respect as well the Ruthenian address is purposeless as regards the government and detrimental to the [other] nations.[94]

The future looked dark. Iosafat Kobrynsky noted: "Spirits are falling; we shall not go far with the black and yellow flower."[95] By the end of 1849, the Ukrainian liberals had become convinced that the government had exploited them for its own purposes and that the Ukrainian cause definitely was lost. Iakiv Holovatsky wrote: "Prokopchyts probably told you how they regard the Ruthenians in Vienna! And I was convinced that they are all so well meaning. However, the opposition party has been so able to undermine our position that I myself was surprised to see how quickly we have fallen."[96] Ultimately, the Polish landed nobility won out by abandoning its aspirations toward independence.

Were there really no possibilities for co-operation between the Ukrainians and the Poles in 1848? The sources permit us to state confidently that such a possibility did exist, but only on the basis of complete equality and democratic principles. Unfortunately, the Poles' agitation and pronouncements did not foster such views in the Ukrainian community. A witness to these events later wrote: "Wise reader! Let these events be the subject of deep reflection for you.... Would all this have happened if, immediately after the constitution was proclaimed, the Poles had not regarded the Ruthenians so lightly, but instead had recognized them as brothers with equal rights, going hand-in-hand with them and exercising the rights and liberties of the constitution?"[97]

Class relationships in those years also were significant. The Polish urban intelligentsia conducted a fierce struggle with the Ukrainians, while the lower strata of society wanted to preserve friendship and harmony. The best proof of this was the joint platform of 3 September 1848 of the peasant Reichstag deputies of both nationalities; the common struggles of journeymen, apprentice craftsmen and the proletariat on the barricades in Lviv in November of 1848;[98] and the Holovna Rada's complaint to the Reichstag that only "Polish reactionaries" denied the national separateness of the Ukrainians, while the "Mazurians" accepted it.[99]

Among the spokesmen for understanding, we can include Jerzy Lubomirski, Leon Sapieha, Karol Paduch, Tadeusz Kilarski, and B. K. Morawski on the Polish side, and Antin Liubych-Mohylnytsky, Kyrylo Vinkovsky, Ivan Hrabianka, the anonymous author of *Warunki zgody między Polską a Rusią* [Conditions for an accord between Poland and Rus'], Fedko znad Peltvy and Vasyl Podolynsky on the Ukrainian side. All of them recognized the necessity for co-operation and the link between national liberation and the liberty of peoples and political rights; all of them criticized the bureaucracy and the alliance with the Habsburg monarchy and opposed tsarist Russia and the German drive to the east.

Vinkovsky's position has not been adequately appreciated. Whereas his "Declaration," published in *Dnewnyk Ruskij*, stressed that he could not envisage the well-being of a Ukrainian nation separated "from our kinsmen of the Polish branch,"[100] he did demand unity "on the basis of complete equality, justice and the free development of nationality." He argued that the Ukrainians should not seek foreign allies; they could find allies in their own country. They should not become clients of common enemies, but, "as a separate, free nation, join with their free, enlightened and resourceful countrymen, together with whom we have fought unyieldingly for our freedom, and thereby gain the respect of the entire world." Only then, Vinkovsky added, could the Ukrainian nation play the role that it deserved on account of its territory, its numerous inhabitants and its capabilities. It could become a "distinct, powerful and very significant member of the family of European nations."

According to Mohylnytsky, the need for unity stemmed from the necessity to overthrow absolutism, to thwart the bureaucracy and to secure rights. Although he did not altogether trust the Poles, he believed that the Ukrainians' own interests dictated living harmoniously with them, because only thus could constitutional liberties become real. Mohylnytsky resolutely condemned national chauvinism. "The Poles," he wrote, "who wish to catch us through cunning are political thieves, whereas the Ruthenians who disrupt fraternal harmony in order to remain eternally the servants of arrogant bureaucrats are complete fools."[101] Likewise, he maintained that freedom had to be attained through work and "united forces, because if we interfere with and hinder one another, later there will be nothing to share."[102]

Ivan Hrabianka posited the necessity of creating a united Galician front against "the masters of power." In his opinion, the Ukrainians, Poles, Armenians and Jews should oppose the government "hand in hand," because only a unity that derived from common purpose could produce results. However, hatred and divisiveness would strengthen enemies and enable them to impose a "uniform yoke" on everyone. Hrabianka was convinced that just as Poland had fallen through oppressing and opposing the freedom of Ukraine, the Ukrainian cause would collapse if the Ukrainian nationality were hostile toward the Polish nationality.[103]

The anonymous author of *Conditions for an Accord* assumed that the greatest enemy of both nations was tsardom, and he offered reasons for "an alliance of joint resistance" linking Poles with Ukrainians.[104] He pointed out that "a Ruthenian ally [would] give Poland more strength than a Ruthenian servant." He realized that it was possible within the boundaries of 1772 "to forge legislative unity, but never national unity." Consequently, "the Poles will be greatly satisfied, if within the natural boundaries of their race they gain independence." He understood, however, that the adherents of a Poland that stretched to the Dnieper were convinced that only then would Poland be capable of opposing Russia. The author was certain that the future Poland "could arise only on principles of popular sovereignty," and this condition must lead to "self-determination by the Ruthenian nationality." Poles, Russians and Hungarians would have to leave the ethnically Ukrainian lands in the future, and if they truly loved Ukraine and did not want to leave, "let them adopt the language and religion [of the area]—and let them become Ruthenians." The Poles had a great role to play in the struggle against germanization in Poznania, Austrian Silesia and along the Oder and Neisse rivers. He closed by pointing out the enormous advantages that could result from Slavic co-operation. "Political considerations have separated the remaining Slavs from Russia for centuries, but as regards language and writing, the greatest advantages will accrue to us if we draw from the rich treasures of the Russian nation. And the Russian nation will someday come to recognize itself and us. We do not doubt that this great nation wishes to be just toward us."

The similarities between *Conditions for an Accord* and *A Ruthenian to the Poles* by Fedko znad Peltvy are striking. According to the latter, there were more adherents among the Galician Ukrainians for an agreement with the Poles than with the Germans. A German alliance would constitute betrayal of both nationalities and all of Slavdom. Only by maintaining the principles of equality could mutual distrust be supplanted, Ukraine forever tied to Poland and the slogan Liberty, Equality and Fraternity made real. Fedko regarded the Ukrainians as "the natural intermediaries between Poland and Muscovy, between West and East," and the agents of their eternal union. Obviously, such a union would be feasible only with a republican and democratic Russia.[105]

Tadeusz Kilarski was decidedly anti-German. Perceiving the danger of applying national sentiments toward political ends, he rightly cautioned against Austria, whose objective was to enfeeble both nationalities. He saw a black future:

> At the same moment when your priests call, "Do not join with the Poles!," in Frankfurt the decree is being passed about the annexation of Poznania to the German Empire! People, look at what they are doing, what they want to do, or look around you at what they have already done! And they will do much if we begin to argue and divide ourselves at their beck and call. Bear in mind that memorable year 1848, when they incorporated Poznania, lest in 1948

they incorporate Lviv and Saint George's.

It was essential to speak the truth to the peasants, saying that "the one who profited from *robot* [the noble] is as guilty as the one who systematically maintained it [the emperor]." Finally, he wrote, "I bid you farewell! And I beseech you that after ousting the Polish language from governmental offices, ... you do not leave any places vacant, because someone will then decree that the Ruthenian dialect is still a small child, that it is necessary to let the German language be its guide until Ruthenian is later introduced, and then Lviv [too will be tied] to Frankfurt."[106] As early as July 1848, Kilarski foresaw the situation that existed after German was introduced into the schools in January of the following year.

We cannot overlook one more pertinent voice in defence of the Ukrainians, that of B. K. Morawski. In an appeal aimed at his fellow Poles, he wrote: "If we wish to be free, we must grant the same freedom that we demand for ourselves to our co-citizens; let not only us but also others be free to think, speak out and act. And so, our freedom must be limited by the freedom of others, and their freedom by our own." Morawski was convinced that the Ukrainians were lost forever to the Poles, and he therefore advised abandoning the fatal thought of reconstructing Poland, which could end tragically on account of Russia's power. Poles should attempt instead "to preserve our constitutional liberties and raise the fortunes of the nation, living with free men among free brothers and free fraternal nations."[107]

Ukrainian political and national thought during the 1848 revolution found its most distinguished representative, however, in the person of Vasyl Podolynsky, who favoured unconditional national and social liberation.[108] He could not imagine the nation's life without freedom. On the basis of the experience of constitutional life up to that point, he concluded that freedom was virtually impossible under a despotic government. The Polish-Ukrainian dispute was purposeless, since each side was partly right. The Ukrainians' desire for liberation was entirely natural; therefore, not to recognize their national separateness was useless. Podolynsky believed in a free and independent Ukraine, although he did not expect it to arise until the resurrection of "the whole of Slavdom, federated and liberal." It is not clear whether he formed the idea of this federation while he was a conspirator (he had been a member of the Free Galicians and the Sons of the Fatherland), or after he read Karol Paduch's "Narodowość polska i ruska na Ukrainie" [The Polish and Ruthenian nationalities in Ukraine] in *Postęp*.[109] Podolynsky urged his compatriots to maintain unity and friendship with the Polish nation, which would strengthen the forces necessary for national liberation.

The Poles wanted to reconstruct their state, although the Ukrainians did not know how they would live in that state, but it would certainly be very good for the Poles. The Ukrainians could only surmise that they would live similarly—on condition, however, that they adopted the Polish language. And it was precisely this issue that drove the Ukrainians away from Poland. The Ukrainians were the age-old inhabitants of that land, and they deserved the natural right, the right of the host. The Poles had the right of settlement and were owed hospitality. On the other hand, the remaining nationalities—Germans, Jews and Armenians—were entitled to the rights of a national minority. The Poles would have to understand this and build Poland not for polonized or educated Ukrainians, because they could overcome their feelings, but for the mass of simple Ukrainians, who could not be polonized. Whether the Poles wished it or not, the Ukrainians desired to be a nation and would become one even though they did not know how to write in Ukrainian. So, until they developed their own language and literature, they would be "Ukrainians using Polish." In his remarkable pamphlet, *Slowo przestrogi* [A word of warning] (September 1848), Podolynsky wrote: "One who does not wish to recognize a Ruthenian is not worthy of being called a Pole," and "One who does not wish to recognize a Pole is not worthy of being called a Ruthenian."

Podolynsky criticized the Holovna Rada for its unfamiliarity with the Ukrainian language, its narrow-mindedness and its pro-Austrian policies. He rightly pointed out that the bureaucracy could not be trusted since, after displacing the Galician Poles, it would begin to persecute the Ukrainian nationality because it was Slavic and, above all, because it had arisen in revolutionary times. Nationalism was foreign to Podolynsky, although, as he wrote, he loved Ukraine the most. He had a fraternal attitude toward Poland and a filial sentiment toward Slavdom. Therefore, if there was to be a Poland, let it be not selfish but tolerant, not unitary but federated. The Ukrainians could accept freedom from any source, but they would not accept an alien nationality.

Podolynsky desired to support his convictions through action and to struggle for the freedom of Hungary. After being detained at the border by a peasant self-defence unit, he was placed in prison. He regained his freedom after Polish noblemen, among whom he apparently enjoyed respect, appeared in court on his behalf. His *Word of Warning* probably did not exert a great influence on the formation of a national consciousness in the Ukrainian community, because it was too threatening for the leaders of the Holovna Rada, the Greek Catholic church and the bureaucracy. The Przemyśl consistory forbade its distribution.

The tragedy of the revolutionary years was that the majority of those who indeed wanted to found mutual relations on just principles (such as Jerzy Lubomirski) could not, or did not want to, propagate their own farsighted concepts.

19. Conclusion

Freedom lasted barely 277 days. How little that is in the life of a nation! Yet virtually every day there were occurrences whose significance was grasped only by persons well versed in politics. The masses for the time being remained on the periphery, eagerly listening for the latest rumours, although they later became involved in the flow of events. It became apparent that this presumably undeveloped people knew its own worth and had its own political sense. The Galician peasants' attitude clearly demonstrated this in 1848 and 1849. Two hundred thousand signatures to the Holovna Rada's memorial on the issue of partitioning Galicia represented an unprecedented success.

The Ukrainian community was not the same at the end of 1848 as it had been before the March events; it was no longer passive, enclosed in its own environment, uninterested, except for a few individuals, in the social, cultural and political life of its own nation and resigned to taking everything that it got by favour of the government. It is true that not everyone immediately found his place in the unfolding events. Hence Kyrylo Khomynsky wrote that in Lviv one could meet "various Ruthenians: Polish, German, Little Russian (so-called *Ruthener*), but very few authentic ones." He expected that soon the true Ruthenians would emerge "from the German Ruthenians," and that the "Polish Ruthenians . . . will have to become true Ruthenians."[1]

And yet this did not occur, or at least not during the period we have been describing. It was precisely during the events of 1848 that the Ukrainian community split into four groups, which contemporaries already called "parties" and which Vasyl Podolynsky splendidly characterized as the "purely Ukrainian," the "Polish-Ukrainian," the "Austro-Ukrainian" and the "Russo-Ukrainian." The first two both sought a free Ukraine, but the purely Ukrainian group desired an independent state, whereas the Polish-Ukrainian group wanted a Ukraine federated with Poland or with the Slavic nations in general. These parties were liberal. The Austro-Hungarian party wanted a Ukraine liberated from the Poles, but not necessarily from foreign bondage; it relied exclusively on Austrian aid. The Russo-Ukrainian party aspired to a Ukraine joined to Russia. Podolynsky did not clarify which programme he regarded as the most valid; he only noted that even if not all the parties were concerned with freedom, certainly each of them was concerned with preserving the Ukrainian nationality. However, as we noted earlier, he could not imagine how a nation could live without freedom.[2]

We have already discussed the activities of the Holovna Rada Ruska and the Sobor Ruskyi, and, therefore, of the Austro-Ukrainian party and the Polish-Ukrainian party. But we have not written about the purely Ukrainian party, since it is not known who, besides Podolynsky, belonged to it, and whether it was perhaps only the creation of the author of *Word of Warning*. Perhaps Antin Liubych-Mohylnytsky could also be counted in its ranks.

A few words ought to be devoted to the Russo-Ukrainian party, even though in 1848-9 it existed more in the minds of the Poles than in reality. More than once the Polish press referred to Bishop Iakhymovych's "Muscovite sympathies," and reports spread from various quarters of Galicia that the Ukrainian clergy was stirring up the peasants with roubles received from the metropolitan, who either wanted to bring in the Muscovites or to barter away the Ukrainian nation to the tsar. It was said that the priests who lived near the Russian border journeyed every week in country wagons to collect the roubles, which they delivered to the Greek Catholic pastors living in the heart of the province.[3] Numerous leaflets and topical poems accused the Holovna Rada of sympathizing with Russia as, for example, "Tęsknota do Rosji" [Longing for Russia] by Leon Jabłoński, or "Pieśń o marach Świętojurskich" [Song about the Saint Georgites' apparitions] by "M. D." However, these charges had no basis in fact.

We would search in vain among the Ukrainians for an organized group of Russophiles. Only a few men, such as Denys Zubrytsky, Ivan Holovatsky, Antin Petrushevych, Bohdan Didytsky and Ivan Naumovych, were favourably inclined toward tsarist Russia. After the abolition of censorship, Ivan Holovatsky could publish "Pinie radostnoho holosa" [Singing of a joyous voice], a verse written in 1845 in honour of Nicholas I. The revolution convinced him that "only the whole of Rus'" could protect itself against the social upheaval that was so foreign to its nature.[4] In actuality, the accusations of sympathy for Russia were based in large part on the written language then used by the Ukrainians. This constituted rather weak proof, because Ivan Holovatsky, Petrushevych, Zubrytsky and Antin Paventsky, as well as the pro-Polish Kyrylo Vinkovsky used similar forms in their writings. It was simply not known how Ukrainian should be written; the works of Shevchenko, Kotliarevsky and other prominent Ukrainian writers in Russia were too rarely seen in Galicia to exert an influence on local knowledge of the pure Ukrainian language.

In 1849, however, a process began among the Galician Ukrainians that led in the 1850s to the formation of the so-called Pogodin colony in Lviv, the seed of the Russophile party. Holovatsky and Didytsky attempted to sneak through the press articles written in rather poor Russian.[5] Didytsky recalled that at that time he had intended to write an article with Naumovych along the lines of the later disquisition "V odin chas nauchitsia Malorusinu po velikorusski" [How the Little Russian can learn the Great Russian language in one hour]. They had already become firm believers in the unity of Galicia's Ukrainians "with the entire remaining Russian world," and "with sorrow and shame" they recalled how the Ukrainian leaders "had been compelled to repudiate our 'unity'" in 1848. Didytsky came to these views under the influence of the Russians, who in 1849 were garrisoned in his native town of Mosty Velyki. An Orthodox priest, with the permission of Didytsky's father, had conducted Orthodox services in the local church. The impressions that he carried away from that period had enabled Didytsky to prepare an outline of the work "Za pol chasa nauchitis chitati slavianskoe evangelie Rusinu po moskovski, a Moskalevi po ruski" [In half an hour a Ruthenian can learn to read the Slavonic gospel in the Muscovite tongue and a Muscovite in Ruthenian].[6] Petrushevych also belonged to the Ukrainian adherents of the Russian language; he had used Russian orthography in a translation into Ukrainian of the metropolitan's pastoral epistle of 12 June 1848, and later he wrote articles and poems in a Russo-Ukrainian jargon.[7]

However, the Russophiles of that time acted in isolation. Only considerably later did a formal Russophile party take shape, and its activities among the Galician Ukrainians were to exert a major influence on opinion about the Ukrainian question in the Poles' historical consciousness (they decidedly overestimated its dimensions). In 1848 the leaders of the Holovna Rada Ruska were labelled "Saint Georgites" [*sviatoiurtsi*], a name that became a synonym for those Ukrainians who were hostile to the Poles and associated with the Greek

Catholic capitulary of Saint George's Cathedral in Lviv. In later years this name lost its original meaning and became associated with the "Old Ruthenian," Russophile movement.[8]

During the revolution of 1848-9 it had not been possible to gain any national rights without political rights, which would have required far-reaching co-operation between the Ukrainian and Polish movements. Moreover, the political situation required co-operation among the forces for liberty in the entire Austrian monarchy and, above all, support for the Hungarian revolution. The Holovna Rada did not take this into account at all, if only because support for the Hungarians would have been equivalent to support for Polish aspirations. The council had chosen another path. It supported the Slavs, thus strengthening the forces of reaction and paving the way for the triumph of the Habsburgs and Russia's victory.

The Poles lost on the Ukrainian issue because they overestimated the effect of the ideas of freedom, progress and socio-political rights and did not appreciate the Ukrainians' national aspirations. It seemed to them that slogans would suffice to sway the Ukrainians to the Polish cause; they deemed far-reaching concessions unnecessary. It was not only the Poles who succumbed to this illusion; the Hungarians did so as well. Such illusions are frequent when national issues are set aside in revolutionary times. Ignoring the Ukrainian question was the Poles' first and fundamental error. When they finally realized this, they established the Sobor Ruskyi, which was doomed to fail because it lacked broad support. Throughout 1848 the notion persisted in the Polish community of subordinating the Ukrainian movement, either by selecting its leaders (a scheme to be furthered by the conversion of Polish-Ruthenian families to Greek Catholicism) or by supporting those elements in the Ukrainian movement that were willing to co-operate.[9]

Instead of taking positive action, the Poles criticized. What did it matter that they were often right? An anonymous Polish author attempted to apprise the Holovna Rada of the inappropriateness and absurdity of its actions:

> You stand on the government's side as its most loyal subjects, who wish to sustain the decrepit structure of the state in its entirety. You extol the benefactions of the former government, which oppressed us all equally. You crawl and humiliate yourselves, and you do all this for very little reward—that is, so that your brothers, the Poles, will be killed off, exterminated or expelled from their fatherland like enemies and aliens and the government turned over to you to sell at a good price, although [the Poles] were raised together with you on one land and are joined to you by blood in thousands of ways.... You hide behind a sense of nationality....

> You crawl abjectly before our and your own enemy, and you are pleased that [the Austrians] now praise you and promise you golden castles in the sky. But you do not perceive that our mutual enemies are only summoning you as blind instruments of their base aims.... Be wary with whom, as you say, you ally yourself eternally... because passion is short and regret is long. Do you think that through your servility you will achieve your aims? One must feel sorry for your short-sightedness. Do you not know that Austria is based only upon its aristocracy and has always supported, supports and will support only it as the sole pillar of its structure?[10]

The Poles realized their mistake too late. As Prince Czartoryski's agent in Istanbul, Franciszek Duchiński, wrote on 28 December 1849 to Wacław Zamoyski: "That we have allowed the Ruthenians in Galicia to take by force from us what we should have given them at their first request—their language—is our unparalleled carelessness.... If we do not want the Ruthenians to make a revolution, then let us Poles make it for the Ruthenians, in response to their just wishes."[11] Apparently, Jerzy Lubomirski's call in June 1848 had returned like a boomerang to its point of release. But, if no one had listened to Lubomirski then, under favourable circumstances, who would hear Duchiński when reaction was victorious?

On numerous occasions both before 1848 and during the revolution, Ukrainian spokesmen pointed out the pronounced similarity of the situation of the Ukrainian nation in Galicia to that of the non-Magyar nationalities in the kingdom of Hungary. Indeed, in both countries the conflict of nationalities was transformed into a social conflict, because in Galicia the Ukrainian nobility had succumbed to polonization and in Hungary the Slavic nobility (with the exception of the Croatian nobility) to magyarization. The Ukrainian intelligentsia and the intelligentsia of the non-Magyar nations (again except for the Croats) stemmed from the common people and consequently were even more anti-Polish or anti-Magyar.

The national movement of the non-Magyar nationalities in the lands of the Crown of Saint Stephen, just as the Ukrainian national movement in Galicia, had begun as a so-called linguistic and cultural renascence. In fact, this pattern was characteristic of the development of nations for this region of Europe. On the other hand, both the liberal Hungarian nobility, standing at the head of the Hungarian national movement, and the liberal Polish nobility and intelligentsia played a dual social and political role: in struggling for their own national liberation, they simultaneously oppressed the nationalities that inhabited territories subject to them. The Hungarian journal *Atheneum* spoke of the Slovaks, Germans, Serbs, Wallachians and other peoples in the kingdom of Hungary as Magyars, whereas the Polish *Dziennik*

Narodowy recognized not only the Mazurians, Kashubs and Silesians as Poles, but also the Lithuanians and the Ruthenians.

Both the Hungarians and the Poles also tried to prove that magyarization and polonization were prerequisites of progress. The leaders of the non-Magyar nationalities initially responded positively to the liberal reforms introduced by the Hungarian nobility, pressing almost exclusively for economic concessions for themselves. Only when the liberal programme was not carried out were nationalistic demands made. However, in Galicia, although as a rule the lesser-known Ukrainian activists supported the programme announced in the Galician Polish address of 18 March, the more prominent Ukrainian leaders rejected it. The Polish national programme in Galicia, just like the independence programme of the Hungarian nobility, found neither approval nor support among the subject peoples. The struggle of the Ukrainian peasants with the Polish *szlachta* in Eastern Galicia and the struggle of the non-Magyar nations with the Hungarian nobility were in fact progressive actions, because they strove to eradicate the remnants of feudalism and foster a sense of social justice among the masses.

The later course of the non-Magyar peoples in Hungary and of the Ukrainians in Galicia depended in large measure on Hungarian and Polish attitudes. Unfortunately, by assuming a nationalist position, the dominant groups attempted to suppress the national aims of their subject peoples. Nevertheless, compromise was still possible until the victory of the counter-revolutionary forces in Prague in June 1848. The defeat of the revolutionary forces on the streets of that city polarized attitudes. On the one hand, it strengthened the nationalist prejudices of the Poles and Hungarians; on the other hand, it moved the non-Magyar nationalities of Hungary and the Galician Ukrainians into the counter-revolutionary camp. In their perception there was no difference between the centralism of Viennese officialdom and Magyar or Polish centralism; the former was even not so directly felt. The result was the war of nationalities in Hungary and intensified Ukrainian-Polish conflict in Galicia in the fall of 1848.[12]

It was precisely then, when Hungary's revolutionary war with the counter-revolution was in full swing, that two articles by Friedrich Engels appeared in the pages of the *Neue Rheinische Zeitung*: "The Magyar Struggle" and "Democratic Panslavism."[13] Assuming worldwide progress, the development of civilization, and the primacy of the idea of revolution over national issues, Engels condemned the actions of the so-called non-historical nations as counter-revolutionary. Among these he included the Galician Ukrainians, the Czechs and the South Slavs. Engels called these nations "remnants of peoples, relics of an extremely complex, thousand-year development." He believed that they would not survive "the worldwide revolutionary storm," because "they had placed themselves at the disposal of Austrian reaction" and become instruments of counter-revolution from the time of the bombardment of Prague. On the other hand, the Germans, Poles and Hungarians, who according to Engels had assumed "the historical initiative" in East Central Europe and in the Danubian region, were "revolutionary nations."

Engels was undoubtedly right from the political point of view. However, his categorical statements about the survival of the "non-historical" nations were proved wrong. Engels simply did not have precise data, and he did not consider the specifics of the nationalities problem in East Central Europe, which differed fundamentally from Western European national development. Consequently, he could not foresee that the German bourgeoisie in the east eventually would succumb to assimilation. Nor did he perceive that there were elements in the national processes of the countries of East Central Europe that would enable the "non-historical" Slavic nations to make a lasting contribution to the "social progress of all of humanity."[14]

The activities of the Holovna Rada in the years 1848 and 1849 evoke mixed feelings. On the one hand, the persistence with which it monitored the Galician and Viennese authorities was impressive. On the other hand, its political short-sightedness was appalling. The Ukrainian leaders tied all their hopes to the government and endorsed its most reactionary policies. As a contemporary noted, "the aim was noble, but the principle erroneous." However, having chosen such a position, the Holovna Rada carried out its programme with iron consistency. It either did not wish to or could not understand that the Habsburg monarchy, existing essentially to defend the interests of the propertied classes, introduced reforms only from necessity, fearing a social revolution that would threaten it with complete collapse. The Holovna Rada also did not want to accept the fact that the Ukrainians were only an object in the government's nationality policy, supported to the extent that they were necessary to keep the Poles in line. After all, the Holovna Rada had written in its memorial of 31 July 1848: "Austria noticed us only in moments of danger, and when it had passed, they immediately forgot about us."[15] Did the Holovna Rada suppose that it would be otherwise this time? Did doubts never seize it, doubts such as found expression in Ivan Holovatsky's words, "The trouble in this is that all of it is a hope and nothing but a hope?"[16]

Out of fear of the peasants and the Ukrainians, the Polish *szlachta* and the Polish liberals did not break with Austria. They feared that if the province was partitioned, the land-owners would be persecuted with the backing of the rural populace. Therefore the Poles, presenting the Ukrainian movement as not so much a national as a social movement, did not doubt that ultimately they would gain the authorities' support. The later history of Galicia demonstrated that they were right.

During the revolution, the Holovna Rada was ready to renounce virtually all of the constitutional gains that the Ukrainians had achieved, with the exception perhaps of the land enfranchisement of the peasants, since the council could not undermine the foundation that justified its own existence. Nonetheless, the Ukrainian peasants made gains not so much because of the Holovna Rada as because of the rivalry between the revolutionary forces and the government for their support. However, one indisputable service of the Holovna Rada Ruska was to awaken the social, political and national energies of the Ukrainian community. The abolition of *robot* paved the way for the eventual rise of a bourgeois Ukrainian nation, in which the whole of the Galician Ukrainian community could embrace national consciousness. But this process demanded enormous political work for several generations.

The opinions of outsiders about a nation are often shaped by its leaders' actions. And so it was that the Holovna Rada Ruska contributed to the Ukrainians in Galicia being dubbed with the none too laudable epithet, "Tyroleans of the East." Instead of leading the people in a struggle for social, political and national rights in alliance with the forces of revolution, it ingrained in them loyalism and allegiance to the throne; instead of teaching the Ukrainians to rely on their own strength and developing in them a sense of their own potential, the council taught them to rely on the Austrian government.

Notes

Abbreviations Used in the Notes

ACz	Muzeum Narodowe w Krakowie, Oddział Czartoryskich
AGAD	Archiwum Główne Akt Dawnych
Bibl. Jagiell.	Biblioteka Uniwersytetu Jagiellońskiego
Bibl. Ossol.	Biblioteka Zakładu Narodowego im. Ossolińskich
BN	Biblioteka Narodowa
IL	Instytut literatury im. T. H. Shevchenka
LBAN	Lvivska biblioteka Akademii nauk URSR
TDIA	Tsentralnyi derzhavnyi istorychnyi arkhiv u Lvovi

1. History, Nationhood and the Slavic Awakening

1. For a general discussion of the nationalities problem in the Habsburg monarchy and East Central Europe, see the works of two contemporary Polish scholars: Henryk Wereszycki, *Pod berłem Habsburgów: Zagadnienia narodowościowe* (Cracow 1975), and Józef Chlebowczyk, *Procesy narodotwórcze we wschodniej Europie środkowej w dobie kapitalizmu (od schyłku XVIII do początków XX wieku)* (Katowice and Warsaw-Cracow 1975). An abridged translation of Chlebowczyk's work was published as *On Small and Young Nations in Europe: Nation-Forming Processes in Ethnic Borderlands of East Central Europe*, Polish Historical Library, no. 1 (Wrocław 1980).
2. Tadeusz Kroński, *Rozważania wokół Hegla* (Warsaw 1960), 105-21; see also Jerzy Szacki, *Ojczyzna, naród, rewolucja. Problemy narodowe w polskiej myśli szlachecko-rewolucyjnej* (Warsaw 1962).
3. Even Soviet scholars have questioned the authenticity of *The Tale of Ihor's Campaign.* See "Obsuzhdenie odnoi kontseptsii o vremeni sozdaniia Slova o polku Igoreve," *Voprosy istorii*, 1964, no. 9: 121-40. A recent English translation is by Robert C. Howes, *The Tale of the Campaign of Igor: A Russian Epic Poem of the Twelfth Century* (New York 1973).
4. English ed.: J. G. Herder, *Outlines of a Philosophy of the History of Man*, trans. T. Churchill (1800; rpt. New York: 1966), 482-4. On Herder's influence on the Slavs, see especially Holm Sundhaussen, *Der Einfluss der Herderschen Ideen auf die Nationalbildung bei den Völkern der Habsburger Monarchie* (Munich 1973); and Konrad Bittner, "J. G. Herders 'Ideen zur Philosophie der Geschichte der Menschheit' und ihre Auswirkungen bei den slavischen Hauptstämmen," *Germanoslavica* 3 (1933): 453-80.
5. See Frank Wollman, "Lidová slovesnost v jazykově literárním obrození Slovanů," *Slavia* 25 (1956): 560.
6. Ján Kollár, *Wybór pism*, ed. Henryk Batowski (Wrocław 1954), 180.
7. See Alexander Belić, *Vukova borba za narodni i književni jezik* (Belgrade 1948).
8. Viktor Kudělka, "Kollárova koncepce slovanské vzájemnosti v jazykověliterárním obrození Slovinců," in *Franku Wollmanovi k sedmdesâtinâm: Sborník prací* (Prague 1958), 115-28.
9. Kozik erroneously wrote at this point that "the Slovaks were predominantly Protestant."
10. The programmes of the Slavic nationalities in Hungary are discussed in Wacław Felczak, *Węgierska polityka narodowościowa przed wybuchem powstania 1848 roku* (Wrocław 1964), 48-63.
11. See Frank Wollman, "Josef Dobrovský a jazykově literární obrození u Slovanů," *Zborník prací filosofické fakulty brněnské university, Řada*

literârněvědna 3, no. 1 (1955): 5-40.

12. On Illyrism, see Jaroslav Šidak, "Der Illyrismus—Ideen und Probleme," in *L'udovít Štúr und die slawische Wechselseitigkeit*, ed. L'. Holotík (Bratislava 1969), 61-89; Wayne S. Vucinich, "Croatian Illyrism: Its Background and Genesis," in *Intellectual and Social Development in the Habsburg Empire from Maria Theresa to World War I: Essays Dedicated to Robert A. Kann*, eds. Stanley B. Winters and Joseph Held (New York 1975), 53-113. On Garašanin, see Charles Jelavich, "Garašanins 'Načertanije' und das grosserbische Programm," *Südost-Forschungen* 27 (1968): 131-47.
13. On Austro-Slavism, see especially Miloslav Novák, "Austroslavismus, příspěvek k jeho pojetí v době předbřeznové," *Sborník archivních prací* 6 (1956): 26-50; Václav Žáček, "K dějinám austroslavismu rakouských Slovanů," *Slovanské historické studie* 7 (1968): 129-79. On Kopitar's contribution to Austro-Slavism, see Stanislaus Hafner, "Das austro-slawische kulturpolitische Konzept in der ersten Hälfte des 19. Jahrhunderts," *Österreichische Osthefte* 5 (1963): 435-44.
14. "Letter Sent by František Palacký to Frankfurt," trans. William Beardmore, *Slavonic and East European Review* 26, no. 67 (April 1948): 303-8.
15. Marceli Handelsman, *Ukraińska polityka ks. Adama Czartoryskiego przed wojną krymską* (Warsaw 1937), 20ff.; Petr A. Zaionchkovsky, *Kirillo-Mefodievskoe obshchestvo 1846-1847* (Moscow 1959).

2. The Galician Ukrainians under Austrian Rule, 1772-1830

1. Egon Vielrose, "Przyczynek do demografii Galicji i Bukowiny w drugiej ćwierci wieku XIX," *Przegląd Statystyczny* 8 (1961): 137-54.
2. Hipolit Stupnicki, *Galicya pod względem topograficzno-geograficzno-historycznym* (Lviv 1849), 16 and tables.
3. See Jan Kozik, "Wpływy polskie na kształtowanie się świadomości narodowej Ukraińców w Galicji," *Studia Historyczne* 10, nos. 1-2 (1967): 88. Cf. H. I. Herbilsky, *Peredova suspilna dumka v Halychyni* (*30-i—seredyna 40-kh rokiv XIX stolittia*) (Lviv 1959), 15. In several towns in Eastern Galicia in 1842 the Jews comprised a majority of the population, 54 per cent in Ternopil and 53.5 per cent in Stanyslaviv, for example. See Karel Vladislav Zap, *Cesty a procházky po halické zemi* (Prague 1844), 185-6.
4. Iakiv Holovatsky, "Velikaia Khorvatiia abo Halytsko-Karpatskaia Rus'," in *Ruska Biblioteka*, vol. 3 (Lviv 1884), 253.
5. Ibid., 254.
6. Stupnicki (*Galicya*, 3, table) estimated the number of nobles in Galicia at 32,200, of whom 8,468 lived in the Sambir district alone.
7. Cf. H. I. Herbilsky (*Rozvytok prohresyvnykh idei u Halychyni v pershii polovyni XIX st.* [*do 1848 r.*] [Lviv 1964], 41), who maintains that the social and national consciousness of the Ukrainian common people was fully

reflected in their songs and proverbs.

8. Holovatsky, "Velikaia Khorvatiia," in *Ruska biblioteka*, 3: 253.
9. The basic studies on social and economic conditions in Eastern Galicia before 1848 are Roman Rozdolski [Rosdolsky], *Wspólnota gminna w b. Galicji Wschodniej i jej zanik* (Lviv 1936); Rozdolski, *Stosunki poddańcze w dawnej Galicji*, 2 vols. (Warsaw 1962); M. P. Herasymenko, *Ahrarni vidnosyny v Halychyni v period kryzy panshchynnoho hospodarstva* (Kiev 1959); F. I. Steblii, *Borotba selian Skhidnoi Halychyny proty feodalnoho hnitu v pershii polovyni XIX st.* (Kiev 1961); and E. M. Kosachevskaia, *Vostochnaia Galitsiia nakanune i v period revoliutsii 1848 g.* (Lviv 1965).
10. Zap, *Cesty a procházky*, 212.
11. I. S. Svientsitsky, *Materialy po istorii vozrozhdeniia Karpatskoi Rusi*, 2 vols. (Lviv 1910), 1: 5-6, 13.
12. Steblii, *Borotba selian Skhidnoi Halychyny*, 26, 29.
13. Ibid., 15 (table); Herasymenko, *Ahrarni vidnosyny v Halychyni*, 222 (table).
14. Steblii, *Borotba selian Skhidnoi Halychyny*, 22 (table). See also Rozdolski, *Wspólnota gminna*, 49.
15. "The Ukrainians in Galicia under Austrian Rule," *Austrian History Yearbook* 3, pt. 2 (1967): 395. See also Wereszycki, *Pod berłem Habsburgów*, 28ff. On developments in Western Galicia, see Józef Buszko, "Wpływy reform józefińskich na charakter walki klasowej na wsi zachodniogalicyjskiej," in C. Bobińska, ed., *Studia z dziejów wsi małopolskiej w drugiej połowie XVIII wieku* (Warsaw 1957), 543-78.
16. Steblii, *Borotba selian Skhidnoi Halychyny*, 56-7. See also Herbilsky, *Rozvytok prohresyvnykh idei v Halychyni*, 23; and Rozdolski, *Stosunki poddańcze*, 1: 143-53.
17. Steblii (*Borotba selian Skhidnoi Halychyny*, 59) set the number of peasants who fled between 1811 and 1848 at 13,919, the majority after 1830. On *robot* in Bukovyna, see Ivan Vahylevych to P. J. Šafařík, 16 April 1839, in V. A. Francev [Frantsev], *Korespondence Pavla Josefa Šafaříka s ruskými učenci*, 2 vols. (Prague, 1927-8), 2: 944.
18. Herbilsky, *Rozvytok prohresyvnykh idei v Halychyni*, 23.
19. Kosachevskaia, *Vostochnaia Galitsiia*, 79.
20. See Steblii, *Borotba selian Skhidnoi Halychyny*, 106-50; Ivan Franko, "Bunt ahrarnyi v Iakubovii Voli 1819 r.," in *Tvory*, 20 vols. (Kiev 1950-56), 19: 590-94; F. Papée, *Skole i Tucholszczyzna* (Lviv 1891); Herbilsky, *Peredova suspilna dumka v Halychyni*, 17-19; Herbilsky, *Rozvytok prohresyvnykh idei v Halychyni*, 23-5.
21. E. M. Kosachevskaia, "Narodnye mstiteli—galitskie opryshki," *Vestnik L.G.U.*, 1947, no. 14; Steblii, *Borotba selian Skhidnoi Halychyny*, 78-96; Herbilsky, *Rozvytok prohresyvnykh idei v Halychyni*, 26, 146. See also Władysław Ochmański, "Zwalczanie zbójnictwa góralskiego przez szlachtę w XVII i XVIII w.," *Czasopismo Prawno-Historyczne* 3 (1951): 193-242; and Adam Przyboś, *Powstania chłopskie w starostwie lanckorońskim i*

nowotarskim w r. 1670 (Cracow 1953).

22. Iakiv Holovatsky, "Podróż po Halickiej i Węgierskiej Rusi," *Dennitsa-Jutrzenka*, 1842, no. 21: 260.

23. M. Sala, *Geschichte des polnischen Aufstandes vom Jahre 1846* (Vienna 1867), 378-81; Iakiv Holovatsky to Osyp Bodiansky, 26 July 1846, in Fedir Savchenko, *Zakhidnia Ukraina v lystuvanni Iakova Holovatskoho z Osypom Bodianskym* (Kiev 1930), 19.

24. Wereszycki, *Pod berłem Habsburgów*, 28.

25. To Bodiansky, 26 July 1846, in Savchenko, *Zakhidnia Ukraina v lystuvanni*, 5.

26. Ivan Harasevych, "O prepodavaniiakh na ruskom iazytsi v vseuchylyshchi Lvovskom zavedenykh vsemylostyviishym Imperatorom Iosyfom II," *Zoria Halytska*, 1851, no. 61: 494. See also Iakiv Holovatsky, *O pervom literaturno-umstvennom dvizhenii Rusinov v Galitsii vo vremia avstriiskogo vladeniia v toi zemle* (Lviv 1865), 12-13; Jan Lewicki, *Ruch Rusinów w Galicji w pierwszej połowie wieku panowania Austrii* (*1772-1820*) (Lviv 1879), 15; and Amvrozii Androkhovych, "Lvivske 'Studium Ruthenum'," *Zapysky Naukovoho tovarystva im. Shevchenka*, 131 (1921): 123-95; 132 (1922): 185-217; 136-7 (1925): 43-105; 146 (1927): 33-118; 150 (1929): 1-80.

27. Lewicki, *Ruch Rusinów w Galicji*, 15.

28. On the Ukrainian schools, see "Materiialy do istorii ruskoho shkilnytstva 1772-1848," *Zbirnyk Istorychno-filosofichnoi sektsii Naukovoho tovarystva im. Shevchenka*, 5: 87-304; and Stefan Tomashivsky, ed., "Materiialy do istorii halytsko-ruskoho shkilnytstva XVIII i XIX vv.," *Ukrainsko-ruskyi arkhiv* 4 (1909).

29. Holovatsky, "Velikaia Khorvatiia," in *Ruska biblioteka*, 3: 256-7.

30. Zap, *Cesty a procházky*, 58; and "Materiialy do istorii halytsko-ruskoho shkilnytstva," 102-10.

31. Holovatsky, "Velikaia Khorvatiia," in *Ruska biblioteka*, 3: 256-7; Iakiv Holovatsky, "Sudba odnogo galitsko-russkogo uchenogo (k biografii Ivana Nikolaevicha Vagilevicha)," *Kievskaia starina*, 1883, pt. 6, no. 3: 453; Tomashivsky, "Materiialy do istorii halytsko-ruskoho shkilnytstva," 1.

32. Havryło Rusyn [Iakiv Holovatsky], "Zustände der Russinen in Galizien," *Jahrbücher für slawische Literatur, Kunst und Wissenschaft* 4 (1846): 367-8. See also Osyp Makovei, "Z istorii nashoi filolohii. Try halytski hramatyky (Ivan Mohylnytsky, Iosyf Levytsky i Iosyf Lozynsky)," *Zapysky Naukovoho tovarystva im. Shevchenka* 51 (1903): 6. On the other hand, Ivan Harasevych (*Zoria Halytska*, 1851, no. 61: 494) blamed the Armenian bishop in Lviv, Symonowicz, who was also dean of the theology faculty, for the termination of lectures in Ruthenian at the university.

33. Iakiv Holovatsky, *Istoricheskii ocherk osnovaniia Halitsko-russkoi Matitsy i spravozdanie pervoho Soboru uchenykh russkikh i liubitelei narodnoho prosvishcheniia* (Lviv 1850).

34. Ivan Zanevych [Ostap Terletsky], "Literaturni stremlinnia halytskykh Ukraintsiv vid 1772 do 1848," *Zhytie i slovo* 2 (1894): 80.
35. Ibid., 78.
36. Vasyl Shchurat, *Na dosvitku novoi doby* (Lviv 1919), 10-16, 21-35. On austrophilism in the Viennese seminary, see V. Shchurat, "V. Kopitar i ep. Iv. Snihursky," *Zapysky Naukovoho tovarystva im. Shevchenka* 125 (1918): 186-7.
37. On intellectual life in Lviv in this period, see Antoni Knot, *Dążenia oświatowe młodzieży galicyjskiej w latach 1815-1830* (Wrocław 1959), 19ff. See also Władysław Zawadzki, *Literatura w Galicji* (*1772-1848*) (Lviv 1879), 29-31.
38. Knot, *Dążenia oświatowe młodzieży galicyjskiej*, 7.

3. Polish Influences

1. Stefan Kieniewicz, "Stosunki polsko-ukraińskie w latach 1820-1870," in *Sesja naukowa w trzechsetną rocznicę zjednoczenia Ukrainy z Rosją* [Warsaw 1956], 133, has argued otherwise: "Ukraine was prepared to remain in a voluntary union with the Russian people."
2. Zawadzki, *Literatura w Galicji*, 49; Klemens Mochnacki [Mokhnatsky], "Pamiętnik spiskowca i nauczyciela," Bibl. Ossol., ms. 12112/II, 7.
3. Zawadzki, *Literatura w Galicji*, 50-52.
4. (Przemyśl 1836), reprinted in M. Vozniak, ed., *Pysannia Markiiana Shashkevycha* (Lviv 1912), 203-4.
5. Shchurat, *Na dosvitku novoi doby*, 106-8.
6. Ivan Holovatsky to his brother Iakiv, 18/30 January-1/13 March 1844, in Kyrylo Studynsky, ed., *Korespondentsiia Iakova Holovatskoho v litakh 1835-1849* (Lviv 1909), 118.
7. On Polish influences on Shashkevych, see C. Studziński [Kyrylo Studynsky], *Geneza poetycznych utworów Marcjana Szaszkewicza*, Rozprawy Akademii Umiejętnosci, Wydział Filologiczny, Ser. 2, no. 12 (Cracow 1898); and Vasyl Shchurat, "Naiblyzhchi zherela tvorchosty M. Shashkevycha," *Uchytel*, 1909, no. 24: 362-8.
8. Ivan Franko, "Panshchyna ta ii skasuvannia 1848 r. v Halychyni," *Tvory*, 19: 649.
9. See Handelsman, *Ukraińska polityka Czartoryskiego*, 85.
10. Mykhailo Tershakovets, "Do zhyttiepysu Markiiana Shashkevycha," *Zapysky Naukovoho tovarystva im. Shevchenka* 105 (1911): 96-7n.
11. *Ruska biblioteka*, 3: xx; Vozniak, *Pysannia Markiiana Shashkevycha*, 228; Shashkevych to T. Wasilewski, 24 May 1835, in Bibl. Ossol., ms. 4364: 173-5; and catalogue of the Tarnowski library in Dykiv, compiled by Stanisław Przyłęcki, ibid., ms. 1830/III.

12. Vozniak, *Pysannia Markiiana Shashkevycha*, 61-2.
13. *Dennitsa-Jutrzenka*, 1842, no. 19: 241-2.
14. Zawadzki, *Literatura w Galicji*, 45.
15. See "Historya *Rozmaitości*, pisma dodatkowego do Gazety Lwowskiej," in Wilhelm Bruchnalski, *Stulecie Gazety Lwowskiej, 1811-1911*, 2 vols. in 4 (Lviv 1911-12), 2, pt. 1.
16. On the role of the Ossolineum in the national life of the Ukrainians, see Shchurat, *Na dosvitku novoi doby*, 56-61, 122-3; and Iakiv Holovatsky, "K istorii galitsko-russkoi pismennosti (neskolko zamechanii na pismo I. Vagilevicha k M. P. Pogodinu)," *Kievskaia starina*, 1883, 646-7.
17. Zorian Dołęga Chodakowski, *O Słowiańszczyźnie przed chrześcijaństwem oraz inne pisma i listy*, ed. Julian Maślanka (Warsaw 1967), 26, 183. On Chodakowski's significance for the Ukrainian national movement, see V. A. Iuzvenko, *Ukrainska narodna poetychna tvorchist u polskii folklorystytsi XIX st.* (Kiev 1961); and Herbilsky, *Rozvytok prohresyvnykh idei v Halychyni*, 97-117.
18. Chodakowski, *O Słowiańszczyźnie*, 200, 208, 210, 219.
19. *Pisma k M. P. Pogodinu iz slavianskikh zemel*, ed. N. Popov (Moscow 1880), 276, 286.
20. Chodakowski, *O Słowiańszczyźnie*, 212, 214-15.
21. Ivan Franko, "Narysy z istorii ukrainskoi literatury v Halychyni," *Tvory*, 16: 154.
22. K. V. Zap to Iakiv Holovatsky, 20 October 1839, and Ivan Holovatsky to his brother Iakiv, 20 February 1844, in Studynsky, *Korespondentsiia*, 20, 112.
23. On Zaleski, see especially K. Ostaszewski-Barański, *Wacław Michał Zaleski* (*1799-1849*). *Zarys biograficzny* (Lviv 1912), pt. 2; and R. F. Kyrchiv, *Ukrainskyi folklor u polskii literaturi* (*period romantyzmu*) (Kiev 1971).
24. Wacław z Oleska, *Pieśni polskie i ruskie ludu galicyjskiego z muzyką instrumentowaną przez Karola Lipińskiego* (Lviv 1833), xxxiv-xxxv, xlii.
25. Ibid., xl.
26. Franko, "Panshchyna ta ii skasuvannia," in *Tvory*, 19: 652.
27. Wacław z Oleska, *Pieśni polskie i ruskie*, xliii.
28. Ibid., xlix.
29. J. Lewicki [Iosyf Levytsky], *Grammatik der ruthenischen oder kleinrussischen Sprache in Galizien* (Przemyśl 1834), 188.
30. Vasyl Shchurat, *Vybrani pratsi z istorii literatury* (Kiev 1963), 109-20.
31. See Henryk Batowski's introduction to Kollár, *Wybôr pism*, xviii; and Karel Krejčí, "První krise českého slovanství (Vliv povstáni listopadového na české národní obrození)," *Slovanský přehled* 20 (1928): 13-22, 108-22, 177-201, 249-72.
32. Polish: Handelsman, *Ukraińska polityka Czartoryskiego*; and Stefan Kieniewicz, *Adam Sapieha* (*1828-1903*) (Lviv 1939). Russian: V. A. Malkin, *Russkaia literatura v Galitsii* (Lviv 1957). Older Ukrainian: Ivan Franko,

"Narysy z istorii ukrainskoi literatury v Halychyni," *Tvory*, 16; Zanevych, "Literaturni stremlinnia halytskykh Ukraintsiv"; Tershakovets, "Do zhyttiepysu M. Shashkevycha." Soviet Ukrainian: Herbilsky, *Rozvytok prohresyvnykh idei v Halychyni*; cf. Mykhailo I. Shalata, *Markiian Shashkevych. Zhyttia, tvorchist i hromadsko-kulturna diialnist* (Kiev 1969), 32-3.

33. 4 December 1844, in Savchenko, *Zakhidnia Ukraina v lystuvanni*, 13.
34. Ludwik Finkel and Stanisław Starzyński, *Historia Uniwersytetu Lwowskiego*, 2 vols. (Lviv 1894), 1: 217-21.
35. Tershakovets ("Do zhyttiepysu M. Shashkevycha," 105: 111-15, and 106: 77-8) took issue with Ustyianovych's contention that Shashkevych was held back with difficulty from joining the insurrectionaries (*Slovo*, 1861, no. 5). Cf. Handelsman, *Ukraińska polityka Czartoryskiego*, 63; and Malkin, *Russkaia literatura v Galitsii*, 14.
36. Ivan Krevetsky, "Falshovanie metryk dlia polskykh povstantsiv z 1830-1831 rr. (Prychynok do kharakterystyky halytsko-ruskoho dukhovenstva pershoi polovyny XIX st.)," *Zapysky Naukovoho tovarystva im. Shevchenka* 77 (1907): 107-13.
37. Bibl. Ossol., ms. 12112/II: 4-7.
38. Kyrylo Studynsky, *Lvivska dukhovna seminariia v chasakh Markiiana Shashkevycha (1829-1843)* (Lviv 1916), xcvi-xcvii, cvi-cxi, cxxvi-cxxvii, cli, ccvii-ccix, ccxxix-ccxxx, 333-7; Studynsky, "Polski konspiratsii sered ruskykh pytomtsiv i dukhovenstva v Halychyni v rokakh 1831-1846," *Zapysky Naukovoho tovarystva im. Shevchenka* 82 (1908): 87-177; Mykhailo Tershakovets, "Materiialy i zamitky do istorii natsionalnoho vidrodzhennia Halytskoi Rusy v 1830 ta 1840 rr.," *Ukrainsko-ruskyi arkhiv* 3 (1907): 106-12.
39. Bibl. Jagiell., ms. 7088: 39-40.
40. "Pamiętnik spiskowca i nauczyciela," Bibl. Ossol., ms. 12112/II: 15-16.
41. Cited in Handelsman, *Ukraińska polityka Czartoryskiego*, 64; and Henryk Bogdański, *Pamiętnik 1832-1848*, ed. Antoni Knot (Cracow 1971), 435-6. See also Ivan Zanevych [Ostap Terletsky], *Znesenie panshchyny v Halychyni: Prychynok do istorii suspilnoho zhyttia i suspilnykh pohliadiv 1830-1848 rr.* (Lviv 1896), 96ff; and Ivan Franko, "Obiavy rusko-polskoho bratania 1842 r.," *Zhytie i slovo*, 1895, pt. 1: 114-16.
42. Julian Horoszkiewicz, *Notatki z życia*, ed. Henryk Wereszycki (Wrocław 1957), 55.
43. Ivan Holovatsky to his brother Iakiv, 6 February 1844, in Studynsky, *Korespondentsiia*, 105.
44. Stefan Kieniewicz, *Konspiracje galicyjskie 1831-1845* (Warsaw 1950), 156.
45. Zanevych, *Znesenie panshchyny v Halychyni*, 77.
46. Ibid., 72. See also Horoszkiewicz, *Notatki z życia*, 71-3.
47. Cited in Herbilsky, *Rozvytok prohresyvnykh idei v Halychyni*, 227. See also Franko, "Panshchyna ta ii skasuvannia," *Tvory*, 19: 601.

48. Cited in Studynsky, "Polski konspiratsii sered ruskykh," 82: 132-3. Cf. Herbilsky, *Rozvytok prohresyvnykh idei v Halychyni*, 232.
49. Kieniewicz, *Polskie konspiracje*, 104, 127.
50. Shchurat, *Na dosvitku novoi doby*, 126; Herbilsky, *Rozvytok prohresyvnykh idei v Halychyni*, 230.
51. *Ukraińska polityka Czartoryskiego*, 69.
52. K. Mochnacki, "Pamiętnik spiskowca i nauczyciela," Bibl. Ossol., ms. 12112/II: 18.
53. "Polski konspiratsii," 80: 53-108, and 82: 87-177. On Ukrainian involvement in the Polish conspiratorial movement, see Shchurat, *Na dosvitku novoi doby*, 96-104, 114-28; Herbilsky, *Rozvytok prohresyvnykh idei v Halychyni*; Józef Krajewski, *Tajne związki polityczne w Galicji* (*1833-1841*) (Lviv 1903); Zygmunt Zborucki, *Proces studentów samborskich 1837-1839* (Lviv 1927); M. Andrusiak, "Ukraiński ruch narodowy i konspiracja polska w Galicji," *Biuletyn polsko-ukraiński* 5 (1936), no. 6; Kieniewicz, *Konspiracje galicyjskie*; and Aleksander Kamiński, *Polskie związki młodzieży 1831-1848* (Warsaw 1968). Valuable source materials are in Tershakovets, "Materiialy i zamitky do istorii natsionalnoho vidrodzhennia," 15-25, 37-43, 49-112, 118-21.
54. Mykhailo Levytsky to Ivan Snihursky, 23 December 1833, in Vasyl Shchurat, ed., "Lysty mytropolyta M. Levytskoho do ep. Snihurskoho i ofitsiialni dokumenty ikh spilnoi diialnosty (1813-1847)," *Ukrainskyi arkhiv* 12 (1924): 82. See also Kieniewicz, *Konspiracje galicyjskie*, 104.
55. Studynsky, "Polski konspiratsii," 80: 88-99; Studynsky, *Lvivska dukhovna seminariia*, clvi-clxxxi.
56. M. Levytsky to Snihursky, 17 April 1835, in Shchurat, "Lysty mytropolyta," 94.
57. Levytsky's letters to Snihursky of 1 January 1836, 16 August 1836, 5 March 1837, ibid., 103-4, 110-11.
58. D. Mokhnatsky's deposition, in Tershakovets, "Materiialy i zamitky do istorii natsionalnoho vidrodzhennia," 146ff.
59. Letters of 5 March and 14 May 1837, in Shchurat, "Lysty mytropolyta," 112, 114.
60. Kieniewicz, *Konspiracje galicyjskie*, 145.
61. Krajewski, *Tajne związki polityczne*, 85-7.
62. Studynsky, *Lvivska dukhovna seminariia*, clxxxii-clxxxiv; Shchurat, *Na dosvitku novoi doby*, 116-18.
63. Cited in Shchurat, *Na dosvitku novoi doby*, 167. Henryk Bogdański described Podolynsky as a political terrorist. In Karol Lewicki, ed., *Pamiętniki spiskowców i więźniów galicyjskich w latach 1832-1846* (Wrocław 1954), 52.
64. Tershakovets, "Materiialy i zamitky do istorii natsionalnoho vidrodzhennia," 22-3.

65. Studynsky, *Lvivska dukhovna seminariia*, clxxvi.
66. Ibid.
67. Ibid., cxxi-cxxii, 152-4, 159-60.
68. See Shchurat, *Na dosvitku novoi doby*, 96-104; Tershakovets, "Do zhyttiepysu Shashkevycha," 105: 106; Studynsky, "Polski konspiratsii," 80: 60ff.; Studynsky, *Lvivska dukhovna seminariia*, c-cvi.
69. Shchurat, *Na dosvitku novoi doby*, 118ff. See also Tershakovets, "Do zhyttiepysu Shashkevycha," 106: 85; Stanisław Schnür-Pepłowski, *Z przeszłości Galicji (1772-1862)*, 2nd rev. ed. (Lviv 1895), 309.
70. Ivan Franko, "M. Shashkevych i halytsko-ruska literatura," *Tvory*, 17: 233; Franko, "Narysy z istorii ukrainskoi literatury v Halychyni," ibid., 16: 154. See also Iakiv Holovatsky, "Sudba odnogo galitsko-russkogo uchenogo," 456.
71. Mykhailo Levytsky to Hryhorii Iakhymovych, 2 January 1848, in Kyrylo Studynsky, ed., "Materiialy do istorii kulturnoho zhytia v Halychyni v 1795-1857 rr.," *Ukrainsko-ruskyi arkhiv*, 13-14 (1920): 270-71.
72. Studynsky, *Lvivska dukhovna seminariia*, ccxxix.
73. Iuliian Romanchuk, ed., *Tvory Markiiana Shashkevycha, Iakova Holovatskoho, Nykoly Ustyianovycha, Antona Mohylnytskoho* (Lviv 1906), 164; *Tvory Markiiana Shashkevycha i Iakova Holovatskoho* (2nd ed.), in *Ruska pysmennist*, vol. 3, pt. 1 (Lviv 1913), 270.

4. The Ruthenian Triad

1. "Materiialy do istorii ruskoho shkilnytstva," 153-4. See also Tomashivsky, "Materiialy do istorii halytsko-ruskoho shkilnytstva," 130.
2. Tomashivsky, "Materiialy do istorii halytsko-ruskoho shkilnytstva," 131. See also "Dolia galitsko-russkogo iazyka," *Dennitsa-Jutrzenka*, 1843, pt. 1: 189.
3. Tomashivsky, "Materiialy do istorii halytsko-ruskoho shkilnytstva," 141.
4. Ibid., 140; Makovei, "Z istorii nashoi filolohii," 7.
5. "Materiialy do istorii ruskoho shkilnytstva," 170-71. See also Tomashivsky, "Materiialy do istorii halytsko-ruskoho shkilnytstva," 142-3; and Zanevych, "Literaturni stremlinnia halytskykh Ukraintsiv," 366-7.
6. "Statuta Societatis Presbyterorum," in "Materiialy do istorii ruskoho shkilnytstva," 258-76. See also Ivan Franko, "Narysy z istorii ukrainskoi literatury v Halychyni," *Tvory*, 16: 147-51; and Shchurat, *Na dosvitku novoi doby*, 50-55.
7. "Statuta Societatis Presbyterorum," in "Materiialy do istorii ruskoho shkilnytstva," 264-5.
8. Ibid., 260; Shchurat, *Na dosvitku novoi doby*, 52.
9. Chodakowski to Ludwik Kropiński, 28 May 1818, in Chodakowski, *O Słowiańszczyźnie*.
10. "Narysy z istorii ukrainskoi literatury v Halychyni," *Tvory*, 16: 150.

11. Reprinted in "Materiialy do istorii ruskoho shkilnytstva," 290-430; and Tomashivsky, "Materiialy do istorii halytsko-ruskoho shkilnytstva," 111-50.
12. Franko, "Narysy z istorii ukrainskoi literatury v Halychyni," *Tvory*, 16: 151.
13. Studynsky, "Materiialy do istorii kulturnoho zhytia v Halychyni," 52-9.
14. Kopitar to Iakiv Holovatsky, 1 February 1839, in Studynsky, *Korespondentsiia*, 15.
15. Makovei, "Z istorii nashoi filolohii," 51: 51-8; Shchurat, *Na dosvitku novoi doby*, 62-7.
16. Makovei, "Z istorii nashoi filolohii," 51: 53. See also Mykhailo Tershakovets, "Vidnosyny V. Kopitara do halytsko-ukrainskoho pysmenstva," *Zapysky Naukovoho tovarystva im. Shevchenka* 94 (1910): 102; and M. Vozniak, "Studii nad halytsko-ukrainskymy hramatykamy XIX v.," ibid., 89 (1909): 113. Cf. Shchurat, "Kopitar i Snihursky," 177.
17. Text of two of Snihursky's sermons in Shchurat, "Kopitar i Snihursky," 188-91.
18. Makovei ("Z istorii nashoi filolohii," 51: 10-12) argues that Mohylnytsky adopted Kopitar's views on the Ukrainian language. Tershakovets ("Vidnosyny Kopitara," 91-2) maintains that Mohylnytsky influenced Kopitar through Snihursky. See also Shchurat, "Kopitar i Snihursky," 175-7.
19. Makovei, "Z istorii nashoi filolohii," 51: 11-12. See also Mohylnytsky's discourse "Vidomist o ruskom iazytsi," in *Ukrainsko-ruskyi arkhiv* 5 (1910): 1-70. This work first appeared in an abridged Polish translation under the title "Rozprawa o języku ruskim," in *Czasopismo Naukowe Księgozbioru Publicznego im. Ossolińskich*, 1829, pt. 3: 56-87.
20. See Herbilsky, *Rozvytok prohresyvnykh idei v Halychyni*, 61.
21. Chodakowski, *O Słowiańszczyźnie*.
22. Iakiv Holovatsky, "Podróż po Halickiej i Węgierskiej Rusi," *Dennitsa-Jutrzenka*, 1842, no. 24: 300. See also Ivan Biretsky to Iakiv Holovatsky, 31 January 1840, and Ivan Holovatsky to his brother Iakiv, 29 October 1847, in Studynsky, *Korespondentsiia*, 23, 209.
23. *Zoria Halytska*, 1850, no. 88: 542. Although it is anonymous, the contents and certain formulations in the article suggest that the author may have been Mykola Ustyianovych.
24. A bibliography of works on and by the Ruthenian Triad is *M. Shashkevych, I. Vahylevych i Ia. Holovatsky. Bibliohrafichnyi pokazhchyk*, eds. M. P. Humeniuk and Ie. Ie. Kravchenko (Lviv 1962). The best brief characterization of the Triad is by Handelsman, *Ukraińska polityka Czartoryskiego*, 80-85.
25. Malkin (*Russkaia literatura v Galitsii*, 17), relying on Holovatsky's memoirs, provides the dates 1830 and 1831-2. However, in his article "Sudba odnogo galitsko-russkogo uchenogo" (p. 456) Holovatsky wrote: "During the ferment of 1833-4 some young persons—students at the university—intended to establish a circle that would be devoted to the rebirth of Galician Ruthenian literature." V. Kotsovsky (*Ruska biblioteka*, 3: xxiii) maintained

that the Triad was founded in 1831. Completely baseless is the contention of M. Stakhiv (*Zakhidnia Ukraina ta polityka Polshchi, Rosii i Zakhodu 1772-1923*, [Scranton, Pa. 1958-9], 1: 48) that the Triad was formed in 1829, when Iakiv Holovatsky was fifteen years old.

26. Iakiv Holovatsky, "Pamiat Markiianu Shashkevychu," *Vinok Rusynam na obzhynky* (Vienna 1846), pt. 1: 57.
27. *Vinok*, pt. 1: 151-2.
28. Tershakovets, "Materiialy i zamitky do istorii natsionalnoho vidrodzhennia," 154ff.
29. Omelian Ohonovsky, *Istoriia literatury ruskoi* (Lviv 1889), vol. 2, pt. 2: 261-2.
30. Ibid., 262. See also "Vospominanie o Markiiane Shashkeviche i Ivane Vagileviche. Iz zapisok Iakova Golovatskogo," *Literaturnyi sbornik*, 1885, no. 1, 11; and *Ruska biblioteka*, 3: xxiii.
31. Ivan Franko, "Krytychni pysma o halytskii intelihentsii," *Tvory*, 16: 35.
32. Vahylevych to Mykhailo Maksymovych, 17 July 1838, in Vladimir Danilov, ed., "Pisma Ivana Vagilevicha k M. A. Maksimovichu," *Russkii filologicheskii vestnik* 68, no. 4 (1912): 441. See also Herbilsky, *Rozvytok prohresyvnykh idei v Halychyni*, 72-3.
33. Franko, "Krytychni pysma o halytskii intelihentsii," *Tvory*, 16: 36.
34. Malkin, *Russkaia literatura v Galitsii*, 17.
35. "Iz zapisok Iakova Golovatskogo," *Literaturnyi sbornik*, 1885, no. 1: 22.
36. Iakiv Holovatsky, "Perezhitoe i perestradannoe," ibid., 135. See also M. Vozniak, "Z romantychnoho periodu folklornykh zaniat Iakova Holovatskoho," in *U stolittia "Zori" Markiiana Shashkevycha (1834-1934)*, 2 parts (Lviv 1936), 1: 74-6.
37. See *U stolittia "Zori,"* 1: 7-27, 29-35, 73-123; 2: 147-216. See also M. Vozniak, *Markiian Shashkevych iak folkloryst* (Lviv 1911); M. Vozniak, "Z folklornykh zaniat Markiiana Shashkevycha," *Zapysky Naukovoho tovarystva im. Shevchenka* 109 (1912): 140-55; Andrii Franko, "Hryhorii Ilkevych iak etnohraf," *ibid.*, 109: 91-122, 110: 123-56, 111: 117-39; Shchurat, *Na dosvitku novoi doby*, 129-33; and Zanevych, "Literaturni stremlinnia halytskykh Ukraintsiv," 439-40.
38. In *Dennitsa-Jutrzenka*, 1842, no. 6: 81.
39. Herbilsky, *Rozvytok prohresyvnykh idei v Halychyni*, 51.
40. Mykola Vereshchynsky to Iakiv Holovatsky, 2 February 1848, in Studynsky, *Korespondentsiia*, 216.
41. Biretsky to Iakiv Holovatsky, 24 and 30 March 1840, ibid., 26.
42. Petrushevych to Iakiv Holovatsky, end of 1843, ibid., 94-5.
43. 18 January 1844, ibid., 97.

5. The Triad's Literary Activities

1. "Syn Rusy ili sobranie stikhotvorov v ruskym iazyku ot kleru Seminarii ieneralnei v Lvihorodi, ruskoho kraiu Metropolii. Rok 1833," reprinted in Kyrylo Studynsky, ed., "Prychynky do istorii kulturnoho zhyttia Halytskoi Rusy v litakh 1833-47," *Zbirnyk Istorychno-filosofichnoi sektsii Naukovoho tovarystva im. Shevchenka*, 11-12: cxiv-cxxv, and Studynsky's comments, iv-ix.
2. M. Vozniak, "Hryhorii Ilkevych iak zbyrach pisen," in *U stolittia "Zori,"* 1: 26.
3. Malkin, *Russkaia literatura v Galitsii*, 13, 15.
4. Studynsky, "Prychynky do istorii kulturnoho zhyttia Halytskoi Rusy," cxi-cxiv.
5. Mykhailo Levytsky to Ivan Snihursky, 3 November 1831, in Shchurat, "Lysty mytropolyta," 61.
6. Tershakovets, "Do zhyttiepysu Shashkevycha," 105: 93.
7. See Kozik, "Wpływy polskie," 101.
8. Makovei, "Z istorii nashoi filolohii," 51: 1-58, 54: 59-96, *passim.*
9. In Tershakovets, "Materiialy i zamitky do istorii natsionalnoho vidrodzhennia," 6-9.
10. Some writers maintained that Michalewicz was in fact the censor for Ruthenian books in Galicia. See, for example, S. Wasylewski, "Michał Michalewicz," in *Stulecie Gazety Lwowskiej*, 1, 2: 12-13.
11. Levytsky's review has not been preserved. Its content is known from the metropolitan's report to the authorities, in Studynsky, "Prychynky do istorii kulturnoho zhyttia Halytskoi Rusy," cxxv-cxxvii.
12. In Tershakovets, "Materiialy i zamitky do istorii natsionalnoho vidrodzhennia," 7.
13. *Literaturnyi sbornik*, 1885, no. 1: 32. Cf. Malkin, *Russkaia literatura v Galitsii*, 22-3.
14. *Literaturnyi sbornik*, 1885, no. 2: 25-6; Studynsky, "Prychynky do istorii kulturnoho zhyttia Halytskoi Rusy," xix.
15. See especially Mykhailo Tershakovets, "Pro naklad 'Rusalky Dnistrovoi'," *Zapysky Naukovoho tovarystva im. Shevchenka* 108 (1912): 117-39.
16. Studynsky, *Korespondentsiia*, 1-2; Studynsky, "Prychynky do istorii kulturnoho zhyttia Halytskoi Rusy," xxxvi-xxxvii.
17. Studynsky, *Korespondentsiia*, 2. See also Studynsky, "Prychynky do istorii kulturnoho zhyttia Halytskoi Rusy," xxxvii, cix.
18. Studynsky, "Prychynky do istorii kulturnoho zhyttia Halytskoi Rusy," cviii; and Tershakovets, "Materiialy i zamitky do istorii natsionalnoho vidrodzhennia," 114-15.
19. G. Petrović to Iakiv Holovatsky, 26 April 1838, and 12 February 1839, in Studynsky, *Korespondentsiia*, 9-10, 16.

20. Fran Kurelac to Iakiv Holovatsky, 23 October 1837, ibid., 7.
21. Rusyn [Holovatsky], "Zustände der Russinen," 372.
22. Studynsky, "Materiialy do istorii kulturnoho zhytia v Halychyni," 74-5.
23. *Vinok*, pt. 1: 54.
24. Iosyf Levytsky, "Listy tyczące się piśmiennictwa ruskiego w Galicji" (Letter no. 1), in Tershakovets, "Materiialy i zamitky do istorii natsionalnoho vidrodzhennia," 210-26.
25. Protocols written by M. Shashkevych, I. Vahylevych and Iakiv Holovatsky, printed in *Zoria*, 1885, no. 1.
26. Cited in *Ruska biblioteka*, 3: xxvii; and Zanevych, "Literaturni stremlinnia halytskykh Ukraintsiv," 443. Cf. *Rusalka Dnistrovaia. Vid davnyny do suchasnosti. Zbirnyk prats z pytan ukrainskoi literatury* (Kiev 1960), 1: 223.
27. Rudnytsky, "Ukrainians in Galicia," 397.
28. The Soviet Ukrainian historian H. I. Herbilsky has contended that *Rusalka Dnistrovaia* was intended to awaken among the Galician Ukrainians the consciousness of their oneness with all Ukrainians and an awareness of their closeness to the "great Russian nation." *Peredova suspilna dumka v Halychyni*, 45; and *Rozvytok prohresyvnykh idei v Halychyni*, 134.
29. To his brother Iakiv, 15/27 Aug. 1841, in Studynsky, *Korespondentsiia*, 56.
30. *Literaturnyi sbornik*, 1885, no. 1: 33.
31. Cited in Ohonovsky, *Istoriia literatury ruskoi*, 2, 2: 372.
32. *Ruska biblioteka*, 3: 61; Vozniak, *Pysannia M. Shashkevycha*, 18, 231-2; *Vinok*, pt. 1: 69.
33. Vereshchynsky to Iakiv Holovatsky, 2 February 1848, in Studynsky, *Korespondentsiia*, 216-17.
34. Ivan Holovatsky to his brother Iakiv, 15/27 August 1841, ibid., 56.
35. Vozniak, "Hryhorii Ilkevych iak zbyrach pisen," in *U stolittia "Zori,"* 1: 25-26; "Puteshestvie Iakova F. G. po Prikarpatskoi Rusi i Vengrii," *Literaturnyi sbornik*, 1886: 33.
36. Both Markiian Shashkevych in *Rusalka Dnistrovaia* and Żegota Pauli in *Pieśni ludu ruskiego w Galicji* acknowledged their debt to Ilkevych.
37. See M. Vozniak, "Do istorii vydannia Ilkevychevykh prypovidok," *Zapysky Naukovoho tovarystva im. Shevchenka* 106 (1911): 175-90. See also Shchurat, *Na dosvitku novoi doby*, 129-33.
38. Ivan Holovatsky to his brother Iakiv, April (?) 1840, in Studynsky, *Korespondentsiia*, 35.
39. Biretsky to Iakiv Holovatsky, 24 March 1840, ibid., 26-7.
40. Ivan Holovatsky to his brother Iakiv, April (?) 1840, ibid., 35.
41. Zdeněk Hájek, "Styky Jakiva a Ivana Holovackých s Josefem Podlipským a Františkem Cyrilem Kampelíkem," in *Franku Wollmanovi k sedmdesátinám: Sborník prací* (Prague 1958), 221-3.

42. Vereshchynsky to Iakiv Holovatsky, 2 May 1840, in Studynsky, *Korespondentsiia*, 38. See also Vozniak, "Do istorii vydannia Ilkevychevykh prypovidok," 185.
43. Studynsky, "Prychynky do istorii kulturnoho zhyttia Halytskoi Rusy," lx; Tershakovets, "Materiialy i zamitky do istorii natsionalnoho vidrodzhennia," 143-4.
44. Ivan Holovatsky to his brother Iakiv, 4/16 June 1841, in Studynsky, *Korespondentsiia*, 52-3.
45. Petrushevych's manuscript is in Bibl. Ossol., ms. 12576/I.
46. Ivan Holovatsky to his brother Iakiv, 5/17 April 1841, in Studynsky, *Korespondentsiia*, 49.
47. Vozniak, "Z romantychnoho periodu folklornykh zaniat Iakova Holovatskoho," in *U stolittia "Zori,"* 1: 79, 87-8.
48. *Literaturnyi sbornik*, 1885, no. 1: 38.
49. See letters of Ivan Holovatsky to his brother Iakiv, 1845-6, in Studynsky, *Korespondentsiia*, 154, 168, 171, 187. The list of subscribers was attached to the first part of *Vinok*.
50. Ivan Holovatsky to his brother Iakiv, 29 October (10 November) 1847, ibid., 210. See also *Literaturnyi sbornik*, 1885, no. 1: 39.
51. 24 February 1848, in Studynsky, *Korespondentsiia*, 219.
52. Ivan Holovatsky to his brother Iakiv, 7/19 May 1847, ibid., 187.
53. Ivan Holovatsky to his brother Iakiv, 4 April 1845, ibid., 142-4.
54. See Ivan Holovatsky to his brother Iakiv, 7/19 May 1847, and Iakiv Holovatsky to Denys Zubrytsky, 11 March 1848, ibid., 188, 224.
55. Vereshchynsky to Iakiv Holovatsky, 2 February 1848, ibid., 216.
56. Petro Holovatsky to his brother Iakiv, 21 January 1847; and Rudolf Mokh to Iakiv Holovatsky, 16 September 1847, ibid., 161, 203-4.
57. 9 September 1847, ibid., 201.
58. Cited in Petro Holovatsky to his brother Iakiv, 21 January 1847, ibid., 161.
59. Liubych-Mohylnytsky to Iakiv Holovatsky, 24 February 1848, ibid., 219.
60. 9 September 1847, ibid., 201.
61. Iakiv Holovatsky to Zubrytsky, 11 March 1848, ibid., 224.
62. Hryhorii Bodnar to Iakiv Holovatsky, 23 March 1849, ibid., 346.
63. Ibid., 286. See also Vereshchynsky to Iakiv Holovatsky, 2 September 1847, ibid., 199-200.
64. See Studynsky, *Lvivska dukhovna seminariia*, ccxlvi, ccxlix; Ohonovsky, *Istoriia literatury ruskoi*, 2, 2: 703-7; M. Vozniak, "Iz korespondentsii R. Mokha," *Zapysky Naukovoho tovarystva im. Shevchenka* 81 (1908): 157-71; Iaroslav Hordynsky, "Kelestyn Skomorivsky i ioho literaturna diialnist," ibid., 128 (1919): 135-71; M. Vozniak, "Virshovi proby Io. Velychkovskoho (Do pytannia avtorstva Shashkevychevoi *Chytanky*)," ibid., 104 (1911): 181-91.

65. See Ivan Franko, "Ruskyi teatr v Halychyni," *Tvory*, 16: 92-105; Franko, "Rusko-ukrainskyi teatr," ibid., 16: 223-39; Franko, "Pysania I. P. Kotliarevskoho v Halychyni," *Zapysky Naukovoho tovarystva im. Shevchenka* 26 (1898): 1-14; M. Vozniak, "Ukrainski dramatychni vystavy v Halychyni v pershii polovyni XIX stolittia (zamitky i materiialy)," ibid., 87 (1909): 70-91, and 88 (1909): 51-93. On the Galician Ukrainian theatre in 1848, see below.
66. Zanevych, "Literaturni stremlinnia halytskykh Ukraintsiv," 2: 443. The full text of *Chytanka dlia ditochok v narodnykh uchylakh ruskykh* is reprinted in Vozniak, *Pysannia M. Shashkevycha*, 148-99.
67. See Iakiv Holovatsky to Doskovsky, 9 September 1847, in Studynsky, *Korespondentsiia*, 201.
68. Kobrynsky to Iakiv Holovatsky, before 22 August 1847, ibid., 214.
69. Ivan Holovatsky to his brother Iakiv, 29 October (10 November) 1847, ibid., 209.
70. Ibid., Ivan Holovatsky to his brother Iakiv, 1 June 1848, and 16/28 March 1849, ibid., 254, 348.
71. Vahylevych in his recollections sharply criticized the literary work of Ivan and Iakiv Holovatsky. See M. Vozniak, "Rozvidky Ivana Vahylevycha pro ukrainsku movu," in *U stolittia "Zori,"* 2: 301ff.
72. 22 June 1847, in Studynsky, *Korespondentsiia*, 192.
73. 13 May 1848, ibid., 242.

6. The Struggle over the Literary Language and Ukrainian Othography

1. Cited in Vozniak, "Rozvidky Vahylevycha pro ukrainsku movu," *U stolittia "Zori,"* 2: 260.
2. Makovei, "Z istorii nashoi filolohii," 51: 51; Vasyl Lev, "Mova poetiv 'Ruskoi Triitsi'," *Zapysky Naukovoho tovarystva im. Shevchenka* 161 (1953): 38.
3. Wollman, "Lidová slovesnost v jazykově literárním obrození Slovanů," 555-84; and Wollman, *Slovanství v jazykově literárním obrození u Slovanů* (Prague 1958).
4. "Vidomist o ruskom iazytsi," in *Ukrainsko-ruskyi arkhiv* 5 (1910): 11. See also Zanevych, "Literaturni stremlinnia halytskykh Ukraintsiv," 2: 202-3; and Makovei, "Z istorii nashoi filolohii," 51: 15-16.
5. Makovei, "Z istorii nashoi filolohii," 51: 17-25. See also Vozniak, "Studii nad halytsko-ukrainskymy hramatykamy," 89: 92-109.
6. Makovei, "Z istorii nashoi filolohii," 51: 17-25; Vozniak, "Studii nad halytsko-ukrainskymy hramatykamy," 90: 109-18, 91: 126-50.
7. Makovei, "Z istorii nashoi filolohii," 51: 44-5.
8. Ibid., 51: 50, 54: 93-96; Tershakovets, "Materiialy i zamitky do istorii natsionalnoho vidrodzhennia," 253-8.

9. Józef Łoziński [Iosyf Lozynsky], *Gramatyka języka ruskiego* (Przemyśl 1846), xxii-xxiii.
10. Kudělka, "Kollárova koncepce slovanské vzájemnosti," 118-20; Makovei, "Z istorii nashoi filolohii," 51: 29-30.
11. Cited in "Avtobiograficheskie zapiski Iosifa Lozinskogo," *Literaturnyi sbornik*, 1885: 117; Makovei, "Z istorii nashoi filolohii," 51: 27. Cf. Malkin (*Russkaia literatura v Galitsii*, 27-28), who erroneously maintains that Lozynsky was an agent of the Polish governor in Galicia. There was no "Polish" governor at that time. See also Herbilsky, *Rozvytok prohresyvnykh idei v Halychyni*, 83-4.
12. Bibl. Jagiell., ms. 5388 II, t. 3: 58-60.
13. Ivan Franko, "Azbuchna viina v Halychyni 1859 r. Novi materiialy," *Ukrainsko-ruskyi arkhiv* 8 (1912): iv-xiv.
14. "Avtobiograficheskie zapiski Lozinskogo," *Literaturnyi sbornik*, 1885: 117.
15. *Ukraińska polityka Czartoryskiego*, 86.
16. *Kievskaia starina* 6 (1883): 647; *Literaturnyi sbornik*, 1885: 20-21. See also Makovei, "Z istorii nashoi filolohii," 51: 35; and M. Vozniak, "Avtorstvo azbuchnoi statti z 1834 r.," *Zapysky Naukovoho tovarystva im. Shevchenka* 136-7 (1925): 109.
17. 27 December 1834 (supplement). Republished in Ukrainian in Ivan Franko, "Azbuchnyi spir v 1859 r.," *Zapysky Naukovoho tovarystva im. Shevchenka* 114 (1913): 103-9.
18. *Kievskaia starina* 6 (1883): 648; *Literaturnyi sbornik*, 1885: 20.
19. Printed in Makovei, "Z istorii nashoi filolohii," 54: 77-81.
20. Bibl. Jagiell., ms. 5388 II, t. 3: 60-61.
21. Makovei, "Z istorii nashoi filolohii," 51: 28.
22. Vasyl Shchurat, "Azbuchna stattia Mykoly Kmytsykevycha," *Zapysky Naukovoho tovarystva im. Shevchenka* 81 (1908): 134-44; M. Vozniak, "Apolohiia kyrylytsi Denysa Zubrytskoho," ibid., 150 (1929): 120-42; Vozniak, "Avtorstvo azbuchnoi statti z 1834 r.," 107-18.
23. 22 April-13 May 1840, in Kyrylo Studynsky, ed., "Z korespondentsii Denysa Zubrytskoho," *Zapysky Naukovoho tovarystva im. Shevchenka* 43 (1901): 26.
24. *Literaturnyi sbornik*, 1885: 20.
25. Reprinted in Vozniak, *Pysannia Markiiana Shashkevycha*, 202-9.
26. Printed in Makovei, "Z istorii nashoi filolohii," 54: 81-6.
27. *Ruskoje wesile opysanoje czerez J. Łozynskoho* (Przemyśl 1835); *Rusalka Dnistrovaia*, 133.
28. Cited in *Literaturnyi sbornik*, 1885: 20.
29. Vozniak, *Pysannia M. Shashkevycha*, 204-5.
30. "Avtobiograficheskie zapiski Lozinskogo," *Literaturnyi sbornik*, 1885: 117.
31. Hájek, "Styky Jakiva a Ivana Holovackých," 217-18.

32. Ivan Holovatsky to his parents, 20 April 1840, in Studynsky, *Korespondentsiia*, 30-35.
33. Vereshchynsky wrote to Iakiv Holovatsky on 2 May 1840, "Father Lozynsky's return [to the fold] is pleasant and proves that he is still a Ruthenian" (ibid., 39).
34. Draft of Iakiv Holovatsky's letter of 5/17 May 1840, ibid., 57-9. See also Hájek, "Styky Jakiva a Ivana Holovackých," 219-20.
35. Ivan Holovatsky to his brother Iakiv, 17/29 May 1840, in Studynsky, *Korespondentsiia*, 39-40.
36. Letter 1, printed in Tershakovets, "Materiialy i zamitky do istorii natsionalnoho vidrodzhennia," 210-26.
37. Letter 2, ibid., 227-41.
38. On the *Biblioteka besid dukhovnykh*, see the materials ibid., 242-51. See also Tershakovets, "Vidnosyny V. Kopitara," 101.
39. Iosyf Levytsky to Metropolitan Mykhailo Levytsky, 16 March 1841, in Studynsky, "Materiialy do istorii kulturnoho zhytia v Halychyni," 381-6.
40. 24 October (5 November) 1844, in Savchenko, *Zakhidnia Ukraina v lystuvanni*, 14.
41. *Dennitsa-Jutrzenka*, 1843, pt. 1: 188-204, pt. 2: 39-45.
42. Letter to the editor and note, ibid., pt. 2: 45.
43. "Das Schicksal der galizisch-russischen Sprache und Literatur," *Jahrbücher für slawische Literatur, Kunst und Wissenschaft*, 1844; Haličer-Russe, "Bemerkungen über den Artikel 'Schicksal der galizisch-russischen Sprache und Literatur'," ibid., 1845, 125-8; "Erwiderung auf die Bemerkungen über den Artikel 'Schicksal der galizisch-russichen Sprache und Literatur'," ibid., 1846: 183-6.
44. Ivan Vahylevych [Wahylewicz], *Gramatyka języka małoruskiego w Galicji* (Lviv 1845).
45. Haličer-Russe, "Bemerkungen über den Artikel," *Jahrbücher*, 1845: 125-8.
46. *Dennitsa-Jutrzenka*, 1843, pt. 1: 188. On the character of this journal, see Jiří Horák, "P. P. Dubrovského *Dennica-Jutrzenka*," in *Z dějin literatur slovanských* (Prague 1948), 340-59.
47. See Vahylevych to Iakiv Holovatsky, 9 November 1843, in Studynsky, *Korespondentsiia*, 92.
48. Zap to Iakiv Holovatsky, 20 July 1846, ibid., 178-9.
49. See Vahylevych to Iakiv Holovatsky, 9 November 1843, and Zap to Holovatsky, 20 January 1844, 19 April 1844, 14 September 1844, ibid., 92, 100, 122, 128.
50. 26 July 1846, in Savchenko, *Zakhidnia Ukraina v lystuvanni*, 19.
51. Bodiansky to Vahylevych, 15 July 1844, in Vozniak, "Rozvidky Vahylevycha pro ukrainsku movu," *U stolittia "Zori,"* 2: 320; Handelsman, *Ukraińska polityka Czartoryskiego*, 81.

52. Vahylevych, *Gramatyka języka maloruskiego*, i-ii, xxii.
53. See Ohonovsky, *Istoriia literatury ruskoi*, 2, 1: 146-57; M. Vozniak, "Proiekt pravopysy Ivana Zhukivskoho na zizdi 'ruskykh uchenykh'," *Zapysky Naukovoho tovarystva im. Shevchenka* 82 (1908): 53-86; Vahylevych to Šafařík, 2 April 1837, in Francev, *Korespondence P. J. Šafaříka*, 2: 938; Iakiv Holovatsky to Mykhailo Malynovsky, 16 November 1848, in Studynsky, *Korespondentsiia*, 311. See also M. Shashkevych's plan for a phonetic orthography, in Vozniak, *Pysannia Markiiana Shashkevycha*, 143-5.
54. See Ivan Holovatsky to his brother Iakiv, 29 October (10 November) 1847, in Studynsky, *Korespondentsiia*, 209.
55. Vozniak, *Pysannia Markiiana Shashkevycha*, 5.
56. Ibid., 203-4.
57. 5/17 May 1840, in Studynsky, *Korespondentsiia*, 59.
58. Ivan Holovatsky to his brother Iakiv, 17/29 May 1840, ibid., 40; Hájek, "Styky Jakiva a Ivan Holovackých," 217-18.
59. Iakiv Holovatsky to his brother Ivan, 5/17 May 1840, in Studynsky, *Korespondentsiia*, 59.
60. 18/30 January-1/13 February 1844, ibid., 105.
61. Vahylevych to Šafařík, 2 April 1837, in Francev, *Korespondence P. J. Šafaříka*, 2: 937.
62. See Dmytro Mokhnatsky's testimony, in Tershakovets, "Materiialy i zamitky do istorii natsionalnoho vidrodzhennia," 167.
63. Romanchuk, *Tvory Shashkevycha, Holovatskoho, Ustyianovycha, Mohylnytskoho*, 4; Lev, "Mova poetiv 'Ruskoi Triitsi'," 86; *Vinok*, pt. 1: 63.
64. 24 September 1848, in Studynsky, *Korespondentsiia*, 296.
65. Biretsky to Iakiv Holovatsky, 1 July 1842, ibid., 64-5.
66. Studynsky, "Materiialy do istorii kulturnoho zhytia v Halychyni," 385.
67. To Vahylevych, 6 Dec. 1845, in Vozniak, "Rozvidky Vahylevycha pro ukrainsku movu," *U stolittia "Zori,"* 2: 323.

7. National and Social Views

1. Bibl. Ossol., ms. 2411/I: "Pisma Jana Wagilewicza. Studia historyczne," 2.
2. Cited in Vozniak, "Z romantychnoho periodu folklornykh zaniat Ia. Holovatskoho," *U stolittia "Zori,"* 1: 109.
3. Ibid., 84.
4. Cited in Vozniak, "Rozvidky Vahylevycha pro ukrainsku movu," *U stolittia "Zori,"* 2: 262*n*.
5. Ibid., 262-3*n*.
6. Tershakovets, "Materiialy i zamitky do istorii natsionalnoho vidrodzhennia," 202-3.

7. Letter of March 1815, Bibl. Jagiell., ms. 2957: 2-5.
8. I. Mohylnytsky, "Vidomist o ruskom iazytsi," *Ukrainsko-ruskyi arkhiv*, 5: 6-7.
9. Ibid., 9-10, 25-36, 60-64.
10. *Grammatik der ruthenischen oder kleinrussischen Sprache*, i.
11. Ibid., iv-ix.
12. Lozynsky, *Gramatyka języka ruskiego*, vii-viii.
13. *Rusalka Dnistrovaia*, ix.
14. *Vinok*, pt. 1: 8-9.
15. Iakiv Holovatsky, *Rosprava o iazytsi iuzhnoruskom i ieho narichiiakh* (Lviv 1849), 14.
16. Ibid., 18-19.
17. Ibid., 27.
18. Ibid., 19, 54.
19. See Władysław Chotkowski, *Historia polityczna Kościoła w Galicji za rządów Marii Teresy*, 2 vols. (Cracow 1909), 2: 408-9.
20. Shchurat, *Na dosvitku novoi doby*, 135.
21. Rusyn, "Zustände der Russinen in Galizien," 378; Kyrylo Studynsky, "Kopitar i Zubrytsky," *Zapysky Naukovoho tovarystva im. Shevchenka* 125 (1918): 147.
22. Ivan Holovatsky to his brother Iakiv, 17/29 October 1842, in Studynsky, *Korespondentsiia*, 69-70.
23. *Rusalka Dnistrovaia*, vi.
24. Iakiv Holovatsky, *Rosprava o iazytsi iuzhnoruskom*, 39.
25. Iakiv Holovatsky, *Istoricheskii ocherk osnovaniia Galitsko-russkoi Matitsy*, 8; Ivan Franko, "Nykola Ustyianovych," *Tvory*, 17: 197.
26. Vahylevych, "Zamitky o ruskoi literaturi," *Ruska biblioteka*, vol. 3: 154.
27. *Rusalka Dnistrovaia*, 115.
28. Vahylevych to M. P. Pogodin, New Year 1839, in *Pisma k M. P. Pogodinu*, 636.
29. *Dennitsa-Jutrzenka*, 1843, pt. 2: 55.
30. Ibid., 52; Svientsitsky, *Materialy do istorii vozrozhdeniia Karpatskoi Rusi*, 1: 151; Vahylevych to Iakiv Holovatsky, 1 July 1844, in Studynsky, *Korespondentsiia*, 126.
31. *Dennitsa-Jutrzenka*, 1843, pt. 3: 125.
32. *Moskvitianin*, 1841, 203-32, 457-67; *Vinok*, pt. 2: 133-206.
33. Iakiv Holovatsky, "Velikaia Khorvatiia," *Vinok*, pt. 2: 138-40.
34. Ibid., 140-42.
35. Iakiv Holovatsky to his brother Ivan, 5/17 May 1840, in Studynsky, *Korespondentsiia*, 58-9.

36. Iakiv Holovatsky, "Velikaia Khorvatiia," *Vinok*, pt. 2: 144-5, 149.
37. *Dennitsa-Jutrzenka*, 1843, pt. 2: 49-50.
38. Ibid., 50-51.
39. Ivan Holovatsky to his brother Iakiv, 17/29 May 1840, in Studynsky, *Korespondentsiia*, 40.
40. 20 July (1 August) 1848, ibid., 278.
41. Vozniak, *Pysannia Markiiana Shashkevycha*, 1-2, 7-9.
42. *Rusalka Dnistrovaia*, ix-xx.
43. Vozniak cites Iakiv Holovatsky to the effect that "the Cossack armies of Khmelnytsky killed none of their captives, but how many unarmed, brave Cossack knights (*lytsari*) fell at the hands of the 'renowned' Polish heroes" ("Z romantychnoho periodu folklornykh zaniat Iakova Holovatskoho," *U stolittia "Zori,"* 1: 90).
44. Antin Liubych-Mohylnytsky, "Slovo o povinnostekh piddanykh," *Vinok*, pt. 2: 16.
45. Vozniak, *Pysannia Markiiana Shashkevycha*, 9-10.
46. *Vinok*, pt. 2: 44.
47. *Rusalka Dnistrovaia*, xii-xiii.
48. Ibid., 97. "Olena" has been the subject of heated controversy among Ukrainian literary historians. See, for example, Zanevych, "Literaturni stremlinnia halytskykh Ukraintsiv," 2: 436; Shchurat, *Na dosvitku novoi doby*, 106; Franko, "Panshchyna ta ii skasuvannia," *Tvory*, 19: 653.
49. See Jiří Horák, "Tři čestí spisovatelé v Haliči," in *Z dějin literatur slovanských* (Prague 1948), 264.
50. Cited in Vozniak, "Rozvidky Vahylevycha pro ukrainsku movu," *U stolittia "Zori,"* 263. Vahylevych wrote articles on the brigands of the Carpathians for *Časopis Českêho Museum*, 1838, 1841.
51. Vozniak, "Z romantychnoho periodu folklornykh zaniat Ia. Holovatskoho," *U stolittia "Zori,"* 1: 93-4; and [Holovatsky,] *Karpatskaia Rus', geograficheskо-statisticheskie i istorichesko-etnograficheskie ocherki Galichiny, severo-vostochnoi Ugrii i Bukoviny. Narodnye pesni Galitskoi i Ugorskoi Rusi sobrannye I. F. Golovatskim*, 4 vols. (Moscow 1878), 3, pt. 2: 709.
52. "Velikaia Khorvatiia," *Vinok*, pt. 2: 172.
53. *Dennitsa-Jutrzenka*, 1842, no. 21: 260.
54. To Iakiv Holovatsky, 24 September 1848, in Studynsky, *Korespondentsiia*, 295.
55. *Vinok*, pt. 2: 184-5.
56. *Dennitsa-Jutrzenka*, 1842, no. 20: 246.
57. Ibid., no. 6: 75-9.
58. Ibid., no. 20: 247.
59. Ibid., 247-8.

60. "Kazky za Zhydiv," *Vinok*, pt. 2: 252-3. See also Luka Dankevych, "Dozhdyk zhydivskii," ibid., pt. 2: 52-4.
61. *Dennitsa-Jutrzenka*, 1842, no. 6: 75. See also ibid., no. 20: 250, and no. 21: 275; and *Vinok*, pt. 2: 346-62. Anti-Semitism was a rather pervasive feature of the Ukrainian awakeners' outlook. See also the examples of Denys Zubrytsky (Studynsky, *Korespondentsiia*, 135) and Luka Dankevych (*Vinok*, pt. 2: 45-54).
62. "Anonimnyi lyst ruskoho popa do tsisaria," in Tershakovets, "Materiialy i zamitky do istorii natsionalnoho vidrodzhennia," 26-37. Iosyf Levytsky is generally acknowledged to be its author.
63. Rusyn, "Zustände der Russinen in Galizien," 376-8.
64. Tershakovets, "Materiialy i zamitky do istorii natsionalnoho vidrodzhennia," 36-7.
65. Pt. 2: 51.
66. 29 November 1844, in Studynsky, *Korespondentsiia*, 135.
67. See *Historia Polski*, vol. 2, pt. 3: *1831-1864* (Warsaw 1959), 68-70.

8. Ties to the Slavic Community

1. Ivan Franko, "Obiavy rusko-polskoho antahonizmu 1831 r.," *Zhytie i slovo*, 1895, pt. 1: 111-13.
2. Kieniewicz, *Adam Sapieha*, 340, 350.
3. Henryk Wereszycki, introduction to Horoszkiewicz, *Notatki z życia*, xxv.
4. Ibid., xxvi.
5. Ibid.; and Kieniewicz, *Adam Sapieha*, 352-4.
6. Wereszycki, introduction to Horoszkiewicz, *Notatki z życia*, xl.
7. *Pamiętniki*, 4 vols. (Cracow 1904), 1: 7. Ziemiałkowski would retain this view in 1848. See Vladimír Hostička, *Spolupráce Čechů a haličských Ukrajinců v letech 1848-1849* (Prague 1965), 56.
8. *Notatki z życia*, 236-7.
9. Zap, *Cesty a procházky po halické zemi*, 57-8.
10. Ibid., 60, 86-7.
11. *Dennitsa-Jutrzenka*, 1842, no. 6: 81.
12. 5/17 May 1840, in Studynsky, *Korespondentsiia*, 58. Cf. Herbilsky, *Peredova suspilna dumka v Halychyni*, 107.
13. Iakiv Holovatsky to Osyp Bodiansky, 26 July 1848, in Studynsky, *Korespondentsiia*, 5, 19.
14. *Vinok*, pt. 2: 230-39.
15. Rusyn, "Zustände der Russinen in Galizien," 18.
16. To his brother Petro, 13/25 May 1848, in Studynsky, *Korespondentsiia*, 248-9.

17. Tershakovets, "Materiialy i zamitky do istorii natsionalnoho vidrodzhennia," 22-3.
18. Shchurat, *Na dosvitku novoi doby*, 112-13.
19. Tershakovets, "Do zhyttiepysu Shashkevycha," 96-7; Shashkevych to T. Wasilewski, 24 May 1835, Bibl. Ossol., ms. 4364/II: 173-4; Vozniak, *Pysannia Markiiana Shashkevycha*, 228; T. Wasilewski to Shashkevych, 20 October 1837, in *Ruska biblioteka*, vol. 3: 63-4.
20. "K istorii galitsko-russkoi pismennosti," 657.
21. See Vahylevych to W. A. Maciejowski, 19 September 1847, Bibl. Ossol., ms. 5819/III: 73. See also Handelsman, *Ukraińska polityka Czartoryskiego*, 69*n*.
22. "Pisma Jana Wagilewicza. Studia historyczne," Bibl. Ossol., ms. 2411/I, book 1: 2.
23. 4 January 1843, in *Pisma k M. P. Pogodinu*, pt. 3: 568.
24. See Ivan Biretsky to Iakiv Holovatsky, 24 and 30 March 1840, in Studynsky, *Korespondentsiia*, 26-7.
25. Iakiv Holovatsky to Vahylevych, 6 December 1845, cited in Vozniak, "Rozvidky Vahylevycha pro ukrainsku movu," *U stolittia "Zori,"* 2: 324. See also Ivan Franko, "Do biohrafii Ivana Vahylevycha," *Zapysky Naukovoho tovarystva im. Shevchenka* 79 (1907): 97-141.
26. See Iakiv Holovatsky's caustic remarks in "Subda odnogo galitsko-russkogo uchenogo," *Kievskaia starina*, 1883: 464-72. See also Stefan Kieniewicz, "Galicja w latach 1846-1848," in *W stulecie Wiosny Ludów 1848-1849*, vol. 1: *Wiosna Ludów na ziemiach polskich* (Warsaw 1948), 313.
27. Maciejowski to Iakiv Holovatsky, 30 October 1838 and 14 November 1839, in Studynsky, *Korespondentsiia*, 14, 19.
28. See Ivan Holovatsky to his brother Iakiv, 18/30 January-1/13 March 1844, and Zap to Iakiv Holovatsky, 19 April 1844 and 25 July 1846, ibid., 112, 114, 123, 176.
29. In *Literaturnyi sbornik*, 1885, no. 1: 13-14. See also M. Vozniak, "Do dzherel ukrainskoho pisennoho zbirnyka Zhehoty Pavli," *U stolittia "Zori,"* 2: 149; and Iakiv Holovatsky, "K istorii galitsko-russkoi pismennosti," *Kievskaia starina*, 1883: 647.
30. Vozniak, "Do dzherel ukrainskoho pisennoho zbirnyka Zhehoty Pavli," *U stolittia "Zori,"* 2: 160-90.
31. Bibl. Jagiell., ms. 5391, vol. 2: 140. See also Vozniak, "Do dzherel ukrainskoho pisennoho zbirnyka Zhehoty Pavli," *U stolittia "Zori,"* 2: 173-5, 190-92.
32. Cf. Herbilsky, *Peredova suspilna dumka v Halychyni*, 106.
33. Cited in Kyrylo Studynsky, "Pavlo Iosyf Shafaryk i Ukraintsi," *Nasha kultura* 7, 1935: 401–12 (published separately, 5-6). See also *Z dejín československo-ukrajinských vzt'ahov* (Bratislava 1957), 316, 535.
34. See M. Vozniak, "Kralodvorskyi rukopys v ukrainskim pysmenstvi," *U stolittia "Zori,"* 1: 128-9; Mykhailo Tershakovets, "Koroledvorska rukopys v

perekladi Markiiana Shashkevycha," *Zapysky Naukovoho tovarystva im. Shevchenka* 68 (1905): 2; Ivan Bryk, "Liubushyn sud v ukrainskim perekladi Kaz. Ios. Turivskoho z 1835 r.," ibid., 128 (1919): 126.

35. Ivan Bryk, "Pereklady serbskykh narodnikh pisen u 'Rusaltsi Dnistrovii'," *Zapysky Naukovoho tovarystva im. Shevchenka* 99 (1930): 213-31; M. I. Holberg, "Pivdennoslovianski zviazky 'Ruskoi Triitsi' (Z istorii pershykh ukrainskykh perekladiv serbskykh narodnykh pisen)," *Mizhslovianski literaturni vzaiemyny*, 1961, no. 2: 225-37.

36. "Puteshestvie Iakova F. G. po Prikarpatskoi Rusi i Vengrii," *Literaturnyi sbornik*, 1886, no. 1: 97. See also Iakiv Holovatsky to his brother Ivan, 5/17 May 1840, in Studynsky, *Korespondentsiia*, 58.

37. Fran Kurelac to Iakiv Holovatsky, 23 October 1837, in Studynsky, *Korespondentsiia*, 7.

38. Ivan Holovatsky to his brother Iakiv, 27 Aug. 1841, 17/29 October 1842, and 8 March 1844, ibid., 56, 66-7, 109.

39. Ivan Holovatsky to his brother Iakiv, 24 July (5 Aug.) 1847, ibid., 196; Iakiv Holovatsky to Osyp Bodiansky, 24 October (5 November) 1844, in Savchenko, *Zakhidnia Ukraina v lystuvanni*, 14.

40. Ivan Holovatsky to his brother Iakiv, 8 March 1844, in Studynsky, *Korespondentsiia*, 109.

41. K. V. Zap to Iakiv Holovatsky, 20 October 1839, Ivan Holovatsky to his brother Iakiv, 15/27 Aug. 1841, 8 March 1844, and 19 March 1845, ibid., 21, 57, 109, 149; Hájek, "Styky Jakiva a Ivana Holovackých," 216. See also Felczak, *Węgierska polityka narodowościowa*, 38ff.

42. See Ivan Bryk, "Iosyf Dobrovsky i ukrainoznavstvo," *Zapysky Naukovoho tovarystva im. Shevchenka* 141-3 (1925): 1-35; Bryk, "Iosyf Dobrovsky i ukrainski hramatyky," in *Josef Dobrovský 1753-1829. Sborník statí* (Prague 1929), 23-43; K. Chekhovych, "Dobrovsky i ukrainska mova," *Slavia* 9 (1930-31): 697-725.

43. In "Vidomist o ruskom iazytsi," *Ukrainsko-ruskyi arkhiv* 5: 1-70. See also Makovei, "Z istorii nashoi filolohii," 51: 11-13.

44. In a review of Ivan Mohylnytsky's *Nauka khristianskaia* (Buda 1815). See also Makovei, "Z istorii nashoi filolohii," 51: 9-10.

45. 2 April 1837, in *Ukrainsko-ruskyi arkhiv* 5 (1910): 21; and Francev, *Korespondence P. J. Šafaříka*, 2: 937.

46. Pp. 138-42. See also Vladimír Hostička, "Pavel Josef Šafařík a Ukrajinci," in *Z dejín československo-ukrajinských vzt'ahov*, 299-300; and Hostička, "Ukrajina v názorech české obrozenecké společnosti do roku 1848," *Slavia* 33 (1964): 562.

47. Pavel Josef Šafařík, *Slovanský národopis*, 4th ed. (Prague 1955), 17-20, 31-39, 146-8.

48. Hostička, "Ukrajina v názorech české obrozenecké společnosti," 561.

49. On Zap's activities in Galicia, see Horák, "Tři čeští spisovatelé v Haliči," 209-73; Vladimír Hostička, "Karel Vladislav Zap a haličští Ukrajinci," in

Kapitoly z dějin vzájemných vztahů národů ČSR a SSSR (Prague 1958), 69-115; and Hostička, "K. V. Zap—přitel ukrajinského lidu," *Slovanský přehled* 43 (1957): 123-4.

50. See Václav Žáček, "Ze styků Čechů a zapadních Ukrajinců v revolučnich letech 1848-1849," in *Z dejín československo-ukrajinských vzt'ahov*, 356. See also Zap to Iakiv Holovatsky, 19 April 1844, in Studynsky, *Korespondentsiia*, 122; and Hostička, "Ukrajina v názorech české obrozenecké společnosti," 568.

51. Cited in Ivan Bryk, ed., "Materiialy do istorii ukrainsko-cheskykh vzaiemyn v pershii polovyni XIX st.," *Ukrainsko-ruskyi arkhiv* 15 (1921): 144.

52. Ibid., 569-70.

53. See Vladimír Hostička, "Havlíčův rozchod z Josefem Bodjanským (K otázce Havlíčkova odchodu z Ruska)," *Slavia* 31 (1962): 613-18; and Herbilsky, *Rozvytok prohresyvnykh idei v Halychyni*, 193-5.

54. Henryk Batowski, *Przyjaciele Słowianie. Szkice historyczne z życia Mickiewicza* (Warsaw 1956), 70-71, 108-10, 197*n*.; Havryło Rusyn, "Zustände der Russinen in Galizien," 376ff. See also Handelsman, *Ukraińska polityka Czartoryskiego*, 77. Leo Thun's works *Über den gegenwärtigen Stand der böhmischen Literatur und ihre Bedeutung* (1842) and *Die Stellung der Slowaken in Ungarn* (1843) were known in Galicia and cited by Iakiv Holovatsky in his writings.

55. Cited in Kollár, *Wybôr pism*, lxvii. On the meaning of Kollár for the Ukrainian awakening, see I. Pañkevyč, "Západnoukrajinské literárne obrodenie a Ján Kollár," in *Z dejín československo-ukrajinských vzt'ahov*, 269-94; Ivan Franko, "Literaturne vidrodzhennia poludnevoi Rusi i Ian Kollár," *Tvory*, 18: 254-63; Franko, "Slovianska vzaiemnist v rozuminni Iana Kollara i teper," *Tvory*, 18: 235-53; Józef Ciągwa, "Słowackie koncepcje wzajemności słowiańskiej w XIX w." *Kwartalnik Historyczny* 77 (1970): 137-49.

56. Herder, *Outlines of a Philosophy of the History of Man*, 482-4; Hájek, "Styky Jakiva a Ivana Holovackých," 219-20; Iakiv Holovatsky to his brother Ivan, 5/17 May 1840, in Studynsky, *Korespondentsiia*, 57-9.

57. Cited in Hostička, "Ukrajina v názorech české obrozenecké společnosti," 562.

58. Kollár, *Wybôr pism*, 36-7. See also Makovei, "Z istorii nashoi filolohii," 51: 28.

59. "Vozrozhdenie Galitskoi Rusi," *Rodimyi listok*, July 1880, no. 2: 28. Cf. Pañkevyč, "Západnoukrajinské literárne obrodenie a Ján Kollár," 275, 278.

60. Cited in Hostička, "Ukrajina v názorech české obrozenecké společnosti," 564. See also Kudělka, "Kollárova koncepce slovanské vzájemnosti," 126.

61. Holovatsky, "Podróż po Halickiej i Węgierskiej Rusi," *Dennitsa-Jutrzenka*, 1842: 299.

62. Cited in Hájek, "Styky Jakiva a Ivana Holovackých," 218.

63. Podlipský thought that the Austrian Slavs should unite in a republican federation on the model of the United States. Kampelík believed that the

Ukrainians would play a major role in the liquidation of the tsarist empire and then, together with the Poles, would liberate the other Slavs. Ibid., 226.

64. Ivan Holovatsky to his brother Iakiv, 13 April 1840, ibid., 217-18. Cf. Herbilsky, *Rozvytok prohresyvnykh idei v Halychyni*, 116; and Pañkevyč, "Západnoukrajinske literárne obrodenie a Ján Kollár," 287.
65. Cited in Hájek, "Styky Jakiva a Ivana Holovackých," 216. See also Ivan Holovatsky to his brother Iakiv, 15/27 Aug. 1841, in Studynsky, *Korespondentsiia*, 56-7.
66. Ivan Holovatsky to his brother Iakiv, 18/30 January-1/13 March 1844, in Studynsky, *Korespondentsiia*, 105.
67. Žáček, "Ze styků Čechů a západních Ukrajinců," 354-5*n*.
68. Vahylevych to Šafařík, 2 April 1837, in Bryk, "Materiialy do istorii ukrainsko-cheskykh vzaiemyn," 21; and Francev, *Korespondence P. J. Šafaříka*, 2: 937-8.
69. Vahylevych to Pogodin, 9 July 1837, in *Pisma k M. P. Pogodinu*, 631. See also Bryk, "Materiialy do istorii ukrainsko-cheskykh vzaiemyn," 22*n*.
70. Hájek, "Styky Jakiva a Ivana Holovackých," 221-3; Podlipský to Iakiv Holovatsky, 12 April 1840, in Studynsky, *Korespondentsiia*, 29.
71. See Studynsky, *Korespondentsiia*, 121-2, 125, 130, 148, 162-6, 178, 181, 377; Francev, *Korespondence P. J. Šafaříka*, 1: 74, 82, 85, 87, 92, 96-8, 102-3. See also Osyp Bodiansky to August Bielowski, 25 June 1857, Bibl. Ossol., ms. 2432/II, vol. 1: 175-8.
72. Vahylevych to Iakiv Holovatsky, 1 July 1843, and Zap to Iakiv Holovatsky, 12 September 1843, 26 February 1844 and 31 May 1844, in Studynsky, *Korespondentsiia*, 86, 88, 120-22, 125. On Havlíček's mission in Russia, see also Hostička, "Ukrajina v názorech české obrozenecké společnosti," 572-3.
73. Francev, *Korespondence P. J. Šafaříka*, 1: 360, 363; 2: 518-19.
74. Šafařík to Koeppen, 6/18 October 1836, and Šafařík to Pogodin, 24 October 1836, ibid., 1: 363, 2: 523. See also ibid., 2: 930-35; and Vahylevych to Šafařík, 3 October 1836, in Bryk, "Materiialy do istorii ukrainsko-cheskykh vzaiemyn," 1-13.
75. Holovatsky, "K istorii galitsko-russkoi pismennosti," *Kievskaia starina*, 1883: 658-62; Francev, *Korespondence P. J. Šafaříka*, 1: lxxxvi; Herbilsky, *Rozvytok prohresyvnykh idei v Halychyni*, 182.
76. "Bojkové, lid ruskoslovanský v Haliči," *Časopis Českêho Museum*, 1841: 30-72.
77. Vahylevych to Šafařík, 3 October 1836, in Bryk, "Materiialy do istorii ukrainsko-cheskykh vzaiemyn," 10, 20-21; Francev, *Korespondence P. J. Šafaříka*, 1: 243, 283; 2: 934, 936; Šafařík to Holovatsky, 24 October 1838, in Studynsky, *Korespondentsiia*, 12.
78. Francev, *Korespondence P. J. Šafaříka*, 1: 243, 464-5.
79. Iakiv Holovatsky to Šafařík, 20 September 1837, ibid., 1: 280-82, 288*n*. See also ibid., 2: 564*n*.

80. Cited in J. Hůrský, "Vznik a poslání Šafaříkova slovanského zeměvidu," in Šafařík, *Slovanský národopis*, 259.
81. Bryk, "Materiialy do istorii ukrainsko-cheskykh vzaiemyn," 25-6, 29-31; Francev, *Korespondence P. J. Šafaříka*, 2: 940-42, 944-5; Hůrský in Šafařík, *Slovanský národopis*, 260.
82. Zap to Šafařík, 10 July 1842, in Bryk, "Materiialy do istorii ukrainsko-cheskykh vzaiemyn," 141-2; Francev, *Korespondence P. J. Šafaříka*, 1: 288-90.
83. Zap to Šafařík, 10 July 1842, in Bryk, "Materiialy do istorii ukrainsko-cheskykh vzaiemyn," 141.
84. As a consequence, the so-called Pogodin Colony, the germ of the later Russophile party, took shape in Lviv in the 1850s.
85. *Ruskalka Dnistrovaia*, iii-vi; *Ruska biblioteka*, vol. 3, 154, 346-7, 349-52.
86. See Handelsman, *Ukraińska polityka Czartoryskiego*, 2.
87. On Kotliarevsky, see the recent biography by P. K. Volynsky, *Ivan Kotliarevsky. Zhyttia i tvorchist* (Kiev 1969).
88. See O. I. Honchar, *Hryhorii Kvitka-Osnovianenko. Zhyttia i tvorchist* (Kiev 1969).
89. A recent biography of Shevchenko is Ievhen P. Kyryliuk, *T. H. Shevchenko. Zhyttia i tvorchist* (Kiev 1959).
90. Mykhailo Hrushevsky, *Iliustrovana istoriia Ukrainy* (Kiev and Lviv 1911), 523.
91. See Biretsky to Iakiv Holovatsky, 31 January 1841, in Studynsky, *Korespondentsiia*, 23-4. See also Ivan Holovatsky to his brother Iakiv, 4 April 1845 and 7/19 October 1845, ibid., 143, 155.
92. See *Rusalka Dnistrovaia*, iii-vi; Vozniak, *Pysannia Markiiana Shashkevycha*, 146-7; Pogodin to Vahylevych, 27 October 1836 and 17 October 1837, and Bodiansky to Vahylevych, 18 March 1838, in Vozniak, "Rozvidky Vahylevycha pro ukrainsku movu," *U stolittia "Zori,"* 2: 308-10.
93. See Studynsky, *Korespondentsiia*, 11-12, 89, 122, 128, 130, 135, 149, 181-2, 353, 386-7.
94. See Pogodin to Vahylevych, 27 October 1836, in Vozniak, "Rozvidky Vahylevycha pro ukrainsku movu," *U stolittia "Zori,"* 2: 308; Zubrytsky to Pogodin, 17 March 1845, in *Pisma k M. P. Pogodinu*, 578; M. Raevsky to Iakiv Holovatsky, 9 November 1849, in Studynsky, *Korespondentsiia*, 403; Bodiansky to Bielowski, 25 June 1857, Bibl. Ossol., ms. 2432/II, vol. 1: 175-8.
95. See Studynsky, *Korespondentsiia*, 88, 123, 298, 302, 416. See also Shchurat, *Vybrani pratsi z istorii literatury*, 148-51.
96. See Studynsky, *Korespondentsiia*, 85, 150, 163.
97. M. Maksymovych, "O stikhotvoreniiakh chervonorusskikh," *Kievlianin*, 1841, book 2: 119-52. See also Shchurat, *Vybrani pratsi z istorii literatury*, 136-7.

98. Svientsitsky, *Materialy do istorii vozrozhdeniia Karpatskoi Rusi*, 145-52; Herbilsky, *Rozvytok prohresyvnykh idei v Halychyni*, 57, 197-8; M. K. Hudzii, *Rosiisko-ukrainske literaturne iednannia* (Kiev 1954), 46; *Pisma k M. P. Pogodinu*, 568, 648.

99. Zap to Iakiv Holovatsky, 12 September 1843, 26 February 1844 and 31 May 1844, in Studynsky, *Korespondentsiia*, 89, 120-21, 125.

100. Iakiv Holovatsky to Bodiansky, 24 October (5 November) 1844 and 12 February 1845, in Savchenko, *Zakhidnia Ukraina v lystuvanni*, 11-12, 14.

101. Zap to Iakiv Holovatsky, 12 February 1846, in Studynsky, *Korespondentsiia*, 164. See also Iakiv Holovatsky to Bodiansky, 26 July 1846, in Savchenko, *Zakhidnia Ukraina v lystuvanni*, 18.

102. Pogodin to Vahylevych, 27 May (8 June) 1836 and 17/26 October 1837, in Vozniak, "Rozvidky Vahylevycha pro ukrainsku movu," *U stolittia "Zori,"* 2: 306, 309.

103. Pogodin to Vahylevych, 27 October 1836 and 5 October 1837, ibid., 308-9; Svientsitsky, *Materialy do istorii vozrozhdeniia Karpatskoi Rusi*, 145-52; Vahylevych to Pogodin, 4/16 October 1840 and 3 January 1842, in *Pisma k M. P. Pogodinu*, 637, 639.

104. *Pisma k M. P. Pogodinu*, 543.

105. I. S. Svientsitsky, *Obzor snoshenii Karpatskoi Rusi s Rossiei v 1-uiu polovinu XIX v.* (Saint Petersburg 1906), 54-5.

106. Pogodin's reports, ibid., 55-8, 63-5.

107. N. P. Barsukov, *Zhizn i trudy M. P. Pogodina*, 22 vols. (Saint Petersburg 1888-1910), 5: 203-4.

108. Svientsitsky, *Obzor snoshenii Karpatskoi Rusi s Rossiei*, 23.

109. Zubrytsky to Pogodin, 10 March 1841, and Vahylevych to Pogodin, 3 January 1842, in *Pisma k M. P. Pogodinu*, 563, 639; *Ruska biblioteka*, 3: 176.

110. Tershakovets, "Materiialy i zamitky do istorii natsionalnoho vidrodzhennia," 114; Vahylevych to Pogodin, 1/13 July 1845, in *Pisma k M. P. Pogodinu*, 648; *Ruska biblioteka*, 3: 186.

111. See Svientsitsky, *Obzor snoshenii Karpatskoi Rusi s Rossiei*, 71-2, 164, 172. See also M. Vozniak, *Iak probudylosia ukrainske narodne zhyttia v Halychyni za Avstrii* (Lviv 1924), 54.

112. Cited in Herbilsky, *Rozvytok prohresyvnykh idei v Halychyni*, 201.

113. Svientsitsky, *Materialy do istorii vozrozhdeniia Karpatskoi Rusi*, 172.

114. Ivan Holovatsky to Sreznevsky, 4/16 May 1846, ibid., 170-71. Cf. Herbilsky, *Rozvytok prohresyvnykh idei v Halychyni*, 201.

115. Lukashevych to Iakiv Holovatsky, 26 September 1839, and Vahylevych to Iakiv Holovatsky, 9 November 1843, in Studynsky, *Korespondentsiia*, 18, 91-2. See also Lukashevych to Vahylevych, 21 September 1843, in Vozniak, "Rozvidky Vahylevycha pro ukrainsku movu," *U stolittia "Zori,"* 2: 310-12.

116. M. Vozniak, *Kyrylo-Metodiivske bratstvo* (Lviv 1921), 128; Handelsman, *Ukraińska polityka Czartoryskiego*, 22*n*.

117. Lukashevych to Vahylevych, 19 January and 6 July 1844, in Vozniak, "Rozvidky Vahylevycha pro ukrainsku movu," *U stolittia "Zori,"* 2: 315, 318.

118. Vahylevych to Maksymovych, 17 Aug. 1838, in *Russkii filologicheskii Vestnik* 68, no. 4 (1912): 413; Maksymovych to Zubrytsky, 22 April-13 May 1840, in Studynsky, "Z korespondentsii Zubrytskoho," 25-8. See also Handelsman, *Ukraińska polityka Czartoryskiego*, 78-9; Herbilsky, *Peredova suspilna dumka v Halychyni*, 100.

119. See Biretsky to Iakiv Holovatsky, 1/13 November 1840, in Studynsky, *Korespondentsiia*, 46. Cf. Herbilsky, *Peredova suspilna dumka v Halychyni*, 100; and Shalata, *M. Shashkevych*, 90, 103.

120. Rusyn, "Zustände der Russinen in Galizien," 378-9.

9. The Crossroads

1. Rusyn, "Zustände der Russinen in Galizien," 378-9.

2. See Stefan Kieniewicz, "Sprawa włościańska w galicyjskim sejmie stanowym (1843-1845)," *Sobôtka* 3 (1948): 168-70.

3. Levytsky to Iakhymovych, 27 April 1848, in Studynsky, "Materiialy do istorii kulturnoho zhytia v Halychyni," 311-12.

4. Zubrytsky to Pogodin, 28 April 1846, in *Pisma k M. P. Pogodinu*, 580.

5. Cited in Handelsman, *Ukraińska polityka Czartoryskiego*, 72.

6. Vahylevych to Maciejowski, 19 September 1847, Bibl. Ossol., ms. 5419/III: 73. See also Handelsman, *Ukraińska polityka Czartoryskiego*, 69*n*.

7. Studynsky, "Prychynky do istorii kulturnoho zhyttia Halytskoi Rusy," lxxxv-lxxxvi; Studynsky, "Kopitar i Zubrytsky," 115-64.

8. Ivan Holovatsky to his brother Iakiv, 17/29 October 1842, in Studynsky, *Korespondentsiia*, 69-70.

9. 18/30 December 1842, ibid., 74-5.

10. 9/21 May 1843, ibid., 79-80.

11. Zubrytsky to Pogodin, 4 January 1843, in *Pisma k M. P. Pogodinu*, 568.

12. See Ivan Holovatsky to his brother Iakiv, 18/30 December 1842, in Studynsky, *Korespondentsiia*, 74.

13. 22 October (4 November) 1843, in Savchenko, *Zakhidnia Ukraina v lystuvanni*, 7.

14. Hostička, "Ukrajina v názorech české obrozenecké společnosti," 572-3.

15. In a letter to his brother Iakiv, 18/30 December 1842, in Studynsky, *Korespondentsiia*, 75.

16. See Studynsky, "Prychynky do istorii kulturnoho zhytia Halytskoi Rusy," lxxxvi. Cf. F. I. Svistun, "Proekt avstro-russkoi literaturnoi vremenopisi v

1842 g.," *Vestnik Narodnogo doma*, 1906: 60-62, 65-70, 80-87, 111-19.

17. Rusyn, "Zustände der Russinen in Galizien," 369-79.
18. See Rudnytsky, "Ukrainians in Galicia," 405-8.
19. *Vinok*, pt. 2: 224, 226, 228.
20. See František Jachim to Iakiv Holovatsky, 24 March 1847, in Studynsky, *Korespondentsiia*, 184.
21. I. V. Sokulsky to Iakiv Holovatsky, 20 October 1847, ibid., 207.
22. To his brother Iakiv, 17/29 May 1847, ibid., 188-9. Iakiv Holovatsky did not reveal to his brother that he himself was the author and admitted that he was in fact Havryło Rusyn only in the 1880s. See *Literaturnyi sbornik*, 1885, no. 1: 40.
23. See Studynsky, *Korespondentsiia*, 204, 207, 210-11.
24. D. Zubrzycki [Zubrytsky], *Granice między ruskim i polskim narodem* (Lviv 1849). On the campaign to partition Galicia, see below.
25. Ivan Holovatsky to his brother Iakiv, 27 July (5 August) 1847, in Studynsky, *Korespondentsiia*, 195.

10. The Dawn

1. Ludwik Jabłonowski, *Pamiętniki*, ed. Karol Lewicki (Cracow 1963), 265-6.
2. *Dziennik Narodowy*, 1848, no. 2: 5.
3. Iakhymovych to Levytsky, 4 August 1847, 17 January 1848, 4 and 10 February 1848; and Levytsky to Iakhymovych, 19 February 1848, in Studynsky, "Materiialy do kulturnoho zhytia v Halychyni," 255, 274, 281-5, 287.
4. Iakhymovych to Levytsky, 10 February 1848, ibid., 283; Iakiv Holovatsky to his brother Petro, 1 April 1848, and Iuliian Vyslobotsky to Iakiv Holovatsky, 9 May 1848, in Kyrylo Studynsky, ed., *Korespondentsiia*, 228, 261. Cf. *Zoria Halytska*, 1848, no. 1: 4.
5. Zubrytsky to Iakiv Holovatsky, 2 March 1848, in Studynsky, *Korespondentsiia*, 222. See also K. Ostaszewski-Barański, "U kolebki prasy ruskiej," in *Rus'*, pt. 3 (Lviv 1911), 268-70; Ivan Bryk, "Pochatky ukrainskoi presy v Halychyni i lvivska Stavropyhiia," *Zbirnyk Lvivskoi Stavropyhii*, 1: 108-9; and Kosachevskaia, *Vostochnaia Galitsiia*, 43.
6. Iakhymovych to Levytsky, 10 February 1848, and Levytsky to Iakhymovych, 19 February 1848, in Studynsky, "Materiialy kulturnoho zhytia v Halychyni," 285, 287.
7. Zubrytsky to Antin Petrushevych, 3 March 1848, LBAN, fond A. S. Petrushevycha, ms. 207/p. 5; and Zubrytsky to Iakiv Holovatsky, 2 March 1848, in Studynsky, *Korespondentsiia*, 222.
8. Ibid.
9. Levytsky to Iakhymovych, 24 February 1848, in Studynsky, "Materiialy kulturnoho zhytia v Halychyni," 290-91.

10. Iakhymovych to Levytsky, 11 March 1848, ibid., 302. Cf. Zubrytsky to Petrushevych, 3 March 1848, LBAN, fond A. S. Petrushevycha, ms. 207/p. 5.
11. Zubrytsky to Petrushevych, 3 March 1848, LBAN, fond A. S. Petrushevycha, ms. 207/p. 5; and M. Vozniak, "Z zarannia ukrainskoi presy v Halychyni," *Zapysky Naukovoho tovarystva im. Shevchenka* 111 (1912): 141.
12. Liubych-Mohylnytsky to Iakiv Holovatsky, 24 February 1848; Iakiv Holovatsky to Zubrytsky, 11 March 1848; and Mykola Vereshchynsky to Iakiv Holovatsky, 27 March 1848, in Studynsky, *Korespondentsiia*, 219, 223-5.
13. Zubrytsky to Iakiv Holovatsky, 28 March 1848, ibid., 226-7.
14. Iakhymovych to Levytsky, 21 February 1848; and Levytsky to Iakhymovych, 24 February 1848, in Studynsky, "Materiialy kulturnoho zhytia v Halychyni," 289-90.
15. Iakhymovych to Levytsky, 27 February and 11 March 1848; and Levytsky to Iakhymovych, 29 February 1848, ibid., 292, 294, 299-300. Cf. Iakiv Holovatsky to Osyp Bodiansky, 20 March 1848, in Savchenko, *Zakhidnia Ukraina v lystuvanni*, 22.
16. See letters to Jan Federowicz, 4 and 8 March 1848, in Ivan Franko, "Prychynky do istorii 1848 r.," *Zapysky Naukovoho tovarystva im. Shevchenka* 88 (1909): 95-6.
17. Z. Zamoyski to Leon Sapieha, Vienna, 16 March 1848, LBAN, fond Sapiehów, ms. 600/IVa, no. 51. Ivan Holovatsky in a letter of 8 June 1848 to his brother Iakiv (Studynsky, *Korespondentsiia*, 255) assessed the events in Vienna quite differently from the Poles. Cf. Władysław Zawadzki, *Dziennikarstwo w Galicji w roku 1848* (Lviv 1878), 19ff.
18. Text reprinted in Marian Tyrowicz, ed., *Galicja od pierwszego rozbioru do Wiosny Ludôw, 1772-1848. Wybôr tekstôw źrôdłowych* (Wrocław 1878), 205-7.
19. F. Ziemiałkowski, *Pamiętniki*, 2: 79. Cf. I. S. Miller, "Na kanune otmeny barshchiny v Galitsii (Iz istorii ideino-politicheskoi borby v polskom obshchestve v 30-40 godakh XIX stoletiia)," *Uchenye zapiski Instituta slavianovedeniia* 1 (1949): 201.
20. *Dziennik Narodowy*, 24 March 1848, no. 1: 2.
21. Ibid., no. 2: 5; and *Vestnik Narodnogo doma*, 1909: 36, which reproduced a contemporary letter from Lviv describing the events of 19-21 March 1848.
22. T. Wasilewski to Jan Federowicz, 3 April 1848, in *Zapysky Naukovoho tovarystva im. Shevchenka* 88 (1909): 105; and Anna z Zamoyskich Sapieżyna to Leon Sapieha, 28 March 1848, LBAN, fond Sapiehów, ms. 583/IVa, in which she wrote, "It is necessary to make a neighbour of the peasant, and not a demanding subject."
23. Appeal of Rada Narodowa of 17 April 1848, in K. Ostaszewski-Barański, *Rok złudzeń (1848). Opowiadanie historyczne* (Zolochiv 1898), 171-2; and

Tyrowicz, *Galicja od pierwszego rozbioru do Wiosny Ludów*, 229-30. See also Adam Czartoryski to Leon Sapieha, 24 March 1848, LBAN, fond Sapiehów, ms. 574/IVa: 216; and Z. Zamoyski to Sapieha, 6 April 1848, ibid., fond Sapiehów, ms. 600/IVa, no. 71.

24. Piotr Stebelski, "Lwów w 1848 r. Na podstawie aktów śledczych," *Kwartalnik Historyczny* 23 (1909): 346-51. For a discussion of the address, see Konstanty Grzybowski, *Galicja 1848-1914. Historia ustroju politycznego na tle historii ustroju Austrii* (Wrocław 1959), 7-8.

25. Z. Zamoyski to L. Sapieha, 6 April 1848, LBAN, fond Sapiehów, ms. 600/IVa, no. 71.

26. A. Gickiewicz to Jan Federowicz, 22 March 1848, in *Zapysky Naukovoho tovarystva im. Shevchenka* 88 (1909): 101-2; *Dziennik Narodowy*, 1848, nos. 6, 9, 11, 23-5, 35, 43; Ostaszewski-Barański, *Rok złudzeń*, 173; Stefan Kieniewicz, "Sprawa włościańska w Galicji w 1848 r.," *Przegląd Historyczny* 38 (1948): 78-9.

27. B. Shchutsky (Szczucki), *Do moikh bratei ludu halytskoho* (Buchach 1848), LBAN, fond Pavlykovskykh, ms. 72-1: 28-9; Ivan Koval z Tovmacha Kavetsky, *Do moikh Bratei Rusyniv* (Tovmach 1848), ibid., fond Naukovoho tovarystva im. T. Shevchenka, ms. 19/1: 438-40.

28. Iakhymovych to Levytsky, 21 March 1848, in Studynsky, "Materiialy kulturnoho zhytia v Halychyni," 303; Kieniewicz, "Sprawa włościańska," 86ff.; J. A. Helfert, *Geschichte der österreichischen Revolution im Zusammenhange mit der mitteleuropäischen Bewegung der Jahre 1848-1849*, 2 vols. (Freiburg im Breisgau and Vienna 1909), 2: 21; *Dziennik Narodowy*, 1848, nos. 4, 5: 15-16, 19-21; LBAN, fond Sapiehów, ms. 602/IVB, nos. 126-8.

29. *Gazeta Lwowska*, 1848, no. 39: 353; J. Załuski to L. Sapieha, 24 March 1848, LBAN, fond Sapiehów, ms. 585/IVa, no. 26; ibid., fond Naukovoho tovarystva im. T. Shevchenka, ms. 19/1: 384-9; *Dziennik Narodowy*, 1848, no. 24: 99-102; I. Krevetsky, *Tsutsylivska trivoha v 1848* (Lviv 1906).

30. Bronisław Łoziński, *Agenor hrabia Gołuchowski w pierwszym okresie rządów swoich* (*1846-1859*) (Lviv 1901), 37, 41.

31. Roman Rozdolski, "Nowe dokumenty do historii zniesienia pańszczyzny w Galicji w r. 1848," *Przegląd Historyczny* 53, no. 1 (1962): 120; *Gazeta Narodowa*, 1848, no. 44: 172. Cf. Karol Widmann, *Franciszek Smolka, jego życie i zawód publiczny. Od roku 1810 do 1849* (Lviv 1886), 177; and Łoziński, *Gołuchowski*, 46.

32. Rozdolski, "Nowe dokumenty," 120-22; Kosachevskaia, *Vostochnaia Galitsiia*, 83-5.

33. Kieniewicz, "Sprawa włościańska," 90; LBAN, fond Sapiehów, ms. 602/IVB, nos. 129-30.

34. *Rada Narodowa*, 1848, nos. 1, 3: 2, 9-10; Stefan Kieniewicz, ed., *Rok 1848 w Polsce. Wybór źródeł* (Wrocław 1948), 261-3.

35. *Rada Narodowa*, 1848, no. 5: 19; *Dziennik Narodowy*, 1848, no. 27: 111-12. See also Kieniewicz, "Sprawa włościańska," 93ff.

36. *Rada Narodowa*, 1848, no. 5: 22; Kyrylo Khomynsky to Antin Petrushevych, late April 1848, LBAN, fond A. S. Petrushevycha, ms. 369/p. 12, no. 443-B; Staniewicz to L. Sapieha, 25 April 1848, ibid., fond Sapiehów, ms. 578/IVa, no. 8.
37. Maurycy Kraiński to L. Sapieha, 5 May 1848, LBAN, fond Sapiehów, ms. 578/IVa, no. 1: 152.
38. Kraśniański to J. Federowicz, 24 April 1848, in *Zapysky Naukovoho tovarystva im. Shevchenka* 88 (1909): 108; *Rada Narodowa*, 1848, no. 13: 47.
39. Kraiński to L. Sapieha, 5 May 1848, LBAN, fond Sapiehów, ms. 578/IVa, no. 1: 152; Staniewicz to L. Sapieha, ibid., no. 9.
40. Andrzej Przybysławski to Michał Czajkowski, 15 July 1848, ACz, ms. 5362: 23. Cf. Kieniewicz, "Sprawa włościańska," 98; Iakhymovych to Levytsky, 27 April 1848, in Studynsky, "Materiialy kulturnoho zhytia v Halychyni," 319.
41. Staniewicz to L. Sapieha, 25 April 1848, LBAN, fond Sapiehów, ms. 578/IVa, no. 8. Cf. Ostaszewski-Barański, *Rok złudzeń*, 179-80.
42. Rozdolski, "Nowe dokumenty," 122.
43. *Polska*, 1848, no. 1: 1-12; Kraiński to L. Sapieha, 5 May 1848, LBAN, fond Sapiehów, ms. 578/IVa, no. 1: 150-51. Cf. G. P[awlikowski], *Prawdy i cele Stowarzyszenia Ziemiańskiego, zawiązanego dnia 3 maja 1848* (Lviv 1848), LBAN, fond Pavlykovskykh, ms. 281a.
44. For a contemporary defence of Stadion, see *Wiener Zeitung*, 1848, no. 235; and *Zoria Halytska*, 1848, no. 18: 75.
45. *Dziennik Narodowy*, 1848, no. 1: 2; K. Ustyianovych, "Istorychnyi moment 18 marta 1848 r.," *Zhytie i slovo* 2, pt. 3 (1895): 467; I. Biretsky to K. V. Zap, 20 May 1848, in Bryk, "Materiialy do istorii ukrainsko-cheskykh vzaiemyn," 94.
46. To Iakiv Holovatsky, 27 March 1848, in Studynsky, *Korespondentsiia*, 226.
47. Petro Holovatsky to his brother Iakiv, 14 April 1848, and Iakiv Holovatsky to his brother Petro, 1 April 1848, ibid., 227, 235, 237.
48. I. Biretsky to Iakiv Holovatsky, 27 April 1848, ibid., 238-9. Cf. *Postęp*, 1848, no. 4.
49. "Zapysky z zhytia natsionalnoho Rusyniv Vasylia Ilnytskoho," LBAN, fond Naukovoho tovarystva im. T. Shevchenka, ms. 25/1-7a: 1.
50. I. Biretsky to Iakiv Holovatsky, 27 April 1848, in Studynsky, *Korespondentsiia*, 238.
51. To his brother Iakiv, 8 June 1848, ibid., 255.
52. Iakhymovych to Levytsky, 21 March 1848, in Studynsky, "Materiialy kulturnoho zhytia v Halychyni," 302.
53. Ibid., 303.
54. Iakhymovych to Levytsky, 23 March 1848, ibid., 307. Nonetheless, a translation was published; see Ivan Levytsky, *Halytsko-Ruskaia bybliohrafiia XIX-ho stoletiia*, 2 vols. (Lviv 1888-95), 1: 32, no. 374. The

Greek Catholic hierachy was concerned over the fate of its extensive latifundia.

55. Iakhymovych to Levytsky, 21 and 23 March 1848, in Studynsky, "Materiialy kulturnoho zhytia v Halychyni," 303, 305-6.
56. Iakhymovych to Levytsky, 20 April 1848, and Levytsky to Iakhymovych, 27 April 1848, ibid., 311-12.
57. Iakhymovych to Levytsky, 28 March 1848, ibid., 323.
58. Levytsky to Iakhymovych, 30 March 1848, ibid., 324.
59. Iakhymovych to Levytsky, 23 and 28 March 1848, ibid., 307, 322.
60. Iakhymovych to Levytsky, 20 April 1848, ibid., 311.
61. Ivan Bryk, "Slavianskyi zizd u Prazi 1848 r. i ukrainska sprava," *Zapysky Naukovoho tovarystva im. Shevchenka* 129 (1920): 164.
62. K. Khomynsky to A. Petrushevych, n.d., LBAN, fond A. S. Petrushevycha, ms. 369/p. 12, no. 195. The role of Stadion's assistant, Josef W. Eminger, in drafting the address is cited in Aleksander Batowski, *Diariusz wypadków 1848 roku*, ed. Marian Tyrowicz (Wrocław 1974), 164.
63. Text of address in *Zoria Halytska*, 1848, no. 2: 7-8.
64. Ibid., 1848, no. 6: 25.
65. To A. Petrushevych, n.d., LBAN, fond A. S. Petrushevycha, ms. 369/p. 12, no. 195. I. Biretsky wrote on 20 April 1848 to his Czech acquaintance K. V. Zap, "At the present time there is nothing else we can demand, nor do we desire more." Bryk, "Materiialy ukrainsko-cheskykh vzaiemyn," 94.
66. *Rada Narodowa*, 1848, no. 25: 96.
67. Ibid.
68. LBAN, fond T. Pavlykova, ms. 2/p. 1, no. 9: 20.
69. K. Khomynsky to A. Petrushevych, circa April 1848, LBAN, fond A. S. Petrushevycha, ms. 369/p. 12, no. 443B; Levytsky to Iakhymovych, 1 May 1848, in Studynsky, "Materiialy kulturnoho zhytia v Halychyni," 312.
70. *Gazeta Lwowska*, 1848, no. 51, 465-6.
71. Kraiński to L. Sapieha, 5 May 1848, LBAN, fond Sapiehów, ms. 578/IVa, no. 1: 151.
72. Iakhymovych to Levytsky, 7 May 1848, in Studynsky, "Materiialy kulturnoho zhytia v Halychyni," 315.
73. See *Zoria Halytska*, 1848, no. 4, 16.

11. The Councils

1. The Polish newpaper *Rada Narodowa* (25 August 1848, no. 100) charged that the Holovna Rada Ruska was created by Stadion, who availed himself of a proposal from Agenor Gołuchowski. This opinion is echoed by Julian Horoszkiewicz (*Notatki z życia*, 246); Florian Ziemiałkowski (*Pamiętniki*, 2: 31); and J. Kalchberg (*Mein politisches Glaubenskenntniss in*

Gedenkblättern aus einer achtzigjährigen Pilgerfahrt [Leipzig 1881]). Iakiv Holovatsky, in a letter to his brother Petro, wrote that the Holovna Rada Ruska was set up as a consequence of machinations by the Austrian bureaucracy (25 May 1848, in Studynsky, *Korespondentsiia*, 248). Holovatsky's view is repeated by Karol Widmann (*Smolka*, 245-6). Bronisław Łoziński denied that the initial proposal came from Gołuchowski (*Gołuchowski*, 126-9). Maurycy Kraiński in a letter to Prince Leon Sapieha conceded that "the Ruthenian committee" was formed "owing to the behaviour of the [Polish] Rada Narodowa" (5 May 1848, LBAN, fond Sapiehów, ms. 578/IVa: 152).

The prevailing view in Ukrainian writings is that the Ukrainians *themselves* established the Holovna Rada Ruska with Stadion's backing. See, for example, Oleksii Zaklynsky, *Zapysky parokha Starykh Bohorodchan* (Lviv 1890; rpt. Toronto 1960), 38-9; A. P. Shankovsky, "Vospominaniia iz nedavnoi byvalshchyny," *Rodimyi Listok*, 1880, no. 3: 41-2; F. I. Svistun, *Prikarpatskaia Rus' pod vladeniem Avstrii 1850-1896*, 2 vols. (Lviv 1896), 1: 267. D. Vintskovsky, *Grigorii Iakhimovich i sovremennoe russkoe dvizhenie* (Lviv 1892), 50. The view that Stadion "invented" the Ruthenians was disposed of by Józef Szujski, *Z wycieczek do Lwowa. Kwestia ruska* (Cracow 1866), 7; and Henryk Lisicki, *Antoni Zygmunt Helcel 1808-1872*, 2 vols. (Lviv 1882), 1: 305-6. A persuasive defense of Stadion appeared in *Wiener Zeitung*, 29 August 1848, no. 235.

2. Ivan Sozansky, "Z literaturnoi spadshchyny Vasylia Ilnytskoho," *Zapysky Naukovoho tovarystva im. Shevchenka* 66 (1905): 15.
3. *Zoria Halytska*, 1848, no. 7: 27.
4. 1 May 1848, in Studynsky, "Materiialy kulturnoho zhytia v Halychyni," 313.
5. *Zoria Halytska*, 1848, no. 7: 27-8; Zaklynsky, *Zapysky parokha*, 44-5. Cf. *Dziennik Narodowy*, 1848, no. 63: 261.
6. *Zoria Halytska*, 1848, no. 2: 9-10; TDIA, fond 180, op. 2, spr. 2, 4-5.
7. LBAN, fond O. Terletskoho, spr. 144-XIII, 13, 22.
8. Ibid., 15.
9. *Zoria Halytska*, 1848, no. 8: 32.
10. TDIA, fond 180, op. 2, spr. 1, 2-3; and spr. 2, 23.
11. *Zoria Halytska*, 1848, no. 7: 28. The proclamation was dated 10 May.
12. Translation from the Polish text in TDIA, fond 180, op. 2, spr. 6: 1-2.
13. Cyrillic-alphabet text, LBAN, fond R. Mokha, ms. 15/p. 2: 1; Latin-alphabet text in Ukrainian, TDIA, fond 180, op. 2, spr. 2: 12-13.
14. LBAN, fond Naukovoho tovarystva im. T. Shevchenka, ms. 19/1: 415.
15. *Rada Narodowa*, 1848, no. 32 (Zalishchyky); LBAN, fond Pavlykovskykh, ms. 254: 83-6 (Stryi). On the Greek Catholic priest who joined the Polish Rada Narodowa in Stanyslaviv, see LBAN, fond Naukovoho tovarystva im. T. Shevchenka, ms. 19/1: 416. On those in Berezhany, LBAN, fond T. Pavlykova, ms. 2/p. 1, no. 7: 19; and *Vestnik Narodnogo doma*, 1909: 40. Cf. *Rada Narodowa*, 1848, no. 7: 28.

16. Iakiv Holovatsky to his brother Petro, 25 May 1848, and Liubych-Mohylnytsky to Iakiv Holovatsky, 10 July 1848, in Studynsky, *Korespondentsiia*, 249, 263.
17. TDIA, fond 180, op. 2, spr. 2: 9-10. See also Levytsky to Iakhymovych, 16 May 1848, and Iakhymovych to Levytsky, 18 May 1848, in Studynsky, "Materiialy kulturnoho zhytia v Halychyni," 316-17.
18. Letter of 18 May 1848, LBAN, fond T. Pavlykova, ms. 2/p. 1, no. 11: 24-5.
19. Ibid., no. 12: 26. The announcement was dated 22 May.
20. Ibid., no. 13: 28.
21. *Rada Narodowa*, 1848, no. 32: 123. Cf. *Dziennik Narodowy*, 1848, no. 101: 425-6.
22. 8 June 1848, in Studynsky, *Korespondentsiia*, 261.
23. LBAN, fond Naukovoho tovarystva im. T. Shevchenka, ms. 19/1: 417; IL, Arkhiv I. Franka, fond 3, ms. 2204. Polish opinion referred to them as "Beiraters." See *Rada Narodowa*, 1848, no. 23: 89; and Ostaszewski-Barański, *Rok złudzeń*, 214-16. The Ukrainian liberals also criticized them. See Iakiv Holovatsky to his brother Petro, 25 May 1848, in Studynsky, *Korespondentsiia*, 249; and Buchynsky to Borodaikevych, LBAN, fond O. Buchynskoho, ms. 230/p. 6.
24. LBAN, fond R. Mokha, ms. 16/p. 2: 1; ibid., fond T. Pavlykova, ms. 64/p. 3: 4-5; 65/p. 3: 18-19; Iustyn Zhelekhovsky, "Avtobiohrafiia," *Vestnik Narodogo doma*, 1909: 200. On the sessions of 2 and 8 June, see ibid., 84-5.
25. See Shankovsky, "Vospominaniia," *Rodimyi listok*.
26. LBAN, fond Naukovoho tovarystva im. T. Shevchenka, ms. 19/1: 418-20. An incomplete version appeared in *Zhytie i slovo* 6 (1897): 119-24. Cf. IL, Arkhiv I. Franka, fond 3, no. 2823.
27. Sozansky, "Z literaturnoi spadshchyny Vasylia Ilnytskoho," 15-16.
28. Text printed in *Zoria Halytska*, 1848, no. 15: 61-2; and no. 17: 71-2.
29. Sozansky, "Z literaturnoi spadshchyny Vasylia Ilnytskoho," 16.
30. Ibid.; and Shankovsky, "Vospominaniia," *Rodimyi listok*, 1881: 72. See also *Dziennik Narodowy*, 1848, no. 61: 254; *Gazeta Narodowa*, 1848, no. 28; *Gazeta Lwowska*, 1848, no. 67; and K. Luchakovsky, *Antin Liubych-Mohylnytsky* (Lviv 1887), 35–7.
31. Zhelekhovsky, "Avtobiohrafiia," *Vestnik Narodnogo doma*, 1909: 190-205; and 1910: 10-14; TDIA, fond 180, op. 2, spr. 4: 75; Iakiv Holovatsky to Kyrylo Blonsky, 1 August 1848, in Studynsky, *Korespondentsiia*, 277-9; and LBAN, fond Pavlykovskykh, ms. 254: 83-5.
32. "Slovo pry ustanovlenii pomenshoi rady narodnoi ruskoi v Hlynianakh," LBAN, fond R. Mokha, ms. 29/p. 2.
33. Compiled from lists in LBAN, fond O. Terletskoho, spr. 144-XIII: 19; and data in TDIA, fond 180, op. 2, spr. 4; and from Iakiv Holovatsky's letters in Studynsky, *Korespondentsiia*, 277, 279, 284.

34. LBAN, fond T. Pavlykova, ms. 65/p. 3: 49, 56, 69-70.
35. LBAN, fond Pavlykovskykh, ms. 254: 84; and Iakiv Holovatsky to Blonsky, 1 August 1848, in Studynsky, *Korespondentsiia*, 278-9.
36. To Petro Holovatsky, 30 October 1848, in Studynsky, *Korespondentsiia*, 303.
37. LBAN, fond O. Terletskoho, spr. 144-XIII: 29.
38. Ibid.: 27; and TDIA, fond 180, op. 2, spr. 4: 50-53.
39. LBAN, fond T. Pavlykova, ms. 67/p. 3: 18, and ms. 65/p. 3: 33; *Vestnik Narodnogo doma*, 1909: 75-6; TDIA, fond 180, op. 2, spr. 4: 76, 109-10, 198. Peasants comprised the majority of members in many councils. See F. I. Steblii, "Selianskyi rukh u Skhidnii Halychyni pid chas revoliutsii 1848-1849 rr.," *Ukrainskyi istorychnyi zhurnal* 1973, no. 6: 33.
40. LBAN, fond R. Mokha, ms. 16/p. 3: 5; and ibid., fond O. Terletskoho, spr. 144-XIII: 39.
41. 7 May 1848, in Studynsky, "Materiialy kulturnoho zhytia v Halychyni," 315.
42. Rozdolsky, "Nowe dokumenty," 124.
43. LBAN, fond O. Terletskoho, spr. 144-XIII: 11.
44. Denys Zubrytsky wrote to Iakiv Holovatsky on 20 May 1848, "We are proceeding in agreement with the government and are enjoying its trust and protection" (Studynsky, *Korespondentsiia*, 245).
45. LBAN, fond T. Pavlykova, ms. 64/p. 3: 1; and ms. 65/p. 3: 13-15.
46. In a letter to Iakiv Holovatsky, 13 May 1848, in Studynsky, *Korespondentsiia*, 243.
47. Liubych-Mohylnytsky to Iakiv Holovatsky, 10 July 1848, ibid., 263-4.
48. TDIA, fond 180, op. 1, spr. 3: 40.
49. Ibid., op. 1, spr. 3: 6; and op. 2, spr. 1: 7-9.
50. LBAN, fond T. Pavlykova, ms. 2/p. 1, no. 10: 22. See also *Vestnik Narodnogo doma*, 1909, 55.
51. LBAN, fond O. Terletskoho, spr. 144-XIII: 30-31.
52. M. Vozniak, "Z-za redaktsiinykh kulis videnskoho Vistnyka ta Zorii Halytskoi," *Zapysky Naukovoho tovarystva im. Shevchenka* 107 (1912): 83-5. Rudolf Mokh spoke in a similar vein on 8 June 1848. LBAN, fond R. Mokha, ms. 29/p. 22.
53. *Zoria Halytska*, 1848, no. 9: 39. See also Mykhailo Kachkovsky to Vasyl Ilnytsky, 7 June 1848, in *Vestnik Narodnogo doma*, 1909: 190; and Buchynsky to Borodaikevych, 14 August 1848, LBAN, fond O. Buchynskoho, ms. 230/p. 6.
54. See Vozniak, "Z-za redaktsiinykh kulis," 83-6.
55. LBAN, fond R. Mokha, ms. 30/p. 2.
56. From Mokh's address of 12 October 1848, ibid.
57. TDIA, fond 180, op. 2, spr. 6: 18-19.
58. Ivan Ilevych to Teofil Pavlykiv, 1848, LBAN, fond T. Pavlykova, ms. 24/p. 2.

59. F. I. Steblii, "Revoliutsiia 1848-1849 rr. na zakhidnoukrainskykh zemliakh," in *Torzhestvo istorychnoi spravedlyvosti* (Lviv 1968), 223.
60. See *Vestnik Narodnogo doma*, 1909: 124. On the attempts to partition Galicia, see chapter 15.
61. LBAN, fond R. Mokha, ms. 12/p. 2: 2; IL, Arkhiv I. Franka, fond 3, no. 2204.
62. *Zoria Halytska*, 1848, no. 3: 14.
63. "Zapysnyk L. Treshchakovskoho vid 1. V. 1848 do 16. XII. 1850," in Studynsky, "Materiialy kulturnoho zhytia v Halychyni," 387.
64. Ibid. See also Levytsky, *Halytsko-ruskaia bybliohrafiia*, 1: 33, no. 293.
65. TDIA, fond 180, op. 2, spr. 6: 9-10. See also Levytsky, *Halytsko-ruskaia bybliohrafiia*, 1: 36, no. 409.
66. LBAN, fond R. Mokha, ms. 25/p. 2.
67. IL, Arkhiv I. Franka, fond 3, no. 715: 1-2.
68. Ibid., no. 2204: 59; *Zoria Halytska*, 1848, no. 3: 11-12. A slightly different version in Polish appeared in *Gazeta Lwowska*, 1848, no. 68, supplement.
69. 27 May 1848, in Studynsky, "Materiialy kulturnoho zhytia v Halychyni," 319.
70. IL, Arkhiv I. Franka, fond 3, no. 2204: 59.
71. *Zoria Halytska*, 1848, no. 4: 15-16. See also LBAN, fond R. Mokha, ms. 16/p. 2: 6.
72. IL, Arkhiv I. Franka, fond 3, no. 2204: 17. Polish text in *Gazeta Lwowska*, 1848, no. 69: 609-10.

12. The Slavic Congress

1. Polish text in Władysław T. Wisłocki, *Kongres słowiański w r. 1848 i sprawa polska* (Lviv 1927), 153-4; Czech in Václav Žáček, ed., *Slovanský sjezd v Praze roku 1848: Sbírka dokumentů* (Prague 1958), 48-9. See also Studynsky, *Korespondentsiia*, 239-41.
2. English text, "Letter Sent by František Palacký to Frankfurt," trans. William Beardmore, *Slavonic and East European Review* 26, no. 67 (April 1948): 303-8.
3. Bryk, "Slavianskyi zizd u Prazi," 177; Žáček, *Slovanský sjezd*, 44; and K. Khomynsky to A. Petrushevych, 18 May 1848, LBAN, fond A. S. Petrushevycha, ms. 369/p. 12, no. 196.
4. Studynsky, *Korespondentsiia*, 241; and Ivan Sozansky, "Do istorii uchasty halytskykh Rusyniv u slovianskim kongresi v Prazi 1848 r.," *Zapysky Naukovoho tovarystva im. Shevchenka* 72 (1906): 120. Zap had in mind the Cabinet Rescript of 8 April 1848.
5. Iakiv Holovatsky to his brother Petro, 25 May 1848, and Iosyf Levytsky of Zabolotiv to Iakiv Holovatsky, 27 May 1848, in Studynsky, *Korespondentsiia*, 248-50.

6. Iakiv Holovatsky to Zap, 19 May 1848, ibid., 244-5; and Sozansky, "Do istorii uchasty halytskykh Rusyniv," 121.
7. Biretsky to Zap, 20 May 1848, in Žáček, *Slovanský sjezd*, 144-6; Bryk, "Slavianskyi zizd u Prazi," 181-2; and Bryk, "Materiialy do istorii ukrainsko-cheskykh vzaiemyn," 92-5.
8. *Zoria Halytska*, 1848, no. 8: 32; and Zaklynsky, *Zapysky parokha*, 46.
9. 20 May 1848, in Studynsky, *Korespondentsiia*, 245.
10. *Zoria Halytska*, 1848, no. 9: 37.
11. Ibid.
12. Ibid.; Kuzemsky to Levytsky of Zabolotiv, 23 May 1848, in Studynsky, *Korespondentsiia*, 247-8; and Sozansky, "Do istorii uchasty halytskykh Rusyniv," 119.
13. TDIA, fond 180, op. 1, spr. 2: 9; Sozansky, "Do istorii uchasty halytskykh Rusyniv," 118-19; Studynsky, *Korespondentsiia*, 246-7. Cf. Bryk, "Slavianskyi zizd u Prazi," 179.
14. Kuzemsky to Levytsky of Zabolotiv, 23 May 1848, in Studynsky, *Korespondentsiia*, 247-8; Sozansky, "Do istorii uchasty halytskykh Rusyniv," 119.
15. Levytsky of Zabolotiv to Iakiv Holovatsky, 27 May 1848, in Studynsky, *Korespondentsiia*, 250. There was no question of Vyrsky being the "fourth delegate" since he apparently favoured co-operation with the Poles. Cf. Iosafat Kobrynsky to Iakiv Holovatsky, ibid., 260; and *Dziennik Narodowy*, 1848, no. 74: 307.
16. Teodor Leontovych believed that a fourth delegate was not sent for financial reasons. TDIA, fond 180, op. 1, spr. 3: 5. See also Hostička, *Spolupráce Čechů a haličských Ukrajinců*, 68.
17. Zaklynsky, *Zapysky parokha*, 47; Bryk, "Slavianskyi zizd u Prazi," 184. The delegation stopped in Cracow to call on the city's military commander, Austrian General Schick. In response to his inquiry how they planned to act at the congress, one of the delegates replied, "My God, it is very simple; on each occasion when the Poles make a proposal, we will vote against it." Cited in *Österreichisches Jahrbuch* 20 (1896): 182. See also Wisłocki, *Kongres słowiański*, 34; and Hostička, *Spolupráce Čechů a haličských Ukrajinců*, 22.
18. Žáček, *Slovanský sjezd*, 39. From the deliberations of the Preparatory Committee on 13 May.
19. Jachim's and Vrba's letters, ibid., 84-5, 147-50; portions of Havlicek's articles are reprinted in Zdeněk Tobolka and Václav Žáček, eds., *Slovanský sjezd v Praze 1848*: *Sbírka dokumentů*, Pt. 1 (all published) (Prague 1952), 256-60.
20. See Hostička, *Spolupráce Čechů a haličských Ukrajinců*, 23*n*.
21. Hryhorii Hynylevych to Holovna Rada Ruska, 30 May 1848, TDIA, fond 180, op. 1, spr. 1: 13-14.
22. Ibid., fond 180, op. 1, spr. 3: 5-8. Text published in Hostička, *Spolupráce Čechů a haličských Ukrajinců*, 68-9.

23. LBAN, fond T. Pavlykova, ms. 24/p. 2; and Hostička, *Spolupráce Čechů a haličských Ukrajinců*, 69-70.
24. Of the sixty-four recorded members of the Polish-Ukrainian section, twenty-three identified themselves as "Ruthenians," including the polonized Ruthenians Leon Sapieha, Jerzy Lubomirski, Jan Dobrzański and Julian Dzieduszycki.
25. Zaklynsky, *Zapysky parokha*, 49-51, 54-5; Bryk, "Slavianskyi zizd u Prazi," 188, 197. Hostička (*Spolupráce Čechů a haličských Ukrajinců*, 27) maintains that Hynylevych made this proposal.
26. Wisłocki, *Kongres słowiański*, 49-51, Žáček, *Slovanský sjezd*, 208-9; Bryk, "Slavianskyi zizd u Prazi," 188. Cf. the notes of Leon Sapieha of the congress, LBAN, fond Sapiehów, ms. 602/IVB, no. 134g.
27. Žáček, *Slovanský sjezd*, 208; Wisłocki, *Kongres słowiański*, 48.
28. Wisłocki, *Kongres słowiański*, 53-4; Žáček, *Slovanský sjezd*, 210.
29. Wisłocki, *Kongres słowiański*, 55-7; Žáček, *Slovanský sjezd*, 211.
30. Wisłocki, *Kongres słowiański*, 58.
31. Ibid., 60.
32. Ibid., 61. Cf. Bryk, "Slavianskyi zizd u Prazi," 190-91; and Hostička, *Spolupráce Čechů a haličských Ukrajinců*, 28*n*.
33. Wisłocki, *Kongres słowiański*, 65-9, 71-2, 77; Žáček, *Slovanský sjezd*, 264-71.
34. Wisłocki, *Kongres słowiański*, 65, 83-8; Žáček, *Slovanský sjezd*, 265, 273-7.
35. The Polish-Ukrainian section's regulations, printed in Wisłocki, *Kongres słowiański*, 178-81; and Žáček, *Slovanský sjezd*, 277-8.
36. Wisłocki, *Kongres słowiański*, 85.
37. Ibid., 72-80, 182-3; Žáček, *Slovanský sjezd*, 268-73.
38. Wisłocki, *Kongres słowiański*, 88-9; Žáček, *Slovanský sjezd*, 278-9.
39. LBAN, fond Sapiehów, ms. 602/IVB: 11. Cf. Zaklynsky, *Zapysky parokha*, 64-5.
40. Wisłocki, *Kongres słowiański*, 90-93; Žáček, *Slovanský sjezd*, 279-80.
41. See discussion of Libelt's proposals in I. I. Udaltsov, "Iz istorii slavianskogo sezda v Prage v 1848 godu," *Uchenye zapiski Instituta slavianovedeniia* 1 (1949): 74-5.
42. "Zbór słowiański w Pradze. Pakt federacyjny z 8 VI 1848," LBAN, fond Lubomirskich, ms. V-13: 68.
43. Władysław T. Wisłocki, *Jerzy Lubomirski 1817-1872* (Lviv 1928), 68.
44. Žáček, *Slovanský sjezd*, 307-10; Wisłocki, *Kongres słowiański*, 99-104.
45. Cf. Seweryn Celarski to Rada Narodowa, 8 June 1848, in Žáček, *Slovanský sjezd*, 343. Robert Hefern wrote to Seweryn Smarzewski, the secretary of the Polish Rada Narodowa in Lviv, on 6 June: "I greatly fear that our messieurs Malisz, Lubomirski, etc. have exceeded the Rada's instructions and that the foolish *szlachta* assembled here without authorization have made a mess of things."

46. *Kongres słowiański*, 105.
47. Ibid., 106-7, 187-9; Žáček, *Slovanský sjezd*, 314-15. Cf. Hostička, *Spolupráce Čechů a haličských Ukrajinců*, 30*n*.
48. Wisłocki, *Kongres słowiański*, 108.
49. The Polish-Ukrainian accord has been variously interpreted by historians. It has been viewed positively by the Pole Wisłocki (ibid., 135); the Czechs Václav Žáček (*Čechové a Poláci roku 1848*, 2 vols. [Prague 1947-8], 2: 186-7) and Vladimír Hostička (*Spolupráce Čechů a haličských Ukrajinců*, 32); and the Ukrainian F. I. Steblii ("Revoliutsiia 1848-1849 rr.," 225). On the other hand, the older Ukrainian historian Ivan Bryk ("Slavianskyi zizd u Prazi," 213) called the accord a "scrap of paper" with no meaning whatsoever. There seems little basis for the opinion of the Soviet historian I. S. Miller ("Revoliutsionnoe dvizhenie i natsionalnaia borba v Galitsii v 1848 g.," in F. V. Potemkin and A. I. Molok, eds. *Revoliutsii 1848-1849*, 2 vols. [Moscow 1952], 1: 410) that "the understanding was only a manoeuver to influence popular opinion. It acquired no practical meaning and the Polish leaders of the national movement completely ignored it."
50. The belief that the agreement stemmed from Czech mediation was expressed by Celarski in a letter to the Rada Narodowa, 8 June 1848, in Žáček, *Slovanský sjezd*, 344; by Hynylevych in a letter to the Holovna Rada, 9 June 1848, ibid., 354; and by Jędrzej Moraczewski, "O kongresie słowiańskim w Pradze," ibid., 326. This view has been echoed in much of the literature on the congress. For example, Zdeněk Tobolka, *Slovanský sjezd v Praze roku 1848* (Prague 1901), 145; Bryk, "Slavianskyi zizd u Prazi," 203-6; Wisłocki, *Kongres Słowiański*, 106; and Hostička, *Spolupráce Čechů a haličských Ukrajinců*, 30-32.
51. See Antoni Helcel to Aleksander Wielopolski, 1 June 1848. in Lisicki, *Helcel*, 1: 513; and Žáček, *Čechové a Poláci roku 1848*, 2: 135.
52. Hostička, *Spolupráce Čechů a haličských Ukrajinců*, 31.
53. Žáček, *Slovanský sjezd*, 116-20, 127-8. Cf. Žáček, *Čechové a Poláci roku 1848*, 2: 105.
54. Žáček, *Slovanský sjezd*, 275, 381-6, 502-10.
55. Ibid., 311-14, 327-36; Wisłocki, *Kongres słowiański*, 109-13, 122-32.
56. Žáček, *Slovanský sjezd*, 313; Wisłocki, *Kongres słowiański*, 112; Wisłocki, *Lubomirski*, 68.
57. Wisłocki, *Lubomirski*, 68.
58. Ibid., 69; Wisłocki, *Kongres słowiański*, 113, 124-5; Žáček, *Slovanský sjezd*, 313, 332.
59. Wisłocki, *Kongres słowiański*, 126; Žáček, *Slovanský sjezd*, 333.
60. Wisłocki, *Kongres słowiański*, 126; Žáček, *Slovanský sjezd*, 332-3. Wisłocki's contention that "the Ruthenians could not figure out which side to support" appears to be without foundation (*Lubomirski*, 70).
61. *Lubomirski*, 91.

62. English text: "Manifesto of the First Slavonic Congress to the Nations of Europe," trans. William Beardmore, in *Slavonic and East European Review* 26, no. 67 (April 1948): 309-13.
63. Žáček, *Slovanský sjezd*, 373-4.
64. Ibid., 379-83.
65. Ibid., 327; Wisłocki, *Kongres słowiański*, 118.
66. Žáček, *Slovanský sjezd*, 328; Wisłocki, *Kongres słowiański*, 118.
67. Žáček, *Slovanský sjezd*, 344.
68. Ibid., 401.
69. Hynylevych to Holovna Rada, 9 June 1848, ibid., 353-6.
70. Ibid., 375-6.
71. Minutes of Rada Narodowa meetings on 16 and 17 June 1848, AGAD, fond 269: 175, 177.
72. See chapter 15.
73. Žáček, *Slovanský sjezd*, 303-4.

13. Elections and the Austrian Reichstag

1. On the elections in Galicia, see Ivan Krevetsky, "Z vyborchoho rukhu u skhidnii Halychyni v 1848 r. (vybir Ivana Kapushchaka)," *Zapysky Naukovoho tovarystva im. Shevchenka* 70 (1906): 73-85; Kieniewicz, "Sprawa włościańska," 101-8; Volodymyr Borys, "Wybory w Galicji i debaty nad zniesieniem pańszczyzny w parlamencie wiedeńskim w 1848 r.," *Przegląd Historyczny* 58 (1967): 28-45; Kosachevskaia, *Vostochnaia Galitsiia*, 87-90.
2. Krevetsky, "Z vyborchoho rukhu," 74.
3. Kieniewicz, "Sprawa włościańska," 103-4. See also the protest of the Rada Narodowa "against the inclusion of Galicia in the Viennese parliament" of 18 May 1848, in *Rada Narodowa*, 1848, no 27; and Lisicki, *Helcel*, 1: 303.
4. Discussed in Kieniewicz, "Sprawa włościańska," 103-4; *Gazeta Narodowa*, 1848, no 52: 203. See also Stanisław Schnür-Pepłowski, *Z przeszłości Galicji 1772-1862* (2nd rev. ed.; Lviv 1895), 548.
5. To Teofil Pavlykiv, June 1848, LBAN, fond T. Pavlykova, ms. 24/p. 2. See also Hostička, *Spolupráce Čechů a haličských Ukrajinců*, 70.
6. Leopold von Sacher-Masoch, *Polnische Revolutionen*: *Erinnerungen aus Galizien* (Prague 1863), 303-4; Krevetsky, "Z vyborchoho rukhu," 74-5.
7. Ostaszewski-Barański, *Rok złudzeń*, 257-8; Kieniewicz, "Sprawa włościańska," 103; Krevetsky, "Z vyborchoho rukhu," 78. Text LBAN, fond Naukovoho tovarystva im. T. Shevchenka, ms. 19/1: 408.
8. There is need to modify the judgement of Polish historian Stefan Kieniewicz that the *Kreishauptmänner* campaigned against the Polish candidates. "Sprawa włościańska," 103. Cf. LBAN, fond T. Pavlykova, ms. 65/p. 3: 38.

9. LBAN, fond Naukovoho tovarystva im. T. Shevchenka, ms. 19/1, 413-14. Reprinted by Ivan Franko in *Zapysky Naukovoho tovarystva im. Shevchenka* 22 (1898): 7-8. See also Krevetsky, "Z vyborchoho rukhu," 75-6.
10. "Nieco o wyborach przez L. Dunina Borkowskiego," *Gazeta Narodowa*, 1848, no. 42: 163-4.
11. LBAN, fond T. Pavlykova, ms. 1-1/p. 1, no. 3: 8-11.
12. *Zoria Halytska*, 1848, no. 5: 21-2; and no. 8: 32-3.
13. To Iakiv Holovatsky, 8 June 1848, in Studynsky, *Korespondentsiia*, 260.
14. Borys, "Wybory w Galicji," 30-32, 42-3.
15. According to a report of the deanery Ruthenian council in Berezhany to the Austrian parliament, in *Vestnik Narodnogo doma*, 1909: 90.
16. To Iakiv Holovatsky, 12 August 1848, in Studynsky, *Korespondentsiia*, 283. These were not isolated incidents. See Kieniewicz, "Sprawa włościańska," 107.
17. Holovna Rada to Andrii Dolnytsky, 18 June 1848, LBAN, fond R. Mokha, ms. 15/p. 2: 3. See also *Zoria Halytska*, 1848, no. 6: 26.
18. *Vestnik Narodnogo doma*, 1909, 86; TDIA, fond 180, op. 1, spr. 4: 49-50.
19. Complaint of the Ruthenian council in Berezhany, 8 June 1848, LBAN, fond T. Pavlykova, ms. 65/p. 3: 8-10.
20. Ibid.: 11-12; and *Vestnik Narodnogo doma*, 1909: 87.
21. LBAN, fond T. Pavlykova, ms. 65/p. 3: 42-5. See also *Vestnik Narodnogo doma*, 1909: 90. The election in Horodok was a case in point. There the name of J. Meyer, the choice of the Poles, was recorded as the selection of the peasants instead of Iosyf Savka's.
22. Ivan Zhukovsky to the Ruthenian deanery council in Hlyniany, 28 June 1848, LBAN, fond R. Mokha, ms. 15/p. 2: 4. See also *Zoria Halytska*, 1848, no. 6: 26.
23. LBAN, fond T. Pavlykova, ms. 2/p. 1, no. 4: 12; and 65/p. 3, 39-40. In Dynów the election was held three times. See Biretsky to Iakiv Holovatsky, 12 August 1848, in Studynsky, *Korespondentsiia*, 283.
24. *Gazeta Narodowa*, 1848, no. 53: 210.
25. LBAN, fond T. Pavlykova, ms. 65/p. 3: 39-40; and *Vestnik Narodnogo doma*, 1909, 108-9.
26. Letter to Iakiv Holovatsky, 8 June 1848, in Studynsky, *Korespondentsiia*, 260.
27. Borysykevych to Ivan Slymakovsky, 9 August 1848, TDIA, fond 180, op. 2, spr. 8: 1-2.
28. LBAN, fond T. Pavlykova, ms. 64/p. 3: 2, 38.
29. Ibid.: 41.
30. *Vestnik Narodnogo doma*, 1909: 110.
31. LBAN, fond T. Pavlykova, ms. 64/p. 3: 5.
32. To Levytsky, 21 June 1848, in Studynsky, "Materiialy kulturnoho zhytia v Halychyni," 327.

33. Kuzemsky to T. Pavlykiv, 28 June 1848, LBAN, fond T. Pavlykova, ms. 8-60/p. 2.
34. See Ivan Franko, *Narys istorii ukrainsko-ruskoi literatury* (Lviv 1910), 126.
35. Iosyf Savka's election was invalidated by the parliament. But on 22 September 1848, in a supplemental election in Vynnyky, Ivan Stavarsky was elected to replace the Pole Pietrowski. The Polish newspaper *Polska* (1848, no. 2: 13) was especially outspoken against seating Savka.
36. The principal sources for identifying the Ukrainian deputies are: *Zoria Halytska*, 1849, no. 2: 9-10, and no. 3: 14; Levytsky, *Halytsko-ruskaia bybliohrafiia*, 1: 31, who added the Galician deputy Jan Federowicz to the list of Ukrainians; LBAN, fond T. Pavlykova, ms. 2/p. 1, no. 4: 12; LBAN, fond Sapiehów, ms. 92/IIB, Miscellanea historyczne i polityczne 1848, no. 1: Okręgi i obwody wyborcze; LBAN, fond Ossolińskich, ms. 7229: 373-6, for an incomplete official list; *Gazeta Lwowska*, 1848, no. 74: 647-8, and no. 78: 695. See also Widmann, *Smolka*, appendix 1; and Schnür-Pepłowski, *Z przeszłości Galicji*, 287-9. Several modern-day historians have suggested that nine, not eight Greek Catholic priests were deputies. Kieniewicz, "Sprawa włościańska," 108; and Borys, "Wybóry w Galicji," 30. The fragmentary nature of the sources largely explains the variety of figures on the number of Ukrainians in the Reichstag. Cf. Zaklynsky, *Zapysky parokha*, 72-3; and Vintskovsky, *Iakhimovich*, 44-5.
37. *Dziennik Narodowy*, 1848, no. 65: 271. See also Kieniewicz, "Sprawa włościańska," 105.
38. Iakhymovych to Levytsky, 27 June 1848, in Studynsky, "Materiialy kulturnoho zhytia v Halychyni," 329.
39. Biretsky to Iakiv Holovatsky, 12 August 1848, in Studynsky, *Korespondentsiia*, 284.
40. To his brother Petro, 13 June 1848, ibid., 262.
41. Kosachevskaia, *Vostochnaia Galitsiia*, 88. See also the complaint by the peasants of the Univ deanery, LBAN, fond R. Mokha, ms. 16/p. 2: 3.
42. Antin Krushelnytsky, "Z dnevnyka hr.-k. parokha 1848-1850 rr.," *Zapysky Naukovoho tovarystva im. Shevchenka* 52 (1903): 5-6. See also the instruction of the Rada Narodowa in Ternopil of 1 June 1848, ibid. 88 (1909): 110-11; and Iakhymovych to Levytsky, 27 June 1848, in Studynsky, "Materiialy kulturnoho zhytia v Halychyni," 329-30.
43. In a letter to Iakiv Holovatsky, 12 August 1848, in Studynsky, *Korespondentsiia*, 283.
44. Józef Putek wrote that the peasants "performed not badly on their first test, but not the best either" (*Pierwsze występy polityczne włościaństwa polskiego 1848-1861* [Cracow 1933], 8). Juliusz Starkel compared the peasant deputies to "sheep-skins to which little constitutional emblems have been pinned" (*Rok 1848* [Lviv 1899], 267). The peasant deputies' attire created quite a sensation on the streets of Vienna. See Anton Springer, *Geschichte Oesterreichs seit dem Wiener Frieden 1809*, 2 vols. (Leipzig 1863-5), 2: 403; and Borys, "Wybory w Galicji," 33.

45. See Henryk Schmitt to his wife, 20 June 1848, in Stefan Kieniewicz, ed., *Henryka Schmitta listy do żony, 1845-1880* (Wrocław 1961), 133.
46. 22 (?) June 1848, TDIA, fond 180, op. 1, spr. 3: 5-6. See also Hostička, *Spolupráce Čechů a haličských Ukrajinců*, 68.
47. *Verhandlungen des österreichischen Reichstages nach der stenographischen Aufnahme*, 5 vols. (Vienna 1848-9), 1: 30, 56; Stanisław Smolka, ed., *Dziennik Franciszka Smolki 1848-1849 w listach do żony* (Warsaw 1913), 6; Schnür-Pepłowski, *Z przeszłości Galicji*, 448; and Kieniewicz, "Sprawa włościańska," 107-8.
48. Holovna Rada to Univ Ruthenian council, 22 September 1848, LBAN, fond R. Mokha, ms. 15/p. 2: 51; and Holovna Rada to Berezhany Ruthenian council, 28 July 1848, ibid., fond T. Pavlykova, ms. 65/p. 3, no. 200: 79.
49. Shashkevych to Kuzemsky, 22 August and 1 September 1848, TDIA, fond 180, op. 2, spr. 5: 5, 45.
50. See Hostička, *Spolupráce Čechů a haličských Ukrajinců*, 37ff.
51. 19 and 25 July 1848, in Studynsky, *Korespondentsiia*, 269-71.
52. *Verhandlungen des österreichischen Reichstages*, 1: 322; 2: 321-2, 328, 737; Hostička, *Spolupráce Čechů a haličských Ukrajinců*, 38; Blonsky to Iakiv Holovatsky, 5 September 1848, in Studynsky, *Korespondentsiia*, 299.
53. *Zoria Halytska*, 3 October 1848, no. 21: 86-7.
54. Blonsky to Iakiv Holovatsky, 25 July 1848, in Studynsky, *Korespondentsiia*, 272.
55. Iakhymovych to Levytsky, 10 August 1848, in Studynsky, "Materiialy kulturnoho zhytia v Halychyni," 338.
56. *Verhandlungen des österreichischen Reichstages*, 2: 163-4.
57. Ibid., 276-7.
58. Ibid., 277-8; Smolka, *Dziennik Franciszka Smolki*, 37-8; Hostička, *Spolupráce Čechů a haličských Ukrajinců*, 39.
59. *Gazeta Powszechna*, 10 October 1848, no. 31; Widmann, *Smolka*, 331-2.
60. In Studynsky, *Korespondentsiia*, 300.
61. Widmann, *Smolka*, 436-8.
62. Ibid., 371-2, 387, 401.
63. To Levytsky, Brno, 23 October 1848, in Studynsky, "Materiialy kulturnoho zhytia v Halychyni," 342-3. See also *Zoria Halytska*, 1848, no. 23: 95.
64. To Iakiv Holovatsky, 16 November 1848, in Studynsky, *Korespondentsiia*, 310.
65. Ibid. Text of appeal in *Gazeta Powszechna*, 26 October 1848, no. 45. See also Widmann, *Smolka*, 431-2.
66. Blonsky to Iakiv Holovatsky, 26 November 1848, and Petro Holovatsky to his brother Iakiv, 1 December 1848, in Studynsky, *Korespondentsiia*, 317-19.
67. Widmann, *Smolka*, 528-32.

68. Iakhymovych to Levytsky, 6 March 1849, in Studynsky, "Materiialy kulturnoho zhytia v Halychyni," 344-5.
69. Martha Bohachevsky-Chomiak, *The Spring of a Nation: The Ukrainians in Eastern Galicia in 1848* (Philadelphia 1967), 49, 72*n*.

14. The Peasant Question

1. See Kieniewicz, "Sprawa włościańska," 65-6; Mykhailo P. Herasymenko, *Ahrarni vidnosyny v Halychyni v period kryzy panshchynnoho hospodarstva* (Kiev 1959), 222, 239-40; F. I. Steblii, *Borotba selian Skhidnoi Halychyny proty feodalnoho hnitu v pershii polovyni XIX st.* (Kiev 1961), 15, 19, 22, 26, 29-31; M. Marassé, *Dzieła ekonomiczno-polityczne i statystyczne*, vol. 1 (Cracow 1887), 352-3, 357-8; and Roman Rozdolski, *Wspólnota gminna w b. Galicji Wschodniej i jej zanik* (Lviv 1936), 49.
2. M. Grabowski, "Wypadki galicyjskie," Bibl. Ossol., ms. 3245/II: 28.
3. *Zoria Halytska*, 1848, no. 2: 7-8.
4. Zubrytsky to Iakiv Holovatsky, 20 May 1848, in Studynsky, *Korespondentsiia*, 246.
5. LBAN, fond R. Mokha, ms. 15/p. 2.
6. Address by Iosyf Lozynsky, in *Zapysky Naukovoho tovarystva im. Shevchenka* 107 (1912): 83-5. See also LBAN, fond O. Buchynskoho, ms. 230/p. 6.
7. Borys, "Wybory w Galicji," 32-41; Kieniewicz, "Sprawa włościańska," 108-18; Kosachevskaia, *Vostochnaia Galitsiia*, 90-99.
8. *Verhandlungen des österreichischen Reichstages*, 1: 511.
9. Ibid., 585-6; Smolka, *Dziennik Franciszka Smolki*, 291-2. See also Putek, *Pierwsze występy polityczne włościaństwa*, 12; J. A. Helfert, *Aufzeichnungen und Erinnerungen aus den jungen Jahren* (Vienna 1904), 54; and Kieniewicz, "Sprawa włościańska," 114.
10. Rozdolski, "Nowe dokumenty," 124-7. Cf. Kosachevskaia, *Vostochnaia Galitsiia*, 93.
11. Marian Tyrowicz, *Julian Maciej Goslar: Zarys życia i materiały biograficzne* (Warsaw 1953), 78-9; Tyrowicz, *Prawda i mit w biografii Juliana Macieja Goslara 1820-1852* (Warsaw 1972), 203-8. See also Jan Kozik, "Nieznane listy Juliana Macieja Goslara z 1848 r.," *Przegląd Historyczny* 66 (1975): 609-20; and Batowski, *Diariusz 1848 roku*, 297.
12. *Verhandlungen des österreichischen Reichstages*, 3: 213-15. Cf. Ivan Franko's assessment in IL, Arkhiv I. Franka, fond 3, no. 609: 1.
13. *Verhandlungen des österreichischen Reichstages*, 1: 631-4; Springer, *Geschichte Oesterreichs*, 2: 420; Borys, "Wybory w Galicji," 39.
14. A. Pirozhyk to Vasyl Harmatii, in *Zapysky Naukovoho tovarystva im. Shevchenka* 88 (1909): 116-17; and *Zhytie i slovo* 6 (1897): 423-4.

15. Borys, "Wybory w Galicji," 34.
16. František Jachim to Iakiv Holovatsky, 8 August 1848, in Studynsky, *Korespondentsiia*, 280.
17. Iuliian Velychkovsky to an unknown addressee, 21 August 1848, TDIA, fond 180, op. 2, spr. 8: 4.
18. *Zoria Halytska*, 1848, no. 18: 76.
19. Ivan Krevetsky, *Ahrarni straiky i boikoty u Skhidnii Halychyni v 1848-1849 rr.* (Lviv 1906); Steblii, "Selianskyi rukh u Skhidnii Halychyni," 30-31.
20. *Zoria Halytska*, 1848, no. 8: 31; and TDIA, fond 180, op. 1, spr. 9: 4, 9.
21. TDIA, fond 180, op. 2, spr. 6: 38; and Iosyf Kropyvnytsky to Iakiv Holovatsky, 5 April 1849, in Studynsky, *Korespondentsiia*, 352.
22. *Zoria Halytska*, 1848, no. 9: 35; and no. 11: 45; TDIA, fond 180, op. 1, spr. 9: 5, 10; LBAN, fond T. Pavlykova, ms. 64/p. 3: 6a, 7b; and Hryhorii Bodnar to Iakiv Holovatsky, 10 September 1848, in Studynsky, *Korespondentsiia*, 287.
23. *Zoria Halytska*, 1848, no. 20: 82. Cf. *Dnewnyk Ruskij*, 1848, no. 9: 35-6.
24. *Zoria Halytska*, 1848, no. 14: 60.
25. Grzybowski, *Galicja 1848-1914*, 29.
26. *Gazeta Narodowa*, 1848, nos. 46, 47: 179-80, 183-4.
27. LBAN, fond R. Mokha, ms. 16/p. 2: 6; and 28/p. 2.
28. Kieniewicz, "Sprawa włościańska," 99.
29. LBAN, fond Naukovoho tovarystva im. T. Shevchenka, ms. 19/1: 425.
30. LBAN, fond R. Mokha, ms. 16/p. 2: 8-10.
31. LBAN, fond T. Pavlykova, ms. 66/p. 3: 50; 64/p. 3: 11a.
32. TDIA, fond 180, op. 1, spr. 4: 40-41, 47-8; spr. 3: 84; spr. 8: 1-16; spr. 10: 117, 159, 173-6.
33. LBAN, fond Naukovoho tovarystva im. T. Shevchenka, ms. 19/1: 446-8; *Zoria Halytska*, 1848, no. 13: 54-6.
34. TDIA, fond 180, op. 1, spr. 9: 1-2.
35. LBAN, fond R. Mokha, ms. 15/p. 2: 25-6.
36. TDIA, fond 180, op. 1, spr. 9: 42-3.
37. Ibid.: 47, 78-111, 121-6.
38. *Zoria Halytska*, 1848, nos. 18-19: 76-8.
39. TDIA, fond 180, op. 2, spr. 6: 13-16; *Zoria Halytska*, 1849, nos. 43-4, 46, 48. Shashkevych presented the Holovna Rada's position to the parliament. *Verhandlungen des österreichischen Reichstages*, 3: 213-15.
40. Blonsky to Iakiv Holovatsky, 16 November 1848, in Studynsky, *Korespondentsiia*, 310-11; "Adresse der Ruthenen an Seine Majestät," ibid., 300-301; "Kurz gefasste Wünsche der Ruthenen," ibid., 301-2.
41. *Zoria Halytska*, 1848, no. 28: 115-16; Staniewicz to Leon Sapieha, 22 November 1848, LBAN, fond Sapiehów, ms. 578/IVa, no. 3.

42. Kieniewicz, "Sprawa włościańska," 125.
43. *Verhandlungen des österreichischen Reichstages*, 4: 146; *Zoria Halytska*, 1848, no. 9: 53; appeal of the Ruthenian council in Kolomyia, 26 December 1848, LBAN, fond R. Mokha, ms. 24/p. 2.
44. Łoziński, *Gołuchowski*, 214; Kieniewicz, "Sprawa włościańska," 125. The increasing incidence of acts of spoliation can be followed in the letters of manorial staff members to Prince Leon Sapieha. LBAN, fond Sapiehów, ms. 577/IVa. See also IL, Arkhiv I. Franka, fond 3, no. 581.
45. *Zoria Halytska*, 1849, no. 9: 52-4.
46. IL, Arkhiv I. Franka, fond 3, no. 30: 29-30; Krevetsky, *Ahrarni straiky i boikoty*.
47. *Zoria Halytska*, 1849, nos. 50-51: 297-9, 303-5.
48. Ibid., no. 53.
49. Ibid., nos. 49, 59: 289-90, 352. Text in TDIA, fond 180, op. 1, spr. 10: 148-51, 153-6.
50. Łoziński, *Gołuchowski*, 211.
51. TDIA, fond 180, op. 1, spr. 9: 55; Ivan Holovatsky to his brother Iakiv, 23 August 1849, and Petro Holovatsky to his brother Iakiv, 27 August 1849, in Studynsky, *Korespondentsiia*, 376, 378; *Zoria Halytska*, 1849, no. 64: 381.
52. TDIA, fond 180, op. 1, spr. 3: 107-12.
53. 27 August 1849, in Studynsky, *Korespondentsiia*, 379.
54. Kosachevskaia, *Vostochnaia Galitsiia*, 106. See also Borysykevych to Iakiv Holovatsky, 20 October 1849, in Studynsky, *Korespondentsiia*, 399.
55. Kieniewicz, "Sprawa włościańska," 126.
56. 19 August 1849, in Studynsky, *Korespondentsiia*, 374-5.
57. Petro Holovatsky to his brother Iakiv, 8 September 1849, ibid., 388. See also Borysykevych to Iakiv Holovatsky, 20 October 1849, ibid., 398.
58. Iakiv Holovatsky to his brother Petro, 28 September 1849, ibid., 391.
59. *Zoria Halytska*, 1849, no. 99: 589-90.

15. The Campaign to Partition Galicia

1. Mykhailo Lozynsky, *Utvorennie ukrainskoho koronnoho kraiu v Avstrii* (Lviv 1915), 17; *Wiener Zeitung*, 1848, no. 205 (Abend Beilage); Ivan Krevetsky, "Sprava podilu Halychyny v rr. 1846-1850," *Zapysky Naukovoho tovarystva im. Shevchenka* 97 (1910): 113-14.
2. Hostička, *Spolupráce Čechů a haličských Ukrajinců*, 66-9; TDIA, fond 180, op. 1, spr. 3: 5-8.
3. See Łoziński, *Gołuchowski*, 138-41; Krevetsky, "Sprava podilu," 94 (1910): 58-62; Lozynsky, *Utvorennie ukrainskoho kraiu*, 7-8. See also Iakhymovych to Levytsky, 17 March 1847, in Studynsky, "Materiialy kulturnoho zhytia v Halychyni," 234.

4. LBAN, fond R. Mokha, ms. 15/p. 2: 8-9; Krevetsky, "Sprava podilu," 94: 68, and 97: 107; Lozynsky, *Utvorennie ukrainskoho kraiu*, 10.
5. LBAN, fond Ossolińskich, ms. 7080/II, Zaleski files, 709. See also Kieniewicz, "Galicja w latach 1846-1848," 329.
6. LBAN, fond A. S. Petrushevycha, ms. 129/6, no. 198.
7. Ibid., fond R. Mokha, ms. 15/p. 2: 9.
8. Łoziński, *Gołuchowski*, 142; Krevetsky, "Sprava podilu," 94: 68; and Lozynsky, *Utvorennie ukrainskoho kraiu*, 10.
9. LBAN, fond R. Mokha, ms. 15/p. 2: 9-11; Krevetsky, "Sprava podilu," 94: 69-91, and 97: 108-9; Lozynsky, *Utvorennie ukrainskoho kraiu*, 11-12.
10. The Holovna Rada had already signalled the necessity of collecting signatures in its circular of 4 June 1848.
11. Appeal of the deanery council in Hlyniany, 31 July 1848, LBAN, fond R. Mokha, ms. 23/p. 2.
12. Ibid.
13. Ibid., fond T. Pavlykova, ms. 64/p. 3: 6-8. Cf. *Dziennik Narodowy*, 1848, no. 127, 533.
14. Krevetsky, "Sprava podilu," 97: 110.
15. Ibid., 94 (1910): 73; Kosachevskaia, *Vostochnaia Galitsiia*, 138.
16. Smolka, *Dziennik Franciszka Smolki*, 22.
17. Shashkevych to Kuzemsky, 28 August and 1 September 1848, TDIA, fond 180, op. 2, spr. 14: 14, 97, 174; Blonsky to Iakiv Holovatsky, 5 October 1848, in Studynsky, *Korespondentsiia*, 300; Mykhailo Malynovsky to Antin Petrushevych, n.d., LBAN, fond A. S. Petrushevycha, ms. 369/p. 6; *Zoria Halytska*, 1849, no. 15: 89; and Krevetsky, "Sprava podilu," 94: 71. See also Kosachevskaia, *Vostochnaia Galitsiia*, 137.
18. To Iakiv Holovatsky, in Studynsky, *Korespondentsiia*, 280-81. See also Hostička, *Spolupráce Čechů a haličských Ukrajinců*, 41.
19. LBAN, fond Ossolińskich, ms. 7080/II, Zaleski files, p. 709. See also Ostaszewski-Barański, *Wacław Michał Zaleski*, 147.
20. Smolka, *Dziennik Franciszka Smolki*, 7, 22.
21. *Dnewnyk Ruskij*, 1848, no. 3: 9. See also Krevetsky, "Sprava podilu," 94: 79.
22. Batowski, *Diariusz 1848 roku*; AGAD, fond 269, Protokoły Rady Narodowej, 26, 27, 29 July and 6 August 1848; LBAN, fond Pavlykovskykh, ms. 73 II: 33. See also Marceli Handelsman, *Ukraińska polityka Czartoryskiego*, 154-5, 157-62.
23. Kyrylo Khomynsky to Antin Petrushevych, 14 August 1848, LBAN, fond A. S. Petrushevycha, ms. 369/p. 12, no. 200.
24. Prokopchyts to Kuzemsky (?), 25 August 1848, TDIA, fond 180, op. 2, spr. 8: 7.
25. *Gazeta Powszechna*, 25 and 26 September 1848, nos. 19-20. See also Rozdolski, "Nowe dokumenty," 127; and Kosachevskaia, *Vostochnaia Galitsiia*, 92, 138.

26. Ostaszewski-Barański, *Zaleski*, 203-5.
27. Cięglewicz's *Rzecz czerwono-ruska 1848 roku* first appeared in the Polish *Dziennik Narodowy* (1848, nos. 130, 133: 545-7, 557-60) and was later published separately as a brochure in Lviv in 1848. A German version, *Die Roth-reussischen Angelegenheiten im Jahre 1848*, was also published in 1848 in Vienna. The German version was subtitled "A Rectification of the Holovna Rada's Memorial of 31 July 1848." Dąbczański's brochure was published in Polish (*Wyjaśnienie sprawy ruskiej*) and German (*Die ruthenische Frage in Galizien*) versions in Lviv in 1848 by the Ossolineum Institute.
28. Dąbczański, *Wyjaśnienie sprawy ruskiej*, 15, 32.
29. Citing the edition of Cięglewicz's work in *Dziennik Narodowy*, 1848, no. 133: 558.
30. Widmann, *Smolka*, 243; and Krevetsky, "Sprava podilu," 94: 82-3.
31. *Zoria Halytska*, 1848, no. 18: 73-4.
32. Krevetsky, "Sprava podilu," 97: 110-14; Lozynsky, *Utvorennie ukrainskoho kraiu*, 14-17. See also *Czas*, 2 December 1848, no. 26; and J. A. Helfert, *Geschichte Oesterreichs vom Ausgange des Wiener Oktober-Aufstandes 1848*, 4 vols. in 6 (Prague 1869-86): 4, 3: 49-50.
33. Łoziński, *Gołuchowski*, 50-56; Ostaszewski-Barański, *Zaleski*, 214-18; Krevetsky, "Sprava podilu," 94: 74ff.
34. Ostaszewski-Barański, *Zaleski*, 222-3.
35. Ibid., 223-9; and LBAN, fond Sapiehów, ms. 92/IIB. Text LBAN, fond Pavlykovskykh, ms. 73 I: 129-50: "Die Frage über die Theilung Galizien," 27 November 1848; and LBAN, fond Sapiehów, ms. 602/IVB, VIII: 144, 1-10. See also Krevetsky, "Sprava podilu," 97: 115-27; and Lozynsky, *Utvorennie ukrainskoho kraiu*, 20-30. Cf. the polemics in *Slawische Central-Blätter*, 1849, nos. 35-6, 47, 102-4.
36. Ostaszewski-Barański, *Zaleski*, 230-33.
37. Ibid., 330. See also A. Z. Helcel to K. Forster, 29 December 1848, ACz, ms. 5654 IV: 140-41, and 5364 III: 37-8.
38. On the issue of Galicia's division in the Constitutional Commission at Kroměříž, see Anton Springer, ed., *Protokolle des Verfassungs-Ausschusses im Oesterreichischen Reichstage 1848-1849* (Leipzig 1885); Paula Geist-Lányi, *Das Nationalitätenproblem auf dem Reichstag zu Kremsier 1848-1849* (Munich 1920), 111-14, 168-79; Robert A. Kann, *The Multinational Empire: Nationalism and National Reform in the Habsburg Monarchy 1848-1918*, 2 vols. (New York 1950), 2: 10-29; Hostička, *Spolupráce Čechů a haličských Ukrajinců*, 55-60; Bohachevsky-Chomiak, *The Spring of a Nation*, 46-9.
39. In a letter to the editor of *Zoria Halytska*, 18 November 1848, in Studynsky, *Korespondentsiia*, 313. See also Blonsky to Iakiv Holovatsky, 16 November 1848, ibid., 310; *Zoria Halytska*, 1848, no. 29: 122; and Hostička, *Spolupráce Čechů a haličských Ukrajinců*, 51-2.

40. Blonsky to Iakiv Holovatsky, 26 November, 3 and 15 December 1848, in Studynsky, *Korespondentsiia*, 317, 320, 323; *Zoria Halytska*, 1848, no. 29, 122; Smolka, *Dziennik Franciszka Smolki*, 163; and Hostička, *Spolupráce Čechů a haličských Ukrajinců*, 53.
41. Hostička, *Spolupráce Čechů a haličských Ukrajinců*, 53-4; Smolka, *Dziennik Franciszka Smolki*, 204-5; Žáček, *Čechové a Poláci 1848*, 2: 323.
42. Springer, *Protokolle des Verfassungs-Ausschusses*, 15.
43. Ibid., 16-17. See also Krevetsky, "Sprava podilu," 95: 58; and Hostička, *Spolupráce Čechů a haličských Ukrajinců*, 56.
44. Springer, *Protokolle des Verfassungs-Ausschusses*, 19-24.
45. Ibid., 24-5. Brestl stated that Iakhymovych's historical considerations had not convinced him that the Poles and Ukrainians did not share a common background, and, in his opinion, the future national status of the individual provinces (*Länder*) should be determined by the inhabitants' ancestry (*Herkunft*). Ibid., 33. See also Krevetsky, "Sprava podilu," 95: 60-61; and Lozynsky, *Utvorennie ukrainskoho kraiu*, 34-5.
46. Springer, *Protokolle des Verfassungs-Ausschusses*, 26-7.
47. Ibid., 30-32.
48. Ibid., 44. These would be Upper and Lower Austria, Bohemia, Moravia with Silesia, Galicia, Tyrol, Styria, Illyria, the Littoral and Dalmatia. See Hostička, *Spolupráce Čechů a haličských Ukrajinců*, 57-8. Bohachevsky-Chomiak (*The Spring of a Nation*, 48) maintained that "Rieger spoke in defense of the division of Galicia."
49. Springer, *Protokolle des Verfassungs-Ausschusses*, 44-5.
50. *Zoria Halytska*, 1849, no. 15: 88-9. Kuzemsky had in mind the directive of the Austrian Ministry of Justice of 28 January 1849. See Grzybowski, *Galicja 1848-1914*, 36*n*.
51. Springer, *Protokolle des Verfassungs-Ausschusses*, 347-8.
52. Ibid., 348-9.
53. Ibid.
54. Ibid., 365.
55. To Levytsky, 6 March 1849, in Studynsky, "Materiialy kulturnoho zhytia v Halychyni," 344-5.
56. Iosyf Kropyvnytsky to Iakiv Holovatsky, 5 April 1849, in Studynsky, *Korespondentsiia*, 352.
57. Steblii, "Revoliutsiia 1848-1849 rr.," 232.
58. Žáček, *Čechové a Poláci 1848*, 2: 322; Hostička, *Spolupráce Čechů a haličských Ukrajinců*, 59-60.
59. *Zoria Halytska*, 1849, no. 7; Krevetsky, "Sprava podilu," 95 (1910): 77. See also D. Zubrzycki [Zubrytsky], *Granice między ruskim i polskim narodem* (Lviv 1849).
60. Łoziński, *Gołuchowski*, 144; Krevetsky, "Sprava podilu," 94: 75-6.

61. Łoziński, *Gołuchowski*, 145; Krevetsky, "Sprava podilu," 94: 76.
62. Łoziński, *Gołuchowski*, 148-9; Krevetsky, "Sprava podilu," 95: 79-80.
63. Steblii, "Revoliutsiia 1848-1849 rr.," 232-3. On Kobylytsia's activities, see Ivan Franko, "Lukian Kobylytsia," *Zapysky Naukovoho tovarystva im. Shevchenka* 49 (1902): 1-40; T. Revakovych, "Lukian Kobylytsia," ibid. 126-7 (1918); T. Balan, *Lukian Kobiliţa* (Chernivţsi 1926); F. P. Shevchenko, *Lukian Kobylytsia. Z istorii antyfeodalnoi borotby selianstva Bukovyny v pershii polovyni XIX st.* (Kiev 1958).
64. *Zoria Halytska*, 1849, no. 15: 88; Antin Petrushevych to Iakiv Holovatsky, 12 April 1849, in Studynsky, *Korespondentsiia*, 354. The article appeared in the journal *Pchola* (7 and 14 May 1849, nos. 1-2). See also Kost Levytsky, *Istoriia politychnoi dumky halytskykh Ukraintsiv 1848-1914*, vol. 1 (Lviv 1926), 51.
65. Printed copy in TDIA, fond 180, op. 1, spr. 6: 25-6.
66. Svientsitsky, *Materialy do istorii vozrozhdeniia Karpatskoi Rusi*, 2: 134-5; *Zoria Halytska*, 1849, no. 86.
67. *Zoria Halytska*, 1849, no. 31: 181-4.
68. On Hungarian Rus', see I. N. Melnikova, "Zakarpatskaia Ukraina v revoliutsii 1848 goda," *Uchenye zapiski Instituta slavianovedeniia* 1 (1949): 241-92; L'. Haraksim, *K sociálnym a kultúrnim dejinám Ukrajincov na Slovensku do roku 1867* (Bratislava 1961). See also Felczak, *Węgierska polityka narodowościowa*, 90-91; and Mikhal Danylak [Michal Danilák], *Halytski, bukovynski, zakarpatski ukraintsi v revoliutsii 1848-1849 rokiv* (Bratislava 1972), 143ff.
69. Cited in Łoziński, *Gołuchowski*, 150.
70. Steblii, "Revoliutsiia 1848-1849 rr.," 233.

16. The National Guard and the Riflemen

1. *Statut über die Organisation der Nationalgarde in dem Österreichischen Kaiserstaate* (Vienna 1848), paragraphs 1, 2, 9; Ivan Krevetsky, "Proby orhanizovannia ruskykh natsionalnykh hvardii v Halychyni 1848-1849 rr.," *Zapysky Naukovoho tovarystva im. Shevchenka* 113 (1913): 125ff.
2. Julian Horoszkiewicz to Leon Sapieha, 15 April 1848, LBAN, fond Sapiehów, ms. 576/IVa, no. 1: 2; *Gazeta Lwowska*, 1848, no. 68. See also LBAN, fond Pavlykovskykh, ms. 72-1: 49-50.
3. Iakhymovych to Levytsky, 31 March 1848, in Studynsky, "Materiialy kulturnoho zhytia v Halychyni," 309.
4. Tyt Burachynsky to Iakiv Holovatsky, 10 April 1848, in Studynsky, *Korespondentsiia*, 234; Petro Holovatsky to his brother Iakiv, 14 April 1848, ibid., 237; Teofil Pavlykiv to the editors of *Gazeta Powszechna*, 19 September 1848, LBAN, fond T. Pavlykova, ms. 2/p. 1: 43-4. See also *Gazeta Powszechna*, 1848, no. 18.

5. "Kronika Ostermana," LBAN, fond Naukovoho tovarystva im. T. Shevchenka, ms. 19/1: 404-5.
6. Bryk, "Materiialy ukrainsko-cheskykh vzaiemyn," 132.
7. Teodor Leontovych to the Holovna Rada's delegation in Prague, 22 (?) June 1848, TDIA, fond 180, op. 1, spr. 1: 5; Hostička, *Spolupráce Čechů a haličských Ukrajinců*, 68ff.
8. Report of Karol Forster, 16 July 1848, ACz, ms. 5654 IV: 63, and 5362 III: 36. See also Handelsman, *Ukraińska polityka Czartoryskiego*, 94.
9. Iakhymovych to Levytsky, in Studynsky, "Materiialy kulturnoho zhytia v Halychyni," 330.
10. *Zoria Halytska*, 1848, no. 9: 36.
11. The Ruthenian council in Kolomyia to the Univ council, 19 July 1848, LBAN, fond R. Mokha, ms. 283/p. 7: 1-2.
12. Zhelekhovsky, "Avtobiografiia," *Vestnik Narodnogo doma*, 1909: 11-12; *Zoria Halytska*, 1848, no. 14: 59-60, and no. 15: 63; *Gazeta Narodowa*, 1848, no. 91. See also Krevetsky, "Proby orhanizovannia hvardii," 103-4.
13. *Zoria Halytska*, 1848, no. 14: 60.
14. *Gazeta Narodowa*, 23 August 1848, no. 98; *Gazeta Powszechna*, 2 and 16 September 1848, nos. 2, 12; *Dziennik Narodowy*, 1848, no. 123: 517; TDIA, fond 180, op. 1, spr. 5: 21.
15. TDIA, fond 180, op. 1, spr. 6: 4-5, 12, 16-17. See also Krevetsky, "Proby orhanizovannia hvardii," 92; and *Gazeta Narodowa*, 1848, no. 139.
16. Mykhailo Malynovsky posited this view in *Zoria Halytska*, 1848, no. 9: 36. It was echoed by Krevetsky, "Proby orhanizovannia hvardii," 84.
17. Kyrylo Khomynsky to Antin Petrushevych, 7 October 1848, LBAN, fond A. S. Petrushevycha, ms. 369/p. 12, no. 203. See also Felczak, *Węgierska polityka narodowościowa*, 140-47.
18. LBAN, fond T. Pavlykova, ms. 65/p. 3: 95-6; LBAN, fond R. Mokha, ms. 15/p. 2: 33-6; *Zoria Halytska*, 1848, no. 21: 85-6; Krevetsky, "Proby orhanizovannia hvardii," 85-9. See also *Vestnik Narodnogo doma*, 1912: 121-2.
19. LBAN, fond R. Mokha, ms. 15/p. 2: 35-6.
20. Ibid.: 33-4.
21. 19 September 1848, in Studynsky, *Korespondentsiia*, 294.
22. Felczak, *Węgierska polityka narodowościowa*, 147.
23. *Zoria Halytska*, 1848, no. 20: 82-3.
24. Ibid., no. 23: 95.
25. Ibid.; Krevetsky, "Proby orhanizovannia hvardii," 90-91.
26. *Gazeta Powszechna*, 1848, no. 36; Krevetsky, "Proby orhanizovannia hvardii," 93-4.
27. *Zoria Halytska*, 1848, no. 25: 105; Krevetsky, "Proby orhanizovannia hvardii," 95.

28. *Gazeta Powszechna*, 25 October 1848, no. 44; *Gazeta Narodowa*, 1848, nos. 150-51; Krevetsky, "Proby orhanizovannia hvardii," 100-101.
29. LBAN, fond R. Mokha, ms. 23/p. 2, no. 58; TDIA, fond 180, op. 1, spr. 6: 34-5, 37-8, 45; *Gazeta Narodowa*, 1848, nos. 152, 154; *Gazeta Powszechna*, 25 October 1848, no. 44; Krevetsky, "Proby orhanizovannia hvardii," 124.
30. LBAN, fond T. Pavlykova, ms. 65/p. 3: 94.
31. Ibid., 109-10, 113; *Vestnik Narodnogo doma*, 1909: 125-6; Krevetsky, "Proby orhanizovannia hvardii," 94.
32. TDIA, fond 180, op. 1, spr. 6: 49-51, 57, 67, 76, 78.
33. *Zoria Halytska*, 1848, no. 27: 110-11. See also Studynsky, *Korespondentsiia*, 300; and Krevetsky, "Proby orhanizovannia hvardii," 95-6.
34. LBAN, fond T. Pavlykova, ms. 65/p. 3: 108; *Vestnik Narodnogo doma*, 1909: 125; *Gazeta Powszechna*, 18 October 1848, no. 38; Krevetsky, "Proby orhanizovannia hvardii," 105-8, 118.
35. Buchynsky to Borodaikevych, 11 January 1849, LBAN, fond O. Buchynskoho, ms. 230/p. 6.
36. LBAN, fond T. Pavlykova, ms. 2/p. 1, no. 5: 13-14; *Vestnik Narodnogo doma*, 1909: 125.
37. LBAN, fond T. Pavlykova, ms. 65/p. 3: 108, and ms. 2/p. 1: 45; TDIA, fond 180, op. 1, spr. 6 (letter to Holovna Rada of 15 November 1848).
38. TDIA, fond 180, op. 1, spr. 6: 67-8.
39. Ibid.: 51, 53-6, 62, 64-6; *Gazeta Powszechna*, 1848, no. 28; Krevetsky, "Proby orhanizovannia hvardii," 124.
40. LBAN, fond T. Pavlykova, ms. 2/p. 1: 45.
41. TDIA, fond 180, op. 1, spr. 6 (letter of the Przemyśl Ruthenian council to the Holovna Rada of 28 January 1849); Krevetsky, "Proby orhanizovannia hvardii," 119-20.
42. Ivan Krevetsky, "Oboronna orhanizatsiia ruskykh selian na halytsko-uhorskim pohranychu v 1848-1849 rr.," *Zapysky Naukovoho tovarystva im. Shevchenka* 63 (1905): 1-26, and 64 (1905): 27-58.
43. *Gazeta Powszechna*, 26 October 1848, no. 45.
44. IL, Arkhiv I. Franka, fond 3, no. 2204: 15.
45. LBAN, fond Naukovoho tovarystva im. T. Shevchenka, ms. 19/1: 515-78 (Osterman's notes). See also *Gazeta Powszechna*, 16 December 1848, no. 50.
46. *Gazeta Powszechna*, 16 December 1848, no. 50.
47. TDIA, fond 180, op. 2, spr. 6: 1-38; *Zoria Halytska*, 1849, nos. 18, 26.
48. *Zoria Halytska*, 1849, no. 3: 16.
49. Text in Ivan Krevetsky, "Batalion ruskykh hirskykh striltsiv 1848-1850 rr.," *Zapysky Naukovoho tovarystva im. Shevchenka* 107 (1912): 52-5.
50. Ibid., 56; LBAN, fond R. Mokha, ms. 15/p. 2: 57. See also *Zoria Halytska*, 1849, no. 29: 169.
51. *Zoria Halytska*, 1849, no. 1: 6. See also ibid., 1848, no. 32: 134.

52. Studynsky, *Korespondentsiia*, 352.
53. To Iakiv Holovatsky, 23 March 1849, ibid., 346.
54. *Zoria Halytska*, 1849, no. 15: 88; no. 29: 170; no. 47: 282. In August, a seventh company was added. Ibid., 1849, no. 69: 409. See also Krevetsky, "Batalion ruskykh striltsiv," 57.
55. *Zoria Halytska*, 1849: 277-8; Krevetsky, "Batalion ruskykh striltsiv," 60-61.
56. Borysykevych to Iakiv Holovatsky, 27 June 1849, in Studynsky, *Korespondentsiia*, 370.
57. Krevetsky, "Batalion ruskykh striltsiv," 61-5. See also *Zoria Halytska*, 1849, no. 69: 409; and Teofil Pavlykiv to Mykhailo Kuzemsky, 19 June 1849, LBAN, fond T. Pavlykova, ms. 2/p. 1, no. 22: 46.
58. *Zoria Halytska*, 1849, no. 47: 279.
59. Krevetsky, "Batalion ruskykh striltsiv," 68-70. See also *Zoria Halytska*, 1849, nos. 71, 81, 93; 1850, nos. 5, 8; 1851, no. 2.
60. Łoziński, *Gołuchowski*, 153-4; Krevetsky, "Batalion ruskykh striltsiv," 72.

17. Education and Culture

1. This attitude was reflected, for example, in V. Kysilevsky to Antin Petrushevych, 1848, LBAN, fond A. S. Petrushevycha, ms. 125/p. 6, no. 156; Iosafat Kobrynsky to Petrushevych, 12 July 1848, ibid., ms. 129/p. 6, no. 198; Hryhorii Bodnar to Iakiv Holovatsky, 10 September 1848, in Studynsky, *Korespondentsiia*, 286. The Ruthenian deanery council in Berezhany wrote to the Holovna Rada on 28 June 1848, "The bondage of the peasants has ended, but their enlightenment is essential if freedom is to work to their advantage." LBAN, fond T. Pavlykova, ms. 65/p. 3: 30.
2. TDIA, fond 180, op. 1, spr. 1: 35.
3. Ivan Antonevych to Iakiv Holovatsky, 8 February 1848; Tyt Burachynsky to Iakiv Holovatsky, 10 April 1848; Father Dasevych to Iakiv Holovatsky, 16 September 1848, in Studynsky, *Korespondentsiia*, 231, 234-5, 290. See also Ziemiałkowski, *Pamiętniki*, 1: 11.
4. Directive of Bishop Iakhymovych, 18 November 1847, in Tomashivsky, "Materiialy do istorii halytsko-ruskoho shkilnytstva," 181-2; Studynsky, "Materiialy kulturnoho zhytia v Halychyni," xli-xlv.
5. Iakhymovych to Levytsky, 1 January 1848, and Levytsky to Iakhymovych, 2 January 1848, in Studynsky, "Materiialy kulturnoho zhytia v Halychyni," 269-70.
6. To Levytsky, 4 January 1848, ibid., 271-2.
7. Iakhymovych to Levytsky, 1 January 1848, and Levytsky to Iakhymovych, 14 January and 2 February 1848, ibid., 269, 272, 274, 281.
8. Iakhymovych to Levytsky, 15 January 1848, ibid., 274-5.
9. *Gazeta Lwowska*, 15 May 1848, no. 57, supplement.

10. See Kosachevskaia, *Vostochnaia Galitsiia*, 133-4.
11. Tomashivsky, "Materiialy do istorii halytsko-ruskoho shkilnytstva," 182.
12. IL, Arkhiv I. Franka, fond 3, no. 2204: 13. See also *Zoria Halytska*, 1848, no. 7: 28; TDIA, fond 180, op. 1, spr. 20: 33-4; and Kosachevskaia, *Vostochnaia Galitsiia*, 132.
13. LBAN, fond R. Mokha, ms. 23/p. 2, no. 35. See also Malynovsky's article in *Zoria Halytska*, 1848, no. 9; and the circular of 30 August 1848 by the *Kreishauptmann* in Kolomyia, in Tomashivsky, "Materiialy do istorii halytsko-ruskoho shkilnytstva," 183-5.
14. See LBAN, fond T. Pavlykova, ms. 65/p. 3: 20 for a report from the Ruthenian council in Berezhany to the Holovna Rada on the need to introduce schooling. See also *Vestnik Narodogo doma*, 1909: 108.
15. Protocol of the meetings of the Ruthenian council in Hlyniany, LBAN, fond R. Mokha, ms. 16/p. 2: 4; and Iosafat Kobrynsky to R. Mokh, 12 October 1848, in *Zapysky Naukovoho tovarystva im. Shevchenka* 81 (1908): 169.
16. 7 July 1848, LBAN, fond R. Mokha, ms. 32/p. 2, and ms. 15/p. 2: 33.
17. LBAN, fond T. Pavlykova, ms. 65/p. 3: 48; *Vestnik Narodnogo doma*, 1909: 111. See also TDIA, fond 180, op. 2, spr. 20: 20-25; and M. Vozniak, *Prosvitni zmahannia halytskykh Ukraintsiv v XIX vitsi* (Lviv 1912), 23-4.
18. Vozniak, *Prosvitni zmahannia halytskykh Ukraintsiv*, 70-71.
19. LBAN, fond T. Pavlykova, ms. 65/p. 3: 103-6; ibid., fond R. Mokha, ms. 15/p. 2: 47-50. See also Blonsky to Iakiv Holovatsky, 25 July 1848, in Studynsky, *Korespondentsiia*, 271. Initially, the *Gubernium* had directed that the learning of Ukrainian would not be compulsory and that teachers of Ukrainian would receive no compensation.
20. Holovna Rada to the Ruthenian councils, 18 September 1848, LBAN, fond R. Mokha, ms. 15/p. 2: 47-50.
21. Ostaszewski-Barański, *Zaleski*, 170; Łoziński, *Gołuchowski*, 159; *Gazeta Lwowska*, 9 October 1848; *Dziennik Narodowy*, 1848, no. 165: 683. See also Smolka, *Dziennik Franciszka Smolki*, 52-4, 64; and TDIA, fond 180, op. 1, spr. 2: 24.
22. 6 October 1848, no. 28. See also *Dnewnyk Ruskij*, 1848, no. 7: 27-8.
23. *Gazeta Lwowska* (11 September 1848, no. 107: 921) printed the Ministry of Education's rescript of 18 August. The preparatory year was introduced in Lviv, Chernivtsi, Przemyśl and Tarnów. See also ibid., 1 December 1848; and Ostaszewski-Barański, *Zaleski*, 176, 236. Cf. the erroneous assessments of the new regulations in Łoziński, *Gołuchowski*, 159-60.
24. TDIA, fond 180, op. 1, spr. 2: 19, 21-2; and op. 2, spr. 20: 148-9; LBAN, fond T. Pavlykova, ms. 65/p. 3: 99. See also Borysykevych to Iakiv Holovatsky, 30 October 1848, in Studynsky, *Korespondentsiia*, 303.
25. LBAN, fond T. Pavlykova, ms. 65/p. 3: 115, 117-18. See also *Zoria Halytska*, 1848, no. 32: 133.
26. Ostaszewski-Barański, *Zaleski*, 172-6.

27. Ibid., 236. *Zoria Halytska* (1848, no. 29: 121-2) made no mention of the Ukrainian delegates' willingness to retain German. However, in a subsequent issue the newpaper maintained that the delegates had requested "that the Ruthenian language and script be introduced in all schools" (nos. 30-31).

28. Ostaszewski-Barański, *Zaleski*, 237-8. Text in Alfred Fischel, ed., *Das österreichische Sprachenrecht*: *Eine Quellensammlung* (Brno 1901), 83.

29. Fischel, *Das österreichische Sprachenrecht*, 84-5. See also Geist-Lanyi, *Das Nationalitätenproblem*, 169-70.

30. In Western Galician gymnasia Ukrainian was accorded the same rights as Polish in Eastern Galicia. See Łoziński, *Gołuchowski*, 269.

31. Smolka, *Dziennik Franciszka Smolki*, 203-4, 206. The Czech newspaper *Lípa slovanskâ* (30 November 1848, no. 18) reported that the Holovna Rada had insisted on the introduction of German. In reply, *Zoria Halytska* (19 December 1848, no. 32) did not deny this contention.

32. *Zoria Halytska*, 1849, no. 59: 353-4; no. 61: 364-6; no. 62: 369-71.

33. LBAN, fond Sapiehów, ms. 602/IVB, VII, 153.

34. *Verhandlungen des österreichischen Reichstages*, 4: 711-13; Smolka, *Dziennik Franciszka Smolki*, 206, 209.

35. *Verhandlungen des österreichischen Reichstages*, 5: 337-8.

36. See Łoziński, *Gołuchowski*, 161, 269.

37. Borysykevych to Iakiv Holovatsky, 13 May 1848, in Studynsky, *Korespondentsiia*, 243. On the congress of Ukrainian scholars, see especially Iakiv Holovatsky, *Istoricheskii ocherk osnovaniia Galitsko-russkoi Matitsy i spravozdanie pervogo Soboru uchenykh russkikh i liubitelei narodnogo prosveshcheniia* (Lviv 1850); Bohachevsky-Chomiak, *The Spring of a Nation*, 50-52; Kosachevskaia, *Vostochnaia Galitsiia*, 128-31; D. Horniatkevych, "Pershyi zizd ukrainskykh uchenykh u Lvovi v 1848," *Vyzvolnyi shliakh*, June-August 1959.

38. Borysykevych to Iakiv Holovatsky, 13 May 1848, Ivan Hurkevych to Iakiv Holovatsky, 27 July 1848, in Studynsky, *Korespondentsiia*, 242-3, 277. Mykhailo Malynovsky presided at the congress, which had forty-five founding members.

39. See Borysykevych to Iakiv Holovatsky, 19 September 1848, ibid., 294; and *Zoria Halytska*, 1848, no. 17: 69-70. The draft statutes, prepared before the congress, stipulated that members must be "of the Greek rite . . . and, in addition, loyal and right-thinking citizens of the constitutional Austrian monarchy."

40. Iakiv Holovatsky to Borysykevych, 17 September 1848, in Studynsky, *Korespondentsiia*, 292.

41. Invitation to attend the congress dated 14 September 1848, ibid., 289. See also M. Vozniak, "Proiekt pravopysy Ivana Zhukivskoho na zizdi 'ruskykh uchenykh'," *Zapysky Naukovoho tovarystva im. Shevchenka* 82 (1908): 53.

42. Holovatsky, *Istoricheskii ocherk osnovaniia Galitsko-russkoi Matitsy*, xvii-xviii.

43. Zhelekhovsky, "Avtobiografiia," *Vestnik Narodnogo doma*, 1909.
44. Sozansky, "Z literaturnoi spadshchyny Ilnytskoho," 21. See also *Zoria Halytska*, 1848, no. 25: 105; and Stefan Kaczała [Stepan Kachala], *Polityka Polaków względem Rusi* (Lviv 1879), 292.
45. Holovatsky, *Istoricheskii ocherk osnovaniia Galitsko-russkoi Matitsy*, 10; Sozansky, "Z literaturnoi spadshchyny Ilnytskoho," 22.
46. Holovatsky, *Istoricheskii ocherk osnovaniia Galitsko-russkoi Matitsy*, 2-9; Sozansky, "Z literaturnoi spadshchyny Ilnytskoho," 9.
47. Sozansky, "Z literaturnoi spadshchyny Ilnytskoho," 22.
48. Ibid. See also Bohachevsky-Chomiak, *The Spring of a Nation*, 51.
49. Holovatsky, *Istoricheskii ocherk osnovaniia Galitsko-russkoi Matitsy*, 98.
50. Vozniak, "Proiekt pravopysy Zhukivskoho," 54. See also Holovatsky, *Istoricheskii ocherk osnovaniia Galitsko-russkoi Matitsy*, xxvii, xcix.
51. Text in Vozniak, "Proiekt pravopysy Zhukivskoho," 70ff.
52. Vereshchynsky to Iakiv Holovatsky, 24 September 1848, in Studynsky, *Korespondentsiia*, 295-6. See also Vozniak, "Proiekt pravopysy Zhukivskoho," 55-6.
53. Levytsky to Iakiv Holovatsky, 20 October 1848, in Studynsky, *Korespondentsiia*, 397; Sozansky, "Z literaturnoi spadshchyny Ilnytskoho," 24. See also Vozniak, "Proiekt pravopysy Zhukivskoho," 56-7.
54. See Zhelekhovsky, "Avtobiografiia," *Vestnik Narodnogo doma*, 1909: 15. The proponents of a phonetic spelling were labelled "samouky" (autodidacts).
55. Text in *Zapysky Naukovoho tovarystva im. Shevchenka* 66 (1905): 142-72.
56. Iakiv Holovatsky, *Rosprava o iazytsi iuzhnoruskom i ieho narichiiakh* (Lviv 1849), 50-53. See also M. Vozniak, "Zmina pohliadiv Iakova Holovatskoho v ioho vlasnomu osvitlenni," in *U stolittia "Zori,"* 2: 217-19.
57. TDIA, fond 180, op. 2, spr. 2: 17; Holovatsky, *Istoricheskii ocherk osnovaniia Galitsko-russkoi Matitsy*, xviii; Kosachevskaia, *Vostochnaia Galitsiia*, 131; Steblii, "Revoliutsiia 1848-1849 rr.," 235.
58. Statutes of the congress of Ukrainians scholars, para. 1, in Studynsky, *Korespondentsiia*, 273.
59. Borysykevych to Iakiv Holovatsky, 20 October 1848, and 20 October 1849, ibid., 303, 398.
60. Statutes of the congress, para. 14, ibid., 274; *Istoriia Lvova. Korotkyi narys* (Lviv 1956), 69; Bohachevsky-Chomiak, *The Spring of a Nation*, 52. See also Borysykevych to Iakiv Holovatsky, 18 November 1848, in Studynsky, *Korespondentsiia*, 314.
61. See TDIA, fond 180, op. 2, spr. 20-23.
62. Borysykevych to Iakiv Holovatsky, 30 October 1848, in Studynsky, *Korespondentsiia*, 303. Shashkevych's appointment was confirmed by the emperor in December 1848 (Blonsky to Petro Holovatsky, 15 December 1848, ibid., 323), but as late as September 1849 he did not have an assigned position in the ministry and functioned only as an informal advisor. See Iakiv

Holovatsky to his brother Petro, 13 September 1849, ibid., 389.

63. Kaczała, *Polityka Polaków względem Rusi*, 397. See also Studynsky, *Korespondentsiia*, 320, 377, 401; Vozniak, "Proiekt pravopysy Zhukivskoho," 62*n*.

64. See Studynsky, *Korespondentsiia*, 377, 403-4, 410.

65. Ivan Holovatsky to his brother Iakiv, 27 October 1849, and to his brother Petro, 17 November 1849, ibid., 401, 404.

66. To Iakiv Holovatsky, 20 October 1849, ibid., 397.

67. *Gazeta Lwowska*, 1848, no. 108: 829-30. See also Borysykevych to Iakiv Holovatsky, 19 September 1848, in Studynsky, *Korespondentsiia*, 294.

68. 13 May 1848, in Studynsky, *Korespondentsiia*, 242.

69. Zubrytsky to Iakiv Holovatsky, 13 September 1848, Borysykevych to Iakiv Holovatsky, 19 September 1848, Zubrytsky to Iakiv Holovatsky, 30 September 1848, ibid., 288, 294, 297.

70. 17 September 1848, ibid., 291-2.

71. Blonsky to Iakiv Holovatsky, 5 October 1848, and Petro Holovatsky to his brother Iakiv, 1 December 1848, ibid., 297-300, 318.

72. Petro Holovatsky to his brother Iakiv, 25 November 1848, ibid., 315; Kolomyia district Ruthenian council to Berezhany district Ruthenian council, 7 December 1848, LBAN, fond T. Pavlykova, ms. 65/p. 3: 119; *Vestnik Narodnogo doma*, 1909: 127.

73. To Iakiv Holovatsky, 26 November 1848, in Studynsky, *Korespondentsiia*, 316.

74. Blonsky to Iakiv Holovatsky, 3 and 8 December 1848, ibid., 319, 322.

75. Petro Holovatsky to his brother Iakiv, 1 December 1848, ibid., 318; Malynovsky to Antin Petrushevych, November (?) 1848, LBAN, fond A. S. Petrushevycha, ms. 202/p. 7, no. 149.

76. Petro Holovatsky to his brother Iakiv, 1 and 4 December 1848, and Volodymyr and Omelian Holovatsky to their brother Iakiv, 10 February 1849, in Studynsky, *Korespondentsiia*, 318, 320, 335.

77. *Try vstupytelnyie prepodavaniia o russkoi slovesnosty* (Lviv 1849), cited in Iuliian Romanchuk, ed., *Tvory Markiiana Shashkevycha, Iakova Holovatskoho, Nykoly Ustyianovycha, Antona Mohylnytskoho* (Lviv 1906), 156.

78. *Istoriia russkoi slovesnosti, preimushchestvenno drevnei*, 4 vols. (Moscow 1846-60). Holovatsky asked Bodiansky to obtain a copy in a letter of 15 April 1849, in Studynsky, *Korespondentsiia*, 416.

79. Oleksander Barvinsky, *Spomyny z moho zhytia*, vol. 1 (Lviv 1912), 102.

80. I. Levytsky, "Iakiv Holovatsky i Panteleimon Kulish," *Dilo*, 1886, no. 48, cited in O. Petrash, "*Ruska Triitsia*." *Markiian Shashkevych, Ivan Vahylevych, Iakiv Holovatsky* (Kiev 1972), 137-8.

81. M. Vozniak ("Proiekt pravopysy Zhukivskoho," 70) argued that "Zhukovsky would have accomplished the obligations of professor of Ukrainian at the

university... with greater advantage for the cultural improvement of Austrian Rus' than did Holovatsky."

82. See Vasyl Petrovych to Teofil Pavlykiv, 7 June 1848, LBAN, fond T. Pavlykova, ms. 8-60/p. 2.

83. See Borysykevych to the editor of *Zoria Halytska*, 18 November 1848, Blonsky to Iakiv Holovatsky, 15 December 1848, Petro Holovatsky to his brother Iakiv, December 1848, Hryhorii Bodnar to Iakiv Holovatsky, 10 May 1849, Iosafat Kobrynsky to Iakiv Holovatsky, 7 June 1849, in Studynsky, *Korespondentsiia*, 313, 322, 327, 359, 363. The organization of the Matytsia was borrowed from the Czech *matica*. See Bohachevsky-Chomiak, *The Spring of a Nation*, 52.

84. To his brother Petro, 19 August, 13 September, 4 October 1849, in Studynsky, *Korespondentsiia*, 374, 390, 395-6.

85. Iakiv Holovatsky to Daniel Hartenstein, 7 April 1849, ibid., 356.

86. See Ivan Franko, "Ivan Hushalevych," in *Tvory*, 17: 346-406.

87. Studynsky, "Polski konspiratsii sered Ruskykh," 88. Franko (*Tvory*, 17: 361) described Hushalevych as "without thought and reactionary in his principles; 'Myr vam brattia' had immediately made him into the poet of the Ruthenian nation in Austria and opened the way for public activities."

88. Shchurat, *Vybrani pratsi z istorii literatury* (Kiev 1963), 148-51.

89. The censor delayed publication. See Malkin, *Russkaia literatura v Galitsii*, 37-8.

90. *Marusia, povist maloruska rozkazana Hrytskom Osnovianenkom* (Lviv 1849). See also *Zoria Halytska*, 1849, no. 55.

91. A similar reading club was located in Lviv. See Iakiv Holovatsky to Osyp Bodiansky, 15 April 1849, in Studynsky, *Korespondentsiia*, 416.

92. Bodnar to Iakiv Holovatsky, 10 May 1849; Kobrynsky to Iakiv Holovatsky, 7 June 1849, ibid., 360, 363; Kobrynsky to Petrushevych, n.d., LBAN, fond A. S. Petrushevycha, ms. 129/p. 6, no. 198; Kobrynsky to Mokh, 12 October 1848, in Vozniak, "Iz korespondentsii R. Mokha," 168.

    On the Ukrainian theatre in Galicia in 1848, see especially H. Khotkevych, *Teatr 1848 roku* (Kharkiv and Kiev 1932); Ivan Franko, "Ruskyi teatr v Halychyni," in *Tvory*, 16: 92-105; Franko, "Rusko-ukrainskyi teatr," ibid., 16: 233-9; Franko, "Pysania I. P. Kotliarevskoho v Halychyni," *Zapysky Naukovoho tovarystva im. Shevchenka* 26 (1898); Franko, "Halytskyi 'Moskal Charivnyk'," ibid., 27 (1899); Vozniak, "Ukrainski dramatychni vystavy v Halychyni," 87-8 (1909); R. F. Kyrchiv, " 'Karpaccy górale' I. Korzheniovskoho v ukrainskykh perekladakh i pererobkakh," *Mizhslovianski literaturni vzaiemyny* 2 (1961): 91-111.

93. Ivan Ozarkevych, "Prychynok do istorii nashoho literaturnoho vidrodzhennia. Stattia nezakinchena" (1886), IL, Arkhiv I. Franka, fond 3, no. 609: 1-3.

94. 7 June 1848, in Studynsky, *Korespondentsiia*, 259.

95. 12 October 1848, in Vozniak, "Iz korespondentsii Mokha," 169.
96. *Zoria Halytska*, 1848, no. 25, 106.
97. Petro Holovatsky to his brother Iakiv, 25 November 1848, in Studynsky, *Korespondentsiia*, 316.
98. See Franko, "Rusko-ukrainskyi teatr," in *Tvory*, 16: 237-9.
99. Steblii, "Revoliutsiia 1848-1849 rr.," 236.
100. Kobrynsky to Iakiv Holovatsky, 8 June 1848, and Petro Holovatsky to his brother Iakiv, 25 November 1848, in Studynsky, *Korespondentsiia*, 259-60, 316.
101. Mokh to Iakiv Holovatsky, 8 August and 13 September 1848, ibid., 281, 287; Ivan Bahrynovych to Mokh, 18 March 1849, LBAN, fond R. Mokha, ms. 121/p. 5; *Zoria Halytska*, 1848, nos. 7, 31; and 1849, no. 89.
102. Ustyianovych to Iakiv Holovatsky, 21 December 1848, in Studynsky, *Korespondentsiia*, 325-6; Ustyianovych to Petro Holovatsky, cited in Khotkevych, *Teatr 1848 roku*, 50; Vozniak, "Ukrainski dramatychni vystavy," 62; Kyrchiv, " 'Karpaccy górale' Korzheniovskoho," 97, 102.
103. *Iermak. Sumohliad v piaty diistviiakh Alekseia Khomiakova*. Trans. into Ruthenian by Tselestyn Dolynianenko (Lviv 1849).
104. *Hryts Maznytsia, abo muzh zamanenyi*. Trans. into Little Russian by Ivan Naumovych (Lviv 1849). The translation originally appeared in *Pchola*, 1849, nos. 4-11.
105. Sozansky, "Z literaturnoi spadshchyny Ilnytskoho," 14; Ustyianovych, *Raievsky i rosiiskyi panslavizm. Spomynky z perezhytoho i peredumanoho* (Lviv 1884), 8.
106. Zhukovsky's proposal of 25 December 1848, TDIA, fond 180, op. 1, spr. 2: 18; Report of Borysykevych, 9 October 1848, ibid.: 24.
107. *Zoria Halytska*, 1848, no. 8.
108. Proposal of 14 February 1849, TDIA, fond 180, op. 1, spr. 1: 14.
109. See Treshchakovsky's proposal of 5 May 1849, ibid., spr. 2: 54.
110. LBAN, fond T. Pavlykova, ms. 66/p. 3: 49; *Vestnik Narodnogo doma*, 1909: 55-6.
111. Motions by Herovsky on 8 May, Ilevych on 20 June, and Borysykevych on 26 June 1848, TDIA, fond 180, op. 1, spr. 1: 43, 45, 51.
112. Berezhany district Ruthenian council to Holovna Rada, 15 June 1848, LBAN, fond T. Pavlykova, ms. 65/p. 3: 16; *Vestnik Narodnogo doma*, 1909: 107.
113. Discussion of Borysykevych's motion, TDIA, fond 180, op. 1, spr. 1: 43.
114. H. Lopatynsky to Holovna Rada, 20 July 1848, ibid., 35.
115. Holovna Rada to Ruthenian council in Perehinsko, 13 September 1848, ibid., 37.
116. Borysykevych to Holovna Rada, 9 October 1848, ibid., spr. 2: 24; "Kurzgefasste Wünsche der Ruthenen," in Studynsky, *Korespondentsiia*, 302.

117. Zhovkva district Ruthenian council to Holovna Rada, 22 March 1849, TDIA, fond 180, op. 1, spr. 1: 22.
118. 27 August 1849, in Studynsky, *Korespondentsiia*, 379.
119. Ibid.
120. Ivan Holovatsky to his brother Iakiv, 27 October 1849, ibid., 401-2.
121. Motions of Paventsky on 20 April, Herovsky on 25 May, and Zhukovsky on 11 October 1849, TDIA, fond 180, op. 1, spr. 1: 25, 33, 55; motion of Malynovsky on 6 October 1848, ibid., spr. 2: 25-6.
122. I. Levytsky to Holovna Rada, 4 February 1849; proposals of Zhukovsky on 2 March and 11 October 1849, ibid., spr. 1: 17, 20, 55.
123. Motions of I. Kulchytsky on 29 July and Treshchakovsky on 8 September 1848, ibid., 27, 33; Kobrynsky to Mokh, 30 September 1848, in Vozniak, "Iz korespondentsii Mokha," 169. The Ruthenian council in Kolomyia accused the metropolitan of not employing Ukrainian in the church's publications.
124. TDIA, fond 180, op. 1, spr. 1: 12, 16; and spr. 2: 30. See also *Gazeta Powszechna*, 18 December 1848, no. 51.
125. Fischel, *Das österreichische Sprachenrecht*, 89-90.
126. See above, 164-7.
127. F. Jachim to Iakiv Holovatsky, 24 March 1847, in Studynsky, *Korespondentsiia*, 183-4; Bryk, "Pochatky ukrainskoi presy," 103.
128. Bryk, "Pochatky ukrainskoi presy," 103.
129. *Zoria Halytska*, 1848, no. 1: 4-5. The Holovna Rada considered *Zoria Halytska* as its own organ.
130. Mykhailo Malynovsky in *Gazeta Lwowska*, 1848, no. 104: 904.
131. Bryk, "Pochatky ukrainskoi presy," 141; *Gazeta Narodowa*, 1848, no. 142; *Gazeta Powszechna*, 1848, no. 34.
132. Ivan Holovatsky to his brother Iakiv, 28 March 1849, in Studynsky, *Korespondentsiia*, 349; Kmytsykevych of Drohobych to Holovna Rada, 2 August 1848, TDIA, fond 180, op. 2, spr. 18: 20-21.
133. To Iakiv Holovatsky, 10 July 1848, in Studynsky, *Korespondentsiia*, 264-5.
134. Lytvynovych to S. Drymalyk, 1848, cited in Bryk, "Pochatky ukrainskoi presy," 128.
135. 13 May 1848, in Studynsky, *Korespondentsiia*, 243.
136. Liubych-Mohylnytsky to Iakiv Holovatsky, 10 July 1848, ibid., 265.
137. Bryk, "Pochatky ukrainskoi presy," 128.
138. 17 September 1848, in Studynsky, *Korespondentsiia*, 293. See also Iakiv Holovatsky to Borysykevych, ibid., 292-3.
139. Gołuchowski's pronouncement of 22 June 1849, in O. Ohonovsky, *Istoriia literatury ruskoi*, 2, 2: 404. The Ruthenian district council in Berezhany suggested that the Holovna Rada seek to have *Zoria Halytska* recognized as a governmental publication. See T. Pavlykiv to Kuzemsky, 19 June 1849, LBAN, fond T. Pavlykova, ms. 2/p. 1: 46.

140. Ivan Franko, "Ivan Hushalevych," in *Tvory*, 17: 346-406 *passim*; Volodymyr Dmytruk, *Narys z istorii ukrainskoi zhurnalistyky XIX st.* (Lviv 1969), 44-6; Levytsky, *Halytsko-ruskaia bybliohrafiia*, 1: 47, 49, nos. 560, 580.
141. Ivan Antonevych to Iakiv Holovatsky, 8 February 1849, in Studynsky, *Korespondentsiia*, 335.
142. To his brother Iakiv, 27 August 1849, ibid., 381-2.
143. Ibid., 382.
144. Ivan Holovatsky to his brother Iakiv, 23 August 1849, ibid., 376. On relations with Ustyianovych, see also Ivan Holovatsky's letters of 19 and 24 November 1849, ibid., 407-11.
145. See Bryk, "Pochatky ukrainskoi presy," 134.

18. Polish-Ukrainian Relations

1. Kieniewicz, *Sapieha*, 340.
2. Henryk Wereszycki, introduction to Horoszkiewicz, *Notatki z życia*, xxv.
3. Kieniewicz, *Sapieha*, 351.
4. *Zoria Halytska* (1849, no. 9: 54) maintained that 2,722,000 Ukrainians lived in the twelve eastern Galician districts, but only 47,000 Poles, concentrated in the Lviv, Przemyśl, Sanok and Sambir districts, inhabited the area. Later *Zoria Halytska* (1849, no. 19: 113) lowered its estimate of the number of Ukrainians to 2,616,799 (including this time Bukovyna).
5. Horoszkiewicz, *Notatki z życia*, xxvii and 236-7. The organ of the wealthy landed nobility, *Polska* (12 December 1848, 300), maintained that the Poles themselves, not Stadion, had caused the Ukrainian question, which the government was using against them.
6. Lubomirski to the Rada Narodowa, 23 June 1848, in Wisłocki, *Lubomirski*, 84-90; Žáček, *Slovanský sjezd*, 348-52. Wisłocki believed that the letter was addressed to Smolka, a view that Handelsman echoed (*Ukraińska polityka Czartoryskiego*, 117*n*). However, the addressee could only have been the chairman of the Rada Narodowa, who at the end of June was Piotr Wasilewski. Lubomirski's views were probably influenced by the émigré Hôtel Lambert. On its objectives for Galicia at this time, see ACz, ms. 5364 III: 45-6; and 5654 IV: 42-3. Toward the end of 1848 the Cracow Pole A. Z. Helcel in the Reichstag pressed for a conciliatory policy by the Poles toward the peasants and the Ukrainians. See his letter of 29 December 1848, ACz, ms. 5654 IV: 140-41; and 5364 III: 37.
7. AGAD, fond 278: 25-6; Handelsman, *Ukraińska polityka Czartoryskiego*, 151. See also Kieniewicz, "Galicja w latach 1846-1848," 311.
8. *Rada Narodowa*, 1848, no. 1: 3-4.
9. AGAD, fond 269: 41, 49; Handelsman, *Ukraińska polityka Czartoryskiego*, 151.

10. *Rada Narodowa*, 1848, no. 15: 55-6; and no. 16: 59-60. The documents were drafted only after considerable debate. See Batowski, *Diariusz 1848 roku*, 181-6; and Handelsman, *Ukraińska polityka Czartoryskiego*, 152.

11. J. Dobrzański, "Stanowisko, które deputowani galicyjscy na sejmie zająć powinni," *Gazeta Narodowa*, 1848, no. 50: 195.

12. Batowski, *Diariusz 1848 roku*, 220-25; Handelsman, *Ukraińska polityka Czartoryskiego*, 153.

13. On the Sobor Ruskyi, see especially the nine issues (all published) of its newspaper *Dnewnyk Ruskij*, which appeared in both Cyrillic and Latin alphabet editions. LBAN possesses scattered copies of both versions, whereas a complete run of the Latin alphabet version may be found in the Österreichische Nationalbibliothek in Vienna. On the Sobor Ruskyi, see also I. P. Filevich, *Iz istorii Karpatskoi Rusi* (Warsaw 1907), 74-80; and N. M. Pashaeva, "Otrazhenie natsionalnykh i sotsialnykh protivorechii v Vostochnoi Galichine v 1848 g. v listovkakh Russkogo Sobora," in *Slavianskoe vozrozhdenie*: *Sbornik statei i materialov* (Moscow 1966), 48-62.

14. AGAD, fond 269: 59; Handelsman, *Ukraińska polityka Czartoryskiego*, 152.

15. *Rada Narodowa*, 1848, no. 17: 63.

16. AGAD, fond 269: 67; Handelsman, *Ukraińska polityka Czartoryskiego*, 152-3.

17. *Dziennik Narodowy*, 10 June 1848, no. 66, 272-3.

18. Volodymyr Borys, "Deiaki pytannia polsko-ukrainskykh vidnosyn pid chas revoliutsii 1848 r. v Halychyni," *Ukrainske slovianoznavstvo* 6 (1972): 76, provides the date 23 May, which is incorrect, since Zubrytsky wrote to Iakiv Holovatsky on 20 May that "an assembly of pseudo-Ruthenians has been formed, composed of deserters from our rite, but we wish to have nothing to do with them" (Studynsky, *Korespondentsiia*, 245).

19. "Widozwa Ruskoho Soboru," in Levytsky, *Halytsko-ruskaia bybliohrafiia*, 1, no. 371. See also Pashaeva, "Otrazhenie natsionalnykh i sotsialnykh protivorechii v Vostochnoi Galichine," 53; and Kieniewicz, "Galicja w latach 1846-48," 312.

20. "Ustaw Soboru Ruskoho," *Dnewnyk Ruskij*, 30 August 1848, no. 1: 2.

21. Stebelski, "Lwów w 1848 r.," 545.

22. Kaczała, *Polityka Polaków względem Rusi*, 291.

23. M. Popel, "Ohłaszenye Mychaiła Popela do wsich rusyniu...," cited in Pashaeva, "Otrazhenie natsionalnykh i sotsialnykh protivorechii v Vostochnoi Galichine," 56.

24. J. H., "Poradnyk hospodarskij," *Dnewnyk Ruskij*, 5 September 1848, no. 2: 8.

25. Ibid.

26. *Dnewnyk Ruskij*, 30 August 1848, no. 1: 2.

27. Ibid., 4 October 1848, no. 6: 21-3; 11 October 1848, no. 7: 25-7; 18 October 1848, no. 8: 29-31; 25 October 1848, no. 9: 33.

28. It is difficult to concur with V. Borys's assessment ("Deiaki pytannia polsko-ukrainskykh vidnosyn," 76) that "the Sobor Ruskyi . . . pretended to act in defence of Ukrainian-Polish understanding, but in reality it considered the Ukrainian populace of Galicia to be a part of the Polish nation and negated the independent development of the Ukrainian nation." Cf. *Dziennik Narodowy*, 1848, no. 162: 671.
29. Miller, "Revoliutsionnoe dvizhenie v Galitsii, " 410. See also Borys, "Deiaki pytannia polsko-ukrainskykh vidnosyn," 81-2.
30. "Obywatele Żółkwi do Rady Narodowej Żółkiewskiej," 15 June 1848, TDIA, fond 180, op. 1, spr. 3: 24. See also *Dziennik Narodowy*, 1848, no. 73: 302-3, and no. 87: 368, regarding similar occurrences in Buchach.
31. The Central Rada Narodowa to Iakhymovych, 30 June 1848, TDIA, fond 180, op. 1, spr. 3: 22.
32. Draft reply, with crossed out passages, of Holovna Rada, 10 July 1848, ibid.: 20-21; declaration of the Ruthenian council in Zhovkva of 3 July 1848, ibid.: 29; texts of Bachynsky's and Krushynsky's remarks, ibid.: 31-3, 36-41.
33. Holovna Rada to Piotr Wasilewski, draft of reply, n.d., ibid., 25-8.
34. AGAD, fond 269: 274; Handelsman, *Ukraińska polityka Czartoryskiego*, 154.
35. Iakhymovych to Levytsky, 14 July 1848, in Studynsky, "Materiialy kulturnoho zhytia v Halychyni," 333.
36. Forster to Hôtel Lambert, 16 July 1848, ACz, ms. 5654: 63.
37. See above, 178.
38. *Dziennik Narodowy*, 1848, no. 2: 5-7; no. 3: 11.
39. Ibid., no. 63: 261-2.
40. Ibid., no. 65: 269.
41. Ibid., no. 66: 272-4.
42. Ibid., no. 67: 279.
43. Ibid., no. 66: 276.
44. Ibid., 27 May 1848, no. 57. See also Borys, "Deiaki pytannia polsko-ukrainskykh vidnosyn," 77-8.
45. *Dziennik Narodowy*, 1848, no. 83: 351.
46. Ibid., no. 95: 399-40, and no. 96: 405.
47. Ibid., no. 78: 331-2.
48. Ibid., no. 106: 446.
49. Ibid., no. 154: 639, and no. 155: 643.
50. Ibid., no. 141: 588. Cf. Ostaszewski-Barański, *Rok złudzeń*, 270, who supported the view taken by *Dziennik Narodowy* in its dispute with the Rada Narodowa's newpaper, *Gazeta Narodowa*.
51. *Dziennik Narodowy*, 1848, no. 146: 608.
52. Ibid., no. 131: 549.

53. Ibid., no. 114: 477-8.
54. E.g., *Postęp*, 22 April 1848, no. 4. See also Biretsky to Iakiv Holovatsky, 27 April 1848, in Studynsky, *Korespondentsiia*, 238.
55. *Postęp*, 6, 8, and 10 June 1848, nos. 21-3.
56. Ibid., no. 9. See also Borys, "Deiaki pytannia polsko-ukrainskykh vidnosyn," 79.
57. Cited in P. Zajcew, *Szewczenko i Polacy* (Warsaw 1934), 54.
58. *Gazeta Powszechna*, 5 September 1848, no. 4.
59. T. Burachynsky to Iakiv Holovatsky, 10 April 1848, in Studynsky, *Korespondentsiia*, 234-5; and Iurii Kmit, "1848 rik i Lvivska ruska dukhovna seminariia," *Zapysky Naukovoho tovarystva im. Shevchenka* 40 (1901).
60. Petro Holovatsky to his brother Iakiv, 14 April 1848, in Studynsky, *Korespondentsiia*, 235.
61. LBAN, fond Dzieduszyckich, ms. IV, misc. 12a: 1-2. Printed in *Dziennik Narodowy*, no. 101, 425-6.
62. Studynsky, *Korespondentsiia*, 248-9.
63. Ibid., 262.
64. Biretsky to K. V. Zap, 20 May 1848, in Žáček, *Slovanský sjezd*, 144; Zhelekhovsky, "Avtobiografiia," *Vestnik Narodnogo doma*, 1909: 199.
65. District Rada Narodowa in Stryi to the central Rada Narodowa, 9 August 1848, LBAN, fond Pavlykovskykh, ms. 254: 84.
66. Studynsky, "Polski konspiratsii sered ruskykh pytomtsiv i dukhovenstva," 82: 119ff.
67. TDIA, fond 180, op. 2, spr. 7, k. 9-12. Copy in *Gazeta Narodowa*, 1848, no. 37: 143.
68. TDIA, fond 180, op. 2, spr. 2: 16-20.
69. Iakhymovych to Levytsky, 21 June 1848, in Studynsky, "Materiialy kulturnoho zhytia v Halychyni," 327; *Zoria Halytska*, 1848, no. 8: 32.
70. *Zoria Halytska*, 1848, no. 4: 17.
71. LBAN, fond Pavlykovskykh, ms. 73 I: 188-91.
72. TDIA, fond 180, op. 2, spr. 1: 5; *Zoria Halytska*, 1848, no. 7: 30; *Dziennik Narodowy*, 1848, no. 74: 306. See also Kyrylo Vinkovsky's declaration in *Dnewnyk Ruskij*, 20 September 1848, no. 4: 13-14.
73. See esp. *Zoria Halytska*, 1848, no. 5: 20-21; no. 6: 23-5; no. 10: 40-42. Among the most noteworthy brochures: T. Polański [Polansky], *Słowo jedno w celu wzajemnego porozumienia się* (n.p. n.d.); "Stefan Rusyn," *Panowie Polacy!* (n.p. n.d.); *Uwagi nad rozprawą o tak zwanych Rusinach w Dzienniku Narodowym lwowskim nr 2 zamieszczoną* (Przemyśl [1848]); Zubrzycki, *Granice między ruskim i polskim narodem*; Fedko znad Peltwi, *Rusin do Polaków* (Lviv 1848).
74. Levytsky to Iakhymovych, 4 June 1848, and Iakhymovych to Levytsky, 19 June 1848, in Studynsky, "Materiialy kulturnoho zhytia v Halychyni," 324-5.

75. *Słów kilka w obronie ruskiej narodowości*, 46, 48, 55; Handelsman, *Ukraińska polityka Czartoryskiego*, 93.
76. TDIA, fond 180, op. 2, spr. 2: 40-41.
77. Ievstakhii Prokopchyts issued a polemical reply to Dąbczański in German, *Die ruthenische Frage in Galizien von Anton Dąbczański, Landrat zu Lemberg. Beleuchtet von einem Russinen* (Lviv 1850).
78. Cited in Krevetsky, "Sprava podilu," 94: 82-3.
79. See *Zoria Halytska*, 1848, no. 15: 65.
80. *Gazeta Lwowska*, 1 September 1848, no. 103.
81. *Gazeta Narodowa*, 18 August 1848, no. 95.
82. *Zoria Halytska*, 22 August 1848, no. 15, 67.
83. Mykhailo Kuzemsky to Iuliian Velychkovsky, 27 September 1848, in Bryk, "Pochatky ukrainskoi presy," 132.
84. TDIA, fond 180, op. 1, spr. 6: 73-4, 79-80.
85. *Gazeta Powszechna*, 19 October 1848, no. 39; *Zoria Halytska*, 1848, no. 24: 101.
86. Kaczała, *Polityka Polaków względem Rusi*, 292.
87. Łoziński, *Gołuchowski*, 50-58; Ostaszewski-Barański, *Zaleski*, 214-20.
88. Letter to *Zoria Halytska*, in Studynsky, *Korespondentsiia*, 312, 314.
89. Ibid., 313.
90. Blonsky to Iakiv Holovatsky, 16 November 1848, ibid., 310.
91. Baranovsky to T. Pavlykiv, 26 December 1848, LBAN, fond T. Pavlykova, ms. 8-60/p. 2.
92. Malynovsky to Petrushevych, n.d., LBAN, fond A. S. Petrushevycha, ms. 202/p. 7, no. 205. See also Zhelekhovsky, "Avtobiografiia," *Vestnik Narodnogo doma*, 1910: 23.
93. Kuzemsky to Iakhymovych, 26 December 1848, in Studynsky, "Materiialy kulturnoho zhytia v Halychyni," xl; Blonsky to Iakiv Holovatsky, 26 November 1848, in Studynsky, *Korespondentsiia*, 317; Metropolitan Levytsky's pastoral letter of 12 July 1848, in Studynsky, "Materiialy kulturnoho zhytia v Halychyni," xxxix; *Zoria Halytska*, 1848, no. 10: 39-40; Petition of the Holovna Rada to Minister F. Stadion, 23 December 1848, in Ostaszewski-Barański, *Zaleski*, 239-40.
94. 11 February 1849, Kroměříž, in Studynsky, *Korespondentsiia*, 338.
95. Kobrynsky to Iakiv Holovatsky, 5 March 1849, ibid., 344.
96. 20 December 1849, Lviv, ibid., 413.
97. Sozansky, "Z literaturnoi spadshchyny Ilnytskoho," 19; LBAN, fond Naukovoho tovarystva im. T. Shevchenka, ms. 25/2: 6. See also Borys, "Deiaki pytannia polsko-ukrainskykh vidnosyn," 82.
98. See F. I. Steblii, "Pershi robitnychi barykady na vulytsiakh Lvova," *Ukrainskyi istorychnyi zhurnal*, 1968, no. 11: 130-31.

99. "Hohe Reichsversammlung. Von der Ruthenischen Hauptversammlung, Lemberg 25 August 1848. Reklamation der Ruthenen in Galizien gegen Einwurf als wenn blos eine polnische Fraktion wären," TDIA, fond 201, op. 4, spr. 269: 2. See also Borys, "Deiaki pytannia polsko-ukrainskykh vidnosyn," 86.

100. "Oswidczenije," *Dnewnyk Ruskij*, 20 September 1848, no. 4. Criticism of Vinkovsky's position appeared in *Zoria Halytska*, 1848, nos. 22-4: 93-4, 97-8, 101-2.

101. Liubych-Mohylnytsky to Iakiv Holovatsky, 10 July 1848, in Studynsky, *Korespondentsiia*, 263-5.

102. [Antin Liubych-Mohylnytsky,] "Vsechestnyi narode zemli Halytskoi," TDIA, fond 180, op. 2, spr. 6: 33-5.

103. Letter to the deanery Ruthenian council in Hlyniany, 3 August 1848, LBAN, fond R. Mokha, ms. 26/p. 2.

104. TDIA, fond 180, op. 2, spr. 7: 3-4. The text was reprinted in Włodzimierz [Volodymyr] Borys, "Głos z 1848 r. w sprawie zgody polsko-ukraińskiej," *Przegląd Historyczny* 62, no. 4 (1971): 717-24. Borys attributed the authorship to T. Leontovych.

105. Borys, "Deiaki pytannia polsko-ukrainskykh vidnosyn," 83-4. One may assume that the anonymous author of *Conditions for an Accord* and Fedko, author of *A Ruthenian to the Poles*, were the same person, Teodor (Fedir, Fedko) Leontovych.

106. Kilarski to Iakiv Holovatsky, 17 July 1848, in Studynsky, *Korespondentsiia*, 267-8. Borys ("Deiaki pytannia polsko-ukrainskykh vidnosyn," 83, and "Głos z 1848 r.," 720) considered him a priest, but the content of his letter suggests that he was a *mandatarius*.

107. "Głos prawego Polaka do braci Polaków. Odezwa B. K. Morawskiego, Lwów 16 września 1848," TDIA, fond 180, op. 2, spr. 6: 29-30.

108. W. Podoliński [Vasyl Podolynsky], *Słowo przestrogi* (Sanok 1848); F. I. Steblii, "*Slovo perestorohy* V. Podolynskoho," *Ukrainskyi istorychnyi zhurnal*, 1966, no. 12: 44-51; Vasyl Shchurat, "Rechnyk nezalezhnosty Ukrainy v 1848 r., Vasyl Podolynsky," in *Na dosvitku novoi doby* (Lviv 1919), 134-78.

109. 1848, nos. 8-9.

19. Conclusion

1. To Antin Petrushevych, 18 May 1848, LBAN, fond A. S. Petrushevycha, ms. 369/p. 12, no. 196.

2. Podoliński, *Słowo przestrogi*, 21-2.

3. TDIA, fond 180, op. 1, spr. 4: 31-3. See also Jędrzej Moraczewski, "O kongresie słowiańskim," in Žáček, *Slovanský sjezd*, 325.

4. Ivan Holovatsky to his brother Iakiv, 8 June 1848, in Studynsky, *Korespondentsiia*, 255-6.
5. Ivan Holovatsky to his brother Iakiv, 19 November 1849, ibid., 407-10.
6. "De-shcho do istorii azbuki i iazyka Galitskoi Rusi (iz svoikh zhytevykh zapisok," *Vestnik Narodnogo doma*, 1906: 29-33.
7. Levytsky to Iakhymovych, 12 July 1848, in Studynsky, "Materiialy kulturnoho zhytia v Halychyni," 332; Petrushevych to Iakiv Holovatsky, 12 April 1849, in Studynsky, *Korespondentsiia*, 354.
8. The name was probably coined by August Bielowski. See IL, Arkhiv I. Franka, fond 3, no. 655: 1.
9. Józef Feldman, *Sprawa polska w roku 1848* (Cracow 1933), 286; Handelsman, *Ukraińska polityka Czartoryskiego*, 118-19.
10. To Borysykevych, 19-20 December 1848, LBAN, fond Narodnoho domu, ms. 277/p. 62: 2.
11. ACz, ms. 5653 IV: 418-19; Handelsman, *Ukraińska polityka Czartoryskiego*, 124-5.
12. On the nationality conflict in Hungary in 1848, see especially Felczak, *Węgierska polityka narodowościowa*.
13. 13 January 1849, no. 194; and 15-16 February 1849, nos. 222-3. Reprinted in Karl Marx and Friedrich Engels, *Werke*, 39 vols. in 41 ([East] Berlin 1959-71), 6: *November 1848 bis Juli 1849*. English translation in Karl Marx, *Political Writings*, ed. David Fernbach, 2 vols. (Middlesex 1973), 1: *The Revolutions of 1848*, 213-45.
14. On Engels's views on the nationalities question in East Central Europe in 1848-9, see especially Józef Chlebowczyk, "Marks i Engels a problem małych narodów w Europie środkowo-wschodniej (w kwestii genezy i rozwoju tzw. narodów niehistorycznych)," *Z Pola Walki* 13, no. 2 (1970): 15-43; and Roman Rosdolsky, "Friedrich Engels und das Problem der 'geschichtslosen' Völker: Die Nationalitätenfrage in der Revolution 1848-1849 im Lichte der *Neuen Rheinischen Zeitung*," *Archiv für Sozialgeschichte* 4 (1964): 87-282, and separate book ed., *Zur nationalen Frage: Friedrich Engels und das Problem der "geschichtslosen" Völker* ([West] Berlin 1979).
15. TDIA, fond 201, op. 4-b, spr. 769: 5; Borys, "Deiaki pytannia polsko-ukrainskykh vidnosyn," 74*n*.
16. To his brother Petro, 17 November 1849, in Studynsky, *Korespondentsiia*, 404.

Appendix I
Prominent Galician Ukrainians

Prominent Galician Ukrainians as their names appear in historical literature in transliteration from Ukrainian and in Polish orthography

Ukrainian	*Polish*
Biretsky, Ivan	Birecki, Jan
Blonsky, Kyrylo	Błoński, Cyryl
Borysykevych, Ivan	Borysikiewicz, Jan
Didytsky, Bohdan	Didycki, Bogdan
Harasevych, Mykhailo	Harasiewicz, Michał
Holovatsky, Iakiv	Głowacki (Hołowacki), Jakub
Holovatsky, Ivan	Głowacki (Hołowacki), Jan
Holovatsky, Petro	Głowacki (Hołowacki), Piotr
Hynylevych, Hryhorii	Ginilewicz, Grzegorz
Iakhymovych, Hryhorii	Jachimowicz, Grzegorz
Ilevych, Ivan	Ilewicz, Jan
Ilkevych, Hryhorii	Ilkiewicz, Grzegorz
Ilnytsky, Vasyl	Ilnycki, Wasyl (Bazyli)
Kapushchak, Ivan	Kapuszczak, Jan
Khomynsky, Kyrylo	Chomiński, Cyryl
Kmytsykevych, Mykola	Kmycykiewicz, Mikołaj
Kobrynsky, Iosafat	Kobryński, Josafat
Kobylytsia, Lukian	Kobyłyca (Kobylica), Łukjan
Kropyvnytsky, Iosyf	Kropiwnicki, Józef
Kuzemsky, Mykhailo	Kuziemski, Michał
Leontovych, Teodor (Fedir)	Leontowicz, Teodor
Levytsky, Iosyf	Lewicki, Józef
Levytsky, Mykhailo	Lewicki, Michał
Levytsky, Venedykt	Lewicki, Benedykt

Lozynsky, Iosyf	Łoziński, Józef
Lytvynovych, Spyrydon	Litwinowicz, Spirydion
Maksymovych, Mykhailo	Maksymowicz, Michał
Malynovsky, Mykhailo	Malinowski, Michał
Mohylnytsky [Liubych-], Antin	Mohylnicki (Mogielnicki) [Lubicz-], Antoni
Mohylnytsky, Ivan	Mohylnycki (Mogielnicki), Jan
Mokh, Rudolf	Moch, Rudolf
Mokhnatsky, Dmytro	Mochnacki, Dymitr
Mokhnatsky, Klyment	Mochnacki, Klemens
Paventsky, Antin	Pawencki, Antoni
Pavlykiv, Teofil	Pawłyków, Teofil
Petrushevych, Antin	Petruszewicz, Antoni
Podolynsky, Vasyl	Podoliński, Wasyl (Bazyli)
Popel, Mykhailo	Popiel, Michał
Prokopchyts, Ievstakhii	Prokopczyc, Eustachy
Shashkevych, Hryhorii	Szaszkiewicz, Grzegorz
Shashkevych, Markiian	Szaszkiewicz, Marcjan
Snihursky, Ivan	Snigurski, Jan
Treshchakovsky, Lev	Treszczakowski, Leon
Ustyianovych, Mykola	Ustyanowicz, Mikołaj
Vahylevych, Ivan	Wagilewicz, Jan
Velychkovsky, Iuliian	Wełyczkowski, Julian
Vereshchynsky, Mykola	Wereszczyński, Mikołaj
Vinkovsky, Kyrylo	Wieńkowski, Cyryl
Zaklynsky, Oleksii	Zakliński (Zakłyński), Aleksy
Zhukovsky, Ivan	Żukowski, Jan
Zubrytsky, Denys	Zubrzycki, Dionizy

Appendix II
Place Names in Galicia

(In the left-hand column, italics indicate that the given place is now located in Soviet Ukraine; in the right-hand column, they indicate that the place is located in Poland.)

Ukrainian	*Polish*
Berezhany	Brzeżany
Bibrka	Bóbrka
Bircha	*Bircza*
Bolekhiv	Bolechów
Bohorodchany	Bohorodczany
Brody	Brody
Buchach	Buczacz
Chernivtsi [Bukovyna]	Czerniowce (Ger. Czernowitz, Rom. Cernăuţi)
Chortkiv	Czortków
Drohobych	Drohobycz
Dyniv	*Dynów*
Halych	Halicz
Hlyniany	Gliniany
Horodok	Gródek
Iabloniv	Jabłonów
Iaroslav	*Jarosław*
Iavoriv	Jaworów
Iaslyska	*Jaśliska*
Kalush	Kałusz
Khodoriv	Chodorów

Kholoiv	Chołojów
Kolomyia	Kołomyja (Ger. Kolomea)
Komarno	Komarno
Kosiv	Kosów
Kryvche	Krzywcze
Kuty	Kuty
Labova	*Łabowa*
Liubachiv	*Lubaczów*
Liutovyska	*Lutowiska*
Lviv	Lwów (Ger. Lemberg)
Maidan	Majdan
Mokriany	Mokrzany
Monastyryska	Monasterzyska
Mykulyntsi	Mikulińce
Naraiv	Narajów
Olesko	Olesko
Oliiv	Olejów
Perehinsko	Perehińsko
Peremyshl	*Przemyśl*
Pidbuzh	Podbuż
Pidhaitsi	Podhajce
Radekhiv	Radziechów
Rohatyn	Rohatyń
Rozdil	Rozdół
Rozhniativ	Rożniatów
Sambir	Sambor
Sianik	*Sanok*
Skalat	Skałat
Skole	Skole
Sniatyn	Śniatyń
Sokolivka	Sokołówka
Solotvyna	Sołotwina
Stanyslaviv (Ivano-Frankivsk)	Stanisławów (Ger. Stanislau)
Stryi	Stryj
Terebovlia	Trembowla
Ternopil	Tarnopol
Tysmenytsia	Tyśmienica
Ustia Zelene	Ujście
Univ	Uniów
Vynnyky	Winniki
Zabolotiv	Zabłotów
Zalishchyky	Zaleszczyki
Zaliztsi	Załoźce

Zatvarnytsia	*Zatwarnica*
Zbarazh	Zbaraż
Zboriv	Zborów
Zhovkva (Nesterov)	Żółkiew
Zhuravno	Żurawno
Zhydachiv	Żydaczów
Zolochiv	Złoczów

Bibliography

1. Archival materials

Archiwum Główne Akt Dawnych [Main archive of old acts] (Warsaw), ms. 269, 277, 278.

Biblioteka Narodowa [National library] (Warsaw), ms. 679, 2886.

Biblioteka Polskiej Akademii Nauk w Krakowie [Library of Polish Academy of Sciences in Cracow], ms. 136451-136880: Zbiór pisemek wyszłych w czasie wypadków w Galicyi w latach 1848-1849 [Collection of leaflets and brochures published during the events of 1848-9 in Galicia], 13 vols.

Biblioteka Uniwersytetu Jagiellońskiego [Library of the Jagiellonian University] (Cracow), ms. 2957, 5388/II, 5390/III, 5391, 7088, 7249/I, 7921/III.

Biblioteka Zakładu Narodowego im. Ossolińskich [Library of Ossolineum National Foundation] (Wrocław), ms. 1830/III, 2411/I, 2432/II, 3245/II, 4364/II, 5819/III, 5829/III, 7994/II, 12044/III, 12112/II, 12576/I.

Instytut literatury im. T. H. Shevchenka [T. H. Shevchenko Institute of Literature] (Kiev), Arkhiv I. Franka [Archives of Ivan Franko], fond 3, ms. 30, 581, 609, 655, 715, 2204, 2823.

Lvivska biblioteka Akademii nauk URSR [Lviv library of the Academy of Sciences of the Ukrainian SSR]:
fond Baworowskich, ms. 1624/I;
fond O. Buchynskoho, ms. 230/p. 6;
fond Dzieduszyckich, ms. IV, misc. 12;
fond Lubomirskich, ms. V-13;
fond R. Mokha, ms. 12/p. 2, 15/p. 2, 16/p. 3, 18/p. 2, 23/p. 2, 24/p. 2, 26/p. 2, 28/p. 2, 29/p. 2, 30/p. 2, 32/p. 2, 121/p. 2, 283/p. 7;
fond Narodnoho domu, ms. 277/p. 62;
fond Naukovoho tovarystva im. T. Shevchenka, ms. 19/1, 25/2;
fond Ossolińskich, ms. 7080/II, 7229;
fond Pavlykovskykh, ms. 72-1, 73 I, 254, 28la;
fond T. Pavlykova, ms. 1-1/p. 1, 2/p. 1, 8-16/p. 2, 8-60/p. 2, 24/p. 2, 64/p. 3, 65/p. 3, 66/p. 3, 67/p. 3;
fond A. S. Petrushevycha, ms. 125/p. 6, 129/p. 6, 202/p. 7, 207/p. 5, 369/p. 6, 369/p. 12;
fond Sapiehów, ms. 92/IIB, 574/IVa, 576/IV, 577/IVa, 578/IVa 583/IVa, 585/IVa, 600/IVa, 602/IVB;
fond O. Terletskoho, spr. 144-XIII, 157-XV.

Muzeum Narodowe w Krakowie, Oddział Czartoryskich [National Museum in Cracow, Czartoryski branch], ms. 5356 III, 5362

III, 5363 III, 5364 III, 5653 IV, 5654 IV.

Tsentralnyi derzhavnyi istorychnyi arkhiv u Lvovi [Central state historical archives in Lviv],

Akty Holovnoi rady ruskoi [Acts of the Supreme Ruthenian Council],

fond 180, op. 1, spr. 1-4, 6-10, 20; op. 2, spr. 1-2, 4-8, 14, 18, 21-3.

fond 201, op. 4, spr. 269; op. 4-b, spr. 7692.

2. Contemporary Newspapers

Czas [Time], 1848-9 (Cracow)

Dennitsa-Jutrzenka [Morning star], 1842-3 (Warsaw)

Dnewnyk Ruskij [Ruthenian daily], 1848 (Lviv)

Dziennik Narodowy [National daily], 1848 (Lviv)

Gazeta Lwowska [Lviv gazette], 1848-9

Gazeta Narodowa [National gazette], 1848 (Lviv)

Gazeta Powszechna [General gazette], 1848 (Lviv)

Jahrbücher für slawische Literatur, Kunst und Wissenschaft, 1846-7 (Leipzig)

Moskvitianin [Muscovite], 1841 (Moscow)

Polska [Poland], 1848-9 (Lviv)

Postęp [Progress], 1848 (Lviv)

Rada Narodowa [National Council], 1848 (Lviv)

Rozmaitości [Variety] 1830s (Lviv)

Slawische Central-Blätter, 1848-9 (Prague)

Wiener Zeitung, 1848-9 (Vienna)

Zoria Halytska [Galician star], 1848-51 (Lviv)

3. Correspondence, Documents, Memoirs, Works

Barsukov, N. P. *Zhizn i trudy M. P. Pogodina* [M. P. Pogodin's life and works]. 22 vols. Saint Petersburg 1888-1910.

Barvinsky, Oleksander. *Spomyny z moho zhytia* [Reminiscences of my life]. Vol. 1. Lviv 1912.

Batowski, Aleksander. *Diariusz wypadków 1848 roku* [Diary of the events of 1848]. Edited by Marian Tyrowicz. Wrocław: Ossolineum, 1974.

Bogdański, Henryk. *Pamiętnik 1832-1848* [Memoirs, 1832-48]. Edited by Antoni Knot. Cracow: Wydawnictwo Literackie, 1971.

Borys, Włodzimierz [Volodymyr]. "Głos z 1848 r. w sprawie zgody polsko-ukraińskiej" [A voice from 1848 on behalf of Polish-Ukrainian accord]. *Przegląd Historyczny* 62, no. 4 (1971): 717-24.

Bryk, Ivan, ed. "Materiialy do istorii ukrainsko-cheskykh vzaiemyn v pershii polovyni XIX st." [Materials on the history of Ukrainian-Czech relations in the first half of the nineteenth century]. *Ukrainsko-ruskyi arkhiv* 15 (1921).

Chodakowski, Zorian Dołęga. *O Słowiańszczyźnie przed chrześcijaństwem oraz inne pisma i listy* [Slavdom before Christianity and other writings and letters]. Edited by Julian Maślańka. Warsaw: Państwowe Wydawnictwo Naukowe, 1967.

Cięglewicz, Kasper. *Rzecz czerwono-ruska 1848 roku* [The question of Red Rus' in 1848]. Lviv 1848. German trans.: *Die Roth-reussischen Angelegenheiten im Jahre 1848.* Vienna 1848.

Dąbczański, Antoni. *Die ruthenische Frage in Galizien.* Lviv 1848. Polish version: *Wyjaśnienie sprawy ruskiej* [Explanation of the Ruthenian issue]. Lviv 1848.

Fedko znad Peltvy. *Rusin do Polaków* [A Ruthenian to the Poles]. Lviv 1848.

Fischel, Alfred, ed. *Das österreichische Sprachenrecht*: *Eine Quellensammlung.* Brno 1901.

Francev [Frantsev], V. A. *Korespondence Pavla Josefa Šafaříka s ruskými učenci* [P. J. Šafařík's correspondence with Russian scholars]. 2 vols. Prague 1927-8.

Franko, Ivan. *Tvory* [Works]. 20 vols. Kiev: Derzhavne vydavnytstvo khudozhnoi literatury, 1950-56.

Herder, J. G. *Outlines of a Philosophy of the History of Man.* Translated by T. Churchill, 1800. Reprint. New York: Bergman, 1966.

Holovatsky, Iakiv. *Istoricheskii ocherk osnovaniia galitsko-russkoi Matitsy i spravozdanie pervogo Soboru uchenykh russkikh i liubitelei narodnogo prosveshcheniia* [Historical sketch of the founding of the Galician-Ruthenian Matytsia and a report on the first assembly of Ruthenian scholars and devotees of national enlightenment]. Lviv 1850.

______.*Karpatskaia Rus'. Geograficheskо-statisticheskie i istorichesko-etnograficheskie ocherki Galichiny, severo-vostochnoi Ugrii i Bukoviny.* [Carpathian Rus': Geographical-statistical and historical-ethnographic sketches of Galicia, northeastern Hungary and Bukovyna] In *Narodnye pesni Galitskoi i Ugorskoi Rusi sobrannye I. F. Golovatskim* [Folk songs of Galician and Hungarian Rus' collected by Ia. F. Holovatsky]. Vol. 3, pt. 2 (Moscow 1878), 557-615.

______."K istorii galitsko-russkoi pismennosti (Neskolko zamechanii na pismo I. Vagilevicha k M. P. Pogodinu)" [Toward a history of Galician Ruthenian literature (Some remarks on the letter of Ivan Vahylevych to M. P. Pogodin)]. *Kievskaia starina*, 1883: 652-7.

______.*O pervom literaturno-umstvennom dvizhenii Rusinov v Galitsii vo vremia avstriiskogo vladeniia v toi zemle* [On the first literary-intellectual movement of the Ruthenians in Galicia during Austrian rule]. Lviv 1865.

______."Podróż po Halickiej i Węgierskiej Rusi" [Journey through Galician and Hungarian Rus']. *Dennitsa-Jutrzenka*, 1842, nos. 6, 9, 20-22, 24: 73-82, 114-18, 245-52, 257-64, 275-6, 293-301. [Originally published in Czech in *Časopis Českêho Museum*, 1841-2].

______.*Rosprava o iazytsi iuzhnoruskom i ieho narichiiakh* [Treatise on the South Rus' language and its dialects]. Lviv 1849.

______."Sudba odnogo galitsko-russkogo uchenogo (k biografii Ivana Nikolaevicha Vagilevicha)" [The fate of a Galician Ruthenian scholar (toward a biography of Ivan Vahylevych)]. *Kievskaia starina*, 1883, pt. 6, no. 3: 453-72.

______."Velikaia Khorvatiia ili Galitsko-Karpatskaia Rus' " [Great Croatia or Galician-Carpathian Rus']. *Moskvitianin*, 1841, pt. 6, nos. 11-12: 213-32, 257-67. Ukrainian version in *Ruska biblioteka*, vol. 3. Lviv 1884.

______."Vospominanie o Markiiane Shashkeviche i Ivane Vagileviche" [Reminiscences of M. Shashkevych and I. Vahylevych]. *Literaturnyi sbornik*, 1885.

Horoszkiewicz, Julian. *Notatki z życia* [Notes from my life]. Edited by Henryk Wereszycki. Wrocław: Ossolineum, 1957.

Inglot, Stefan, ed. *Maurycego Kraińskiego regestry materiałów do historii zniesienia stosunku poddańczego w Galicji* [Maurycy Kraiński's file of materials on the history of the abolition of serfdom in Galicia]. Cracow: Nakładem Polskiej Akademii Umiejętności, 1948.

Jabłonowski, Ludwik. *Pamiętniki* [Memoirs]. Edited by Karol Lewicki. Cracow: Wydawnictwo Literackie, 1963.

Kieniewicz, Stefan, ed. *Rok 1848 w Polsce. Wybór źródeł* [1848 in Poland: Selected sources]. Wrocław: Ossolineum, 1948.

Kollár, Ján. *Wybór pism* [Selected writings]. Edited by Henryk Batowski. Wrocław: Ossolineum, 1954.

Krushelnytsky, Antin. "Z dnevnyka hr.-k. parokha 1848-1850 rr." [From the diary of a Greek-Catholic priest in 1848-50]. *Zapysky Naukovoho tovarystva im. Shevchenka* 52 (1903): Miscellanea, 2-19.

[Levytsky, Iosyf.] "Dolia galitsko-russkago iazyka" [The fate of the Galician-Ruthenian language]. *Dennitsa-Jutrzenka*, 1843, pt. 1: 188-204; pt. 2: 39-45.

———.*Grammatik der ruthenischen oder kleinrussischen Sprache in Galizien*. Przemyśl 1834.

Levytsky, Ivan. *Halytsko-ruskaia bybliohrafiia XIX-ho stoletiia* [Galician-Ruthenian bibliography of the nineteenth century]. 2 vols. Lviv 1888-95.

Lewicki, Karol, ed. *Pamiętniki spiskowców i więzniów galicyjskich w latach 1832-1846* [Memoirs of Galician conspirators and prisoners, 1832-46]. Wrocław: Ossolineum, 1954.

Lozynsky, Iosyf. "Avtobiograficheskie zapiski Iosifa Lozinskogo" [Autobiographical notes of Iosyf Lozynsky]. *Literaturnyi sbornik*, 1885.

———.*Gramatyka języka ruskiego* [Grammar of the Ruthenian language]. Przemyśl 1846.

———."Rozprawa o wprowadzeniu abecadła polskiego do piśmiennictwa ruskiego" [Discourse on the introduction of the Polish alphabet into Ruthenian writings]. *Rozmaitości*, 1834, no. 29: 228-30.

———.*Ruskoje wesile* [The Ruthenian wedding]. Przemyśl 1835.

"Materiialy do istorii ruskoho shkilnytstva 1772-1848" [Materials on the history of Ruthenian education, 1772-1848]. *Zbirnyk Istorychno-filosofichnoi sektsii Naukovoho tovarystva im. Shevchenka* 5: 87-304.

Mohylnytsky, Ivan. "Rozprawa o języku ruskim" [Discourse on the Ruthenian language]. *Czasopismo Naukowe Księgozbioru Publicznego im. Ossolińskich*, 1829. Reprinted in Lviv 1848.

Ukrainian trans. as "Vidomist o ruskom iazytsi." In *Ukrainsko-ruskyi arkhiv* 5 (1910): 1-70.

Pisma k M. P. Pogodinu iz slavianskikh zemel [Letters to M. P. Pogodin from the Slavic lands]. Edited by N. Popov. Moscow 1880.

Podolynsky, Vasyl [Podoliński, Wasyl]. *Słowo przestrogi* [A word of warning]. Sanok 1848.

Romanchuk, Iuliian, ed. *Tvory Markiiana Shashkevycha, Iakova Holovatskoho, Nykoly Ustyianovycha, Antona Mohylnytskoho* [Works of Markiian Shashkevych, Iakiv Holovatsky, Mykola Ustyianovych and Anton Liubych-Mohylnytsky]. Lviv 1906.

Rozdolski [Rosdolsky], Roman. "Nowe dokumenty do historii zniesienia pańszczyzny w Galicji w r. 1848" [New documents on the abolition of *robot* in Galicia in 1848]. *Przegląd Historyczny* 53, no. 1 (1962): 119-27.

Rusalka Dnistrovaia. Vid davnyny do suchasnosti [The nymph of the Dniester. From older times to the present]. Kiev 1960.

Rusyn, Havryło [Holovatsky, Iakiv]. "Zustände der Russinen in Galizien." *Jahrbücher für slawische Literatur, Kunst und Wissenschaft* 4 (1846): 361-79.

Sacher-Masoch, Leopold. *Polnische Revolutionen: Erinnerungen aus Galizien.* Prague 1863.

Šafařík, Pavel Josef. *Slovanský nārodopis* [Slavic ethnography]. 4th ed. Prague: Nakladatelství Československé Akademie Věd, 1955.

Savchenko, Fedir, ed. *Zakhidnia Ukraina v lystuvanni Ia. Holovatskoho z O. Bodianskym* [Western Ukraine in the correspondence of Iakiv Holovatsky with Osyp Bodiansky]. Kiev 1930.

Shankovsky, A. P. "Vospominaniia iz nedavnoi byvalshchiny" [Recollections of the recent past]. *Rodimyi listok*, 1880-81.

[Shashkevych, Markiian]. *Pysannia Markiiana Shashkevycha* [Markiian Shashkevych's writings]. Edited by M. Vozniak. Lviv 1912.

Shchurat, Vasyl, ed. "Lysty mytropolyta M. Levytskoho do ep. Snihurskoho i ofitsiialni dokumenty ikh spilnoi diialnosty (1813-1847)" [Letters of Metropolitan Mykhailo Levytsky to Bishop Ivan Snihursky and official documents of their joint activities, 1813-1847]. *Ukrainskyi arkhiv* 12 (1924).

Smolka, Stanisław, ed. *Dziennik Franciszka Smolki 1848-1849 w listach do żony* [Diary of Franciszek Smolka from 1848-49 in his letters to his wife]. Warsaw 1913.

Sozansky, Ivan. "Z literaturnoi spadshchyny Vasylia Ilnytskoho" [From the literary heritage of Vasyl Ilnytsky]. *Zapysky Naukovoho tovarystva im. Shevchenka* 66 (1906): 1-59.

Springer, Anton, ed. *Protokolle des Verfassungs-Ausschusses im Oesterreichischen Reichstage 1848-1849*. Leipzig, 1885.

Studynsky, Kyrylo, ed. *Korespondentsiia Iakova Holovatskoho v litakh 1835-49* [Iakiv Holovatsky's correspondence, 1835-49]. Lviv 1909.

———."Materiialy do istorii kulturnoho zhytia v Halychyni v 1795-1857 rr." [Materials on the history of cultural life in Galicia, 1795-1857]. *Ukrainsko-ruskyi arkhiv* 13-14 (1920).

———."Prychynky do istorii kulturnoho zhyttia Halytskoi Rusy v litakh 1833-47" [Contributions to the history of cultural life in Galician Rus', 1833-47]. *Zbirnyk Istorychno-filosofichnoi sektsii Naukovoho tovarystva im. Shevchenka*, vols. 11-12.

———."Z korespondentsii Denysa Zubrytskoho" [From Denys Zubrytsky's correspondence]. *Zapysky Naukovoho tovarystva im. Shevchenka* 43 (1901): 1-66.

Tershakovets, Mykhailo, ed. "Materiialy i zamitky do istorii natsionalnoho vidrodzhennia Halytskoi Rusy v 1830 ta 1840 rr." [Materials and notes on the history of the national rebirth of Galician Rus' in the 1830s and 1840s]. *Ukrainsko-ruskyi arkhiv* 3 (1907).

Tomashivsky, Stefan, ed. "Materiialy do istorii halytsko-ruskoho shkilnytstva XVIII i XIX vv." [Materials on the history of Galician-Ruthenian education in the eighteenth and nineteenth centuries]. *Ukrainsko-ruskyi arkhiv* 4 (1909).

Tyrowicz, Marian, ed. *Galicja od pierwszego rozbioru do Wiosny Ludów, 1772-1848: Wybór tekstów źródłowych* [Galicia from the first partition of Poland to the Spring of the Nations, 1772-1848: Selected sources]. Wrocław: Ossolineum, 1956.

Vahylevych, Ivan. *Gramatyka języka małoruskiego w Galicji* [Grammar of the Little Russian language in Galicia]. Lviv 1845.

Verhandlungen des österreichischen Reichstages nach der stenographischen Aufnahme. 5 vols. Vienna 1848-9.

Vinok Rusynam na obzhynky [A wreath for the Ruthenians at the harvest feast]. 2 parts. Vienna 1846.

Vozniak, Mykhailo, ed. "Iz korespondentsii R. Mokha" [From Rudolf Mokh's correspondence]. *Zapysky Naukovoho tovarystva im. Shevchenka* 81 (1908): 157-71.

Žáček, Václav, ed. *Slovanský sjezd v Praze roku 1848: Sbírka dokumentů* [The Slavic Congress in Prague in 1848:

Collection of documents]. Prague: Nakladatelství Československé Akademie Véd, 1958.

Zaklynsky, Aleksei [Oleksii]. *Zapysky parokha Starykh Bohorodchan* [Records of the pastor of Stari Bohorodchany]. Lviv 1890. Reprint. Toronto: Ukrainske vydavnytstvo "Dobra knyzhka," 1960.

Zaleski, Wacław [Wacław z Oleska]. *Pieśni polskie i ruskie ludu galicyjskiego z muzyką instrumentowaną przez Karola Lipińskiego* [Polish and Ruthenian songs of the Galician people with instrumental music written by Karol Lipiński]. Lviv 1833.

Zap, Karel V. *Cesty a procházky po halické zemi* [Journeys and excursions through Galicia]. Prague 1844.

Zhelekhovsky, Iustyn. "Avtobiografiia" [Autobiography]. *Vestnik Narodnogo doma*, 1909-10.

Ziemiałkowski, Florian. *Pamiętniki* [Memoirs]. 4 vols. Cracow 1904.

Zubrytsky, Denys [Zubrzycki, Dionizy]. *Granice między ruskim i polskim narodem* [The boundary between the Ruthenian and Polish nations]. Lviv 1849. German translation: *Grenzen zwischen der russinischen und polnischen Nation in Galizien.* Lviv 1849.

4. Selected Secondary Works

Androkhovych, Amvrozii. "Lvivske 'Studium Ruthenum' " [The Lviv "Studium Ruthenum"]. *Zapysky Naukovoho tovarystva im. Shevchenka*, 131 (1921): 123-95; 132 (1922): 185-217; 136-7 (1925): 43-105; 146 (1927): 33-118; 150 (1929): 1-80.

Batowski, Henryk. *Przyjaciele Słowianie. Szkice historyczne z życia Mickiewicza* [Slavic friends: Historical sketches from Adam Mickiewicz's life]. Warsaw: Czytelnik, 1956.

Bergmann, Moses. "Der polnisch-ruthenische Antagonismus in Galizien in den Jahren 1848-1867. Zur Geschichte des Kampfes der Ruthenen um ihre nationale Gleichberechtigung." Diss. Phil., University of Vienna, 1924.

Bohachevsky-Chomiak, Martha. *The Spring of a Nation: The Ukrainians in Eastern Galicia in 1848*. Philadelphia: Shevchenko Scientific Society, 1967.

Borys, Volodymyr. "Deiaki pytannia polsko-ukrainskykh vidnosyn pid chas revoliutsii 1848 r. v Halychyni" [Some questions concerning Polish-Ukrainian relations in Galicia during the revolution of 1848]. *Ukrainske slovianoznavstvo* 6 (1972): 74-87.

______."Wybory w Galicji i debaty nad zniesieniem pańszczyzny w parlamencie wiedeńskim w 1848 r." [Elections in Galicia and the debate over the abolition of *robot* in the 1848 Viennese parliament]. *Przegląd Historyczny* 58 (1967): 28-45.

Brock, Peter. "Ivan Vahylevych (1811-1866) and the Ukrainian National Identity." *Canadian Slavonic Papers* 14, no. 2 (1972): 153-90.

Bryk, Ivan. "Iosyf Dobrovsky i ukrainoznavstvo" [Josef Dobrovský and Ukrainian studies]. *Zapysky Naukovoho tovarystva im. Shevchenka* 141-3 (1925): 1-35.

______."Iosyf Dobrovsky i ukrainski hramatyky" [Josef Dobrovský and the Ukrainian grammars]. In *Josef Dobrovský 1753-1829: Sborník statí* [Josef Dobrovský 1753-1829: Collection of articles], 23-43. Prague 1929.

______." 'Liubushyn sud' v ukrainskim perekladi Kaz. Ios. Turivskoho z 1835 r." ['Libuša's prophecy' in the 1835 Ukrainian version of K. I. Turivsky]. *Zapysky Naukovoho tovarystva im. Shevchenka* 128 (1919): 121-33.

______."Pochatky ukrainskoi presy v Halychyni i lvivska Stavropyhiia" [The beginnings of a Ukrainian press in Galicia and the Lviv Stavropygian Institute]. *Zbirnyk Lvivskoi Stavropyhii* 1 (1921): 99-143.

———. "Slavianskyi zizd u Prazi 1848 r. i sprava ukrainska" [The Slavic Congress of 1848 in Prague and the Ukrainian question]. *Zapysky Naukovoho tovarystva im. Shevchenka* 129 (1920): 141-217.

Chlebowczyk, Józef. *Procesy narodotwórcze we wschodniej Europie środkowej w dobie kapitalizmu (od schyłku XVIII do początków XX wieku)* [Nation-forming processes in East Central Europe in the period of capitalism (from the close of the eighteenth to the beginning of the twentieth century)]. Katowice: Śląski Instytut Naukowy; Warsaw-Cracow: Państwowe Wydawnictwo Naukowe, 1975.

Chotkowski, Władysław. *Historia polityczna Kościoła w Galicji za rządów Marii Teresy* [Political history of the church in Galicia during the rule of Maria Theresa]. 2 vols. Cracow 1909.

Danylak, Mikhal [Danilák, Michal]. *Halytski, bukovynski, zakarpatski ukraintsi v revoliutsii 1848-1849 rokiv* [Galician, Bukovynian and Transcarpathian Ukrainians in the revolution of 1848-9]. Bratislava: Slovenské pedagogické nakladatel'stvo, 1972.

Dmytruk, Volodymyr T. *Narys z istorii ukrainskoi zhurnalistyky XIX st.* [Outline history of Ukrainian journalism in the nineteenth century]. Lviv: Vydavnytstvo Lvivskoho universytetu, 1969.

1848 rik v Halychyni: Anotovanyi pokazhchyk rukopysnykh materialiv bibliotek [1848 in Galicia: An annotated index of manuscript materials in libraries]. Lviv: Lvivska biblioteka Akademii nauk URSR—Viddil rukopysiv, 1953.

Felczak, Wacław. *Węgierska polityka narodowościowa przed wybuchem powstania 1848 roku* [The Hungarian nationalities policy before the outbreak of the 1848 insurrection]. Wrocław: Ossolineum, 1964.

Feldman, Józef. *Sprawa polska w roku 1848* [The Polish question in 1848]. Cracow 1933.

Feldman, Wilhelm. *Stronnictwa i programy polityczne w Galicyi 1846-1906* [Political parties and programs in Galicia, 1846-1906]. 2 vols. Cracow 1907.

Filevich, I. P. *Iz istorii Karpatskoi Rusi* [From the history of Carpathian Rus']. Warsaw 1907.

Finkel, Ludwik and Starzyński, Stanisław. *Historia Uniwersytetu Lwowskiego* [History of Lviv University]. 2 vols. Lviv 1894.

Franko, Andrii. "Hryhorii Ilkevych iak etnohraf" [Hryhorii Ilkevych as an ethnographer]. *Zapysky Naukovoho tovarystva im. Shevchenka* 109 (1912): 91-122; 110 (1912): 123-56; 111

(1912): 117-39.
Franko, Ivan. "Azbuchna viina v Halychyni 1859 r. Novi materiialy" [The alphabet war in Galicia in 1859. New materials]. *Ukrainsko-ruskyi arkhiv* 8 (1912).
______."Azbuchnyi spir v 1859 r." [The conflict over the alphabet in 1859]. *Zapysky Naukovoho tovarystva im. Shevchenka* 114 (1913): 81-116; 115 (1913): 131-51; 116 (1913): 87-125.
______."Do biohrafii Ivana Vahylevycha" [Toward a biography of Ivan Vahylevych]. *Zapysky Naukovoho tovarystva im. Shevchenka* 79 (1907): 97-141.
______.*Narys istorii ukrainsko-ruskoi literatury* [Outline history of Ukrainian-Ruthenian literature]. Lviv 1910.
______."Pysannia I. P. Kotliarevskoho v Halychyni" [I. P. Kotliarevsky's writings in Galicia]. *Zapysky Naukovoho tovarystva im. Shevchenka* 26 (1898): 1-14.
Geist-Lányi, Paula. *Das Nationalitätenproblem auf dem Reichstag zu Kremsier 1848/1849*. Munich 1920.
Glinka, L. *Gregorio Jachymovyč, metropolita di Halyč, ed il suo tempo* (*1840-1865*). 2d ed. Rome: PP. Basiliani, 1974.
Grodziski, Stanisław. *Historia ustroju społeczno-politycznego Galicji 1772-1848* [History of Galicia's socio-political system, 1772-1848]. Wrocław: Ossolineum, 1971.
______.*W Królestwie Galicji i Lodomerii* [In the Kingdom of Galicia and Lodomeria]. Cracow: Wydawnictwo Literackie, 1976.
Grzybowski, Konstanty. *Galicja 1848-1914. Historia ustroju politycznego na tle historii ustroju Austrii* [Galicia 1848-1914: History of the political structure against the background of the Austrian system]. Wrocław: Ossolineum, 1959.
Hájek, Zdeněk. "Styky Jakiva a Ivana Holovackých s Josefem Podlipským a Františkem Cyrilem Kampelíkem" [Iakiv and Ivan Holovatsky's ties with J. Podlipský and F. C. Kampelík]. In *Franku Wollmanovi k sedmdesâtinam. Sborník prací* [To Frank Wollman on his seventieth birthday. Collection of articles], 213-27. Prague: Státní pedagogické nakladatelství, 1958.
Hallemann, Jakob. "Die Entstehung der ruthenischen Nationalbewegung in Galizien." Diss. Phil., University of Vienna, 1934.
Handelsman, Marceli. *Ukraińska polityka ks. Adama Czartoryskiego przed wojną krymską* [The Ukrainian policy of Prince Adam Czartoryski before the Crimean War]. Warsaw 1937.
______."Wpływy polskie na Rusinów galicyjskich w trzeciem i

czwartem dziesięcioleciu XIX w." [Polish influences on the Galician Ruthenians in the 1820s and 1830s]. *Ziemia Czerwieńska* 2, no. 1 (1937): 52-67.

Helfert, Josef Alexander. *Geschichte der österreichischen Revolution im Zusammenhange mit der mitteleuropäischen Bewegung der Jahre 1848-1849.* 2 vols. Freiburg im Breisgau and Vienna 1909.

______.*Geschichte Oesterreichs vom Ausgange des Wiener Oktober Aufstandes 1848.* 4 vols. in 6. Prague 1869-86.

Herasymenko, Mykhailo P. *Ahrarni vidnosyny v Halychyni v period kryzy panshchynnoho hospodarstva* [Agrarian relations in Galicia during the crisis of the *robot* economy]. Kiev: Vydavnytstvo Akademii nauk URSR, 1959.

Herbilsky, Hryhorii I. *Peredova suspilna dumka v Halychyni* (*30-i—seredyna 40-kh rokiv XIX stolittia*) [Advanced social thought in Galicia from 1830 to the mid-1840s]. Lviv: Vydavnytstvo Lvivskoho universytetu, 1959.

______.*Rozvytok prohresyvnykh idei v Halychyni u pershii polovyni XIX st.* (*do 1848 r.*) [The growth of progressive ideas in Galicia in the first half of the nineteenth century (to 1848)]. Lviv: Vydavnytstvo Lvivskoho universytetu, 1964.

Horák, Jiří. *Z dějin literatur slovanských. Statí i rozpravy* [From the history of Slavic literatures: Articles and essays]. Prague 1948.

Horniatkevych, D. "Pershyi zizd ukrainskykh uchenykh u Lvovi v 1848" [The first congress of Ukrainian scholars in Lviv in 1848]. *Vyzvolnyi shliakh*, June-August 1959.

Hostička, Vladimír. "Havlíčkův rozchod z Josefem Bodjanským (K otázce Havlíčkova odchodu z Ruska)" [Havlíček's break with Osyp Bodiansky (on the question of Havlíček's departure from Russia)]. *Slavia* 31, no. 4 (1962): 613-18.

______."Karel Vladislav Zap a haličtí Ukrajinci" [K. V. Zap and the Galician Ukrainians]. In *Kapitoly z dějin vzájemných vztahů národů ČSR a SSSR* [Chapters in the history of mutual relations between the peoples of Czechoslovakia and the USSR], vol. 1, 69-115. Prague: Nakladatelství Československé Akademie Věd, 1958.

______."Pavel Josef Šafařík a Ukrajinci" [P. J. Šafařík and the Ukrainians]. In *Z dejín československo-ukrajinských vzt'ahov* [From the history of Czechoslovak-Ukrainian relations], 295-318. Bratislava, 1957.

______.*Spolupráce Čechů a haličských Ukrajinců v letech 1848-1849* [Co-operation between Czechs and Galician Ukrainians in

1848-9]. Prague: Nakladatelství Československé Akademie Věd, 1965.

______."Ukrajina v názorech české obrozenecké společnosti do roku 1848" [Ukraine in the opinion of the Czech awakeners to 1848]. *Slavia* 33, no. 4 (1964): 558-78.

Istoriia Lvova. Korotkyi narys [History of Lviv: A brief outline]. Edited by Ie. K. Lazarenko et al. Lviv: Vydavnytstvo Lvivskoho universytetu, 1956.

Iuzvenko, V. A. *Ukrainska narodna poetychna tvorchist u polskii folklorystytsi XIX st.* [Ukrainian folk poetry in Polish folklore studies of the nineteenth century]. Kiev: Akademiia nauk URSR, 1961.

Kaczała, Stefan [Kachala, Stepan]. *Polityka Polaków względem Rusi* [Polish policy toward Rus']. Lviv 1879.

Kamiński, Aleksander. *Polskie związki młodzieży 1831-1848* [Polish youth associations, 1831-48]. Warsaw: Państwowe Wydawnictwo Naukowe, 1968.

Kann, Robert A. *The Multinational Empire: Nationalism and National Reform in the Habsburg Monarchy 1848-1918.* 2 vols. New York: Columbia University Press, 1950.

Khotkevych, H. *Teatr 1848 roku* [The theatre of 1848]. Kharkiv and Kiev 1932.

Kieniewicz, Stefan. *Adam Sapieha* (*1828-1903*). Lviv 1939.

______."Galicja w latach 1846-1848" [Galicia, 1846-8]. In *W stulecie Wiosny Ludów 1848-1849* [On the hundredth anniversary of the Spring of the Nations, 1848-9]. Vol. 1, *Wiosna Ludów na ziemiach polskich* [The Spring of the Nations on Polish lands], 269-346. Warsaw: Państwowy Instytut Wydawniczy, 1948.

______.*Konspiracje galicyjskie 1831-1845* [Galician conspiracies, 1831-45]. Warsaw: Książka i Wiedza, 1950.

______."Sprawa włościańska w Galicji w 1848 r." [The peasant question in Galicia in 1848]. *Przegląd Historyczny* 38 (1948): 61-128. Rev. ed. as *Pomiędzy Stadionem a Goslarem* [Between Stadion and Goslar]. Wrocław: Ossolineum, 1980.

______."Sprawa włościańska w galicyjskim sejmie stanowym (1843-1845)" [The peasant question in the Galician Estates Diet, 1843-45]. *Sobótka*, 3 (1948): 168-90.

______."Stosunki polsko-ukraińskie w latach 1820-1870" [Polish-Ukrainian relations, 1820-70]. In *Sesja naukowa w trzechsetną rocznicę zjednoczenia Ukrainy z Rosją* [Scholarly session commemorating the 300th anniversary of the unification of Ukraine with Russia], 131-57. Warsaw:

Państwowe Wydawnictwo Naukowe, 1956.

Knot, Antoni. *Dążenia oświatowe młodzieży galicyjskiej w latach 1815-1830* [Educational aspirations of Galician youth, 1815-30]. Wrocław: Państwowe Wydawnictwo Naukowe, 1959.

Kosachevskaia, E. M. *Vostochnaia Galitsiia nakanune i v period revoliutsii 1848 g.* [Eastern Galicia on the eve of and during the revolution of 1848]. Lviv: Izdatelstvo Lvovskogo universiteta, 1965.

Kozik, Jan. "Czeskie i południowosłowiańskie powiązania 'Ruskiej Trójcy' " [Czech and South Slavic ties of the "Ruthenian Triad"]. *Studia Historyczne* 11, no. 3 (1968): 323-41.

______."Galizische Ukrainer im konstituierenden Reichstag von Wien und Kremsier (1848-1849)." In *Studia Austro-Polonica*, vol. 1, pp. 129-55. Cracow: Nakładem Uniwersytetu Jagiellońskiego, 1978.

______."Kwestia włościańska w Galicji wschodniej w polityce Hołownej Rady Ruskiej 1848-1849" [The peasant question in Eastern Galicia in the policy of the Holovna Rada Ruska, 1848-9]. *Zeszyty Naukowe Uniwersytetu Jagiellońskiego*, vol. 364; *Prace Historyczne*, no. 50, pp. 63-93. Cracow 1974.

______."Stosunki ukraińsko-polskie w Galicji w okresie rewolucji 1848-1849. Próba charakterystyki" [Ukrainian-Polish relations in Galicia during the revolution of 1848-9: An attempt at a description]. In *Z dziejów współpracy Polaków, Ukraińców i Rosjan* [From the history of co-operation among Poles, Ukrainians and Russians], 29-53. Cracow: Nakładem Uniwersytetu Jagiellońskiego, 1975.

______."Wpływy polskie na kształtowanie się świadomości narodowej Ukraińców w Galicji" [Polish influences on the formation of national consciousness among the Ukrainians in Galicia]. *Studia Historyczne* 10, no. 1-2 (1967): 87-112.

Krajewski, Józef. *Tajne związki polityczne w Galicji 1833-1841* [Clandestine political associations in Galicia, 1833-41]. Lviv 1903.

Krevetsky, Ivan. *Ahrarni straiky i boikoty u Skhidnii Halychyni v 1848-1849 rr.* [Agrarian strikes and boycotts in Eastern Galicia, 1848-9]. Lviv 1906.

______."Batalion ruskykh hirskykh striltsiv 1848-1850 rr." [Battalion of Ruthenian highlander riflemen, 1848-50]. *Zapysky Naukovoho tovarystva im. Shevchenka* 107 (1912): 52-72.

______."Falshovanie metryk dlia polskykh povstantsiv z 1830-31 rr. (Prychynok do kharakterystyky halytsko-ruskoho dukhovenstva pershoi polovyny XIX st.)" [Falsification of certificates for Polish insurrectionaries in 1830-31 (A contribution to the description of the Galician-Ruthenian clergy in the first half of the nineteenth century)]. *Zapysky Naukovoho tovarystva im. Shevchenka* 77 (1907): 107-13.

______."Oboronna orhanizatsiia ruskykh selian na halytsko-uhorskim pohranychu v 1848-1849 rr." [The organization of defence by Ruthenian peasants in the Galician-Hungarian borderland in 1848-9]. *Zapysky Naukovoho tovarystva im. Shevchenka* 63 (1905): 1-26; 64 (1905): 27-58.

______."Proby orhanizovannia ruskykh natsionalnykh hvardii v Halychyni 1848-1849" [Attempts to organize Ruthenian national guards in Galicia in 1848-9]. *Zapysky Naukovoho tovarystva im. Shevchenka* 113 (1913): 77-146.

______."Sprava podilu Halychyny v rr. 1846-1850" [The issue of partitioning Galicia, 1846-50]. *Zapysky Naukovoho tovarystva im. Shevchenka* 93 (1910): 54-69; 94 (1910): 58-83; 95 (1910): 54-82; 96 (1910): 94-115; 97 (1910): 105-54.

______."Z vyborchoho rukhu u skhidnii Halychyni v 1848 r. (Vybir Ivana Kapushchaka)" [The electoral campaign in Eastern Galicia in 1848 (The election of Ivan Kapushchak)]. *Zapysky Naukovoho tovarystva im. Shevchenka* 70 (1906): 73-85.

Kyrchiv, R. F. *Ukrainskyi folklor u polskii literaturi (period romantyzmu)* [Ukrainian folklore in Polish Romantic literature]. Kiev: Naukova dumka, 1971.

Kyryliuk, Ievhen P. *T. H. Shevchenko. Zhyttia i tvorchist* [Taras Shevchenko: His life and work]. Kiev: Derzhavne vydavnytstvo khudozhnoi literatury, 1959.

Levytsky, Kost. *Istoriia politychnoi dumky halytskykh Ukraintsiv 1848-1914* [History of the political thought of the Galician Ukrainians, 1848-1914]. Vol. 1. Lviv 1926.

Lewyzka, Irena. "Das Jahr 1848 und die Ukrainer in Österreich." Diss. Phil., University of Vienna, 1925.

Lisicki, Henryk. *Antoni Zygmunt Helcel 1808-1872*. 2 vols. Lviv 1882.

Łoziński, Bronisław. *Agenor hrabia Gołuchowski w pierwszym okresie rządów swoich (1846-1859)* [Count Agenor Gołuchowski in the first period of his administration, 1846-59]. Lviv 1901.

Lozynsky, Mykhailo. *Utvorennie ukrainskoho koronnoho kraiu v Avstrii* [The formation of a Ukrainian crown land in Austria]. Lviv 1915.

Luchakovsky, K. *Antin Liubych-Mohylnytsky, ieho zhytie, ieho znachenie* [Antin Liubych-Mohylnytsky, his life and his significance]. Lviv 1887.

Makovei, Osyp. "Z istorii nashoi filolohii. Try halytski hramatyky (Ivan Mohylnytsky, Iosyf Levytsky i Iosyf Lozynsky)" [From the history of our philology: Three Galician grammars (I. Mohylnytsky, I. Levytsky and I. Lozynsky)]. *Zapysky Naukovoho tovarystva im. Shevchenka* 51 (1903): 1-58, 54 (1903): 59-96.

Malkin, Viktor A. *Russkaia literatura v Galitsii* [Russian literature in Galicia]. Lviv: Izdatelstvo Lvovskogo universiteta, 1957.

Miller, I. S. "Nakanune otmeny barshchiny v Galitsii (Iz istorii ideino-politicheskoi borby v polskom obshchestve v 30-40 godakh XIX stoletiia" [On the eve of the abolition of serfdom in Galicia (From the history of the ideological-political struggle in Polish society in the 1830s and 1840s)]. *Uchenye zapiski Instituta slavianovedeniia* 1 (1949): 119-240.

———."Revoliutsionnoe dvizhenie i natsionalnaia borba v Galitsii v 1848 g." [The revolutionary movement and the national struggle in Galicia in 1848]. In *Revoliutsii 1848-1849* [The revolutions of 1848-9]. Edited by F. V. Potemkin and A. I. Molok. 2 vols. Moscow: Izdatelstvo Akademii nauk SSSR, 1952.

Ohonovsky, Omelian. *Istoriia literatury ruskoi* [History of Ruthenian literature]. Lviv 1889.

Ostaszewski-Barański, K. *Rok złudzeń (1848). Opowiadanie historyczne* [Year of illusions, 1848: A historical narrative]. Zolochiv 1898.

———.*Wacław Michał Zaleski (1799-1849). Zarys biograficzny* [Wacław M. Zaleski, 1799-1849: A biographical outline]. Lviv 1912.

Paňkevyč, I. "Západnoukrajinské literárne obrodenie a Ján Kollár" [The Western Ukrainian literary revival and Jan Kollar]. In *Z dejín československo-ukrajinských vzt'ahov* [From the history of Czechoslovak-Ukrainian relations], 269-94. Bratislava 1957.

Pashaeva, N. M. "Otrazhenie natsionalnykh i sotsialnykh protivorechii v Vostochnoi Galichine v 1848 g. v listovkakh Russkogo Sobora" [The reflection of national and social contradictions in Eastern Galicia in 1848 in the leaflets of the Sobor Ruskyi]. In *Slavianskoe vozrozhdenie: Sbornik statei i materialov* [The Slavic renaissance: Collection of articles and materials], 48-62. Moscow: Nauka, 1966.

Petrash, Osyp. *Ruska Triitsia* [The Ruthenian Triad]. Kiev: Dnipro, 1972.

Rozdolski, Roman. *Stosunki poddańcze w dawnej Galicji* [Serf relations in old Galicia]. 2 vols. Warsaw: Państwowe Wydawnictwo Naukowe, 1962.

———. *Wspólnota gminna w b. Galicji Wschodniej i jej zanik* [The village commune in old Eastern Galicia and its decline]. Lviv 1936.

Rudnytsky, Ivan L. "The Ukrainians in Galicia under Austrian Rule." *Austrian History Yearbook* 3, pt. 2 (1967): 394-429.

Sala, M. *Geschichte des polnischen Aufstandes vom Jahre 1846*. Vienna 1867.

Schnür-Pepłowski, Stanisław. *Z przeszłości Galicji 1772-1862* [From Galicia's past, 1772-1862]. 2d rev. ed. Lviv 1895.

Shalata, Mykhailo I. *Markiian Shashkevych. Zhyttia, tvorchist i hromadsko-kulturna diialnist* [M. Shashkevych: Life, work, and public-cultural activities]. Kiev: Naukova dumka, 1969.

Shchurat, Vasyl. *Na dosvitku novoi doby* [At the dawn of a new era]. Lviv 1919.

———. *Vybrani pratsi z istorii literatury* [Selected works from the history of literature]. Kiev: Vydavnytstvo Akademii nauk URSR, 1963.

———. "V. Kopitar i ep. Iv. Snihursky" [Jernej Kopitar and Bishop Ivan Snihursky]. *Zapysky Naukovoho tovarystva im. Shevchenka* 125 (1918): 165-200.

Šidak, Jaroslav. "Der Illyrismus—Ideen und Probleme." In *L'udovít Štúr und die slawische Wechselseitigkeit*, edited by L'. Holotík, 61-89. Bratislava: Vydavateľstvo Slovenskej akadémii vied, 1969.

Sommergruber, Josef. "Die nationalpolitischen Verhältnisse in Galizien 1848-1867." Diss. Phil., University of Vienna, 1941.

Sozansky, Ivan. "Do istorii uchasty halytskykh Rusyniv u slovianskim kongresi v Prazi 1848 r." [On the participation of the Galician Ruthenians in the Slavic Congress in Prague in 1848]. *Zapysky Naukovoho tovarystva im. Shevchenka* 72 (1906): 112-21.

Stebelski, Piotr. "Lwów w 1848 r. Na podstawie aktów śledczych" [Lviv in 1848 on the basis of investigatory files]. *Kwartalnik Historyczny* 23 (1909): 303-61, 507-64.

Steblii, F. I. *Borotba selian Skhidnoi Halychyny proty feodalnoho hnitu v pershii polovyni XIX st.* [The struggle of the Eastern Galician peasantry against feudal oppression in the first half of the nineteenth century]. Kiev: Vydavnytstvo Akademii Nauk URSR, 1961.

———. "Revoliutsiia 1848-1849 rr. na zakhidnoukrainskykh zemliakh"

[The Revolution of 1848-9 in Western Ukraine], 217–38. In *Torzhestvo istorychnoi spravedlyvosti* [The triumph of historical justice]. Lviv: Vydavnytstvo Lvivskoho universytetu, 1968.

_____.“Selianskyi rukh u Skhidnii Halychyni pid chas revoliutsii 1848-1849 rr.” [The peasant movement in Eastern Galicia during the revolution of 1848-9]. *Ukrainskyi istorychnyi zhurnal* 16, no. 6 (1973): 28-38.

_____.“*Slovo perestorohy* V. Podolynskoho” [*Word of Warning* by Vasyl Podolynsky]. *Ukrainskyi istorychnyi zhurnal*, 1966, no. 12: 44–51.

Studynsky, Kyrylo. “Kopitar i Zubrytsky” [Kopitar and Zubrytsky]. *Zapysky Naukovoho tovarystva im. Shevchenka* 125 (1918): 115-64.

_____.*Lvivska dukhovna seminariia v chasakh Markiiana Shashkevycha (1829-1843)* [The Lviv theological seminary during the time of Markiian Shashkevych, 1829-43]. Lviv 1916.

_____.“Pavlo Iosyf Shafaryk i Ukraintsi” [Pavel Josef Šafařík and the Ukrainians]. *Nasha kultura* 7 (1935): 401–12.

_____.“Polski konspiratsii sered ruskykh pytomtsiv i dukhovenstva v Halychyni v rokakh 1831-1846” [Polish conspiracies among the Ruthenian seminarians and clergymen in Galicia, 1831-46]. *Zapysky Naukovoho tovarystva im. Shevchenka* 80 (1907): 53-108; 82 (1908): 87-177.

Stulecie Gazety Lwowskiej, 1811-1911 [The hundredth anniversary of *Gazeta Lwowska*, 1811-1911]. Edited by Wilhelm Bruchnalski. 2 vols. in 4. Lviv 1911-12.

Stupnicki, Hipolit. *Galicya pod względem topograficzno-geograficzno-historycznym* [Galicia: Topography, geography, history]. Lviv 1849.

Svientsitsky, I. S. *Materialy po istorii vozrozhdeniia Karpatskoi Rusi* [Materials for the history of the rebirth of Carpathian Rus’]. 2d ed., 2 vols. Lviv 1910.

_____.*Obzor snoshenii Karpatskoi Rusi s Rossiei v l-uiu polovinu XIX v.* [Survey of the relations of Carpathian Rus’ with Russia in the first half of the nineteenth century]. St. Petersburg 1906.

Svistun, F. I. *Prikarpatskaia Rus’ pod vladeniem Avstrii* [Subcarpathian Rus’ under Austrian rule]. 2 vols. Lviv 1896-7; reprinted in 1 vol., Trumbull, Conn. 1970.

Tershakovets, Mykhailo. “Do istorii vydannia Ilkevychevykh prypovidok” [On the publication history of Ilkevych’s *Galician*

Proverbs]. *Zapysky Naukovoho tovarystva im. Shevchenka* 106 (1911): 175–90.

———. "Do zhyttiepysu Markiiana Shashkevycha" [Toward a biography of Markiian Shashkevych]. *Zapysky Naukovoho tovarystva im. Shevchenka* 105 (1911): 92-115, and 106 (1911): 77–134.

———. "Pro naklad 'Rusalky Dnistrovoi' " [About the number of printed copies of *Rusalka Dnistrovaia*]. *Zapysky Naukovoho tovarystva im. Shevchenka* 108 (1912): 117-39.

———. "Vidnosyny V. Kopitara do halytsko-ukrainskoho pysmenstva" [Jernej Kopitar's ties to Galician-Ukrainian literature]. *Zapysky Naukovoho tovarystva im. Shevchenka* 95 (1910): 107-54.

Udaltsov, I. I. "Iz istorii slavianskogo sezda v Prage v 1848 godu" [From the history of the Slavic Congress in Prague in 1848]. *Uchenye zapiski Instituta slavianovedeniia* 1 (1949): 57-84.

Ustyianovych, K. "Istorychnyi moment 19. marta 1848 r." [A historical moment—19 March 1848]. *Zhytie i slovo* 2, pt. 3 (1895).

U stolittia "Zori" Markiiana Shashkevycha (*1834-1934*) [The hundredth anniversary of M. Shashkevych's *Zoria* (1834-1934)]. 2 parts. Lviv 1936.

Vielrose, Egon. "Przyczynek do demografii Galicji i Bukowiny w drugiej ćwierci wieku XIX" [A contribution to the demography of Galicia and Bukovyna in the second quarter of the nineteenth century]. *Przegląd Statystyczny* 9 (1961): 137-54.

Vintskovsky, D. *Grigorii Iakhimovich i sovremennoe russkoe dvizhenie* [Hryhorii Iakhymovych and the contemporary Ruthenian movement]. Lviv 1892.

Vozniak, Mykhailo. "Apolohiia kyrylytsi Denysa Zubrytskoho" [Denys Zubrytsky's apologia for the Cyrillic alphabet]. *Zapysky Naukovoho tovarystva im. Shevchenka* 150 (1929): 120-42.

———. "Avtorstvo azbuchnoi statti z 1834 r." [The authorship of the 1834 article regarding the alphabet]. *Zapysky Naukovoho tovarystva im. Shevchenka* 136-7 (1925): 107-18.

———. "Do vyiasnennia natsionalnykh pohliadiv Iakova Holovatskoho" [Toward an explanation of Iakiv Holovatsky's national views]. *Zapysky Naukovoho tovarystva im. Shevchenka* 121 (1914): 133-72.

———. *Iak probudylosia ukrainske narodne zhyttia v Halychyni za Avstrii* [How Ukrainian national life in Galicia was awakened under Austrian rule]. Lviv 1924.

_____.*Kyrylo-Metodiivske bratstvo* [The brotherhood of Saints Cyril and Methodius]. Lviv 1921.

_____.*Markiian Shashkevych iak folkloryst* [M. Shashkevych as a folklorist]. Lviv 1911.

_____. "Proiekt pravopysu Ivana Zhukivskoho na zizdi 'ruskykh uchenykh'" [Ivan Zhukovsky's proposal regarding orthography at the congress of Ruthenian scholars]. *Zapysky Naukovoho tovarystva im. Shevchenka* 82 (1908): 53-86.

_____.*Prosvitni zmahannia halytskykh Ukraintsiv v XIX vitsi* [Educational aspirations of the Galician Ukrainians in the nineteenth century]. Lviv 1912.

_____. "Studii nad halytsko-ukrainskymy hramatykamy XIX v." [Studies on nineteenth-century Galician-Ukrainian grammars]. *Zapysky Naukovoho tovarystva im. Shevchenka* 89 (1909): 111-43; 90 (1909): 33-118; 91 (1909): 126-50.

_____. "Ukrainski dramatychni vystavy v Halychyni v pershii polovyni XIX stolittia" [Ukrainian dramatic performances in Galicia in the first half of the nineteenth century]. *Zapysky Naukovoho tovarystva im. Shevchenka* 87 (1909): 70-91; 88 (1909): 51-93.

_____. "Z folklornykh zaniat Markiiana Shashkevycha" [Regarding Markiian Shashkevych's folkloristic endeavours]. *Zapysky Naukovoho tovarystva im. Shevchenka* 109 (1912): 140-55.

_____. "Z-za redaktsiinykh kulis videnskoho *Vistnyka* ta *Zori Halytskoi*" [Behind the editorial scenes of the Viennese *Vistnyk* and *Zoria Halytska*]. *Zapysky Naukovoho tovarystva im. Shevchenka* 107 (1912): 73-109.

_____. "Z zarannia ukrainskoi presy v Halychyni" [The beginnings of the Ukrainian press in Galicia]. *Zapysky Naukovoho tovarystva im. Shevchenka* 111 (1912): 140-59.

Wereszycki, Henryk. *Pod berłem Habsburgów. Zagadnienia narodowościowe* [Under the sceptre of the Habsburgs: The nationalities problems] Cracow: Wydawnictwo Literackie, 1975.

Widmann, Karol. *Franciszek Smolka, jego życie i zawód publiczny. Od roku 1810 do 1849* [Franciszek Smolka, his life and public career, 1810-49]. Lviv 1886.

Wisłocki, Władysław T. *Jerzy Lubomirski 1817-1872*. Lviv 1928.

_____.*Kongres słowiański w r. 1848 i sprawa polska* [The Slavic Congress of 1848 and the Polish question]. Lviv 1927.

Wollman, Frank. "Josef Dobrovský a jazykově literární obrození u Slovanů" [Josef Dobrovský and the Slavs' linguistic-literary rebirth]. *Zborník prací filosofické fakulty brněnské university*, Řada literárněvědna 3, no. 1 (1955): 5-40.

———. "Lidová slovesnost v jazykově literárním obrození Slovanů" [The folk literary genre in the Slavs' linguistic-literary rebirth]. *Slavia* 25 (1956): 555-84.

———.*Slovanství v jazykově literárním obrození u Slovanů* [The theme of Slavdom in the Slavs' linguistic-literary rebirth]. Prague: Státní pedagogické nakladatelství, 1958.

Žáček, Václav. *Čechové a Poláci roku 1848* [Czechs and Poles in 1848]. 2 vols. Prague: Slovanské ústav, 1947-8.

———. "K dějinám austroslavismu rakouských Slovanů" [Toward a history of Austro-Slavism among the Austrian Slavs]. *Slovanské historické studie* 7 (1968): 129-79.

———. "Ze styků Čechů a západních Ukrajinců v revolučnich letech 1848-1849" [The ties of Czechs and Western Ukrainians in the revolutionary years 1848-9]. In *Z dejín československo-ukrajinských vzt'ahov* [From the history of Czechoslovak-Ukrainian relations], 351–74. Bratislava 1957.

Zaionchkovsky, Petr A. *Kirillo-Mefodievskoe obshchestvo 1846-1847* [The Cyril and Methodius society, 1846-7]. Moscow: Izdanie Moskovskogo Gosudarstvennogo Universiteta, 1959.

Zajcew, Paweł. "Szewczenko i Polacy" [Shevchenko and the Poles]. *Biuletyn Polsko-Ukraiński* 3, no. 10 (1934): 2-21.

Zanevych, Ivan [Terletsky, Ostap]. "Literaturni stremlinnia halytskykh Ukraintsiv vid 1772 do 1848" [Literary strivings of the Galician Ukrainians, 1772-1848]. *Zhytie i slovo* 1 (1894): 207-15, 354-70; 2 (1894): 69-80, 198-204, 428-51; 3 (1895): 99-110, 274-85, 430-61; 4 (1895): 112-60, 272-302, 385-454.

———.*Znesenie panshchyny v Halychyni. Prychynok do istorii suspilnoho zhyttia i suspilnykh pohliadiv 1830-1848 rr.* [The abolition of *robot* in Galicia. A contribution to the history of social life and social views, 1830-48]. Lviv 1896.

Zawadzki, Władysław. *Dziennikarstwo w Galicji w roku 1848* [Journalism in Galicia in 1848]. Lviv 1878.

———.*Literatura w Galicji* (*1772-1848*) [Literature in Galicia, 1772-1848]. Lviv 1879.

Zborucki, Zygmunt. *Proces studentów samborskich 1837-1839* [The trial of the Sambir students, 1837-9]. Lviv 1927.

Index of Names

Adelung, 151
Andrusiak, Hryhorii, 243, 253
Anhelovych, Antin, 26–7
Ankwicz, Andrzej, 52
Antonevych, Ivan, 217

Bach, Alexander, 262, 324
Bachynsky (priest), 342
Bakunin, Mikhail, 224–5, 227–8, 232–3, 235
Balahur, Iatsko (pseud. of Iakiv Holovatsky), 78
Ban, Matija, 12
Bandtkie, Jerzy Samuel, 111
Bantysh-Kamensky, Dmytro, 150–51
Baranovsky, I., 353
Bednarz (pseud. of Hryhorii Bodnar), 80
Bem, Józef, 299
Berehulsky, Iosyf, 40, 43
Bernolák, Anton, 5
Berwiński, Ryszard, 227, 235
Bezborodko, Oleksander, 147
Bielowski, August, 33, 117, 121, 133, 156, 345
Biletsky, Iosyf, 27
Bilynkevych, Porfyrii, 60
Bilynsky, Ivan, 62, 134
Biretsky, Ivan, 60, 62, 63, 75, 78, 107–8, 133, 138, 145–6, 150, 186–7, 216–17, 245
Blonsky, Kyrylo, 28, 56, 101, 118, 134, 151, 181, 242–3, 246–9, 317, 320, 353
Bodiansky, Osyp, 37, 62, 76, 99, 103, 143, 145, 148–54, 159, 166–7
Bodnar, Hryhorii, 43, 49, 78, 80, 181, 299, 319
Bodnar, Mykhailo, 247, 282
Bodnarenko (pseud. of Hryhorii Bodnar), 80
Bogdański, Henryk, 39, 47
Bolesław the Bold, 133
Bolesław the Wrymouth, 38, 118
Bordolo, Jan, 330
Borkowski-Dunin, Józef, 139
Börne, Ludwig, 49
Borovykovsky, Levko, 77, 104, 148, 320
Borysykevych, Ivan, 82, 179, 194–5, 203, 206–7, 216–17, 224–31, 234–5, 241–2, 275, 278, 280, 282, 290, 292, 300, 305, 309, 315–16,

320, 324, 326–7, 353
Brandys, Wojciech, 227
Brauner, František, 280
Brestl, Rudolf, 276, 278
Brocki, Eugeniusz, 30, 121
Brodziński, Kazimierz, 31
Bryk, Ivan, 143
Brylynsky, Iosyf, 349
Buchwald, Feliks, 226–7
Bulvynsky, Mykhailo, 47, 60
Burachynsky, Denys, 217
Burke, Edmund, 4
Bychynsky, Iosyf, 295
Byron, George Gordon Noel, 49, 80

Catherine II, 340
Čelakovský, František, 75
Celarski, Seweryn, 226, 228, 234
Chłędowski, Walenty, 30
Chodakowski, Zorian Dołęga (pseud. of Adam Czarnocki), 33–4, 54, 58, 61, 115, 117
Chojecki, Edmund, 227, 235
Cięglewicz, Kasper, 40, 42, 227, 231, 270–71, 338, 341, 351
Čop, Matija, 6, 87
Cybulski, Józef, 345
Cybulski, Wojciech, 225
Czajkowski, Michał, 31
Czarnocki, Adam, *see* Chodakowski, Zorian Dołęga
Czartoryski, Prince Adam, 11, 232, 365

D., M. (journalist), 362
Dąbczański, Antoni, 243, 270–71, 338, 349, 351
Dalibor (pseud. of Ivan Vahylevych), 60, 71
Daniel II (Archbishop), 145
Dankevych, Luka, 78, 80, 124, 202, 289, 319
Danylovych, Ivan, 78
Davydovych, Ihnatii, 53
Didytsky, Bohdan, 329, 362–3
Doblhoff, Anton, 248, 269
Dobner, Gelasius, 9
Dobriansky, Adolf, 284, 318
Dobriansky, Antin, 78
Dobriansky, Oleksander, 243, 247–50
Dobrovský, Josef, 9–10, 54, 57, 59, 84, 87, 111, 135, 137
Dobrzański, Jan, 177, 224, 230, 346
Dolynchuk, Ivan, 282
Dolzhikov, P., 322
Dombrovytsky (priest), 295
Doskovsky, Ivan, 78–9
Dovbush (brigand), 22, 121
Drašković, Prince Janko, 11
Drymalyk, Sylvester, 242, 244, 328
Dubrovsky, Petr, 11, 98, 100, 102
Duchiński, Franciszek, 365
Dukhnovych, Oleksander, 284
Dumas, Alexandre, 49
Dunin-Borkowski, Count Leszek, 30, 164, 248, 308
Dutkevych, A., 244
Dvořáček, Jan, 143
Dylewski, Marian, 269, 308
Dynets, Iosyf, 243, 247, 250
Dzieduszycki, Aleksander, 338
Dzieduszycki, Julian, 227, 229, 338
Dzieduszycki, Włodzimierz, 338
Dzierzkowski, Józef, 177, 269
Dzivakovsky, Andrii, 243, 247, 315
Dzvinka, Stepan, 121

Engels, Friedrich, 366–7
Erben, Karel, 153
Ersch, Johann G., 49
Ettmayr (Hofrat), 273

Fedko znad Peltvy, 355, 357
Fedorovych (deputy), 248
Ferdinand I, 171, 177, 194, 196, 212–13, 248
Ferdinand II, 202
Fichte, Johann Gottlieb, 4, 28
Forster, Karol, 289, 343
Francis I, 47, 168
Franko, Ivan, 31, 34, 48, 54, 60, 329

Franz Josef, 261, 273

Gaj, Ljudevit, 10–11, 137
Garašanin, Ilija, 11–12
Goethe, Johann Wolfgang von, 28, 49, 179
Gogol, Nikolai, 95, 151, 320, 322
Golejewski, Antoni, 338
Gołuchowski, Agenor, 206, 243, 260–62, 266, 281–2, 284, 290, 296, 300, 303, 306, 308, 315, 324–5, 330, 334
Gonta, Ivan, 340
Gorczyński, Adam, 227
Goslar, Julian Maciej, 253
Goszczyński, Seweryn, 30, 32, 132, 136
Grech, Nikolai, 100, 103–4
Gregory XVI (Pope), 49, 99
Gruber, Johann G., 49
Grzybowski, Witalis, 225

H., F. (journalist), 339, 340–42
H., R. (journalist), 345
Hakman, Eugene (Bishop), 282–3
Halka (pseud. of Mykola Kostomarov), 77
Hammerstein, Wilhelm, 295, 298, 300, 352
Handelsman, Marceli, 42, 88
Hanka, Václav, 5, 143
Hankevych, I., 302
Hankevych, Mykhailo, 243, 247–50, 348
Hannibal, 191
Harasevych, Mykhailo (Canon), 26–7, 32, 113, 342
Harmatii, Vasyl, 243, 247
Hartenstein, Daniel, 150
Hauer, Franz, 52
Havlíček-Borovský, Karel, 12, 139–40, 143, 152, 159, 166, 219, 246, 315
Hegel, Georg Wilhelm Friedrich, 4, 49
Helcel, Antoni Zygmunt, 226–7, 229–30, 233–4
Herder, Johann Gottfried, 5, 80, 140
Herovsky, Ivan, 179, 290
Hlynsky, Teofan, 313
Hnidkovsky, Mykhailo, 62, 101, 243, 247
Hodža, Michał Miloslav, 136–7
Hoi, Stepan, 243, 247, 250, 253–4
Holovatska, Mariia, 62
Holovatsky, Iakiv, 17, 23, 25, 32, 37, 48–9, 55, 58–63, 65–71, 73–83, 88, 95–100, 102–9, 112–19, 121–4, 130–46, 150–53, 156–9, 162, 164–72, 180–81, 186–7, 198, 200, 202, 207, 216–17, 236, 244, 246, 248, 262, 268, 292, 299, 309, 312–14, 316–22, 324–5, 327–9, 348, 353, 355
Holovatsky, Ivan, 31, 34, 60, 62, 73–9, 81, 95–8, 102, 105–6, 112, 117, 131, 136–7, 141–2, 156, 161, 164–6, 171, 173, 187, 325, 327, 329–30, 362–3, 367
Holovatsky, Petro, 79–80, 131, 262, 316, 320–21, 324, 326, 330, 348, 354
Hordynsky, Mykola, 44–5
Hornbostl, Theodor, 248
Horoch, Kalist, 227
Horoszkiewicz, Julian, 39–41, 129, 334, 338
Hoshovsky, Mykola, 110–11
Hostička, Vladimír, 232
Hrabianka, Ivan, 355–6
Hrebinka, Ievhen, 148, 150–51, 158, 318, 320, 341
Hrechansky, Dezyderii, 43, 48
Hromnytsky, Ivan, 27
Hromovych, Ievhen, 295
Hryhoruk, Iosyf, 243, 247, 253
Hrynevetsky, Modest, 32, 34, 55, 58
Hubicki, Marian, 247
Hulak, Mykola, 150
Hulak-Artemovsky, Petro, 77, 104, 148–50
Hurkevych, Ivan, 179, 309, 315, 325–6
Hůrský, Josef, 145

Hushalevych, Ivan, 207, 241, 316, 319, 329
Hynylevych, Hryhorii, 217, 220–22, 224–30, 234, 266

Iablonsky, H., 311–12
Iakhymovych, Hryhorii (Bishop), 46–7, 80, 103, 114, 129, 163, 179, 187–95, 198, 200, 205, 211–12, 247–50, 252, 243–5, 247–50, 252, 276–8, 280, 282, 288–9, 295, 302–3, 320, 339, 342–3, 350, 362
Iaminsky, Iuliian, 60
Ianovsky, Amvrozii, 241, 307
Iaroslav (pseud. of Iakiv Holovatsky), 60, 71
Iazykov, Nikolai, 151
Ilevych, Ivan, 224, 238, 288
Ilkevych, Hryhorii, 32, 34, 60–61, 66, 74–6, 81, 95, 98, 104, 134, 143, 158
Ilnytsky, Ivan, 78, 181
Ilnytsky, Stepan, 201
Ilnytsky, Vasyl, 201–2, 311
Iuzychynsky, Antin, 309

Jabłonowski, Józef, 338
Jabłonowski, Karol, 303
Jabłonowski, Ludwik, 338
Jabłoński, Bartłomiej, 32
Jabłoński, Kajetan, 100, 134
Jabłoński, Leon, 362
Jachim, František, 139, 142, 219, 268
Janiszewski, Jan, 226
Janosik (brigand), 22
Jelačić, Josip, 228–9, 247, 295
Jordan, Jan Petr, 11, 98, 102–3, 167, 171
Joseph II, 19–21, 23, 49, 124, 168–9, 251, 253, 256, 258, 260–61
Jungmann, Josef, 10

Kachala, Stepan, 339
Kachanovsky, Danylo, 53
Kamiński, Jan Nepomucen, 30, 32, 80, 153, 156
Kampelík, František, 75, 95, 106, 143
Kant, Immanuel, 28
Kapuściński, Józef, 352
Kapushchak, Ivan, 243–4, 253
Karadžić, Vuk S., 5, 10, 36, 59, 87, 97, 106, 136–7, 153, 172
Karamzin, Nikolai, 151
Kashubynsky, Ippolit, 191
Kaušić, Matias, 276, 279
Kempis, Thomas à, 46
Kerechynsky (physician), 179
Khmelnytsky, Bohdan, 68, 118, 340
Khomiakov, Aleksei, 80, 97, 151, 322
Khomynsky, Iakym, 179
Khomynsky, Kyrylo, 190, 361
Khomynsky, Vasyl, 241
Kieniewicz, Stefan, 128, 334
Kilarski (*mandatarius*), 63
Kilarski, Tadeusz, 355, 357–8
Kireevsky, Petr, 97, 153
Kirste, Vasyl, 282
Kłosoń (priest), 204
Kmytsykevych, Iuliian, 43
Kmytsykevych, Lev, 43
Kmytsykevych, Mykola, 29, 43, 45, 131
Kmytsykevych, Teofil, 43
Kniazevich, D., 153
Kobrynsky, Iosafat, 60, 78, 80–81, 108, 200, 217, 240, 242, 266, 301, 320–21, 355
Kobylytsia, Lukian, 248, 279, 282
Koeppen, Petr, 144
Kollár, Ján, 5, 8–9, 12, 36, 69, 72, 75, 102, 106, 135–6, 139–41, 319
Komarnicki, Bolesław, 338
Komarnicki, Ludwik, 338
Komarnicki, Michał, 338
Komarnickis (noble family), 122
Kompanevych, V., 153,
Konarski, Szymon, 149
Konstantynovych, Iosyf, 44
Konstantynovych, Ivan, 241
Konysky, Hryhorii (Bishop), 147
Kopitar, Jernej, 10, 12, 25, 55–7,

67–70, 77, 84–7, 91, 110, 114, 117, 135, 138, 140, 163, 166–7
Korecki, Leon, 44, 344
Korsun, Oleksander, 104
Korzeniowski, Józef, 322
Kościuszko, Tadeusz, 271
Kossak, Mykhailo, 326, 329, 331
Kossuth, Lajos, 283
Kostetsky, Platon, 162
Kostomarov, Mykola, 5, 77, 147–8, 150–51, 341
Kosynsky (hetman), 30
Kotkiewicz, Karol, 40
Kotliarevsky, Ivan, 10, 33, 77, 85, 97, 104, 107, 114–15, 143, 146–8, 150–51, 158, 318, 320–21, 329, 341, 363
Kotsovsky, Volodymyr, 48
Kotula, Andrzej, 227
Kotzebue, August von, 49, 321
Koubek, Jan, 136
Kozanovych, Mykhailo, 73, 80, 201, 319
Kozar, Panko, 243, 250, 253
Kozlovsky, Mykhailo, 37, 304
Kraiński, Maurycy, 192, 224, 227
Kral, Antoni, 282
Krasuski (official), 204
Krauss, Philip, 248
Kropotkin, Prince Dmitrii, 153
Kropyvnytsky, Iosyf, 299
Krukhovsky, Ivan, 243, 247
Krushynsky, Iosyf, 207, 342
Krynytsky, Ivan, 207
Krynytsky, Onufrii, 188, 306, 338
Kryzhanovsky, Romuald, 338
Kucharski (priest), 303
Kudlich, Hans, 254
Kulchytsky, I., 179
Kulchytsky, Markyl, 62, 134
Kulczycki, Ignacy, 177
Kulczyński, Hipolit Ignacy, 39–40
Kulish, Panteleimon, 5, 150, 341
Kurakin, Prince Aleksei, 329
Kurelac, Fran, 136
Kushchykevych, Venedykt, 44–5
Kushlyk, N., 60
Kuzemsky, Mykhailo, 102, 189, 191, 194–5, 200, 218, 241, 243, 261–3, 275, 278, 281, 299, 302, 306, 310, 315, 319, 323, 325–6
Kuzmány, Karol, 136–7, 141
Kvitka-Osnovianenko, Hryhorii, 77, 97, 114, 148, 150–51, 158, 165, 300, 318, 320, 341

Lamennais, Félicité Robert de, 32, 49, 91
Lapchynsky, Mariian, 45
Latour, Count Theodor, 248, 296
Laube, Heinrich, 49
Lavrovsky, Iuliian, 315, 350
Lavrosky, Ivan, 27–8, 34, 55–8
Leitner (theatre director), 321
Lelewel, Joachim, 5, 115–17, 120
Leontovych, Pavlo, 80, 319
Leontovych, Teodor, 179, 195, 207, 222–3, 241, 245, 288, 309, 326, 351
Lesiuk, Stefan, 243–4
Levytsky (priest), 171
Levytsky, Hryhorii, 243, 247, 323
Levytsky, Iosyf, 10, 25, 28, 36, 49, 55–6, 62, 68, 71, 85, 87, 89–90, 93–4, 98–104, 108, 111, 140, 156, 167, 218, 271, 311, 313, 316, 318
Levytsky, Ivan, 43
Levytsky, Mykhailo (Metropolitan), 34, 44, 46, 51–3, 55, 57, 60, 67, 77, 99, 101–3, 110, 162, 167, 172, 179–80, 188–9, 192–3, 205, 269, 295, 302, 350, 354
Levytsky, Venedykt, 46, 68–71, 75–6, 86, 89, 101–2, 180
Lewickis (noble family), 122
Lezhohubsky, Sylvester, 203, 242, 294
Libelt, Karol, 224–7, 229–31, 234
Likhutin, M.D., 19
Linde, Samuel Bogumil, 10, 59, 100, 133

Linhart, Anton, 10
Lipiński, Karol, 35
Löhner, Ludwig, 247
Lomnytsky, Ivan, 243, 247, 275
Lomonosov, Mikhail, 89
Lopatynsky, Viktor, 60
Lototsky, Ivan, 315
Lovytsky, Iosyf, 60
Lozynsky, Antin, 43
Lozynsky, Iosyf, 10, 28, 32, 36, 55–8, 60, 62, 67, 72–3, 85–91, 93–6, 101–2, 104, 112, 207–8, 211, 309, 313, 318, 320, 329
Lubomirski, Prince Jerzy, 220, 224–8, 232–4, 334–5, 355, 360, 365
Lucca, Prince of, 77
Luchakovsky, Oleksa, 43
Luchkai, Mykhailo, 34, 60, 302
Luka z Rakova (pseud. of Luka Dankevych), 80, 319
Lukashevych, Platon, 60, 135, 148, 150, 157
Łukasiewicz, Lesław, 225
Luzhetsky, Antin, 43, 78
Lytvynovych, Mykhailo, 70
Lytvynovych, Spyrydon, 127–8, 164, 241–2, 244, 262, 327–8

Maciejowski, Wacław Aleksander, 132, 134, 145, 151, 163
Maksymovych, Mykhailo, 33, 61, 92, 97, 104, 134–5, 143, 148, 150–51, 157–9, 165
Malczewski, Antoni, 30
Malisz, Karol, 225, 227, 232
Malynovsky, Mykhailo, 70, 78, 124, 164, 179, 191, 195, 216, 241, 289, 306, 309, 315, 317, 325–6, 354
Maria Theresa, 21, 23
Markevych, Mykola, 78, 151
Marusiak (brigand), 22, 121
Mauss, Józef, 37
Mayer, Kajetan, 276
Mazepa, Ivan, 30, 340
Mažuranić, Ivan, 5
Mazurkiewicz, Matiasz, 242
Metlynsky, Amvrosii, 77, 104, 148, 151, 320
Metternich, Prince Clemens Lothar, 28, 169, 177
Michałewicz, Mikołaj, 32, 68–9
Mickiewicz, Adam, 5, 27, 31, 149
Midowicz, Józef, 227, 232
Mikhalyts (writer), 302
Miklošić, Fran, 77, 106, 165–6, 171
Milikowski, Jan, 32, 78, 150–51
Miloradov, Olimpii, 224
Milovuk, Josip, 136
Minasiewicz (Canon), 52
Mirosław z Horodenki (pseud. of Hryhorii Ilkevych), 32
Mohyla (pseud. of Amvrosii Metlynsky), 77
Mohylnytsky, (Liubych-), Antin, 46–7, 60, 77–9, 119–20, 181, 187, 198, 202, 319, 327–9, 355–6, 362
Mohylnytsky, Ivan, 28, 32–4, 51–7, 67, 85, 101–2, 109–11, 137, 152
Mokh, Rudolf, 46, 60, 78–80, 202, 207–8, 309, 311–13, 319, 321–2, 328
Mokhnatsky, Dmytro, 38, 44, 47, 60
Mokhnatsky, Klyment, 38–9, 42, 47
Molière (Jean Baptiste Poquelin), 322
Monastyrsky, A., 306
Moraczewski, Jędrzej, 235
Morawski, B. K., 355, 358
Morgosh, Vasyl, 282
Moszczański, Karol, 106, 137, 142
Muchynsky, M., 66
Muravev, Count Mikhail, 155
Muravev-Apostol, Sergei, 149
Mykhalsky, Dorotei, 55
Mynchakevych, Mykhailo, 46, 62
Myroslav (pseud. of Hryhorii Ilkevych), 60

Nadezhdin, Nikolai, 153
Nalyvaiko, Severyn, 118
Napadiievych, Mykola, 47

Napoleon, 6, 19, 27, 58
Naumovych, Ivan, 362–3
Nazarevych, Petro, 53
Nestor the Chronicler, 86, 92, 111, 133, 157, 329
Neuberg, Jan, 220
Neustern, Baron de, *see* Mykhailo Harasevych
Nicholas I, 77, 155, 362
Njegoš, Petr, 5
Nowicki, Napoleon, 44
Nychyporuk, Hryhorii, 243–4, 247, 253

Obradović, Dositej, 10
Obrenović, Prince Mihajlo, 136
Okhrymovych, Iosyf, 60
Olshavsky, Ivan, 56
Ossoliński, Józef Maksymilian, 32
Ostrozhynsky, Iosyf, 60
Ostyslavsky, Ivan, 27
Ozarkevych, Ivan, 151

Paduch, Karol, 347, 355, 358
Padura, Tomasz, 30, 32
Palacký, František, 5, 12, 117, 135, 138, 140, 216, 234, 246, 276–8
Paparas (noble family), 122
Pasichynsky, Roman, 46–7, 60
Paskevich, Prince Ivan, 124, 127
Paslavsky, Havrylo, 302
Paslavsky, Petro, 56
Pauli, Ignacy, 134
Pauli, Żegota, 74, 90, 134–5
Paventsky, Antin, 195, 241, 257, 309, 326, 330–31, 363
Pavlo z Shutkova (pseud. of Pavlo Leontovych), 80, 319
Pavlović, Todor, 136
Pavlovsky, Oleksander, 33, 59, 104, 148, 150
Pavlykiv, Teofil, 240, 294
Pawlikowski, Gwalbert, 88, 273–4
Pelcl, František Martin, 10
Pergen, Count J. Antoni, 113
Pestel, Pavel, 149
Peter I, 340
Petrenko, Mykhailo, 148
Petrović, Georgij, 69–70, 136, 141
Petrushevych, Antin, 62–3, 180–81, 283, 350–51, 362–3
Petrushevych, Stepan, 62, 76, 151
Petryshyn, Hryn, 243, 247
Pichler, Caroline, 49
Pichler, Karel, 151, 220
Piller, Piotr, 328
Pillersdorf, Baron Franz, 206, 212
Pinkas, Adolf, 276, 278–9
Pleshkevych, Semen, 47, 60
Podlipský, Josef, 75, 95, 106, 143
Podolynsky, Vasyl, 45, 131, 187, 355, 358–9, 361–2
Pogłodowski, Zenon, 227, 229–30, 232, 338
Pogodin, Mikhail, 12, 34, 48, 92, 94–5, 97, 113, 116, 133, 143–4, 149–55, 158–9, 166, 314, 363
Pokynsky, Ivan, 60
Pol, Wincenty, 28
Poletyka, Hryhorii, 147
Poliansky, Toma, 241
Popel, Mykhailo, 40–41, 43, 338–9
Popović, Jovan, 136
Poremba, Michał, 326, 329
Posatsky, Konstantyn, 243, 247, 253, 315
Potockis (noble family), 122
Prešeren, France, 5–6, 87, 141
Prokopchyts, Ievstakhii, 201, 243, 270, 316, 318, 355
Proskurnytsky, Ivan, 78
Puchmajer, Antonín, 87
Pushkin, Aleksandr, 149
Pysarevsky, S., 322

Radetzky, Count Johann Joseph, 352
Radykevych, A., 207
Raevsky, Mikhail (Archpriest), 151
Rajačić, Josip (Patriarch), 77, 172
Rajić, Jovan, 10
Rajski, Tomasz, 344

Rakowiecki, Ignacy, 59
Ranke, Leopold, 98
Rastislav, 116
Ratz, Kasper, 278
Richardson, Samuel, 49
Rieger, František, 219, 246, 276–9
Rittersberg, Ludvik, 143
Riurik, 116, 343
Rościszewski, Adam, 153
Rotteck, Karl, 49
Rozheiovsky, Teodor, 195
Rüdiger, Fedor, 300
Rudnytsky, Ivan L., 21
Ruslan (pseud. of Markiian Shashkevych), 60, 68, 71, 74
Rusyn, Havryło (pseud. of Iakiv Holovatsky), 167, 171
Ruthene (pseud. of Iosyf Lozynsky), 211
Ryshko, Ivan, 243–4, 247, 253
Rzewuski, Leon, 347

Saar, Matylda, 321
Sacher-Masoch, Leopold von, 180
Šafařík, Pavel J., 5, 9–10, 34, 59, 110, 112–13, 115, 117, 135, 138–9, 141–6, 153, 216, 313, 319
Sakharov, Ivan, 97
Sanguszko, Władysław, 162
Sapieha, Prince Leon, 129–30, 162, 192, 226–7, 229, 232, 334, 338, 355
Savchynsky, Hryhorii, 181
Savka, Iosyf, 241–3
Savych, Mykola, 150
Schelling, Friedrich von, 28, 49
Schiller, Friedrich von, 27–8, 49, 80, 179
Schlecer, August, 86
Schlegel, Friedrich von, 28, 49
Scholl, Joseph, 278
Schwarzenberg, Prince Felix, 276
Scott, Sir Walter, 49, 80
Seletsky, Ivan, 43–4
Semash, Stepan, 326
Semenovych, S., 62
Seroichkovsky, Havrylo, 47
Shakespeare, William, 49
Shankovsky, Petro, 200–02
Shashkevych, Antin, 43, 47, 62
Shashkevych, Hryhorii, 200–01, 243, 246–8, 250, 253–4, 259, 262, 268, 275, 315, 317
Shashkevych, Markiian, 30–31, 33, 36–8, 43–4, 46–9, 59–60, 62–3, 66, 68–74, 76, 78, 80–81, 84, 89, 92–5, 98, 101–5, 107, 114–15, 118–20, 127, 132, 134–6, 141–3, 146, 150, 158, 194, 318
Shchurat, Vasyl, 27, 48
Sheptytsky, Lev (Bishop), 113
Shevchenko, Taras, 5, 10, 30–31, 77, 115, 148, 150–51, 157, 318, 320, 341, 347, 363
Shevyrev, Stepan, 100, 151, 318
Shpyhotsky, Oleksander, 77
Shukhevych, Iosyf, 80, 319
Shushkevych, Andrii, 240
Siemieński, Lucjan, 33, 132
Skomorovsky, Iosyf, 60
Skomorovsky, Tselestyn, 47, 78, 80, 188, 319, 347
Słotwiński, Konstanty, 33
Slymakovsky, Ivan, 241, 309
Smarzewski, Seweryn, 335–6
Smolka, Franciszek, 245, 248, 250, 268–9, 271, 275, 279, 307–8, 321
Snihursky, Ivan (Bishop), 28, 53, 55–6, 58, 70, 76, 78, 88, 173
Sobieski, Jan III, 270
Sokulsky, Iosyf, 101
Sofia (Archduchess), 300
Sopikov, Vasilii, 151
Sosnovsky, Lev, 309
Sozansky, Vasyl, 53
Sreznevsky, Ivan, 143, 150–51
Sreznevsky, Izmail, 5, 77, 106, 148, 156, 159, 165–6
Sroczyński, Marian, 294
Stadion, Count Franz, 178–80, 184–8,

191–2, 206, 210–12, 215, 217–19, 243–4, 246–7, 253–4, 266, 277, 281, 287–8, 295, 302–3, 308–9, 316, 324, 326, 334, 343
Stadnicki, Kazimierz, 303
Stalmach, Paweł, 229
Stanisław (Bishop), 133
Stanisław August, 58
Stankiewicz (family), 167
Stavarsky, Ivan, 250
Stecki, Ludwik, 227
Štorch, Karel, 143
Striletsky, Iosyf, 56
Strobach, Anton, 248, 250
Stroinovsky (counsellor), 262
Studynsky, Ivan, 47
Studynsky, Kyrylo, 42
Štúr, L'udovít, 5, 141, 235
Supiński, Józef, 344
Suski (lawyer), 194
Szajnocha, Karol, 43
Szczucki, Baltazar, 257

Tangl, Karlman, 308
Tarnowski, Count Jan Feliks, 31, 132, 144
Tavrashkevych, Danylo, 43
Tavrashkevych, Petro, 43
Telykhovsky, Roman, 27
Terletsky, Mykhailo, 188, 217
Terletsky, Mykola, 78
Thun, Count Leo, 12, 140, 172, 218
Tomíček, Jan Slavomír, 142–3
Topolia, Kyrylo, 148
Torbatsky, Mykola, 55
Tovarnytsky (store-keeper), 179
Treshchakovsky, Lev, 60, 211, 278, 323
Trylovsky, Ivan, 53
Tsertelev, Mykola, 148, 150
Tsybuliak, Stepan, 204
Turchmanovych, Ivan, 53
Turkuls (noble family), 122
Turowski, Kazimierz, 43, 45, 121, 153
Tymniak, Mykhailo, 62, 78

Uherek, E., 294
Ustyianovych, Mykola, 37, 47, 60, 69, 73, 78, 101, 114, 146, 188, 202, 241, 257, 309–13, 319, 321–2, 329–30
Uvarov, Count Sergei, 154–5, 161

Vahylevych, Ivan, 34, 46, 48–9, 59–60, 62, 66–7, 71–2, 74, 78, 81, 83, 92, 94, 101–4, 109–10, 112, 114–15, 117, 120, 132–4, 138, 142–6, 150, 152–8, 162–3, 198, 302, 306, 316–18, 338
Velychkovsky, Iuliian, 47, 80, 179, 203, 254, 319, 326
Velymyr (pseud. of Viktor Lopatynsky), 60
Vendzilovych, Ivan, 60
Venelin, Iurii, 151
Verbytsky, Mykhailo, 321
Vereshchynsky, Mykola, 60, 63, 69, 74–5, 77–9, 96, 98, 107, 122, 186, 242, 244, 313
Vinkovsky, Kyrylo, 178–9, 182, 186, 243, 247–50, 338, 343, 350, 355–6, 363
Vitoshynsky, Ivan, 207, 321
Vocel, Jan, 142
Voigt, Mikuláš Adaukt, 9–10
Volney, Constantin, 49
Volodymyr, Saint, 295
Voltaire, François Marie Arouet de, 179
Voltigi, J., 86
Vostokov, Aleksandr, 10, 104, 151
Vozniak, Mykhailo, 134
Vrba, Čeněk, 219
Vyhovsky, Ivan, 340
Vyrsky, Tadei, 217–18
Vyslobotsky, Iuliian, 188, 262, 326
Vytvytsky, Stepan, 302

Wacław z Oleska (pseud. of Wacław Zaleski), 34, 61, 101–2, 140, 156
Walewski, Antoni, 224–5, 232–4

Wasilewski, Piotr, 294, 343
Wasilewski, Tadeusz, 31, 132, 162, 269
Widmann, Józef, 303
Wielopolski, Aleksander, 169
Wisłocki, Władysław, 231, 234
Wiśniewski, Wiktor, 293
Wiśniowiecki, King Michał Korybut, 270
Wiśniowski, Teofil, 352
Wollman, Frank, 84

Zabila, Viktor, 148
Zachariasiewicz, Jan, 347
Zajączkowski, Józef, 240, 242–3, 245
Zaklynsky, Oleksii, 194, 217, 224–5, 227, 229, 231, 234, 241, 275
Zaleski, Józef Bohdan, 30–32
Zaleski, Wacław, 34–5, 61, 74, 87–8, 93, 101–2, 129, 134, 140, 156, 270, 273, 281, 293, 295–6, 305, 317
Zalizniak, Maksym, 340
Zamoyski, Wacław, 365
Zap, Karel, 12, 18, 25, 103, 130, 135–9, 142–3, 145–6, 151–3, 156, 159, 216–17, 225
Zaremba, Erazm, 226, 228, 230
Zarytsky, Ivan, 309
Zawadzki, Aleksander, 153
Zgierski, Alojzy, 40
Zhukovsky, Ivan, 104, 179, 194–5, 241, 309, 312–13, 315–17, 324, 326
Ziemiałkowski, Florian, 129, 276
Zubrytsky, Denys, 32, 45, 47–8, 76, 78, 81, 89, 91–2, 94–5, 102, 116, 124, 133, 145, 153, 155–6, 158, 162, 166, 171, 179–81, 186, 195, 216–17, 362–3
Zygmunt III, 340

Subject Index

Academic Committee, 338
Academic Gymnasium, 27
Academic Legion, 188, 352
Adamiv, 241
Adriatic Sea, 154–5
Agrarian reforms, 20–21, 184–5, 203, 260–63
Agriculture, textbooks on, 80–81; as subject in journals, 180, 210
Alcoholism, 123–4, 139
Alphabet, Latin, 36, 52, 75, 85–9, 93–8, 101, 105, 135, 140, 143, 165–6, 179, 301–2, 325; Cyrillic, 36, 70, 75, 87–9, 91–7, 118, 140, 143, 165, 171, 179, 324, 344, 346; Old Slavonic, 133, 310; Polish, 87–9, 91, 102; *see also* Language; Orthography
America, 272, 330
Archeological Commission (St. Petersburg), 144, 154
Arctic, 113, 314
Armenians, 122, 294, 356, 359
Asia, 97, 312
Assimilation, 108, 128, 333–4, 367
Association of the Polish People, *see* Stowarzyszenie Ludu Polskiego
Atheneum, 365
Augsburger Allgemeine Zeitung, 210
Austria, bureaucracy, 16, 21–2, 163, 178, 183, 198, 237, 250, 279, 290, 340, 342, 346, 348, 355–6, 359, 360; Council of Ministers, 184–5, 206; Ministry of Education, 293, 305–8, 315, 317; Ministry of Justice, 261; monarchy, 10, 12, 67, 115, 131, 170–71, 178, 182, 195, 210, 246, 249, 261, 268, 270, 273, 278, 289, 297, *see also* Habsburg monarchy; nationalities policy, 9, 101, 113–14, 142, 163–4, 170–71, 178, 206, 279, 282, 308, 353, 357, 359, 367; police, *see* Police; press code, 329; relations with Russia, 67–8, 113, 154–5; religious policy, 23–4, 26–7; state structure, 216, 220, 223–4, 270–71, 276–9
Austro-Constitutional Association, 200
Austrophilism, 23, 27, 47, 202
Austro-Slavism, 10, 12, 140, 207, 230, 232, 284

Bachórz, 107–8
Baltic Sea, 128
Barbareum, 23, 27
Baroque, 5
Basilian gymnasium, 25, 305
Basilian Order, 55, 188
Battalion of Ruthenian Mountain Riflemen, 284, 297, 299, 300
Bautzen, 11
Beirat, 191–2, 199–201, 302–3
Belgrade, 11
Belorussia (Belorussians), 7, 42, 95, 111–12, 341
Berezhany, 27, 59, 199, 203–4, 238, 240–43, 245, 256, 293–6, 299; district, 22, 62; Ruthenian Council, 191, 198, 203–4, 206, 224, 238, 240–43, 246, 256, 288, 294, 304–6
Bernardines, 25
Beskyd, 78, 112
Bessarabia, 334
Biala river, 16
Bible, 326
Bibrka, 203, 294
Bircza, 203
Black Sea, 45, 78, 112–13, 128, 133, 314
Bochnia, 273
Boh river, 112, 149
Bohemia (Bohemians), 7–10, 139, 155, 218–19, 249, 268, 276
Bohemian charter, 220
Bohorodchany, 203
Boiky, 144
Bolekhiv, 203, 257, 294, 306
Booksellers, 32, 78, 108, 134, 143, 150, 163, 319–20
Book smuggling, 150–51
Bosnians, 7
Bourgeoisie, 6, 8, 16, 367
Bratislava, 76, 141
Bratslav, Palatinate of, 111
Brest, Union of, 101, 336
Brigands, 22, 30, 62, 120–21
Brno, 248–9
Brody, 143, 150, 294, 319; district, 296; Ruthenian council, 203–4
Brotherhood of Saints Cyril and Methodius, 12, 29, 149–50, 157, 161
Buchach, 25, 294, 299, 305; Ruthenian council, 203, 255
Budapest, 69, 71, 76, 94, 136–7, 141
Buh river, 41, 78, 112
Bukovyna, 6–8, 15, 21, 34, 79, 169, 203, 210, 224, 243, 247, 297, 300; population of, 16–17, 145, 279; separation of, 277–9, 282
Bulgarians, 7, 11, 117
Byzantium, 117

Calvinism, 284
Carbonari, 44, 91, 132
Carinthia (Carinthians), 86, 140, *see also* Slovenes
Carniola, 86
Carpathian mountains, 22, 42, 45, 112, 115–16, 121, 144, 157
Časopis Českêho Museum, 136, 142–4
Catholicism, *see* Greek Catholic church; Roman Catholic church
Caucasus, 112
Censors (censorship), 66–72, 74–7, 85–6, 94, 99, 101, 150–51, 157, 166, 178, 182, 187, 322, 330, 360, 362
Českâ Včela, 143
Chair of Ukrainian language and literature, 82, 168, 212, 303, 305, 316–17
Chernihiv, 111, 149, 155
Chernivtsi, 80, 145, 203, 282, 320
Chortkiv, 22, 34, 62, 70, 118, 202–3, 205, 207; district, 107, 257
Chteniia, 153
Citizens' Committee, 184
Class conflict, 54, 162, 355–6, 358
Clerical Society, *see* Societas Presbyterorum
Commission for the Study of Ancient

Documents, 154
Committee of Forty, 184
Committee of Four, 201
Composers, 321
Congress of Ukrainian scholars (1848), 107, 112, 146, 309–15, 317, 321, 352
Constantinople, 115, 117
Constituent Assembly, 229
Constitutional Commission, 275–6, 278–9, 282
Constitutional government, 177
Corpus Christi celebrations, 289
Cossacks, 30, 62, 97, 118, 121, 147, 157, 311, 321, 340
Courland, 91
Cracow, 114, 131, 133, 135, 171, 253, 273, 279, 281; Grand Duchy of, 281; gubernia, 223, 277; insurrection of 1846, 22, 131, 162, 169, 184, 263
Crimea, 91
Croatia (Croats), 5–7, 11, 69, 76–7, 86, 116, 122, 137, 140, 152, 169, 220, 271, 365, *see also* Illyria
Crown of Saint Stephen, 8, 365
Cyril, Saint, 96, 313
Cyrillic alphabet, *see* Alphabet, Cyrillic; font, 69; script, 80–81, 88
Czasopismo Naukowe Księgozbioru Publicznego im. Ossolińskich, 33
Czech Museum, 11, 136, 142–4
Czechs, 5–7, 9, 13, 36, 96, 117, 151, 154, 169, 216, 220–22, 235, 248–9, 265, 268, 276, 279, 366; relations with Poles, 219, 232, 246–7, 353; relations with Russians, 37, 140; relations with Ukrainians, 75, 95, 110, 135–6, 138–9, 142–4, 146, 159, 219, 232, 246–7, 254, 275, 307, 347

Dacians, 115
Dalmatia, 23, 169
Danica, 11
Danube river, 96, 171
Danubian basin, 16, 115, 279, 367
Deanery councils, 197–211, 223, 238, 293–4, 353, *see also* Holovna Rada Ruska; Ukraine, national councils
Deliatyn, 243
Demyche, 18
Denationalization, 17–18, 167, 189, 198, 304, 311, 322
Deputies, Croatian, 271, 276; Czech, 247–8, 250, 275; Polish, 219, 246–7, 253–4, 268, 271, 355; Slovenian, 271; Ukrainian, 211, 217–19, 243–9, 252–5, 270, 275, 278, 280, 282, 315, 355, *see also* Ukraine, peasants
Dennitsa-Jutrzenka, 11, 100, 102–3, 167
Desna river, 78, 112
Dictionaries, 10, 34, 36, 46, 57, 86, 99, 153–4
Dnewnyk Ruskij, 134, 269, 317, 338–9, 356
Dnieper river, 41, 49, 97–8, 112, 121, 133, 147, 341, 343, 357
Dniester river, 41, 78, 112, 122, 157, 171, 299
Dominican gymnasium, 305–6, 308, 316–17
Don river, 78, 112
Donets river, 78, 112
Drohobych, 202–3, 241, 289
Dykiv, 31, 132, 144
Dynów, 203, 240–41
Dziennik Môd Paryskich, 177
Dziennik Narodowy, 219, 337–8, 343–6, 348, 351, 365–6

Education, *see* National enlightenment; Schools
Elbe river, 171
Elections, 221, 223–5, 237–50, 252–4
Emancipation, 29, 301, 327
Eneida, 147, 150–51, 320, 329
Enfranchisement, 208, 253, 263, 368

England, 334
Enlightenment, 3–4, 21
Equality, 4, 6, 43, 209, 211, 226, 268, 271, 322, 335, 349, 356–7
Ethnography, 62, 112, 157, 165, 313, 328
Etymology, 57, 90, 312
Europe, 3, 6–8, 12, 48, 95, 97–8, 106, 137, 141, 173, 177, 196, 231, 233–4, 272, 346, 353, 365, 367

Federalism, 29, 42, 110, 131, 149–50, 154, 183, 225–6, 230–1, 233–4, 248, 265, 276, 346, 349, 358
Feudalism, 3–4, 16, 19–21, 117, 131, 182, 184, 211, 263, 334, 366, *see also Robot*; Serfdom
Folk idiom, 84–6, 90, 99–101, 103, 107, 114, 138, 147–8, 152, 164, 242, 309
Folklore, 5–6, 33–6, 61–2, 107, 115, 137, 328
Folk songs, 6, 33, 66, 68, 72, 74, 76, 85–6, 99, 109, 115, 118, 121, 134–5, 148, 152, 311, 341
Folk tales, 65, 165
Forests, 19, 195, 251, 254, 259
France, 44, 177, 181, 330, 353
Frankfurt, 12, 215–16, 357–8
Free Galicians, *see* Vilni Halychany
French Revolution, 6, 98, 105, 117

Galicia, boundary of, 15, 145; ethnic composition of, 16–17, 145; internal migration in, 21; Kingdom of, *see* Kingdom of Galicia and Lodomeria; partition of, 211, 220–22, 229–30, 232, 235, 246, 250, 253–4, 263, 266–78, 280–82, 350–52, 354, 361, 367; population of, 16–17, 112
Galician committee, 227, 229, 231
Galician estates diet, 162, 182, 185, 189, 208, 244, 266, 269, 273, 279
Galician-Ruthenian Matytsia, *see* Halytsko-Ruska Matytsia
Galician School Council, 306, 317
Gazeta Lwowska, 328
Gazeta Narodowa, 352
Gazeta Powszechna, 305, 346–7
General Confederation of the Polish Nation, *see* Konfederacja Powszechna Narodu Polskiego
Gente Rutheni, natione Poloni, 18, 338
Germanization, 9, 11, 16, 24–6, 28, 170, 249, 307, 309, 336, 341, 357
Germany (Germans), 8, 12, 17, 41, 49, 69, 96, 131, 146, 155, 163, 184, 186, 194, 211, 216, 219–20, 222–4, 228, 246, 249, 269, 308, 321, 346, 353, 359, 365, 367
Gniezno, 116
Gospels, 111
Greece, 97
Greek Catholic church, 6–7, 17–18, 23–4, 34, 58, 70, 72, 79, 113, 155, 198, 205, 289, 325, 339, 359–60, 364; clergy, 7, 23–4, 26–7, 33, 38, 44, 52, 55, 60–61, 78, 96, 99, 108, 168, 179, 190–91, 198, 200, 202, 207, 210–12, 217, 224, 231, 243–4, 273–4, 302, 335, 348, 362; consistories, 25–6, 52–3, 57, 71, 79, 99, 124, 181, 188–9, 191, 195, 199–200, 217, 255, 303, 307, 309, 311, 315–17, 335–6, 346, 360; hierarchy, 26, 38, 44, 46, 51, 53, 55, 61, 77, 99, 103, 162–3, 167, 171–2, 181, 186, 188, 190–92, 205, 235, 244, 302, 311, 315, 325, 333, 349, 352; seminary (seminarians), 23, 25, 27, 31, 38, 43–6, 56, 59, 66, 68, 71, 80, 100, 119, 132, 163, 168, 178, 181, 187, 195, 212, 224, 288, 320, 346–7; *see also* Rite, Greek
Gubernium, 20, 52, 57, 179, 229, 241, 256, 288
Gymnasia, 24–5, 82, 147, 305–6, 308, 315–19, 340

Habsburg monarchy, 6, 11, 15, 19, 21, 49, 56, 106, 111, 116, 118, 163, 202, 216, 249, 355, 364, 367, *see also* Austria
Hadiach, Union of, 340
Haidamaks, 121, 340
Haliczanin, 30, 36, 121
Halych, 167; Principality of, *see* Principality of Halych and Volodymyr; Ruthenian council, 203–4
Halycho-ruskyi vistnyk, 329
Halytska Pchola, see Pchola
Halytsko-Ruska Matytsia, 11, 309–10, 314–15, 317, 325–6, 329
Historicism, 5
Histories, popular, 320, 329
Hlubichok, 295
Hlyniany, 202–3, 205, 207, 267
Holovna Rada Ruska, 140, 171, 186, 193–207, 209–11, 215–18, 220–25, 235, 237–8, 240–46, 250, 252, 254–5, 257–63, 266–8, 270–73, 275, 278, 280–84, 287–94, 296–300, 304–7, 309, 311, 315, 317, 321, 323–6, 329–31, 333, 336–8, 342–4, 348–55, 359, 361–2, 364, 367–8
Horodenka, 243
Horodok, 203, 241, 243
Horozhanna, 22
Horshova, 257
Hotel George, 177
Hôtel Lambert, 232–3
Hrazhdanka, 93–4
Hrodna, 145
Hrushiv, 171
Hungary, 6, 8–9, 11, 15, 23, 92, 101, 116, 183, 228, 247, 271, 337, 359, 365–6; censorship in, 69, 71; Holovna Rada Ruska and, 283–5, 290–93, 296–300; Ivan Holovatsky in, 136–7, 142; Jelačić's intervention in, 247–8; revolution in, 283, 296–7, 364; Russian intervention in, 22; Ukrainian language in, 101, 112; *see also* Magyars; Rus', Transcarpathian
Husiatyn, 199
Hutsuls, 22, 62, 121

Iabloniv, 243
Iavoriv, 243, 295–6
Illyria (Illyrians), 6, 9, 12, 75, 115, 137, 166, 246, 249
Imperial Academy of Sciences, 153–4
Imperial Society of Russian History and Antiquity, 154
Incunabula, 58
Indemnification, 184–5, 247, 253–4, 260–61
India, 115
Innsbruck, 212
Irish question, 334
Islam, 7, 340
Istanbul, 365
Italy, 140, 177, 181, 293, 352

Jagiellonian Library, 90, 135
Jagiellonian University, 111
Jahrbücher für slawische Literatur, Kunst und Wissenschaft, 11, 98, 103, 167, 171
Jarosław, 203, 223
Jaśliska, 203
Jasło district, 259, 273, 281
Jesuits, 25, 39, 97, 113, 170, 334, 350
Jews, 8, 54, 76, 123–4, 155, 168, 204, 207, 239–40, 254, 294, 304, 320, 322, 356, 359
justiziarii, 20–21

Kalush, 203, 205, 294
Kamianka, 149
Kamianka Voloska, 296
Kaniv, 122
Karlovci, 77
Karlovy Vary, 155
Kashubs, 344, 366
Kazan, 91

Kharkiv, 98, 148, 334; university, 147, 340
Kharkovskii Demokrit, 147–8
Khmeleva, 76
Khodoriv, 203, 294, 304
Kholoiv, 203
Kiev, 97–8, 107, 116, 149–50, 157, 319, 322, 341; district, 149, 334; Palatinate of, 111; university, 147
Kievlianin, 151, 158
Kingdom of Galicia and Lodomeria, 16, 113, 279, 281
Klekotyn, 321–2
Klymets, 297
Kobzar, 148, 151
Koliivshchyna, 131, 340
Kolo Ruske, 45
Kolomyia, 60, 66, 70, 74, 203, 205, 243–4, 256, 289, 294, 299, 320, 328; district, 62, 76, 107, 296, 299, 320; Ruthenian council, 203, 205, 218, 256, 289, 294, 328; theatre, 321
Komarno, 203
Konfederacja Powszechna Narodu Polskiego, 43
"Kormchaia kniga," 144
Košice, 136, 300
Kosiv, 203
Kosmach, 121
Kozivka, 242
Krakowiak, 108
Královédvorský rukopis, 5, 30, 136, 142
Kreise, 20, 240–43, 256, 259–61, 296, 303–4
Kreishauptmänner, 239, 241–3, 256–7, 288, 294–5, 303, 321
Kremianets, 34, 58
Kremnica, 300
Kretivtsi, 242
Kroměříž, 249, 271, 274–5, 279–80, 308, 353
Kryvche, 241
Kuban river, 112
Kuty, 243–4
Květy, 139, 143

Łabowa, 203
Land disputes, 255–63
Landessprache, 52–3
Land-owners' Society, *see* Stowarzyszenie Ziemiańskie
Language, Belorussian, 113, 137–8; Beskydian, 157; Carniolian, 111; Church Slavonic, 12, 23–4, 32, 48, 51, 54, 56–7, 62, 70–71, 83–4, 87, 89–90, 92–3, 113, 132, 144, 152, 157, 310, 312–13, 318, 323, 326; Czech, 9, 111, 140, 166; Galician-Ruthenian, 99–102, 269; German, 3, 9, 28, 46, 51, 92, 130, 275, 301, 303, 305–8, 324, 346, 353, 358; Hungarian, 9, 284; Illyrian, 9, 111, 140, 166; Kiev-Pereislav, 114; Latin, 9, 25, 46, 51, 99, 117, 324; Little Russian, 100, 102, 104, 111–13, 153, 164, 334, 363; Old Bulgarian, 83; Old Serbian, 9; Polish, 5, 9, 17, 46, 52, 57, 83, 90, 92, 96, 111, 113, 129, 140, 158, 301, 310, 322, 344, 359, as official language, 267, 305, 324, 358, in schools, 275, 293, 303, 305, 307–8; Romanian, 145; Russian, 9, 56–7, 62, 71, 83, 85, 90, 92, 100, 102, 111, 113, 138, 140, 148–9, 154, 158, 310, 314, 363; Ruthenian, 23–4, 26, 52, 99–104, 112–13, 152, 158, 180, 199, 311; Sanskrit, 97; Serbian, 137; Serbo-Croatian, 9; Slavo-Ruthenian, 23, 25–6, 51–2, 84–5, 100, 137; Slovak, 5; Slovenian, 111; South Rus', 83, 103, 111–14, 153, 158, 312;

Ukrainian, admired, 67, 311; as dead language, 86, 108, 301; as limited, 94–5, 102, 111, 149, 158, 274, 305–6; as official language, 204, 212, 221, 229, 232, 322–4; as

Polish dialect, 128–9, 231, 270, 342–4; as Russian dialect, 148; Chair of (Lviv), 82, 168, 212, 303, 305, 316–17; defended, 33, 46, 54, 56–7, 71, 113, 137–8, 336, 341, 346, 348; government documents in, 171, 189; ignored, 316, 323, 359; in schools, 51–3, 183, 189, 212, 221, 224, 229, 232, 234, 277, 293, 302–10; lectures in, 46–7; literary language, 35, 54, 56–7, 70–71, 83–4, 86, 90, 99–102, 106–7, 136, 138, 147, 158, 173, 180, 312; publications in, 24, 34, 38, 53–6, 60–61; purity of, 86, 363; rebirth of, 48, 147, 322; studied, 109, 111, 132, 305; suppressed by church, 26, 52, 70, 99, 306, 311; translations into, 31, 46, 61, 80, 99, 111, 132, 136, 141, 165;

see also Alphabet; Linguistic conflicts; Orthography; Ukraine, grammar

Language of instruction, Czech, 24; German, 24–5, 51, 306, 358; Polish, 24–5, 51–2, 182, 221, 293, 303, 309; Slavo-Ruthenian, 25–6, 51–2; Ukrainian, 168, 189, 212, 221, 224, 232, 253, 278, 293, 302–5, 307

Language of official documents, 323–4

Łapichłopstwo, 254

Lastivka, 148

Learned societies, 11, 43, 56

Learned Society, *see* Towarzystwo Uczonych

Łęchowie, 343

Lędzianie, 343

Leipzig, 11, 27, 98, 143, 167

Lekhia (Lekhites), 116, 283

Liakhy, 17–18, 31–2, 39, 41, 75, 133–4, 200, 244, 246, 251, 277, 324, 327, 330, 347–8, 353

Libraries, 31–2, 56, 58, 73, 144, 351

Libuše, prophecy of, 117

Linguistic conflicts, in Bohemia, 9; in Croatia, 86; in Galicia, 5, 9, 26, 28, 48, 52, 57, 71, 83–108, 140, 143, 153, 301–8, 312–13, 322–4; in Hungary, 9; in Moravia, 9; in Russian Ukraine, 148; in Serbia, 9, 86; in Slovakia, 5; in Slovenia, 6, 9, 86–7, 140; *see also* Alphabet; Language; Orthography; Ukraine, grammar

Linguistics, 10, 61, 100, 104, 115

Lisnyky, 191

Literacy, 65

Literature, German, 36, 48–9, 59; Greek, 106; Old Rus', 318; Old Slavonic, 98; Polish, 27–8, 30–37, 48, 59, 93, 130, 341; Roman, 106; Russian, 37, 93, 100, 180, 318; Ruthenian, 49, 58–9, 70, 157; Serbian, 77–8, 87, 93, 136–7; Slavic, 87; Slovak, 5, 9, 36, 140, 314; Slovene, 5–6, 9–10, 140; Ukrainian, 30–37, 69–74, 76–8, 84, 86, 93–5, 98, 100, 102–3, 105–6, 114–15, 136, 142, 146–8, 157–8, 168–9, 181, 277, 310, 312, 319

Lithuania (Lithuanians), 17, 42, 78, 145, 230, 334–5, 344, 346–7, 351, 366

Lithuanian Statute, 92

Little Russia (Little Russians), 6, 78, 102, 110–12, 114, 140, 147, 150–51, 165, 341

Ljubljana, 11

Lodomeria, *see* Kingdom of Galicia and Lodomeria

Lubaczów, 203, 241

Lublin, 145

Lusatian Sorbs, 7, 11, 314

Lutowiska, 241

Lviv, 20, 23–7, 30, 32, 34–5, 37–8, 41, 43, 46, 48–9, 51–2, 55–6, 58–9, 67–9, 71, 73–5, 79–80, 102–3, 107, 118, 124, 132, 134, 143–4, 146, 150–53, 156, 163, 166, 177, 182,

200, 209–10, 219–21, 231, 249, 253, 259, 269, 272, 280, 283, 287, 289, 292–3, 295–6, 298–9, 302, 309, 317, 321, 325, 337–8, 344–5, 348, 352–5, 358, 361, 363; academy, 305; Chronicle, 157; diocese, 25, 80, 210, 302; gubernia, 223; gymnasia, *see* Gymnasia; municipal council, 325; seminary, *see* Greek Catholic church; university, 23–6, 32, 38, 48, 56, 58–9, 68, 82, 146, 305, 308, 316, 326

Magyarization, 249, 365–6
Magyarones, 137
Magyars, 12, 139, 141–2, 220, 228, 233, 249, 282, 334, 357, 364–7; relations with Poles, 219, 247–8, 282; relations with Slovaks, 141, 172–3; *see also* Hungary; Rus', Transcarpathian
Maidan, 241
Maksymovychivka, 158
Mandatarii, 20–21, 63, 239, 241–2, 255, 259, 272
Manifestos, 234–5, 248, 271
Manorial lands, 19–21, 54, 122, 162, 182–3, 254, 256, 261–3, 333
Mariampil, 243
Matica Ilirska, 11
Matica Serbska, 11
Matica Slovenska, 11
Matica Srpska, 11
Matice Česká, 11, 310
Mazovian dialect, 344
Mazuria (Mazurians), 131, 184, 231, 246, 254, 281, 293, 345, 355, 366
Meadows, 19, 121, 195, 251, 254
Medyka, 88
Mekhitarist priests, 76
Messianism, 140, 312
Młoda Sarmacja, 43, 45
Mokriany, 203
Moldavia, 279
Monasteries, 55, 102, 144, 153, 188, 329
Monastyryska, 243
Montenegro (Montenegrins), 5–7, 97, 121
Monumenta Serbica, 145
Moravia (Moravians), 7, 9, 36, 117, 220, 248–9, 275
Moscow, 62, 143, 147, 152, 166, 228, 318–19
Moskovskii nabliudatel, 144, 152
Moskvitianin, 116, 152
Mosty Velyki, 363
Muscovitism, 102, 165, 362
Muscovy (Muscovites), 31, 41, 76, 97, 334, 340, 357, 362; *see also* Russia
Mykulyntsi, 243
Mykytyntsi, 76

Načertanije, 11
Naraiv, 22, 203, 241, 294
Nassau regiment, 249
Nation, 4, 27, 345; as subject in historiography, 10; defined, 109–10
National anthems, 202, 271, 289, 319
National aspirations, of Poles, 4–5, 29–30, 230; of Serbs, 8; of Slavs, 5–6, 8, 28; of Ukrainians, 59–61, 67, 72, 84, 105–6, 114, 132, 135, 138, 142, 211, 218, 285, 328, 343, 364
National awakening, 3–6, 9, 30, 37, 53, 66, 73, 113, 118, 135, 173, 235, 321
National chauvinism, 323, 356
National conflicts, in East Central Europe, 8; in Galicia, 66–7, 127, 135, 139, 333, 365–6; in Hungary, 365–6
National consciousness, 5–6, 8; in Europe, 141; in Galicia, 18, 22, 24, 28, 42–3, 59, 65, 67, 69–70, 72, 80–81, 95, 110, 149, 172–3, 187, 191, 236, 251, 281, 315, 320, 327–8, 341, 359, 368; in Russian

Ukraine, 15, 95
National demands, 42–50, 53, 226, 229, 235, 266
National development, 98, 149, 267, 271–2, 347, 365
National enlightenment, 104–8, 301, 310, 312, 339
National guard, *see entries under* Poland; Ukraine
National independence, 4, 9, 39, 42–3, 45, 60–61, 110, 118, 146, 183, 190, 196, 201, 219, 226, 231, 233, 266, 340, 347, 355, 357–8, 362
Nationalism, 28, 58, 78, 141, 359
National liberation, 40, 72, 148, 355, 358–9, 365
National movements, 7–13, 84, 172; *see also entries on individual nationalities*
National oppression, 7, 16–17, 119–20, 130, 139, 228
National programmes, 42–50, 66–7, 72, 112, 231, 233–4, 266
National question, 66, 84, 109, 230, 234, 251, 283, 339, 345
National Reading Club, 320
National rebirth, 58–60, 325
National rights, 105, 139, 178, 191, 280, 335, 359
National spirit, 109, 278
Nationhood, 13, 111, 223
Neisse river, 357
Neman river, 133
Neue Rheinische Zeitung, 366
New Testament, 77
Nizhyn, 147
Nobility, Croatian, 365; Czech, 7–8; Hungarian, 8–9, 16, 365–6; Polish, 8, 16–18, 22, 27, 29, 39–40, 42, 96, 118–19, 121–2, 129–31, 133, 139, 145, 148–9, 162, 168–9, 183–5, 191, 220, 251, 260, 334, 340, 350–51, 355, 365–7; Russian, 8; Serbian, 7; South Rus', 83; Ukrainian, 8, 17–18, 122, 189, 270, 336, 340, 351, 365
Normans, 115
Novgorod, 97, 106, 116
Novoselytsia, 297
Novyny, 329

October Revolution (1848), 248–9, 292
Oder river, 357
Odessa, 147, 334
Oesterreichischer Beobachter, 87
Old Believers, 224
Olesko, 87, 203
Oliiv, 241
Olomouc, 123, 248–9, 258, 274–5, 298, 320
Ondava river, 112
Order of Leopold, 103
Orsk, 150
Orthodoxy, 6–7, 77, 96, 169, 282, 345
Orthography, 36, 70–71, 74–5, 81, 83–108, 143, 148, 151, 157–8, 166, 180, 310, 312–13, 329; *see also* Alphabet; Language; Ukraine, grammar
Ossolineum, 27, 32, 38, 133, 150, 345
Oświęcim, Duchy of, 281
Ottoman Empire, 7, 154

Pacific ocean, 113, 154, 314
Paliivshchyna, 131
Pamiętnik Lwowski, 33
Pannonia, 12, 96, 116
Pan-Slavism, 4, 12–13, 164–5, 366
Papal Curia, 55
Paris, 36, 232
Parma regiment, 249
Pastures, 19, 195, 251, 254
Pątnik Lwowski, 30
Patriarchy, 96–7, 116–17
Patrons, 58, 69, 102, 136
Pchola, 180–81, 320, 326, 329
Peasants, *see* Ukraine, peasants
Pechora river, 91
Perehinsko, 203, 301, 323
Petitions, 177–8, 182–6, 188–91, 194,

207, 213, 252–4, 257, 260–61, 265, 267–9, 272, 278–9, 282, 284, 308, 323–4, 346, 348, 361
"Philomaths," 91
Phonetic spelling, 89–90
Piarists, 25
Pidbuzh, 203
Pidhaitsi, 203, 294
Pidlyssia, 37, 132
Pistyn, 76
Podillia, 21, 111, 113, 122, 146, 149, 334
"Podnistrianka," 157
Pokuttia, 62, 107, 217, 223
Poland (Poles), Commonwealth, 16–17, 38, 335, 347; émigrés, 11, 38, 232, 299; history, 117; independence, 77, 183, 284; insurrection of 1830–31, 37–8, 66, 127–8, 149, 273, 333; insurrection of 1846, *see* Cracow; intelligentsia, 4–5, 8, 128, 134, 295, 333–4, 343, 355; journals, 11, 28, 30, 32–3, 35–6, 76, 87, 89, 91, 100, 102–3, 121, 132, 134, 164, 167, 177, 219, 269, 305, 317, 328, 337–9, 343–8, 351–2, 356, 358, 365–6; Kingdom of, 271, 335; landlords, 184–6; Lyceum, 34; magnates, 129, 334; messianism, 4–5; National Council, *see* Rada Narodowa; national guard, 178, 181, 185, 229, 232, 287–9, 296; national movement, 6, 8, 27–8, 46, 128–9, 177–8, 182–4, 187, 230–31, 233, 246, 270–74, 366; nobility, *see* Nobility, Polish; partition of, 15–16, 23, 29, 233; population, 138; propaganda, 183, 244; relations with Czechs, 219, 232, 246–7, 353; relations with Magyars, 247–8, 282; relations with Russians, *see* Russia, relations with Poles; relations with Ukrainians (literary), 30–37, 79, 95, 132; relations with Ukrainians (poltical), 28–30, 37–50, 66, 68, 88, 106, 119, 127–8, 131, 134–5, 139, 141–2, 155, 161, 170, 178, 182, 184, 186–9, 194, 196, 198–9, 211, 217, 220–22, 225–34, 244–7, 263, 265, 270–72, 280, 283, 288–9, 295, 333–66; religion, 7; revolutionaries, 38–46, 106, 119, 128, 132, 149, 184, 253, 263, 272, 347, 352–3, 367; Slavism, 12; *see also Lekhia; Liakhy;* Polonization
Polanians, 117, 343
Police, 33, 41, 67, 69–70, 72, 75, 114, 164, 180, 325; Russian, 22
Polish Committee, 227
Political demands, 177–8, 182, 189–90, 220–22, 235, 253, 265–6
Political prisoners, 178, 188
Political programmes, 11–12, 39–42, 106, 119, 140, 149–50, 169–70, 177–8, 191, 196, 220–21, 252, 334–7, 344, 348–9, 355–62
Północ, 36–7
Polonization, 17, 24, 26, 101, 122, 133, 145, 147, 167, 183, 249, 278, 305, 308, 340, 347, 365–6
Poltava, 147, 149, 155, 334, 340
Popelnyky, 217
Poprad river, 112
Population, 16–17, 112, 138, 145, 279
Postęp, 346–7, 358
Potutory, 242
Poznań, 224
Poznania, 215, 226, 273, 341, 357
Prague, 76, 123, 143–4, 151, 153, 182, 215–19, 221, 223–5, 229–30, 235, 237, 245, 248, 266, 268, 274–5, 277, 288, 334, 338, 366–7; agreement, 215, 228–9, 231–5, 288, 342, 350
Principality of Halych and Volodymyr, 7, 34, 38, 113, 115, 118, 133, 189, 266
Printing shops, 58, 69, 76, 188, 326, 328, 352

Pripet river, 78, 112
Proclamations, 194–6, 203, 205, 209–10, 215–16, 260, 290–91, 294, 303, 335–6, 339, 345
Protestantism, 7
Proverbs, 74–6
Przemyśl, 32, 38, 43, 51, 53, 55–6, 58, 69, 76, 86, 92, 99, 140, 173, 205, 217, 243, 300, 316, 321–2, 326; consistory, 52, 360; diocese, 25, 210; district, 62, 108; Ruthenian council, 203, 207
Przyjaciel Ludu, 76, 132

Rada Narodowa, 185–6, 188, 190, 192, 194, 198–200, 205–6, 224, 235, 237, 239–40, 256, 269, 274, 293, 334–9, 342–3, 346, 348–9, 352–3
Radekhiv, 243
Radymychians, 343
Radyvyliv, 150
Rakiv, 80, 319
Rectors, 27–8, 46–7, 56, 68, 71, 78, 80, 145, 181, 187, 308
Reichstag, 195, 221, 235–7, 239, 241–2, 245–50, 253, 257–8, 268–9, 275, 278–80, 287, 306, 308, 340, 354
Religion, as attribute of nationality, 97; Austrian policy, 23–4, 26–7; in East Central Europe, 6–7; in Galicia, 6–7, 16–17, 276–7; persecution, 189, 336; *see also* Rite and entries on individual denominations
Renaissance, 5
Revolution of 1848, 11–12, 16, 45, 123–4, 167, 172, 177–8, 181–3, 265, 287, 302, 358, 364
Revolutionary parties, 241, 245, 342
Riflemen, 284, 297, 299–300
Rite, Greek, 6–7, 18, 26, 92, 117, 128, 154, 190, 194, 196, 199, 274, 303, 315, 345; Latin, 17–18, 117, 133, 195, 204, 336
Robot, 19, 21–3, 29, 39–43, 53, 60, 62, 107, 119–20, 122–4, 131, 148, 162, 170, 173, 178, 181–5, 188, 191, 208, 244, 247, 251–3, 255, 257–8, 260, 262–3, 267, 279, 284, 299, 304, 322, 335, 339, 354, 358, 368; *see also* Feudalism; Serfdom
Rohatyn, 203, 294
Roman Catholic church, 7, 17, 96, 99, 168, 333; consistories, 24, 52–3, 303; *see also* Rite, Latin
Romania (Romanians), 8, 16, 220, 279, 282–3
Romanticism, 3–5, 30, 63
Rome, 97, 191
Rozdil, 203
Rozhirche caves, 144
Rozhniativ, 243
Rozhniv, 217
Rozmaitości, 28, 32, 35–6, 87, 89, 91, 121, 124
Rus', 7, 31, 35, 39, 60, 72, 78, 83, 85, 91–2, 94, 96–7, 104, 110, 112, 115–18, 120–22, 128, 146, 151, 181, 187, 222, 227, 230–31, 233–4, 283–4, 292, 297, 310–11, 324, 333–4, 336, 339–41, 343, 346–7, 349, 351–2, 355, 363
Black, 111; Red, 85, 266, 270, 341, 348, 351; South, 60, 83, 97, 110, 112; Transcarpathian, 6–8, 15–16, 41, 62, 74, 110, 235, 277, 283–4; White, 85, 111
Rusalka Dnistrovaia, 32–3, 60, 68–75, 86, 89–90, 94, 98, 100, 103, 110, 112, 114–15, 118, 120, 136, 141, 143–4, 146, 151, 157, 163, 319
Rusini, 17, 110
Ruska Pravda, 92, 118
"Ruska Zoria," 60
Ruslany, 47
Rusnaky, 110–11
Rusniaki, 110–11, 145
Russia, army, 22; centralization, 170; education, 152, 154; embassy (Vienna), 77, 143, 151; history,

116; imperialism, 141, 161, 279; migration to, 21–2; propaganda, 114, 166; relations with Austrians, 67–8, 113, 154–5; relations with Poles, 12, 37, 41, 128–9, 183, 232–4, 271–2, 282, 334–5, 344–5; relations with Ukrainians, 15, 22, 41, 67–8, 75–6, 89, 95–7, 100, 106, 113–14, 128–9, 131, 138–9, 143, 146–59, 161, 169, 187, 206, 268, 314, 318, 320, 330, 334, 355, 357, 362–4; revolutionaries, 149, 224, 233; songs, 97; statehood, 6, 151, 155; *see also* Muscovy; Pan-Slavism; Slavophiles
Russification, 113, 147, 164, 325
Russinen, 168
Russische Partei, 44, 60
"Russkaia Pravda" (programme), 149
Russophiles, 47–8, 91–2, 153, 318, 325, 331, 362–4
Rustical lands, 19–20, 183, 253–6, 260–61
Rusyny, 17, 110–12
Ruthenen, 17, 111, 361
Ruthenian Assembly, *see* Sobor Ruskyi
Ruthenian Circle, *see* Kolo Ruske
Ruthenianism, 169, 173, 200, 334, 347
Ruthenians, as Austrian subjects, 27, 47, 68, 91, 119, 131, 159, 168, 170, 190, 212–13, 244, 289, 352; as distinct nationality, 18, 47, 63, 66, 95, 110–11, 113, 116, 178; as invention of Stadion, 334; attitudes to Russia, 154–5, 159; emblems of, 201, 222, 229; identified, 110–11; self-identification, 17, 47, 66; *see also* Ukraine
Ruthenian Triad, 10, 33, 40, 42–3, 46, 49–51, 57, 59–63, 65–7, 69–74, 80–81, 83–4, 86, 90, 96, 101–5, 107, 109–10, 112, 114, 116, 119–20, 122, 127, 130, 132, 134–8, 140–41, 146, 152–3, 157, 163, 172, 180–81, 186, 191, 200, 206, 301, 313, 319, 333
Ruthenization, 321
Ruthenophobes, 327
Rzeszów, 139, 273, 281

Sącz, 107, 134, 273, 281
Saint Barbara's Church, 56
Saint George's Capitulary, 193, 364
Saint George's Cathedral, 195, 354, 364
Saint George's hill, 200
Saint George's Monastery, 55, 102
Saint Georgites, 269, 294, 330, 341, 344, 346, 352, 362–3
Saint Onufrii's Monastery, 144, 153
Saint Petersburg, 67, 144, 149, 157, 319
Sambir, 18, 38, 43, 203, 205, 241, 299, 321, 339; district, 22
San river, 15–16, 78, 112–13, 308, 314
Sanok, 203, 243, 294; district, 62, 107, 259, 281, 295
Sava river, 171
Scandinavia, 116, 343
Schools, 24–6, 34, 51–5, 99, 129, 149, 155, 168–9, 178, 197, 211–12, 255, 301–11, 315–17, 323, 341, 353–4, 358; convent, 25; parish, 24–5, 46, 51–2, 55, 58, 88, 107, 302–3; primary, 46, 183, 189, 212, 301–3, 305; trivium, 24–5, 52, 60, 302–3, 307
Seim river, 112
Self-determination, 195, 234, 357
Self-government, 203, 255
Senica, 300
Separatism, 8, 67, 130, 140, 170, 217, 231, 279, 300, 334, 345
Serbia (Serbs), cultural activity, 10–13; orthography, 36, 86, 89; relations with Magyars, 8, 228, 365; relations with Russians, 154; relations with Ukrainians, 136–7, 172; religion, 7, 77, 137, 172; revolution, 98; social structure, 7; songs, 73, 78, 97, 136; statehood, 6;

uskoks in, 121
Serbian Chronicle, 144
Serfdom (serfs), 3, 19–21, 31, 39, 41, 43, 122, 148–50, 170, 242, 252, 257, 260; *see also* Feudalism; *Robot*
Servitudes, 182, 185, 207, 253–5, 258–9, 262
Shutkiv, 80, 319
Sianky, 204
Siberia, 345
Sich, 121, 340
Silesia (Silesians), 36, 117, 249, 334, 357, 366
Skalat, 203, 241
Sklo, 108
Skole, 243
Slavdom, 41, 48–9, 56, 95–7, 104, 117, 130, 133, 141, 143–4, 156, 164–5, 225, 312, 319, 337, 357–9
Slavery, 97, 106, 122
Slavic Club, 275
Slavic Committee, 227–8
Slavic Congress, 215–20, 223–37, 246, 265–6, 269, 277, 334, 338
Slavic studies, 56, 84, 115, 146, 313
Slavophiles, 5, 72, 97–8, 113, 116, 140
Slavs, South, 6, 10–12, 49, 87, 95, 136, 220, 225, 228, 234, 246, 248, 275, 277, 366
Slawische Central-Blätter, 275
Slawische Jahrbücher, 102
Slovakia (Slovaks), in Bratislava, 76; language and literature, 5, 9, 36, 140, 314; national movement, 13, 137; relations with Austrians, 6, 220; relations with Magyars, 141, 172, 228, 235, 337, 365; relations with Poles, 334; relations with Russians, 154; relations with Ukrainians, 137, 172, 290; religion, 7; social structure, 7
Slovenia (Slovenes), language and literature, 5–6, 9–10, 140; national movement, 13; orthography, 86; relations with Poles, 271; relations with Ukrainians, 110; religion, 7; social structure, 7
Slovo o polku Ihorevi, 5, 92, 118, 133, 153, 329
Słowianin, 121
Sniatyn, 203, 243–4
Sobor Ruskyi, 222, 224, 243, 267, 269, 311, 316–17, 327, 337–9, 342–3, 349–50, 352–3, 362, 364
Social change, 106, 117; liberation, 40, 72, 96, 148, 297, 358; oppression, 7, 16–17, 41, 120, 122–3, 130, 139, 189, 251, 336; stratification, 19; struggle, 84
Societas Presbyterorum, 53–6, 105
Society of Galician Antiquities, *see* Towarzystwo Starożytności Galicyjskich
Society of United Slavs, 149
Sokal, 243
Sokolivka, 241
Solotvyna, 243–4
Sons of the Fatherland, 358
Sprachzeichen, 24
Srbske Narodne Novine, 136
Staaten Bund, 220, 223
Stanyslaviv, 32, 205, 239, 294, 299, 328; Beirat, 200–01; district, 19, 25, 62, 200, 296; Ruthenian council, 203–4, 270
Stari Myslytyntsi, 296
Statehood, 4, 29
Stavropygian church, 32; Institute, 24, 41, 69, 164, 178–81, 189, 311, 326, 329, 352
Štokavian dialect, 87, 137
Stowarzyszenie Ludu Polskiego, 42–5, 128
Stowarzyszenie Ziemiańskie, 186, 206, 344
Stryi, 22, 202, 241, 296, 299, 321; district, 62, 289; Ruthenian council, 203, 205, 306
Stube, 24

Studena, 297
Styria, 86, 249
Supreme Ruthenian Council, *see* Holovna Rada Ruska
Sviatoiurtsi, *see* Saint Georgites
Sweden, 116
Switzerland, 351
Syn Rusy, 65–9
Szczebrzeszyn, 145
Szlachta, *see* Nobility, Polish

Tarnów, 124, 253, 273
Tatars, 118, 120, 340
Teachers, 304–7, 311, 315–16, 325
Terebovlia, 34, 203
Ternopil, 22, 268, 295, 321; district, 296; gymnasium, 316; Ruthenian council, 203–5, 294
Terrorism, 45, 192, 265, 283
Theatre, 80, 147, 320–22
Theocracy, 231
Third Department, 22
Tisza river, 92
Tobacco, 81
Toloka, 122
Torun, 297
Towarzystwo Starożytności Galicyjskich, 43
Towarzystwo Uczonych, 43
Transcarpathia, *see* Rus', Transcarpathian
Transylvania, 23, 334
Tulchyn, 149
Turka, 203–4, 243
Turkey (Turks), 15, 340
Tygodnik Peterburski, 164
Tyrol, 249, 278
"Tyrolians of the East," 27, 368
Tysmenytsia, 243

Ukraine (Ukrainians), education, *see* Schools; grammar, 25, 30, 36, 49, 55–6, 58–9, 65, 67, 71, 85–6, 99–100, 103–4, 150, 157, 302, 310; history, 61, 314; in France, 44; in Hungary, 6, 112, 138, 228, 235, 283, 290, *see also* Rus', Transcarpathian; in Russia, 6, 112, 138, 146–59; intellectual life, 32, 48, 55–6, 60–61, 79, 81, 98, 181; intelligentsia, 7, 60, 128, 162, 206, 284, 301, 309, 319, 322, 339, 347–8, 365; journals, 61, 76, 114, 142, 147–8, 164–5, 179–81, 186, 194, 310, 320, 325–30; messianism, 312;

nation, 57, 60–61, 73, 75, 84, 88, 91, 95–6, 102, 107, 109, 111–14, 118, 128, 138, 163, 171, 187, 190, 201, 211, 233, 280, 311, 337; autonomy of, 217, 266, 277; bourgeois, 368; enemies of, 146, 148, 284, 355; immortality of, 78; new stage of development, 167, 244; non-existent, 270, 314, 355; rebirth of, 58–9, 121; self-determination of, 195; *see also* Nation, National;

national councils, 200–11, 252, 266–7, 294, 296, 301, 303, 324–5, 348–9, 353, *see also* Deanery councils, Holovna Rada Ruska, and entries on individual towns and villages; national guard, 222, 229, 232, 238, 287–96, 298–9, 352; national movement, 23, 28, 31, 47, 40, 47, 59–64, 86, 109, 117–19, 129, 139, 146, 149, 161, 163, 171–3, 179, 190–92, 198, 209, 215, 235, 251, 266, 292, 334, 344–5, 352–3, 364–5, 368; national question, 142, 163, 231, 234, 236, 282, 329, 333–4, 363–4; national thought, 58, 60, 144, 150, 347–52, 355–60; nobility, *see* Nobility, Ukrainian;

peasants, anti-clericalism of, 244; deputies, 243–8, 252–5, 270, 275, 282, 315, 355; economic conditions of, 16, 18–23, 170, 251–63; grievances of, 20–21, 42, 207–8, 254, 267; illiteracy of, 78, 107, 210, 244–5; loyalty to Austrian monarchy, 21–3, 159, 170, 185; peasant question, 162, 185, 248, 251–63, 345; resistance, 21–3, 41, 131, 149, 181, 184, 340; status of, 7–8, 17–23;

poetry, 61, 65, 73; population, 16–17, 112, 138, 145, 279; publications, 24, 34, 38, 53–6, 58, 60–61, 68–70, 74, 76, 78, 80, 92, 99, 121, 134–5, 143, 148–9, 151, 165–6, 315, 319–20; relations with other nationalities, *see* entries for individual nationalities; religion, *see* Greek Catholic church, Orthodoxy; revolutionaries, 42–50, 98; self-identification, 17; social structure, 17–18; songs, 36, 38, 61–2, 76, 97, 108, 140, 147, 152, 157, 165

Ukrainization, 234, 289, 309, 316–17

Ukrainophilism, 159

Ukrainskii vestnik, 147

Ukrainskii zhurnal, 147

Uniate church, *see* Greek Catholic church

Union of Welfare, 149

Univ, 294; Ruthenian council, 202, 256, 304

Urals, 45

Uskoks, 121

Ustia Zelene, 203

Varangians, 115

Vasylkiv, 149

Viatychians, 343

Viche, 117

Vienna, 20, 23, 27, 52, 55–6, 60, 67, 69–71, 74, 76–7, 86, 95, 123, 133, 136–7, 141, 143, 151, 156, 163–7, 171, 180–82, 188, 191, 206, 211–12, 224, 237, 240–42, 244–5, 247, 253, 258, 262, 267–8, 283–4, 292–3, 295, 302, 307, 317, 320, 329, 334–5, 353, 355; Congress of, 28, 177; uprising, 248–9; Vienna-Przemyśl Circle, 56–7

Világos, 300

Vilni Halychany, 45, 358

Vilnius, 91

Vinok Rusynam na obzhynky, 76–9, 112, 116, 124, 131, 156, 170–71, 173, 180–81, 319

Vistnyk dlia Rusyniv avstriiskoi derzhavy, 329–30

Vistula river, 16, 78, 171, 343

Vltava river, 171

Voinyliv, 243

Vojvodina, 7–8

Volga river, 91

Volhynia, 19, 21, 34, 99, 111–12, 146, 149, 334

Volhynian Chronicle, 180

Volodymyr, Principality of, *see* Principality of Halych and Volodymyr

Vychliana, 304

Wadowice, 273

Wallachia (Wallachians), 220, 279, 365

Warsaw, 11, 98, 124, 127, 151

White Mountain, 7

White Sea, 45, 91

Wiara river, 112

Wiener Allgemeine Literatur Zeitung, 56

Wiener Zeitung, 306, 351

Wieprz river, 112

Wisłoka river, 145

"Young Europe," 91

Young Sarmatia, *see* Młoda Sarmacja

Zabolotiv, 218

Zagreb, 76, 137

Zalishchynsky, 199, 243

Zaliztsi, 203

Zamość, 37
Zaporozhskaia starina, 5
Zator, Duchy of, 281
Zatwarnica, 203
Zbarazh, 203, 241–2
Zbora estate, 167
Zboriv, 203
Zbruch river, 15, 63, 73, 111
Zelenohorský rukopis, 5
Zhovkva, 22, 243, 289, 343; district, 62, 296; Ruthenian council, 202–3, 205, 207, 294, 342
Zhupanie, 297
Zhuravno, 203
Zhurnal Ministerstva narodnogo prosveshcheniia, 152
Zhydachiv, 243
Ziewonia, 33, 36
Zolochiv, 62, 73, 203, 241, 243, 304
Zoria (miscellany), 33, 66–8, 71, 84, 114, 163
Zoria Halytska, 58, 190, 195, 203, 210, 235, 245–6, 255, 257–8, 271, 281, 284, 289, 292, 297–8, 322, 326–7, 329–31, 348, 350–52
Związek Węglarzy Polskich, 44

$16.30